AMERICA'S ATLANTIC COAST LIGHTHOUSES
A TRAVELER'S GUIDE

By Jeremy D'Entremont

FIFTH EDITION
From an original Edition
by Colonel Kenneth G. Kochel, U.S.Army(Ret)

LIGHTHOUSE DIGEST
P.O. Box 1690
Wells, Maine 04090

AND

KENNETH KOCHEL PUBLISHING
P. O. Box 14023
Clearwater, Florida 33766

AMERICA'S ATLANTIC COAST LIGHTHOUSES
A TRAVELER'S GUIDE

FIFTH EDITION

First Edition, 1994
Second Edition , completely revised, 1996
Second Edition, second printing, 1997
Third Edition, revised, 1998
Fourth Edition, revised, 2000
Fifth Edition, 2001

A NOTE FROM THE AUTHOR

The earlier editions of this book have been faithful and invaluable companions on many of my own lighthouse odysseys, and it is my hope that this updated volume will continue to win friends among professional and amateur pharologists. I have updated the histories of the lighthouses in the book, and I have added new cruise and tour information. I have also included website and email addresses as often as possible, knowing that many of you, like me, use the internet as a valuable trip planning tool. Also new with this edition is the addition of photographs of many of the lighthouses.

I wish to express my deepest gratitude to Tim Harrison, editor of *Lighthouse Digest*, for his faith, patience, friendship and tireless work in the lighthouse preservation field. I also extend my thanks to the many lighthouse preservation groups, tour operators, Coast Guard personnel, and other individuals who have provided valuable assistance. I hesitate to single any of these out, not wishing to slight anyone, but I feel I must mention Bob Muller for his generous help with the section of this book covering the lighthouses of Long Island, New York. Shirley Sabin of the Nauset Light Preservation Society also went above and beyond the call of simple proofreading, and her help is truly appreciated. Without exception, every person I approached was cheerfully generous with time and information. Suffice it to say that every individual or organization mentioned in this book is worthy of special thanks.

As I worked on this revision, the theme that cropped up over and over again from Florida to Maine was one of successful preservation stories. Locally and nationally, individuals and organizations are finding ways to get the job done. They're moving lighthouses, patching them, painting them, even relighting them. But the struggle is far from over. It will take much more hard work and vigilance, as well as a great deal of money, to preserve our historic beacons.

A five minute walk from my home takes me within view of North America's first light station, Boston Light, as well as dramatic Graves Light. Not that I need extra inspiration. It is the work of authors like Edward Rowe Snow, Elinor DeWire, F. Ross Holland, Bill Caldwell and Kenneth Kochel that drew me into the rich field of lighthouse history. These authors have laid the groundwork for other lighthouse researchers of the present and future.

It is your continued love for our lighthouses that will help insure their preservation. Support lighthouse preservation organizations in any way you can, and happy lighthouse hunting!

Jeremy P. D'Entremont
March 2000

PHOTO CREDITS

CONTENTS

ABOUT THE GUIDE

The book includes most standing Atlantic Coast lighthouses. It provides directions and transportation guidance to reach or view the lighthouses, short histories with emphasis on lighthouse construction, restoration and preservation, information on museums and exhibits displaying lighthouse equipment and memorabilia, commentaries and advisories. Although the text is oriented from Florida to Maine, lighthouse chapters are geographically stacked and their directions so ordered to facilitate travel either north or south.

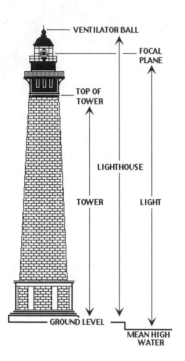

TERMINOLOGY. A lighthouse is the entire structure which, with its optic, displays a continuous or intermittent signal for guiding navigators. Although a light is also a lighthouse, use of light herein is confined to its definition as an illuminating device or the signal emitted by the device.

A lamp is a device; it is the producer of the artificial light signal. Although an illuminant can be either a device or a lamp, it also refers to the substance used to power the lamp, such as, whale oil or kerosene.

An optic is any one of the lenses, prisms or mirrors of an optical instrument. In this context, a Fresnel lens together with its lamp and illuminant is often referred to as an optic.

A beacon can be used to identify either an illuminated or an unlighted (daybeacon) aid to navigation.

MEASUREMENTS. There are several ways to express lighthouse heights. The traveler should be aware that erroneous reporting of lighthouse heights happens. The most common error is taking the U.S. Coast Guard's published height of the light above water and using it as the overall height of the lighthouse, including the tower, lantern, roof and ventilator ball.

The height of a lighthouse is measured from its base to the top of its ventilator ball.

The height of the light above mean high water (HAW) is measured from the water's surface to the optic's focal plane.

The height of the tower is measured from its base to the top of the shaft, usually directly under the watchroom or lantern deck.

LIGHTHOUSE NAMES. Although lighthouse name changes have been accepted at various levels of government, the selections for the guide's chapter headings are primarily based on the names listed in the National Register of Historic Places and those officially accepted by the U.S. Coast Guard.

SCHEDULES. Schedules change with the annual calendar and for many other reasons. Even after you have secured a brochure or printed schedule, it is advisable to call ahead to verify open and departure times.

Weather and sea conditions may not prevent the departure of a sightseeing cruise, but they surely can disappoint the lighthouse seekers. Lighthouse sighting information as presented in excursion brochures may be true for a calm and clear day, but fog, squalls and sea chop can interfere with or prevent the comfortable viewing and photographing of lighthouses. Occasionally, when squally weather or swift tides prevail, the captain may alter his course, leaving your lighthouse far away and out of sight. If you are in doubt about the day's weather conditions and how they might affect your lighthouse viewing, ask the captain or a responsible official (not ticket sellers!) the following questions:

ABOUT THE GUIDE

*"What lighthouses do you pass, how close do you pass to them
and how clearly will I be able to see them?"*

The author has found that each tour operator or boat captain so questioned, unhesitatingly gave a forthright answer.

Oh yes, if weather conditions cause you to decide not to take a scheduled (non-cancelled) boat departure or to exchange it for another day, make sure you understand the operator's refund policy before you purchase the first ticket.

For cruises take along Dramamine or sea bands for the wrist, raincoats, jackets and/or sweaters and non-skid footwear to wear while aboard cruise boats. For both land and sea viewings be sure to carry binoculars. Don't forget sun screen, sunglasses, and insect repellant.

In his extensive lighthouse travels the author has consistently found that if the traveler is confronted with municipal recreation areas or parks that charge admission fees to bathers, picnickers and campers, a polite request to enter for a few minutes only to view and photograph a lighthouse usually receives a favorable no cost response from gate attendants.

Certain light stations, although their lighthouses are clearly visible from outside the property's perimeter, are closed to the general public, being privately or institutionally owned. The inclusion of these private stations in the guide must not be construed as an invitation to enter the restricted grounds to view and photograph the lighthouses.

AMERICAN HOLIDAYS.

New Years Day	January 1
Martin Luther King, Jr. Day	January 15 or first Monday after
Presidents Day	Third Monday in February
Easter Day	Sunday, usually falls in April
Memorial Day	Last Monday in May
Independence Day	July 4
Labor Day	First Monday in September
Columbus Day	Second Monday in October
Thanksgiving Day	Third Thursday in November
Christmas Day	December 25

ARCHITECTURAL DEFINITIONS. See the sketch on the following page.

Acanthus. Leaves of a Mediterranean plant.

Architrave. Lowest architectural member of an entablature which rests on the top of a column. Also the molding around a door or rectangular opening.

Ashlar. Building stone squared and finished.

Astragal. Projecting strip or narrow half round molding on the edge of a window or door.

Baluster. Vertical post that supports a railing.

Balustrade. A row of balusters supporting a rail. Also called a railing.

Boss. An ornamental projecting block.

Boston Granite. Solid granite block shaped and squared.

Console. Projection from a wall that forms a bracket. Over doors and windows it supports the cornice.

Corbel. Wall bracket or progressively stepped up masonry that serves to support a cornice or an over-hanging member.

Cornice. Uppermost projecting portion of an entablature. Also the crowning horizontal molding of wall or building.

Coving. Architectural member with a concave cross section.

Dormer. Vertical window with its own gable which protrudes from a sloping roof.

Entablature. Consists of an architrave, a frieze (horizontal band painted or decorated with sculpture or moldings) and a cornice.

Fluting (flutes). Shallow concave channels cut vertically into the shaft of a pilaster.

Freestone. Any stone, such as soapstone or brownstone, that can be cut freely without splitting.

Gabion. A basket or cage filled with earth or rocks used in building a support or abutment.

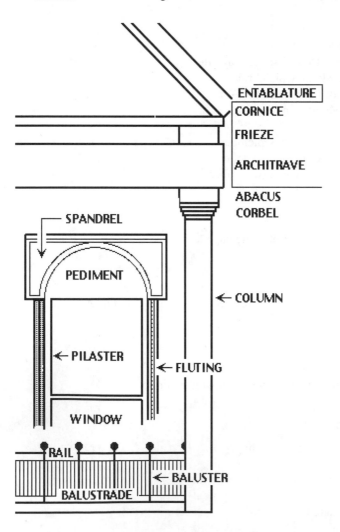

Gable. Triangular end of pitched roof framed by sloping sides.

Lintel. A horizontal architectural member that carries the load above a door or window.

Mullion. A slender vertical or horizontal member that forms a division between glass or decorative units of a window or door.

Necking. A reference to heavy molding.

Ovolo. One quarter of a circle.

Pediment. A triangular or arched space formed by the sloping sides and the horizontal cornice of a gabled building. Used mostly above doors and windows.

Pilaster. An upright architectural member that is rectangular and is structurally a pier. Also called a column.

Quoin. A large masonry block used to reinforce the corner of a wall.

Spandrel. The space between cornices, sometimes ornamented, above the pediment.

Voussoir. A radiating wedge.

LIGHTHOUSE CONSTRUCTION

"Remove not the ancient landmark, which thy fathers have set."
Proverbs 22:28

THE COLONIAL PERIOD (1716-1790). Mariners and their ships discovered America, charted our shores, brought colonists to the new world and set in motion the founding of a great nation. Early in America's emergence as a maritime power, businessmen, traders and ship owners, sometimes independently of governing bodies, began the task of building coastal and intracoastal waterway lighthouses.

On August 7, 1789, the First United States Congress passed its first public works act, establishing a national Lighthouse Service under the Treasury Department. Under the auspices of this 9th Congressional Act of 1789, 12 Colonial plus four other aids formed the nucleus of America's lighthouse system.

1716.	Boston (MA). Destroyed 1776. Rebuilt 1783. Ceded in 1790.
1746.	Brant Point (MA). Built 1746. Rebuilt 1759. Destroyed by fire 1774. Rebuilt 1777. Destroyed by a storm and rebuilt 1786. Destroyed by storm and rebuilt 1788. Ceded between 1788 and 1795.
1749.	Beavertail (RI). Built 1754. Rebuilt 1762 and 1779. Ceded 1793.
1760.	New London Harbor (CT). Rebuilt 1801. Ceded 1790.
1764.	Sandy Hook (NJ). Ceded circa 1791.
1765.	Cape Henlopen (DE). Rebuilt 1783. Ceded 1789.
1767.	Morris Island (SC). Ceded 1790.
1769.	Plymouth (MA). Rebuilt 1783. Ceded 1790.
1771.	Portsmouth Harbor (NH). Ceded 1791.
1771.	Cape Ann (MA). Ceded 1790 or 1791.
1784.	Nantucket (MA). Ceded 1790.
1788.	Newburyport Harbor (MA). Ceded 1790.

Tybee Island (GA). An octagonal daymark established between 1736 and 1742. Officially recognized as an aid to navigation in 1748. Possibly an active lighted aid as early as 1773. Correspondence indicates that a lighthouse was active and manned in 1789. Although ceded in 1791, there is no known government documentation of that act. First congressional appropriation occurred in 1817.

Portland Head (ME). Construction begun in 1787. Ceded unfinished in 1790. Light established 1791.

Cape Henry (VA). First lighthouse to be constructed by the new Federal Government. Under construction 1790. Lighthouse ceded 1791. Light established 1792.

Bald Head (NC). Under construction 1792. Completed in 1794. Ceded in 1796.

THE LIGHTHOUSE SERVICE. Between 1789 and 1820 management of the lighthouse establishment was bounced around Washington's fledgling bureaucracy between the Treasury Department and the Commissioner of Revenue. In 1820, with high hopes for a more efficient organization, Congress returned the service to the Secretary of the Treasury and told him to reestablish it under a new service head. The Secretary chose an auditor, Stephen Pleasonton.

Without further discussion of Pleasonton's career, one might characterize the Lighthouse Service as being the domain of a miserly bookkeeper without any maritime experience who, for over 20 years, delegated to a mariner without engineering experience the task of constructing and equipping America's lighthouses. By 1840 the press, the Treasury Secretary and even Congress began to question the way he was running the Lighthouse Service. Although besieged with accusations of felonious conduct and severely criticized in investigation reports, Plcasonton managed to stay in office for 32 years.

1

AMERICA'S ATLANTIC COAST LIGHTHOUSES

THE COLONIAL REVIVAL PERIOD (1790-1852). America's colonial lighthouses were designed after the basic structural demands followed in Europe - structural strength, resistance to wind, maximum possible height to allow their lights to be seen over the curvature of the earth and the use of the least amount of flammable construction materials.

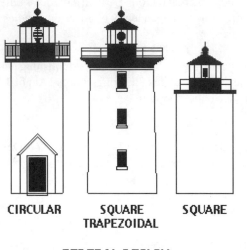

CIRCULAR   SQUARE   SQUARE
            TRAPEZOIDAL

FEDERAL DESIGN

After 1789 practically all congressional appropriations were committed to the establishment of landfall (coastal) lighted aids. Although maritime interests demanded the marking of shoals, reefs and ledges, little was done to promote or fund such construction. The marking of sandbars or soft seabeds was to come later. Perhaps one reason for this hiatus was the fact that the few people in America with any formal architectural or engineer training were not interested in lighthouse design and construction. As a matter of fact, college education in engineering did not begin until the establishment of the U.S. Military Academy in 1802. During the 1850-80 period, West Point graduates were very much a part of the lighthouse construction business, designing and supervising the building of a string of lighthouses from Florida to Massachusetts.

Builders of lighthouses, employing the same vernacular construction methods used from as early as 1760, built simple structures based on the geometric form known as the "fustrum of a cone." The round or polygonal towers had thick masonry walls, few windows and no stylistic ornamentation. They were of moderate height and utilitarian in design, constructed using local materials (wood, cut or rubblestone, brick or granite) and erected by local masons and carpenters using building specifications disseminated as contractor solicitation ads published in local newspapers.

The keeper's dwelling was also simplistic in design: rectangular or square in form with centered door and plain windows, four-sided hip roof with perhaps one window dormer with its own gable extending outward through a sloping roof and one or two tall brick chimneys.

THE PRE-LIGHTHOUSE BOARD PERIOD (1847-1852). A very important change in the operations of the Lighthouse Service occurred in 1847 when Congress, still seething over I. W. P. Lewis' (Winslow's nephew) 1842 report on Massachusetts and Maine lighthouses, told the U.S. Army's Corps of Topographical Engineers to take over the construction of several lighthouses being built by Pleasonton's organization. With this opportunity, Corps architects began the quest for new designs, different materials and better construction techniques.

THE LIGHTHOUSE BOARD (1852-1910). After Congress established the Lighthouse Board in 1852, research and development became the responsibility of a centralized planning staff already involved in the formulation of new lighthouse designs and construction engineering techniques. All sorts of ideas came off the drafting tables.

One innovation which became an important step in the continuing effort to build offshore masonry towers was the introduction of the foundation built with colossal blocks of granite cemented and shackled together, then bolted to the bedrock and filled with a rubblestone and a high quality cement mix. The cast-iron, concrete-filled caisson foundation was next to appear, followed by the cast-iron superstructure. Also introduced was the economical use of proven designs to erect new light towers.

Before metal's architectural triumph, however, stylistic references and elaborations began to appear in American lighthouse design. Adherence to the functional needs of lighthouse construction gave way to the building of imposing and decorative structures with integrated or attached light towers, each exhibiting some degree of borrowed detailing from a number of architectural revivals.

LIGHTHOUSE CONSTRUCTION

While the American revivals were essentially different from the European types, America's lighthouse architects chose to incorporate certain Old World designs and ornamental signatures in their structures. Although there have been attempts to classify America's lighthouses as belonging to specific revivals, only three can be directly related to a particular revivalistic style. They are New York's Race Rock and Stratford Shoal (Gothic) and Maine's Portland Breakwater (Greco-Classical).

THE FEDERAL DESIGN PERIOD (1853-1909). During this period, lighthouse design borrowed the simplicity of the post-Colonial period, but with one important variation. Architects chose to adhere to the cube (cubic probity) in designing functional but unadorned light towers. The circular towers are usually short structures. Some of the square towers have four trapezoidal elevations; a few display corbel supports for the lantern deck. The only elaborations are the covered entry ways (not an exclusive addition), perhaps one to three windows and, for the square towers, a curved cornice that extends up and out from the corbel, resulting in a slightly larger lantern deck.

VICTORIAN-GOTHIC

The keeper's dwellings usually have roofs that are marked by steeply pitched gables in singles or pairs and arranged systematically. Most gables are centered and some show decorated edges (vergeboards) along their roof projections. Exteriors are vertical planes, using the board and batten technique. There is an extensive use of moldings. Although windows vary in size and shape, they are often arched within peaked gables.

The Franklin Island Lighthouse, built in 1807 during the Colonial Revival period (1790-1852) of lighthouse construction, probably served as the design model for the circular Federal Design (1853-1909) light towers. Other similarly shaped lighthouses are Long Island Head (1819), Libby Island (1824), Moose Peak (1828), Browns Head (1832) and Straitsmouth (1835). The square design was an innovation of the Lighthouse Board's architects. Nineteen circular and 17 square Federal Design lighthouses were built, all in New England.

THE ITALIANATE INFLUENCE. This styling shows a masonry structure with roofs that have low pitches with wide eaves supported by large brackets, sometimes surmounted with a cup-shaped (cupele) decorated with flower clusters (involcre). Italianate windows are tall vertical openings on the second story, usually with arched hood moldings. Doors mimic the window designs.

America's lighthouse designers borrowed from the Italian form, but did so on a selective basis and often with alterations for all of the revivals. Nevertheless, the Italianate influence is quite often seen in gabled windows, protruding doors, service galleries and even ventilators. The detailing includes fluting, acanthus leaves and moldings, intricately designed gallery support brackets and fancy balusters.

THE VICTORIAN AND GOTHIC REVIVALS (1867-1870). It was quite common to have architects draw into their building designs contemporary variations of the basic Victorian form. Two commonly seen designs are the Stick and Queen Anne two-story houses with either integrated or attached light towers. Roofs are usually steeply pitched and gabled. Exteriors are coursed brick or textured and patterned with wooden shingles or clapboards. Many have one-story extended porches with ornate corner brackets and turned spindlework for supporting posts, newels and balusters. New Jersey's Hereford Inlet (1874) and Sea Girt (1896) Lighthouses display a marked adherence to the Victorian Revival genre.

AMERICA'S ATLANTIC COAST LIGHTHOUSES

The Victorian-Gothic lighthouse, usually a 2 1/2-story structure, has thick walls of coursed solid (Boston style) granite ashlar or rough hewn ashlar faced with dressed granite (Victorian style). Walls have reinforcing corner quoins. Except for the appearance of semi-elliptical attic openings, windows and protruding doors are rectangular with either arched or curved pediments. Slate covered roofs are moderately sloping and show extended cornices. The tower emerges from the front elevation and, with beveled corners, appears octagonal in shape. There is no stylistic ornamentation. Examples:

SECOND EMPIRE

New York	Old Field Point	1868
	Plum Island	1870
Connecticut	Great Captain Island	1868
	Sheffield Island	1868
	Morgan Point	1868
Rhode Island	Block Island North	1867

SECOND EMPIRE REVIVAL (1870-1874). Here again the lighthouse is a dwelling with an integrated tower. The one physical feature that identifies a lighthouse as architecturally Second Empire is the steeply sloping mansard roof with dormer windows, showing either arched or curved pediments and foot-scrolled surrounds. The tower, like its Victorian-Gothic cousin, emerges from the mansard roof with beveled corners that give it a polygonal appearance. Atlantic Coast examples:

New York	Long Beach Bar	1871
	North Dumpling	1871
	Stepping Stones	1877
Connecticut	Penfield Reef	1874
Rhode Island	Rose Island	1870
	Pomham Rocks	1874

THE IRON PERIOD (1843-1909). The era of the cast-iron lighthouse first emerged when engineers erected Connecticut's Black Rock Harbor screwpile lighthouse in 1843. That project was soon followed by the building of another screwpile structure on Delaware Bay's Brandywine Shoal (1847) and the piling supported, lattice-styled platform on Massachusetts' Minot's Ledge (1848-50). Although these last two lighthouses were destroyed during storms, their use of cast iron would permit the construction of two large skeletal light towers in the Florida Keys. Early onshore cast-iron towers include Boston Harbor's Long Island Head (1844), Lake Champlain's Juniper Island (1846) and Cape Cod's Monomoy Point (1849).

Major George H. Elliot, the Lighthouse Board's Executive Secretary has been credited with the development, in the late 1860s, of two far reaching cast-iron designs, the caisson and the light tower.

The cast-iron foundations were made of curved plates with flanges extending toward the inside of the curve and knees molded in for reinforcement. The plates are bolted into horizontal rings and the rings fastened vertically to form a large circular tube. After having been anchored to the seabed and forms for storage rooms or cisterns built inside, the caisson was usually filled with concrete. As strong and stable as its granite predecessor and easily manufactured, transported and installed, the cast-iron pier quickly became the standard foundation for offshore and breakwater lighthouses.

While styling remained a popular blueprint pastime, improved forged, rolled and cast metal processes, galvinization, hardened bolts and welding gave architects new opportunities to come up with designs calling for iron structures with coffee pot, skeletal, truncated, tall and slender or spider-legged shapes. Although far less stylish than the masonry lighthouses, the towers and platforms became the standard for inexpensive, sturdy and storm resistant aids to navigation.

LIGHTHOUSE CONSTRUCTION

One of the new designs, reportedly Major Elliot's second contribution, was the tall, segmented cast-iron light tower. Two were built -- one on South Carolina's Hunting Island, the other on Florida's Cape Canaveral. Thereafter, except for the construction of Virginia's Cape Henry in 1881, the authorities chose to mass produce the shorter and larger diameter coffee pot (caisson - see Massachusetts' Duxbury Pier, 1871) and truncated (landfall) light towers.

Before succumbing to the stodgy cast-iron tower the Lighthouse Board, in one last architectural splurge in 1876-77, decided to build two Second Empire prototypes, New Haven's Southwest Ledge and Delaware Bay's Ship John Shoal. Each consists of a one-story, cast-iron dwelling surmounted by a second story mansard roof and lantern. Both rest on concrete filled cast-iron piers.

While skeletal towers lacked the surface (except for door surrounds) to display ornamental detail, Lighthouse Board designers could not resist embellishing the otherwise drab truncated or coffee pot towers. The first cast-iron towers appeared with a style featuring elaborations that included arched windows and door openings, projecting pedimented window hoods, deeply molded window surrounds and a plain projecting surround at the entrance. One of the towers was the Essex Range Lighthouse built in 1875 in Ipswich, Massachusetts. It is now located in Edgartown Harbor on Martha's Vineyard.

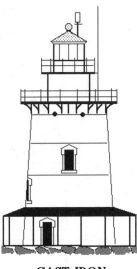

Later the lighthouses were given another architectural detail, one calling for rectangular window openings with plain, shallow-molded arched hoods resting on brackets and entrances capped with arched hoods resting on unadorned consoles and pilasters.

In the 1900s, architects changed the design a wee bit to provide more comfortable work and living areas. To do so they enlarged the diameter of the superstructures and both widened and roofed the first level galleries. Also added were more windows at each level with fancier trim and molded cornices in place of brackets. Connecticut's Peck Ledge (1906) shows these design features.

CAST-IRON

Peck Ledge Lighthouse, CT - U.S. Coast Guard photograph

LAMPS, ILLUMINANTS AND LENSES

LAMPS. The lamp used in America's earliest lighthouses was the spider lamp, a simple device consisting of a shallow brass pan (oil reservoir) with four to eight adjustable solid round wicks (no chimneys) circling inside the pan. The lamp was awfully sooty, difficult to keep burning in cold weather and drafty towers, and not a very effective beacon. Also, while increasing light intensity, it threw off toxic fumes which cut down the length of time keepers could remain inside the lantern. Inefficient as it proved to be, the spider lamp remained in service until 1812.

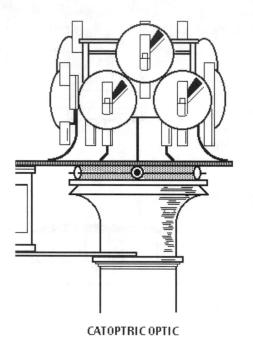

CATOPTRIC OPTIC

In 1781 Amee (Ami) Argand (1755-1803), a Swiss chemist, invented a lamp that burned with the brightness of seven candles by the use of two cylinders of brass, one inside to feed oil to the lamp's circular wick and an outside tube to allow oxygen to pass upward and around the wick. His smokeless lamp used half the amount of oil burned in the spider lamp. The optic received some magnification from a parabolic reflector, which had a slide mechanism attached to the lamp's frame allowing the lamp to be lowered through the reflector to trim the wick. Later versions were made with concentric woven wicks that carried extra air to the flame. The Argand lamp and parabolic reflector were first installed in an English lighthouse in 1789. By the turn of the century the lamp was in widespread use in both Great Britain and France. It is believed that the first reflector lamps, possibly Argands, were installed in Massachusetts' two 1809 Newburyport Harbor towers. The Argand lamp made expressly for use in the home is now a scarce, expensive and highly prized collectible.

In 1784 Borda of Dieppe invented the catoptric (reflective) optic, consisting of a small metal or glass revolving apparatus of five or more parabolic reflectors molded from copper-silver alloy sheets. This device was combined with the Argand lamp, using 18-inch reflectors.

In 1812 the U.S. Government purchased, for $20,000, a patented "reflecting and magnifying lantern" from a former ship captain from Wellfleet, Massachusetts. Winslow Lewis' (1770-1850) catoptric optic consisted of 10 whale oil-burning lamps each fitted with a parabolic reflector. Later, Lewis placed round green glass or plano-convex lenses in front of the lamps. Interestingly, when Winslow Lewis came forth with his imitation of the Argand in 1810, his friend and future benefactor as chief of the Lighthouse Service, Stephen Pleasonton, was in charge of diplomatic and international patent accounts in the Department of State and Patent Office. Although Lewis' "invention" was a copy of an improved Argand catoptric optic that had been placed in England's South Stack Lighthouse in 1809, it had serious flaws. The green bullseyes cut the range of the light. The reflectors were more spherical than parabolic and were backed with a silver coating that with cleaning soon rubbed off. Lamps and reflectors were not firmly attached to the frame, and as a result were often jostled out of focus. And although most of Lewis' lamps were fixed, those that revolved had uncovered brass gears that were too soft and quickly wore out trying to rotate the heavy chandelier. They also were easily fouled by dust and grit. Lewis was so successful in selling his patented crude copy of the Argand that he not only installed the lamps and furnished the whale oil, but also secured government contracts to design and build lighthouses. Between 1812 and 1817, all 49 of America's lighthouses had been fitted with Lewis' lamps. It took another 45 years to remove them.

The LePaute lamp, a modified Argand, became the first lamp for the newly adopted Fresnel lens. Basically, the 4-foot tall apparatus consisted of a cylindrical reservoir base topped with a standpipe leading vertically up to five concentric wicks that burned with a solid flame. During its operation, a heavy gravity-fed piston within the reservoir forced the oil up through the standpipe to the wicks. Unburned oil draining down into the reservoir acted as a coolant for the lamp. The piston, by the way, had to be cranked to its starting position once or twice a night.

LAMPS, ILLUMINANTS AND LENSES

Adaptations, all improvements of the LePaute lamp, followed. One was the Carcel lamp. Another variation was the Hains lamp, which did not require heating of the fuel. The Franklin lamp provided for the heating process by wrapping the reservoir around the chimney. Another popular model was the Funck lamp, developed by an employee of the Lighthouse Service's main supply depot. Even George G. Meade introduced a five-wick lamp that also fed oil to the wicks via a hydraulic pump.

In the early 1900s the Bureau of Lighthouses began installing two different lighting devices. First came the acetylene gas lamp, which could be installed inside a Fresnel without having to alter the lens. The acetylene system also allowed the attachment of an astronomic switch that turned the light on at sunset and off at dawn.

The second invention was the kerosene-fed incandescent vapor lamp, whose design was similar to today's Coleman lantern. The lamp's mechanism consisted of a fuel tank from which kerosene was mixed with pressurized air and pumped through lines and control valves to the lamp. The system greatly increased light intensity (candlepower) and brilliance, and was used at remote sites as late as the 1940s.

Today the trend in lighthouse lighting is solarization, especially the recent installations where heavy-duty solar panels are placed outside of the lantern and bolted to the lens' frame, tower and balustrades. Inside the lantern there is a heavy-duty 2,900-ampere bank of batteries. The lamp is a 110-watt tungsten/ halogen lamp that emits a light intensity equal to the 1,000-watt alternating current lamp it is replacing. The Coast Guard rightly claims both ecological and financial gains for this lighting device - the elimination of diesel oil as an illuminant and savings in fewer tender service requirements.

ILLUMINANTS. The first fuel for America's lamps was fish oil. By the late 18th century the principal fuel was spermaceti oil from the sperm whale. There were difficulties in using this illuminant. There had to be a thick mixture for summer and a thinner strain for winter months. Low temperatures caused the oil to congeal and its consistency had to be maintained by warming. This process was accomplished by a stove built inside the lantern. As the whale population declined and the price of sperm oil increased, unscrupulous suppliers botched the oil's burning qualities by mixing the sperm oil with such fillers as fish oil, animal fats and other whale oils. In turn, the Lighthouse Service set out to find alternative fuels.

There were many attempts to come up with readily available, less costly and suitable illuminants. As early as 1803 porpoise oil was tried at North Carolina's Cape Hatteras Lighthouse. It was decided that whale oil was more efficient than that supplied by the porpoise. In 1817 the use of coal gas, manufactured from bituminous coal and tree resin, was undertaken at the Beavertail Lighthouse in Rhode Island. Although the project showed considerable promise for this new illuminant, the Treasury Department caved in to the demands of the whaling community and shelved the idea. In 1841 a similar coal gas experiment was to be repeated at three Delaware Bay lighthouses. That project also was tabled.

During the 1850s the Lighthouse Board became interested in colza or rapeseed oil. This oil is made from any of the coles, such as cabbages, turnips and rapeseed or grape pomace. It allowed the wick to burn longer and with less soot, and was widely used in France where widespread plantings of grapes and cabbages enabled the French to manufacture colza on a large scale. American farmers, although offered farm productivity grants, refused to provide the quantities of coles required for the oil's manufacture.

In the search for a whale oil substitute, lard oil emerged in the 1850s as the principle illuminant. Delivered to lighthouse keepers in blocks (butts), the lard had to be heated (usually on the first floor), quickly toted up the stairs, dumped into the lamp reservoirs and the wick lighted before the oil cooled -- a nightly, sometimes twice nightly, uphill slalom.

In the 1860s natural gas was first tested at the Presque Island Lighthouse at Erie, Pennsylvania, and later at the Jones Point Lighthouse on the Potomac River. Condensation and delivery problems canceled both experimental projects. In the 1870s, the Lighthouse Board began experimenting with kerosene, then known as mineral oil. By 1878 kerosene was being used as an illuminant for minor aids to navigation. In 1883 the first-order Fresnel in New Jersey's Highlands Lighthouse was the first lens of that order to burn kerosene.

Twelve years after Thomas A. Edison electrified the Statue of Liberty in 1886, the two Highlands beacons became electrically powered. There are certain tradeoffs for electricity's contributions to lighthouse operations. One is automation. In many cases, without the presence of their keepers, lighthouses have become easy prey for vandals. Also, as large high-intensity lamps are installed, the Fresnel lenses are retired. Many of these priceless relics have been damaged during removal or later lost or stolen and in some instances deliberately destroyed.

By the late 1800s kerosene wick lamp made its debut. In 1908 acetylene, a gaseous hydrocarbon, first appeared as an illuminant for the incandescent oil vapor lamp.

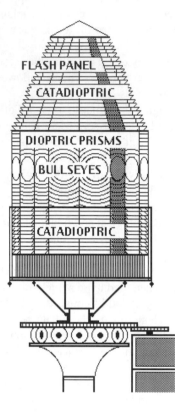

THE FRESNEL LENS. In 1822 Augustin Jean Fresnel (fra nel') (1788-1827), a French physicist, introduced his magnificent invention to the world. The lens is shaped like a bullet. Directly over and under the central glass drum are curved dioptric prisms and above these curved catadioptric prisms. Around the fixed (stationary) lens' waist is a central drum of convex glass; the revolving optic employs a series of convex bullseye lenses.

The lenticular principles of physics applied in the Fresnel lens are refraction (the bending of light) and reflection. As each light ray enters and passes through the catadioptric prism the ray undergoes a refraction and a reflection; upon leaving the prism it is again refracted. The dioptric prism effects two refractions of the light ray, one within the prism and the second as the ray exits the prism. By positioning the prisms around the outside of the lens so that all emerging light rays are parallel to each other, the lens is capable of collecting up to 90% of the lamp's light and concentrating it into an intense horizontal beam.

The factors that make this invention so unique are the practical application of the principles of visible light, the lens' delicate balance and ease of rotation and its flawless manufacture. Fresnel's lenses were designed and made with precise mathematical measurements. The prisms were hand ground from perfectly molded lead crystal. The parts were then fitted together with an equally precise attention to detail. Finished and resting in its brass frame and cradle, the Fresnel lens is an exquisite addition to the world's classical art forms.

Fixed lenses could be made to flash by placing moving screens (eclipsers) in front of the optic. The rotating or revolving Fresnel optic's vertical segments of dioptric and catadioptric prisms and bullseyes are called "flash panels." Like the fixed lens these panels bend and reflect light, but the bullseyes and curved prisms also funnel the light rays into vertical segments or pencil beams similar to the spokes of a wheel. This emission produces the light's flashing characteristic. Some lenses have as many as 24 flash panels.

Some of the larger of the ordered lenses were divided into two separated halves. They are called "bivalve" or "clam shell" lenses.

To warn mariners away from offshore hazards such as reefs, ledges and sand bars, a colored light sector is sometimes employed. The light sector is an arc of light seen as a ship approaches the lighthouse. Flash panels are used in the revolving Fresnel lens. Lighthouses with fixed lenses, on the other hand, can display a hazard identification sector by having the optic's light pass through suspended colored panels or through the lantern's colored glass panes. Colored panels moving around a fixed white light also were used to produce an alternating characteristic.

To achieve even greater magnification of the light emitted from his invention, Fresnel attached to the outside of the lens a rectangular set of prisms (condensing panel) that produced a greater degree of reflection and refraction along a narrow path. This lens was used primarily as a range light. Condensing panels also have been used to produce a flashing characteristic.

THE FRESNEL ORDERS. To provide further utility to his lens, Fresnel designed different strengths, or orders, which offered the lighthouse architect six choices of light intensities.

LAMPS, ILLUMINANTS AND LENSES

First-order. This lens, the most powerful and largest of the six, was installed in primary landfall (coastal) lighthouses to give warning to the approach of land. Inside diameter = 72 7/16".

Second-order. Aids marking coastal headlands and the approaches to bays and sounds usually received this lens. Inside diameter = 55 1/8".

Third-order. This lens was assigned to aids covering wide bays and located on large lakes, coastal inlets and their entrances. Inside diameter = 39 3/8".

Fourth, Fifth and Sixth-orders. These lenses, including a mesoradial 3 1/2-order, mark prominent headlands, points and shoals in large bays and sounds. They also are used to give warning of existing obstructions in rivers or mark piers and wharves. Inside diameters: fourth = 19 11/16"; fifth = 14 3/4"; sixth = 11 3/16".

There is one active (and huge) hyperradial lens in the United States. That one, on Makapuu Point, Oahu, Hawaii, has an 8 1/2' diameter and an overall height of 24 feet.

At the beginning of 1998 the Coast Guard was maintaining 14 active landfall first-order Fresnel lenses.

Atlantic Coast:	Gulf Coast:	Pacific Region:
Block Island Southeast	Pensacola	Destruction Island
Bodie Island		Heceta Head
Cape Henry		Makapuu Point
Currituck Beach		Point Conception
Jupiter		Yaquina
St. Augustine		
Seguin Island		
Tybee Island		

LIGHT CHARACTERISTICS.

Lights are classified according to their rhythm and color. How far out to sea a light can be seen depends on the light's intensity, the height of the light's focal plane above mean high water and meteorological visibility.

Intensity dictates the light's nominal range, which is defined as the maximum distance a beacon can be seen in clear weather without regard to the curvature of the earth, height of the light or elevation of the helmsman's eye. Distances herein are nautical miles (nm).

FIXED - A CONTINUOUS AND STEADY LIGHT.

EQUAL INTERVAL (ISOPHASE) - ALL DURATIONS OF LIGHT AND DARKNESS ARE EQUAL.

OCCULTING - ECLIPSE IS REGULARLY REPEATED. GROUP AND COMPOSITE VARIATIONS

FLASHING - PERIOD'S TOTAL DURATION OF LIGHT SHORTER THAN TOTAL DARKNESS. FLASHES OF EQUAL DURATION. GROUP & COMPOSITE VARIATIONS.

CONTINUOUS QUICK - REGULARLY REPEATED FLASHES AT NOT LESS THAN 80 PER MINUTE. ALSO INTERRUPTED QUICK.

ALTERNATING - SHOWS DIFFERENT COLORS ALTERNATINGLY. SHOWN ARE WHITE (W) AND RED (R).

FLORIDA
CAPE FLORIDA

TO KEY BISCAYNE

In Miami, at the intersection of I-95's Exit 1 and US 1 ("Key Biscayne" sign), take the William Powell Bridge (toll east only) and causeway to Key Biscayne.

South Crandon Boulevard, the main road leading to the state recreation area, requires a $1 toll.

Continue on South Crandon Boulevard and follow the posted "State Park" signs to the park entrance.

BILL BAGGS CAPE FLORIDA STATE RECREATION AREA

PARK OPEN. All year, daily 8 to sunset.

ADMISSION FEES. Three basic fees: (1) Pedestrian, bicyclists and extra passengers, (2) vehicle with driver and (3) vehicle with maximum of 8 passengers. Discounts for Florida seniors 65+, Florida residents participating in food stamp program and those entering the park one hour before closing. Under 6 free.

STATION OPEN. Guided tours of the light station (nominal fee) are conducted Wednesday through Sunday at 10 AM and 1 PM. Be sure to arrive 30 minutes early to sign up on the tour list as there is a 10-person maximum. Children younger than eight are not allowed to climb the tower. Visitors are led through the furnished air-conditioned cottage and the cookhouse, now an air-conditioned video mini-theater.

Bill Baggs Cape Florida State Recreation Area, 1200 South Crandon Boulevard, Key Biscayne, FL 33149

Phone (305) 361-5811 or (305) 361-8779.

Website: http://www.dep.state.fl.us/parks/BillBaggs/billbaggs.html   Email: capefla@gate.net

CAPE FLORIDA LIGHTHOUSE (EYE OF MIAMI)

Following congressional appropriations of $24,000 between 1822 and 1824, a contract was let that called for the building of lighthouses on Cape Florida, at Key West and in the Dry Tortugas. After several mishaps and delays, the Cape Florida Lighthouse was finally completed in December 1825. The lighthouse is the oldest building in south Florida. The beacon marked Florida Reef and guided ships around the reef into the Cape Florida channel.

In December 1835, the Second Seminole War erupted in the Fort Dallas (Miami) area after a U.S. Army unit, marching north from Tampa (Fort Brooke) to Ocala (Fort King) under the leadership of Major Francis Dade, was massacred near Brooksville. That war, by the way, was the longest and costliest of the Indian wars in the United States.

A few months later Cape Florida's lightkeeper lost his wife and children during an Indian raid. Emotionally drained, the keeper departed for Key West with neighboring families, leaving the lighthouse unattended. Soon after his departure a replacement keeper arrived.

Then, in the late afternoon on July 23, 1836, the new keeper and his assistant began their historic battle to save the lighthouse. The conflict started when a band of warring Seminoles opened the skirmish with rifle fire; the keeper returned fire and held the Indians at bay. At nightfall the war party reached the base of the tower and set fire to the entrance door and the ground floor window.

The flames soon reached the inside; and, fed by leaking oil cans (over 200 gallons of whale oil were stored inside the tower), engulfed the entire ground floor. After the two defenders reached the watchroom, they tried to chop down part of the wooden stairway. Unable to do so and having been forced out onto the balcony, the keeper threw a barrel of gunpowder down the stairwell. The ensuing explosion dropped the burning stairs. Finally, the Seminoles believing both men to be dead, set fire to the keeper's house and departed in his sloop. The wounded assistant was roasted alive. The keeper, with parts of his feet burned or shot off and suffering severe body and head burns, endured twelve agonizing hours in the hot July sun before being rescued by the crew of a passing naval vessel, the *Motto*.

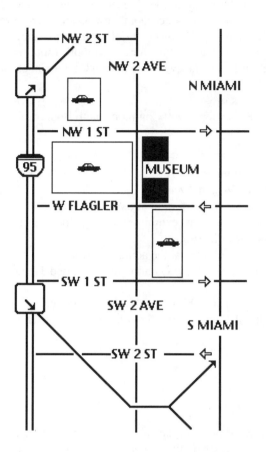

The walls of the 60-foot tall tower completed in 1825 are four feet thick at its base, tapering to 18 inches at the top. Upon examination of the burned-out lighthouse, a Lighthouse Service inspector reported that the builder fraudulently doubled his profits by constructing hollow brick walls.

Although the report created somewhat of a furor in Washington, the government's condemnation ignored the fact that the hollow wall technique for building masonry light towers had been used before. The walls provided extra strength and ventilation.

Congress authorized the rebuilding of the tower in 1837; but because of the presence of hostile and warring Seminoles in the nearby Everglades, work on the lighthouse was delayed until 1846. In 1855 the tower was redesigned by then Lieutenant George C. Meade. The tower was reinforced at its base and raised to 95 feet.

Cape Florida's first signal was a fixed white light generated from 17 whale oil-fed lamps each backed by a 21-inch reflector. It had a range of 16 nautical miles. This system was replaced by a second-order Fresnel lens in 1855.

In the summer of 1861, the same Confederate raiding party that put the Jupiter Inlet light out of commission hit Cape Florida and damaged the lighting apparatus and its lens. The 1855 second-order Fresnel lens was repaired in 1866 and reactivated the following year.

Cape Florida's light was extinguished in 1878, when the Fowey Rocks light was established south of the cape. The lens and illuminating apparatus from Cape Florida were shipped to the Lighthouse Depot at Staten Island, New York. One hundred years later, on July 4, 1978, the light was reactivated by the Coast Guard as a navigational aid.

OWNER. State of Florida since 1966. Managed by the Department of Natural Resources.

PRESERVATION. Listed in the National Register of Historic Places.

Except for the replacement of the original wooden stairs with a cast-iron stairway, the Cape Florida lighthouse was allowed to deteriorate, with broken lantern windows, a badly rusted staircase, watchroom and lantern, and disintegrating interior and exterior brickwork.

In Miami the Dade Heritage Trust decided to do something about Florida's oldest lighthouse. In 1989 the Trust began a fund-raising campaign and produced a video to help promote an awareness of the need to save the structure. It also contacted state authorities in an attempt to rouse their interest in preserving the tower. The only response from the state was a $30,000 grant for an engineering survey.

In 1990 the Trust's request for a special category grant received no consideration. As a result, the request did not reach the legislature. The request was resubmitted in 1991; but because of Florida's burgeoning fiscal requirements, it was tabled. In 1992 the Department of Historic Resources acted on the Trust's request and sent it to the Florida Historic Preservation Advisory Council. The Council recommended that the request be forwarded to the state legislature. As a result, sufficient funds were earmarked for a $450,000 contract to repair the exterior brickwork, using 24,000 replacement (dark red to buff pink) bricks manufactured by a Tennessee company. After the repair of the brickwork the tower was given a coat of stucco and covered with a coat of white paint.

The nearly $2 million restoration was further financed with (1) $280,000 in state and matching funds to pay for a 103-step iron staircase fabricated in Alabama and installed in 1994, (2) a special category grant of $261,000 for the replication of a 24-foot tall lantern by a Jacksonville, Florida firm, (3) $200,000 raised from corporate and private donations Florida's Department of Environmental Protection, and a $750,000 grant from the State's Department of State's Division of Historical Resources. The tower was fully restored by February 1999.

The entire restoration included: new lantern dome, replacement of the second-order Fresnel lens with a modern plastic optic, new lantern glazed with ballistic-proof storm panes, replacement of the watchroom, new historically-correct cast-iron stairway with a new supporting central column, new windows, repairs to the tower's brick walls, replacement of the stairway's cast-iron support base and interior lighting. The project was completed in time for the symbolic (not certified by the Seventh Coast Guard District as a private aid) relighting of Cape Florida on the eve of the Miami Centennial on July 27, 1996.

For further information contact the Bill Baggs Cape Florida State Park or

- Division of Recreation and Parks, Department of Environmental Protection, 3900 Commonwealth Boulevard, Tallahassee, FL 32339-3000. Phone (904) 488-6563.

HISTORICAL MUSEUM OF SOUTHERN FLORIDA   **See map on page 11.**

If northbound on I-95, take the NW 2nd Street exit and turn right at NW 2nd Avenue.

If southbound, take the Miami Avenue exit, backtrack on SE 2nd Street and turn right at SW 2nd Avenue.

The museum is located in Miami's Metro-Dade Cultural Center. It has among its exhibits depicting Florida's historic past Carysfort Reef's first-order Fresnel lens that was removed from the tower in 1960.

Parking tickets for the lot on NW 2nd Avenue (west of the center) are validated at the admission desk.

OPEN. All year. Mondays through Saturdays 10 to 5 (Thursdays to 9). Sundays noon to 5. Closed January 1, Thanksgiving Day and December 25.

ADMISSION FEES. Non-members only. Discounts for groups (20+) and children 6-12. Under 6 free.

- The Historical Museum of Southern Florida, Metro-Dade Cultural Center, 101 West Flagler Street, Miami, FL 33130

Phone (305) 375-1492

Website: http://www.historical-museum.org

FLORIDA LIGHTHOUSE ASSOCIATION

The Florida Lighthouse Association, Inc., founded in 1996, is a not-for-profit organization chartered by the State of Florida for the preservation of Florida's lighthouses and maritime heritage. Membership is open to all, worldwide, as well as Floridians. The group publishes a quarterly newsletter, the FLA FLASH. They also hold quarterly meetings at various lighthouse locations throughout the state, along with special programs and tours.

This very active organization has accomplished a great deal in just five years. They have made financial contributions to the Cape St. George, St. Johns River, and St. Marks lighthouses, and are raising funds for the Crooked River Lighthouse to help the Carrabelle Lighthouse Association begin the restoration. They encouraged the United States Navy to refuse a commercial venture's request to move the 1859 St. Johns River Lighthouse from its historic location.

The Florida Lighthouse Association also runs tours to many of Florida's lighthouses that are normally closed to the public. Tours are sometimes also offered to lighthouses in neighboring states.

For more information:

- The Florida Lighthouse Association, P.O. Box 340028, Tampa, FL 33694-0028
Website: http://www.floridalighthouses.org
Email: info@floridalighthouses.org

FOWEY ROCKS

FOWEY ROCKS LIGHTHOUSE
CHARACTERISTIC: Flashing white 10s (2 red sectors)
HAW: 110'
RANGES: White 15; red 10 nm

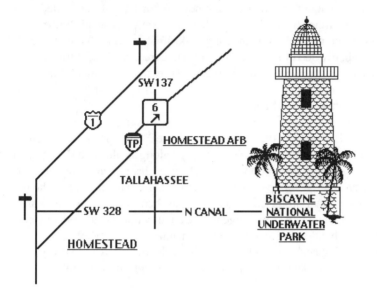

Fowey Rocks, unseen from the mainland, lies about 10 miles south of Cape Florida. The tower is a driven-pile and disc structure supported by eight wrought-iron pilings passed through large stabilizing iron discs resting on a concrete foundation and driven vertically into the hard coral reef. The keeper's house sits on a platform about 23 feet above the water. This lighthouse and its similarly designed Florida Reef cousins all have withstood the destructive forces of countless hurricanes, attesting to the sound construction design of the driven-pile and screw-pile skeletal towers.

Fowey Rocks' first-order Fresnel lens and the same order lens still active in Delaware Bay's Ship John Shoal Lighthouse were first exhibited at Philadelphia's 1876 Centennial Exposition prior to their installations. Fowey Rocks' light was established on June 15, 1878.

In 1931 Fowey Rocks's kerosene powered classical lens was electrified, its candlepower increased and a flashing characteristic established using a metal screen that revolved inside the lens. The light was automated in 1974 and its old Fresnel has been replaced by a high intensity optic powered by solar charged batteries. That system was installed after an unsuccessful testing of a windmill driven generator.

OWNER. U.S. Coast Guard.
PRESERVATION. Not listed in the National Register of Historic Places.

BOCA CHITA KEY TOWER See above map.

East of Homestead in the Biscayne National Underwater Park lies the 32 acre island of Boca Chita Key. The lighthouse is the work of Mark C. Honeywell of the Honeywell Corporation who owned the island from 1937 to 1945. The 65-foot tall tower is constructed of pockmarked limestone (not coral rock) and is topped with a beehive lantern resting on an corniced gallery. There are 54 steps to the service balcony.

Mr. Honeywell placed an optic in the lantern to enable his boat captain to use it as a harbor aid. Not having been told about the new "light" and thus in use as an uncharted aid, the Bureau of Lighthouses promptly told Marc H. to extinguish it.

In 1992 Hurricane Andrew tore the island and its properties to smithereens and in 1996 vandals did a hurricane's amount of damage to practically everything on the island. Since then the National Park Service has spent $2 million to remove the debris, build a new dock, refurbish the light tower and the island's structures, install a power plant and prepare picnic and camping areas with restrooms, tables and grills.

There is a daily schedule for transportation for campers, scuba divers and snorkelers. There is no regularly scheduled ferry service to the island for casual visitors and picnickers. Call for availability or schedule. The boat departs from the concession stand next to the visitor center. No pets on the island.

FEES: Varied round trip transportation fees. Mooring fee for private boats. No other fees.
Biscayne National Underwater Park, PO Box 1270, Homestead, FL 33030
Phone (305) 230-1100 Fax (305) 230-1120
Website: http://www.nps.gov/bisc/

13

CARYSFORT REEF

FLORIDA KEYS NATIONAL MARINE SANCTUARY. In 1990 the 250-mile long Florida Reef, America's only barrier coral reef and the third largest in the world, was officially designated the Florida Keys National Marine Sanctuary, a 3,500-square mile expanse of islands and water stretching from north of Key Largo to the Dry Tortugas 75 miles west of Key West.

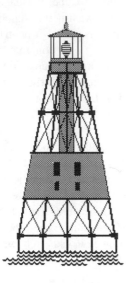

It is important to point out that the Keys are not just barren atolls sprinkled with palms and bushes and encircled by mangroves. There are exotic trees and shrubs, such as Jamaican dogwood, gumbo limbo, mahogany, wild lime, wild coffee and pigeon plum. The extremely hardwood of the Keys' lignum vitae tree was used during World War II to make mechanical bearings. Key Largo's 10,000 acre Hammock State Botanical Site contains about 2,000 acres of the largest stand of the West Indian tropical hardwoods remaining in the United States.

The Keys also support much valuable wildlife. For example, America's only crocodile inhabits Key Largo's 7,000 acre Crocodile Lake National Wildlife Refuge. In 1994 a new habitat, or "crocominium," was developed along an elevated Card Sound Road. There is a series of 14 shallow ponds (stocked with fish and crabs) and connecting 4-foot deep sections dotted with peat and sand mounds for basking and the laying of eggs. There are many other protected critters, such as the rarest butterfly on Earth, the Schaus' swallowtail, the white crown pigeon, the small wood rat and the tiny cotton mouse (Key Largo), banded tree snails, the rare mangrove turtle (Key Vaca), miniature key deer and the ring neck snake (Big Pine Key), the rice rat (Cudjoe Key) and the cotton rat (Lower Keys). America's only freshwater mud turtle is found throughout the Keys.

TO THE UPPER KEYS. Take any route out of the Miami area that leads to US 1 and Florida City. From there follow US 1 to Key Largo.

The previously reported location for viewing the Carysfort Reef Lighthouse is now behind a fence protecting a state wildlife refuge. There are no longer any public roads off Card Sound Road leading to the ocean.

CARYSFORT REEF LIGHTHOUSE.
CHARACTERISTIC: Group flashing white 60s (3 red sectors)
HAW: 100' **RANGES**: White 15; red 13 nm
By 1842 the lightship that had been on station since 1825 was so riddled with dry rot that it had to be replaced. Despite the complaints of sea captains that the ship's lights could not be seen and that the lightship was often off station, the Carysfort Lightship remained in service until 1852, when it was transferred to duty on Narragansett Bay's Brenton Reef.

The foundation level of the Carysfort Lighthouse consists of a central and eight peripheral vertical iron screw piles that describe an octagon 50 feet wide. The structure rises as a five-story octagonal pyramid to the lantern's service deck. A two-story keepers' quarters, contained in a circular enclosure, is 24 feet above the foundation level. The skeletal tower is braced with lateral iron straps (girts) and iron diagonal and radial tiebars. The overall height of the brown lighthouse is 112 feet.

Refer to the graphic on the following page. Carysfort Reef consists of a hard upper crust, primarily elkhorn and staghorn corals, over a sand layer. This seabed condition virtually dictated the use of screw piles for the foundation construction. The screw piles were 13-inch hollow iron shafts with a zinc-tipped 22-inch diameter auger-like bit of two complete turns. Nine main shafts were screwed through the coral and into the sand crust to a depth of 10 feet. The piles were capped with four-foot diameter iron discs that weighed 1,692 pounds.

The main support piles (nine-inch diameter), inserted inside the hollow shafts, rise to a height of almost 16 feet. At that elevation the peripheral piles were capped with angling sockets that accept the lower chords, girts and radial beams connecting them to the central pile.

CARYSFORT REEF

The completion of the tower designed by I. W. P. Lewis began in 1848 but was delayed for four years due to foul weather, a lack of funds and the death of the construction superintendent. In 1851 Lieutenant George G. Meade, assigned to the U.S. Army's Corps of Topographical Engineers, was dispatched to Florida to complete the project. Lieutenant Meade later used and improved upon the disc pile Carysfort Reef model in overseeing the construction of the lighthouses at Sombrero Key (1853-56) and Sand Key (1852-53), both located in the Lower Keys.

The light was established on March 10, 1852, using a whale oil-powered revolving first-order Fresnel lens with 16 flash panels, manufactured by Henri LePaute. The optic had a focal plane of 100 feet above the water and was powered by a single oil lamp. In 1931 the number of flash panels was reduced to four by replacing every fourth one with a metal screen. Sometime before the turn of the century the light's illuminant was changed to kerosene. Storage was obtained by strapping 14 holding tanks to the underside of the living quarters deck.

The beacon was electrified in 1926. The first-order Fresnel was replaced by a third-order lens when the light was automated in 1960.

In 1975 Carysfort Reef became one of the first of America's solar powered lights. The Coast Guard installed an 80-watt solar panel to harness sunlight for its conversion into low voltage direct current. The converted electricity, stored in batteries, powers a medium-intensity xenon lamp inside the third-order lens.

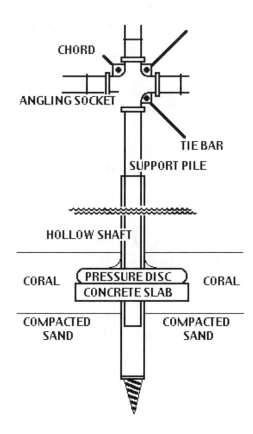

OWNER. U.S. Coast Guard.

PRESERVATION. Listed in the National Register of Historic Places.

In mid-1996, the Coast Guard sandblasted and painted the tower's exterior, repaired worn and torn turnbuckles and tie bars and restored the lantern's roof. This was the tower's first overhaul in over 40 years. Apparently the interior is not to be refurbished, leaving it to further succumb to the elements (no windows or shutters to prevent corrosion) and vandalism (no caretakers to provide protection).

ALLIGATOR REEF

TO UPPER MATECUMBE KEY. Pull out of the campground and head south (left) on CR 905A to US 1 in Key Largo. The Overseas Highway from Florida City to Key West is the southernmost section of US 1. The 126-mile highway follows the railbed of the Florida East Coast Railway built in 1904-21 and destroyed by the 1935 Labor Day hurricane. There are 42 bridges, one seven miles long

The first viewing location for the Alligator Reef Lighthouse extends from the southern end of Upper Matecumbe Key (MM 80), across the Tea Table Channel bridge to the north end of Lower Matecumbe Key (MM 77). The best offroad spot to photograph the lighthouse is at MM 79.[1]

ALLIGATOR REEF LIGHTHOUSE (GATOR).
CHARACTERISTIC: Group flashing white 60s
(two red sectors)
HAW: 136' **RANGES**: White 16; red 13 nm

Although Alligator Reef, as early as 1857, had been selected as the best location for a lighthouse, Congress waited until1870 to pass its appropriation bill. The project began in 1871. The cast-iron components for this white skeletal structure were forged in Cold Spring, New York. It is an octagonal and pyramidal driven-pile tower. There is a small keeper's apartment nestled within the framework. The 12-inch wrought-iron piles were passed through the center hole of a cast-iron disc resting on a concrete slab and pounded into the sand and coral bed to a depth of 10 feet. The light tower cost $83,000.

The September 1935 hurricane, which tore the Keys to shreds and wiped out the railroad to Key West, raked Alligator Reef Lighthouse with a 20-foot wall of water and swept across Upper Matecumbe Key, leaving little standing and killing over 400 residents. "Old Gator" withstood the full force of that storm surge. And again in 1960, according to newspaper accounts, Hurricane Donna gave the Coast Guard watch a few breathless moments. Just before the storm surge hit the tower, the crew had climbed up into the lantern and lashed themselves to the framework. They and their charge survived.

We think we have pollution problems -- pity America's early lightkeepers. When the offshore sentinels were built, a collection system used in many of America's lighthouses allowed rainwater to be gathered via gutters and spouted down into cement-lined galvanized cisterns. Health problems arose in the Keys after the lead in the paint used to prevent rust and erosion leached out of the coatings. As a result, the rainwater ran over the exposed surfaces carrying the lead into the cisterns. The problem was subsequently solved by using a gate arrangement which allowed the first spate of rainwater to wash the tower and send it overboard before shunting the less contaminated water into the cisterns. Further steps to alleviate the problem called for more frequent cleaning of the cisterns and the use of unleaded paints. Unfortunately, it took 70 years to eliminate the health hazard.

In 1931 the light tower's original fourth-order Fresnel lens was modified by replacing every 5th and 6th of its 24 flash panels with metal screens. The optic is now solar powered.

---

1. Those small green and white numbered posts along the road's shoulders are mile markers (MM). They begin at the corner of Fleming and Whitehead Streets in Key West and end with MM 126 near Florida City. Although the reconstruction of the Overseas Highway and the laying of a new water main to Key West destroyed many of the markers, Florida Keys' Chambers of Commerce claim they will be replaced. Meanwhile, the accompanying Florida Keys maps continue to show the location of each key and major municipalities next to their respective mile marker, beginning with MM 106 on Key Largo and MM 4 on Stock Island.

ALLIGATOR REEF

OWNER. U.S. Coast Guard.
PRESERVATION. Not listed in the National Register of Historic Places.

TO THE MIDDLE KEYS. In the southern portion of the Upper Keys one can see the Tennessee Reef beacon's platform, which consists of a small black house atop a skeletal tower on piles. Sightings of the aid can be made between Craig Key (MM 72) and the north end of Long Key (MM 70).

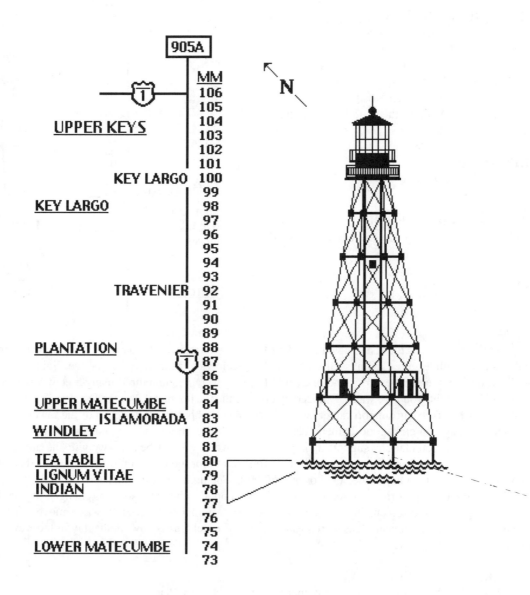

SOMBRERO KEY

ACROSS THE MIDDLE KEYS. Upon arrival on the Conch Keys, the motorist has reached the Middle Keys. The Tennessee Reef's tower and platform again can be spotted between Long Key (MM 66) and Conch Key (MM 63).

TO SOMBRERO BEACH STATE PARK. The Sombrero Key tower is visible from a side road in Marathon on Vaca Key. At MM 50 (traffic signal with the route marked by a small sign on the right) turn left into FL 931 (North Sombrero Road). Continue on North Sombrero and connecting Sombrero Beach Road to the park (2.0 miles). Free parking. Walk to the shoreline. The lighthouse lies off to the right.

OPEN. Sunrise to sunset.
FREE ADMISSION.
Phone: (305) 292-4560

SOMBRERO KEY LIGHTHOUSE.
CHARACTERISTIC: Group flashing white 60s (3 red sectors)
HAW: 142'
RANGES: White 15; red 12 nm

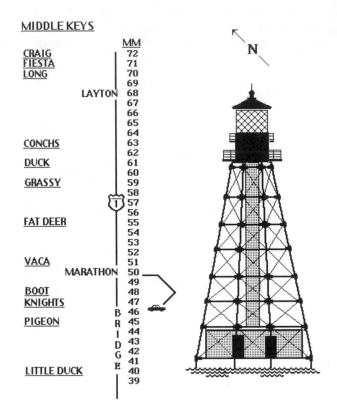

This reef lighthouse was the last to be built under Meade's supervision. It is a brown driven pile tower, octagonal and pyramidal in shape, with a central cylindrical stairwell. Sombrero Key is the tallest of the reef light towers. To achieve a longer underwater life, the eight exterior and one central pilings were manufactured using a new American metallurgical process, in which wrought-iron pipe was galvanized by dipping the red hot metal into melted zinc. Then, because the reef's compacted and hard surface can support rather heavy loads, Meade chose to anchor each of the tower's nine 12-inch piles by passing each through an eight-foot diameter cast-iron disc resting on a concrete bed poured 10 feet below the reef's surface. The discs and foundations support and spread the tower's vertical bearing weight; the angled pilings provide lateral strength. Ergo, an incredibly strong and durable foundation for the reef's tallest lighthouse. The cost? With construction delayed in 1856 by a hurricane, a tad over $150,000. The light was established on March 17, 1858.

In 1931 Sombrero Key's original fixed first-order Fresnel optic's characteristic was changed to five flashes every 15 seconds by placing revolving screens inside the lens. The lens (original cost $20,000) was removed in 1984, when solar charged batteries and a high intensity lens were installed. The Fresnel lens is now on display in the Key West Lighthouse Museum.

OWNER. U.S. Coast Guard.
PRESERVATION. Not listed in the National Register of Historic Places.

In 1980, with the influx of Cubans fleeing Castroville, the Coast Guard restored the vandalized keepers' quarters and established manned radar and observation posts in the Alligator Reef, Sombrero Key and American Shoal Lighthouses.

AMERICAN SHOAL

ACROSS THE LOWER KEYS. The Sombrero Key Lighthouse can be seen again while crossing the Seven Mile Bridge between Knight Key (MM 46) and Little Duck Key (MM 40). The best offroad viewing spot is between MM 46 (to the south) and MM 47 (to the southeast).

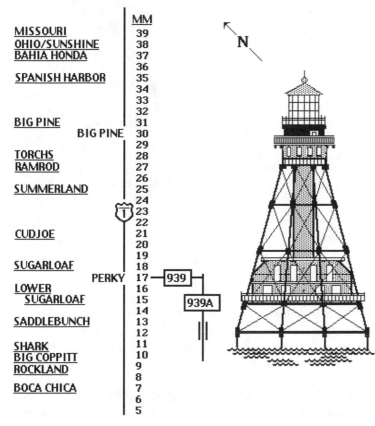

LOWER KEYS

	MM
MISSOURI	39
OHIO/SUNSHINE	38
BAHIA HONDA	37
	36
SPANISH HARBOR	35
	34
	33
	32
BIG PINE	31
BIG PINE	30
	29
TORCHS	28
RAMROD	27
	26
SUMMERLAND	25
	24
	23
	22
CUDJOE	21
	20
	19
SUGARLOAF	18
PERKY	17—939
LOWER	16
SUGARLOAF	15
939A	14
SADDLEBUNCH	13
	12
SHARK	11
BIG COPPITT	10
ROCKLAND	9
	8
BOCA CHICA	7
	6
	5

Once across the Seven Mile Bridge, the motorist is in the Lower Keys. Big Pine Shoal Light 22's (flashing white 4s) platform and small red building can be seen beginning at the south end of Spanish Harbor Key Bridge (MM 34) and across the bridge to the north end of Big Pine Key (MM 32).

Continue on to Sugarloaf Key and at MM 17 (opposite the Sugarloaf Lodge) turn left and follow FL CR 939 (Sugarloaf Boulevard) for 2.5 miles to its terminus at a T-head intersection. Turn right into FL CR 939A and drive southwest along Sugarloaf Beach for another 2.5 miles to a small concrete bridge from which the lighthouse can be seen directly seaward to the southeast.

AMERICAN SHOAL LIGHTHOUSE.
CHARACTERISTIC: Group flashing white 15s (2 red sectors)
HAW: 109' RANGES. White 13; red 10 nm

With congressional approval, a contract was awarded in 1879 to a Trenton, New Jersey firm to fabricate the iron structure. Within 13 months, the tower was manufactured, put together at the factory to insure it met design specifications, shipped to Key West, transshipped to the construction site on nearby Looe Key and erected on American Shoal. Cost: $125,000. The lighthouse, almost a duplicate of Fowey Rocks, is a brown disc and screw pile tower with an octagonal, pyramidal shape. It has a white central tubular stairwell. The former keeper's house, a brown octagonal structure, rests on a platform about 40 feet above the water.

When activated, American Shoal's optic was a revolving bivalve first-order Fresnel lens whose 24 flash panels produced one flash every five seconds. This lens was removed when the light was automated. The optic has been solar charged since 1963.

OWNER. U.S. Coast Guard.
PRESERVATION. Not listed in the National Register of Historic Places.

SAND KEY

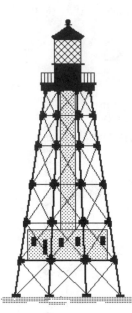

TO SAND KEY BY BOAT. This skeletal light tower is located on Sand Key about 8.5 miles south southwest of Key West. It is visible distantly from Key West's Mallory Square wharf. There are many charter boats available in Key West for a trip to the lighthouse. For a list charter boat services and fees:

- Key West Chamber of Commerce, 402 Wall Street, Key West, FL 33040.

Phone (305) 294-2587. In USA toll-free (800) 527-8539.

BY AIR. See the Key West map on page 24 for the location of the Key West International Airport.

The Island City Flying Service offers a 30 to 40-minute reef sightseeing tours originating from the Key West International Airport. The flight takes the passenger out to Sand Key, circles westward for a short distance into the Gulf of Mexico and then returns to the airport.

FARES. One round trip fare for three passengers. Charter flights are also available at an hourly rate.

- Island City Flying Service, Key West International Airport, 3471 South Roosevelt Boulevard, Key West, FL 33040.

Phone (305) 296-5422.

SAND KEY LIGHTHOUSE.

CHARACTERISTIC: Group flashing white 15s (4 red sectors)
HAW: 105'   **RANGES**: White 13; red 8 nm

The first lighthouse on Sand Key was completed in 1826 and lighted on April 15, 1827. The revolving optic was powered by 14 oil lamps, each fitted with a 21-inch reflector. With the beacon some 70 feet above the water, its beam could be seen out to a distance of 20 nautical miles. The brick tower (65 feet from base to optic) withstood many hurricanes, including the recorded storms of 1835, 1841 and 1842. On October 10, 1846 a devastating hurricane swept across the small island, leveling the lighthouse.

Congress appropriated funds for a new lighthouse in 1847, but construction was delayed when Washington forced Stephen Pleasonton's controversial Lighthouse Service to suspend operations until its demise in 1852. Although a lightship was assigned to mark the reef, she proved to be a poor substitute for the destroyed lighthouse. Many ships were reported to have been wrecked during her tenure on station.

In 1852 a contract was signed with the John F. Riley Iron Works, a Charleston, South Carolina firm, to manufacture the tower designed by I. W. P. Lewis. Just after the pilings had been set, construction of the tower ceased for lack of funds. In March 1852, as he was finishing the task of overseeing the building the Carysfort Reef Lighthouse, George G. Meade was ordered to supervise the construction of Sand Key. By the end of 1852, money and laborers became available to continue the project.

This screw pile lighthouse is of the same design and construction as the other primary reef lights, but with two exceptions. Its shape is square, vice octagonal, and there are 12 supporting piles bored into the reef. As in the construction of the other primary reef lighthouses, the peripheral piles (12 inches in diameter) were passed through wrought iron discs anchored to concrete foundations. Then, the eight-inch diameter iron piles were booted with drilling bits and bored 10 feet into the compacted coral and sand reef. The skeletal tower is composed of slanting cast-iron pipe columns with supporting wrought-iron tension and compression members. The overall height of the structure is 132 feet. The tower tapers from a 50-foot square at its foundation to a 19-foot square cast-iron deck that supports the circular watchroom and lantern.

With Meade's penchant for details the keeper's house turned out to be one of the better equipped and more comfortable keepers' quarters on the Florida Reef. The central column contains a spiral stairway (17 feet in diameter) that extends from the quarters deck to the circular watchroom on the observation deck. A ladder provides access to the circular lantern. The lantern is enclosed with triangular (plate glass) storm panes arranged in three tiers.

SAND KEY

The light was reestablished on July 20, 1853, using a fixed first-order classical lens powered by a whale oil-fed lamp. In 1931 the optic's power source was converted to acetylene gas, and with the addition of a double flasher its characteristic changed to two flashes every 10 seconds. The Fresnel lens was removed when the light was automated in 1941. Before its destruction, the lantern held a 300-watt solar system powering a high-intensity xenon lamp that did not require magnification.

OWNER. U.S. Coast Guard.

PRESERVATION. Listed in the National Register of Historic Places.

Although this historic lighthouse bears the scars of many hurricanes with at least one packing 150 mile-an-hour winds, it was a raging fire that almost destroyed it on November 12, 1989. The fire started in the unoccupied keepers' quarters among flammable materials stored there by the contractor refurbishing the compartment. Flames and heat spread rapidly up through the central stairway tube where the heat of the fire destroyed the optic and lantern. The tube collapsed through the living quarters, leaving a badly damaged superstructure.

After a substitute optic was placed on a temporary structure some 200 yards away, local preservationist groups urged the Coast Guard to restore the tower to its original condition. In 1991, after a structural survey determined the tower to be repairable, the Coast Guard announced its intention to restore the lighthouse at a cost of about $500,000. In early 1996 the contractor stopped work on the tower due to severe weather. He resumed work in June. The project was completed in 1997 with the laying of a lantern floor and the installation of a $10,000 state-of-the-art modern optic.

Key West Lighthouse

KEY WEST
GARDEN KEY - DRY TORTUGAS

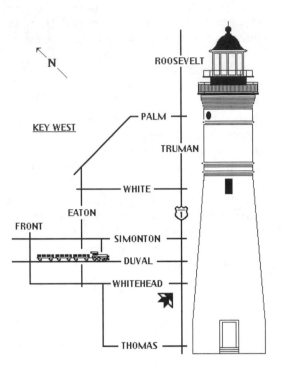

THE ISLAND. Upon leaving Stock Island (MM 4.0), bear right into North Roosevelt Boulevard. Follow it and connecting Truman Avenue across Whitehead Street and turn right into a small parking lot (free) behind the compound.

In 1815 Juan Pablo Salas was presented Cay Hueso (Bone Key) by the governor of Spain's Florida Territory for his valued military service. In 1821, following the end of Spanish rule in Florida, Senor Salas sold the island not once, but twice, and departed for Havana. The second sale to John Simonton for $2,000 was upheld, since Salas did not personally sign the first contract. With the island in the hands of an American, the Federal Government, in response to lobbying efforts of Simonton and friends, decided to formally claim the island. They sent Lieutenant Matthew C. Perry to plant the flag in 1822.

Meanwhile, unwarned ships were being wrecked all along the Florida Keys and, in turn, salvage operations mushroomed. It was a bustling, expanding and profitable business. In 1825, in order to stop salvaged goods from being shipped to and sold in the Bahamas and Cuba, Washington outlawed the transfer of wreckers' loot to foreign ports. That did it. Key West, already a big flea market for salvaged cargoes, became the auction house for such materials.

By 1836 many of the Bahamian wreckers moved wives, kids and entire houses from their home islands to Key West. While all this activity was financially fine for the wreckers, the suffering ship owners pressed Washington to build more lighthouses along the reef and out into the Gulf of Mexico. The wrecking business peaked between 1850 and 1860. Thereafter, as the number of lighthouses and other aids to navigation increased, the wrecking business proportionately waned. Today's salvage operations center around sunken treasures. [1]

KEY WEST LIGHTHOUSE MUSEUM. The museum is located in the former keeper's bungalow constructed in 1887. It holds exhibits of furniture of the 1890s Key lighthouses, Key West's maritime history, archaeological artifacts found buried on the station and a fourth-order bullseye lens on loan from Chicago's Museum of Science and Industry.

Inside the compound in a separate building (entrance is through the gift shop) stands the towering first-order Fresnel lens last active in the Sombrero Key Lighthouse. Visitors may climb the tower's 88 steps to the service balcony and another ten into the lantern. From the gallery there is a panoramic view of Key West, the Gulf of Mexico and the Florida Strait.

OPEN. All year, daily 9:30 to 5:00. Closed December 25.
ADMISSION FEES. Children free to age 7. Discount for children 7-12.
- Key West Lighthouse Museum, 938 Whitehead Street, Key West, FL 33040.
Phone (305) 294-0012.
Website: http://www.kwahs.com/lighthouse.html

---

1. It should be pointed out that the salvaging work of wreckers or mooncussers (a moonlit night was bad for salvaging) was not confined to Key West, It flourished all along the Atlantic Coast. On North Carolina's Outer Banks, for example, Nags Head received its name from wreckers who led ponies with lanterns tied to their necks around buildings to create the flashing light of a coastal lighthouse. Ship captains would steer clear of this false warning and end up bashed on a reef. Block Islanders used the same ruse to lure ships by tying lanterns on poles or on cows' tails and marching themselves or their animals around a shed or building.

KEY WEST, GARDEN KEY & DRY TORTUGAS

KEY WEST LIGHTHOUSE (WHITEHEAD POINT).

The first lighthouse on Key West was constructed in 1825 on what was then known as Whitehead Point. According to the 1838, 1845 and 1848 Lists of Lighthouses, the 65-foot tall tower's lantern held a fixed optic consisting of 15 lamps, each backed by a 15-inch reflector. With its beacon 83 feet above the sea the light could be seen out to a distance of 17 nautical miles. This lighthouse was destroyed on October 10, 1846 by a hurricane that also destroyed the old Sand Key tower and practically leveled Key West.

On March 3, 1847, Congress appropriated $12,000 for the construction of the present lighthouse farther inland. The tower's brick walls are four and one-half feet thick at its base, tapering to two and one-half feet at the lantern's deck. The spiral stairway's steps are cast-iron wedges welded to wall studs and to a cast-iron centerpost. The new light was reestablished on January 15, 1848.

On March 3, 1893, Congress reaffirmed previous appropriations by earmarking $4,500 for a 20-foot increase in the height of the tower. The project, completed in 1894, was necessary to raise the optic above trees that were masking its light on the northwest. At the same time, the watchroom section was enlarged to provide a service gallery. The overall height of the lighthouse is now 86 feet. [2]

In 1858 Key West's old lighting apparatus, consisting of 15 oil-burning lamps with 15-inch reflectors, was removed. In 1872 the lighthouse received a new lantern in order to accommodate a single oil-fed hydraulic lamp and a Henri LePaute third-order Fresnel lens. On February 5, 1895, the light's characteristic was changed to fixed white with three red sectors. In 1908 the Fresnel lens was given an incandescent oil vapor lamp. Then on January 1, 1915, Key West became one of the first of America's lighthouses to have an acetylene gas lamp. That power system was the only one available to establish a flashing light characteristic without removing or altering the 1873 third-order lens. That event, by the way, retired the resident keepers because the system's automatic light switch eliminated the need to manually turn the light on and off. Key West was electrified in 1933. The third-order optic was decommisioned as an official aid on December 1, 1969.

Although it was relighted on July 15, 1972, the Seventh Coast Guard District states that the light has not been certified as a private aid.

OWNER. Leased to Monroe County in 1966. Subleased in 1972 to the Key West Art and Historical Society, 3501 Roosevelt Boulevard, Key West, FL 33040. Phone: (305) 296-3913.

Website: http://www.kwahs.com/

PRESERVATION. Listed in the National Register of Historic Places as part of the Key West Historic District.

In 1873, after years of "failing health," the lighthouse was rejuvenated with the installation of a new cast-iron lantern with copper dome and ventilator ball. The lantern's glass panes were separated by narrower vertical holding dividers (mullions). In 1899 the lighthouse was scrubbed down and repainted.

By the mid-1980s the light tower was in need of a major overhauling. Work on the tower began in October 1988. At a cost of $217,000, funded by the Monroe County Tourist Development Council, the National Park Service's Bicentennial Lighthouse Fund and private donors, the tower's old paint was removed, the masonry walls were repaired and repainted in the original black and white daymark colors. For its protection from weather phenomena and vandalism, the lens and its photoelectrically controlled halide lamp are now surrounded by a laminated glass screen. At the same time, all of the lantern's storm panes were reglazed with glass reinforced with wire. After the expenditure of $265,000 during the first restorative phase, the lighthouse was reopened to the public on its 150th birthday - February 4, 1989.

The Key West Art and Historical Society, with an additional grant of $222,000 from Florida's Division of Historical Resources, restored the keepers' dwelling (complete with 1889-1914 period furnishings), the main walkway, privy, oil house and cistern. That project was completed in November 1990.

TO FORT JEFFERSON. The Dry Tortugas National Park, encompasses 64,700 acres (40 acres of dry land) seven islands, including Garden Key (Fort Jefferson and lighthouse) and Loggerhead Key (Dry Tortugas Lighthouse).

BY FERRY. The narrated cruise aboard the 100-foot Lydia yacht *Yankee Freedom* (two lower enclosed air-conditioned decks; plus sundeck) leaves Key West and sails past the Boca Grande National Bird Sanctuary, Marquessas Key and across Rebecca Channel to Garden Key.

A complimentary breakfast is served. Food, beverages (including full bar), picnic lunches and snorkeling equipment rentals and fresh water showers available on board. Only campers may board with coolers.

---

2. Reports on the height of the Key West Lighthouse are a bit confusing. In 1838 the Lighthouse Service reported that the structure was 65 feet tall. Then in 1872 the Lighthouse Board reported that the tower had been raised five feet. In 1891 the Board recommended that the 60-foot tall lighthouse be raised 20 feet and the watchroom heightened by three feet.

AMERICA'S ATLANTIC COAST LIGHTHOUSES - FLORIDA

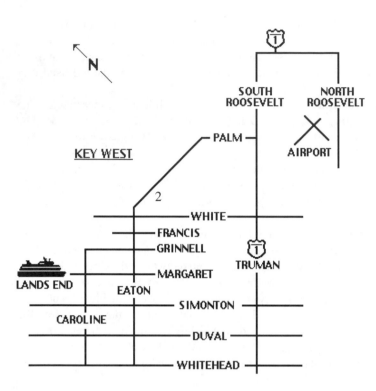

See also the map on the next page.

SCHEDULE.
End of October to May, Mondays through Saturdays at 8. Boarding at 7:30. Returns 6:30 to 7.

May to end of October (low season) sailing days varied.

FARES. Fares are subject to fuel charges. Passenger discounts for seniors 62+ and children 16 and younger. Camper fares higher. Credit cards accepted.

- Dry Tortugas & Fort Jefferson Ferry from Key West, PO Box 5903, Key West, FL 33040.

Phone (305) 294-7009. In USA toll-free (800) 634-0939.

Website: http://www.fastcatferry.com/

BY AIR. See also the map on the next page.

There are two seaplane companies that service Fort Jefferson. Both take the same route. The 70-mile trip takes about 40 minutes, permitting a 2-hour layover before heading back to Key West.

The low-level flight over the Gulf keys to the Dry Tortugas is quite an experience. The waters are clear and blue. Sharks, large loggerhead turtles, manta rays and porpoise are easily seen.

Bird watchers can spot the magnificent frigate bird on Frigate Island and other birds on the wing or resting on shoals and channel markers. The flights pass over the wrecks of Spanish galleons and Mel Fisher's "Treasure Salvors" salvage site. As the aircraft approaches Garden Key, there is the fascinating panorama of Fort Jefferson as it looms into view. The Dry Tortugas Lighthouse on nearby Loggerhead Key is visible during the planes' landing pattern. The return flights are flown at a higher altitude to provide a wider view of the area.

While at the fort be sure to take the self-guided 40-minute tour that provides first an audio/slide presentation and then a detailed walk around the fort. Garden Key's swimming beach is of brilliant white coral sand and there is some fantastic snorkeling only 60 yards offshore in five feet of water. Call ahead for flight availability, minimum passenger load, departure times, equipment carry-on restrictions and cancellation policies.

- Key West Air Service, 5603 West Junior College Road, Key West, FL 33040.
  Phone (305) 294-6978. In USA toll-free (888) 359-3678. Fax (305) 292-5205.

FARES. Half-day, full day and camper fares. Minimum of three passengers. Discounts for seniors 62+, children 7-12 and 2-6. Under 2 free. Credit cards accepted.
- Seaplanes of Key West, Key West International Airport, 3471 South Roosevelt Boulevard, Key West, FL 33040.
  Phone (305) 294-0709. In USA toll-free (800) 950-2359.

FORT JEFFERSON.[3] Garden Key, since the 1600s, was a favorite haunt for freebooters, scum and cutthroats, who plied their trade in the Gulf, among the Keys and off Cuba. After Florida's annexation in 1821, the Federal Government decided to rid the area of the buccaneers. Once a naval presence had been established in Key West, Garden Key and the other Tortugas islands were liberated. Fort Jefferson was the largest link in a chain of American coastal fortifications built from Maine to Texas in the 1800s.

---

3. Since 1986, sonic booms created by fighter aircraft have caused large sections of the fort's weakened brick walls to peel off and drop into its moat. Although the National Park Service has requested relief, the flights have continued. Meanwhile, certain damaged sections may be closed to visitors.

KEY WEST, GARDEN KEY & DRY TORTUGAS

FORT JEFFERSON.[3] Garden Key, since the 1600s, was a favorite haunt for freebooters, scum and cutthroats, who plied their trade in the Gulf, among the Keys and off Cuba. After Florida's annexation in 1821, the Federal Government decided to rid the area of the buccaneers. Once a naval presence had been established in Key West, Garden Key and the other Tortugas islands were liberated. Fort Jefferson was the largest link in a chain of American coastal fortifications built from Maine to Texas in the 1800s.

Begun in 1846 with slave labor and although worked on for some 30 years, this massive, hexagonal citadel was never completed. With its 8-foot thick brick walls rising 50 feet above the key, the "Gibraltar of the Gulf" was built to hold 450 25-ton smooth bore Rodman cannons on three levels with sufficient interior space and facilities to house a 1,500-man garrison. The largest of the Rodmans, a 20-inch caliber monster weighing more than 57 tons was capable of belching a 1,000-pound cannonball out to a distance of more than five miles.

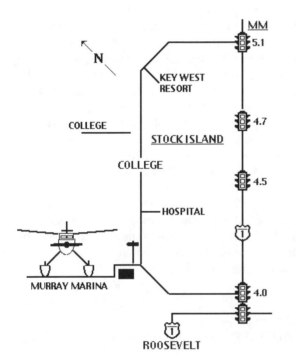

By 1861 most of the slaves had been replaced by Union Army deserters and Confederate war prisoners. Fort Jefferson's most famous prisoner was Samuel Mudd, who innocently set the broken leg of John Wilkes Booth, President Abraham Lincoln's assassin. Dr. Mudd spent the first two years of his incarceration in chains in a dark and stinking cell. He was pardoned in 1869 after he volunteered his medical services to fight a yellow fever epidemic. His cell is open to visitors.

- Dry Tortugas National Park, PO Box 6208, Key West, FL 33041
Phone (305) 242-7700 (8 to 4).
Website: http://www.nps.gov/drto/
Email: EVER_Reception_Desk@nps.gov

---

3. Since 1986, sonic booms created by fighter aircraft have caused large sections of the fort's weakened brick walls to peel off and drop into its moat. Although the National Park Service has requested relief, the flights have continued. Meanwhile, certain damaged sections may be closed to visitors.

GARDEN KEY LIGHTHOUSE (FORT JEFFERSON; TORTUGAS HARBOR).

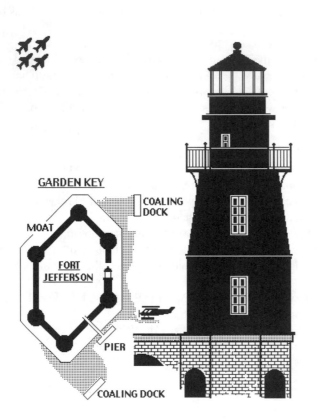

The first Garden Key Lighthouse was built in 1825 to the east of Garden Key on land that was then known as Bush Key and later became Fort Jefferson's parade ground. The tower was of brick construction and 75 feet tall. Its lantern held a lighting apparatus that produced a fixed white light from 17 oil-burning lamps, each with a 21-inch reflector. The optic was 70 feet above sea level and its range was 16 nautical miles.

In 1874, after a damaging hurricane in October 1873 and another fever outbreak, the U.S. Army withdrew its forces. The hurricane also damaged the lighthouse, requiring its beacon to be transferred to a cast-iron pole and downgraded to a fourth class harbor light. Meanwhile, the U.S. Navy continued to use the surrounding waters as an anchorage. In support of naval operations, the present 37-foot tall cast-iron lighthouse was built in 1876 atop the fort's southeast parapet. Its light was reestablished on April 5, 1876.

The hexagonal lighthouse and its kerosene-powered fourth-order Fresnel lens (1858) were decommissioned in 1912. In recognition of the fort's historic importance, the National Park Service turns on the lighthouse's small light each evening. The foundation outlines of the old lighthouse and its keeper's quarters can still be seen on the parade ground.

OWNER. National Park Service. Managed by the Dry Tortugas National Park.

PRESERVATION. Listed (1971) in the National Register of Historic Places as part of Fort Jefferson National Monument.

DRY TORTUGAS LIGHTHOUSE (LOGGERHEAD KEY)
CHARACTERISTIC: Flashing white 20s
HAW: 151' **RANGE**: 24 nm

The first light tower on Loggerhead Key, 2.6 miles west of Garden Key, was completed in 1826 and toppled by a hurricane in 1856.

The 157-foot tall brick structure was set on a framework of wood or grillage. (For an explanation of this technique see the CAPE HATTERAS and CURRITUCK BEACH chapters.) The tower's diameter at its base is 23 feet, tapering to a topside diameter of 13.5 feet. Inside the ends of the stairway's 226 granite steps are imbedded in the interior wall and a central brick column.

Badly damaged by hurricanes in October 1873 and September 1875, the tower's top nine feet were completely rebuilt. The excellence of this restoration work cancelled plans to build a new tower. It is a conical brick tower with its top half painted black and the lower half white.

The second and present lighthouse was first lighted on July 1, 1858. Its lantern held a second-order bivalve Fresnel lens, consisting of two 160-degree panels placed back to back and about 14 inches apart.

In August 1925, Dry Tortugas' status was changed from a watched to an unmanned aid. At the same time, the kerosene-powered optic was refitted with an automated acetylene lamp.

The classical lens was removed when the light was automated in 1986.

OWNER. U.S. Coast Guard.
PRESERVATION. Not listed in the National Register of Historic Places.

REBECCA SHOAL LIGHTHOUSE (destroyed).

Although started in 1854, weather, storms and rough seas delayed work on a skeleton tower that was to be used as an unlighted daybeacon. In 1858 a storm tore out all the construction work that had been accomplished.

Until the lighthouse was finished the channel was marked by a buoy, poles and a 75-foot tall skeletal tower. Before leaving Florida, George G. Meade had prepared a design for a lighthouse on Rebecca Key. Work on the structure began in 1858 but was almost continuously disrupted by tropical storms and hurricanes. The lighthouse, finally completed in 1886, was a 2 1/2-story house with window dormers, resting on a large square platform supported by driven cast-iron pilings. The lantern rested on the roof and was surrounded by a balustraded miradore, or widow's walk.

The aid's oil-powered fourth-order Fresnel optic was established on November 1, 1886. In August 1925 the Bureau of Lighthouses reported that Rebecca Shoals' illuminant had been changed from kerosene to acetylene, its light automated and the watch crew removed.

Today the lighthouse is gone, the victim of a 1953 hurricane. It has been replaced by a white square skeletal tower resting on a platform supported by pilings. Its lighted beacon marks the main channel between the Gulf of Mexico and the Florida Strait. The present aid is a familiar sight to crews participating in the Southern Ocean Racing Conference's annual 403-mile race from St. Petersburg to Fort Lauderdale as they head east on their inbound run to the finish line at the Port Everglades Channel off Fort Lauderdale.

HILLSBORO INLET

TO POMPANO BEACH. The lighthouse stands on three acres of land that can be reached only by crossing the restricted entry Hillsboro Country Club. The best place from which to view and photograph the lighthouse is on the beach south of the inlet. Public access to the beach is via NE16th Street.

NE 16th is 0.1 mile north of FL 844 (NE 14th Street) and 4.4 miles south of FL 810 (Hillsboro Boulevard).

From NE 16th Street's metered (one free handicapped space) parking lot, there is about a half-mile walk to the inlet.

If a parking space can be found on the one-way road, which passes under the drawbridge, the lighthouse can be viewed and photographed from the bridge.

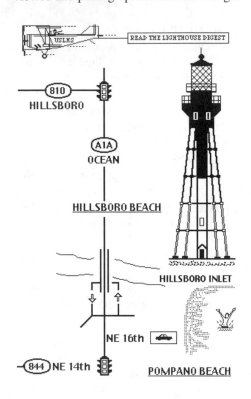

HILLSBORO INLET LIGHTHOUSE. (BIG DIAMOND)
CHARACTERISTIC: Flashing white 20s
HAW: 136' **RANGE**: 28 nm

The Hillsboro Inlet Lighthouse is an octagonal, pyramidal and skeletal cast-iron structure built in Chicago. Before it reached Florida, the tower was assembled as an exhibit at the St. Louis 1904 Exposition. After the fair closed, it was dismantled and shipped to Pompano Beach.

Reconstruction of the lighthouse and the building of a one-story wood framed keeper's house were completed in 1907. The 132-foot tall tower's foundation consists of eight peripheral screwpiles anchored in bedrock and at ground level, tied to the central tubular pile. The central cylinder houses the 175-step spiral stairway leading to the watchroom.

The station still retains several buildings used by former Lighthouse Bureau and Coast Guard personnel until the light was automated in 1974. The 1907 keeper's residence is now occupied by a caretaker. Other structures, all built in 1942, include a three-story building that once housed offices, living quarters, a mess and recreational facilities for assigned Coast Guard personnel, a garage and a generator shed.

In 1907 the lantern was fitted with a $90,000 kerosene-powered Fresnel first-order lens. The rotating optic showed a flash every 10 seconds. In November 1931, the Lighthouse Bureau reported that with the electrification the optic's intensity had been increased from 630,000 to 5.5 million candlepower. At the same time, a new motor was installed to slow the bivalve lens to one rotation every 40 seconds, producing a characteristic of one flash every 20 seconds.

In 1966 a more efficient electric lamp was installed That modification again increased the optic's luminous intensity and extended its range to 28 nautical miles. In 1992 the rotating mechanism failed and the Coast Guard decided not to repair it. Instead of removing the lens, the Coast Guard installed a modern plastic lens on the outside of the lantern. Then in 1996, because of the health hazard to maintenance crews, the mercury float was removed. In 1997 the Coast Guard decided it was time to remove the classic lens and put the operating optic inside the lantern. The service suggested it be placed on public display in a museum. That idea was challenged by municipalities Lighthouse Point, Pompano Beach and Fort Lauderdale, who advocated leaving the historic lens in the lighthouse.

One of the goals of the nonprofit Hillsboro Lighthouse Preservation Society has been the restoration and repair of the Hillsboro Light's original Fresnel lens and its reactivation in the lighthouse. The group helped convince the Coast Guard to renovate the lens and lighthouse at a cost of $143,000 in 1998. On January 28,1999, the restored lens was illuminated as hundreds watched. Unfortunately there was a problem with the ball bearing assembly for rotating the lens, which replaced the earlier mercury float. The external light had to be reactivated while the problem was solved. A new bearing assembly was constructed and installed, and the light was successfully put back into operation at a ceremony on August 18, 2000.

- Hillsboro Lighthouse Preservation Society, 1819 N.E. 24th Street, Lighthouse Point, FL 33064.
Phone: (954) 942-7263 or (954) 781-7458.
Website: http://www.castlesbythesea.com/lighthou.htm

OWNER. U.S. Coast Guard.
PRESERVATION. Listed in the National Register of Historic Places.

JUPITER INLET

TO JUPITER. The lighthouse is located within Jupiter Lighthouse Park. Its entrance, marked with a sign, is off CR 707 (Beach Road). CR 707 is 1.3 miles north of FL 706 (Indiantown Road) and 0.4 mile south of the Tequesta & Waterway intersection. Free admission and parking.

FLORIDA HISTORY CENTER & MUSEUM. This complex, located in Burt Reynolds Park south of the US 1 & FL A1A junction in Jupiter, includes the museum, the DuBois Pioneer Home (1886) in nearby DuBois Park, an outdoor Seminole Living History Village, a turn-of-the-century Florida "cracker" house. The museum is dedicated to the preservation, conservation and education about Florida history and restoration of historic structures and local artifacts. Permanent and temporary exhibits, lecture presentations and educational programs are available throughout the year.

CENTER & MUSEUM OPEN. All year, Tuesdays through Fridays 10 to 5. Closed on national holidays.

TOWER OPEN. All year, Sundays through Wednesdays 10 to 4 . Lease stipulations require that climbers sign a liability waiver. Children must be at least 48 inches tall. Visitors are allowed no more than 15 minutes in the lantern room. There is a paved, gradually sloping walkway up to a viewing area below the lighthouse. High riser steps lead up to the entrance.

ADMISSION FEES. Museum discounts for seniors 55+ and children 6-18; free for members. A nominal donation requested for the lighthouse tour. No discounts.

- Florida History Center and Museum, 805 North US Highway One, Jupiter, FL 33477.

Phone: Center & Museum (561) 747-6639. Lighthouse (561) 747-8380. Fax (561) 575-3292.

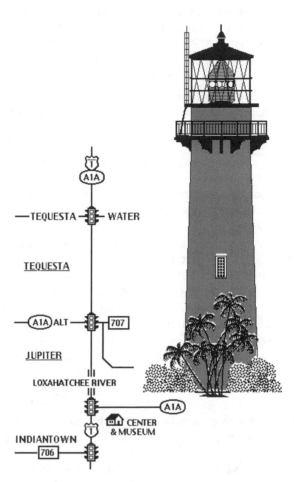

JUPITER INLET LIGHTHOUSE.
CHARACTERISTIC: Group flashing white 30s
HAW: 146' **RANGE**: 25 nm

On January 30, 1852, the Lighthouse Service recommended that a first class light with a focal plane 150 feet above the sea be established near Jupiter. The change of command from Stephen Pleasonton to the Lighthouse Board on October 9, 1852, delayed the submission of a funding request until March 3, 1853. Congress appropriated $35,000 for a lighthouse on a 61-acre portion of the Fort Jupiter reservation, a military camp that had been established during the Seminole War period.

Of note is the fact that the opposing generals during the Gettysburg Campaign in 1863 strode across Florida's lighthouse history. Captain Robert E. Lee was a member of the original survey team for the light station, and Lieutenant George G. Meade was one of the tower's designers and its construction supervisor. Although Lt. Meade, then chief of administrative affairs of the Seventh Lighthouse District, submitted the design of the lighthouse to the Lighthouse Board, his subordinate, John W. Nystrem, was the chief architect responsible for the final design and blueprint drawings. Construction arrangements were supervised by Meade until May 31, 1856, when his singular job with the Seventh District ended and he was reappointed the administrative chief for both the Seventh and Fourth Lighthouse Districts. This dual role required Meade's presence in Philadelphia. By mid-1855 construction materials had been manufactured and readied for shipment. With Jupiter Inlet sanded shut and closed to shipping, barges from the Indian River Inlet had to be sent down the Indian River and through the Jupiter Narrows, a 35-mile route that involved shallow water lightering across 21-inch depths and overland portage of 500 tons of construction materials.

In 1856 work on the tower ceased after surveyors over at Fort Myers trespassed on Seminole Chief Billy Bowlegs' property, destroyed his garden and banana grove and tore down his home. A Seminole retaliatory attack ignited the Third Seminole War. Construction resumed in 1858. In 1859 the heat and humidity of summer and insect molestation further delayed the completion of the structure. By the time the 105-foot brick tower was completed and its beacon placed in operation, the cost of the project had risen to nearly $61,000. The lighthouse is built on a 46-foot tall knoll with the top six feet consisting of oyster shells.

The Jupiter Inlet tower is a conical red brick (now painted red) structure that has walls that taper in thickness from 31.5 inches at its base to 18 inches at the watchroom deck. The main entrance is outlined in brick with a semicircular arch showing a radiating wedge (voussoir) of brick. The lantern is enclosed with glass storm panes sectioned in three tiers.

Jupiter Inlet's presently active first-order Fresnel optic was commissioned on July 10, 1860. In August 1861, a group of armed Jupiter Inlet men (one of whom was an assistant keeper) either decided or were ordered to darken the light to deny its use by Union naval ships and to allow the South's blockade runners to operate in unlighted waters. They arrived at the lighthouse and ordered the keeper to turn off the light. The keeper refused. The posse then went to work removing the lamp and first-order Fresnel lens and hiding them in Jupiter Creek west of the lighthouse. With this accomplished, the raiding party headed for Cape Florida to put that beacon out of commission. The lens' parts were later recovered and the beacon was reactivated on June 28, 1866. Twenty years later, when the illuminant was changed over to kerosene, the lantern received six new plate glass storm panes.

In September 1928, several months after an automated electric arc light replaced the kerosene-fed lamp and its clockwork powered rotation system removed, a raging hurricane hit the area. With an electrical outage, the keeper was unable to start his emergency generator. With his father suffering from a badly infected hand, the keeper's 16-year old son volunteered to go aloft with the old kerosene lamp. There, the lad kept the light burning and, by counting the time interval of rotation, moved the lens by hand. For four hours, while the young man worked the lens, the hurricane swayed the tower, blew out mortar between the rows of bricks and caused the Fresnel lens' bullseye to explode. For two more days, until a neighbor brought his generator to the site, the keeper's family, including his wife, took turns rotating the lens. After the storm, the keeper gathered up as many of the pieces of shattered French-made prisms as he could find and shipped them off to Charleston, South Carolina. There they were reassembled, cemented and then molded together with supporting wire. The crisscross patchwork is still visible on Jupiter Inlet's working first-order lens.

The optic in operation today is the original lens powered by a 1,000-watt quartz-iodine bulb.

OWNER. U.S. Coast Guard. In the mid-1970s, the lighthouse was leased to the Loxahatchee Historical Society. The lease was transferred in 1994 to the Florida History Center and Museum.

PRESERVATION. Listed in the National Register of Historic Places. In 1995 the Florida's legislature appropriated $137,000 as the state's contribution to a matching federal grant of $800,000 to do restorative work on the light tower. Later the state's Bureau of Historical Preservation provided a grant of $48,000 for the restoration. The contract was signed in March 1996.

On April 28, 2000, a relighting ceremony was held after the completion of the restoration. The extensive restoration to the interior of the tower brought the structure back to its condition in the period of the mid to late 1800s. The lens was also refurbished under the jurisdiction of the United States Coast Guard.

CAPE CANAVERAL

VIEWING THE LIGHTHOUSE. The lighthouse is located inside the Cape Canaveral Air Force Station adjacent to the J. F. Kennedy Space Center. Unfortunately, a previous arrangement whereby the public could contact the Coast Guard Station Port Canaveral for permission to enter the base to visit the lighthouse has been scrubbed.

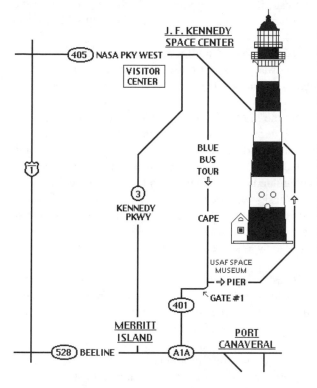

KENNEDY SPACE CENTER. There is a fleeting view of the lighthouse while aboard one of two bus tours originating at the Kennedy Space Center's Visitor Center located on FL 405 (NASA Parkway West) about 7 miles east of US 1 and 11 miles east of I-95. If traveling north on FL A1A take FL 3 (Kennedy Parkway South) to the Visitor Center. The Blue Tour is the bus ride to take to view the lighthouse. It travels through the Cape Canaveral Air Force Station with its historic rocket control facilities and launch sites and stops briefly at the Air Force Space Museum. Bus tickets should be purchased upon arrival, because they are preassigned departures and show times.

The bus passes, but does not stop at the lighthouse. For the best view sit on the left side of the bus. The driver, if informed of your interest in photographing the lighthouse, might obligingly slow the bus to permit some quick camera shots of the tower.

OPEN. All year, daily 9 to dusk (except Christmas and launch days).

BUS TOURS. Depart daily every 15 minutes 9:30 until 2 hours before dusk.

FREE ADMISSION. Fees for tours and IMAX theater.
-Visitors Center, Kennedy Space Center, FL 32899. Phone (407) 452-2121. Launch information (407) 867-4636.
Website: http://www.kennedyspacecenter.com/

IN THE CITY OF CAPE CANAVERAL. Distant sightings are possible from Cape Canaveral's beach access stiles located at the ends of several avenues with presidential names, beginning with Washington (south) to Polk (north). The avenues are all east of FL A1A (Ridgewood Avenue).

U.S. AIR FORCE SPACE MUSEUM. The lighthouse cannot be seen from the grounds of the museum, and visitors are not allowed to walk or drive to the lighthouse while visiting the museum. Drive to Gate #1 and the security guard will issue a pass to the museum. Do not attempt to drive to the lighthouse.

OPEN. For drive-ins all year, weekends only 10 to 4. For blue bus tours all year, daily 10 to 2.
Closed during launch periods.

FREE ADMISSION.
- U.S. Air Force Space Museum, 45th SPW/PA, Patrick AFB, FL 32925.
Phone (407) 853-3245.

CAPE CANAVERAL LIGHTHOUSE.
CHARACTERISTIC: Group flashing white 20s
HAW: 137' **RANGE**: 24 nm
The construction of the first Cape Canaveral lighthouse began in 1843 and was completed in 1847. The light was first lighted on January 27, 1848. The tower was a 60-foot tall brick structure with a cast-iron lantern. Its lighting apparatus consisted of 15 whale oil lamps each backed with a 21-inch reflector. With the lantern's focal plane 65 feet above the sea (55 feet from base to optic), the revolving light could be seen 16 nautical miles at sea. In 1893 the Lighthouse Service reported that "The old brick tower, which was built in 1847, was blown up with dynamite to be used in making concrete for the foundation of the tower at the new site." Today, the old tower's circular red brick and mortar base (with protruding iron rods) lies almost hidden in the nearby undergrowth.

On September 12, 1862, Mills Burnham, the light's keeper since 1853, in a letter addressed to the Confederate States of America's Treasury Secretary in Richmond reported that he had cached "...200 gallons of sperm oil, the reflectors fifteen in number with all the brushes and cleaning material..." He also stated that the only parts taken to St. Augustine and turned over to Union authorities were "...the lamps and clock..." After the war, Burnham returned the buried equipment to the Federal Government. Because of that act and his past experience, Burnham was reappointed as the light's keeper and continued to serve until his death on April 4, 1885.[1]

There are serious gaps and omissions in Cape Canaveral's recorded history, and because of the lack of historical continuity it may be that the beacon reported lighted on May 10, 1868 was not in the present cast-iron tower. Based on much serious research the following paragraph is a contrarian's scenario of what might have occurred between 1865 and the early 1870s.

In 1865 the Cape Canaveral light was probably reestablished in the old brick tower, using the original multi-lamp optic that Captain Burnham had dug up and returned to the Federal Government. In 1868, in order to accommodate the installation of a newly acquired first-order Fresnel lens, a 145-foot tall wood framed lighthouse was erected. Although there are some references to the wooden tower's short-lived stability due to deterioration by infestation, it is believed the structure was purposely built as a temporary means to keep the cape lighted, while planning and contracting efforts for a new and permanent tower were underway. The development of the design for a cast-iron tower, built of prefabricated curved sections in the form of a truncated cone was developed in the late 1860s by Major George H. Elliot, the Lighthouse Board's Executive Secretary. The first of the coffee pot-styled cast-iron lighthouses, Duxbury Pier, was constructed in Plymouth's harbor in 1871. Then in 1872, South Carolina's Hunting Island was surveyed to find a site for a new light tower. Assuming that Major Elliot would have preferred to be present in the United States when his new and untested design for a towering cast-iron lighthouse went into production, the Lighthouse Board's Engineering Committee probably coordinated its approval and the issuing of production and construction contracts to coincide with Elliot's return from a lighthouse inspection trip to Europe in late 1873. Construction of the new 140-foot tall Hunting Island Lighthouse began in late 1873 and its light established on July 1, 1875. Also, a Lighthouse Board design drawing of August 16, 1876 depicts a proposed cast-iron Dry Tortugas tower showing a more ornate architectural styling similar to the Ponce De Leon Inlet Lighthouse. Finally in 1876, there were at Cape Canaveral several personnel changes (resignations, promotions, and new appointments) among the assistant keepers that suggest keeper Burnham was responding to or preparing for a change in his lightkeeping responsibilities. Consequently, the year of completion of the cast-iron Cape Canaveral tower is believed to have occurred not in 1868, but probably during the 1873-76 period.

Erosion of the lighthouse site began in the early 1880s and by 1886 the sea had encroached to within 70 feet of the tower. In 1892 Congress approved its relocation 1.25 miles inland. The dismantling, transfer and reassembly work began on June 30, 1893. The relocated beacon was relighted on July 25, 1894.

Because passing ships were outlined by its beam, the light was darkened during World War II to deny German submarines a shooting gallery target. Prior to its blackout, however, a ship was torpedoed off the cape. Shades of Key West and Block Island! Her flotsam brought out hordes of wreckers to salvage a shipload of Scotland's finest malt beverage.

Interestingly, the 168-foot tall lighthouse was used as an observation post during the earliest years of America's rocket testing and missions. The gallery was a favorite spot of rocket scientist Werner von Braun during launchings. The lighthouse is equipped not only with an automated seaward beacon, but also radio beacon and other electronic equipment needed to support NASA activities.

Cape Canaveral's first-order Fresnel lens was removed in 1993. It is on display in a specially built building in the Ponce De Leon Inlet Lighthouse compound.

---

1. There have been accusations that the Confederacy ordered all or most of the Fresnel lenses under its control to be destroyed or rendered useless. Contrarily, there are bits and pieces from historical records that support the premise that instead of ordering their destruction, the South followed a policy of saving the classical lenses and optics for reinstallation after having won the War Between the States. Cape Florida's lens was damaged, not destroyed. Jupiter Inlet's lens was cached and later recovered. Although pro-Confederate Irish-Jasper Greens dynamited the Tybee Island tower, the raiders first removed the lens. Cape Hatteras' lens was removed and forwarded to a depot in Tarboro, North Carolina, where it was carefully crated and presumably shipped to a safer holding area. Cape Henry's first-order Fresnel optic was similarly removed unharmed.

CAPE CANAVERAL

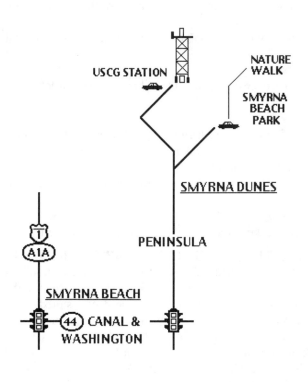

OWNER. U.S. Coast Guard.

At this writing (early 2000), ownership of the lighthouse is in transition from the Coast Guard to the Canaveral Air Force Station. The Air Force hopes to eventually open the tower to the public on occasion.

PRESERVATION. Not listed in the National Register of Historic Places.

In 1996 the Coast Guard gave the tower a complete refurbishing. The $300,000 project included sandblasting (removal of lead based paint) and repainting of the tower, replacing the lantern's roof, installing bullet-proof glass panes and replacing the main service gallery.

TO SMYRNA DUNES ON US 1. See map at left. There is the opportunity to take the short drive to Smyrna Dunes for a spectacular cross-inlet view (via nature boardwalk) of the majestic Ponce De Leon Inlet Lighthouse. The old tower standing in the Coast Guard Station Ponce De Leon Inlet (open to the public) once held the Ponce De Leon Inlet beacon.

OPEN. All year, daily sunrise to sunset.
FREE ADMISSION.

Cape Canaveral Lighthouse

PONCE DE LEON INLET

TO PONCE INLET. In Port Orange, south of Daytona Beach:

-> East on Dunlawton Avenue and drive over the high-rise bridge crossing the Halifax River. At the second traffic light, you will see the Atlantic Ocean ahead.

-> Turn right (south) on Atlantic Avenue and continue through the village of Wilbur-by-the-Sea and four additional miles to a four-way stop sign.

-> Turn right (west) on Beach Street. Go to the next four-way stop.

-> Turn left (south) on Peninsula Drive. In two blocks you will see the entrance to the lighthouse on your left.

From Interstate I-95 North or South:

-> Exit from I-95 at Port Orange, Route 421 (exit no. 85, south of Daytona Beach), and go east on Dunlawton Avenue.

-> Continue on Dunlawton Avenue through the intersection with U.S. Route 1 and over the high-rise bridge crossing the Halifax River. At the second traffic light, you will see the Atlantic Ocean ahead.

-> Turn right (south) on Atlantic Avenue and continue through the village of Wilbur-by-the-Sea and four additional miles to a four-way stop sign.

-> Turn right (west) on Beach Street. Go to the next four-way stop.

-> Turn left (south) on Peninsula Drive. In two blocks you will see the entrance to the lighthouse on your left.

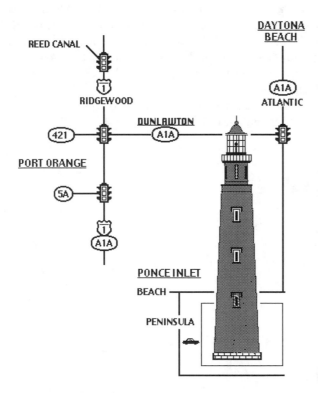

LIGHTHOUSE MUSEUM COMPLEX. In 1972 the Ponce de Leon Inlet Lighthouse Preservation Association was incorporated to aid in restoring the light station. Besides the lighthouse, the head keeper's dwelling has been restored and is now the Museum of the Sea, which features ship navigation instruments and other exhibits. One of the two assistant lightkeepers' houses is also a museum. The other assistant keeper's residence is furnished as it was in the 1890s. In 1987 the tower's interior received a complete refurbishing. In 1990 the vandalized and burned out brick oil storage building, the largest built in the United States, was completely restored and now contains the old fuel tanks and aids to navigation.

The Lens Exhibit Building displays Cape Canaveral's magnificent rotating first-order and Ponce De Leon Inlet's third-order lens, plus an exhibit showing the evolution of lighthouse illuminating devices. The first-order Fresnel weighs in at 6.4 tons and from pedestal base to the top of its bullseye lens stands a majestic 17 feet tall. A mezzanine allows visitors to see the lens at its focal plane. A wheelchair lift is available to the upper level. Visitors may climb the tower's 203 steps to the main service gallery.

OPEN. Daily 10 to 5 (last museum/lighthouse admission at 4). May 1 through Labor Day: 10 to 9 (last admission at 8).

ADMISSION FEES. Discount for children under 11.

- Ponce de Leon Inlet Lighthouse Preservation Association, 4931 South Peninsula Drive, Ponce Inlet, FL 32127. Phone (904) 761-1821.
Website: http://www.ponceinlet.org/ Email: lighthouse@ponceinlet.org

PONCE DE LEON INLET LIGHTHOUSE (MOSQUITO INLET).
CHARACTERISTIC: Flashing white 10s
HAW: 159' **RANGE**: 17 nm

The first Mosquito Inlet lighthouse was built at New Smyrna Beach side of the inlet. It was completed by Winslow Lewis in early 1835. Because the government failed to order the whale oil and as a result of an October 1835 storm which undermined and tilted the brick tower, the optic, a multi-lamp and reflector device suspended on a chandelier, was removed and never placed in operation.

PONCE DE LEON INLET

In December 1835, during the Second Seminole War, a band of Seminoles raided the peninsula and practically destroyed the inoperative lighthouse. In April of 1836 it toppled into the sea.

Plans for the construction of the present 175-foot tall lighthouse and congressional funding extended from 1882 to 1886. In between those years work on the tower was interrupted several times by storms, mosquitos, disease and an earthquake that created two cracks along the brickwork from below the upper windows to its base.

The 175-foot tall tower is firmly anchored on a foundation that has a diameter of 45 feet and is 12 feet thick. A molded brick (laid in stringer courses) water table encircles the top of the foundation, which is constructed of red brick. The tower's architectural design differs markedly from other southern lighthouses. For example, it has granite embellishments in the keystones of the window arches, as well as granite lintels and sashes. The granite step-up entrance has the look of classical styling, although its pediment lacks that genre's decorative frieze. Note also the area of the watchroom underneath the lantern where there are four vertically spaced windows. Each window centers itself among a round of eight non-supporting pilasters resting on and capped by corbels of coursed brick. All of these architectural treatments give the tower a handsome appearance and distinguish it from being a mere utilitarian structure.

Ponce De Leon Inlet's first optic consisted of a five-wick kerosene-fed hydraulic lamp and a first-order Fresnel lens manufactured by Barbier and Fenestre in 1867. It was established on the evening of November 1, 1887. In 1933, after electrification, the first-order lens was removed and replaced by a third-order Fresnel.

In May 1970 the Coast Guard, citing high maintenance costs, moved the beacon to a steel tower at Smyrna Dunes. On December 15, 1983 with high-rise building construction threatening to mask the Smyrna Dunes light, the Coast Guard recommissioned Ponce de Leon Inlet's unmanned lighthouse. Today the light is generated by an automated rotating lantern.

OWNER. Town of Ponce Inlet since June 20, 1972. Managed by the Ponce de Leon Lighthouse Preservation Association.

PRESERVATION. Listed (September 2, 1972) in the National Register of Historic Places. Declared a National Historic Landmark on August 6, 1998.

By summer of 2001 a $1.14 million dollar restoration of the lighthouse was near completion. The restoration project by International Chimney Corp. included work on the main and lantern galleries, as well as repainting the dome to its original black color. The tower's iron staircase inside was cleaned and repainted, and the outside granite steps were repaired. The last phase of the restoration was the abrasive blasting and repainting of the inside and outside of the tower. A new Administration/Maintenance building is now open, providing the staff with much-needed office space, an exhibit design area, and storage space.

Ponce de Leon Inlet Lighthouse

ST. AUGUSTINE

NORTH OR SOUTH ON FL A1A. If traveling north on FL A1A, Old Beach Road is at the intersection where FL A1A turns left. If traveling from Old St. Augustine, follow FL A1A (Anastasia Boulevard) past the alligator farm to the intersection.

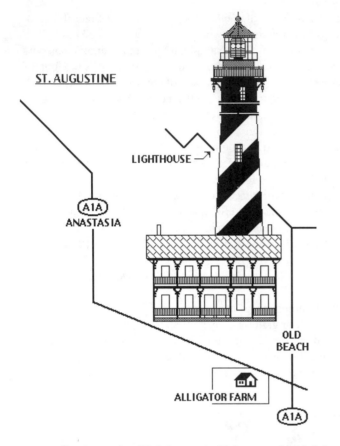

ST. AUGUSTINE LIGHTHOUSE & MUSEUM. A major and expensive restorative effort, begun in 1980 by members and friends of the Junior Service League of St. Augustine, has resulted in a superbly restored keepers dwelling that today houses this fine museum. It was dedicated on April 16, 1988. The dwelling's first floor contains exhibits, a period room and a video theater that tells the story of the lightkeepers and the light they tended. Upstairs in the Anastasia Gallery there are displays that illustrate the cultural and natural history of coastal Florida. Guided tours of the lighthouse (219 steps to the service gallery) provide visitors with a beautiful panoramic view of St. Augustine and its coastline.

OPEN. Tuesday through Friday 9 to 6, Saturday and Sunday 9 to 7. Rest of the year, daily 9:30 to 5. Hours are seasonal so please check these times regularly. Guided tours of the tower and the grounds begin at 9 AM Tuesday through Sunday, and cycle every 1/2 hour. Closed Easter Day, Thanksgiving Day, December 25 and during high winds or storms.

ADMISSION FEES. Museum only; under 12 free. Museum and lighthouse fee with discounts for seniors 55+ and children 7-12. Children are allowed inside the base of the lighthouse where they will see the keeper's office, the old oil storage area and weight well. They also are able to look up through the center of the spiraling staircase. Children less than seven years old and less than 48 inches tall are not allowed to climb the tower.

- St. Augustine Lighthouse and Museum, 81 Lighthouse Avenue, St. Augustine, FL 32084.
Phone (904) 829-0745. Fax (904) 829-0745.
Website: http://www.staugustinelighthouse.com

ST. AUGUSTINE LIGHTHOUSE.
CHARACTERISTIC: Fixed and flashing white 30s
HAW: 161' **RANGES:** Fixed 19; flashing 24 nm

The first beacon on Anastasia Island was a wooden lookout tower built in 1586 by St. Augustine's Spanish settlers. Subsequently, according to historians, a wooden and coquina[1] watch tower was in existence after the completion of the Castillo de San Marcos fort in 1695, during the tenure of Governor Manuel de Montiano from 1737 to 1749, and in 1740 when General James Oglethorpe occupied the island.

During the British occupation (1763-1784) the tower was reinforced and remodeled.

Following Florida's annexation in 1821, the tower underwent additional repair work during the 1823-24 period. The U.S. Government took possession of the 30-foot tall tower in 1824, and after officially commissioning it as an aid to navigation, St. Augustine became Florida's first official light. That harbor lighthouse had 10 of Winslow Lewis' whale oil lamps each fitted with a 14-inch parabolic reflector. At an elevation of 73 feet the beam could be seen out to a distance of 16 nautical miles. In 1855 after having been raised to 52 feet, the tower was outfitted with a fourth-order Fresnel lens. That optic was taken out of service by the Confederacy and the aid was not relighted until 1867. Although for years it withstood the undermining of the encroaching sea, the tower finally keeled over in 1880.

---

1. A cement-like mixture of crushed oyster shells burned to produce lime, sand or coral and water. Also called tabby.

ST. AUGUSTINE

On May 16, 1872, with an initial Congressional appropriation of $60,000, the Lighthouse Board bought five acres of land for the new station. Although the tower's foundation was finished on July 28, 1872, the construction of a protecting jetty north of the site delayed work on the tower. With an additional $20,000 of congressional funds earmarked for a keeper's dwelling and for the completion of the jetty project, work on the light tower began.

The conical brick tower, resting on an octagonal foundation, has the same one-story entry building shielded by a bracketed gable hood seen at North Carolina's Bodie Island and Currituck Beach Lighthouses. The entry with its marble floor was used to store lard butts but not kerosene.

St. Augustine Lighthouse's construction design, exterior detailing at the watchroom level and the fancy gallery support brackets are almost identical to the Outer Banks towers at Cape Hatteras, Bodie Island and Currituck Beach. The tower has six cast-iron decks all connected by a spiraling cast-iron stairway that leads to the watchroom deck below the lantern. The 165-foot tall lighthouse and the station's keepers' dwelling (a two-story brick duplex built in 1875 atop a coquina foundation are the oldest brick structures in St. Augustine. The station's construction cost $105,000.

St. Augustine's first-order Fresnel optic was lighted on October 15, 1874. First fueled by lard oil and later kerosene, the beacon was electrified in 1936. At that time, a motor-driven gear box replaced the original hand wound weighted clockwork mechanism used to rotate the optic. It was automated in 1955.

In December 1986, a boy with a high-powered rifle took two pot shots at the lantern. The rifle fire shattered the lantern's glass storm panes and tore a gaping hole through the lens' mid-section, destroying 19 of the lens' 320 prisms. On September 6, 1991, the Coast Guard turned off the light and the rotating mechanism and removed the lens. This was done to prevent further damage from irregular rotations and resulting vibrations. The repair cost was initially estimated to be as high as $250,000.

OWNER. U.S. Coast Guard (lighthouse). Victorian duplex and grounds were sold in 1971 to St. Johns County for $29,000. Leased in 1981 for 99 years to the Junior Service League of St. Augustine.

PRESERVATION. Listed (1981) in the National Register of Historic Places.

In 1969 the light station was declared surplus property and put up for sale. The next year, during purchasing negotiations between the Federal Government and St. John's County, a "suspiciously" set fire gutted the keepers' dwelling.

For ten long years the lighthouse grounds stood neglected. Finally in 1980 the Junior Service League of St. Augustine and others began to lay the groundwork for its restoration and preservation. First order of business was to have the light station accepted into the National Register of Historic Places. The initial restoration plan of 1984 called for two phases. The first involved closing the roof and securing the building, followed by the restoration of the structure's interior and porch. The duplex's restoration cost $500,000, of which $200,000 came from state funds.

Later the Junior Service League raised another $25,000 to add safety rails, stair supports and an interior lighting system for the tower. At the same time the adjoining fuel storage building was restored to become an office for the lighthouse administrators.

In November 1990 the Junior Service League raised $15,000 that, with an additional $15,000 from the National Park Service's Bicentennial Fund, has been spent on repairs that match the architectural specifications required to restore the tower to its 1874 engineering standards.

In 1991 Florida's Historic Preservation Advisory Council recommended that the state appropriate $300,000 for the lens' repair. Faced with the problem of finding sources of income to support Florida's burgeoning fiscal requirements, Tallahassee tabled many non-essential fundings, reducing budgetary outlays for historic preservation projects from $12 million to $3 million. Finally in 1992, Tallahassee released $360,000 for the lens' rehabilitation and other minor repairs. In another program $80,000 was made available through a state grant and matching funds.

Taking measurements, the first step and the most difficult part of the job, was accomplished using a portable robot originally designed for medical purposes. The robot, basically an image digitizer, was able to scan the undamaged prisms and electronically measure their shapes. The measurements, in the form of computerized drawings, were then used to mold new bullseyes and prisms. With its repaired first-order lens back in the lantern, St. Augustine Lighthouse was relighted on May 22, 1993.

The final restoration phase involved the sandblasting, repointing, treating and painting of the tower's brickwork. That job was completed in April 1994. Also completed is a brick wall that replicates the one that originally surrounded the station.

<u>WILLIAM TROTTER LIGHTHOUSE MARITIME STUDIO</u>. This studio, located off FL A1A in Jacksonville Beach, displays a unique collection of scale models, lighthouse and ship paintings, photographs, blueprints, architectural drawings and lighthouse artifacts.

OPEN. All year, Tuesday through Saturday 10 to 4. Guided tours are available upon request.

FREE ADMISSION.

- William Trotter Lighthouse Maritime Studio, PO Box 50186 (1011 North 3rd Street), Jacksonville Beach, FL 32250. Phone (904) 241-8845.

St. Augustine Lighthouse

ST. JOHNS
ST. JOHNS RIVER

NORTH TO MAYPORT ON FL A1A. At the FL A1A & FL 101 (Main Street) intersection continue straight ahead on FL 10 to the main gate. Signs direct visitors to the security office.

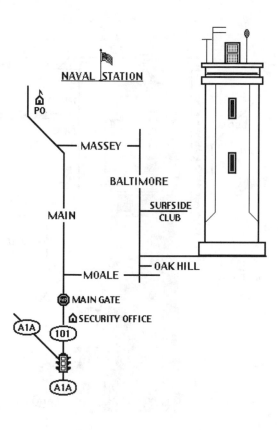

SOUTH ON FL A1A. Take the St. Johns River ferry that operates between Fort George Island and Mayport (tolls charged for vehicles) with crossings every 30 minutes. Phone (904) 246-2922.

Before heading for the naval station, leave the ferry landing area and continue straight ahead into Broad Street. The St. Johns River Lighthouse is located a short distance down Broad and close by the station's perimeter fence. There is a fence walk-through for visitors to freely enter the base and view the lighthouse.

SOUTH ON I-95. Depart I-275 (FL 9A) via either the FL 113 or Monument Road Exits (or the FL 10 Exit, if open to traffic). Then:
-> FL 10 (Atlantic Boulevard),
-> FL A1A (Mayport Road),
-> Left (north) at FL A1A to the naval station.

THE NAVAL STATION. The station is home port to more than 30 naval ships, including the aircraft carrier *J. F. Kennedy* and is the East Coast base for the Navy's newest generation of anti-submarine helicopters.

OPEN. All year, daily during daylight hours.

FREE ADMISSION. The general public is now allowed to the enter the base without having to secure a pass. Free guided tours of one of the ships berthed at the naval station are offered every Saturday and Sunday.

- Public Affairs Office, Naval Station, Box 280032, Mayport, FL 32228-0032.
Phone (904) 270-5226. For a recorded message about the stations' weekend visitation schedules call (904) 241-6289.

CONTINUE ON STATION. Leave the Security Office parking lot. Then:
-> Pass through the Main Gate and motor straight ahead on Main Street,
-> Right at Moale Avenue,
-> Left at Baltimore Avenue,
-> Pass Oak Hill Street on the right,
-> Right and up a short hill into an office compound.

After viewing the light tower, return to Baltimore Avenue and turn right. Turn right again at the one way entrance to the Surfside Club. An excellent spot from which to photograph the tower is to the right and rear of the club.

ST. JOHNS LIGHTHOUSE (MAYPORT).
CHARACTERISTIC: Group flashing 20s
HAW: 83' **RANGE**: 22 nm
This 64-foot tall light tower was constructed in 1954 using concrete blocks finished with an exterior coating of cement. Its optic is a Crouse-Hinds FB-61 lens.
OWNER. U.S. Navy.

ON TO THE ST. JOHNS RIVER LIGHTHOUSE. Note the above reference to the unrestricted opportunity to walk through the fence off Broad Street in Mayport.

If you care to drive over to the lighthouse, return to Baltimore Avenue and turn right. Then:

-> Left at Massey Avenue,
-> Right at Main Street,
-> Pass a McDonald's, a post office and Bravo Piers on the right,
-> At the north end of the pier area, the road curves to the right. Part way through the curve there is a stop sign at Main's intersection with Perimeter Road,
-> Left at Perimeter Road and continue to the St. Johns River Lighthouse.

VISITING THE LIGHTHOUSE. At this writing the future of this lighthouse is in limbo. The Florida Lighthouse Association fought a plan to sell the lighthouse to private developers, who proposed to move it, and the plan was dropped. The U.S. Navy, in coordination with local and state tourist and preservation entities, announced in 1997 that the service would turn the property over to the newly organized Mayport Lighthouse Association, which planned to restore the light station to its original appearance and open the tower to the public. That transfer has still not taken place.

The Navy has stated their committment to preserve the lighthouse and has worked with the Florida State Historic Preservation Office to establish a maintenance program.

Meanwhile, the nonprofit Mayport Waterfront Partnership has received an estimate from International Chimney on the cost of moving the lighthouse to a more accessible site on city property. For now, the site may be open to the public on weekends only.

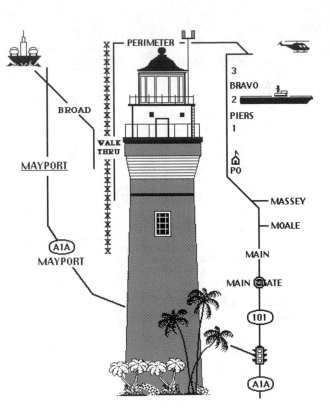

ST. JOHNS RIVER LIGHTHOUSE.

This pretty lighthouse was built in 1829 for the then hefty sum of $24,500. Its light was established the following year. Threatened by the encroaching sea, the tower was moved inland in 1835. Raised to 65 feet, the lighthouse was refitted with its original Lewis multiple lamp lighting device. The Lighthouse Service's 1848 List of Lighthouses notes that the whale oil-fed lamp, at 80 feet above the water, displayed a fixed white light that was visible out to 16 nautical miles.

In 1852 another $10,000 was funded by Congress to secure the tower from shifting sands and erosion. A year later sand dunes had piled up so high that ship captains could not see the light. Even the keeper's house was almost buried in sand. Saddled with many other pressing actions, the newly created Lighthouse Board decided to solve the problem temporarily by erecting two range beacons across the sand bar seaward of the endangered structure. Three years later, with $15,000 of newly appropriated funds, a new conical tower and front range beacon were constructed. On January 1, 1859, the new St. Johns River light was relighted using an oil-powered third-order Fresnel lens showing a fixed white light.

Not much news about the St. Johns River Lighthouse is found in official documents until 1864, when it was reported that Federal gunboats engaged in the blockading of southern ports used the light to navigate past the changeable and narrow channel on their forays down the St. Johns River. The Confederacy decided that the light be darkened. Instead of removing the optic, a former keeper decided to do the job by shooting out the light. After the war and until it was again placed in operation, small warning lanterns were placed on top of the tower.

ST. JOHNS & ST. JOHNS RIVER

Although the lighthouse was rebuilt in 1887 to its present height of 81 feet, it was recommended in 1889 that it be replaced by another lighthouse on Fort George Island. That plan never materialized. Instead, the beacon's candlepower rating was increased in 1912 with the installation of an incandescent kerosene vapor lamp. The light, electrified in the early 1920s, was discontinued on January 15, 1929 when it was replaced by the lightship *Brunswick*.

An interesting fact about this lighthouse is that its base is buried some 20 feet below the present elevation of the land around it. This was done, reportedly, when the surrounding land had to be raised and leveled off for the laying of the station's runways. How does one get into the tower? Through the lower window facing Broad Street. And if you look closely at the bottom of the tower's south side you will see the outline of the top portion of the previously attached keeper's house.

OWNER. U.S. Navy.
PRESERVATION. Listed in the National Register of Historic Places.

St. Johns River Lighthouse

AMELIA ISLAND

TO FERNANDINA BEACH. The Amelia Island Light Station and its lighthouse are not open to the public. While summer foliage masks the lighthouse, its top third can be seen and photographed from points along FL A1A (Atlantic Avenue) between the entrance to Fort Clinch (Park Drive) and North Wolfe Street. At this writing in the summer of 2001 there is discussion of opening the station to the public twice each month.

SOUTH ON I-95. Depart at Exit 129. Then:
-> US 17 -> Yulee -> FL A1A. North Wolfe is about 0.6 mile east of North 14th Street.

AMELIA ISLAND LIGHTHOUSE.

CHARACTERISTIC: Flashing white 10s (red sector)

HAW: 107' **RANGES**: White 23, red 19 nm

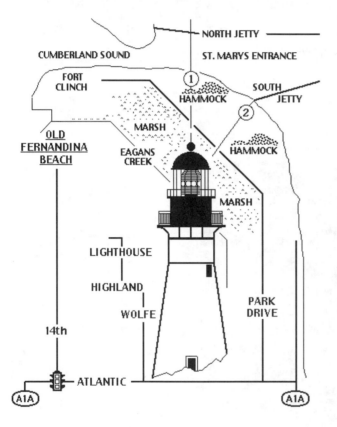

This lighthouse was first built on the southern tip of Georgia's Cumberland Island in 1819-20. In 1838, while northern Little Cumberland Island's tower was under construction, the island's southern tower was dismantled, shipped to and reassembled on Amelia Island.

Upon its arrival in Florida in 1839, the brick tower was reassembled on a piece of plantation land purchased by the Federal Government in 1820. The tower was 50 feet tall. Its base was 25 feet in diameter, tapering to 12 feet across at the top. It shows the plain and unadorned architectural features of the Colonial Revival Period.

Most accounts say the increase in height to 64 feet was accomplished when the tower was rebuilt in 1839. One report, however, has the additional height being added in 1903. The 12-foot addition is the cylindrical section inserted between the top of the conical tower and its watchroom. When established, the lighting device was a rotating chandelier which held 14 whale oil lamps each backed with a 15-inch reflector.

In 1903 the tower was refurbished and possibly heightened to permit the addition of a cast-iron service gallery. The original balcony was a wooden walkway resting on hand hewn soapstone supports imbedded in the tower's masonry walls. The removed green soapstone fragments were used to form the foundation for the existing walkway at base of the tower.

The lighthouse has a unique 68-step gray granite stairway imported from New England. The stairway underwent repairs in 1885 and again in 1905 to repair a crack that was caused by one of the keepers winding the weight-driven clock mechanism too tight, causing the cable to snap and whiplash the granite step.

In 1857 the old multiple lamp optic was removed and replaced with a single lamp and a third-order Fresnel lens manufactured by the Parisian firm of Barrier, Bernard and Turrene. In 1881 the lantern was enlarged and another lighting system introduced. This time the lamp's illuminant was kerosene and the third-order lens was rigged to be rotated by a clockwork mechanism resembling the workings of a grandfather clock. The chain drum had to be rewound every four hours. The light was electrified in 1935.

OWNER. The City of Fernandina Beach took ownership of the light station from the Coast Guard in March 2001. A group called the Amelia Lighthouse and Museum, Inc., has formed to seek restoration and public access. The U.S. Coast Guard Auxiliary has been involved with the maintainance of the lighthouse for several years.

PRESERVATION. Not listed in the National Register of Historic Places.

AMELIA ISLAND

NORTH AND SOUTH CHANNEL RANGE LIGHTS.

Prior to the construction in 1880 of the north and south jetties, there were two channel entrances into the port of Old Fernandina. A lighthouse was erected east of Fort Clinch at the entrance to the North Channel (#1 on map). The aid was a two-story wood framed building surmounted by a square wooden tower. When established, the lard oil-powered North Channel light ranged with Amelia Island's elevated beacon.

The south channel was similarly marked, again using the Amelia Island light. The South Channel range beacon, however, was placed on a dolly that ran along a short rail track extending from the east side of the marsh towards the beach at South Jetty (#2 on map). To facilitate the servicing of this moveable aid by the Amelia Island's keeper, a causeway of oyster shells was laid across the bayou to the beach hammock. Traces of the causeway can be seen from atop the Amelia Island tower. The ruins of South Channel's brick oil house lie deep within Fort Clinch State Park's hammock with no readied access to them.

Amelia Island Lighthouse

GEORGIA
LITTLE CUMBERLAND ISLAND

This lighthouse has a significant place in America's lighthouse history. It stands within a Natural Wilderness Area that divides a semi-circular line of private beach home sites. Neither the residential area nor the lighthouse is open to the public, since only property owners may land on the island. The ferry service out of St. Marys, Georgia to the Cumberland National Seashore is not a means to gain access to Little Cumberland Island. The lighthouse cannot be seen from Jekyll Island.

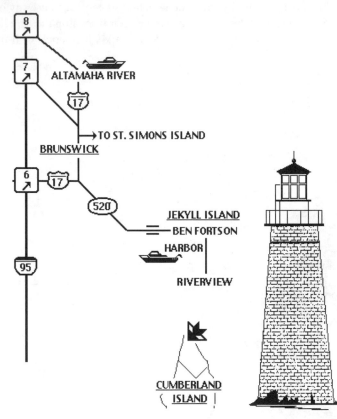

VIEWING THE LIGHTHOUSE. A charter boat captain offers the lighthouse seeker the opportunity to view and photograph the lighthouse.

TO JEKYLL ISLAND. Leave I-95 at Exit 6 and follow US 17 towards Brunswick. At the juncture of US 17 & GA 520, bear right and follow GA 520 across the Jekyll Creek bridge to the island's collection station (nominal vehicle toll). Continue straight ahead on Ben Fortson Parkway for a short distance and turn right into South Riverview Drive. At Harbor Drive turn right and continue to the Jekyll Harbor Marina. Captain Vernon Reynolds' cruisers (23-foot Aquasport with twin outboards, 25-foot Chris Craft cabin cruiser with inboard power and 24-foot Carolina skiff with outboard power) are docked at the Jekyll Harbor Marina. The narrated 10-mile round trip takes about 1 1/2 hours. Captain Reynolds can also provide a charter to view the St. Simons Island Lighthouse from the water.

SCHEDULE. On demand.
FARES. Per passenger fare; inquire for current rates.
- Coastal Expeditions, 3202 East Third Street, Brunswick, GA 31520.
Phone (912) 265-0392.

LITTLE CUMBERLAND ISLAND LIGHTHOUSE.
Although Congress appropriated funds for a lighthouse on the southern end of the Cumberland Island as early as April 1802 and several times thereafter, the station's construction contracts were not signed until July 1819. Then the Federal Government specified that Winslow Lewis was to build a round, brick and lime mortar tower that was to have a 25-foot diameter at its base, tapering to 12 feet beneath the lantern deck. The station's keepers dwelling was to be a small one-story brick structure. Lewis completed the two projects (although the diameters were a constant one foot short of the contract's specifications) in one year for $17,000. The multiple lamp/reflector optic, with a focal plane 74 feet above the sound, was lighted on July 4, 1820. In 1838 the lighthouse was moved to Florida, reassembled and renamed the Amelia Island Lighthouse. The 1820 keepers house no longer exists.

While the southern lighthouse was being transferred, the present brick conical tower was erected on the island's northern end. The tower was given a wooden staircase that extended up to an access hole bored in the lantern's circular soapstone deck. Unfortunately the tower's cross-supporting wooden beams embedded in its brick walls eventually succumbed to dry rot deterioration. The station's keepers were also provided with two wood and brick dwellings, an outdoor privy and a well.

LITTLE CUMBERLAND ISLAND

Over the ensuing years the station underwent several construction changes and additions. In 1879 the dry rot-riddled tower was extensively renovated. The weakened timbers were replaced with cast-iron stringers. A cast-iron plate that had replaced the soapstone deck was itself replaced by wooden flooring. The wooden deck did not last and in 1881, a new cast-iron lantern and deck had to be manufactured. A brick oil house was added in 1890 and a boathouse in 1896. In 1901 the lighthouse was again refitted with a new cast-iron lantern deck. Finally, in 1915 the light was decommissioned and the lighthouse abandoned. In 1968 the keeper's residence was destroyed and the station's fog signal house demolished.

The light was first activated on June 26, 1838. In 1857 the old multiple lamp optic was replaced with a single whale oil-powered lamp and a Henri LePaute manufactured third-order Fresnel lens. The new optic displayed a fixed white light 71 feet above the water. Damaged and darkened during the Civil War, the aid was reactivated on September 1, 1867, using its original, but repaired, third-order lens.

OWNER. Little Cumberland Island Association since 1961.
PRESERVATION. Listed in the National Register of Historic Places.

In December 1919, a five year revocable commercial (usage) license was issued to a private individual. In January 1924, after the lease had been terminated, the lighthouse and the station's six acres were sold to R. L. Phillips & Company of Brunswick for $800. The station remained unused and unattended for the next 37 years.

In 1967 after acquiring the 60-foot tall lighthouse, the Little Cumberland Island Association dismantled two buildings and sold the bricks to association members. The proceeds from the sale were to be used to repair the tower's walls and to replace the tower's supposedly removed spiral stairs and rusted lantern. But after having dug through a huge sand pile to reach the tower's entrance, they found the tower's brickwork to be in excellent condition. The staircase, although damaged by water leaking though the roof, was still intact. With that good fortune the Association decided to build a new stairway, emplace new windows and add a new lantern and roof.

During the 1994-95 period, the Association stabilized and completely restored the old light tower. The exterior of the tower was further renovated in 1998, restoring its original appearance.

ST. SIMONS ISLAND

TO ST. SIMONS ISLAND. In Brunswick on US 17 (Glynn Avenue) just past the visitor center turn east at a "St. Simons-Sea Land" sign and drive across the St. Simons (F.J. Torras) Causeway (vehicle toll eastbound only). Upon reaching the island bear right into Kings Way. Then:

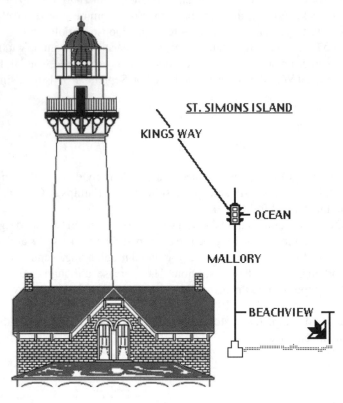

-> Motor through the Frederica Road & Retreat Avenue intersection (traffic signal) to Mallory Street and turn right,

-> Left at Beachview Drive (last street before The Pier),

-> Pass the post office,

-> Right into 12th Street.

The lighthouse grounds and museum are handicapped accessible.

MUSEUM OF COASTAL HISTORY. The Coastal Georgia Historical Society has been instrumental in the restoration of the lighthouse and the keepers' residence and in making them available to the public. Following its restoration the dwelling was opened as the museum. In 1984 the Society signed a lease with the Coast Guard to allow visitors to climb to the top of the tower. With the lease, the Society assumed full responsibility for the care and maintenance (less beacon) of the light station property.

The museum displays a replica of a lantern set with a fourth-order Fresnel lens from Michigan's Manisteque Harbor Lighthouse. It also has an exhibit depicting the island's colorful past and the life of a turn-of-the-century lighthouse keeper and his family. Visitors may climb the tower's 129 steps to the observation gallery.

OPEN. All year, Mondays through Saturdays 10 to 5. Sundays 1:30 to 5. Closed selected holidays.

ADMISSION FEES. Discount for children 6-11; under 6 free. Group rates for school and special tours require a reservation.

- Museum of Coastal History, Coastal Georgia Historical Society, PO Box 21136 (101 12th Street), St. Simons Island, GA 31522-0636.

Phone (912) 638-4666.

Website: http://www.glynncounty.com/stsimonslight/

Email: ssilighthouse@thebest.net

ST. SIMONS ISLAND LIGHTHOUSE.

CHARACTERISTIC: Fixed and flashing white 60s

HAW: 104' **RANGES**: Fixed 18; flashing 23 nm

The lighthouse stands on the site of Fort St. Simons, a coastal defense station built in 1737-38 by General James Edward Oglethorpe to protect Fort Frederica (1736) from a naval incursion up the Frederica River. Designed primarily to defend against an impending Spanish move northward out of Florida, it was hastily abandoned once Spaniards began their advance into Georgia. In 1742, although defeated in a battle fought at Fort Federica (on the island's north side), the Spanish forces were able to advance upon and destroy both Fort St. Simons and Jekyll Island before withdrawing. Their departure left coastal Georgia in the hands of the British.

The original St. Simons Island lighthouse was built during 1807-10 by James Gould from Massachusetts. The tower was octagonal in shape with the lower portion built of tabby (coquina). The top 12.5 feet were constructed of red sandstone brick. The 75-foot tall tower's base had a 25-foot diameter, tapering to ten feet at its top. The light was first established in 1811 by Mr. Gould, who held the head keeper position until 1837.

ST. SIMONS ISLAND

The tower and keeper's house were destroyed in 1862 by departing Confederate troops to prevent the light from being used as a navigational aid by Union ships. The site of this destroyed lighthouse is located about 30 feet south of the present light tower.

Although work on a new tower began in 1867, the presence of malaria prevented work being done during the spring and summer months. The tower's completion was delayed until September 1, 1872. The 100-foot tall conical tower has a base diameter of 25 feet and tapers to ten feet below the watchroom deck. Note the molded cast-iron windows with their acanthus leaves treatments. The service gallery's handsome design and ornamentation, with its knobbed balustrades and supporting deck brackets, are typical of the period.

The keepers' dwelling shows both Georgian (the symmetry of America's antebellum manors) and Victorian (decorative eaves) stylistic borrowings. The building was designed and built by Charles Cluskey, a noted Irish student of the Greek Revival architectural school. Both the tower and dwelling are made of handmade Savannah gray brick. The brick oil house was added in 1890, when the fuel for the lamps was changed from lard oil to kerosene.

St. Simons' first optic was a bit unusual for an American lighthouse. It consisted of 15 whale oil-fed lamps suspended from chains within the cast-iron lantern that was 10 feet tall and 8 feet across. In 1857 the lantern received a newer model oil lamp and a third-order double-convex Fresnel lens. With the improvement, the beacon became a primary seacoast aid.

The presently operating L. Sautter & Company third-order Fresnel lens was first established in 1872. It is now electrified (1934) and automated (1953).

In a letter of November 13, 1942 from the District Coast Guard Officer, 6th Naval District, Charleston to the Coast Guard Commandant described this classical lens as having four panels each fitted with 15 prisms in the central drum, 11 prisms above and 4 below. The lens itself did not rotate. Its flashing characteristic was achieved by a belt of four 45-degree panels that revolved around the fixed lens and covered seven of the top eleven prisms and all of the central drum's prisms. The letter writer also reported that the lens' description was the only one (no sketches or blueprints) on file in the District Office.

This lighthouse, as is found in the recorded and related histories of many other American lighthouses, harbors its own ghost. It seems that after 1880, when an assistant keeper murdered his boss, the footsteps of the slain keeper ascending the steps to service his light and descending to the kitchen have been heard by succeeding residents of the keeper's dwelling. Not surprisingly, the smell of kerosene permeates the stairwell after each such ghostly visit.

OWNER. U.S. Coast Guard (lighthouse). Dwelling and grounds were sold to Glynn County in 1972. The lighthouse became part of the museum when the lighthouse was leased to the Coastal Georgia Historical Society in 1984. The optic is maintained by the local Coast Guard Auxiliary.

PRESERVATION. Listed (April 13,1972) in the National Register of Historic Places.

During the 1989-90 period, the Society received a $5,000 state grant for renovation work. In 1989 after multiple coats of paint and asphalt were removed, the exterior of the tower was restored. During the cleaning of the lantern a copper dome and shiny brass mullions were uncovered. Two of the tower's windows of modern design were replaced with new windows fabricated according to original architectural specifications.

In 1990 another project was completed. The passageway between tower and house (dismantled in 1953) was rebuilt, a public restroom and a ramp for the disabled were added and the second floor's assistant keeper's quarters returned to its 1812-1900 motif.

A most impressive restoration!

SAPELO ISLAND

SAPELO ISLAND. The Sapelo (sap' uh lo) Lighthouse and its front range light tower are located on the southeastern end of Sapelo Island within the Sapelo Island National Estuarine Research Reserve. Georgia's Department of Natural Resources' State Parks Division manages the reserve with its salt marsh ecosystems, maritime climax forests, Hog Hammock, a community of descendants of slaves from 19th century island plantations, the University of Georgia's Marine Institute, the Reynolds Mansion and the Spalding tabby sugar mill ruins.

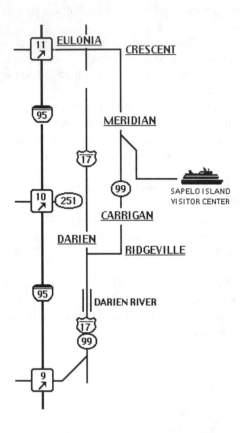

VISITING THE ISLAND. In the past, the land tour of the island has not featured the light towers. The lighthouse is located about one mile from the closest viewing point and then only the top of the tower is visible above the intervening trees. The lighthouse has been restored and there are plans to include it as part of public tours of the island.

VISITING THE LIGHTHOUSE. Here is another way to get to the island and visit the lighthouse. Michael Gowen's SouthEast Adventure Outfitters will handle all aspects of the boat/land visit. The ferry is handicapped-accessible, but the vehicles on the island are not. Seniors should have no problem, since there is little walking required.

SCHEDULE. All year. Call or check website for schedule.
FARES. Ferry ticket plus additional fare, depending on length of tour. Three-day prior reservation required to secure ferry tickets.
- SouthEast Adventure Outfitters, 313 Mallory Street, St. Simons Island, GA 31522.
Phone (912) 638-6732.
Website: http://www.gacoast.com/navigator/sea.html

TO MERIDIAN LANDING AND VISITOR CENTER. See above map. The center contains exhibits and shows a film and an interpretive video.
OPEN: On tour days 8:30 to 12:30.
TOUR FARES. Reservations required. Discounts for children 6-18.
SCHEDULE. Guided tour takes four hours. Public tours on Wednesday (8:30 - 12:30) and Saturdays (9:00 - 1:00) September through May. Also on Fridays, June through August.

- Sapelo Island Visitor Center, PO Box 15, Sapelo Island, GA 31327.
Phone (912) 437-3224. Fax (912) 485-2141.
Website: http://www.cr.nps.gov/goldcres/sites/sapelo.htm

SAPELO ISLAND LIGHTHOUSE (1820).

Between 1808 and 1820, Congress appropriated and reappropriated funds to build a lighthouse on an islet just off the southern tip of the island at the mouth of Doboy Sound, but nothing was accomplished until Winslow Lewis obtained two contracts. Both were financed by appropriated and reappropriated funds totaling $17,000. One contract of September 14, 1819 was for the construction of an 80-foot tall brick and stone light tower and a small keeper's abode. The other contract of January 20, 1820 covered the aid's lighting apparatus.

In 1855 the lighthouse was given a fourth-order Fresnel lens to replace Lewis' original revolving apparatus, consisting of 15 lamps each equipped with a 15-inch reflector.

The light station received extensive damage in 1867, but was back in operation on April 15, 1868. The restoration work on the light tower included new window frames and sashes, new door frame and door, repaired stairway, a new lantern and a new optic. The keeper's dwelling was also rebuilt. The tower was painted with alternating horizontal bands of red and white.

SAPELO ISLAND

In 1890 the station received a brick oil house. Only its ruins remain. The keeper's dwelling was destroyed and the base of the main tower even more severely eroded by a hurricane and tidal surge in 1898.

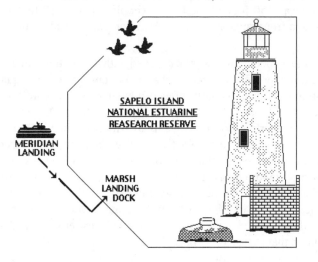

OWNER. Lighthouse, range tower and land were sold to the State of Georgia in April 1992. Managed by the Georgia Department of Natural Resources, Parks & Historic Sites.

PRESERVATION. Not listed in the National Register of Historic Places.

In 1969 the State of Georgia purchased the northern 75% of the island from the widow of Richard J. Reynolds, Jr., the tobacco heir, and turned the land into a wildlife refuge. In 1976 a second state purchase from the Sapelo Island Research Foundation gave the State a divided interest in the southern part of the island, but not the old light station. Isolated and neglected, both towers had fallen into disrepair.

In 1989 the lighthouse was described as "deteriorating badly." In 1991, after years of litigation, the State entered into an agreement to purchase for $500,000 full rights to 206 acres of dry ground and marsh, including the old light station property.

In 1997 the Georgia Department of Natural Resources announced that the lighthouse would be fully restored and repainted in its original red and white stripes. The restoration began in November 1997 and was completed in August 1998, culminating in a dedication and relighting ceremony on September 6, 1998.

The final amount for the restoration was $494,838. Funds were provided by the Georgia Department of Transportation ($176,000) and the Georgia General Assembly ($100,000). The balance was obtained from private donations to the Sapelo Island Restoration Foundation.

Future plans include the installation of a hard surface road to the lighthouse and adjacent structures, installing exhibits in the fuel storage buildings, constructing a trail from the lighthouse to the site of the steel tower, and reconstructing the dock the lighthouse keepers used to access the Island. There are also plans to include the restored lighthouse in public island tours.

Tax-deductible contributions may be forwarded to:

- Sapelo Island Restoration Foundation, 205 Butler Street SE, Suite 1252, Atlanta, GA 30334.

Phone (404) 656-3500.

Website: http://www.state.ga.us/dnr/parks/lighthouse/

SAPELO ISLAND FRONT RANGE LIGHT (1868).

In 1857 an outer beacon was established to range with the main light. In 1867-68 when repairs were being made to the light station, a new front range beacon was erected. The aid was a 50-foot tall skeletal tower placed on a 100-foot long tramway some 660 feet east of the lighthouse. Both the main and front range lights were activated on April 15, 1868.

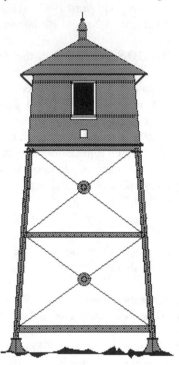

By 1877 the wooden tower was so decayed with dry rot that Congress appropriated $2,500 for the construction of a 25-foot tall tapered and square tower, consisting of four diagonally braced tubular legs, a square house with a pointed hip roof topped by a ventilator ball. The shed rests on a cast-iron deck, whose supporting exterior I-beams are trimmed with gingerbread molding. Over its remaining years of active service, the front range beacon was moved numerous times to offset erosion and changes in the channel.

In 1899 the Lighthouse Board reported that "In February the front beacon was dismantled and the range discontinued." In the absence of information concerning the existence of a third range tower, it is reasoned that the dismantling referred to the removal of the 1877 tower's lens and the Funck-Heap lamp that replaced the beacon's Hains lamp in 1893.

PRESERVATION. Not listed in the National Register of Historic Places.

SAPELO ISLAND LIGHTHOUSE (1905).

In 1900 the Board began deliberations on the feasibility of building a new light station farther inland. In 1902 the Board reported that, on June 28, 1902, $40,000 had been appropriated for "... the construction of a combined light tower and keeper's dwelling in the vicinity of the old one."

By 1904 the Lighthouse Board had decided on the new light tower's design, completed land surveys and contracted for the manufacture of a 103-foot tall skeletal steel tower, similar in design to those constructed at Hillsboro Inlet (1907), Cape Charles (1894) and Marblehead, Massachusetts (1895). The new tower's beacon was activated on September 18, 1905.

Faced with a steady decline of commercial shipping in and out of Doboy Sound, the second Sapelo Island light was deactivated in 1933. In 1940 the iron tower was dismantled and shipped to South Fox Island, Michigan. Its concrete foundation footings are still visible.

COCKSPUR ISLAND

EAST ON US 80. Take US 80 east out of Savannah to the Fort Pulaski National Monument. The lighthouse can be clearly seen and photographed from atop Fort Pulaski. There is a closer and unobstructed view from a location just east of the Lazaretto Creek bridge off US 80. Once over the bridge turn left into a dirt road and follow it for a short distance to a few boat docks. Fishermen's trucks at the docks can make a turnaround a bit tight for large vehicles. The docks are a short walk from the highway.

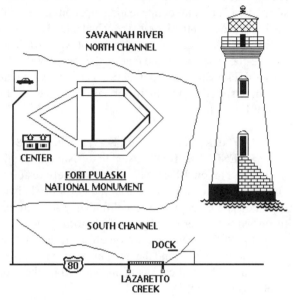

FORT PULASKI NATIONAL MONUMENT. Fort Pulaski is the third fortification to have been built in 1794 and destroyed by a hurricane ten years later. Fort Pulaski's construction took18 long years (1829-1847). Imposing as this citadel is, it did not play a prominent role in the Civil War.

The Visitor Center presents various historical exhibits. For the adventurous lighthouse seeker, the lighthouse can be reached on foot from the fort. The walk involves wading across a tidal creek. Check with the park's rangers before heading out to visit the tower. If you go, use insect repellant.

OPEN.
Memorial Day to Labor Day, daily 8:30 to 6:45.
Other times of the year until 5:15.
Closed January 1 and December 25.
The Visitor Center is open 9 to 5 daily.
ADMISSION FEES. All year. Under 17 free. Family rate.

- Fort Pulaski National Monument, PO Box 30757, Savannah, GA 31410-0757.
Phone (912) 786-5787.
Website: http://www.nps.gov/fopu/local/

COCKSPUR ISLAND LIGHTHOUSE (SOUTH CHANNEL).

This lighthouse, on a small oyster bed just east of the main island, once marked the south channel of the Savannah River. According to some historians, a beacon may have been established on the island as early as 1772. Little is known about this aid. In 1820 the State of Georgia ceded Cockspur Island to the Federal Government with the understanding that the island would be used for the construction of aids to navigation.

Meanwhile on April 9, 1831, The *Savannah Georgian* reported that the State had appropriated $3,000 to establish a beacon on the north channel's White Oyster Beds. On April 22, 1831, the Collector of Port called for proposals to build a beacon 35 feet high with an 18-foot square base tapering to 9 feet at the top. References to the White Oyster Beds tower ceased around 1893, although there is a January 11, 1902 letter from Secretary of the Treasury to the Speaker of the House of Representatives requesting an appropriation to build a dwelling on the parapet of Fort Pulaski for the keepers of the "Cockspur and Oyster Beds Range, Georgia, Light Station." While the White Oyster Beds beacon was reported in 1934 to be still standing, it has since disappeared.

On April 16, 1836, another item in the *Savannah Georgian* mentioned a proposal to build a brick and stone lighthouse on "Grass Island at east end of Cockspur Island." Additionally, there are three recorded references to Congressional appropriations of $4,000 in 1834, with the same amount reappropriated in 1837. In 1837 another $3,000 was authorized for "two small beacon-lts. on Cock-spur Island." Despite the availability of federal funds, construction petitions were not submitted to Congress until 1848. The lighthouse was built and its light established in 1849. The first official reference to the Cockspur Island Lighthouse was in the Government's 1851 List of Lighthouses.

Between 1876 and 1905 the tower, house and boat landing were repaired several times. The tower was abandoned in 1949.

In 1856 the Lighthouse Board reported that the tower had been rebuilt, a fourth-order Fresnel lens had replaced the original multiple lamp apparatus and the keeper's dwelling repositioned on a brick foundation. In 1893 the optic's Hains lamp was replaced by the newer and more efficient Funck-Heap lamp. Dark during the Civil War, the light was reestablished in 1868. In 1909, the aid was discontinued due to the poor navigability of the South Channel.

An interesting bit of history surrounding the Cockspur Island Lighthouse occurred in 1862, when Union forces from Hilton Head Island landed on Tybee Island and moved on Fort Pulaski. The Union commander ordered the garrison to surrender. The Confederate leadership, confident the fort could withstand an artillery attack, refused. What the garrison did not know was that the Union Army had added ten experimental rifled artillery guns to its order of battle. The bombardment of Fort Pulaski began on the morning of April 10. The battle did not last long. After seeing artillery rounds rip through the fort's 2-foot thick walls and fearing the loss of 400 defenders should artillery projectiles penetrate the gunpowder magazine's 4-foot thick walls, the Confederate garrison capitulated the next day. In doing so, the lighthouse was saved from almost certain destruction, for the tower stood in the direct line of fire from the Union guns positioned along the Savannah River east of Lazaretto Creek.

OWNER. National Park Service since 1958.

PRESERVATION. Listed in the National Register of Historic Places as part of the Fort Pulaski National Monument.

The National Park Service completely restored the structure in 1978. Although financially strapped by a $4,000 budget, a maintenance crew from the Fort Pulaski National Monument went to work in 1991 and gave the Cockspur Island Lighthouse a much needed facelift. They scraped, repointed, refilled and painted both the interior and exterior walls and furnished the lantern with plexiglass storm panels.

In 1995 a new preservation effort began. The tower's lantern was removed for cleaning and painting. Upon closer examination it was found that the lantern cap had several structural cracks, so a decision was made to fabricate a new replica of the cap. The replica was manufactured by the Flotech Corporation of Jacksonville, Florida. It was set in place on the lighthouse on May 18, 2000.

Other repairs in 2000 included the reconstruction of the exterior staircase (the original was washed away in 1999 high tides), pressure washing and some repointing of the exterior brickwork, applying two coats of whitewash to the exterior, and cleaning the interior.

TYBEE ISLAND [1]

TO TYBEE ISLAND. From the Fort Pulaski National Monument continue east on US 80. At Tybee Island's first traffic caution light turn left into Campbell Street and continue to the parking area in front of Fort Screven.

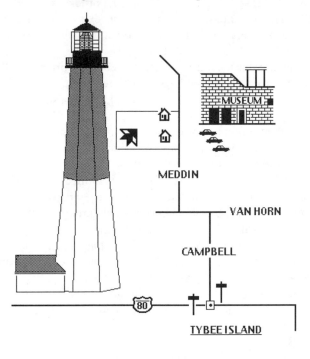

TYBEE ISLAND LIGHTHOUSE & MUSEUM

The museum is located in Battery Garland (1898), one of Fort Screven's coast artillery positions. It displays Tybee Island artifacts and memorabilia from Colonial times through World War II. An old submarine periscope allows the visitor to view the lighthouse's lantern and service gallery.

The head keeper's quarters (1867) is now the complex's visitor center, which contains a gift shop and exhibits depicting the history of the lighthouse, including a collection of photographs dating from 1862 and sketches of the early colonial lighthouse. The second assistant's cottage (1861) serves as a video theater for a film about the history of the lighthouse. Visitors may climb the tower's 178 steps leading to the main service gallery. The maximum number of people allowed in the lighthouse at one time is ten.

COMPLEX OPEN.

April to early September, daily (except Tuesdays) 9 to 6. September through March, daily (except Tuesdays) 9 to 4. Closed January 1, Thanksgiving Day and December 25

ADMISSION FEES. One admission for both lighthouse and museum. Discounts for groups, seniors 62+ and children 6-12. Under six free.

- The Tybee Island Lighthouse and Museum, PO Box 366 (30 Meddin Drive), Tybee Island, GA 31328.

Phone: Lighthouse (912) 786-5801. Museum (912) 786-4077. Fax (912) 786-6538.

To schedule a tour call Tina Lewis at 912-786-5801 Wednesday through Sunday. Reservations are required for guided tours.

Website: http://www.tybeelighthouse.org/

TYBEE ISLAND LIGHTHOUSE (TYBEE; TYBEE MAIN).

CHARACTERISTIC: Fixed white

HAW: 144' **RANGE**: 19 nm

In 1732, after the founding of the Savannah Settlement, General James Edward Oglethorp ordered the building of a coastal landmark at the mouth of the Savannah River. The first Tybee Island unlighted daylight marker, a 90-foot tall cedar piles and brick structure, was completed in 1736. Badly damaged by 1740-41 storms, it was replaced in 1742 with a wooden, shingled and roofed 94-foot tall tower. The second tower was almost completely rebuilt in 1757. The third tower, finished in 1773 at a different location, was a 95-foot tall brick structure that was lighted with spermaceti (whale oil) candles.

Between 1773 and 1791 there exists a serious gap in historical data concerning the lighthouse. There are no known official Georgian historical annals, no federal recognition as being one of the original colonial lighthouses, no record of any Congressional appropriations to build or maintain the property. Stranger still, there is no documentation to show that the lighthouse was ceded by Georgia to the Federal Government possibly as early as December 1791.

The first factual reference to the Tybee Island Light happened in a letter written on November 14, 1789 by John Habersham of Savannah to Alexander Hamilton, Secretary of the Treasury. On November 13, 1795, Mr. Habersham again wrote to Secretary Hamilton. In that missive Habersham reviewed his correspondence concerning the beacon and informed Secretary Hamilton that the light had been an active aid in 1791, with an assigned keeper and equipped with spermaceti candles.

---

1. The Savannah aid to navigation, an 80-foot tall Texas tower located at the mouth of the Savannah River, was destroyed in late November 1996 when rammed by an ocean freighter.

The first officially recorded Congressional appropriation for the light station was a $1,200 grant issued on March 3, 1817. The first official reference to the lighthouse occurred in the 1838 List of Lighthouses. The first official reference to the structure's year of construction (1793) appeared in 1852. With no factual information to deny its existence, the lighthouse can be reasonably recognized as having served as an active aid to navigation during the American Revolutionary War and was one of the original colonial lights ceded to the Federal Government under the Act of 1789.

For several years after its establishment, there were attempts to improve the light's intensity. Sometime prior to 1838, the candles were replaced by a fixed optic consisting of 15 oil-fed lamps each backed by a 15-inch reflector. In 1841 16-inch reflectors were introduced. In 1857 the light's candlepower was greatly increased with the installation of a single-lamp and a second-order Fresnel lens.

Before we leave the early 1800s, let it be known that the lighthouse property was also a very, very popular dueling station. Seems that insulted or warring gentlemen from South Carolina would cross the state line to freely settle their disputes with pistols at "x" paces. Interestingly, the only witness to these shootouts was the lighthouse keeper.

On December 3, 1861, during the Union occupation of Tybee Island, Confederate troops, later identified as a Confederate raiding party of sixteen Savannah-based Irish-Jasper Greens, removed the lens before detonating a gunpowder charge that destroyed the interior stairway and the inside of the lantern housing. In 1866 Union troops not only brought with them a cholera epidemic to disrupt repair work being done on the lighthouse, but also did further damage to the structure. By then the tower was not only inoperable; it was a burned-out, vandalized wreck. In 1867, after withdrawing the sick and undisciplined Union detachment, the Federal Government resumed work on the tower. Using the 1773 tower's solid bottom, Savannah brick, cast-iron sheeting and wrought-iron bars, workmen brought the lighthouse back to active duty. Its walls are 12 feet thick at its base, tapering to an 18-inch thickness at the top. The overall height of the lighthouse is 154 feet. The distance from the tower's base to the lantern's deck is 145 feet. The station also received a new keepers' residence. The lantern, which still retains the first-order Fresnel lens made by Henri LePaute of Paris and installed in 1867, is 20 feet tall with 16 storm panes. The light was reestablished on October 1, 1867.

A hurricane in 1871 produced cracks in the walls. The tower's vibrations during storms of 1878-79 enlarged the cracks. Then in 1886, an earthquake caused more damage to the tower and displaced the lens. With repairs the tower remains a solid, sturdy structure.

In 1884 the light's power source was switched from lard oil to kerosene. Electrified in 1933, the first-order classical lens now magnifies one 120-volt, 1,000-watt light bulb.

We cannot leave Tybee Island without some reference to the light's keepers. Enter Henry Jackson, today a retired member of the Tybee Island community and yesterday a child of one of the keepers. Henry possesses past keepers' logs and is an eager conversant with life among the wickies. As a youngster, Henry had to huff and puff up the tower's 178 staircase each morning to cover the lens, a precautionary measure to insure that the sun's hot rays would not damage the lens' huge and delicate prisms. In the afternoon, he again would climb the stairs to uncover the lens. Henry's early years were not devoid of the usual childhood antics. For example, he would write the names of movie stars in the lighthouse's visitors book, a definite "no-no" in his father's no-frills approach to recording station activities.

One other amusing anecdote from the old keepers' logs concerns an earlier lightkeeper. Seems this individual was a bit prone to stuffing his log with extraneous happenings. On one fine day, for example, our keeper found a huge snake at his doorstep. A bit frightened and not willing to take on a large ophidian menace alone, the keeper called for help. He recorded in his log that his neighbors responded with alacrity carrying with them every possible handled weapon at their disposal. With whacks and thwacks the anti-snake posse did the errant reptile in. The keeper, in his concluding passage, wrote that the snake was no less than 14 feet long and that the reptile's demise was one of Tybee Island Light Station's greatest moments.

OWNER. U.S. Coast Guard (lighthouse). Dwellings and grounds leased to the Tybee Historical Society (Tybee Museum Association) in 1987.

PRESERVATION. Listed (May 25, 1982) in the National Register of Historic Places as part of the Fort Screven Historic District.

TYBEE ISLAND

During the 1990-91 period the Tybee Island Historical Society received grants to restore the light tower's anteroom, the outdoor summer kitchen and a storage building. The interior of the unused part of anteroom was stripped to reveal its original brick walls and wooden rafters. The summer kitchen was completely renovated. All three cottages' exteriors were painted and essential repairs made to their interiors. In 1995 three landings in the tower were repaired.

In 1996 damaged brick corbels that anchor the gallery's support brackets were repaired.

In 1997 the tower had to be closed to the public to allow a thorough inspection of the damage to the brickwork by moisture and to cast iron parts by rust. In 1996, although Georgia's legislature voted to grant $105,000 for the repair work, the governor vetoed the bill.

The Tybee Island Historical Society moved forward by raising funds from public and private sources, with major help coming from Harbour Lights (makers of collectible lighthouse models) and their Collectors' Society. Children of the lighthouse's last keeper, George Jackson, were active in the fundraising. In July 1998 bids were taken, and Internatonal Chimney Corporation, lighthouse movers and restorers at so many other locations, were brought in for the restoration. Internatonal Chimney's crew was augmented by Scottish masons, Irish painters and local craftsmen.

The restored lighthouse was relighted on March 1, 1999. A Scotsman in full dress played "Amazing Grace" on the bagpipes from the lighthouse's gallery, and Grace Jackson Weaver, daughter of the last keeper, helped throw the switch for the relighting. More restoration work is planned on the station's buildings. The buildings will be restored to the 1919-39 period, with total costs estimated at $1.2 million. Your help is welcomed.

- The Tybee Island Lighthouse and Museum, PO Box 366, Tybee Island, GA 31328.

Phone (912) 786-5801. Fax (912) 786-6538.

Website: http://www.tybeelighthouse.org/

Tybee Island Lighthouse

SOUTH CAROLINA
HILTON HEAD[1]
HAIG POINT

TO HILTON HEAD ISLAND. Enter Hilton Head Island on US 278. The Hilton Head Range Rear Lighthouse stands on the grounds of the Palmetto Dunes residential community and resort. It cannot be visited without specific permission. Although the Haig Point Lighthouse is closed to visitors, it is plainly visible while cruising Calibogue Sound.

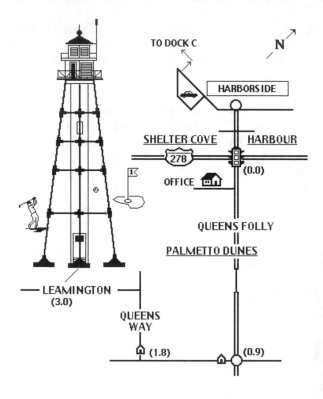

VISITING THE HILTON HEAD LIGHTHOUSE.

While the following information does not insure that permission to visit will be granted, send or call requests to:

- Director of Advertising and Public Relations, Greenwood Development Corporation, PO Box 5628, Hilton Head Island, SC 29938.

Phone (843) 785-1106. Fax (843) 842-8509

Ask to see the lighthouse. If permission is granted, instructions on where to go to pick up your entry permit will be provided. That office will issue an entry pass for the resort area. The accompanying map is not an invitation to you to drive into Palmetto Dunes without permission. If you do, you will be stopped at the first security gate.

HILTON HEAD (RANGE REAR) LIGHTHOUSE
(LEAMINGTON).

Although Congress first appropriated funds in 1854 for a lighthouse and beacon on Hilton Head Island, nothing was done until 1863, when Union forces occupying the island established an offshore anchored lightship and erected a system of range lights to guide ships into Port Royal Sound. After the end of the Civil War, the lightship was transferred and by 1869 the beacons were no longer active.

In 1876 Congress appropriated $40,000 for range lights. By 1877 the Lighthouse Board had come up with the plans, but haggling over the cost of the land held up construction. The contract was finally signed in 1879. In the following year, the contractor completed the construction of the rear range light tower, a nearby keeper's residence and at a distance of one mile forward of the rear range structure, a house with a tower perched atop it. The house was converted into a movable structure in 1884 to enable the beacon to be adjusted as shifting sands and channel dictated its relocation. Several moves were made during the 1890s.

Not much more is known about the lighthouse until the World War II period. Then, two houses were built on the former light station to house personnel, who manned a maritime observation post atop the tower. The houses were badly damaged in a 1948 hurricane. In 1949 the residents no longer employed as watch personnel moved out, claiming that the houses were haunted and hexed by the ghost of the daughter of a former keeper who drowned during an 1898 storm. Soon after their departure, the houses were moved to Harbour Town, renovated and turned into a delicatessen. Fortunately for the new owner, the lady ghost chose to remain with the lighthouse.

The system was taken out of service and the rear range lighthouse abandoned in 1932. All that remains of the light station is the rear range tower and its brick oil house built in 1892.

---

1. That 90-foot tall red and white banded tower standing at the entrance to Harbour Town's small harbor is <u>not</u> the Hilton Head Lighthouse. It was built in 1970 by the developers of the Sea Pine Plantation as a property enhancement for the small harbor, surrounding real estate and gold course.

The lighthouse is a 95-foot tall skeletal cast-iron tower with a central column containing a 112-step cast-iron stairway. The tube was originally sheathed in wood to give it a cylindrical form. Later in 1913 when both lighthouses were renovated, the tube's wood exterior was sheathed with steel sheeting. Windows appear alternatingly at landings two through five. The hexagonal watchroom and lantern are of wood construction. The watchroom's narrow balcony is cast-iron. Six concrete foundation blocks form a hexagon some 30 feet in diameter. The tower's supporting legs are bolted to the concrete bases and rise in five stages, with cast-iron channels connecting the columns at each juncture. Wrought-iron tie bars with pinned connections provide diagonal bracing at each stage. The center tube is attached to the vertical members by tension bars.

The optic first installed in the rear range tower is believed to have been a Fresnel lens. Records show that the optic's light was generated by two Hains lamps that did not require preheating of the oil. The beacon's height above water was 87 feet. Its range was 15 nautical miles. In 1893 the Hains lamps were replaced by a more efficient Funck-Heap kerosene lamp.

OWNER. Greenwood Development Corporation.
PRESERVATION. Listed in the National Register of Historic Places.

Photographs taken in 1980 show a rather shabby tower with heavily rusted cast iron support members and paint peeling off its wooden components. In fact, it had a downright ugly appearance. In 1985 the Greenwood Development Corporation completely refurbished the lighthouse. Today, despite its age and hurricane scars, the tower is structurally sound and superbly restored.

VIEWING THE HAIG POINT LIGHTHOUSE. Captain Mark Maurer operates two narrated cruises down Broad Creek and out into Calibogue Sound that enable the traveler to see the lighthouse. Both excursions depart from Dock C, Shelter Cove Harbour. The entrance to this marina is opposite the entrance to Palmetto Dunes.

- Adventure Cruises,Inc, Suite G Harbourside III, Shelter Cove Harbour, Hilton Head Island, SC 29928.
Phone (843) 785-4558.
Website: http://www.hiltonheadisland.com/adventure.htm

The Dolphin Watch Nature Cruise aboard the *Holiday* (two decks, lower with mid-deck enclosed area), a narrated one hour and 45 minute cruise down Broad Creek and out into Calibogue Sound, provides distant viewing of the Haig Point Lighthouse. Call for current schedule.

FARES. Tickets are sold at dock beginning 1/2 hour before departure. Discounts for families and children 3-12. Under 3 free.

The Daufuskie Island Nature Cruise is for you lighthouse seekers also interested in seeing Daufuskie (daw fuss' key) Island. This narrated two hour and fifteen minute tour should please all. The *Adventure* (two decks; lower enclosed) passes the lighthouse. If you tell the skipper of your interest in the lighthouse, he may sail closer to the point as he enters the Cooper River.

After docking at the Freeport Marina, passengers may take the guided safari tour (extra fare; child's fare). The jungle bus stops at the old winery, the ancient Union Baptist Church and the famous old schoolhouse. Pat Conroy wrote about his teaching experiences in the schoolhouse in his novel *The Water Is Wide*. The story was later made into the movie *Conrack*.

You may also rent a 4-passenger golf cart (per day fee) and explore the island on your own. Reservations are not required. You will not be able to visit the lighthouse.

Daufuskie's famous deviled crabs, other foods and beverages are sold at the Freeport Marina Gazebo.

Call for the latest cruise schedule.

FARES. Discount for children 3-12. Under 3 free. Guided land tour of Daufuskie Island extra charge with discount for children

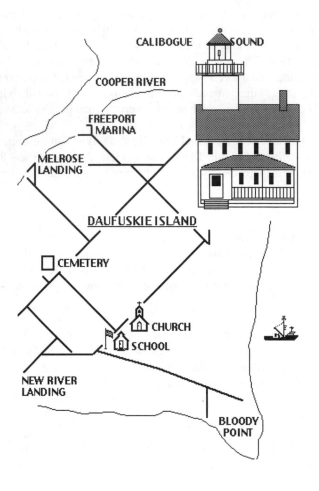

DAUFUSKIE ISLAND. This island, known as the "Place of Blood," earned its name from the fierce fighting between Native American Indians (with a few pirates thrown in) and the Spanish, French and English colonists. The colonists arrived on the island as early as 1526 and by the 1750s had established their plantations. Reportedly, the last and bloodiest battle (c. 1715) between the Native Americans and the New World settlers was at Bloody Point, where the last of the island's Indian population was annihilated. The plantations thrived producing cash crops of rice, sugar cane, timber and cotton. The Union blockade of the island during the Civil War signaled the end to plantation prosperity.

After the war, the island and its freemen or "Gullah" inhabitants (now down to about 60 residents) became locked in the past. Gullah is the name of an historic African-English language spoken among "Geechee" African Americans in the rural low country of northern Florida, Georgia and South Carolina. The language is characterized by words borrowed from the King's English, American vernacular and African Benta. It has its own sentence structure. To most English-speaking persons the language is barely understandable and sounds distinctly West Indian. For example, the Gullah sentence, "Bunk up get your hind cut," translates into "Bend over and take a whipping." Gullah added the words "yam" and "goober" to the American lexicon.

HAIG POINT (RANGE REAR) LIGHTHOUSE (DAUFUSKIE ISLAND).
CHARACTERISTIC: Flashing white 14s **HAW**: 47'

The first beacons on Haig Point were front and rear range lights erected and established in 1872. They were then known as the Daufuskie Island Front and Rear Range Lights. The front beacon was placed atop an offshore pole. The rear light, as seen today, rests atop the Victorian dwelling's rather tall integrated tower. The original optic was a kerosene-fed lamp and a fifth-order Fresnel lens. Both were deactivated in 1934.

OWNER. International Paper Realty Corporation of South Carolina, PO Drawer 7319, Hilton Head Island, SC 29938.

Phone (803) 686-4244.

PRESERVATION. Listed in the National Register as part of the Daufuskie Historic District.

The 25-foot tall lighthouse remained unattended and boarded up until its present owner restored it, added antique furniture and turned the lighthouse into a restaurant and a bed and breakfast lodge for members of the Haig Point Club. In October 1986, Haig Point was reactivated as a private aid. The light, produced by a modern optic, marks the confluence of the Cooper River (Intracoastal Waterway) with Calibogue Sound.

HILTON HEAD & HAIG POINT

BLOODY POINT (FRONT RANGE) LIGHTHOUSE

In the early 1800s, Bloody Point had two operational range lights. By placing candles on an offshore pole and in the keeper dwelling's attic windows, the front beacon and the house on the beach at Bloody Point became Daufuskie Island's first aids to navigation. This rudimentary arrangement, in common usage in the 1700s, was established to warn mariners entering Calibogue Sound from the south. It is not known how long this candlelight arrangement continued in operation, but it is conceivable that oil-burning lamps were introduced in the early 1800s.

The beacon was reestablished in 1883 with a kerosene-fed lamp displayed in a dormer window on the upper story of a new keeper's cottage. A rear range light was established on a triangular white metal tower. The light was produced by a locomotive headlight, which was kept in a "lamp room" during the day. The lamp room was an 8 by 10 foot brick building. Each night the keeper would run the light up on rails to a height of 81 feet.

The light was extinguished in 1922 and the house sold to a private party. The eventual owner was Arthur A. (Papy) Burn, who had been the station's last assistant keeper. Burn occupied the cottage for 40 years, and converted the old lamp room into a successful winery that became known as the Silver Dew WInery. He stored the wine in the station's old oil house.

The owner today is Joe Yocius, a real estate broker. Mr. Yocius has done extensive restoration of the buildings and has done much to preserve the history of this unique station.

The house cannot be seen from the safari bus, but, if moving about the island on a golf cart, stop and walk to the property's entrance for a look at the old ex-lighthouse.

For more information you can visit Joe Yocius' excellent website.
Joe Yocius
Dunes Marketing Group, W.M. Byrne BIC
P.O. Box 21326
Hilton Head Island, SC 29925
Phone (800) 258-5202
Website: http://www.lowcountryjoe.com
Email: Info@LowCountryJoe.com

Hilton Head Lighthouse

59

HUNTING ISLAND

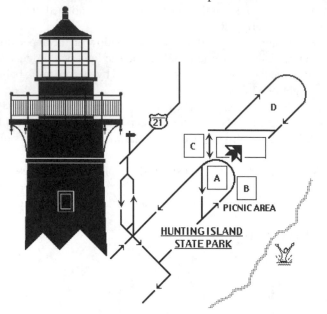

TO HUNTING ISLAND STATE PARK. Take US 21 out of Savannah. The lighthouse is located within the Hunting Island State Park some 16 miles east of Beaufort (byoo' fert). The park is a 5,000-acre barrier island dedicated to both human recreational needs and wildlife preservation.

Enter the park and stay on the main paved road. Follow the "North Beach" signs and lighthouse symbol signs posted along the winding road past the "A" to the "C" parking areas. The lighthouse compound adjoins lot "C." The lighthouse grounds are handicapped accessible.

The park's visitor center has exhibits on the island's history, its environment and the lighthouse. Visitors may climb the 181 steps to the top of the lighthouse.

PARK OPEN. All year, daily 6 to sunset.

TOWER OPEN. All year daily 10 to 4.

ADMISSION FEE. April to October, daily per vehicle. Lighthouse climb free.

- Hunting Island State Park, 2555 Sea Island Parkway, St. Helena Island, SC 29920.

Phone (843) 838-2011.

Website: http://www.huntingisland.com/

HUNTING ISLAND LIGHTHOUSE (HUNTING ISLAND STATE PARK)

In August 1854, Congress authorized the construction of a lighthouse on the north end of the island, about 0.25 mile from the surf. This tower was to replace a lightship stationed in St. Helena Sound. By 1859 work on the 95-foot wooden (some references say it was a brick structure) tower was completed. The lantern was outfitted with a second-order Fresnel lens, producing a beam of light visible out to a distance of 17 nautical miles. The beacon became operational in July 1859. The lighthouse was destroyed by Confederate troops (not beach erosion) in 1862.

An 1872 land survey discovered that some 150 acres on the island's north end had been washed away. As a result of the topographic change, the site for the second light tower was selected about one mile south of the 1854 tower, but again only 0.25 mile from the sea. When completed, the light station consisted of the tower, a 2 1/2-story wood framed keeper's dwelling, a brick oil house and two outbuildings. The new beacon was activated on July 1, 1875.

Shore erosion forced the lighthouse's displacement in 1889. Having been constructed of cast-iron sections, the 140-foot tall lighthouse was unbolted, taken apart, moved 1.25 miles south to its present location and reassembled. It was relighted on October 1, 1889. A year later, the keeper's dwelling and support buildings were moved to the present compound. A dock and tram railroad were also built for the delivery of supplies and barrels of oil to the station.

After the light's decommissioning on June 16, 1933, the house was razed and the fog signal building destroyed. The tower, oil house and two storage sheds remain.

Hunting Island and Cape Canaveral have a special niche in America's lighthouse history. Their construction as tall, tapering light towers, using prefabricated cast-iron plates, introduced the fourth of America's cast-iron architectural designs. The brick-lined tower is secured to its concrete base by anchor bolts. It cost $102,000 to build.

Hunting Island's optic consisted of a kerosene-powered incandescent oil vapor lamp intensified by a second-order Fresnel lens. The light's focal plane was 121 feet above mean high water and could be seen out to a distance of 18 nautical miles.

OWNER. State of South Carolina. Managed by the Department of Parks, Recreation and Tourism.

PRESERVATION. Listed in the National Register of Historic Places.

HUNTING ISLAND

Sadly, for many years the unattended lighthouse was open to visitors who slathered graffiti throughout the interior and mutilated the historic structure's windows so thoroughly that they had to be removed. Weathering etched and crusted the open cast-iron tower. Worse still is the plight of the second-order classical lens that once rested inside at the entry level. It has been so badly vandalized that it is probably beyond restoring.

Fortunately, preservationists' clarion calls for action were heard, and in 1992 the State went to work on the structure. The interior's cast-iron stairs, landings, watchroom deck, rails and other iron work were sandblasted, primed and painted. New windows were fabricated using the design and dimensions of the old windows. The tower has been sealed from the intrusion of the maritime atmosphere.

Although budget limitations prevented the continuation of the restoration project, the manager contracted for the painting of the inner brick walls and tower's exterior. The latter was coated with an improved industrial (acrylic) coating. Both projects were completed in 1993.

Hunting Island Lighthouse

MORRIS ISLAND

TO FOLLY BEACH. If northbound and before reaching the Ashley River bridge, turn right off US 17 into SC 171. If southbound and a short distance west of the Ashley River bridge, turn left into SC 700. Continue on SC 171 to Folly Beach and, at the second traffic signal one block before a hotel at the end of Center Street, turn left into East Ashley Street. Continue for 3.3 miles to the entrance of an abandoned Coast Guard LORAN station.

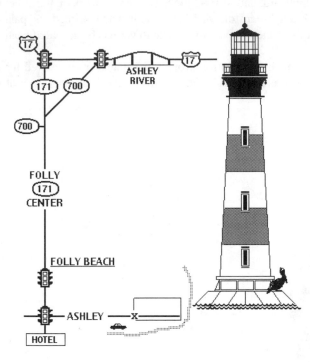

Although vehicular traffic is denied entry by a locked barrier, pedestrians are allowed to walk the 0.25 mile to the beach for a spectacular view of the lighthouse.

Across Charleston Bay one can see the towering Charleston Lighthouse on Sullivans Island. At the gate's turnaround there is free off-road parking. On weekends this parking lot is usually full. If it is, park on one of the side streets and walk the short distance to the station's entrance.

MORRIS ISLAND LIGHTHOUSE (OLD CHARLESTON; CHARLESTON MAIN; CHARLESTON; MIDDLE BAY).

The first Morris Island tower was an octagonal brick structure built in 1767 on one of three small islands (Cumming's Point, Morrison's, and Middle Bay) that now form Morris Island. The height of the light above the tower's base was 102 feet. That lighthouse was one of the twelve Colonial lighthouses turned over to the new Federal Government under the terms of the Act of 1789. A small plaque attached to the present tower's foundation block, states that the "first stone of this beacon" was laid on May 30, 1767.

Although there is one official report that alludes to the construction of a new tower in 1837 on Lighthouse Island near Fort Sumter, that event apparently did not happen. The original tower was again repaired in 1845; and in 1857, it received a first-order Fresnel lens. The new optic was lighted on January 1, 1858.

In December 1860, Congress was notified that South Carolina had seized all lights along her coast. The following year the Confederacy ordered the destruction of the Morris Island tower and the caching of its classical lens. At that time some 164 lights along the Atlantic and Gulf coasts from Virginia to Texas were darkened. Only a few lights in Florida remained operational.

After the taking of Charleston in 1865, the harbor had to be resurveyed, because silting had totally changed the navigability of the main channel. With old channels closed and new ones appearing and in use, the Lighthouse Board decided in 1873 to build a new lighthouse on Morris Island. Construction began in 1874 and the lighthouse is believed to have been finished in 1876.

A hurricane (1885) and a powerful earthquake (1886) damaged the lens and cracked the masonry wall. Repaired, the old tower has withstood both time and wear.

Interestingly, the original tri-island complex was large enough to house a small self-sufficient community with pigs and chickens and garden plots. By the late 1800s, there were 15 buildings, including the station's three Italianate wood framed keeper dwellings and a one-room schoolhouse. Transportation about the island was accomplished via a system of connecting boardwalks and one automobile. In 1938, when the light was automated, the keepers and their families left the island.

MORRIS ISLAND

The conical brick tower is 150 feet tall and rests on an 8-foot thick concrete base formed between foundation pilings and laid atop the foundation ruins of the 1767 tower. It has a base diameter of 33 feet, tapering to nearly 17 feet at its top. The tower's protruding cast-iron windows, located on the east and west sides, show projecting pedimented hoods (segmentally arched lintels and spandrels) and molded surrounds. The main entrance is similarly designed. The watchroom's ornate gallery can be reached via an interior spiral cast-iron stairway with nine landings, six with windows.

Based on an 1832 Lighthouse Service report that the revolving multi-lamp optic's focal plane was 125 feet above sea level, the repairs done on the tower in 1800 apparently included the installation of a larger lantern and a new rotating lighting apparatus.

When Morris Island was reestablished on October 1, 1876, the lantern held a lard oil-powered lamp and a revolving first-order Fresnel lens 155 feet above the sea. That lens may have been the lighthouse's original 1857 Fresnel .

PRESERVATION. Listed (June 28, 1982) in the National Register of Historic Places.

The light was discontinued in 1962 when the new Charleston light was established on Sullivans Island. After the lighthouse and its magnificent first-order Fresnel lens were sold at auction, the efforts of the Charleston Preservation Society were instrumental in preventing its demolition.

Jetties were constructed in 1896 to protect the island, and they have caused the complete erosion of the shoal protecting Morris Island from the sea. As a result, the island has disappeared and the tower stands in water at high tide. This lighthouse, standing alone and leaning a bit from the ravages of time, storms and an earthquake, is still a majestic sight to behold.

According to 1982 Charleston County records, the lighthouse was purchased in 1966 for $25,000 by S. E. Felkel, Yelsen Land Company, Inc., Goose Creek, South Carolina. In 1995 Mr. Felkel forfeited the structure in a foreclosure suit brought against him. It was later sold to Columbia logger Paul Gunter.

In 1999 a nonprofit organization, Save the Light, Inc., was successful in purchasing the lighthouse for $75,000. The group's sole purpose is to preserve the lighthouse.

Initial engineering studies have been completed, and estimates put the cost of Morris Island Lighthouse's long term preservation at $1.5 million to $2 million. The South Carolina Legislature allocated $500,000 for preservation of the lighthouse. The SC Natural Resources Board voted on April 21, 2000 to buy the lighthouse for $1 and lease it back to Save The Light Inc. for preservation. Engineers are now evaluating the foundation of the lighthouse to determine what needs to be done to save it.

Robert New, co-chairman of Save the Light, believes that $1 million can be raised through the continued fundraising campaign. This "colonial" lighthouse could become the "Pride of Charleston."

- Save The Light Inc., PO Box 12490, Charleston, SC 29422.

Phone: (843) 795-8911.

Website: http://www.savethelight.org/

CHARLESTON

TO SULLIVANS ISLAND. In Mount Pleasant take SC 703 south across the Sawyer Memorial Bridge (free) to Sullivans Island. At a stop sign and a "Ft. Moultrie" sign, turn right into Middle Street. Drive about 0.4 mile and turn left at Sta [Station] 18 1/2. You will not have to search for this lighthouse. Just look up and to your left. Then drive the two city blocks to the station.

Visitors may enter the station but not the light tower.

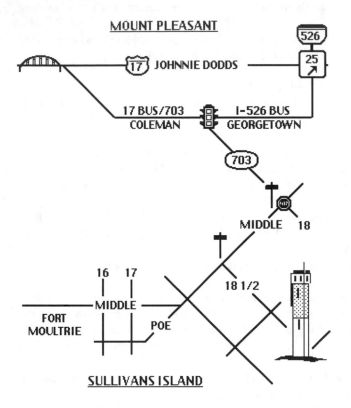

CHARLESTON LIGHTHOUSE (SULLIVANS ISLAND).
CHARACTERISTIC: Group flashing white 30s
HAW: 163'   **RANGE**: 26 nm

The Charleston Lighthouse, built in 1962, is a mighty imposing structure. Unlike its concrete Oak Island cousin this triangular 140-foot tall tower is constructed of steel and clad in aluminum siding. It is the only elevator-serviced lighthouse in the United States.

Its optic, whose light marks the northside entrance to Charleston Harbor, can generate a high intensity beam ranging from 1.2 million to a high of 28 million candlepower.

OWNER. U.S. Coast Guard.

FORT MOULTRIE NATIONAL MONUMENT. Just west of the lighthouse on West Middle Street is Fort Moultrie. The original Fort Moultrie was only half completed when on June 28, 1776, a British naval flotilla of nine warships appeared and opened fire on its defenders. South Carolina volunteers fought off a British landing party and saved the fort. That battle, which occurred six days prior to the signing of the Declaration of Independence, was one of the first decisive victories of the emerging Revolution. Edgar Allen Poe was once stationed at Fort Moultrie as a sergeant major. Thus, it is not surprising that he chose the Sullivans Island locale for his story "The Gold Bug." Osceola, the famous Seminole chieftain and betrayed warrior, died while unjustly incarcerated in the fort and is buried within the compound.

OPEN.
Memorial Day to Labor Day, daily 9 to 6.
Other times of the year, daily 9 to 5.
Closed December 25.
The Visitors Center offers a 20-minute movie on Fort Moultrie's history and a more comprehensive 1 1/2-hour slide show.
FREE ADMISSION.
Phone (843) 883-3123.

CAPE ROMAIN

NORTH OR SOUTH ON US 17. The two Cape Romain Lighthouses are located in the Cape Romain National Wildlife Refuge, a stretch of barrier islands, salt marshes and open water encompassing 65,000 acres. A wilderness area of 25,000 acres is included in the refuge. The refuge office is located about 20 miles north of Charleston on US 17. The former headquarters and visitor center were destroyed in 1989 during Hurricane Hugo. The new Seewee Visitor and Environmental Education Center is now open to the public. The construction project was a joint venture of the U.S. Fish and Wildlife Service and the U.S. Forest Service.

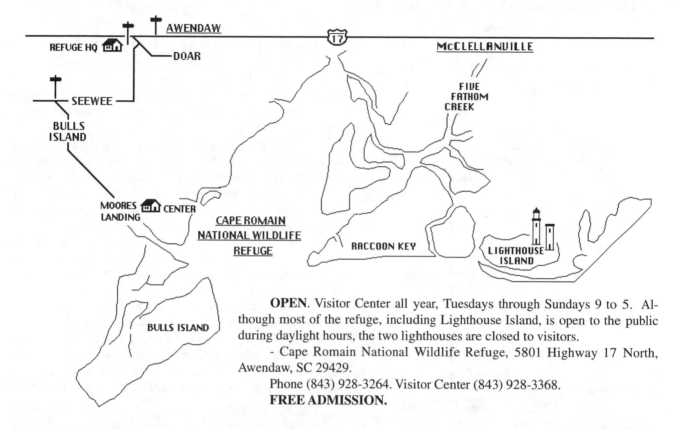

OPEN. Visitor Center all year, Tuesdays through Sundays 9 to 5. Although most of the refuge, including Lighthouse Island, is open to the public during daylight hours, the two lighthouses are closed to visitors.

- Cape Romain National Wildlife Refuge, 5801 Highway 17 North, Awendaw, SC 29429.

Phone (843) 928-3264. Visitor Center (843) 928-3368.

FREE ADMISSION.

REFUGE CRUISES. The U.S. Fish and Wildlife Service has granted Ann Goold's Coastal Expeditions exclusive rights to transport passengers by boat within the refuge. Although there is a scheduled service to Bulls Island from Moores Landing, the only way a traveler can get to Lighthouse Island and the light towers is by a subcontracted charter boat that may depart from either Moores Landing or from McClellanville's waterfront (see next map). The ferry transport will be a "six-pack" craft carrying six passengers. Disembarking is accomplished by beaching the boat and hopping off -- sometimes into the water. The day's favorable spot to beach the boat could involve a short walk along the beach. Crossing time from Moores Landing is 45-60 minutes; from McClellanville 25-30 minutes.

FARES. Minimum four-hour round trip. $25.00 per hour per passenger.

- Coastal Expeditions, Inc., PO Box 556, Sullivan's Island, SC 29482.

Phone (843) 881-4582.

CAPE ROMAIN LIGHTHOUSE (1827).

After Congressional approval and an appropriation of $10,000 in 1823, the first lighthouse on Cape Romain (South Carolina's second) was erected, in 1827, on the northeast key (now Lighthouse Island) of the Raccoon Keys, southwest of the mouth of the Santee River. The beacon's mission was to warn ships off the Cape Romain shoals nine miles to the southeast and to help southbound ships keep out of the northerly flow of the Gulf Stream.

This structure is a 65-foot tall conical, brick tower without ornamentation. The work was contracted to Winslow Lewis, who spent $7,475 of appropriated funds to complete the task. The tower's base is 30 feet in diameter with its walls tapering to 15 feet at the lantern's deck. Simple pegged windows appear on the east and west sides. The lantern deck was reached via a wooden spiral stairway. "Light" and "1827" are carved into the ground level doorway's wooden lintel.

Lewis equipped the tower with his "patent lamps, reflectors, &c." for another $950. The fixed light had a focal plane 87.5 feet above sea level and a range of 18 nautical miles. In 1847 the tower was refitted with another fixed optic consisting of 11 lamps each backed with a 21-inch parabolic reflector.

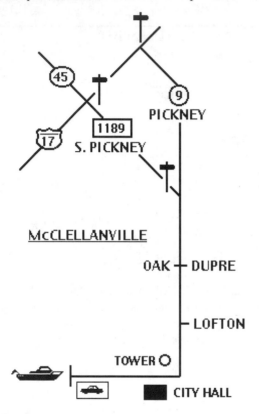

CAPE ROMAIN LIGHTHOUSE (1857).

In 1851, findings of an investigation gave the old lighthouse a fourth-order rating and recommended that a new first-order aid be built. By 1937 the abandoned tower had been stripped of its lantern, painted red for daymark purposes and relegated to being a storage shed.

The second lighthouse was completed in 1857 by slave labor and first lighted on January 1, 1858. The 150-foot tall natural brick tower is octagonal and pyramidal in shape. While under construction, it was discovered that the tower's walls were irregularly sloped. Despite orders to correct the problem, the tower was completed with a noticeable tilt.

Between 1869 and 1873, the tower's walls began to crack, causing it to lean even more. By 1891 the tilt had thrown the lens out of plumb. With repairs and adjustments the light remained active.

The focal plane of its first-order Fresnel lens was 161 feet above the ocean and its light could be seen out to a distance of 19 nautical miles. In 1861, as was the case for many other southern lights, the Confederacy removed the lens before badly damaging the tower and its lantern. In 1866 the tower and the neglected keeper's dwelling were repaired and the beacon was relighted.

The Fresnel lens was removed in 1931, when the island received a generator to supply electricity to a newly installed lighting system consisting of a 500-watt bulb and a bullseye lens that had two of its eight panels darkened. The optic made one revolution every minute and had a range of 19 nautical miles. In 1937 the lower wattage apparatus was supplanted by a fixed 1,000-watt optic that required attention only once every three months. As a result the keepers were removed.

In 1947, after the removal of its first-order lens, the light tower was downgraded to daymark status. Sea buoys now mark the shoals off the cape.

OWNER. U.S. Fish and Wildlife Service since 1947.
PRESERVATION. Both lighthouses are listed in the National Register of Historic Places.

CAPE ROMAIN

Over their many inactive years the lighthouses of Cape Remain were reduced to empty, decaying and virtually forgotten historic structures. The older tower stands without its lantern. The newer and taller lighthouse's windows had been smashed, its interior violated and the ground floor door torn off its hinges. Although the newer tower's spiral cast-iron stairway to the watchroom remains intact, its lantern, (sans its storm panes, but retaining its circular and conical brass roof) still holds the Fresnel lens' revolving brass pedestal. All other buildings, including the keeper's dwelling, oil house and outbuildings were dismantled after the light was discontinued in 1947.

Since 1988, the U. S. Fish & Wildlife Service and volunteers have spent a considerable amount of time, effort and money in cleaning the structures, making certain interior repairs, replacing the windows and main door, and securing both towers.

During 1994-95, the government authorized and funded a restoration project for both towers. Their exteriors were repointed to provide greater stability and repainted. The newer tower's window sashes were replaced and the lantern reglazed with new storm panes. The older tower has a solid barn red coating. The newer lighthouse's upper half sports alternating white and black vertical stripes around its eight sides; its watchroom and lower half are white.

BULL ISLAND LIGHTHOUSE (BULL BAY) (destroyed).

The mid-19th century Bull Island Lighthouse was constructed as a 1 1/2-story wooden house with a octagonal tower built into the roof's mid-section. The circular lantern was equipped with a fourth-order Fresnel lens and a whale oil-fed lamp. The Lighthouse Bulletin of April 1913 reported that the beacon had been discontinued. Not long after its deactivation the lighthouse was destroyed by a storm. Reportedly, the ruins can be seen at low tide off Cape Romain Wildlife Refuge's Bulls Island.

GEORGETOWN

NORTH OR SOUTH ON US 17.   The Georgetown Lighthouse is located on the southern tip of North Island, a barrier island located between Winyah Bay and the Atlantic Ocean. A boat cruise to the North Island beach and lighthouse departs from Georgetown's Sampit River waterfront. The boat landing is a floating dock at the Harborwalk Seaport located off Front Street at the end of Broad Street.   Free parking is available in the lots shown as "P" on the map.

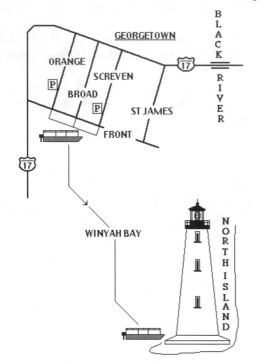

LIGHTHOUSE CRUISES. Captain Sandy Vermont offers cruises by appointment to the Georgetown Lighthouse and/or the Cape Romain Lighthouse. A round trip to the Georgetown Lighthouse takes around three hours; a round trip to the Cape Romain Lighthouse is about five hours. Captain Sandy will combine both lighthouses in an all day excursion. The maximum number of passengers is twelve.

SCHEDULE. By appointment only. The cruise to the lighthouse area on North Island depends on good weather and favorable winds. If winds are high, Captain Vermont may choose to land his passengers farther north and away from the lighthouse.

FARES. Call for information. Reservations required.

- Captain Sandy's Tours, Inc., PO Box 2533, Pawleys Island, SC 29585. Phone (843) 527-4106.

Another local company offers a three-hour tour on a 49-passenger pontoon boat leaving from Georgetown. The trips focus on the Georgetown Lighthouse, shelling, and the natural environment of the Carolina "low country."

SCHEDULE. Cruises are offered twice daily (except Sunday). Call for dates and times.

- Carolina Rover, 735 Front St., Georgetown, SC. Phone: (843) 546-8822.

GEORGETOWN LIGHTHOUSE.
CHARACTERISTIC: Group flashing white 15s
HAW: 85' **RANGE**: 15 nm

In response to Congress passing, on August 7, 1789, the act that established a national lighthouse service, patriot Paul Trapier donated a tract of land on North Island for the construction of a lighthouse. Although the South Carolina legislature agreed to turn the land over to the Federal Government in the fall of 1795, the final bill of agreement was not approved until December 19, 1796. Because of certain restrictions and stipulations attached to the bill, Congress requested that the legislature pass a rewritten act of cession. The new act was forwarded to Washington in early 1798. Because of the three-year delay, Congress had to reappropriate the funds for the lighthouse's construction. This was done and $7,000 was available for contract proposals. The construction contract was signed on November 19, 1798 and work began on the lighthouse at the entrance to Winyah Bay.

The 72-foot tall pyramidal wooden tower was built atop an octagonal brick foundation with a 26-foot base diameter, narrowing to 12 feet at the top. The structure was of cyprus construction, shingled and painted. The cast-iron framed lantern was six feet in diameter and rested on a cyprus deck covered with flagstones. It was topped with a ventilator-equipped copper dome. There were five flights of stairs (124 steps) leading up to the lantern deck. Also added to the new light station was a small two-story wood framed house, cisterns for the storage of whale oil and a well. The beacon was first lighted on February 14, 1801.

The lighthouse collapsed during a storm in August 1806. Congress appropriated $20,000 on February 10, 1807 for a new brick or stone light tower and reappropriated the same sum on February 26, 1810. Variations in contractor proposals delayed the project's start until 1811. Although a plaque on the lighthouse announces that "This Light House Was Erected - 1811," the new tower was completed in 1812 for slightly less than $17,600. This structure resembled its predecessor, except that it was built of brick and had a larger lantern. The stairway's steps and their supporting centerpost have been cut from stone.

The present brick lighthouse is the 87-foot tall 1812 tower that was rebuilt in 1857 to receive a Fresnel lens and again in 1867 to repair damage inflicted during the Civil War.

GEORGETOWN

The first two lighthouses were fitted with multi-lamp/reflector optics. The 1812 lighthouse displayed a fixed white light that was 89 feet above mean high water. The tower retains its fourth-order Fresnel lens installed in 1857.

A ghost in the lighthouse? Yes, according to a former Belle Island Coast Guard Station Chief. One evening, two of his subordinates set up a tape recorder at the top of the tower stairs and turned it on. The recorder taped the footsteps of the descending men and the slamming and the locking of the door as they left the tower. The tape remained silent until it began recording the steps of someone descending the stairs, stopping on the ground floor and then returning up the stairs to the lantern. The next morning, when the two (none would enter alone) retrieved their recorder, the door to the tower was closed and locked. There was no evidence that a living being had been inside the tower and the recorder was undisturbed.

The light station consists of the lighthouse, several one-story buildings, a bayside dock and a radio tower.

OWNER. The station had been leased since 1988 to the South Carolina Department of Youth Services, but on February 16, 2001 the South Carolina Department of Natural Resources voted to make the station part of the Heritage Trust Program's Tom Yawkey Wildlife Reserve. The transfer will hopefully lead to improved protection for South Carolina's oldest light station, which has had problems with vandalism. The DNR already owned the rest of the island, which was willed to the state in 1976 by the late Boston Red Sox owner Tom Yawkey.

PRESERVATION. Listed in the National Register of Historic Places.

Bald Head Lighthouse

NORTH CAROLINA
OAK ISLAND

TO SOUTHPORT: Three main routes lead to Southport.
1. North on US 17 and in Supply, NC, east on NC 211.
2. From Wilmington east on US 17 then south on NC 133.
3. From Wilmington south on US 421 and the Fisher-Southport ferry. See the FEDERAL POINT chapter.

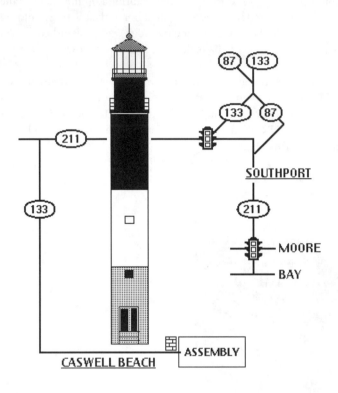

TO CASWELL BEACH. In Southport from NC 211 take NC 133 south. The Oak Island Lighthouse is located in Caswell Beach at the end of NC 133. Enroute and while crossing the Elizabeth River Bridge, both lighthouses will appear off to the left. Continue into Caswell Beach and after a sharp left turn, continue eastward to the Coast Guard station.

A short distance farther east is the North Carolina Baptist Assembly. Along the wall to the left of the entrance is the former site of the earlier Oak Island range light tower.

See also the Cape Fear Range Lights in the FEDERAL POINT chapter.

OAK ISLAND LIGHTHOUSE (CASWELL),
CHARACTERISTIC: Group flashing white 10s
HAW: 169' **RANGE:** 24 nm

The tower is 148 feet tall and is of reinforced concrete construction. The structure has a 16-foot deep concrete base that rests on a reinforced concrete foundation placed atop piles driven to a depth of 125 feet into bedrock. Its exterior is covered with a precolored enamel-like coating that needs no painting. The process, often referred to as the slip (slurry) method, adds a hardy weatherproofing glaze, while reducing long-term maintenance costs. The method has been used on concrete bridge supports, unadorned buildings and storage silos. After the tower was completed, a U.S. Marine Corps heavy-lift helicopter picked up the massive lantern and settled it in place.

The light was established on May 15, 1958. Eight 480-volt high intensity mercury arc bulbs normally flash 1.4 million candlepower; and, when visibility drops below 19 nautical miles, its beam can be increased to 14 million candlepower. The intense heat in the lantern room forces Coast Guardsmen to wear protective clothing.

The lighthouse, by the way, sways as much as three feet in a 60 mile-per-hour gale.

OWNER U.S. Coast Guard.

BALD HEAD
CAPE FEAR LIGHTHOUSES

IN SOUTHPORT. The Bald Head Lighthouse, located on Bald Head (aka Smith) Island south of Southport. Access to the world class resort and exclusive residential enclave is reached by ferry boat that departs from the Indigo Plantation Marina.

If you are not bound for Bald Head Island, an unobstructed distant viewing of the lighthouse is possible from Bay Street along Southport's waterfront.

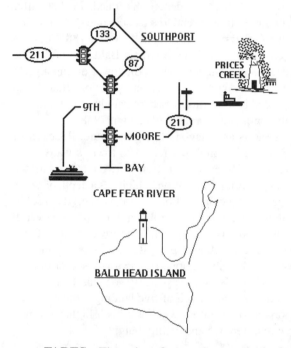

TO BALD HEAD ISLAND. In Southport turn west off NC 211 into West 9th Street and follow the road and signs through the main gate into Indigo Plantation Drive to the ferry landing.

Vehicles are not transported to the island. There is an all day fee for parking in the company's secured lot. A free parking area is located near the entry gate across from Indigo Village's townhouses.

FERRY SERVICE. On weekends and throughout the summer season, golfers, island visitors and returning homeowners keep the passenger ferries booked solid.

SCHEDULE. Crossing time is 15 minutes. All year, daily leaving Indigo Plantation on the hour 8 to 6.

From Bald Head Island, daily on the half-hour 8:30 to 6:30. Except no 11:30 departures and mid-day departures Mondays through Fridays at 12:20.

FARES. There is a ferry only round trip fare with no island transportation and a guest round trip ticket, which includes transportation to your rental unit. Reservations must be made in advance and reconfirmed not less than three days prior to visiting day. Round trip discount for children under 12.

- Bald Head Island Management's Information Center is located at 5079 Southport-Supply (NC 211) Highway, Southport, NC 28461.

Phone: Information, rental and ferry reservations in USA toll-free (800) 234-1666 (9 to 5).

Indigo Plantation Marina (910) 457-5003 (9 to 5).

ISLAND TOUR. There is also a narrated 1 1/2-hour Bald Head Island historic tour by open air tram that features Old Baldy, the old lifesaving station, the concrete foundation of the former Cape Fear Lighthouse, Captain Charlie's Station (he was Cape Fear's only keeper) and the old boathouse. The lighthouse is open (free) to the public daily from sunrise to sunset. There are 108 steps to the lantern. The price of the tour includes mainland parking, round trip ferry service and lunch on the island.

Phone: Reservations (910) 457-5003.

BALD HEAD LIGHTHOUSE (OLD BALDY; CAPE FEAR).

In 1784 the North Carolina General Assembly levied a tonnage tax on shipping to finance the construction of a lighthouse on Smith Island. In 1790 Mr. Smith, the island's owner, granted, by warranty deed, 19 acres for the lighthouse. Work on the structure did not begin until after Congress appropriated an extra $4,000 in construction funds in 1792. The lighthouse was finally finished and lighted on December 5, 1794. Not much is known about the first tower, although we do know that the structure, after having been undermined by erosion, was "wrecked" by a "waterspout" during the War of 1812.

In April 1816, Congress appropriated $15,000 for the construction of a second light tower. The contractor, unwilling to use the poor quality brick used in the old tower and unable to transport them one mile through a heavy coppice of thickets and trees, lost money on the project. Although the stone lintel over the tower's entrance bears the inscription: "R. Cochran/ Founder/ A.D. 1817/D.S. Way, Builder," the light was established in 1818.

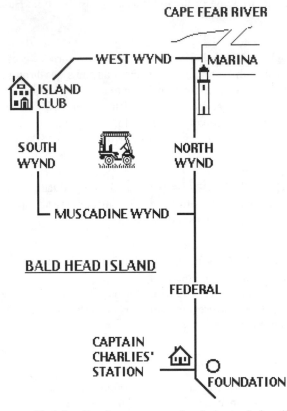

With the construction of a second lighthouse at Federal Point in 1866, Bald Head was decommissioned. In 1880, after the Federal Point light was rendered useless due to the closing of New Inlet, Old Baldy was relighted. From 1881 to 1885 extensive jetty work was done to protect Bald Head from the sea's encroachment. The jetty saved the tower during a great hurricane in 1883. With Cape Fear in operation, Bald Head was downgraded to a fourth-order harbor light, deactivated in 1935 and discontinued as a radio beacon in 1958.

Bald Head is an octagonal brick structure. Its exterior walls are finished in rough plaster. The tower's walls taper from a thickness of five feet at its base to two feet beneath the lantern deck. The brick foundation, which has a depth of seven feet, is topped with a course of brown sandstone. Its base diameter is 36 feet, tapering to 14.5 feet at the top. The overall height of the lighthouse is 90 feet. The tower's entry has a sand-stone elliptical arch whose keystone is marked with projecting stone block inlays (quoins). The tower's interior contains a 108-step wooden stairway (not the original) that spirals around the interior wall. Each of five landings above ground level supports a room with a window. Each higher room is smaller in circumference and ceiling height.

Each landing has a rectangular, balustraded well cut in its center, forming a continuous open space from the lantern's trapdoor to the ground floor. The lantern deck is a single stone covered with marble slabs. Its 15-inch extension (lip) is supported by a cornice formed by a single course of sand-stone. The small lantern was placed on the tower after it had been downgraded to a harbor light. The offset allows the lantern to be reached via a topside trap door.

The light station also received a one-story (two rooms) brick keeper's dwelling with a gabled roof and two attached "shed rooms." The latter were probably functioned as a kitchen and a workroom.

In 1834 the lighthouse was reported to have been outfitted with 15 whale oil lamps and reflectors. Its fixed white light was visible out to a distance of 18 nautical miles. The beacon was extinguished by the Confederacy in 1861. It was relighted after the war, but again darkened in 1866, when the Federal Point light became active. After Federal Point was rendered obsolete by the construction of a breakwater in 1870, Old Baldy was brought back into service. Bald Head remained a primary aid until its status was downgraded to a lesser harbor light in 1903.

OWNER. Old Baldy Foundation since 1985.
PRESERVATION. Listed in the National Register of Historic Places.

A group of concerned citizens organized the nonprofit Old Baldy Foundation to take care of the lighthouse. During 1990-92, Old Baldy underwent a refurbishing that involved the replastering of the tower's exterior, the replacing of the main door and the copper dome of a previously manufactured lantern and the rebuilding of the interior staircase. The restoration project was made possible through grant monies and contributions received during the Foundation's "Steps To The Top" drive. The project was completed in time to open the tower to the public in 1993. In 1995 the Foundation announced that $125,000 had been raised to restore Old Baldy's interior.

BALD HEAD & CAPE FEAR LIGHTHOUSES

The foundation has built the Smith Island Museum of History, a replica of one of the original lighthouse keeper's cottages. The museum houses historic artifacts and a Historic Tour of Bald Head Island. Contributions welcomed.
- Old Baldy Foundation, Inc., Bald Head Island, Southport, NC 28461.
Phone (910) 799-4640.
Website: http://www.oldbaldy.org
Email: keeperscottage@oldbaldy.org

CAPE FEAR LIGHTHOUSE (destroyed).

While work progressed to save Bald Head Lighthouse, the sea was preparing for the light's decline as an important navigation aid. By 1889 a rock and sand shoal had formed as a continuation of Cape Fear, extending seaward some 20 miles to the southeast. This shoal became as dangerous to ocean shipping as the shoals off Cape Hatteras. The lightship *Frying Pan* was placed on station in 1894, but the ship's light did not have the elevation to give an early warning to passing ships. Neither could Old Baldy. The lightship was retired in 1964 and replaced with a screw pile platform some 40 miles southeast of Cape Fear. The old ship is now part of a nautical antique shop complex in Salisbury, Maryland.

In July 1, 1898, Congress granted $35,000 for a new lighthouse on Smith Island. In March 1901 in a supplemental appropriation, $35,000 was set aside to be used, if required, to complete the construction task. On August 31, 1903, the 161-foot tall Cape Fear Lighthouse was commissioned on the southeast corner of Smith Island. The new aid was constructed as a 150-foot octagonal, skeletal steel tower and enclosed watchroom. A central cylinder housed the ascending stairway. Its optic, an incandescent oil vapor lamp and a first-order Fresnel lens, had a focal plane of 159 feet above the sea and could be seen out to 19 nautical miles.

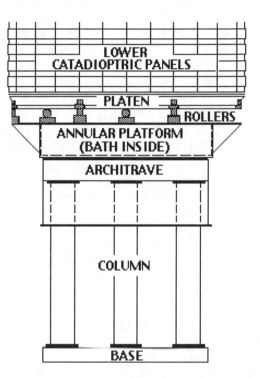

On May 22, 1920, Cape Fear's first-order Fresnel lens received a mercury float, a new load-bearing device that replaced the worn wheeled chariot installed in 1903. At that time the float was the largest ever built in the United States.

The mercury float consisted of a circular cast-iron tub (bath) filled with mercury and an inner annular (ring) platform with an outside diameter of 4.5 feet, an inside diameter of three feet and a depth of 13 inches. The inner platform, with 1/16-inch clearances on the sides and bottom and thus resting snugly inside the mercury-filled outer bath, was able to support the Fresnel optic. The float's rotation, one revolution every four minutes, was controlled by a new type D first-order clock.

The lens was bolted to a platen (table) with a diameter of 6-feet, 2-inches. The platen, in turn, rested on an annular platform. The lens was held vertically by a steel track fastened to the underside of the platen, bearing on six conical, hardened horizontal (weight-bearing) rollers, which bore on the outer periphery of the same track. Six vertical (stabilizing) rollers, equally spaced between the horizontal rollers, centered the platen. The lens was revolved by means of a 36-inch bronze internal gear fixed atop the lens' platen and driven by a 6-inch spur gear connected to the clock by a long, vertical drive shaft provided with universal joints.

The entire mechanism was supported by a cast-iron architrave casting with four leveling wedges. Four cast-iron columns supported the architrave casting. The columns, each about seven feet long and flanged on both ends, were bolted to the molded architrave and cast-iron base.

Access to the interior of the lens was by means of a ladder extending upward from the column supporting base to a platform supported on an inner rim cast integral with the mercury tub. This platform also supported a vertical stanchion that held the vapor lamp.

Cape Fear became obsolete when the present Oak Island Lighthouse became operational on May 15, 1958. Then on September 12, 1958, after the dismantled Fresnel lens and its mercury float and associated optical equipment had been removed and sold to a private party, the 55-year old tower was severely damaged by the first dynamite explosion and finally toppled by a second set charge. In 1967 the lens was reported to have been stored in a warehouse in Wilmington. The dismantled lens was purchased in the early 1970s by Mr. Michael Labriola, an antique dealer, for "a couple hundred dollars." Since then the lens' magnificent prisms have been sold for "two to five dollars" each. [2]

SOUTHPORT - FORT FISHER FERRY. To reach the ferry landing follow NC 211 (North Howe Street) south to East Moore Street. Turn left (east) and continue on East Moore to the ferry landing. Ferry carries 38 cars. Crossing time is 30 minutes.

SCHEDULE. Dates change annually. Call or check website for current dates and times. At this writing there are between eight and 16 crossings per day depending on the time of year.

FARES. Various vehicle, cycle and foot passenger one way fares. Vehicles longer than 20 feet higher fares.

- North Carolina Department of Transportation, Ferry Division, 113 Arendell Street, Morehead City, NC 28557.

Schedule information in USA toll-free (800) 293-3779. (1-800 BY FERRY). West of the Mississippi call (252) 726-6446.

Southport information in USA toll-free (800) 368-8969.

Website: http://www.ncferry.org

PRICES CREEK LIGHTHOUSE (ruins). As the ferry departs Southport, go to the port side of the vessel and look for a light-colored brick tower on a spit of land just north of the ferry landing. If not masked by summer foliage, the ruins of the crumbling walls of Prices Creek's keeper's house can also be seen. At this writing in August 2001 there is an ongoing debate about the future of the Price's Creek tower. The site and tower are owned by Archer Daniels Midland, Inc. One of the possibilities discussed is the proposed relocation of the lighthouse to Southport.

FORT FISHER STATE HISTORIC SITE. The ruins and archeological findings of three Federal Point lighthouses lie within the Fort Fisher State Historic Site, about one mile north of the Southport-Fort Fisher ferry landing and at the southern end of US 421.

On December 23, 1865, Union forces launched their first naval and infantry assault against Fort Fisher. Three days later they withdrew without having penetrated the fort. Determined to take the fort, the Federals returned to Hampton Roads, Virginia, regrouped, resupplied their forces and sailed back up the Cape Fear River. On January 14, 1866, a 3,300-man infantry regiment, under the supporting fires of the greatest naval bombardment of the Civil War, was able to land and attack the fort. The following day the Confederates capitulated.

The victory at Fort Fisher was followed by the capture of Wilmington on the 22nd of January, resulting in the isolation of the South from the outside world. With the loss of Fort Fisher and with no way to move supplies to Wilmington, the Confederacy destroyed or severely damaged Bald Head, Federal Point, the Horseshoe Shoal lightboat inside New Inlet and all of the range lighthouses on the Cape Fear River.

Encroachment by the sea has destroyed many of the battlements. A revetment (see map) protects the remaining encampment.

---

2. In front of Mr. Labriola's antique shop is a homemade brick tower. On top of the tower are the lower (catadioptric) lens panels, platen and rollers, annular platform and mercury tub. The display is decorated with a string of Christmas lights. The internal bronze gear is also on the tower. Next to the tower is a birdhouse that rests atop one of the architrave's 7-foot tall supporting columns. The other three columns, as well as the cast-iron base, lie among other collectibles in his backyard. It took ten men to move the base off the delivery truck. Mr. Labriola is willing to sell all of his collection.

To reach his store and residence from US 421 in Wilmington, take US 76 east via Dawson Street (one-way) and Oleander Drive to a water slide on the right. Across the street is the home-made light tower.

- Mr. Michael Labriola, 5323 Oleander Drive, Wilmington, NC 28403. Phone (910)791-2406

BALD HEAD & CAPE FEAR LIGHTHOUSES

OPEN.
April to October, Mondays through Saturdays 9 to 5. Sundays 1 to 5.
November to March, Tuesdays through Saturdays 10 to 4. Sundays 1 to 4.
Closed Thanksgiving Day and December 24-25.
FREE ADMISSION.
- Fort Fisher State Historic Site, PO Box 169, Kure Beach, NC 28449.
Phone (910) 458-5538.
Website: http://www.ah.dcr.state.nc.us/sections/hs/fisher/fisher.htm

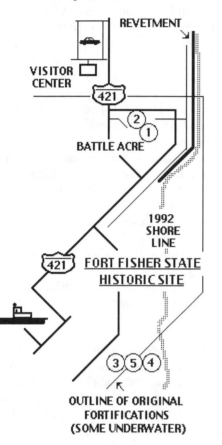

FEDERAL POINT LIGHTHOUSES (destroyed & dismantled).

One range beacon and two lighthouses constructed on the southernmost point of Fort Fisher (about eight miles north of Bald Head) were responsible for guiding ships through New Inlet into the Cape Fear River.

The first beacon on Federal Point was installed in a 51-foot tall wooden tower completed north of New Inlet in September 1816 for $1,300. The light was established in March 1817. Although historical records on this tower are sketchy at best, it is possible that two range beacons were established. One light, located in the dwelling's tower, served as the rear range aid. The front range beacon was placed on a simpler and shorter structure. Two uncovered sites (#3 and #4 on map) near a lighthouse built in 1866 (#5 on map) could have been occupied by these early range lights. The tower burned down on April 13, 1836.

Construction of a second lighthouse began in July 1837 with nearly $4,900 in appropriated funds. It was completed and established as an aid to navigation in December 1838. This light tower was equipped with one of Winslow Lewis' fixed lighting apparatuses (11 lamps and 14-inch reflectors) that reportedly had a range of 15 nautical miles. The light tower and keeper's residence received a major overhaul from 1843 to 1845. In 1863 both were destroyed by Confederate troops.

A few years ago archaeological diggings in the depression located within the Battle Acre near the Battle Monument (#1 on map) area uncovered what is believed to be the foundation ruins (#2 on map) of the 1837-38 keeper's house. The tower's site, although normally close to the house, has not been found. It could be underwater off the shoreline to the east of the house ruins.

The third lighthouse on Federal Point was built in 1866 (see the sketch on the following page). It was located about 600 yards south of the Battle Acre ruins. The structure was a two-story wooden salt box with gabled roof surmounted by a short tower, wide octagonal service gallery and cast-iron lantern. The lighthouse endured until 1881, when New Inlet was altered by severe storms in 1879-81 and finally closed by a rock breakwater built by the U.S. Army's Corps of Engineers. As best as can be determined, the fate of the 1866 Federal Point Lighthouse is unrecorded. It is believed, however, that the former site of the lighthouse lies between the earlier range beacons (#3 and #4 on the Fort Fisher map).

75

CAPE FEAR RANGE LIGHTS. In August 1848, Congress approved the establishment of a 26-mile series of range lights and a lightboat along the Cape Fear River from below Wilmington to Folly Beach. The appropriation included funds for range lights on the Upper Jetty (a few miles south of Wilmington), on Campbells (Big) Island, Orton Point, Prices Creek and Oak Island. A lightship on Horseshoe Shoal, located between Prices Creek and New Inlet just south of Fort Fisher, was established in 1851.

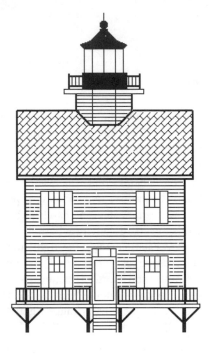

Work on the Upper Jetty aid was delayed for want of sufficient funds to build two light towers. When finally established in 1856, the range station consisted of a wood framed keeper's dwelling surmounted by an integrated tower (similar to the above sketch) and a front range light tower. The Campbells Island (centered in the river) and the Orton Point (west side) light towers were simple wooden structures completed in 1850. The rear range light established at Prices Creek was housed in a wooden tower that rested atop a square two-story brick keeper's house. That beacon was aligned to range with an optic placed atop a circular, pyramidal brick tower. The front range tower was later raised about six feet and capped with a square concrete lantern deck. All that is left of the rear range lighthouse are parts of the dwelling's walls. The abandoned and deteriorating front range tower is the structure seen while aboard the Southport-Fort Fisher ferry.

By 1863 all five range stations had been darkened and their towers either destroyed or rendered inoperable by the Confederacy. In 1867 the Federal Government declared the beacons to be abandoned properties.

In 1866 the roof of the old Oak Island keeper's house was used to hold a reestablished range light. Later, perhaps as late as 1879, a new rear range tower appeared. It was a tri-sectional structure consisting of a square brick base, a wooden, skeletal tower and a tapered, gingerbread ornamented enclosure that supported both lantern and optic. After receiving storm damage in 1883 and later rendered useless due to a realignment of the main channel, the Oak Island range light was discontinued in July 1884. The wooden tower was destroyed in 1958 when a brush fire got out of control and engulfed the structure. Today the bottom courses of brick are visible outside the wall of the North Carolina Baptists Assembly compound (old Fort Caswell).

FORT FISHER - SOUTHPORT FERRY. Ferry information is on page 74. About a mile south of Fort Fisher just beyond the end of US 421 is the ferry terminal. As the ferry departs Southport, go to the port (left) side of the vessel and look for the light colored brick tower on a spit of land just north of the ferry landing.

CAPE LOOKOUT

TO BEAUFORT. In Beaufort (bow' fert) ON US 70 (Cedar Street) turn south into Turner Street. The intersection is marked by "Beaufort Waterfront" and "Museum" signs. Motor down Turner to its dead end at Front Street and turn right to the museum.

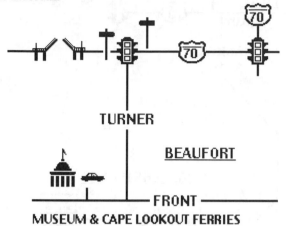

NORTH CAROLINA MARITIME MUSEUM. This museum is widely recognized for its coverage of maritime and coastal natural histories. It has free parking and is handicapped accessible.

One of many, many interesting exhibits is a fourth-order Fresnel lens made in Paris by Henri LePaute in 1892. The lens was installed when the Maryland Point Lighthouse was constructed in 1892. It remained in the lighthouse at least until 1909, and possibly up to the time that the light tower was dismantled in the mid-1960s.

OPEN. All year, weekdays 9 to 5. Saturdays 10 to 5. Sundays 1 to 5. Closed January 1, Thanksgiving Day and December 25.

FREE ADMISSION.

- North Carolina Maritime Museum, 315 Front Street, Beaufort, NC 28516.
Phone (252) 728-7317
- Website: http://www.ah.dcr.state.nc.us/sections/maritime/

TO HARKERS ISLAND. The Cape Lookout Lighthouse is located on Core Banks Island within the National Park Service's Cape Lookout National Seashore. It can be reached via passenger ferries operating out of Harkers Island. See the following map.

Between Otway and Smyrna at a "Cape Lookout National Seashore" sign turn south off US 70 into Harkers Island Road. Continue into the town of Harkers Island.

CAPE LOOKOUT NATIONAL SEASHORE. The Seashore's headquarters and visitor center are located on Shell Point at the eastern end of the island. The lighthouse can be seen across Back Sound from the Shell Point parking area (free) across the street from the center.

OPEN. All year, daily 8 to 4:30. Closed January 1 and December 25.

FREE ADMISSION.

- Cape Lookout National Seashore, 131 Charles Street, Harkers Island, NC 28531. Phone (919) 728-2250 (recording during non-duty hours). Fax (919) 728-2160.

Website: http://www.nps.gov/calo/

FERRY SERVICE TO CAPE LOOKOUT. Several companies located in Beaufort and on Harkers Island are sanctioned by the Cape Lookout National Seashore to ferry visitors to the lighthouse. All operate on a "demand" (no schedule) basis. Reservation required. The shortest trip is one taken from Harkers Island. If you go, be sure to take along water and don't forget a sun hat and insect repellant.

- **Outer Banks Ferry Service** sails out of Beaufort's waterfront. Children half price.
- Outer Banks Ferry Service, 328 Front Street, Beaufort, NC 28516. Phone (919) 728-4129.
- **Beaufort Belle Tours** is also docked on the Beaufort waterfront. Children half price.
- Beaufort Belle Tours, 300 Front Street, Beaufort, NC 28516. Phone (919) 728-6888.
- **Barrier Island Transportation Company's** *Pristine Mistress* (two open decks) sails from Harkers Island Fishing Center and carries up to 60 passengers. Crossing time is 45 minutes. No pets. No minimum passenger load. Discount for motel guests. Free parking.
- Harkers Island Fishing Center, PO Box 400 (1002 Island Road), Harkers Island, NC 28531. Phone (919) 728-3907. Fax (919) 728-6405.
- **Sand Dollar Transportation** operates in the same manner. Its motor launch departs from Barbour's Harbour Marina on Island Road. Reduced fare for children. Separate daily parking fee.
- Sand Dollar Transportation, Barbour's Harbour Marina, Harkers Island, NC 28531. Phone (919) 728-6181.

AMERICA'S ATLANTIC COAST LIGHTHOUSES - NORTH CAROLINA

HARKERS ISLAND MOTELS.

Harkers Island Fishing Center	(919) 728-3907
Calico Jack's Inn & Marina	(919) 728-3575
Fisherman's Inn	(919) 728-5780
Sea Level Inn	(919) 225-3651

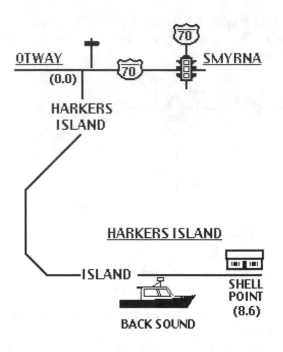

CAPE LOOKOUT LIGHT STATION. Both the lighthouse and the ocean are a one-half mile walk from the ferry dock. There is a jitney service (fares) from the dock east to the beach and south to the cape's Cape Point (2.75 miles). The 1873 brick keeper's duplex displays posters and photographs depicting the lighthouse's history. Restrooms are located at the house. The dwelling is open March to November and is staffed by both rangers and volunteers.

CAPE LOOKOUT LIGHTHOUSE.
CHARACTERISTIC: Flashing white 15s
HAW: 156' **RANGE**: 25 nm

Although it was authorized by Congress in 1804, the first lighthouse was not completed until 1812. It was a strange arrangement with two nested towers. The inside one was a brick tower. The outside structure was a wood framed and shingled building. Together the structures stood 96 feet tall. Not so strange was the fact that the fixed light, some 104 feet above the water, was not an effective aid. In 1845 the tower was painted with red and white horizontal bands to improve its visibility as a daymark.

In 1856 Congress appropriated $45,000 to build the present 169-foot tall lighthouse. The conical 150-foot tall brick tower is laid in courses of one-to-five common bond and has two elevated entry doors and ten windows spaced alternatingly in vertical rows of three and two around the tapering shaft. All openings have stone lintels and juniper wood frames. The walls of the tower diminish in thickness skyward from eight feet at the base to two feet at the lantern deck. A cast-iron stairway, installed in 1867, has wedge-shaped steps that wind around a series of fluted vertical columns. There are five semicircular landings. The 201-step stairway is marked with a plaque inscribed with "L. Sautter & Co./ Constructeurs/ A.Paris." The lantern deck rests on a stepped up and outward cornice of coursed brick corbel. There are no cast-iron gallery braces such as those seen on the Cape Hatteras, Bodie Island and Currituck Beach towers.

In 1873 the station received a new keeper's residence, a generator, and two oil houses, all of brick construction. At the same time, the tower was first painted with its distinctive black-and-white diamond design.

In 1850 the lighthouse keeper first reported that shifting sands had banked to a height above the top of the keeper's house. Although the action of the sea threatened to topple the structure, the authorities went ahead and installed a first-order Fresnel lens. That light was established on November 1, 1859.

Although it had been mishandled by a raiding party the year before, the Confederacy, in 1862, removed and further damaged the first-order Fresnel lens. A less powerful optic, installed in 1863 by Union troops, was put out of action two years later, when Confederate raiders dynamited the tower's interior. In 1867 the lighthouse was refurbished and refitted with another first-order Fresnel lens.

In 1950, after the optic was automated, the Coast Guard removed its watch personnel. The first-order lens was removed in 1972 and placed in storage in Portsmouth, Virginia. In 1994 the lens was installed in the relocated Block Island Southeast Lighthouse. The transfer has not set well among Tar Heel conservationists, curators, historians and Carteret County's commissioners, who complained that the Coast Guard should have consulted both the National Park Service and North Carolina authorities before moving the lens north. The commissioners fired off a letter to the Coast Guard, expressing their chagrin over the transfer of the lens and requested the Coast Guard to return it to North Carolina. Now installed and operating in the Block Island Southeast Lighthouse, the lens appears to have become a permanent Rhode Island resident.

CAPE LOOKOUT

OWNER. U.S. Coast Guard. Managed by the National Park Service.
PRESERVATION. Listed in the National Register of Historic Places.

For more than 40 years the lighthouse was subjected to the damaging effects of the weather and hurricanes, neglect and vandalism. By 1991 the tower's exterior paint was peeling away uncovering cracked bricks. Windows were rotting with their panes of glass broken, and the light's lantern showed a slight tilt. In 1992 the Coast Guard renovated the aging structure. The project included removing the exterior paint using a high-pressurized water system, remortaring the courses, replacing broken windows and spraying all metals and masonry parts with two coats of a waterproofing paint over a coat of primer. The tower's windows were replaced with authentically crafted replicas made of treated lumber and glazed with a more durable glass.

In 1933 a hurricane created the Barden Channel between the Core Banks and the Shackleford Banks. The resulting swift current began to wash away the sands around the base of the lighthouse. Since then, this action has caused the shoreline to recede to within 250 feet of the tower. If this erosion continues and no major effort is made to save the tower, the sea will eventually claim it. Proposed solutions range from dredging a new relief channel to the building of a new lighthouse.

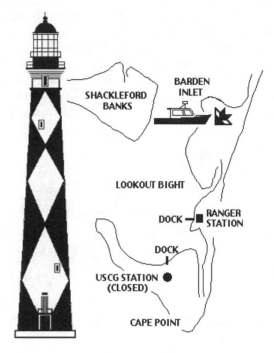

OCRACOKE

NORTH CAROLINA'S SCREW PILE LIGHTHOUSES. In earlier days lighthouses also existed in North Carolina's Pamlico, Croatan and Albermarle Sounds. These inland waterway aids were constructed along a basic design, calling for hexagonal or rectangular keepers' houses with gabled roofs. The light towers were either built atop or attached to the side of the dwellings. The house rested on a wide balustraded platform equipped with boat davits, an outdoor privy and a landing platform slung underneath. The superstructure was supported by pilings screwed into the seabed. Stability was acquired by cross channeling and taut turnbuckles. The first floor of the living quarters usually consisted of three small rooms (living, bedroom and kitchen) with a few closets. The second floor had two small rooms. One room, with an access dormer to the station's externally mounted fog bell, housed the bell's striking machinery. The other room served as a workroom and for the storage of tools and equipment.

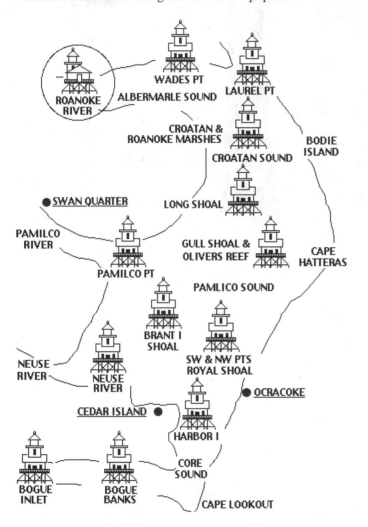

Between 1856 and 1891, sixteen (plus one on Horseshoe Shoal in the Cape Fear River inside New Inlet) screw pile structures were erected. Although examples of the screw pile design exist in the Chesapeake Bay region, all of those in the sounds were once thought to have been either dismantled or destroyed. Today only the Roanoke River Lighthouse remains. It is now located in Edenton, North Carolina in a well-preserved condition. Its lantern still holds the original fourth-order Fresnel lens. Hopefully, the Washington County Historical Society and the Port O'Plymouth Roanoke River Museum in Plymouth, North Carolina will be able to purchase the historic structure. If the sale goes through, the lighthouse will be moved onto the museum's grounds and opened to the public.

Although some historians suggest that the first beacon at the confluence of the Roanoke River and Albermarle Sound may have been established as early as 1835, Roanoke River was one of four screw piles built in 1867. The structure was destroyed by fire in 1885, rebuilt, damaged by ice in 1886 and rebuilt the following year. Another damaging ice storm occurred in 1918. The four beacons were discontinued in 1940. In 1955 Elijah Tate purchased the Wade's Point, Roanoke Marshes and Roanoke River Lighthouses. His attempt to salvage and moved the first two ended in losing both in a barging accident and a storm. The Roanoke River Lighthouse was then given to Emmet Wiggins who successfully moved it to Edenton and turned it into his private residence.

FERRY TO OCRACOKE. Throughout the year there is daily ferry service to Ocracoke from Cedar Island (50 cars) and Swan Quarter (28 cars). Crossing time from Cedar Island is 2 hours 15 minutes; from Swan Quarter 2 hours 30 minutes. Reservations are strongly recommended.

The Driftwood Motel and Restaurant adjacent to the ferry terminal in Cedar Island is open all year. Phone (919) 225-4861.

For the handicapped the boarding officer will position your vehicle near the stairs to the upper lounge deck. Ask the ticket agent who collects the fare for "handicapped access" boarding.

OCRACOKE

SCHEDULES. Subject to change.
For current schedules call or check website.

FARES. Various vehicle, cycle and foot passenger one-way fares. Vehicles longer than 20 feet higher fares.

- North Carolina Department of Transportation, Ferry Division, 113 Arendell Street, Morehead City, NC 28557.
Website: http://www.outer-banks.com/ferry/
Phone: for Morehead City (919) 726-6446 or (919) 726-6413.
For general information in USA toll-free (800) BY-FERRY

For reservations contact these terminal offices between 6 and 6:
Cedar Island   In USA toll-free (800) 856-0343 or (919) 225-3551
Swan Quarter   In USA toll-free (800) 773-1094 or (919) 926-1111.
Ocracoke   In USA toll-free (800) 345-1665 or (919) 928-3841.

OCRACOKE VILLAGE. Ocracoke's (oak ruh coke) earliest history reaches back to June 23, 1585, when Sir Walter Raleigh, on his way to eventually colonize Roanoke, Virginia, stopped over to explore and map the island. The first settlement by mariners was recognized in 1715 by the Colonial Legislature. The town was incorporated in 1753. During the Revolutionary War and while the British Navy effectively blockaded northern ports, ship captains slipped past the thinly deployed southern British fleet and sailed their ammunition and supplies through Ocracoke Inlet to the eastern shores of Pamlico Sound. There, the cargoes were unloaded and hauled overland to General George Washington's troops.

After Independence, Ocracoke's importance began to ebb. To this was added the almost total destruction of the village's docks and warehouses during a raging storm in 1810. The Civil War further compounded Ocracoke's maritime decline with sunken vessels blocking the inlet. The inhabitants, in turn, turned to fishing to gain their livelihood. In 1942 the outside world dramatically altered Ocracoke's tranquil existence. World War II drew German submarines into the Atlantic's shipping lanes and the U.S. Navy into Silver Lake. Electric power and telephones soon followed. Even a highway was built across the island.

In 1957 the island's isolation was forever broken with the inauguration of a mainland ferry service. Despite these changes, "Pony Island" retains much of its old world charm.

TO THE LIGHTHOUSE. See the following map.

In Ocracoke about 0.6 mile north of the ferry landing or 12 miles south of the Hatteras Inlet ferry dock turn west into Lighthouse Road. Continue on Lighthouse for another 0.7 mile to the light station and its small off-road parking area (free). Visitors are permitted to enter, but not climb the tower.

OCRACOKE

SHELL CASTLE ISLAND LIGHTHOUSE (destroyed). The area's first lighthouse was erected on Old Rock Island, one of five islets lying west of Ocracoke Inlet. Although Old Rock (later named Shell Castle Island and now known as Beacon Island) was nothing more than a partly submerged, though stable oyster bed some 800 yards long and 20 yards wide, the island's importance grew with the increasing volume of shipping passing through Ocracoke Inlet.

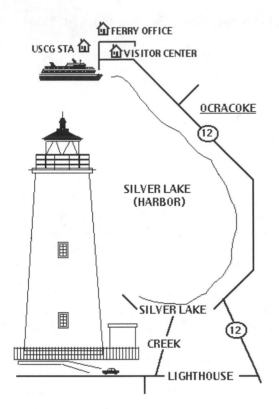

In 1789 the island was purchased by a local merchant and a Washington, D.C., nabob who had shipping interests in Pamlico Sound. Despite the island's isolation and small size, the island's owners decided to build a transshipment point on the barren outcropping. And, during the 1790s the entrepreneurs just about controlled the maritime trade through Ocracoke Inlet.

Ignoring or overlooking a previous letter of instruction (March 1792) to the Secretary of the Treasury to build a driven-pile lighthouse on Royal Shoal farther west of the inlet, as well as the purchase (1790) on Ocracoke Island of one acre of land for the purpose of erecting a lighthouse, Congress, on May 13, 1794, approved the construction of the Shell Castle Island Lighthouse. The aid was to complement the first of Cape Hatteras' lighthouses and was positioned to warn vessels passing through Ocracoke Inlet into Pamlico Sound. The pyramidal wood framed and shingled tower was about 55 feet tall. The station was also provided a one-story wood framed keeper's house and a shed for the storage of whale oil. Lightning and a resulting fire destroyed the tower and keeper's dwelling in August 1818. According to some historians, Shell Castle Island's single oil-burning spider lamp was first lighted in 1798; others claim the date of illumination was 1803, the year Cape Hatteras became operational.

OCRACOKE LIGHTHOUSE.
CHARACTERISTIC: Fixed white
HAW: 75' **RANGE**: 14 nm

Although the North Carolina General Assembly authorized the building of a lighthouse on Ocracoke Island in 1789 and then followed up on that decision with the purchase on September 13, 1790 of one acre for the new tower, construction was delayed by debate on whether another tower should be built on Shell Castle or elsewhere. By 1822 the use of Shell Castle Island for another lighthouse was eliminated with the shifting of the main channel through Ocrtacoke Inlet. After a $14,000 lightship substitute (1820) proved unable to assume the warning role, Congress, on May 7, 1822, voted to spend as much as $20,000 to build the present Ocracoke Lighthouse. Unfortunately the 1790 deed for the one acre purchase stipulated that the construction of the intended lighthouse had to be completed by 1801. Thus, before work could begin on the Ocracoke aid, Congress had to purchase a new plot of land. The purchase of the station's present two acres was finalized in December 1822.

The 75-foot tall lighthouse was completed in 1823 at a cost of $11,360. By 1824 the station consisted of the brick and cement-coated light tower, a two-story brick dwelling and two storage buildings.

In 1856, a year after the tower and keepers' residence had been thoroughly renovated, a fourth-order Fresnel lens replaced the octagonal lantern's original multi-lamp device. The classical lens was removed in 1861 and subsequently lost. Three years later, the lantern received a new fourth-order Fresnel lens; and in 1899, a third fourth-order optic. Before its electrification, the light's lamps first burned whale oil, then lard oil, then kerosene in the late 1870s. The beacon was automated in 1955.

OCRACOKE

OWNER. U.S. Coast Guard. Managed by the National Park Service since 1994.
PRESERVATION. Listed in the National Register of Historic Places.

In 1989 the Coast Guard and the National Park Service began work on painting the light tower and making repairs to its door and windows. The old wooden windows were removed and plastic ones substituted. The Ocracoke Preservation Society protested, claiming that in accordance with statutes regarding the restoration of historic structures, the windows should have been restored to their original specifications. After many letters and consultations the Coast Guard agreed to remove the ersatz windows and metal door and replace them with authentically fabricated wooden ones. The stairway's metal treads were also exchanged for replicated wooden steps. Future restorative work will entail the repointing of the brick tower.

In 1987 the National Park Service began a $270,000 project to restore the keeper's house. The dwelling's interior was refurbished in 1990; restoration of the exterior was completed in 1993. The historic house is now used as living quarters for Park Service personnel. It is not open to the public.

HATTERAS INLET FERRY. Reservations are not required. The ferry carries 30 cars. Crossing time is 40 minutes.

SCHEDULE. Daily trips hourly from 5 AM to midnight, with additional trips May to October. Prior loading of commercial vehicles occurs on some trips from June through Labor Day. Call to confirm schedule.

FREE TRANSIT.

Phone: for schedule information in USA toll-free (800) 293-3779.

Website: http://www.outer-banks.com/ferry/

Okracoke Lighthouse

CAPE HATTERAS

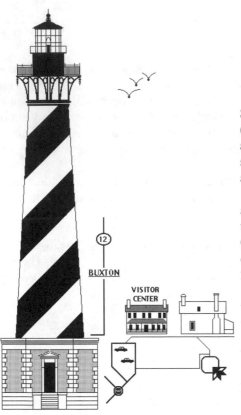

NORTH OR SOUTH ON NC 12. In Buxton turn off NC 12 at a "Cape Hatteras" sign and drive to the station's parking areas. Spaces for the handicapped are located in the parking lot on the left. Parking (free) is limited to two hours 10 to 4.

CAPE HATTERAS VISITOR CENTER. The Cape Hatteras Light Station consists of the light tower (1870), the brick head keeper's quarters (1892), the assistant keepers' duplex (built in 1854 and expanded in 1892), and a brick oil house (1892) that now contains a standby generator. The sand covered ruins of the 1802 light tower, destroyed in February 1871, are located 200 yards south of the lighthouse.

The assistant keepers' duplex, completely restored in 1985, serves as the visitor center and the Museum-by-the-Sea with exhibits on the history of the Outer Banks, including the lighthouse and lifesaving services, German submarine activity during both World Wars, relics of shipwrecks on Diamond Shoals, photographs and lighthouse memorabilia. There are 268 steps to the lighthouse service gallery.

The station was rededicated and opened on May 5, 2001 following the historic move of the tower. The rededication took place in conjunction with a Cape Hatteras Lighthouse Keepers Descendants Homecoming.

An incident in June 2001 when a small support segment of the stairs broke off caused the tower to be closed to the public. An engineering study found similar problems throughout the stairs, no doubt exacerbated by the fact that more than 200,000 people climb the tower each year. At this writing it looks like the tower will remain closed until at least the start of the 2002 season so that the stairs can be repaired and made safe.

VISITOR CENTER OPEN.
All year, daily 9 to 5.
Closed December 25.
TOWER OPEN.
Easter Sunday to Columbus Day daily 10 to 2.
[Memorial Day to Labor Day, daily 9:30 to 4.]
FREE ADMISSION. Visitor Center free. Budget restrictions may result in a fee being charged to climb the lighthouse.

- Cape Hatteras National Seashore, Route 1, Box 675, Manteo, NC 27954.
Phone (919) 473-2111.
. Visitor center and museum (919) 995-4474.
Website: http://www.nps.gov/caha/

THE CAPE. The tip of the Cape Hatteras, Cape Point, is due north of Cat Island in the Bahamas and 300 miles east of the north Florida coast. What makes the cape and its environs so dangerous to maritime shipping is the interactions of shoals, visibility, wind and ocean current. Offshore, Diamond Shoals, a menacing mass of shifting underwater sand bars, is more often than not enshrouded with haze. The sea lane around the cape also comes into play. Southbound passage via the Virginia Coastal Current becomes difficult as ships enter into the fast moving northerly Gulf Stream. To add further resistance, prevailing winds from the southwest force vessels back north. Thus, as ships try to overcome the effects of wind and current, they tend to be set onto the shoals. Since the 1500s the waters off Cape Hatteras have claimed more than 600 errant vessels. No wonder the area is known as "The Graveyard of the Atlantic."

Three different lightships have marked Diamond Shoals. The first dropped anchor in 1824, but was broken up during a gale three years later. The second, the *Diamond*, took its position in 1897 and remained on station until 1918, when a German gunfire sank it. The third, also named *Diamond*, remained active until 1967, when the present Texas-type tower replaced it. The tower, a square superstructure resting on four steel pilings, is painted orange and white with the word "Diamond" showing on all four sides. The light was fully automated on September 7, 1977.

On a clear day the Diamond Shoals tower, some 13 miles off Cape Point, can be seen from Cape Hatteras.

CAPE HATTERAS

CAPE HATTERAS LIGHTHOUSE.
CHARACTERISTIC: Flashing white 7.5s
HAW: 191' RANGE: 24 nm

The original Cape Hatteras Lighthouse, first given to congressional debate in 1794, was finally approved for construction in 1797. The obtaining of the property, the process of securing a contractor, and sickness among the laborers delayed the tower's completion until October 1803. The octagonal brick and dark sandstone lighthouse was 90 feet tall. Its 12-foot tall lantern held 18 oil-fed lamps each backed with a 14-inch reflector. In clear weather the fixed light could be seen at sea for 18 nautical miles. The tower was damaged by a storm in 1806 and again during the War of 1812. In response to the complaints by ship captains that the tower was not tall enough nor was its light of sufficient intensity to warn them off Diamond Shoals, Congress between 1845 and 1848 took steps to upgrade the light's effectiveness. And still the sea captains complained.

During 1853-54, extra courses of brick were added to the structure, increasing the beacon's height above the sea to 150 feet. A rotating first-order Fresnel lens was installed that was turned by a weighted series of gears. With these improvements, the Cape Hatteras light was transformed into an effective and dependable aid. Also, the tower's lower half was whitewashed and its upper half painted red. During the tower's reconstruction, the assistant keepers' duplex was built.

In 1867, after cracks were found in the 1854 tower, Congress appropriated $75,000 for the reconstruction of the damaged walls. This project was tabled after engineer surveys recommended the building of a new tower using granite foundation stones mined in Vermont and bricks made in Virginia.

In 1935, in anticipation of the toppling of the Cape Hatteras tower due to erosion, the Coast Guard abandoned the tower and transferred it to the National Park Service. In 1936 a new Cape Hatteras light was established atop a skeletal steel tower about 2,000 yards to the northeast at Buxton Woods. This beacon, at an elevation of 166 feet above the sea, flashed a beam out to 19 nautical miles. Fortunately the erosion stopped, the beach filled in and the Cape Hatteras Lighthouse was brought back into service on January 23, 1950. The Buxton Woods steel tower was used by the National Weather Service until it closure in 1995.

CONSTRUCTION. When constructing a coastal lighthouse, especially a massive structure like Cape Hatteras, the first and foremost engineering challenge is to make sure the tower has a strong, solid and lasting foundation. To this end, a multitude of strengthening techniques have been used, e.g., granite bases, driven iron piles, screw piles with or without load bearing discs, deeply poured reinforced concrete slabs with anchoring bolts and cement-filled cast-iron caissons. At Cape Hatteras engineers discovered that the sand, 9 to 10 feet below the surface, was compacted and hard as rock. This phenomenon was first noticed in the Florida Keys, where George G. Meade used the screw pile-and-disc technique to build the light towers on Carysfort Reef (1852) and Sand Key (1853) and the driven pile and disc designed Sombrero Key Lighthouse (1858).

As a result of this finding, the tower's floating foundation was laid in the following manner. First, a 6-foot deep dry cofferdam was excavated. Then, iron pilings were driven six feet into the compacted sand. Huge yellow pine timbers were cross laid on top of the pilings in alternating rows. On top of the grillage and at ground level, the first octagonal course of dressed 18-inch thick granite blocks was laid, using cement mixed with granite chips and rubble stone. Since wood resists decay under water, the dam was then allowed to fill with seawater. Four more granite block courses were laid with each row stepped up to the start of the tower's base. For another 10 feet, granite blocks were placed at the octagonal corners (groins) and blocked in with brick. At that elevation the bricklayers began laying the tower's 13-inch thick walls.

Patterned after the Cape Lookout lighthouse, Cape Hatteras' tower has a circular stairway with its seven semicircular landings rising 175 feet from the tower's base to the watchroom deck. There are nine openings (two doors and seven windows); each opening has a lintel and sill of stone. The 208-foot tall structure is America's tallest brick lighthouse. Its construction and accessories cost $150,000. The light was first exhibited on December 16, 1870.

OPTICS. Over the years Cape Hatteras' lighthouses have had a variety of whale oil, lard oil, kerosene and electrically powered optics

CAPE HATTERAS

1803-54.   Three variations of Winslow Lewis' lamp/reflector device.

1856-62.   New first-order Fresnel lens.

1862-63.   Second-order lens.

1863-1936. Second first-order lens.

1950-72.   Dual aerobeacon.

1972.   Single high-intensity lens.

In 1862, after having dynamited the tower, Confederate troops withdrew from the station and forwarded the classical lens to a depot in Tarboro, North Carolina. There the lens' parts, less larger cast-iron castings, were carefully wrapped and packed into 45 boxes. Although correspondence exists that suggests the crates and castings were to be moved to a safer place by railroad box car, the lens was never recovered.

In April 1987, the National Park Service reported that thieves had entered the Little Kinnakeet Station Boathouse (north of Buxton) and had broken off and absconded with four panels of Cape Hatteras' first-order Fresnel lens. In December 1988 the missing panels were found hidden in a nearby marsh. The thieves were later apprehended. This is the lens that, while still located in the tower, was mutilated by vandals in 1935. At that time several hundred glass prisms were removed, many of the brass sections of the lens were bent or broken, and its rotating mechanism was damaged. While no longer repairable as a unit, the National Park Service has salvaged one-half of the top one-third of the lens.

PRESERVATION. Listed in the National Register of Historic Places.

The sea was in constant motion around the tower. The waters slowly, but steadily were encroaching over the beach towards its base. While the surf was about 1,300 feet from the tower in 1870, the sea's wash moved to within 300 feet by 1919 and 100 feet in 1935. Although it receded for a spell, the ocean was about 200 feet away in 1993. In 1995 that distance shortened to 150 feet.

1930.   900 feet of interlocking steel sheet pile groins were emplaced. This effort was followed by the building of a barrier sand dune system all along the entire length of Cape Hatteras Island.

1933.   More steel sheet pile groins.

1935.   Dikes, breakwaters and wooden revetments.

1966   312,000 cubic yards of fine sand, pumped from Pamlico Sound, later disappeared.

1967.   Large sand-filled nylon bags. Only a few of these bags remain.

1969.   Reinforced concrete and steel sheet pile groins set to protect both the lighthouse and a nearby naval facility. These have been partially destroyed by storms.

1971.   Another 200,000 cubic yards of sand replenishment.

1973.   Another 1.3 million cubic yards of sand.

1975.   12-foot high steel fence joined to the remaining portions of the 1969 concrete breakwater.

1980.   A severe winter blizzard in March destroyed the old foundation ruins. At the same time, the storm broke through the steel and concrete jetty and began a serious erosion of the beach in front of the lighthouse. In an emergency effort (October) to plug the gap, rubble was dumped into the breach and the groin nearest the lighthouse was extended some 150 feet. By December the sea had washed completely around the extension, requiring the placing of yet another extension. This effort pushed the sea back to about 100 feet from the lighthouse.

1980.   250 units of artificial seaweed, called "Seascape," were dropped offshore in about 10 feet of water. The units were polypropylene devices consisting of hollow gravel filled tubes with connecting fronds designed to gather suspended sand particles and link the with the underwater sand bar. In November the area, further eroded by another storm, required additional applications of the devices, the dumping of more rubble and a 150-foot extension landward of the previously reinforced groin.

1983.   Granite stone groin.

1984.   The south groin was covered with a scour protection mat (rip-rap sleeve).

1984.   The lighthouse was closed to the public to allow engineers and other experts to survey the extent of newly found cracks in the tower's walls and cast-iron sections, moisture in the interior and eroded staircase anchoring brackets. As a result of the study, the National Park Service and the U.S. Army's Corps of Engineers began design work for the construction of a 23-foot high seawall around the tower's base. The estimated cost was reported to be $5.7 million. That project never materialized.

CAPE HATTERAS

1986.   2,700 additional units of artificial seaweed.

1992.   More large nylon bags of sand.

1994.   One of the three groins emplaced in 1969 was destroyed by Hurricane Gordon. It was rebuilt at a cost of $356,000. Another $500,000 was spent on building offshore an 8-foot high wall of 400 sandbags. Each bag weighed two to three tons.

1996.   Another 300 bags of sand.

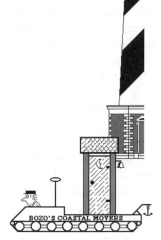

NO, NO, CHOMLEY! THE CONTRACT SAYS "LIGHTHOUSE".

RELOCATION. In 1987 a citizens' group, calling itself the "Move The Lighthouse Committee," voiced its protestations, saying the lighthouse should be relocated. The National Park Service contracted with the National Academy of Sciences (NAS) for an independent study of the best long term protection for the lighthouse. In April, 1988, NAS presented its final report, "Saving Cape Hatteras Lighthouse from the Sea." The report recommended that the Lighthouse be relocated. The National Park Service began work on an Environmental Assessment of Alternatives.

Meanwhile, in 1990 the Save Cape Hatteras Lighthouse Committee donated $10,000 for repairs to the lighthouse roof. The repair work was performed by International Chimney Corporation of Buffalo, New York.

In 1998 the Ad Hoc Committee of Faculty at North Carolina State University updated the 1988 NAS report. The new report endorsed the NAS report, saying that if the Cape Hatteras Lighthouse is to be preserved, it must be moved, and moved immediately. $2 million was appropriated to begin planning and request for quotes.

After a series of proposals, a contract was awarded to International Chimney Corporation, which had previously moved the Block Island Southeast Lighthouse, Highland (Cape Cod) Lighthouse, and Nauset Lighthouse.

In October 1998, Congress appropriated $9.8 million for the project, which was estimated at a total of $12 million. The two keeper's dwellings, oil house and cisterns were to be moved as well as the tower, which was to be moved 2,900 feet to the southeast.

The Save Cape Hatteras Lighthouse Committee opposed the planned relocation, saying the price tag was too high, and argued instead for a $6.4 million groin and beach nourishment project designed to slow erosion. It is estimated that the lighthouse move will preserve the tower for at least 100 years, while a fourth groin would only have protected the lighthouse for a maximum of 20 years. Groin proponents admitted that the lighthouse would eventually have to be relocated, with an inflated price tag. As a result the plans for an immediate move won out.

The light was extinguished on March 1, 1999, in preparation for its journey, which began at 3:05 PM, June 17, 1999, when the lighthouse was moved four inches to the southeast. Here, basically, is how America's tallest lighthouse was moved by International Chimney Corporation, lighthouse movers par excellence:

The first step was to excavate the site for the crew and equipment. In addition to preparing a work space around the lighthouse, a road had to be excavated and repaired for the move. Crushed stone was laid across the move corridor.

Then the lighthouse foundation had to be removed and replaced with structural steel supports in preparation for the move. Main beams were out into place with hydraulic jacks. These beams with their jacks lifted the lighthouse to allow roll beams to be put into place. Once the roll beams were in place, the move began, Five push jacks all pushed at the same rate to slowly move the lighthouse in 5-foot increments. Track steel was leapfrogged from back to front as the lighthouse continued its trip to the new site.

A total of 9,000 crib blocks, six inches by six inches by four feet, were used to support the tower during the move. Each block weighed 58 pounds and was handled 16 to 18 times by workers as the lighthouse was moved.

The lighthouse was moved as much as 355 feet in a single day, and was pushed its final 79 feet on July 9, 1999 at 1:23 PM. The roll beams, main beams and other support materials were removed, and on August 17 the full weight of the lighthouse was lowered into its new location. The keeper's dwelling and other outbuildings were secured in their new sites. Cape Hatteras Lighthouse now sits on a concrete pad foundation 1,600 feet from the shoreline -- a little more than the distance it stood from the sea when it was built in 1870.

The old site was filled and graded, and the move corridor was returned to its natural condition.

At 4 PM on Saturday, November 13, 1999, the National Park Service held a relighting ceremony. The event was attended by thousands, gathered to celebrate a monumental and successful effort to save a magnificent example of American architecture and engineering.

CAPE HATTERAS

NORTH OR SOUTH ON NC 12. Rodanthe is about 23 miles north of the Cape Hatteras Lighthouse and 17 miles south of the Bodie Island aid. In Rodanthe we will deviate slightly from our coastal lighthouse tour of lighthouses to take a look at this restored station.

CHICAMACOMICO LIFESAVING STATION. In 1848 the Federal Government decided to financially support a growing lifesaving effort operated by volunteers. But it was not until 1871 that a professional lifesaving service was formed and placed under the Secretary of the Treasury's Revenue Marine Bureau. From its beginning the new service had a bunch of problems. Money was scarce. Training and equipment were substandard. Some of the service's personnel had never seen an ocean; some were incompetent political appointees. After two terrible shipwrecks at Currituck Beach and Nags Head, the service was given independent status. Under its new superintendent, Summer Kimball, the service developed into a dedicated and proficient saver of lives with many, many acts of heroism by both individuals and crews.

When you visit the Chicamacomico station you will become familiar with the service's tools of its trade, such as, the surfboat, the breeches buoy, the beach cart and the Lyle gun.

This restored outpost of the old U.S. Lifesaving Service is one of 23 Outer Banks stations established during the period 1874-1909 and closed in 1954.

The first station in Rodanthe was established in 1874. The present station was built in 1911. Most of America's lifesaving stations were designed by George Tolman during the 1894-1907 period. His structures are architecturally classified as being of the Duluth or Great Lakes genre. The design of the Chicamacomico station was developed by architect Victor Mendleheff, who also blueprinted the replacement structures at the Outer Banks' Poyners Hill, Kitty Hawk and Nags Head stations.

The old station contains two small museums devoted to the Lifesaving Service. The 1874 station in the rear of the property displays other lifesaving gear and the self-bailing surfboat used in the rescue of the crew from the oil tanker *Mirlo*, torpedoed by a German submarine in August 1918.

OPEN. May to September, Tuesdays, Thursdays and Saturdays 11 to 5.

FREE ADMISSION. Donations cheerfully accepted.

DEMONSTRATION. Mid-June to Labor Day only on Thursdays at 2. During the Historic Beach Apparatus Drill, surfmen dressed in 1890s uniforms ready a Lyle gun, then fire its lifeline towards an onshore mast where a visiting volunteer waits in a breeches buoy. After the lifeline wraps itself around the spar, the surfmen attach it to the mast and the lucky "mariner" slides to safety.

- Chicamacomico Historical Association, Inc., Box 5, Rodanthe, NC 27968.

Phone (919) 987-1552.

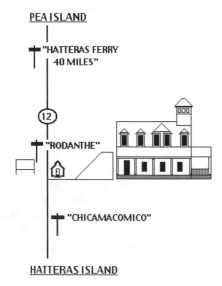

RESTORATION. In 1982 the independent and nonprofit Chicamacomico Historical Association began the station's restoration in 1982. As of 1996 the group was still working on the project. The interior of the 1911 building was about 80% complete. The 1874 boathouse needed restoration work done on it. The station's other five out-buildings were in good shape, but not fully restored. Memberships in the Chicamacomico "Lifesavers Club" support the Association's work.

Some of the crew from International Chimney Corporation at work

This view from the old foundation shows how much progress had been made in the first 12 days of the move

BODIE ISLAND

<u>NORTH ON NC 12</u>. The Bodie (pronounced "body") Island Lighthouse is located off NC 12 about 17 miles north of Rodanthe and four miles north of the Oregon Inlet Bridge.

<u>OR SOUTH</u>. The lighthouse is 5.8 miles south of Whalebone Junction.

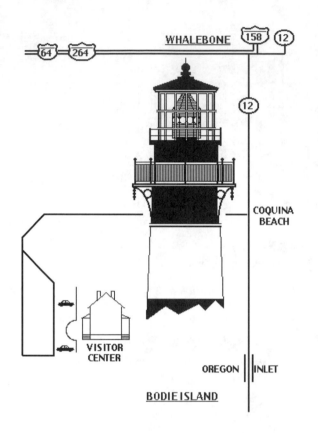

BODIE ISLAND VISITOR CENTER. The station's duplex keepers' dwelling, after its $430,000 restoration to its 1893 condition, was opened in 1992 as a visitor center. One side features a small museum with exhibits on lighthouse history, technology and preservation. There is a panel from Cape Hatteras' first-order lens, the clockwork mechanism, a 1,000 watt bulb from Bodie Island and an oil reservoir from the Currituck Beach Lighthouse. The other side contains the information desk and gift shop staffed by Eastern National Park and Monument Association employees and volunteers from the Outer Banks Lighthouse Society. National Park interpretive rangers have been withdrawn due to funding cuts.

Visitors may enter the lighthouse (access may be curtailed due to danger of falling debris), but not climb its stairs. The station grounds are handicapped accessible.

OPEN. Memorial Day to Thanksgiving Day, daily 9 to 5. [Memorial Day to Labor Day until 6].

FREE ADMISSION.
- Cape Hatteras National Seashore, Route 1, Box 675, Manteo, NC 27954.
Phone: Seashore (919) 473-2111.
Visitor Center (919) 441-5711.

<u>BODIE ISLAND LIGHTHOUSE</u> (PEA ISLAND).
CHARACTERISTIC: Group flashing white 30s
HAW: 156' **RANGE**: 18 nm

In 1837 Stephen Pleasonton, the Lighthouse Service chief, dispatched a young Naval officer on a fact-finding survey of the coastal Virginia and the Outer Banks. His report urged the establishment of a first class aid on Pea Island. Eleven years later, the area's first lighthouse was constructed on the island. The lighthouse, keeper's house, cisterns and two sheds cost a little over $11,000. Even at that price the structure was a bummer. The tower simply did not look like a lighthouse.

The 54-foot tall brick tower had a 17-foot diameter base with a dumpy conical design that produced at the top a 12-foot diameter floor for the 10-foot diameter lantern. Its appearance was not its only fault. Forbidden by Stephen Pleasonton's field inspector to sink pilings, the contractor was forced to lay the foundation in unstable soil. As was to be expected, it wasn't long until one side of the base began to sink, throwing the tower out of plumb.

The lantern was fitted with a rotating chandelier holding one of Winslow Lewis' lighting devices, consisting of 14 oil-fed lamps and reflectors. The optic was rotated by a weight-powered mechanism, much like a grandfather clock. As the foundation began to settle, the erratic rotation of the optic gave each revolution of the light a varying characteristic.

Although there were attempts to right it, the old tower was finally abandoned (and lost to the sea) and a second lighthouse erected on Pea Island. The 80-foot tall brick tower was fitted with a cast-iron lantern and a third-order Fresnel lens. The light was established on July 1, 1859. That tower was blown up by the Confederacy in 1861.

BODIE ISLAND

Work on the present 166-foot tall lighthouse began in 1871 when the contractor, after finishing his work at Cape Hatteras, moved his equipment, materials and storage sheds to the Bodie Island construction site. He opted to apply the same foundation laying technique he used for Cape Hatteras. In less than a year he completed the job at a cost of $140,000.

The new optic, a lard oil-powered first-order Fresnel lens, was first displayed on October 1, 1872. When the beacon was electrified in 1931, the keeper and his assistant were withdrawn. The Fresnel lens, now automated, still projects its strong warning beam.

The keeper of the new Bodie Island Lighthouse reported an experience similar to that of many other light keepers, especially the keeper of the Saddleback Ledge Lighthouse in Maine. It seems that shortly after the Bodie Island beacon was turned on, a flock of wild geese decided to fly into the lantern. In the process several glass storm panes were smashed and the lens damaged. After the goose attack, the keeper screened the exterior glass panes.

OWNER. National Park Service since July 2000. The dwelling and grounds were deeded to the National Park Service in 1953.

PRESERVATION. Not listed in the National Register of Historic Places.

In July 1997, the U.S. Coast Guard announced that it had contracted with the Golden Eagle Contractor of Virginia Beach to restore the lighthouse. The following work was completed in late 1997.

Phase I: Repairing the wooden windows, replacing and sealing of the lantern's storm panes, repairing the 214 stair treads, repointing the interior brickwork, sealing of interior masonry cracks and repairing the exterior cast-iron cracks at the gallery and lantern levels.

Phase II: Surface preparation and painting of the interiors of the watchroom, gallery and lantern (not the tower's interior) and the tower's exterior walls and attached oil house.

A great deal of restoration is still needed. In fact, in April 2000 the Park Service erected a fence around the base of the tower to protect visitors from being struck by falling material. A total restoration has been estimated at $1.7 million. The Save America's Treasures Historic Preservation Fund has granted $200,000, and another another $200,000 was included by Congress in the National Park Service budget for 2000-01.

Bodie Island Lighthouse

91

CURRITUCK BEACH

TO COROLLA. This lighthouse is located just south of Corolla on NC 12. In Kitty Hawk, where US 158 makes a sweeping curve and US 158 NC 12 (Business) rejoins US 158, turn north into NC 12. Continue on for about 20.5 miles to Corolla Village Road. Turn left at a lighthouse sign. Free parking across the street from the light station.

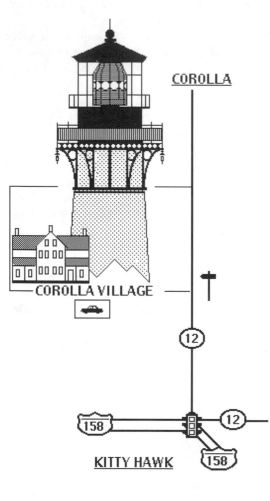

OPEN. Easter weekend to Thanksgiving Day, daily 10 to 6. Closed rest of year and during high winds and thunderstorms.

The keepers' duplex will be opened to the public after its restoration has been completed.

ADMISSION FEE. Visitor Center at base of tower free. Fee to climb the tower's 214 steps and walk out onto the service gallery. Children under five free.

- Currituck Beach Lighthouse, PO Box 361, Corolla, NC 27927. Phone: (252) 453-4939.
Website: http://www.currituckbeachlight.com

CURRITUCK BEACH LIGHTHOUSE
(WHALEHEAD; WHALESHEAD).
CHARACTERISTIC: Flashing white 20s
HAW: 158' **RANGE**: 18 nm

The 163-foot tall Currituck Beach Lighthouse is of the same structural design as Cape Lookout (basic), Cape Hatteras and Bodie Island. Finished in 1875, it was the last lighthouse to be built in North Carolina.

Like the Cape Hatteras tower, Currituck Beach's red brick tower stands on a brick foundation which rests on a subterranean mix of pilings, grillage (framework of timbers) and stone. The stone bed is 6.75 feet deep. The walls are 5.7 feet thick at the base, tapering to three feet at the watchroom deck. The tower's outer diameter at its base is 28 feet; inside 16.5 feet.

The 158-feet tall tower shows three windows placed vertically facing the ocean; two face Currituck Sound. Each window has been proportionately reduced in size to conform to the height and taper of the conical tower. The windows are embellished with segmented arches, molded brick frames and granite keystones and corners. Four narrow casement windows surround the tower on the first of two watchroom decks.

A semicircular cast-iron stairway leads to the deck below the watchroom, followed by two flights of spiral stairway to the watchroom and an intermediate deck just below the lantern, where the rotating mechanism was housed. The spacious gallery, extending from the mechanism room, is supported with long decorative cast-iron brackets with dangling pendants that begin at a heavy molded necking and slope upward to the deck. The lantern, serviced from a narrower gallery, is polygonal with a copper roof and an acorn-shaped copper ventilator. Interestingly, the lightning rod's spindle is connected to the lantern's framework, which explains why the tower is closed to visitors during thunderstorms.

Adjoining the tower's base is a small, one-story brick building that has been used both as a repair shop and storeroom for oil storage tanks. The wood framed keepers' two-story dwelling, completed in 1876, is located on the west side of the tower.

The 12-foot tall lantern still holds the lighthouse's original first-order Fresnel lens. When first established, the lard oil-fed optic was rotated by a weight-activated clockwork that is now displayed in the Bodie Island visitor center. The weights descended through the middle of the tower.

CURRITUCK BEACH

OWNER. U.S. Coast Guard (lighthouse). Dwelling and grounds leased to the Outer Banks Conservationists in 1981.

PRESERVATION. Listed in the National Register of Historic Places.

In 1939 the Coast Guard automated the light and removed its personnel. Although an Act of Congress transferred the station (less tower) to North Carolina's Wildlife Resources Commission in 1952, not much was done to maintain or protect the station's property.

When the 2.5-acre station was finally leased to the nonprofit Outer Banks Conservationists, it was in terrible shape. The ornately Stick-styled keepers' duplex was falling apart, its porches had collapsed, vines were growing through its walls and the interior was cruelly vandalized.

In 1981 work began on refurbishing the duplex's exterior. That project is almost complete. The rehabilitation of the interior has been a mammoth undertaking. Plaster walls and pine floors had to be completely repaired, stolen wainscotings have been replaced, and the mahogany balustrades, which were stolen from both sets of stairs, were replaced. Another smaller assistant keeper's house, believed to have been moved onto the station around 1920, was almost a total loss; it has been renovated and now serves as a gift shop. A storehouse was returned to its original condition in 1994.

In 1999 a detailed inspection was performed on the tower's ironwork, especially the brackets beneath the gallery decking. This inspection was the first step in a $400,000 renovation completed in about three months by International Chimney Corporation. Repairs and enhancements were made to the gallery deck, handrails, brackets, roof, exterior of the lantern room, lantern deck and ventilation system. Plexiglas panels in the service room windows were replaced with replicas of the original wooden windows. The exterior door to the gallery deck was also removed and replicated. All the repairs were completed before the opening of the lighthouse in the spring of 2000.

- Outer Banks Conservationists, Inc., PO Box 1891, Manteo, NC 27954.

Phone (252) 453-4939.

Currituck Beach Lighthouse

VIRGINIA
CAPE HENRY

TO FORT STORY IN VIRGINIA BEACH. Just past 82nd Street turn right off US 60 into continuing Atlantic Avenue and motor to Fort Story's west gate. "Fort Story" and "Cape Henry Lighthouse" signs mark the turn. Stay on Atlantic Avenue to the lighthouses.

Motorists driving vehicles without Department of Defense bumper decals may be requested by the gate guard to show their vehicle operator's licenses before being allowed to enter the post. After December 31, 2001 the guard stations will be staffed throughout the day. All visitors will be required to show identification to receive passes to visit the area. The Army is also considering a plan to build a visitor center at the east entrance. The center would provide a place for visitors to receive passes and might include historic exhibits.

SOUTH ON US 60. About 0.4 mile east of the entrance (traffic signal) to Seaside State Park turn left into VA 305 (marked with a "Ft. Story" sign) and continue on to the east gate. Stay on the main road through Fort Story to the lighthouses. There is ample free parking.

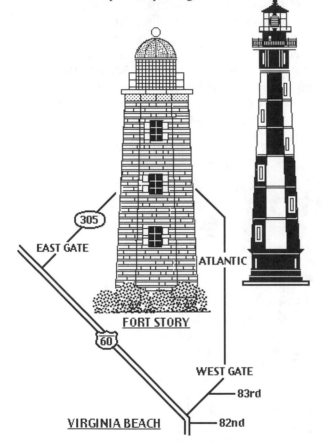

VISITING OLD CAPE HENRY. There is a series of steps up a knoll to the base of the tower. The climb up to old Cape Henry's lantern traverses a winding staircase with 205 steps.

OPEN. April 1 through October, daily 10 to 5.

ADMISSION FEES. Discounts for seniors 65+ and children 7-18.

- Administrator, Old Cape Henry Lighthouse, 4401 Wishart Road, Virginia Beach, VA 23455.

Phone (757) 422-9421.

Off-season (757) 460-1688 recording.

CAPE HENRY LIGHTHOUSE (1791).

Although both Virginia and Maryland agreed in 1773 to cooperatively build a lighthouse on Cape Henry, the lack of transports to deliver the building materials and the Revolutionary War delayed its construction. Then in 1790, at the request of the State, Congress appropriated $24,000 for the erection of a lighthouse on the southside entrance to Chesapeake Bay. Virginia ceded the land to the Federal Government and then sold it the sandstone (ballast) stockpiled for the earlier planned lighthouse. By the time work began on the lighthouse, however, the stones had sunk so deeply into their marshy resting place that their extraction was considered to be too difficult, time consuming and expensive.

The construction contract was signed on March 31, 1791 by the Secretary of the Treasury, Alexander Hamilton, and a "brick layer" who happened to be the famous builder of lighthouses, John McComb.

This 90-foot tall lighthouse was the first to be authorized (1790), completed (1791) and established (1792) under the auspices of the First United States Congress. The aid cost a little over $15,000. The lighthouse stands near the shore where English colonists, in 1607, first set foot in Virginia.

An 1872 inspection reported the old tower to be unstable and unsafe. It was recommended that a new and more powerful aid be built. Six years later Congress appropriated $75,000 for the construction of a new Cape Henry light tower. Although old Cape Henry's light was extinguished in early December 1881, the tower was used for many years as a daymark and for coastal survey triangulations.

The octagonal tapered stone tower is faced with sandstone ashlar. The lantern's domed roof is covered with hammered copper sheets. The lantern's small glass panes are representative of window treatments for early Colonial lighthouses.

CAPE HENRY

OWNER. Association for the Preservation of Virginia Antiquities since 1930. Maintained by the City of Virginia Beach.

PRESERVATION. Listed in the National Register of Historic Places.

This lighthouse and its 1.8-acre parcel had been privately owned since 1930, but its deterioration, caused by erosion and an unlocked door permitting unauthorized entry and vandalism, was not halted until its restoration was completed in 1972.

CAPE HENRY LIGHTHOUSE (1881).

CHARACTERISTIC: Flashing morse code "U" white 20s (red sector)

HAW: 164' RANGE: White 17; red 15 nm

This lighthouse is not open to the public.

At a cost of $125,000, the present 163-foot tall lighthouse was constructed of prefabricated cast-iron plates bolted together into a tall, tapered shape. The interior is lined with brick. Cape Henry's architectural design is almost identical to the lighthouses built on South Carolina's Hunting Island and Florida's Cape Canaveral. The tower's lantern was fitted with a first-order Fresnel lens that was first lighted on December 15, 1881.

In 1912 the original lard oil-burning lamp was replaced by an incandescent mineral oil (kerosene) vapor lamp. The presently active first-order optic was electrified in 1923.

In 1929 Cape Henry became the second American lighthouse to house a radiobeacon. New Jersey's Sea Girt had the first operational radiobeacon in 1921. Cape Henry's antenna is located about 80 yards from the tower. The radiobeacon broadcasts its "CB" signal out to a distance of 150 nautical miles.

OWNER. U.S. Coast Guard.

OLD COAST GUARD STATION MUSEUM.

This excellent and interesting museum is housed in a restored 1903 lifesaving station. It is located on the beach at the foot of 24th Street off Atlantic Avenue.

The museum is dedicated to preserving the history of the Lifesaving Service and the U.S. Coast Guard. There are exhibits depicting the services' operations along the Virginia coast and a fine collection of maritime artifacts and photographs. There is also an audiovisual presentation.

OPEN. Memorial Day to October 1, Mondays through Saturdays 10 to 5. Sundays noon to 5. Rest of the year, Tuesdays through Saturdays 10 to 5. Sundays noon to 5. Closed January 1, Thanksgiving Day and December 25.

ADMISSION FEES. Discounts for seniors 60+, active duty military and children 6-18. Also group rates.

- Old Coast Guard Station Museum, PO Box 24, Virginia Beach, VA 23548.

Phone (757) 422-1587.

Email: old_coast@va-beach.com

THIMBLE SHOAL

NORTH ON US 60. From Fort Story or the Chesapeake Bay Bridge and Tunnel take US 60 (Ocean View Avenue) west. In Norfolk's suburb of Ocean View and just past Granby Street (US 460) turn right into a bayside park marked with a "Norfolk Public Park" sign.

Thimble Shoal Lighthouse is nicely positioned offshore for viewing and photographing.

SOUTH ON I-64. In Norfolk take I-64's Exit 272 to US 60. Park is located a few blocks east of the US 60 and VA 168 (Tidewater Drive) interchange.

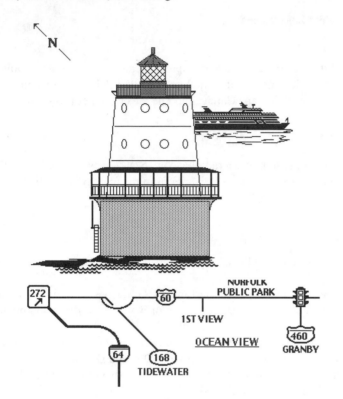

THIMBLE SHOAL LIGHTHOUSE.
CHARACTERISTIC: Flashing white 10s
HAW: 55' **RANGE**: 18 nm

The first lighthouse on Thimble Shoal, a screw pile structure built in 1870, was destroyed by fire in 1880. Using the undamaged pilings of the destroyed lighthouse, as well as its lantern and the fourth-order Fresnel lens recovered by divers, a new screw pile lighthouse was built and put into operation within two months of the fire.

The second Thimble Shoal Lighthouse also was not to be spared. One reason for its demise was the fact that a rather fragile structure was placed on a sealane heavily used by large ocean-going vessels. In 1891 a ship rammed the platform and caused a great deal of damage. In 1898 a coal scow hit it. On December 27, 1909, a large sailing vessel under tow collided with the tower. The jolt upset a stove and started a fire that totally destroyed the structure. The ship stayed afloat and drifted clear. That was the end of the screw pile design for Thimble Shoal.

The Treasury Department, in late 1912, approved a construction contract calling for a truncated cast-iron tower. The 40-foot tall lighthouse superstructure rests on a 300-ton caisson foundation that was assembled ashore, towed to the shoal, sunk and filled with concrete. The tri-level (portholes show the location of the levels) tower is made with bolted and welded cast-iron plates. The smallish lantern is serviced by an extra large tower gallery; another balcony circles the superstructure's keepers' quarters below. Construction of this light tower cost around $90,000.

The light was reestablished on December 1, 1914, using the original fourth-order Fresnel lens. The lens was removed when the aid was automated in 1964.

OWNER. U.S. Coast Guard.
PRESERVATION. Not listed in the National Register of Historic Places.

In 1988 the Coast Guard refurbished the lighthouse. Rusted metal was replaced or reinforced before the entire structure was sandblasted, primed and repainted.

In September 1996 the Coast Guard undertook a major refreshening of the lighthouse's interior and exterior painted surfaces. Surfaces were chipped, but not sandblasted, before applying new coats of paint. According to the Coast Guard the structure needs additional work done on it, but funds were not available to complete a more thorough job. Deficiencies reported are a cracked entry-level concrete walkway and rusted out rain spouts and gutters.

OLD POINT COMFORT

TO FORT MONROE. Take I-64 to Hampton and depart the interstate at Exit 268 (VA 169). Then:
-> VA 169 (Mallory Street),
-> Right at VA 143 (County Street),
-> Continue on VA 143 (Water Street) to the main gate.

While entry into Fort Monroe is free and no passes are required, the visitor may be stopped and requested to show a driver's license or military identification card.

Enter Fort Monroe on Ingalls Road, continue straight ahead to Fenwick Road and turn left. There are free parking spaces opposite the lighthouse.

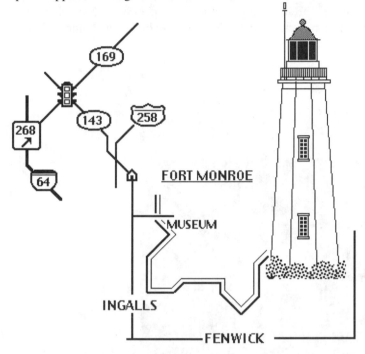

FORT MONROE. The Jamestown settlers named Old Point Comfort in 1607, and in 1609 they built a small stockade called Fort Algermourne. The redan was destroyed by a storm in 1626. A third fortress erected in 1727 was leveled by a hurricane in 1749. That early fort played a small yet significant part in America's lighthouse history, because as early as 1749 it is recorded that a sentry was stationed on the ruins and instructed, when spotting an approaching ship, to light a bonfire as an aid to navigation.

The present Fort Monroe was built after the War of 1812. Construction began in 1818. The stones used to build the fort were cut from quarries in Richmond, Virginia. Slaves began the construction task, but were later replaced by military prisoners and paid civilian laborers.

Edgar Allen Poe, as he did at South Carolina's Fort Moultrie, served as a sergeant major in 1828. Lt. Robert E. Lee supervised the final construction of the moat revetments and outworks.

CASEMENT MUSEUM. Contains Confederate President Jefferson Davis' cell, cannons, Monroe's history, Civil War artifacts and military uniforms. The 1.25-mile walk around the fort's elevated perimeter offers great views Hampton Roads area, including the Thimble Shoal Lighthouse and Fort Wool.

OPEN. All year, daily 10:30 to 4:30.
Closed January 1, Thanksgiving Day and December 25.
FREE ADMISSION.
- Casement Museum, PO Box 341, Fort Monroe, VA 23651.
Phone (757) 727-3391.

OLD POINT COMFORT LIGHTHOUSE.

CHARACTERISTIC: Group flashing red 12s (white sector)
HAW: 54' **RANGE**: White 16 nm; red 14 nm
Although Congress as early as 1798 authorized the construction of a lighthouse on Old Point Comfort, it was not completed until 1802.

The British occupied the lighthouse in 1812 and used it as an observation platform. During the Civil War the tower was badly battered by naval gunfire. After the war, the tower was restored to its present condition.

This 54-foot tall lighthouse's architectural design is a fine example of the Colonial Revival period of lighthouse construction. It is a conical masonry (sandstone) tower of utilitarian styling with few windows and without ornamentation. The octagonal tower's unique spiral stairway, one of the very few remaining today, consists of a series of wedge-shaped stones, whose broad ends are embedded in the wall and the smaller ends are anchored to a center post.

OLD POINT COMFORT

In 1838 the Lighthouse Service reported that, in February 1836, the lantern's ceiling had been damaged by a fire ignited by the heat from its 10 whale oil lamps. Sometime in the mid-1850s the tower received its presently active classical lens.

OWNER. U.S. Coast Guard (lighthouse). The 1900 Victorian-styled keeper's house, now the family residence of Fort Monroe's Command Sergeant Major, has been owned and maintained by the U.S. Army since 1973.

PRESERVATION. Listed on the National Register of Historic Places.

ANOTHER VIEW OF THIMBLE SHOAL. The viewing spot is about 1.4 miles from the Old Point Comfort Lighthouse. Continue north on Fenwick Road and a short distance from Battery Ruggles turn right into an unmarked paved lane. Motor to Gulick Drive and park. Walk up the ramp to the top of the seawall. The red tower lies about 2 miles offshore.

Old Point Comfort Lighthouse

NEWPORT NEWS MIDDLE GROUND

This side trip portion of the Atlantic Coast lighthouse tour includes bayside viewings of this lighthouse, a cruise that passes it and two stopovers to view Fresnel's classical lenses.

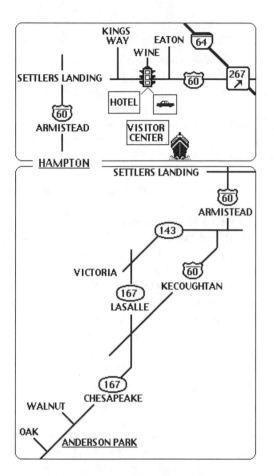

TO THE HAMPTON HARBOR CRUISE. From Fort Monroe follow VA 143 (Water and County Streets) through the I-64 underpass into US 60/VA 143 (Settlers Landing Road).

If traveling on I-64, take Exit 267 (Hampton University) to Settlers Landing.

A short distance past the drawbridge at Wine Street (on the right) turn left into the entrance to the Radisson Hotel. Bear left and up into a municipal parking garage (free). There is a short walk to the Hampton Visitor Center and boat dock located behind the garage and hotel.

HARBOR CRUISE. The *Miss Hampton II* (two open decks) sails west along the Fort Monroe shoreline and across Hampton Roads to Fort Wool, where passengers can debark for a ranger-led tour of the pre-Civil War fortress. Before returning to port, the motor vessel moves along the two-mile long waterfront of the Norfolk Naval Base. The narrated tour takes three hours. Reservations recommended. The cruise provides views of Old Point Comfort (about 150 feet), Thimble Shoal (2-3 miles) and Newport News Middle Ground (1.5 miles).

SCHEDULE. Mid-April to late October, daily cruises. Call for times.

FARES. Discounts for seniors 65+ and children 6-12. Under 6 free.

- Miss Hampton II Harbor Cruises., 764 Settlers Landing Road, Hampton, VA 23669.

Phone (757) 722-9102. In USA toll-free (888) 757-BOAT. Fax (757) 722-9113.

TO ANDERSON PARK. From the Hampton cruise take US 60 (Settlers Landing Road) west and south to VA 167 (Lasalle Avenue). Follow VA 167 south on Lasalle and southwest on Chesapeake Avenue. Anderson Park is about 2.5 miles from where Lasalle ends and VA 167 takes a right turn into Chesapeake. The Newport News Lighthouse can be seen from the park's fishing pier.

OPEN. All year, daily sunrise to sunset.

FREE ADMISSION.

CHESAPEAKE CHAPTER OF THE U.S. LIGHTHOUSE SOCIETY This active group focuses on the restoration and preservation of the lighthouses and lightships of Virginia and Maryland. They offer periodic lighthouse cruises and land tours in the Chesapeake area and elsewhere. Check their website or call for the latest tour information.

- Chesapeake Chapter, USLHS. PO Box 1270, Annadale, VA 22003-1270.

Website: http://www.cheslights.org

NEWPORT NEWS MIDDLE GROUND LIGHTHOUSE.
CHARACTERISTIC: Equal interval white 6s
HAW: 52' **RANGE**: 9 nm

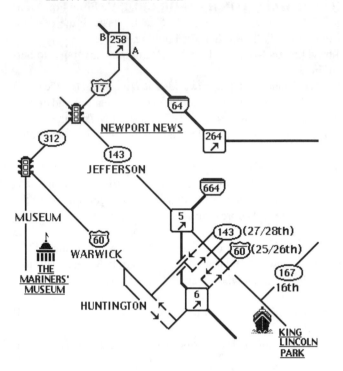

This aid marks the shallow shoal that lies south of the Newport News Channel. It is a coffee pot-styled, cast-iron lighthouse constructed in 1891. The red 35-foot tall superstructure with its three interior decks rests on a red concrete-filled caisson sunk in 15 feet of water. The caisson contains the usual cisterns for water and fuel storage.

In 1979 a ship hit the lighthouse and caused damage to the lower part of the caisson, allowing sea water to enter.

OWNER. U.S. Coast Guard.

PRESERVATION. Eligible for listing in the National Register of Historic Places.

TO THE MARINERS' MUSEUM. From Waterman's Wharf cruise dock follow Jefferson Avenue northwest to Museum Drive and turn left. Museum Drive is marked with a large museum sign. Continue to the museum's parking lots (free).

If traveling on I-64, take Exit 258A to US 17 (J. Clyde Morris Boulevard). Continue southwest on VA 312 (J. Clyde Morris) and cross US 60 (Warwick Boulevard) into Museum Drive.

This museum is dedicated to the builders of ships and to other craftsmen who captured the lore of the sea and man's maritime adventure over the past 3,000 years. Just inside the museum's entrance on the left is the Chesapeake Bay Gallery and its centerpiece, Cape Charles Lighthouse's original first-order Fresnel lens and its rotating mechanism. A fifth-order lens is also on display.

There are ten additional galleries, including the newer Great Hall of Steam, the Carvings Gallery and the William Francis Gibbs Naval Architect Gallery. Photographs, costumes, tools, weapons, miniature models, paintings, and an array of international small craft are attractively displayed. Guided tours upon request.

OPEN. All year, daily 10 to 5.
Closed Thanksgiving Day and December 25.
ADMISSION FEES. Discounts for seniors 60+, active duty military and students (any age). Under 5 free.

- The Mariners' Museum, 100 Museum Drive, Newport News, VA 23606-3759.
Phone (757) 596-2222. In USA toll-free (800) 581-7245. Fax (757) 591-7310.
Website: http://www.mariner.org/ Email: marketing@mariner.org

NEWPORT NEWS MIDDLE GROUND

WHITE SHOAL (destroyed). This screw pile lighthouse was built in 1855 on a shoal offshore of the Lion Bridge in Newport News. It was later criticized by the Lighthouse Board as being poorly constructed. The hexagonal house-cum-tower was then rebuilt in 1871 and given a fixed white light magnified by a fifth-order Fresnel lens. The lighthouse was later sold at auction. In 1973 the abandoned structure began to show its disintegration. In 1990 broken pilings and a hunk or two of its platform were clearly visible. By 1995 the ruins had disappeared.

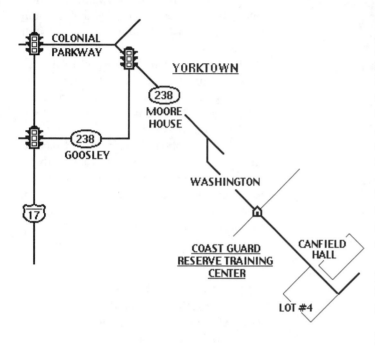

TO THE COAST GUARD RESERVE TRAINING CENTER. Even if you are only a wee bit interested in lighthouses, you must visit this center's fabulous collection of lenses, beacons, cans, buoys, nuns and daymarks. There is an outside static display of aids to navigation that the whole family will enjoy. Inside the Aids to Navigation Facility, Canfield Hall, there is a superb display of Fresnel lenses that can be closely inspected and photographed.

Take US 17 (George Washington Highway) north towards Yorktown. At either VA 238 (Goosley Road) or the Colonial Parkway turn right at Moore House Road and continue on connecting Washington Road to the center's main gate.

Active duty and retired military personnel with proper Department of Defense identification are allowed to visit the station after checking in with the station's gate security officer.

Non-military visitors must first call the center's Public Affairs Office to arrange for entry into the station.

From the main entrance continue straight ahead (southeast) to parking lot #4. Canfield Hall and its static aids display are next to the parking area. Just inside the building's main entrance is a lobby displaying these classical lenses.

First-order	Fourth-order (2) rotating drum	Fifth-order fixed drum
Second order bivalve	Fourth-order fixed drum	Sixth-order
Third-order drum		

OPEN. All year, daily 8 to 4.
FREE ADMISSION.
- U.S. Coast Guard Reserve Training Center, Yorktown, VA 23690.
Phone: Security/Operations (757) 898-2314. Public Affairs Office (757) 898-2337.
Website: http://www.uscg.mil/hq/rtc/

CAPE CHARLES

NORTH OR SOUTH ON US 13. This lighthouse, located on Smith Island east of Kiptopeke, can be seen while crossing over US 17's 17.6-mile long Chesapeake Bay Bridge-Tunnel (vehicle toll).
- Chesapeake Bay Bridge & Tunnel District, PO Box 111, Cape Charles, VA 23310.
Phone (757) 624-3511 ext 20 or (757) 331-2960.
Website: http://www.cbbt.com

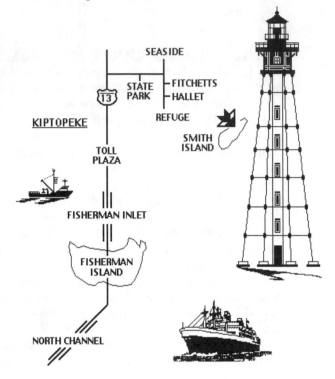

On the way north to Virginia's Eastern Shore there is a continuing panoramic sighting of the distant tower from the top of the North Channel Bridge, over the Fisherman Inlet Bridge and along the causeway to the toll booths. Look for the skeletal tower with its black top (lantern and watchroom) and white substructure. There is no stopping enroute, so slow down to view the lighthouse.

The southbound motorist will have to stretch his or her neck a bit to view the lighthouse. The tower is to your left rear as you leave the toll gate and drive to and up onto the Fisherman Inlet Bridge and while crossing over the North Channel Bridge. [1]

CAPE CHARLES LIGHTHOUSE
(SMITH ISLAND; SMITHS ISLAND)
CHARACTERISTIC: Flashing white 5s
HAW: 180' **RANGE**: 24 nm

In 1828 the first Cape Charles Lighthouse was a brick tower built on Smith Island at a cost of about $7,400. In 1852 the Lighthouse Board had this to say about the lighthouse: "The tower has an elevation of only fifty-five feet [probably the distance from the tower's base to the optic's focal plane], placed on a very low coast, giving the light, if in other respects good, a range of not more than twelve nautical miles, which it can seldom reach in consequence of the very inferior illuminating apparatus."

In 1856 Congress authorized the construction of a new light tower about 1.25 miles southwest of the first tower. Work on the structure began in 1858. By 1862, with work slowed by weather and the slow arrival of constructions materials, only 83 feet had been raised. At that point in time, a Confederate raiding party destroyed the old tower and absconded with most of the building materials stockpiled for the tower under construction.

In 1864 Congress reappropriated $20,000 for the completion of the tower and assigned a military detachment for its protection. The 150-foot tall lighthouse with its first-order Fresnel lens was commissioned on May 7, 1864.

As it has happened to so many other landfall lighthouses, the sea doomed the structure. The average annual encroachment in 1883 (first reported in 1857) was 30 feet. In 1885 Congress ordered the building of three large stone jetties as bulkheads to stem the erosion. Four more jetties were built in 1891. At the same time Congress contracted for another lighthouse to be erected about one mile inland of the second tower.

---

1. According to a ranger from the U.S. Fish and Wildlife Refuge located east of Kiptopeke, the top of the lighthouse can be seen through a "small window" from a high ground on one of the refuge's nature trails. The refuge can be reached from US 13 by turning east (just north of the toll booths) into the paved road to the Kiptopeke State Park. Continue east past the entrance to the park to a T-head and turn right on paved Seaside Road. Continue south past Fitchetts Road (on the left) and straight ahead into the refuge's unpaved entrance road. The refuge's entrance is marked with a "Wildlife Trail and Visitor Information - Other Areas" sign. Phone (757) 331-2760.

CAPE CHARLES

The building of the third light tower, an octagonal, skeletal cast-iron structure, was finished in December 1894 at a cost of $150,000. The 191-foot tall lighthouse's eight vertically sloping legs are tied together with bolt-anchored tension and compression rods all tightened with turnbuckles. In the structure's center is a large diameter tube that contains the staircase that spirals to the watchroom.

Also added to the station was an L-shaped 2 1/2-story, brick Victorian-styled keeper's residence with gabled roof, a brick oil shed and an outdoor privy. All except the privy remained until the keeper's quarters was destroyed by a brush fire on July 13, 2000.

Barrier, Bernard & Turrene's revolving first-order mercury-float lens was late in arriving from Paris, delaying the light's establishment until August 14, 1895. That lens, one of the only two numerical flash lenses installed in American lighthouses, was first exhibited at Chicago's 1893 Columbian Exposition. The classical lens had a "4-5" flash; Minot's Ledge still shows its "1-4-3" characteristic. The first-order Fresnel lens was removed in 1963 when the light was automated and the presently active modern lens substituted. It is now beautifully displayed in The Mariners' Museum in Newport News, Virginia.

OWNER. U.S. Coast Guard. The island is owned by the Nature Conservancy.

PRESERVATION. Not Listed in the National Register of Historic Places.

HOG ISLAND LIGHTHOUSE (dismantled).

The first lighthouse on barrier Hog Island was built in 1854. The beacon, which marked the entrance to Great Machipongo Inlet, served as an intermediate aid to navigation for the otherwise unlighted coastal expanse between Assateague and Cape Charles. The original conical tower was constructed of stone and, although fitted with a fourth-order Fresnel lens, the optic's low elevation raised questions about the aid's effectiveness. The station also had a 1 1/2-story stone keeper's house that had two dormers built into its gabled roof. In 1888 the Lighthouse Board decided to build a 150-foot tall skeletal cast-iron tower and equip it with a first-order Fresnel lens. The tower's design was identical to that of the Cape Charles Lighthouse. The Hog Island light was reestablished on January 31, 1896. Hog Island succumbed to the erosive power of the sea. It was torn down in 1948.

KILLICK SHOAL LIGHTHOUSE (dismantled).

This screw pile lighthouse was built off Wallops Island (now a NASA station) west of the western tip of Chincoteague Island, Virginia. The beacon marked the southern entrance to Chincoteague Inlet. Killick Shoal's design was considerably different from its Chesapeake screw pile contemporaries. The superstructure consisted of a two story, square clapboard house (painted white with black trim) surmounted on one side of the roof (from peak to eave) by a square tower, a wide service balcony and lantern. The lighthouse was replaced by a 20-foot tall steel tower.

ASSATEAGUE

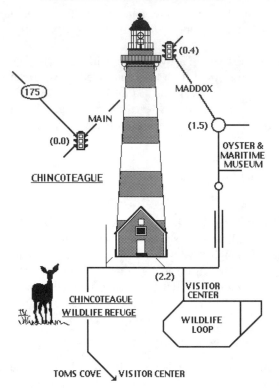

NORTH ON US 13. Just north of Oak Hall take VA 175 east across the causeway and drawbridge to Chincoteague (shing' go teeg).

SOUTH ON MD 12/VA CR 679. In Wattsville turn left at VA 175.

CONTINUE ON. In Chincoteague turn left at Main Street and right at Maddox Boulevard. Continue straight ahead through a traffic rotary. Note the entrance to the Oyster & Maritime Museum (see below).

Then continue on the main road around a toll booth until you reach a parking area (on the right) marked with a lighthouse symbol sign. There is a 0.25-mile path up a knoll and through the woods to the lighthouse. A generous application of insect repellant is advisable.

Note the location of the Oyster and Maritime Museum on the map.

CHINCOTEAGUE NATIONAL WILDLIFE REFUGE. This refuge is Virginia's part of the 37-mile long ocean barrier called the Assateague National Seashore. The preserve of almost 10,000 acres, is a veritable kaleidoscope of 316 identified resident and migratory birds. Wild ponies, white-tailed deer, Sika oriental elk, 'possums, Del Marva Peninsula squirrels, red foxes and a grand assortment of other furry creatures roam the wide marshes and loblolly trails. Along the 3.2-mile Wildlife Loop you will thoroughly enjoy watching some of the refugee's denizens. Access to the loop is restricted to hikers and bikers before 3 PM. Vehicles may travel the loop from 3 PM to dusk.

The Visitor Center (free) is handicapped accessible. Pick up a free brochure with map.

OPEN.
April and October, daily 6 AM to 8 PM.
May through September, daily 5 AM to 10 PM.
November through March, daily 6 AM to 6 PM.
ADMISSION FEE. From Memorial Day weekend to Labor Day there is a vehicle fee, good for seven days. National Park passes for seniors 62+, the handicapped and blind apply.
- Chincoteague National Wildlife Refuge, 8231 Beach Rd., Box 62, Chincoteague, VA 23336-0062.
Phone (757) 336-6122.
- Assateague Island National Seashore, 7206 National Seashore Lane, Berlin, MD 21811.
Phone: (410) 641-1441
Website: http://www.nps.gov/asis/

ASSATEAGUE LIGHTHOUSE.
CHARACTERISTIC: Group flashing white 5s
HAW: 154' **RANGE**: 22 nm
In 1831 Congress authorized the building of a lighthouse on Assateague Island. Fifty acres of land were purchased in 1832 and work on the new lighthouse began. The structure, completed in late January 1833, proved to be an inefficient warning aid. With a height of 45 feet, the tower was too short and its Winslow Lewis' chandelier-arranged multi-lamp/ reflector optic too dim to warn ships off the barrier shoals.

In 1852 the Lighthouse Board announced its intentions to raise the tower to 150 feet and to install a new optic. Construction of the new lighthouse did not begin until 1860 and then was suspended during Civil War. In 1865 work resumed; the lighthouse was completed and established on October 1, 1867. According to an inscription above the tower's entry vestibule, the lighthouse was "Rebuilt in 1866-67."

ASSATEAGUE

The keeper's houses west of the tower were constructed in 1910. The brick oil house was added in the late 1800's.

The lighthouse is 142 feet tall and stands on a mound of crushed oyster shells that is 22 feet above mean high water. The mound was donated by Chingoteague's oystermen. From its 27.5-foot diameter base, the tower's conical shape has been formed by a tapering exterior brickwork coursed in running bond. The tower's interior is cylindrical in shape and is laid all in header bond. While the walls are thick and solid, the tower had a dumbwaiter arrangement alcoved into the wall. The lift was used to hoist cans of fuel to the watchroom.

Entry into the tower is through a small advance building. A cast-iron stairway winds around a center post which is marked with plate inscribed with "Barbier and Fenestre, Paris, 1866." Arched openings behind each tower window allow sunlight into an otherwise dark stairway.

The lantern was fitted with a fixed first-order Fresnel lens and a whale oil-powered Argand lamp. The optic displayed a fixed beam visible out to 14 nautical miles. In 1933, after two generators were installed next to the lighthouse, the Fresnel lens was powered by a cluster of three 100-watt light bulbs, controlled by an astronomic on-off switch. The lantern now holds two rotating airport-type beacons. Each beacon is in the shape of a large drum, with a 1,000-watt bulb inside. The drums are aligned about 12 degrees apart to produce the double flash every five seconds.

OWNER. U.S. Coast Guard.

PRESERVATION. Listed in the National Register of Historic Places.

The Coast Guard has seen to it that the Assateague tower is kept in top-notch condition.

OYSTER & MARITIME MUSEUM (AND THE ASSATEAGUE LENS).

The museum features the oyster farming and seafood industries with permanent exhibits on the island's history and marine specimens. There are also demonstrations by wildlife artists and carvers.

After the installation of the new lighting system in 1961, the first-order Fresnel lens was donated by the Coast Guard to the Eastern Shore of Virginia Historical Society. On November 6, 1976, the Society transferred ownership of the lens to this Chincoteague museum. For 24 years the lens sat unattended out in the open. Meanwhile some local citizens and organizations such as the Chincoteague Natural History Association and the Chincoteague Taxpayers Committee tried to secure the lens. The latter, specifically organized to influence the Coast Guard to recover ownership of the lens for display within the refuge, was accepted as a chapter of the U.S. Lighthouse Society. The war of the lens ended when the Coast Guard refused to become further involved in the squabble, disassembled the lens and moved it to the museum.

In 1996 the museum, with a $50,000 bank loan, finished construction of a front building wing to be used exclusively for the display of the huge lens. Now it needs additional financial help to complete the restoration task. For example, the lens' three silver reflectors must be replated and some 17 prisms must be replaced. The museum's director reports that at least $50,000 will be needed to complete the restoration of the lens.

OPEN.

June through August, daily 10 to 5. Spring and Fall, weekends 10 to 5. Closed during winter months.

ADMISSION FEES. Discounts for seniors and children under 13.

- Oyster and Maritime Museum, PO Box 352 (7125 Maddox Boulevard), Chincoteague, VA 23336.
Phone (757) 336-6117.
Website: http://www.chincoteague.com/omm/

DELAWARE
FENWICK ISLAND

NORTH ON MD 528. Motor through Ocean City, Maryland and turn left into 142nd Street and right at Lighthouse Avenue.

SOUTH ON DE 1. Just past DE 54 turn right into 146th Street and continue to the lighthouse.

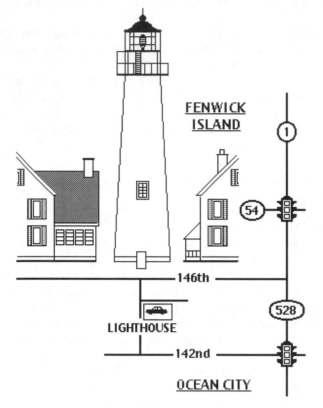

MUSEUM AND GIFT SHOP. A small museum shas been established at the base of the tower. The old generator building is now a gift shop. Due to insurance costs the public is not allowed to climb the stairs to the top.

OPEN. A handful of days June through September. Call or check website for the current schedule. The schedule is also usually posted at the lighthouse during the summer months.

FREE ADMISSION. Donations welcomed.

- Friends of Fenwick Island Lighthouse, Inc., PO Box 6, Selbyville, DE 19975-0006.

Phone (410) 250-1098 during the summer months. (302) 436-8410 in the winter.

Website: http://www.beach-net.com/lighthousefi.html

FENWICK ISLAND LIGHTHOUSE.
CHARACTERISTIC: Occulting white 13s
HAW: 83' **RANGE**: 8 nm

The Fenwick Island Lighthouse was authorized by Congress in 1856. A Lighthouse Board report of 1858 states that the construction of Fenwick Island "...commenced in the season of 1857." In 1859 the Board announced that "Fenwick Island was lighted on 1st August last." The cost of the land and station, including a keeper's house and several outbuildings, amounted to $23,750. The keeper's house was provided with gutters and spouts that delivered rain water to basement cisterns.

The first (east side) of two keepers' dwellings was built in 1858 and served two families. Overcrowded conditions brought about the construction of the second and larger house on the west side in 1882. After its completion, the two keepers' families moved into the newer house, leaving the older structure for the assistant keepers. The keepers' quarters received a telephone in 1898, which facilitated communicating with the nearby lifesaving station. Both houses were sold to private parties in 1940.

The great-grandfather of Paul Pepper was appointed Fenwick Island's third keeper in July 1869 with annual salary of $400. He and his family lived on the first floor of the older house. Paul's grandfather was the assistant keeper and lived on the second floor. Paul's father, Fred, and most of his siblings were born in the old house. Fred Pepper had fond memories as a boy growing up in the lighthouse service. He was wont to tell of how the family would get to its homestead in Georgetown. The "Fenwick Ditch" (upper Assawoman Bay) did not have a bridge (now DE 54) across it, and so the Pepper family used a small flat scow and rope to pull themselves and their horse and carriage to the mainland. From there they would ride to Selbyville and then catch the train to Georgetown. Paul's father was fond of telling about the many times they returned (usually after midnight) to find their scow had been borrowed and left on the opposite bank. The family's solution was to have Fred swim across "The Ditch" to retrieve the scow.

FENWICK ISLAND

The 87-foot tall lighthouse is of double wall construction. The painted outer wall is conical in shape formed by coursed bricks (15 stretcher to one header course) laid to a base diameter of 27 inches and tapering to 18 inches at the top. The inner tower is cylindrical in shape and has brick walls uniformly nine inches thick. The diameter of the inner tower is about eight feet. The 75-foot tall tower has a spiral cast-iron staircase that leads to the watchroom. The entire structure rests on a 12-foot deep rubble stone and masonry base. Of the five windows that circle the tower, the top one is at the watchroom level. Atop the watchroom is a standard ten-sided cast-iron lantern, protected by a network of mesh-covered rods.

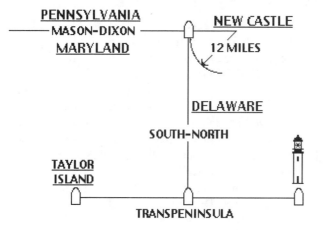

The first optic placed in the tower's lantern was its presently active third-order Fresnel lens powered by a single whale oil lamp. In 1879, with its conversion from lard oil to kerosene, the characteristic of the optic was changed to fixed white with an additional white flash produced by three revolving eclipser panels attached to a small dolly that rolled (six bronze guides and 12 smaller wheels) around the lens on a track some 17 inches in diameter. Rotation was accomplished by a weight-activated clockwork whose weights descended within a tube imbedded in the interior wall. One interesting item remaining in the tower is the central galvanized iron tube (eight inches in diameter) used to hoist cans of kerosene to the watchroom.

OWNER. The lighthouse was deeded to the State of Delaware and leased to the Friends of Fenwick Island Lighthouse on September 12, 1981. The dwellings are privately owned.

PRESERVATION. Listed in the National Register of Historic Places.

When Fenwick Island was deactivated in December 1978, the Coast Guard stripped the structure of all wiring, removed the Fresnel lens and withdrew its personnel. At that time Mr. Paul Pepper and friends began their campaign to save the lighthouse. This nonprofit organization was able to secure a $15,000 grant from the state for the purpose of restoring the badly deteriorated lighthouse. Additionally, the Friends recovered the third-order Fresnel lens and reestablished the light on May 26, 1982.

During the 1989-90 period vents were installed in the tower to reduce moisture buildup, surrounding steps and walks were replaced and the lighthouse repainted. The paint job is usually contracted for every six years at a cost of $20,000. In 1995 the Friends asked for bids on some repair work and the painting of the tower's exterior in 1996. All of the bids came in over the Friends' budget. Fortunately, the State of Delaware in 1997 provided $75,000 to complete the project

THE TRANSPENINSULAR LINE. This "crown stone" in front of the lighthouse marks the beginning of the Transpeninsular Line of 1751. It is not, as is commonly reported, a Mason-Dixon Line marker. The Fenwick Island marker was in place 13 years before Messrs Mason and Dixon reached America's shores. The stele is carved on both sides. On its south face is the coat of arms of the Lords Baltimore, the Calvert family of Maryland. The north side shows the coat of arms of the Penn family of Pennsylvania and the "Three Lower [eastern] Counties Upon Delaware." The stone is the first to have been set by the surveying team (two surveyors from each colony) ordered by the 1750 British Chancery Court to settle the near century-long boundary dispute between the Calverts and the Penns. The line, as planned, ran from Fenwick Island westward to Taylor Island. From its midpoint a south-to-north line was surveyed to intersect with another line running due west from New Castle. The survey team completed its work in 1763. But then, enter Charles Mason and Jeremiah Dixon, two English astronomers hired to assist the American team. Between 1764 and 1767 they officially resurveyed the south-to-north line separating Delaware and Maryland and then extended the New Castle line westward to establish the east-to-west Mason-Dixon line separating Maryland from Pennsylvania. The boundary stone is now listed in the National Register of Historic Places as part of the Delaware State Line.

DELAWARE BREAKWATER EAST
HARBOR OF REFUGE

TO CAPE HENLOPEN STATE PARK. The park, located east of Lewes and 0.5 mile past the Cape May-Lewes Ferry terminal at the end of US 9, is the best onshore place for viewing these towers.

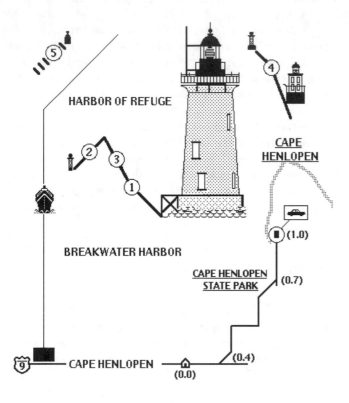

OPEN. All year, daily 8 to sunset.

ADMISSION FEES. Memorial Day to Labor Day, daily Delaware and out-of-state vehicle + passenger fees. Free rest of year.

CONTINUE IN THE PARK. Enter the park on the main concrete road and, just past a "Point Parking Lot" sign on the right, bear left at the next side road. Follow this winding road to a T-head intersection and turn left. Continue north bearing right into a one way road that loops around a ship reporting building. Turn right into an unpaved parking area

- Cape Henlopen State Park, 42 Cape Henlopen Drive, Lewes, DE 19958.

Phone (302) 645-8983.

Website: http://www.destateparks.com/chsp.htm

HARBOR CRUISE. Of the several cruises in and out of Lewes Harbor one is recommended for the lighthouse seeker. The cruise vessel departs from Fisherman's Wharf located off US 9 Business just before the Lewes-Rehobeth Canal drawbridge.

The two-hour narrated Evening Sunset Cruise of Lewes Harbor and the Delaware Breakwater area offers excellent views of the Delaware Breakwater and Harbor of Refuge Lighthouses.

SCHEDULE.
May 30 to September 1 daily at 7 PM. Call to confirm time.
FARES. Discounts for children under 12.
- Fisherman's Wharf, PO Box 150, Lewes, DE 19958. Phone (302) 645-8862 or (302) 645-8541.
Website: http://www.lewes-beach.com/whalewatch.html

THE HARBORS. The Lewes port of call consists of two separate harbors, each served by a lighthouse. The inner basin is the Delaware Breakwater Harbor; the outer one is the Harbor of Refuge. The brown tower off to the west northwest (left) is the Delaware Breakwater Lighthouse, whose red sector covers the inner harbor's shallows around the lighthouse. The white and black tower to the north is the Harbor of Refuge's Harbor of Refuge Lighthouse, whose red sectors cover The Shears to the northwest and the Atlantic Ocean's Hen and Chickens Shoal to the southeast off Cape Henlopen.

In 1822 Congress authorized a study of the feasibility of constructing a "harbor of refuge" at Lewes. The study was undertaken by General B. Bernard, a former French officer and then the Chief of the U.S. Army's Corps of Topographical Engineers, Major J. G. Totten, former professor of mathematics at the U.S. Military Academy and Commodore W. Banbridge, an expert on coastal fortifications. The trio recommended the building of a large permanent harbor. Congress authorized and funded the project in 1825, but because unspent monies had to be returned to the Treasury at year's end, completion of the project was delayed as each year's reappropriation had to be again requested and congressionally approved.

DELAWARE BREAKWATER EAST & HARBOR OF REFUGE

The Lewes harbor complex began to emerge in 1828-1839 period, when two portions of the inner breakwater were constructed. They consisted of the 2,100-foot long rubble stone main breakwater (#1 on map) and the 1,700-foot long ice breaker pier (#2 on map). Both breakwaters are constructed of some 835,000 tons of Brandywine granite boulders, weighing from one-half to six tons each. The stones were barged in from New Castle, Delaware and dumped overboard. Each pier is 120 feet wide at its base and 20 feet wide at the capped walkway. During the 1883-98 period the breakwater #1 and the ice breaker pier #2 were connected by a rubble stone closure (#3 on map) that has a base width of 145 feet and 20-foot wide dressed stone cap.

The Delaware Breakwater Harbor proved to be an effective and popular safe haven. Unfortunately its 400-acre expanse was usually overcrowded with ships seeking refuge from storms. Although the construction of breakwater (#4 on map) began as early as 1892, Congress formally authorized the building of "The National Harbor of Refuge" in 1896. Breakwater #4, built atop a shoal known as The Shears, is 8,040 feet long, 40 feet wide and is formed by dressed granite stones weighing up to 13 tons. Also added in 1901 was the 1,300-foot long series of ice breaker piers (#5 on map), located northwest of breakwater #4. Both barriers cost over $2,000,000. Harbor of Refuge's breakwater #4 possesses an historic significance in that the design and construction techniques used to build it were used for most of America's breakwaters constructed after 1901.

DELAWARE BREAKWATER WEST & EAST LIGHTHOUSES.

In 1834 the U.S. Army established a temporary light on the west end of the breakwater #1. Although the blueprints for a lighthouse had been readied for construction in 1834, the aid was finally built on the west end of the breakwater #1 in 1848. The lighthouse was a two-story wood framed building with a mid-roof tower and lantern. The beacon was locally referred to as the "Breakwater Beacon Light."

In 1876 the Western Union Telegraph Company was given permission to occupy the lighthouse and use it as a telegraph station. After the new lighthouse was built in 1885 Western Union moved its telegraph operations into a small building built next to the new lighthouse. That building has been removed.

In 1880 the Philadelphia Maritime Exchange moved into the unoccupied lighthouse and used it as a reporting station for incoming and departing ships. The maritime exchange building, turned over to the Coast Guard in 1954, was later dismantled.[1]

Recognizing that the construction of the closure #3 would render the 1848 lighthouse obsolete, the present light tower was erected in 1885 on the east end of breakwater #1.

The 49-foot tall tower rests on a cylindrical concrete foundation. It has been constructed using four tiers of cast-iron plates bolted together. The brick-lined tower tapers from a 22-foot diameter base to 18 feet at the watchroom deck. The watchroom atop the tower is 11 feet in diameter. There are five interior decks. The entry level housed a generator. When occupied, the second level contained the galley. Living quarters were on the third deck. The top deck was used to store supplies. The watchroom rests on the last deck. The overall height of the lighthouse is 56 feet.

The first Lewes lighthouse had a multi-lamp, oil-fueled optic placed atop the construction superintendent's shed located on the west end of the breakwater #1. That beacon, established in 1834, was listed in the 1838 Light List as the "Breakwater Beacon Light." That optic was later transferred to the 1848 lighthouse.

Although it is not known what kind of optic was first placed in the 1885 tower, we do know that it was reequipped with a fourth-order Fresnel lens in 1908. The lighthouse was deactivated in 1996.

OWNER. Delaware River and Bay Authority.

PRESERVATION. Listed in the National Register of Historic Places as part of the National Harbor of Refuge and Delaware Breakwater Harbor Historic District.

The lighthouse was completely refurbished in 1992 following some 40 years of unattended weathering and damage by vandals. Some further restoration of the exterior took place in 1999.

---

1. The January 1996 issue of *Lighthouse Digest* (page 26) shows a drawing that appeared in the *Philadelphia Sunday Press* on March 12, 1893. The drawing depicts two buildings. One is a two-story house topped with what looks like a lantern. That structure most likely was the 1848 lighthouse located on the west end of breakwater #1. Although the only other structure on the breakwater was a Western Union shanty built in 1885 next to the present east end lighthouse, the second building in the sketch, showing two poles that could have supported a wire antenna, is probably the artist's rendering of the telegraph station, although misrepresented as being located next to the old west end lighthouse.

In 1996, the Government Services Administration announced that the lighthouse is available for title transfer to the state or a local government. If no governmental office will take it, the GSA intends to auction it off to the highest bidder.

HARBOR OF REFUGE LIGHTHOUSE (HARBOR OF REFUGE BREAKWATER).
CHARACTERISTIC: Flashing white 5s (2 red sectors)
HAW: 72' **RANGES**: White 23; red 20 nm

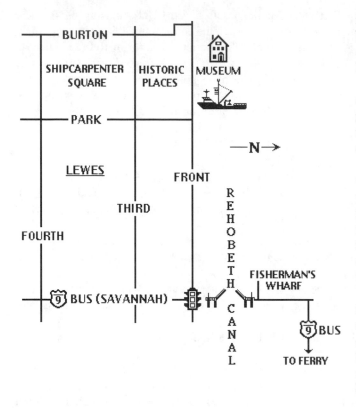

The first lighthouse built on <u>breakwater #4</u> was a cast-iron structure completed in 1896. In February 1920 a storm badly damaged the station's landing wharf and washed away all of its outbuildings and tore off 40 feet of the main gallery deck.

In January 1928 the Lighthouse Board reported that as of November 15, 1926, the damaged lighthouse had been rebuilt by strengthening the structure, raising the height of the optic and placing the fog signal on the tower's third deck.

The tower's foundation is a cast-iron caisson shell with a three-foot lining of poured concrete. A concrete wall surrounds the caisson. The cylindrical structure is a four-level tower 25 feet in diameter. The entry deck holds the station's fog signal machinery and air tanks. Most of the tower's interior is filled with a central tube eight feet in diameter that contains the spiral staircase leading to the watchroom. The lighthouse is 66 feet tall.

Following the tower's restructuring, the lantern was fitted with a fourth-order Fresnel lens and an incandescent oil vapor lamp. The optic's flashing characteristic was accomplished by a revolving four-panel screen that rolled on ball bearings and was driven by clockwork actuated by weights strung within the tower's hollow central cast-iron column. The new light was reestablished on November 2, 1927.

OWNER. In 1999 a new nonprofit organization, the Delaware River and Bay Lighthouse Foundation, Inc., received a lease from the Coast Guard Fifth District Office on the Harbor of Refuge Lighthouse. The Coast Guard will continue to maintain the beacon.

- Delaware River and Bay Lighthouse Foundation, Inc. PO Box 991, Boyertown, PA 19512.
Phone: (610) 473-9783.
Website: http://www.delawarelights.org/
Email: btrapani@fast.net

PRESERVATION. Listed in the National Register of Historic Places as part of the National Harbor of Refuge and Delaware Breakwater Harbor Historic District.

In 1999 the exterior of the tower was completely restored by the Coast Guard. The Delaware River and Bay Lighthouse Foundation plans to restore the interior. They first intend to conduct an engineering study to determine what interior structural deterioration needs attention. There are also preliminary plans to create a maritime museum of the Delaware River and Bay and to eventually make the lighthouse available to the general public for educational tours.

LEWES HISTORICAL SOCIETY COMPLEX.
This collection of old buildings dating from the 18th century is located within and north of Shipcarpenter Square. Within the square is the Thompson Country Store, farm houses, a blacksmith shop and creamery.

DELAWARE BREAKWATER EAST & HARBOR OF REFUGE

On the waterfront at the foot of Park Street is the lightship *Overfalls*, formerly the *Boston* and a sistership of the original *Overfalls* that was stationed at the entrance to Delaware Bay 1892-1961. The *Overfalls* was built in 1938 and served on the Cornfield Point (CT) Station 1938-57, the Cross Rip Station (MA) 1958-62 and the Boston Station 1962-72. Acquired in 1973 by the Lewes Historical Society, the vessel has been serving as a maritime museum. In 1997 the society announced that the rusting vessel was for sale, claiming that her needed repairs and upkeep will be too much of a drain on its finances.

Across the street from the lightship is the old lifesaving station's boathouse (1884), which now contains exhibits of old maps and charts and other maritime artifacts.

OPEN. Mid-June through Labor Day, Tuesdays through Fridays 11 to 4. Saturdays 11 to 1.

ADMISSION FEES. One admission fee covers all of the exhibits in Shipcarpenter Square. Additional fees for some of the other historic places. Children under12 free. Self-guided and guided tours extra.

- The Lewes Historical Society, 119 West Third Street, Lewes, DE 19958.
Phone (302) 645-8719.
Website: http://www.beach-net.com/lewestour/ltour15.html

CAPE HENLOPEN LIGHTHOUSE (destroyed).

The first lighthouse was built in 1767 with funds raised by a lottery. In 1777 the tower was almost totally destroyed by a fire set by British marauders. It was rebuilt in 1784 by Pennsylvanians in the architectural style of New Jersey's Sandy Hook light tower. The lighthouse and grounds were ceded to the Federal Government in 1789. By 1851, its 13 whale oil-burning lamps had been replaced by 18 larger and brighter ones. In 1856 the multi-lamp optic was replaced by a first-order Fresnel lens and a single oil lamp. The light had a focal plane some 180 feet above the sea. The rebuilt octagonal fieldstone (rocks scrounged from surrounding areas) was a solid structure requiring only minor repairs during its watch tenure. Unfortunately, the tower rested on a shallow foundation laid atop loose sand. Cape Henlopen withstood 142 years of erosion, wear and fatigue. Its major battle was one against the winds' fickleness in first moving sand away from it (1788-1851) and then blowing large mounds of beach grit towards and against the structure (1851-1872). Finally, after many years of battling the shifting sands to a standstill with windbreaks and vegetation plantings, the encroaching sea took over. In 1924 with the weakened tower hopelessly endangered, its optic was extinguished and removed. During a raging coastal storm on April 13, 1926, the historic lighthouse toppled into the sea.

In 1994 the Delaware Coast Press began a quest for contributions to be used to build a replica of the Cape Henlopen Lighthouse. That project under the guidance of the Rehobeth Beach Historical Society has not materialized. Since then, the town of Lewes has decided to demolish its facsimile of the Cape Henlopen Lighthouse and fabricate a new one.

LEWES - CAPE MAY FERRY.

The ferry operates daily throughout the year, carrying 100 cars and 800 passengers. Crossing time is 70 minutes. Handicapped-licensed vehicles will be granted priority boarding. Inform the toll booth operator and he will direct you to the priority loading lane. As you drive onto the ferry, inform the boarding officer (ticket taker) of your handicap priority. **SCHEDULE.** At least six daily departures; the number varies with the season. Call or check website for current schedule.

FARES. Vehicle/driver + passenger fares. Under 5 free. No same day reservations.

- Cape May-Lewes Ferry, Lewes Terminal, PO Box 517, Lewes, DE 19958.
Phone (302) 644-6030. Schedule times in USA toll-free (800) 643-3779.
For reservations 24 hours in advance (extra non-refundable fee) in USA toll-free (800) 64-FERRY.
Website: http://www.capemay-lewesferry.com/

NEW JERSEY
CAPE MAY

EAST ON US 9. From the ferry landing take US 9 (Ferry Road) east. Then:
-> Right at CR 626 (Seashore Street and Broadway),
-> Right at CR 606 (Sunset Street),
-> Left at CR 629 (Lighthouse Road).

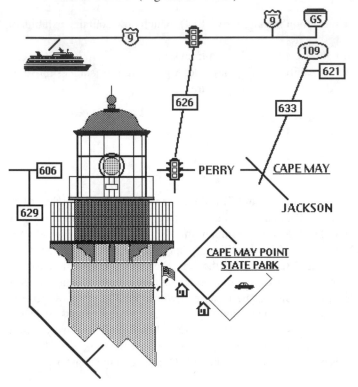

SOUTH ON NJ 109. In Cape May:
-> CR 633 (Lafayette Street),
-> Right at Jackson Street,
-> Left at West Perry Street,
-> Cross CR 626 (Broadway),
-> Into CR 606 (Sunset Boulevard),
-> Left at CR 629 (Lighthouse Street).

VISITING THE LIGHTHOUSE. Visitor orientation takes place in the restored oil house. A unique feature for lighthouses is the showing of a narrated videotape that takes the visitor on the climb up the tower. There is also a panorama of captioned photographs of landmarks seen from the gallery above them. For non-climbers the exhibit has a notebook containing all of the staircase's informational panels.

For the hale and hearty there are 199 diamond-patterned steps to the watchroom's balcony (19 more to the lantern deck). Along the way at each landing (about 30 steps apart) climbers will find panels of historic interest. At the top you will experience a breath-taking view of the Jersey coast from the Atlantic Ocean around the cape to Delaware Bay.

OPEN. Open daily April through November and on weekends most of the rest of the year. Call for the latest schedule. Open 9 AM to 8 PM late June to Labor Day, shorter hours other months.

ADMISSION FEES. Visitors' Orientation Center and ground floor of lighthouse free. Tower fee. One child climbs free with adult. Discount for other children 3-12.

- Mid-Atlantic Center for the Arts, PO Box 340 (1048 Washington Street), Cape May, NJ 08204
Phone (609) 884-5404 or toll-free (800) 884-5404. Lighthouse (609) 884-8656.
Website: http://www.capemaymac.org/
Email: mac4arts@jerseycape.net

CAPE MAY LIGHTHOUSE.
CHARACTERISTIC: Flashing white 15s
HAW: 165' **RANGE**: 24 nm

Although we are left with no official documentation dated prior to the Act of 1789, which provided for the transfer of Colonial lights to the newly established Federal Government, there is sufficient evidence to believe an active light tower existed on Cape May Point.

Based on a map printed in 1744 and showing the location of a "flash light," the British may have established a beacon on the cape. A Cape May County recorded deed, dated September 23, 1785, conveys "a tract of land for the purpose of erecting a beacon for the benefit of navigation." There are at least two other references to the presence of a lighthouse. One is a travel advertisement published in a Philadelphia newspaper in July 1801 that mentioned a "lighthouse" as one of Cape May's tourist attractions. Another reference is a family history that states a child was born in the lighthouse in 1817.

CAPE MAY

Cape May's first official recognition as an aid to navigation occurred on May 7, 1822, when Congress authorized the initial expenditure of $5,000 for the building of a lighthouse. Another congressional appropriation of $5,750 was authorized on March 23, 1823. The optic installed in the tower was one of Winslow Lewis' rotating Argand-styled optics that, with its focal plane 88 feet above the sea, was reported (exaggerated) to have had a range of 27 nautical miles. The aid was first lighted in October 1823.

According to the 1849 Light List, the 68-foot tall brick tower was "Removed, and rebuilt in 1847, 400 yards N.E. from old site." The 1851 Light List reported that the 78-foot tall lighthouse retained Winslow Lewis' original lighting apparatus consisting of 15 lamps on three planes. The original 16-inch parabolic reflectors, however, had been exchanged for ten 15-inch parabolic and five 14-inch spherical reflectors. The revolving catoptric beacon had the same 88-foot height above the water.

A U.S. Statement of Appropriations reported that on May 3, 1857, the government allocated $40,000 "For rebuilding and fitting with first-order apparatus the lighthouse at Cape May entrance to Delaware Bay." The present 170-foot tall lighthouse was built during the 1857-59. U.S. Army topographical engineers involved in building the tower were Captain William F. Raynolds, Captain W. B. Franklin and finally Major Hartman Bache. The light was activated on October 31, 1859.

The 147-foot tall brick tower rests on a 12-foot deep, pyramidal foundation of stone blocks. It is of double wall construction. The exterior wall has a base diameter of 27 feet, tapering to 13.5 feet. Its thicknesses range from 3.75 feet at its base to 1.5 feet at the watchroom deck. The 0.75-foot thick inner wall is cylindrical in shape with a constant diameter of 10.5 feet.

Today the station consists of the lighthouse, one (1860) of four keepers' residences built in 1847 and 1860 (2) and 1903, and a brick oil house (1893). The 1847 tower was demolished in 1862. Its foundation ruins can be seen at low tide.

Cape May's original optic consisted of an Argand whale oil lamp and a Henri LePaute first-order Fresnel lens. The lens, rolling on a multi-wheeled chariot, made one 360-degree revolution every eight minutes. The movement was regulated by a clockwork powered by descending weights. One rewind allowed the clock to run for eight hours.

In 1878 one multi-wicked Funck hydraulic-lift lamp was introduced. First installed in 1902, the lens was refitted with a newer incandescent oil vapor lamp. The optic was electrified in 1938. In 1946 it was reequipped with a modern 36-inch rotating aerobeacon that forced the retirement of the large classical lens.

OWNER. Dwelling and grounds leased to State of New Jersey in 1986 and subleased to the Mid-Atlantic Center for the Arts (MAC). Lighthouse deeded to State of New Jersey in September 1992. Optic is maintained by the U.S. Coast Guard.

PRESERVATION. Listed in the National Register of Historic Places.

In 1986 MAC's Lighthouse Committee proceeded to lay out a comprehensive 10-year restoration schedule. It opened the ground floor to visitors in July 1987, then the tower on May 28, 1988. In 1989 with public donations, contributions from private industry and a grant from the New Jersey Historic Trust, MAC installed electric lights in the tower's interior, added a new handrail, restored the vestibule doors and windows and repaired the watchroom gallery. In 1990 the oil house was restored and converted into a visitor center. In 1992, ownership of the light station was transferred from the U.S. Coast Guard to the New Jersey Department of Environmental Protection's Division of Parks and Forestry. Since 1993 MAC has received more than $1.5 million in state funds and grants to complete the restoration of the lighthouse.

In 1994 the tower's lantern and dome were rehabilitated and its exterior brickwork coated with a green enamel-like substance. The process, often called the slip (slurry) method, was used to weatherproof the Oak Island Lighthouse in North Carolina. Of particular interest was the process used in accomplishing the rehab job. Since the supports were embedded in the tower's walls to a depth of four feet, the lantern could not be removed. Thus, after the dome was removed by helicopter and shipped to Buffalo, New York, for its restoration, a huge cylindrical metal can was placed over the lantern to protect the tower's interior from precipitation and to allow renovation work to continue during inclement and cold weather. The lantern received new safety glass storm panes, eliminating the need for the wire mesh blanket used to protect the old panes from bird bombardments. Finally, the light tower was painted in an historically accurate beige mortar color and its upper cast-iron lantern in red. The lighthouse was reopened to the public in August 1994.

Future restoration projects involve the rehabilitation of the interior of the tower's two-story entry vestibule and watchroom plus landscaping the grounds.

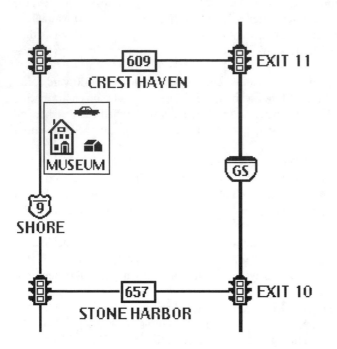

DELAWARE BAY LIGHTHOUSE CRUISE.

The MAC-sponsored Delaware Bay Lighthouse Adventure departs from Miss Cris Fishing Center, 3rd Avenue & Wilson, Cape May aboard the *Cape May Whale Watcher.* Advance reservations suggested.

Lighthouses seen on the cruise include Brandywine Shoal, Cape May, Delaware Breakwater, Fourteen Foot Bank, Harbor of Refuge and Miah Mauli.

SCHEDULE. Around six or eight cruises between May and September. Call or check website for the schedule.

FARES. Discount for children 3-12.

- Mid-Atlantic Center for the Arts, PO Box 340 (1048 Washington Street), Cape May, NJ 08204. Phone (609) 884-5404.

Website: http://www.capemaymac.org/

JOHN HOLMES HOUSE AND MUSEUM. See above map.

This museum, located in Cape May Courthouse off US 9 and west of the Garden State Parkway (toll-free from Cape May), is rich in artifacts from medical and pharmaceutical history, Indian relics, old household utensils, ship models and genealogical records.

One of the museum's principal displays is the first-order Fresnel lens formerly installed in the Cape May Point Lighthouse. The lens is in a barn located behind the main house.

MUSEUM OPEN.

April to mid-June, Tuesdays through Saturdays 10 to 4.

Mid-June to mid-September, Mondays through Fridays 10 to 4.

Mid-September through November, Tuesdays through Saturdays 10 to 4.

December through March, Saturdays only.

TOURS. Guided tours every 40 minutes daily, beginning at 10:10 with the last tour at 3 PM. Groups can arrange tours at other times.

ADMISSION FEES. Include museum tour. Discount for children under 12; under 2 free.

- The Cape May County Historical and Genealogical Society, 504 US Route 9, Cape May Courthouse, NJ 08210. Phone (609) 465-3535.

Delaware Breakwater Lighthouse

Cape May Lighthouse

HEREFORD INLET

TO NORTH WILDWOOD. Enter North Wildwood on Ocean Drive's CR 621 (Atlantic Avenue) and one block after CR 621's turn west into 26th Street, then right at Central Avenue and continue to the lighthouse, located between 1st and Chestnut Avenues. On street parking is free.

If southbound on CR 62 or eastbound from the Garden State Parkway on NJ 147 to CR 621, continue straight ahead on Spruce Street into connecting Central Avenue.

From the Garden State Parkway, take Exit 6 to North Wildwood, look for signs or turn left onto 1st Avenue soon after you get into town.

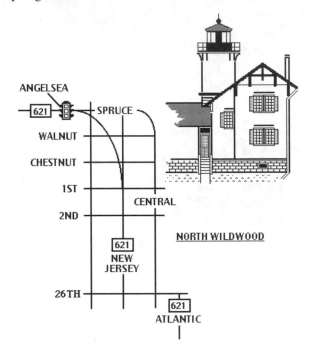

HEREFORD INLET LIGHTHOUSE AND GARDENS. This center was first opened to the public on July 1, 1984 in the partially refurbished keeper's residence. With financial assistance from the New Jersey State Council on the Arts and Cape May County's Cultural and Heritage Commission, prize-winning paintings have been purchased and are on display along with other maritime memorabilia, antiques and Hereford Inlet's 1874 fourth-order Fresnel lens. The landscaped Lighthouse Cottage and Herb Gardens have won many awards and are visited by thousands each year.

OPEN.

February to April, weekends 9 to 5.

May to mid-October, daily 9 to 5.

October to December, weekends 9 to 5.

FREE ADMISSION. Donations help purchase supplies.

- Hereford Inlet Lighthouse, First and Central Avenues, North Wildwood, NJ 08260.

Phone (609) 522-4520.

Website: http://www.herefordlighthouse.org

HEREFORD INLET LIGHTHOUSE.
CHARACTERISTIC: Flashing white 10s
HAW: 57' **RANGE**: 24 nm

In 1849 a lifesaving station was activated to serve the increasingly heavy traffic passing through the wide Hereford Inlet linking the Atlantic Ocean with the intracoastal waterway. This strategic location, then known as the fishing village of Angelsea on Five Mile Beach, was selected by Congress on June 10, 1872 for the construction of a harbor lighthouse on 1.5 acres purchased in 1873 for $150. The lighthouse was built by the U.S. Army's Corps of Topographical Engineers under the supervision of Lt. Colonel W. F. Raynolds, who also supervised (as a Captain) the construction of New Jersey's Absecon and Barnegat Lighthouses. The light was activated on May 11, 1874.

This lighthouse is almost identical in design to those on New Jersey's Tucker Beach (destroyed), Oregon's Point Adams and California's East Brother Island in San Francisco Bay and Point Fermin near San Pedro. The wooden building shows the exterior ornamentation of the Stick style of construction popular in the latter half of the 1800s. Typical Stick treatments are seen in the supports under the roof, the fancier brackets supporting the overhanging lantern deck and the decorative porch posts. The two-story living quarters has five fireplaces. Surmounting the house is the square tower. The overall height of the house and tower is 49.5 feet.

Hereford Inlet has had its share of damaging incidents. The structure's foundation was nearly washed away in the late 1890s. At the turn of the century, two interior fires threatened to put an end to the lighthouse. In 1914, after its foundation had again been extensively damaged during an August 1913 storm, the lighthouse was moved about 150 feet inland to its present location.

The fourth-order Fresnel lens, installed in 1874 and removed when the light was deactivated, now rests in the museum. Hereford Inlet's presently active lens, another fourth-order Fresnel, was installed in 1986.

HEREFORD INLET

OWNER. State of New Jersey. Managed by the North Wildwood's Hereford Inlet Lighthouse Commission since September 2, 1982.

PRESERVATION. Listed (September 20, 1977) in the National Register of Historic Places.

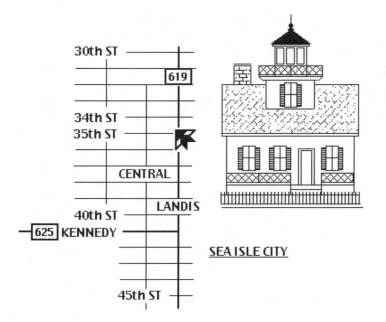

SEA ISLE CITY

Shortly after its deactivation in 1964, the station was transferred to the control of the New Jersey Marine Police. In 1982 the New Jersey Department of Environmental Protection turned the stewardship of the light station over to the City of North Wildwood. By the time North Wildwood was officially recognized as its benefactor, the neglected lighthouse was a weatherworn, shabby-genteel structure. Mayor Lewis G. Vinci, desirous of preserving North Wildwood's newly acquired historic place, appointed a Lighthouse Commission to oversee the lighthouse's restoration and preservation. The restoration, made possible by state and county funding and public donations, is a beautiful piece of work. Another project, sponsored by the State of New Jersey and its Green Acres Trust, was the conversion of the station's grounds into a park with gardens and gazebo overlooking the inlet.

After the restoration was completed, the City and the Lighthouse Commission were able to convince the Coast Guard to reestablish the beacon as a private aid in April 1986.

In July 1996, the New Jersey Historic Trust and the City of North Wildwood equally shared a contribution of $101,712 for the replacement of the roof, windows and missing decorative woodwork.

In 1999 the 3,000 pound lantern room was removed from the lighthouse for a two-month restoration. The $190,000 restoration project also included the repair of water damage to the tower caused by leaks. Funds for the restoration project came from a $70,000 grant from the New Jersey Historic Trust with the remaining $120,000 paid for by the City of North Wildwood and the Hereford Inlet Lighthouse Commission. City officials have said they need to raise another $500,000 for additional renovations to the historic monument.

TO SEA ISLE CITY. The Ludlam Beach Lighthouse, originally located on the beach at the end of 30th Street, no longer retains its former lighthouse configuration. The house (less tower) is located on CR 619 at 3414 Landis Avenue.

LUDLAM BEACH LIGHTHOUSE (reconfigured).

The original Ludlam Beach Lighthouse was commissioned on November 3, 1885. The structure consisted of a wood framed keeper's dwelling surmounted by a short square tower whose service gallery barely cleared the roof's peak. The aid's kerosene-powered fourth-order Fresnel lens displayed a flashing white light that derived its rotation from a weight-powered clockwork mechanism. The beacon had a focal plane of 36 feet above the water and could be seen out to a distance of about 12 nautical miles.

The station was continuously subjected to damage by storms and hurricanes. Not even a heavy timber, rock and concrete bulkhead could protect it from storm surges. The lighthouse's end began in 1914, when a storm ripped away most of the protective bulkhead. The next nail in its coffin occurred in 1923 when an accidental tipping of a kerosene lamp caused a fire that did considerable damage to the dwelling's interior. The lantern had not been touched by the fire so the lighthouse, with repairs, remained active. Finally, a storm tore off the roof in 1924. With that last incident the Bureau of Lighthouses closed the station and sold it to a private party.

117

ABSECON [1]

TO ATLANTIC CITY. There are several route options to reach Atlantic City. They all lead to Atlantic Avenue. Head north on Atlantic to Rhode Island Avenue, turn right (one-way) and continue to Pacific Avenue. The lighthouse is located on the corner of Rhode Island and Pacific.

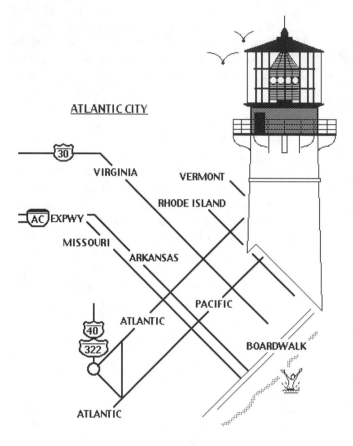

ABSECON LIGHTHOUSE.
CHARACTERISTIC: Flashing white 15s
HAW: 165' **RANGE**: 24 nm

Since as early as 1779, hundreds of ships have been recorded as having been wrecked along Absecon Beach and on the shoals off Egg Harbor. In 1840, after years of petitioning the U.S. Government to sponsor the construction of a lighthouse, the U.S. Navy surveyed the Absecon site. The navy rejected the proposal. An 1846 resolution by the New Jersey legislature, calling for the building of a lighthouse, was summarily ignored by Washington. Finally, after 26 years of trying to convince Congress that a lighthouse was needed, Dr. Jonathan Pitney, regarded as the "father of Atlantic City," was able to secure enough congressional votes for the appropriation of $35,000 for the construction of the present Absecon Lighthouse.

Major Hartman Bache was assigned to the project. He was replaced by Lt. George G. Meade, the tower's architect, who was dispatched from his Philadelphia post to get the construction underway. The lighthouse was completed in late 1856 under the supervision of another topographical engineer, Captain W. F. Raynolds. The $52,000 station was also provided two keepers' dwellings (one a duplex), outbuildings and an oil house. Absecon was lighted on January 15, 1857.

The tower, with its nearly 600,000 coursed bricks, has a base diameter of a bit over 26 feet, with its walls tapering to a 12-foot diameter at the watchroom deck. The interior is cylindrical with a 10-foot diameter from the base to the lantern. That constant dimension leaves the walls at the tower's base over eight feet thick.

In the 1870s sea erosion reached the light station, resulting in the lighthouse being washed by storm-driven waves. Later, sand began to fill in around the protective jetties built in 1876-78, resulting in a geological expansion that permitted the building of homes and apartment buildings north and east of the station.

The lantern still contains its original L. Sautter first-order Fresnel lens last powered by a kerosene-fed multi-wick, hydraulic-lift Funck lamp. With a focal plane of 167 feet above mean high water, the fixed optic's range was 20 nautical miles.

OWNER. Deeded to Atlantic City in 1948. Later turned over to the State of New Jersey and leased to Atlantic City Coastal Museum. Now under management of the Inlet Public/Private Association.

PRESERVATION. Listed in the National Register of Historic Places.

---

1. This aid was first known as the "Abscombe Light on Tuckers Beach." Later, the new 171-foot tall brick lighthouse took its present name from Absecon Island (now Atlantic City) and Absecon Inlet.

ABSECON

On July 11, 1933, the light was decommissioned and the tower, scheduled for demolition, was abandoned. Although public opposition saved the lighthouse from destruction, the Lighthouse Bureau stripped the station of its keepers' house and the old lifesaving station.

In 1963 Atlantic City appointed a committee, the Atlantic City Coastal Museum, as the station's conservator. The committee arranged for the repainting of the light tower (red band on white), the building of a replica of the original keeper's dwelling to house a museum and the relighting of the beacon as a private aid.

The state, in a lease agreement, conveyed to the Atlantic City Coastal Museum the responsibility for the station's general maintenance. The state paid for any repairs and the utilities bill. By 1983 the scene had changed somewhat. The station's grounds had been cleared and given an orderly appearance and the lighthouse wore a new coat of paint.

The Atlantic City Coastal Museum, down to a one man stewardship, struggled to find the ways and means to take care of the unattended lighthouse property, which, despite periodic cleanups, was soon again slathered with graffiti and restrewn with trash. The State's Department of Environmental Protection through its Wharton State Forest at Hammonton responded to the Museum's requests for repairs and maintenance assistance. The Atlantic City Boys and Girls Club, as well as the Inlet Public Private Association, a neighborhood improvement group, also assisted in clearing the station and painting out the graffiti.

Since 1933 the lighthouse has mostly been an abandoned and decaying structure. Water seepage into its double walls has created some serious damage to both mortar and bricks. Paint continues to peel off the interior walls. Puddles of rain water lie on the lantern deck. Although the Fresnel's prisms are chipped from heat generated by its oil lamps, the first-order lens is in fine shape. In September 1993, the Inlet Public Private Association decided to take on the preservation project. In 1994-95 the Association completed a historic structures report that confirmed previous estimates that the entire lighthouse from base to ventilator ball requires a complete overhaul. The $50,000 survey was paid for from a community development grant.

The lighthouse was relighted in January 1996 as a prelude to its complete restoration and the building of a replica of the old keepers' dwelling to be used as an interpretive center and museum. In 1997 there was available some $2,470,922 for the combined projects. Contributors include the federal government's Transportation Enhancement Program, the New Jersey Historic Trust and the Atlantic City Casino Reinvestment Development Authority.

According to contractor Integrated Construction Enterprises, there was severe corrosion of metals in the lantern, and the masonry joints were deteriorated throughout the tower. After the lead-based coatings were removed, the structure was selectively repointed. Some of the metal castings were replaced, and new windows and doors were installed and the tower was repainted. The Fresnel lens assembly was removed, cleaned and reinstalled. New electrical, lighting, fire alarm, and security systems was installed.

In August 1871 the tower was first painted white with a red band around its middle. In August 1893 the color combination was changed to an orange-black-orange motif. In 1948 the tower was given a white-blue-white coat of paint. In 1983 the tower was repainted with a reddish orange midsection. As a part of the 1925-33 period to be used for the interpretive center the tower has been painted with trisecting yellow-black-yellow bands. Note that the color "yellow" (some call it "ochre") vice "orange" was selected from Bureau of Lighthouses' engineering descriptions held in the National Archives.

In July 1998 the newly rebuilt keeper's dwelling, finished a few days earlier, was swept by fire. The metal door in the passageway to the tower was closed, preventing damage to the tower, but the house was a total loss.

At this writing in August 2001 the Inlet Public-Private Association has nearly completed the rebuilding of the keeper's quarters for a second time. The building should open to the public in October, after exhibits have been set up. The reconstructed keeper's quarters will house the museum, gift shop, and visitor center for the light station.

- Inlet Public/Private Association, 300 Atlantic Avenue, Suite 102, Atlantic City, NJ 08401.
Phone (609) 441-9272.

BARNEGAT

TO BARNEGAT LIGHT. Take NJ 72 east to Ship Bottom on Long Beach Island. In Ship Bottom turn left and drive to the town of Barnegat Light on the northern tip of the island.

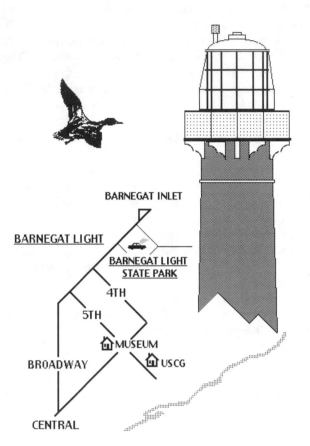

BARNEGAT LIGHTHOUSE STATE PARK. The lighthouse is located inside the park.

PARK OPEN. All year, dawn to dusk.
LIGHTHOUSE OPEN.
The park is open 8 AM to 10 PM every day all year. The lighthouse is open 9 AM to 4:30 PM every day from Memorial Day through Labor Day, weekends only in May, September and October.
PARK FEE. Memorial Day to Labor Day, daily vehicle parking fee. Fee not collected on Tuesdays, except holidays.
LIGHTHOUSE FEE. Nominal climber's fee (217 steps) when parking fee not collected. Under 12 free.
- Barnegat Lighthouse State Park, PO Box 167 (Broadway and Bay Street), Barnegat Light, NJ 08006.
Phone (609) 494-2016.
Website: http://www.state.nj.us/dep/forestry/parks/barnlig.htm

BARNEGAT LIGHTHOUSE (OLD BARNEY; JEWEL OF THE NIGHT).
The first lighthouse at Barnegat Inlet was built by Winslow Lewis in 1835 for $6,000. It was 50 feet tall. Although planned to be a coastal aid, the beacon's low elevation and its subdued brightness from one of Winslow Lewis' multi-lamp optic reduced the light to fifth-class status. In other words, it was but a harbor light of limited range responsible for marking Barnegat (Sea Dog) Shoals on the southside entrance to Barnegat Inlet.

After having inspected the lighthouse in September 1855, Lt. George G. Meade reported to the Fourth Lighthouse District in Philadelphia that the tower had been poorly built with inferior materials, the mortar was disintegrating and the tower's bricks were popping out. His survey concluded that the light tower was in "very bad condition." Meade included in his report designs for a new tower with an estimated cost of $30,000. He also suggested the purchase of a first-order Fresnel lens for $16,000. Despite his report, the Lighthouse Board opted to refurbish the tower and installed a new fourth-order Fresnel lens. One year later, after Meade's inspection, the tower was hit by a storm surge and toppled into the inlet. The Board quickly reestablished the beacon on a temporary wooden tower built farther inland. Later, after numerous complaints from ship captains, the Lighthouse Board resurveyed the site and decided Barnegat Inlet required a new lighthouse.

Construction of the Barnegat tower began in 1857 at a site some 900 yards south of Lewis' old tower. Captain W. F. Raynolds of the U.S. Army's Corps of Topographical Engineers completed the construction task in 1858 at a cost of $45,000. The 172-foot tall brick structure (150 feet from base to focal plane) stands on a 28-foot deep stone foundation. Its walls are hollow and were so designed to provide both strength to and insulate the tower. The conically shaped exterior wall is 4.5 feet thick at the tower's base, tapering to 1.5 feet at the top. Its diameters range from 28 feet at the bottom to 14 feet at the top. The cylindrically shaped interior wall is 9 inches thick with a 10.5-inch interior. Inside, in the center of the tower, there is a vertical pipe that supports a wall-anchored and cantilevered stairway leading to the watchroom. The tube was also used as a passageway for descending weights. The lighthouse and two work sheds at its base cost the government $45,000, the priceless Fresnel lens $15,000 and the land $600. Three very fine Victorian keepers' cottages, built in 1889 for $12,000, were either swept out to sea or dismantled between 1919 and 1940.

BARNEGAT

Barnegat was relighted on January 1, 1859, using a first-order Fresnel optic manufactured in France in 1847 by Henri LePaute's Saint-Gobain crystal foundry. The lens was rotated by gears moved by a 150-foot weight that descended by cable inside the central column to a distance of 65 feet. The lens was powered by a kerosene lamp consisting of five circular wicks with the outer wick having a diameter of five inches. The other four had diminishing diameters and were nested inside the next larger wick. The lamp was fed from a 10-gallon reservoir and burned 4.5 (summer) to 7.5 (winter) gallons of kerosene each night. With a focal plane of 163 feet above sea level, the flashing light's nominal range was 20 nautical miles, although ship captains reported discerning the light's loom at 25 miles from ships' bridges and 30 miles from crows' nests.

In 1927, because it was threatened by erosion, the Barnegat Lightship (now docked in Camden, NJ) was stationed offshore and Barnegat's classical optic was removed and carted off to be displayed in Staten Island's Tompkinsville Lighthouse Depot. The lighthouse was then fitted with an 800-pound gas-fired blinking lamp. Ten acetylene gas drums at the base of the tower held enough fuel to keep the lamp burning for six months. In a matter of weeks electricity reached Long Beach Island. Ergo, another change. The gas lamp was removed and a 250-watt bulb substituted. Although the lamp had been positioned inside the lantern 13 feet higher than the gas lamp's focal plane, the electric lamp was visible for only eight nautical miles. In 1944 the "Grand Old Champion of the Tides" was retired from service.

OWNER. State of New Jersey since 1926. Managed by Department of Environmental Protection and Energy.
PRESERVATION. Listed in the National Register of Historic Places.

In 1934 with Old Barney being seriously threatened by the erosive action of the sea, a subterranean coffer dam was constructed around the base of the tower. The device consisted of two wrought iron rings braced by tie rods and filled with concrete to a depth of 20 feet. Outside of the reinforced concrete circle another sheet metal ring was driven to a depth of 30 feet, providing a protective barrier some 20 feet above mean high water.

In August 1988, after parts of the gallery's railing had fallen, the lighthouse was closed to the public and actions were initiated to determine its stability. Shortly thereafter, the Department of Environmental Protection and Energy acquired $400,000 in waived construction improvement funds and a federal contract to survey and restore the lighthouse. The task was not an easy one. The exterior walls were repointed and repainted. All metal fixtures were coated with high-performance, low-maintenance anti-corrosives. With the safety of Old Barney's visitors in mind, extensive repairs were made to the spiral staircase (reanchored and more balustrades added to prevent tots from falling though), its main center post (stabilized and leveled), the watchroom deck (stabilized and cracks repaired) and the lantern's metal grill replaced with protective panes of clear plexiglass around the observation gallery. The restoration work cost $666,000. The tower was again opened to the public on June 8, 1991.

The surging tides of Barnegat Inlet have opened a 50-foot hole in the floor of the inlet near the northwest side of the lighthouse. In 2001 the Army Corps of Engineers spent $1.38 million to stabilize the lighthouse, placing 160 stone-filled "mattresses" — each four inches thick, six feet wide and 20 feet long — in the deepest part of the slope to shore up the eroded rock. After the mattresses were in place, the project contractor, the Jay Cashman Co. of Boston, moved in nearly nine tons of riprap (crushed rock) with individual boulders weighing from 250 to 5,500 pounds.

Also, a Corps of Engineers survey has shown that the tower is leaning about 22 inches away from the vertical. The engineers say the tower is stable, however.

BARNEGAT LIGHT HISTORICAL SOCIETY & MUSEUM. This museum is housed in a one room schoolhouse built in 1903 and exhibits a varied collection of historical memorabilia from the town and the immediate Jersey shore area. Of particular interest is Old Barney's first-order Fresnel lens. The lens contains 1,024 prisms and 24 bullseyes, each nine inches thick. The optic (eight feet in diameter and 15 feet tall) rests in a bronze cradle. The whole assembly weighs over five tons.

The museum is owned by the Borough of Barnegat Light, but its directorship is under the auspices of the nonprofit Barnegat Light Historical Society.
OPEN.
July and August, daily 2 to 4. June and September, weekends only 2 to 4.
FREE ADMISSION. Donations welcomed.
- Barnegat Light Historical Society, PO Box 386 (Fifth Street and Central Avenue), Barnegat Light, NJ 08006.
Phone (609) 494-8578.
Website http://www.nealcomm.com/nonprof/blhist.htm

SINBAD - THE COAST GUARD'S FAMOUS MASCOT Sinbad, a mutt who retired from the Coast Guard as "top dog," was picked up off the streets by the crew of the Coast Guard cutter *Campbell* and smuggled aboard in 1937. From that year until his transfer to the beach and retirement on 1948, Sinbad's career was an interesting one. He had his own bunk and personnel file that documented his deeds, promotions and courts-martial. At musters Sinbad would report with his life jacket in his mouth, and, when his name was called, he would drop the jacket and bark his presence. He was prone to get drunk ashore, for which he was often busted to seaman first by convened disciplinary boards.

During World War II, the *Campbell* took on six German submarines, ramming and sinking the last one. After three days without power the cutter, with its engine room flooded, was towed back to port. During the ordeal part of the crew and Sinbad stayed aboard and kept the vessel afloat.

On September 15, 1989, more than one hundred of Sinbad's Coast Guard friends gathered in Barnegat Light to honor his reburial with a color guard, the playing of taps, a rifle salute and the dedication of a headstone at the foot of the flag pole in front of the old Barnegat Light Coast Guard Station on East 5th Street. Hanging on a bulletin board just inside the main entry are photographs of Sinbad.

A lifesized statue of Sinbad was donated to the USCG Campbell Association and then given to the new USCG *Campbell* (W-909) where it is mounted on the bulkhead wall of the mess deck. And to highlight the effect old Sinbad had as a morale builder, his statue was placed atop the pile of one of the larger drug confiscations in the Caribbean by the crew of the new *Campbell*.

TUCKER BEACH LIGHTHOUSE (TUCKER ISLAND; LITTLE EGG HARBOR) (destroyed)
This lighthouse was located on Tucker Beach off the southern tip of Long Beach Island. In 1849 the light was activated in a brick tower located a short distance away from the station's keeper's dwelling. Its 1854 fourth-order Fresnel lens was deactivated in 1859 and relit in 1868 in a newly constructed T-shaped, two-story building with a centrally located tower that resembled the Stick style of residential architecture.

By 1877, the eight-mile long island had dwindled to a one-mile long sand bar. With its foundation seriously eroded by the sea, the lighthouse topped over on October 12, 1927. The entire Coast Guard station disappeared in 1935. By 1940 almost all of the sand bar had been washed away. In 1952, it disappeared completely. Strange as it may seem, in 1990 the sea receded just enough to uncover the remains of the lighthouse engulfed in the large sand bar.

In 1996 the Town of Tuckerton announced its plan to build a $2.5 million replica of the Tucker Beach Lighthouse as the centerpiece of a revitalized waterfront area, the Tuckerton Seaport. The lighthouse will be used as an interpretive center with displays on the lighthouses of the Jersey Shore and their keepers. A grand opening is expected in the spring of 2000.

Tuckerton is located on US 9. From the Garden State Parkway's Exit 58 take NJ 539 south.

- Tuckerton Seaport, PO Box 52, Tuckerton, NJ 08087.

Website: http://www.tuckertonseaport.org

Sea Girt Lighthouse

SEA GIRT

TO SEA GIRT. If northbound on the New Jersey Garden State Parkway, take Exit 88 to NJ 70.

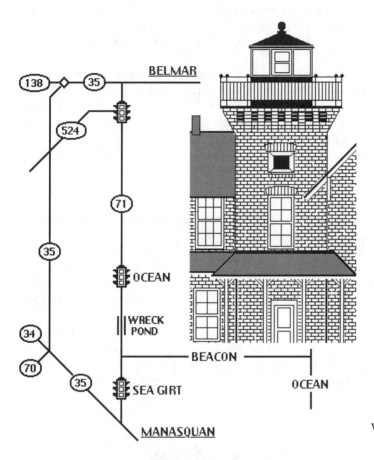

Then:
-> North on NJ 70,
-> Southeast on NJ 35,
-> North on NJ 71 to Sea Girt.
If southbound on the parkway, take Exit 98 to NJ 138. Then:
-> East on NJ 138 and NJ 35,
-> South on NJ 71 to Sea Girt,
If traveling south on NJ 36, continue through Long Branch. Then:
-> West to NJ 35,
-> South on NJ 71 to Sea Girt.

SEA GIRT LIGHTHOUSE MUSEUM.

This beautifully restored lighthouse is a superb example of civic pride in action. It contains a small museum displaying historic artifacts and memorabilia. In August 1983, the lighthouse was furnished a fourth-order Fresnel and reactivated as a private aid.

OPEN. Sundays, June to November, 1 to 4.

FREE ADMISSION. Donations accepted.

- Sea Girt Lighthouse Citizens Committee, Inc., PO Box 83, Sea Girt, NJ 08750.

Phone (908) 974-0514.

Website: http://www.lonekeep.com/seagirtlighthouse/

SEA GIRT LIGHTHOUSE.

Although Congress on March 2, 1889, appropriated $20,000 for the construction of the Sea Girt Lighthouse, it took seven years to acquire the land. Construction of the lighthouse, its oil house, a well and a windmill were completed in 1896.

The Sea Girt Lighthouse is neither an ornate structure nor a towering landmark. It is a two-story brick and mortar Victorian-styled house with attached square tower, standing among similarly designed residential homes. The light filled the gap of navigational aids between the Barnegat Lighthouse, 26 miles to the south, and the Highlands Lighthouse some 19 miles to the north.

At an elevation of 52 feet above the water, the kerosene-fed lamp magnified by a fourth-order Fresnel lens flashed a one second red beam visible for 15 nautical miles. The lens was powered by a clockwork mechanism that had to be rewound every five hours and 15 minutes. The light was activated on December 10, 1896.

RADIO BEACONS. Sea Girt and New York's Fire Island and Ambrose Lightships hold distinguished places in lighthouse history. These aids to navigation were the first in the world to operate a successful radiobeacon system.

The first experiments with maritime use of radio waves occurred as early as 1888. In 1912 the French lighthouse service established radio fog signals at three of its light stations. The signals were transmitted on an experimental 80-meter (30s) wave length. By 1916 radio compasses were introduced. Then, after scientists came up with the principle of amplification using an electron tube, the Bureau of Lighthouses in cooperation with the Bureau of Standards began a series of radio transmission tests using 125-meter wave lengths. The first occurred in 1917, when tests were run using an automatic radio fog signal transmitter at the Highlands (Navesink) Lighthouse and a radio compass (radio direction finder) on the tender *Tulip*. This experiment was followed in 1919 with the installation of radio fog signal transmitters at three Chesapeake Bay lighthouses and an improved radio compass on the tender *Arbutus*.

In 1920 "very satisfactory" results were gained using the *Tulip's* radio direction finding equipment with wireless transmitters placed on the Sea Girt and Ambrose Channel stations and on the *Ambrose* and *Fire Island* lightships. The network was retested in February 1921, before being placed in regular operation on the following 1st of May. The transmissions gave the sea captain the capability of determining his position by radio triangulation, the plotting on a navigation chart the locations and bearings of the radio transmitters.

Fire Island's automatic wireless signalling apparatus broadcasted two dashes. The *Ambrose* signal was one dash and Sea Girt's three dots. To give the reader an idea of how this system worked, Sea Girt's signal would be transmitted for two minutes. One minute later *Fire Island* would send its dashes for another two minutes. Finally, after another one minute break, *Ambrose* would broadcast its dashes. The round-robin signalling would begin all over again every ten minutes. In 1928, Sea Girt's radiobeacon was transferred to the lightship *Barnegat*.

During World War II the lighthouse was used to house Coast Guardsmen assigned to patrol the area's beaches. The light was discontinued in 1945. Thereafter the property was used as a library, Civil Defense headquarters and a meeting place for local organizations.

OWNER. Purchased by the Borough of Sea Girt on August 10, 1956 for $11,000. Leased to the Sea Girt Lighthouse Citizens Committee on August 31, 1981.

 PRESERVATION. Not listed in the National Register of Historic Places.

In 1980 the Borough of Sea Girt decided that the cost of the lighthouse's upkeep was too expensive and considered selling the deteriorating structure. The following year a spirited group of people from various Sea Girt organizations formed the Sea Girt Lighthouse Citizens Committee and began the task of raising the money needed to restore the lighthouse.

The first stage involved rebuilding the porches, stairways and underpinnings, recycling much of the original construction materials, while keeping to earlier construction techniques. By 1982 the second stage was underway, when the lighthouse received a new roof, restored copper gutters and downspouts and repointed exterior brick walls. The completed third stage involved refurbishing the interior, repairing the windows and shutters and scraping off 88 years of paint and varnish.

Sandy Hook Lighthouse

SANDY HOOK

NORTH ON NJ 36. From the Sea Girt Lighthouse take NJ 71 -> NJ 35 -> NJ 36 to the Sandy Hook Unit of the Gateway National Recreation Area.

EAST ON NJ 36. From the Highlands site return to NJ 36 via Highland Avenue and Portland Road. Cross over the drawbridge and follow the "Sandy Hook" signs through the cloverleaf to the park.

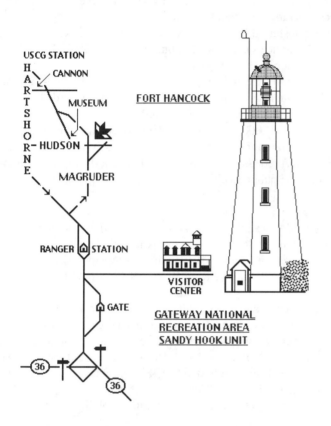

SANDY HOOK UNIT. This 1,665-acre wildlife refuge with its beaches and sports fields make it a popular playground for the region's urbanites.

The Spermaceti Cove Visitor Center is housed in the restored Sandy Hook Lifesaving Station built in 1894. It is one of many such stations established every 3.5 miles all along the Jersey Coast. The center's museum displays an unusual assortment of lifesaving gear. See also the CHICAMACOMICO LIFESAVING STATION chapter.

OPEN. All year, daily sunrise to sunset. Visitor Center open all year, daily 10 to 5.

ADMISSION FEE. Memorial Day weekend to Labor Day, daily beach parking fee. Other times free. No charge to visit Fort Hancock.

- Gateway National Recreation Area, Sandy Hook Unit, PO Box 530, Highlands, NJ 07732.

Phone (732) 872-5970. Emergencies (732) 872-5900. Website: http://www.nps.gov/gate/

Additional website for the lighthouse: http://www.shore.co.monmouth.nj.us/lighthouses/sandyhook.htm

TO FORT HANCOCK. After passing through the toll gates stay on the main road north past the Spermaceti Cove Visitor Center, the Sandy Hook Ranger Station and follow the "Ft Hancock" and "Lighthouse" signs to the lighthouse.

Fort Hancock is the last of several coastal defense forts erected on Sandy Hook to protect shipping entering New York Harbor.

If you have not seen a Rodman cannon, there is one of the shell belchers at Fort Hancock located within a triangular intersection near the end of Hartshorne Road, once called "Officers' Row." Fort Hancock's story is told in exhibits at the Fort Hancock Museum (west of the lighthouse on Hudson) and the History House (last restored house north on Hartshorne). Both are open July and August, daily 1 to 5. Rest of year, weekends 1 to 5. Free self-guiding folder.

SANDY HOOK LIGHTHOUSE (NEW YORK; REFUGEES' TOWER; LIGHTHOUSE FORT).

OPEN. The lighthouse grounds are open to the public the year round.

TOURS. Tours of the light tower are conducted by volunteers from the New Jersey Lighthouse Society. June to mid-November, weekends 12 to 4. Call Gateway to verify schedule.

CHARACTERISTIC: Fixed white
HAW: 88' **RANGE**: 19 nm

Although the Colonial Assembly of New York authorized, in May 1761, the holding of two lotteries to finance the construction of a lighthouse, the take from the first game of chance was short of estimated cost of three thousand pounds. In turn, a group of New York merchants chipped in with enough money to buy a four-acre plot. The following year another lottery, plus tonnage taxes levied on ships entering New York Harbor, brought in enough money to erect the Sandy Hook Lighthouse. The light was established on July 11, 1764.

The tower's octagonal base, with its almost 9-inch thick walls, is 29 feet across. The tower tapers to a 15-foot diameter at the lantern deck. The interior is lined with coursed brick. The overall height of the lighthouse is 85 feet.

The original light was produced by 48 oil "blazes" (probably a shallow round pan with 48 wick guides soldered atop its lid) occupying a space seven feet high and 15 feet in circumference. This early light was visible out to a distance of 15 nautical miles. In 1827 the old lamp was removed and a Lewis multi-lamp and reflector optic installed. In 1842 reflectors with 21-inch diameters replaced the smaller ones. The presently active third-order Fresnel lens was installed in 1857. The light was automated in 1962. Sandy Hook is America's oldest operating lighthouse.

OWNER. In 1996 the ownership of the lighthouse was transferred by the U.S. Coast Guard to the National Park Service. Managed by the Sandy Hook Unit of the National Park Service's Gateway National Recreation Area.

PRESERVATION. Listed (June 1964) in the National Register of Historic Places.

Except for a new cast-iron lantern fitted in 1880, until recently the only major repair work on the 103-foot tall lighthouse was completed way back in 1863. In 1987 the Coast Guard gave the tower's exterior a much needed coat of paint. In 1988 the tower's interior and its decorative stone gargoyle rain spouts were repainted.

The old tower finally got a $600,000 restoration in the spring of 2000. Among other improvements, the tower was pressure-washed and repainted, and a new door was installed. The interior stairway and lantern deck were also repaired. Worchester-Eisenbrandt, Inc., a Baltimore, MD firm, did the work. A rededication was held in June 2000 with Revolutionary War re-enactors on hand, and the tower was again opened for the public to climb.

SANDY HOOK RANGE LIGHTS (relocated; dismantled).

During the period 1804-17 appropriations were made to build two additional light towers and effect some repairs to Sandy Hook. The new wooden towers were erected on the northern tip of Sandy Hook. The Atlantic's East beacon ranged with channel buoys in the Sandy Hook Channel. The West aid ranged with buoys marking the juncture of the Sandy Hook Channel with the Raritan East Reach and Terminal Channels. See also the LOWER NEW YORK BAY RANGE LIGHTS chapter.

Plagued with a destructive fire, damage from artillery fire, storms and erosion, the East beacon was moved several times. Ater having been redesignated the North Hook Light in 1881, it was transferred to a truncated cast-iron lighthouse erected south of the original lighthouse's location. In 1917 the tower was dismantled to remove it from the line of fire of a new coast artillery battery and stowed in Staten Island's Thomkinsville Depot. The North Hook beacon was then installed on a simple skeletal steel tower. The dismantled cast-iron tower was later rebuilt at Jeffreys Hook, where it has become known as the Little Red Lighthouse under New York City's George Washington Bridge.

The West beacon, also threatened by erosion, was moved farther south, renamed the South Hook light and made to range with Sandy Hook.

Both range lights were discontinued in 1923.

HIGHLANDS

WEST ON NJ 36. In Highlands just after crossing over the drawbridge on NJ 36 take the cloverleaf right and downhill to Bay Avenue and turn right. Then:
-> Right at Highland Avenue,
-> Left into a steep, narrow uphill road. The turn is marked with a "Twin Lights State Historic Site" sign. Carefully follow the road up onto the parking apron.
EAST ON NJ 36. Before reaching the drawbridge turn right at Portland Road and right again at Highland.

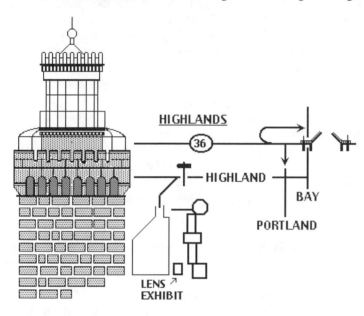

TWIN LIGHTS STATE HISTORIC SITE <u>MUSEUM.</u> In 1988 the Division of Parks and Forestry teamed up with the Twin Lights Historical Society to redesign the exhibits at the lighthouse. In 1994 the Society received a $100,000 grant from the State to fabricate and install the new displays. On May 18, 1996, the museum unveiled four topical exhibits covering the history of the Highlands Lighthouse, lighthouse technology, piloting and navigation and the U.S. Lifesaving Service.

SITE OPEN. All year, daily 9 to sunset.
MUSEUM AND NORTH TOWER OPEN. Memorial Day weekend to Labor Day, daily 10 to 5.

Other times of the year, Wednesdays through Sundays 10 to 5.

Closed January 1, Thanksgiving Day and December 25.

FREE ADMISSION. Donations welcomed.
- Twin Lights State Historical Site, Lighthouse Road, Highlands, NJ 07732.
Phone (732) 872-1814.
Website: http://www.shore.co.monmouth.nj.us/lighthouses/twinlights.htm

HIGHLANDS LIGHTHOUSE (TWIN LIGHTS; TWIN LIGHTS OF NAVESINK; HIGHLANDS OF NAVESINK; NAVESINK TWIN LIGHTS).
CHARACTERISTIC: Occulting white 10s
HAW: 246' (north tower)
As early as 1746, the Highlands bluff was used as an observation platform by militiamen who lit signal fires to warn New York City residents of marauding pirates and foreign privateers. Samuel Smith, in his *The History of New Jersey* published in 1765, wrote that New York merchants had erected a "commodius lighthouse for the security of navigation." A British report of 1776 mentions that two loyalists had been able to slip by the sentry stationed near "the lighthouse." With these references in mind it is altogether possible that the first beacon on the bluff was established as early as 1756. Further, there are references to the rebuilding of a lighthouse in 1786 and its destruction in 1788. In 1828 a small keeper's house and two blue split stone octagonal towers about 320 feet apart were erected on the bluff. One of the whale oil-fueled optics exhibited a fixed characteristic, the other a flashing light. The optics were built and installed by David Melville, who in 1817 experimented with and developed a new illuminant at Rhode Island's Beavertail Lighthouse. Each beacon had a focal plane of 246 feet above the bay.

In 1838 Congress passed legislation that approved the importation of "...one or two Fresnel lenses for comparison and investigation..." With this incentive, the Lighthouse Service sent Commodore Matthew C. Perry to Paris to purchase two Fresnel lenses. In 1841 a fixed first-order optic was placed in the north tower. The south tower received a revolving second-order lens. By the late 1850s, while both towers were in relatively good condition, the wood framed keeper's dwelling and the station's support buildings were all badly deteriorated. Around 1860 the Lighthouse Board decided to build a new station.

The present towers, their connecting storage galleries and keepers' quarters were completed on May 1, 1862 at a cost of $74,000. The structures are constructed of freestone (brownstone) mined from quarries located at Belleville, New Jersey. While the 1828 towers were twins and thereby gave the site its "Twin Lights" name, the second pair of towers are not alike. The northern tower is octagonal and the southern one square. Reportedly the two lights were designed for the purpose of uniqueness and importance with an appearance altogether different from other lighthouses.

In 1883 the north (octagonal) tower became America's first first-order optic to be powered by mineral oil (kerosene). The lens' focal plane was a wholesome 254 feet above sea level. On June 2, 1898, the north light was discontinued and the south (square) tower was fitted with one of the largest lenses ever manufactured. The Fresnel hyper-radial first-order bivalve (clam shell) lens was constructed in France in 1893 for the World's Columbia Exposition in Chicago. With the permission of the French Lighthouse Board, it was transferred to Navesink in 1898. The lens has a 9-foot diameter and weighs over seven tons. Its clockwork mechanism, powered by a 700-pound descending weight, made the 360-degree revolution in 10 seconds. The south tower's Fresnel optic was the first electrically powered primary light on the American coast. The electric arc lens produced millions of candlepower. Although the visible geographic range of the light was 22 nautical miles, airborne observers reported seeing the optic's loom (indistinct reflection) at a distance of 70 nautical miles. In 1931 the lens was fitted with an electric lamp cluster (three 500 watt lamps), increasing its candlepower output and making the lighthouse beacon the most powerful in the United States. In 1951 the classical lens was removed and exhibited in the Boston Museum of Science. It was returned on March 1, 1979. The aid was automated 1949 and deactivated in 1953. The lens was shipped to Boston's Museum of Science, where it was on exhibit for 25 years.

In 1962 the north (octagonal) tower was relighted as a private aid using a 500-watt blinking lamp inside a sixth-order Fresnel lens manufactured in 1882. The beacon is turned on from dusk to dawn.

OWNER. Deeded to the Borough of Highlands since 1954. Turned over to the State of New Jersey in 1960 and designated an historic site. Managed by the Department of Environmental Protection and Energy's Division of Parks and Forestry.

PRESERVATION. Listed in the National Register of Historic Places as Twin Lights.

In 1978 both towers and keepers' dwelling underwent major repairs. The $1 million project included cleaning and repointing the exterior masonry, repainting woodwork, replacing the lantern's storm panels, construction of public restrooms and landscaping of the grounds. In 1979 the first-order lens that had been removed in 1953 was returned and put on display in the power generating building.

In early 1991, after a couple of vandals entered the building and broke or damaged several of the prisms, the building housing the lens was closed to the public. The lens was repaired over several years; only one prism was too badly damaged to be repaired. Renovations totalling $120,000 (new windows, drainage system, exterior and interior brick walls cleaned and repaired, roof repairs, a security system and a new double door) were made to the former power generating building built in 1909.

The last phase of the restoration project was the installation of the lens and placement of exhibits about the Fresnel lens. The lens exhibit is once again open to the public.

LOWER NEW YORK BAY RANGE LIGHTS

Before departing the Highlands Lighthouse walk out onto the overlook (200 feet above sea level) and enjoy the magnificent panoramic view of Raritan Bay, New York's Manhattan skyline, Lower New York Bay, Sandy Hook and the Long Island coast. On a clear day several of Lower New York Bay's light towers can be seen and recognized.

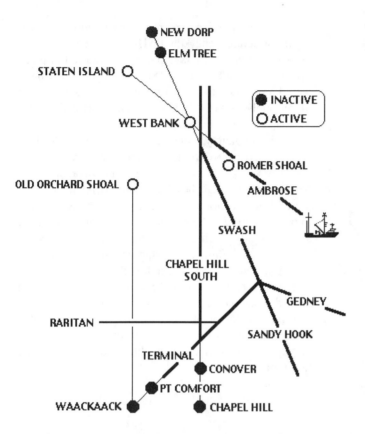

There have been several pairings of range lights established to guide mariners through Lower New York Bay's channels.

On New York's Staten Island there were two range sets (see their respective chapters):

1. New Dorp Rear and Elm Tree Front to range on Swash Channel.

2. Staten Island Rear and a rebuilt West Bank Front to range on the newly dredged Ambrose Channel.

In New Jersey there were three sets of range lights.
WAACKAACK REAR (dismantled)
POINT COMFORT FRONT (dismantled)

Both lighthouses were located in Keansburg. When first established in 1856, Waackaack had a second-order Fresnel and Point Comfort had a third-order lens. They ranged on the old Gedney and today's Sandy Hook and Terminal Channels.

The Waackaack tower was an hexagonal wooden one that duplicated the architectural design used for the Conover Front and Elm Tree Front structures.

The Point Comfort Front lighthouse was a two-story, wood frame building with a rather tall square tower surmounting it at mid-roof. The house plan (sans tower) of the Point Comfort building was the same used for all of New Jersey's range keepers' residences.

NEW WAACKAACK REAR (dismantled)
OLD ORCHARD SHOAL (FRONT).

These beacons ranged on the waterway through Princes Bay. The new Waackaack Rear tower that had been built for display at the 1893 World's Columbian Exposition was a cast-iron replacement for the older wooden tower. The tower no longer exists. See also the OLD ORCHARD SHOAL chapter.

CHAPEL HILL REAR
CONOVER FRONT.

The Chapel Hill (in Chapel Hill) and the Conover (in Leonardo) range beacons ranged on what is now the Chapel Hill South Channel. Today the Chapel Hill Lighthouse is a private residence located just west of the Bay View (Chapel Hill) Cemetery and east of the U.S. Naval Weapons Station Earle. Concealed by a thick stand of trees, it can be seen best during the fall and winter months. Viewing points are located at the southern end of Hosford Avenue (turn south off NJ 36) and along connecting Stillwell Road. It is a simple two-story wood framed and clapboard house surmounted by a square tower that rises uninterrupted to form a windowed lantern above an attached service gallery. Its design is similar to the sketch shown in the NEW DORP chapter.

Chapel Hill is not listed in the National Register of Historic Places. In 1996 the property was on the real estate market at an asking price of $480,000.

The Conover Front Range tower stands on the beach between North Leonard and Roop Avenues. The best advantage point to view and photograph the tower is on the beach located east (right) of North Leonard and just before the street's sharp left turn into Beach Avenue.

It is a skeletal steel tower built in 1856. Originally equipped with a third-order Fresnel lens, the lantern is now empty.

The foundation of Conover's keepers house can be seen behind the tower between North Leonard and Roop.

OWNER. U.S. General Services Administration (surplus federal property).
PRESERVATION. The tower is not listed in the National Register of Historic Places.

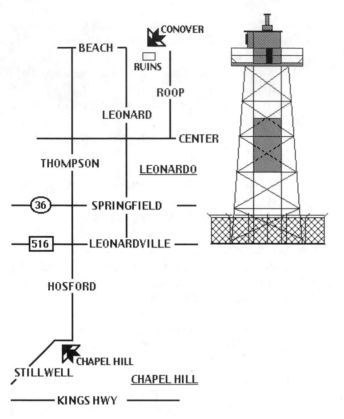

Two parties have expressed an interested in saving the structure. The Atlantic Highlands Historical Society would prefer to have the tower restored in place. The New Jersey Lighthouse Society, on the other hand, would have liked to move the tower to the state-owned marina at the end of Concord Avenue, one block west of the map's Thompson Avenue.

Unfortunately, there are a lot of problems that have to be solved before the tower can be restored. One is that New Jersey wants to sell the marina to a private party. No one, however, has shown an interest in buying it. Then there is the question of how and to whom ownership is to be transferred. The state does not want the structure and apparently is reluctant to act as the broker in accepting and then finding a township or group to accept the property. On top of that glitch is the restoration itself. The tower is badly rusted and covered with multiple coats of lead based paint. Scraping off the old paint poses an environmental problem in the paint's disposal. And as far as the bottom line is concerned, no entity has the money or wants to spend available funds on the restoration project.

GREAT BEDS

NORTH TO PERTH AMBOY (GREAT BEDS). Follow NJ 36 and 35 into Perth Amboy. Then:
-> Right at Smith Street,
-> Right at Front Street,
-> Continue past the Armory Restaurant to the free municipal parking area.
The Great Beds Lighthouse lies about 0.9 mile to the southeast.

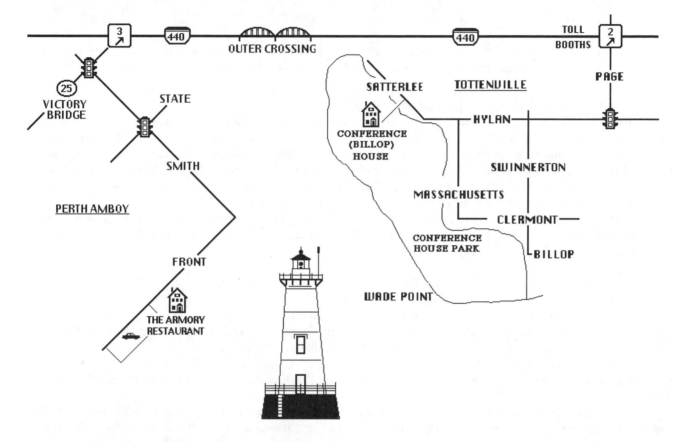

SOUTH FROM STATEN ISLAND. From Conference House Park in Tottenville take Hylan Boulevard north to Page Avenue and turn left. Then:
-> Enter NY 440,
-> Cross over the Outerbridge Crossing (free westbound only),
-> Depart NJ 440 at Exit 3 (NJ 35/Victory Bridge Avenue),
-> Left at Smith Street,
-> Right at Front Street to the parking area.
GREAT BEDS LIGHTHOUSE.
CHARACTERISTIC: Flashing red 6s
HAW: 61' **RANGE**: 6 nm
Before the Great Beds Lighthouse could be constructed with $33,500 in congressional funds, its ownership had to be decided. That was accomplished on April 8, 1880, when New York ceded to the Federal Government the shoal lying about 0.75 mile off Staten Island's Ward (Wards) Point. The light was established on November 15, 1880.

This structure is a boilerplate, caisson-supported replica of the cast-iron towers built during the 1871-1915 period. The 60-foot tall lighthouse's interior is lined with brick.

When built the lantern received a kerosene lamp and a fourth-order Fresnel lens. That lens was removed when the light was automated in 1945 and refitted with a modern lens.
OWNER. U.S. Coast Guard.
PRESERVATION. Not listed in the National Register of Historic Places.

NORTH TO STATEN ISLAND (GREAT BEDS). In Perth Amboy take Smith Street north. Then:
-> Right at to NJ 35 (Victory Bridge Avenue),
-> Enter NJ 440 at its Exit 3,
-> Cross over the Outer Bridge Crossing (vehicle toll eastbound only),
-> Depart NY 440 via Exit 2 to Page Avenue,
-> Right on Page,
-> Right at Hylan Boulevard,
-> Continue to Hylan's end at Satterlee Street. Park on any unrestricted street and walk (free) across the grounds of Conference House Park to the shore. The Great Beds Lighthouse lies off to the southwest.

NATIONAL LIGHTHOUSE CENTER AND MUSEUM
After a selection process that lasted one year, in 1998 a coalition of lighthouse organizations from around the U.S. chose Staten Island to be the site of a new National Lighthouse Center and Museum. The 10-acre site for the museum, along the North Shore Esplanade just east of the St. George Terminal of the Staten Island Ferry, was the center of operations for the U.S. Lighthouse Service from 1867 to 1939. The location offers panoramic views of New York Harbor and includes an 850 foot pier and five major buildings. One of the buildings is the former U.S. Lighthouse Service Administration Building, a New York City Landmark. All the buildings are in need of major renovation.

When completed the museum will feature exhibits and interactive displays on the world's lighthouses, lenses, lamps and other technology, and personal histories of keepers and their families. There are also plans for an archive for the research of American lighthouse history.

The Staten Island Ferry is a free 25-minute ride from Manhattan. Frequent departures all year. For schedule information call (718) 727-2508. For more information see page 140.
To reach the future site of the National Lighthouse Center and Museum by car:
- From Verazzano-Narrows Bridge: Take the first exit to Bay Street and continue north on Bay Street to St. George Ferry Terminal. After the ferry terminal, Bay Street becomes Richmond Terrace.
- From New Jersey (Goethals Bridge): Continue on Route 278 to Clove Road exit. Go north (left) on Clove Road to Richmond Terrace. Turn right on Richmond Terrace (along the Kill vam Kull) and continue to the St. George Ferry Terminal.
- From New Jersey (Outerbridge Crossing): Take West Shore Expressway (440) to Staten Island Expressway (278) and continue east to Clove Road exit. Go north (left) on Clove Road to Richmond Terrace. Turn right on Richmond Terrace (along the Kill vam Kull) and continue to the St. George Ferry Terminal.
At this writing over $5 million has been committed to the project; as much as $20 million will be needed to complete construction. Donations are needed to help make this important center a reality.

- National Lighthouse Center and Museum, One Lighthouse Plaza, Staten Island, NY 10301.
Website: http://www.lighthousemuseum.org
Email: info@lighthousemuseum.org

PRINCES BAY

NORTH OR SOUTH ON HYLAN BOULEVARD. The Princes Bay Lighthouse is located on the bluff overlooking Princes (Princess) Bay and adjacent to the Mount Loretto Mission of the Immaculate Virgin, a child-caring institution. Regulations relative to its youth population make the Mission's grounds off limits to the general public. However, the lighthouse can be seen in the fall and winter when the surrounding trees have shed their leaves. Look for the Mission's sign on Hylan Boulevard.

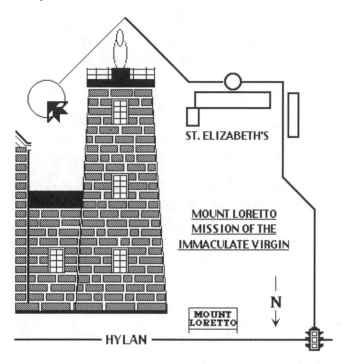

PRINCES BAY LIGHTHOUSE (PRINCESS BAY). The bluffs' first light tower, a wooden structure, was erected in 1826. The station was also provided with a small wooden keeper's house. At the beginning of the Civil War, the weatherworn lighthouse was deemed ready for renovation or replacement. The Lighthouse Board opted for a new tower.

The tower, completed in 1864, is built of shaped brownstone blocks. Its optic, transferred from the old tower, was reached via a circular cast-iron stairway that spirals around a centerpost. In 1868 the present two-story, Gothic-styled brownstone keeper's dwelling was built and attached to the tower by a one-story, roofed access.

Princes Bay's first optic consisted 10 lamps and reflectors, producing a fixed white light. In 1840 after an 1837 naval inspection, two extra lamps and reflectors were introduced into the middle of the existing optic. This arrangement gave the aid an almost 180 degree warning sector.

In 1857 the old optic was discarded and replaced by a whale oil-powered 3 1/2-order Fresnel lens. A flashing signal was accomplished by an eclipser that revolved around the optic.

In 1890 the 3 1/2-order Fresnel was replaced by a smaller rotating fourth-order lens. The kerosene-fed optic produced a white five second flash. The light was deactivated on August 31, 1922 and its lantern and optic removed. A statue of the Virgin Mary now graces the tower's top.

OWNER. The Mission since April 1926.
PRESERVATION. Not listed in the National Register of Historic Places.

NORTH ON HYLAN BOULEVARD (PRINCES BAY). There is another location from which the Princes Bay Lighthouse can be seen across Princess Bay. The location is down a dirt lane sometimes filled with fishermen's cars and trucks. Parking may also be hard to find. Try it anyway.

-> To reach the bayside spot turn south (right) off Hylan Boulevard at Seguine Avenue (traffic signal). Seguine is located northeast of Bayview Avenue (on the right).

-> Continue south on Seguine until you reach its end at the Princess Bay Yacht Club and the narrow, unimproved lane to the shore. The lighthouse can be seen off to the west (right).

OLD ORCHARD SHOAL

NORTH OR SOUTH ON HYLAN BOULEVARD. Old Orchard Shoal Lighthouse is located offshore of the Gateway National Recreation Area's Great Kills Park (free). Enter the park off Hylan Boulevard and stay on the main road through the large parking area to the 1st Beachhouse Parking Lot (free). The lighthouse (upper half white, lower half brown) can be observed with binoculars lying about three miles off to the southeast.

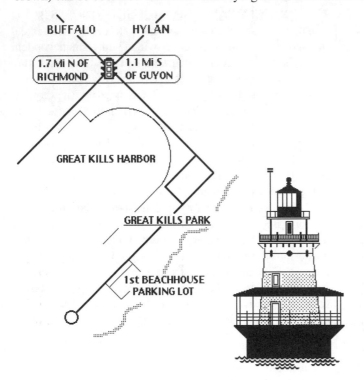

OLD ORCHARD SHOAL LIGHTHOUSE.
CHARACTERISTIC: Flashing white 6s (red sector)

HAW: 51'   **RANGES**: White 7; red 5 nm

In order to give warning of the presence of Old Orchard Shoal to ships and towed barges plying the narrow north-south sealane off Staten Island, the Lighthouse Board decided to set up a pair of range lights in 1891. See also the LOWER NEW YORK BAY RANGE LIGHTS chapter. Congress approved the request and allocated $60,000 for the project. The tower was completed two years later.

The rear range beacon was placed in a newly built Waackaack skeletal steel tower in Keansburg, NJ. The front range light was established, on April 25, 1893, in the new Old Orchard Shoal Lighthouse.

The lighthouse is a cast-iron "coffee pot" resting on a concrete-filled cast-iron caisson. Its superstructure is 35 feet tall.

Old Orchard Shoal's original optic consisted of a fourth-order Fresnel lens and a kerosene-fed lamp. Later the lens was fitted with an incandescent kerosene vapor lamp. The Fresnel optic was removed in 1955 when an automated modern lens was installed. It is no longer a range light.

OWNER. U.S. Coast Guard.

PRESERVATION. Not listed in the National Register of Historic Places.

STATEN ISLAND
WEST BANK - ROMER SHOAL

NORTH ON HYLAN BOULEVARD. Continue on Hylan Boulevard to Guyon Avenue and turn left. Then:

-> Left at Amboy Road,
-> Right at Clarke Avenue,
-> Right at Richmond Road,
-> Left at Lighthouse Avenue (pillars on the corners).

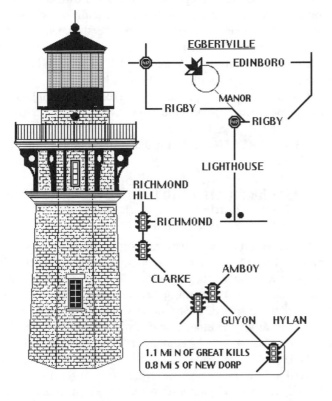

SOUTH ON HYLAN. From the New Dorp Lighthouse take Richmond Road west past New Dorp Lane and at the next traffic signal bear right and continue on Richmond. Then:

-> Pass Spruce Street (on the right) and Kensico Avenue (left),
-> Right at Lighthouse Avenue.

CONTINUE ON. Manor Court, the cobblestone lane that leads up to and circles the base of the lighthouse has been closed to both vehicular and foot traffic.

To view the lighthouse turn right at Rigby Avenue and continue east then north for 0.4 mile to Edinboro Road. Turn left. The lighthouse and former keepers' residence (50 yards east of the tower) are about 0.8 mile down Edinboro.

STATEN ISLAND (RANGE REAR) LIGHTHOUSE.
CHARACTERISTIC: Fixed white
HAW: 231' **RANGE:** 18 nm

This lighthouse is such an imposing edifice one may wonder why it was not built as a coastal aid. Its design, construction and styling are decidedly different from America's Atlantic Coast lighthouses. The buff colored bricks used to build the 90-foot tall octagonal tower were manufactured from a glass-like silica compound formed by heat and fusion. The brackets that support the watchroom gallery are larger and heavier than the cast-iron supports used in earlier American lighthouses. The tower rests on a gray limestone foundation. The aid was established on April 15, 1912, using a bivalve second-order range lens manufactured by the Chance Brothers foundry in Birmingham, England. The Chance Brothers lens is indeed a relic. There were only 75 such lenses installed in America's lighthouses. Each half of the lens consisted of a large central bullseye encircled by rows of prism reflectors, which intensified the incandescent kerosene oil vapor lamp's output by a whopping 233% into a fixed narrow beam visible only on the range line. Today the automated light, using half of the original lens, ranges with the West Bank Lighthouse some 5.5 miles to the east.

Joseph N. Esposito, lighthouse historian and preservationist and for more than nine years the caretaker of New York's Staten Island Lighthouse, was recognized on April 18, 2001 by the Coast Guard in a citation awarded for meritorious service as he stepped down from the volunteer position. Reflecting on the end of his lighthouse duties, Esposito says, "I feel like I've lost a dear friend."

OWNER. U.S. Coast Guard (lighthouse). Keeper's dwelling is privately owned.
PRESERVATION. Eligible to be listed in the National Register of Historic Places.

WEST BANK (RANGE FRONT) LIGHTHOUSE.

CHARACTERISTIC: Equal interval white 6s (red sector)
HAW: 69' **RANGES**: White 16 nm; red (12 nm); white high intensity 23 nm

West Bank's foundation is a pneumatic cast-iron caisson filled with concrete. The original superstructure contained five levels, each formed by curved cast-iron plates bolted together. The windows, typical of the period, are rectangular in shape and are treated with shallow-molded arched hoods. The lighthouse was built in 1900 and its light established on January 1, 1901. In 1908, after the opening of the newly dredged Ambrose Channel, the tower was raised two levels (to 55 feet) to facilitate its ranging with the Staten Island light. When first established, West Bank's fourth-order Fresnel lens was powered by an incandescent oil vapor lamp, showing a fixed white light and a red sector. The optic was automated in 1985.

OWNER. U.S. Coast Guard.

PRESERVATION. Not listed in the National Register of Historic Places.

ROMER SHOAL LIGHTHOUSE (ROMER SHOALS).

CHARACTERISTIC: Group flashing white 15s
HAW: 54' **RANGE**: 15 nm

The first navigation aid, a 25-foot granite daymark for the Swash Channel, was surveyed and built in 1838 by Winslow Lewis on a site thought by him to be the principal location of Romer Shoal. Not so, reported two naval officers who made their second survey at the same time construction of the tower was about to be completed. The daymark was at the wrong side of the shoal and at least a mile off the center of the hazard. Mariners were warned not to head for the tower, but to bear away from it as they sailed through the channel. In 1886, with the misplaced tower showing signs of deterioration and a bit out of plumb, the Lighthouse Board erected a skeletal steel tower on the other side of Swash Channel. The 25-foot tall tower rested on a circular caisson and held a fifth-order Fresnel lens powered by compressed gas. Tanks held enough of the illuminant to keep the light burning for three months. At 41 feet above sea level, the beacon could be seen for some 10 nautical miles. Unfortunately the unattended device proved to be a fragile one, requiring frequent repairs. Not satisfied with its performance, the Board decided to build a new aid, a cast-iron lighthouse resting on a cast-iron, concrete-filled caisson. When completed in 1898, it was fitted with a kerosene-powered fourth-order Fresnel lens that showed a flashing white light. The light's current characteristic was established in 1924. In 1939 the Coast Guard increased the light's intensity with the installation of an incandescent oil vapor lamp. In 1966 the Coast Guard withdrew its watch crew after having automated a newly installed modern lens.

OWNER. U.S. Coast Guard.

PRESERVATION. Eligible to be listed in the National Register of Historic Places.

Romer Shoal is in poor condition, having been severely damaged by storms. It lost its access ladder during a 1992 storm. The structure's condition was considered much too costly to repair. As a result of that early estimate, the Coast Guard contemplated razing the coffee pot and replacing it with a skeletal steel tower. After a thorough 1994-95 structural survey, however, Coast Guard engineers found the tower structurally sound and determined that it can be rehabilitated at a lesser cost. The Coast Guard then announced that it was ready to restore the tower's exterior walls and make other repairs, such as replacing the ladder, strengthening the caisson, converting to solar power and removing unneeded submarine cable, fuel tanks, generator and the disappearing canopy over the main deck's walkway. That project was to be completed in 1997. Fiscal restraints, however, tabled most of the restoration items.

Recent developments have created a new possible future for the Romer Shoal Lighthouse. Holly Stephenson, wife of National Lighthouse Center and Museum Project Director Henry Stephenson (see page 132), noticed the striking similarity between Romer Shoal Lighthouse and the experimental lighthouse shown in photographs of the old Lighthouse Depot on Staten Island. Wayne Wheeler of the U.S. Lighthouse Society did some research and is convinced that the two structures are one in the same. This has led to a long range plan to relocate the structure back to its original home on Staten Island as part of the National Lighthouse Center and Museum.

NEW DORP

NORTH ON RICHMOND ROAD. Follow Richmond Road through the double Amboy Avenue and New Dorp Lane intersections to Altamont Street and turn left.

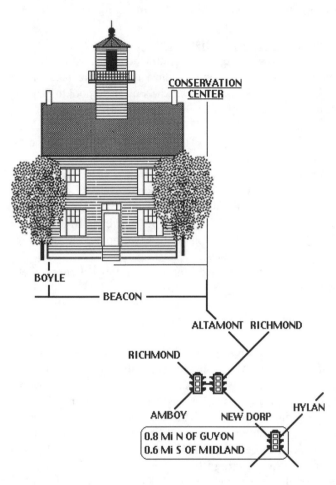

NORTH OR SOUTH ON HYLAN BOULEVARD. See map.

The New Dorp Lighthouse is nestled within a forested area and is fairly well hidden from the property's entrance road off Altamont Street and from Beacon and Boyle Streets. The best viewing times are during the fall and winter months. The property is not open to the public.

NEW DORP LIGHTHOUSE (SWASH CHANNEL RANGE REAR). The New Dorp and Elm Tree beacons ranged on Swash Channel. See also the LOWER NEW YORK BAY RANGE LIGHTS chapter.

The lighthouse is a 1 1/2-story wooden structure surmounted by an unusually tall narrow, square tower that rests on the front side of the structure's hip roof. It extends upward through the service gallery to form a windowed lantern. Access to the lantern was via an outside ladder.

New Dorp's design duplicates the range lighthouses built in New Jersey at Chapel Hill and Point Comfort in Keansburg. New Dorp and Elm Tree's wooden towers were built for about $60,000, a sum appropriated by Congress in 1852. Both lighthouses were completed and established in 1856. The 80-foot tall New Dorp continued active until 1964, when it was stripped, boarded up and served to vandals.

Both New Dorp and Elm Tree were originally fitted with whale oil-powered second-order classical lenses. In 1891 both Fresnels were removed and replaced with sixth-order bullseye lenses similar to, but much smaller than, Staten Island Lighthouse's lens. In 1907 the beacons' kerosene light sources were changed to incandescent kerosene vapor lamps.

OWNER. Private owner since 1974.

PRESERVATION. Listed in the National Register of Historic Places. The owner has restored the structure to its original condition.

ELM TREE LIGHTHOUSE (SWASH CHANNEL RANGE FRONT - dismantled).

The Elm Tree Lighthouse, a hexagonal wooden tower, was located at the southeast end of New Dorp Lane. It was of the same design as the old Waackaack (Keansburg) and the extant Conover (Leonardo) range towers. It was dismantled in 1939 and its range responsibility transferred to the former Miller Air Field's control tower.

FORT WADSWORTH

NORTH ON HYLAN BOULEVARD. Follow Hylan Boulevard across the I-278 overpass to Bay Street (not shown on map), turn right and continue into the park.

NORTH ON STATEN ISLAND EXPRESSWAY (I-278). Take the Bay Street Exit to traffic light. Turn left and continue to Bay Street.

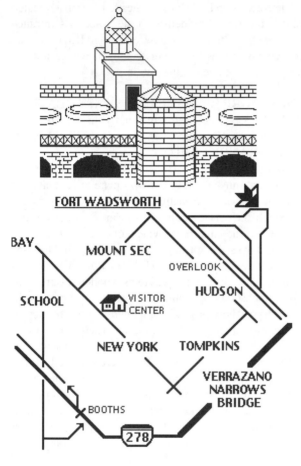

SOUTH FROM BROOKLYN. Take I-278 across the Verrazano Narrows Bridge (toll westbound only). After reaching Staten Island and just beyond its unused toll booths take I-278's Fort Wadsworth & School Street Exit. Follow School to Bay Avenue, turn right and continue through the park's entrance to the visitor center on the left.

VISITOR CENTER. The center presents exhibits on the fort's history and an introductory video. Visitors may then take the 1.5 mile trail that introduces Wadsworth's major fortifications and the lighthouse. Construction to improve the park may temporarily close parts of the trail while work progresses.

OPEN. All year. Fridays 1 to 5. Weekends 10 to 5.

TOURS. By reservation only. A two-hour walk conducted by a park ranger. Weekends at 2.

- Gateway National Recreation Area, Floyd Bennett Field, Building 69, Brooklyn, NY 11234.

Phone (718) 354-4500.

Website: http://www.nps.gov/gate/

FORT TOMPKINS LIGHTHOUSE (disassembled).

The Fort Wadsworth story begins with a lighthouse built on Fort Tompkins, an Army post located adjacent to Fort Wadsworth.

The Fort Tompkins Light was first established in 1828, after Congress granted $30,000 for the construction of a 40-foot tall light tower, its lighting device (a Winslow creation) and a wood frame keeper's house. Fort Tompkins received a fourth-order classical lens in 1855. During the Civil War, construction of new facilities and damage to the lantern from the fort's coast artillery firings resulted in the decision to move the beacon elsewhere.

With an appropriation of $1,500 another lighthouse was constructed inland of its former site. With that small amount of dollars, the architects came up with a lulu of a lighthouse. The new 2 1/2-story wood framed dwelling-cum-tower structure was an architectural jewel. It was rakishly Victorian in its gingerbread detailing and bold cornices and profoundly Second Empire with its high mansard-styled slate roof and sharply outline windows. The similarly decorated square tower had an elegant lantern service deck protected by a railing centered with fancy cast-iron balusters. The octagonal lantern was capped with a pitched ogee dome. With the fourth-order Fresnel transferred from the dismantled 1828 tower, the new beacon was activated on December 20, 1873.

FORT WADSWORTH LIGHTHOUSE.

With another new artillery battery threatening its existence and its warning capability hindered by its inland location, the Fort Tompkins fourth-order Fresnel lens was transferred, in March 1903, to a semi-circular brick tower erected against the side of the fort and next to a brick building (shown in sketch with entry door) that stands on Fort Wadsworth's outer rampart. With a focal plane 75 feet above the bay, Fort Wadsworth's alternatingly flashing white and red light could be seen out to a distance of 13 nautical miles.

FORT WADSWORTH

Before its discontinuance in 1965, the optic's (incandescent oil vapor lamp and fourth-order lens) characteristic was changed to an alternating white with green sector. Fort Wadsworth Light was extinguished after construction of the Verrazano Narrows Bridge. Its apparently abandoned lantern (empty and without glass panes) is slowly succumbing to the elements. As of August 2001 it is on *Lighthouse Digest's* "Doomsday List" of endangered lighthouses.

OWNER. National Park Service. Managed by the Gateway National Recreation Area.

PRESERVATION. This redan, originally a U.S. Army coast artillery post, was last used by the U.S. Navy as a headquarters, billeting and residential homeport base. In 1993, with the Navy having announced its intention to pull out of the station in 1995, the National Park Service began planning to take over the site, as it was ordered to do in 1972 by Congressional edict. In June 1994 the Secretary of the Interior decided that only the fortifications were of sufficient historical interest for acceptance as a national monument. The other one-third, comprising Wadsworth's office and service buildings as well as a new 400-person dormitory, was to be turned into a housing site for New York's homeless. That was the federal solution for the utilization of the smaller portion of Fort Wadsworth. Both of New York's U.S. Senators, the state's governor, New York City's mayor, Staten Island's borough president and the area's property owners voiced their opposition to the idea and quashed the proposal.

Finally, on October 1, 1995, Fort Wadsworth was divided into three parts. The fort and lighthouse went to the National Park Service's Gateway National Recreation Area. The housing billets were assigned to the Coast Guard. The administration buildings were given to the U.S. Army.

Although not listed in the National Register of Historic Places, it will become either eligible for or included in the register as a part of the Fort Wadsworth National Monument.

Fort Wadsworth Lighthouse

ROBBINS REEF

TO ST. GEORGE. This lighthouse lies about one mile offshore from the Staten Island Ferry Plaza (ferry and marine museum). The terminal is located on Richmond Terrace (Bay Street connection). On weekdays when parking lots at or near the terminal are full, vehicles are double parked along Richmond Terrace. On weekends parking is usually available. Nevertheless, try to get into one of the plaza's two municipal parking lots (24-hour fee).

Lot #P1 is at the bottom of the one way ramp leading to the ferry loading lanes. Lot #P2 is located on the terminal's west side. If unable to find a parking spot at or near the plaza, try one of the less crowded side streets.

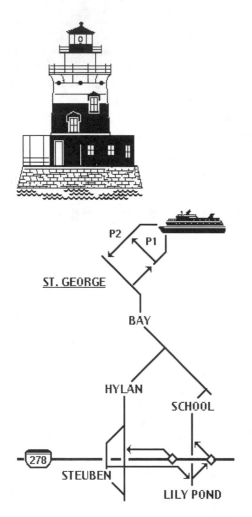

ROBBINS REEF LIGHTHOUSE.
CHARACTERISTIC: Flashing green 6s
HAW: 56' **RANGE**: 7 nm

The pier to the left of the present lighthouse is where Robbins Reef's first lighthouse stood. Finished in 1839, the 66-foot octagonal stone tower contained sufficient room to house the keeper's family.

On July 10, 1883, the Robbins Reef light was reestablished in a newly constructed cast-iron tower that has arched windows with projecting pedimented hoods and deeply molded surrounds. Except for the semicircular living quarters that wrap around its base and the coursed granite block foundation, the brown and white lighthouse resembles its coffee pot contemporaries.

Originally equipped with a Lewis lighting device (nine lamps with 14-inch reflectors), the optic was changed in 1849 to 15 lamps with 16-inch reflectors and in 1855 to a whale oil-fed lamp and a fourth-order Fresnel lens. When the newly installed modern lens was automated in 1966, the Coast Guard removed the classical lens and its watch personnel.

Kate Walker, a petite lady possessed of considerable inner strength and physical stamina, heeded the words of her dying husband to "mind the light." She did so with unfailing devotion to her job. Kate spent 34 years (1885-1919) in the shadow of the burgeoning Manhattan skyline, yet seldom ventured into the Big Apple. For all of her keeper years on the reef, her daytime chores included the cleaning of the lens, polishing brass, painting, keeping her log current, checking the oil level and tending her garden and on school days rowing her two children to and from Staten Island. Her nocturnal tasks began with the sounding of retreat on Governor's Island, a few miles across the harbor. With that cannon boom she checked the lantern, replenished the oil, cranked up the steam engine to run the fog horn, trimmed wicks, and in winter, cleared the ice off the lantern's glass panes. Oh yes, she is officially credited with having saved at least 75 lives!

OWNER. U.S. Coast Guard.
PRESERVATION. Not listed in the National Register of Historic Places.

STATEN ISLAND FERRY. One of New York City's better sightseeing bargains is the low cost passenger fare for a ferry trip across New York's Upper Bay to Manhattan's South Ferry in Battery Park. Refreshments are available on board. The upper deck views of the Robbins Reef Lighthouse, Governors Island, the Statue of Liberty, Ellis Island and the lower Manhattan skyline are superb. At Battery Park, near the ferry terminal, one can board excursion boats for visits to the Statue of Liberty and Ellis Island. The ferry operates all year with daily daytime half hour service. Crossing time is 25 minutes. Phone (718) 727-2508.

One bit of advice. On weekdays avoid the morning (8-10) and late afternoon (4-6) rush hours when hundreds of commuters head for or leave their places of employment in New York City.

ROBBINS REEF

STATUE OF LIBERTY (THE LIGHTHOUSE).

About two miles northeast of the Robbins Reef stands America's Statue of Liberty. What is not widely known is that "Liberty Enlightening the World" was once a commissioned lighthouse. In 1877 Congressional approval for the President's acceptance of France's gift specified that the structure would be maintained as a beacon. When Ms. Liberty was in place in 1886, a lantern was formed in the torch by cutting windows in the torch's side and inserting window panes. Under the supervision of Thomas Alva Edison, workers installed an electric arc light. The beacon was discontinued in 1902 and turned over to the old War Department. A public outcry over its being extinguished gave the light new life. The War Department reconsidered and continued to operate the beacon for a few more years.

Staten Island Lighthouse

CONEY ISLAND

NORTH TO LONG ISLAND. Take I-278 across the Verrazano Narrows Bridge (no toll eastbound) to Brooklyn. Take the lower level's left lane for Exit 2 east to the Belt Parkway. Just before reaching the parkway's Exit 4 (Bay & 8th Streets), there is a bayside turnout where one may park (free) to distantly view the lighthouse. The tower can also be seen enroute between the parkway's Exits 4 and 5.

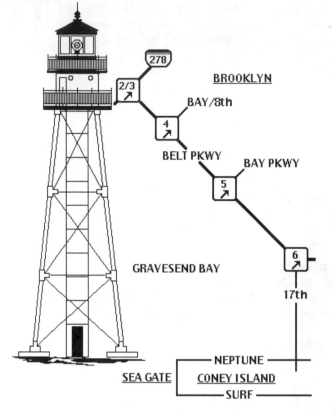

WEST ON THE BELT PARKWAY. The southbound motorist can reach the waterside park by crossing the parkway at Exit 4.

The white pyramidal skeletal Coney Island tower is tucked away in the restricted residential community of Sea Gate.

CONEY ISLAND LIGHTHOUSE (NORTON POINT).

CHARACTERISTIC: Flashing red 5s

HAW: 75' **RANGE**: 16 nm

This lighthouse is located on Norton Point at the eastern tip of Coney Island and stands guard at the entrance (The Narrows) to Upper New York Bay and warns of the shoals in Gravesend Bay.

It is a 70-foot tall skeletal cast-iron tower. When established on August 1, 1890, the Coney Island Range Light Station consisted of two skeletal towers. In 1896 the front range beacon was dismantled and the present two-story wood framed keeper's residence built.

Coney Island's original optic was a kerosene-powered fourth-order Fresnel. The light station became fully automated in 1979 and ten years later its fourth-order lens was removed.

The light's present keeper, Frank Shubert, a 57-year veteran from seaman on the tender *Tulip* in 1937 to a tour in the U.S. Army during World War II to lightkeeper since 1960. Unwilling to retire and leave his beloved aid, Captain Shubert has been granted his wish to remain on active duty. The octogenarian climbs the 87 steps to the lantern each day to perform the required maintenance chores.

OWNER. U.S. Coast Guard.
PRESERVATION. Not listed in the National Register of Historic Places.

SOUTH STREET SEAPORT MUSEUM. Coney Island's fourth-order Fresnel lens is displayed in the Museum's Visitor Center on 12 Fulton Street by the East River in New York City's lower Manhattan.
OPEN.
April 1 to September 30, daily 10 to 6 (Thursdays until 8)
Rest of year, daily 10 to 5, closed Mondays.
ADMISSION FEES. Discounts for seniors, students and children 2-11.
Phone (212) 748-8600.
Website http://www.southstseaport.org/

FIRE ISLAND

EAST ON LONG ISLAND. Take the Long Island Expressway (I-495) to Sagtikos State Parkway south (Exit 53) or Southern State Parkway to Robert Moses Causeway (Exit 40) south. Go to the end, following signs for Robert Moses State Park. At a traffic circle, bear left and park in Field 5 (state charges a fee seasonally), then walk approximately one mile following the dirt road or boardwalk nature trail to the lighthouse. There are no parking facilities at the lighthouse, but universally accessible parking is available for cars with handicap plates.

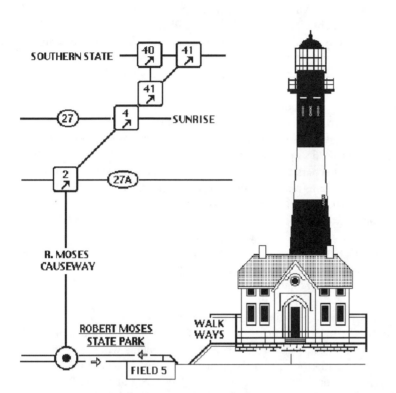

KEEPERS' QUARTERS. The restored keepers' house is now a visitor center and museum featuring memorabilia from the original 1826 light station and its 1858 lighthouse, including its original fourth-order Fresnel lens. Other topical exhibits include the whaling, fishing and shellfishing industries, shipwrecks, the Lifesaving Service, the Coast Guard, the effects of the 1938 hurricane, the Surf Hotel and other early community developments.

In 1986, after the relighting of the lighthouse, the Fire Island Lighthouse Preservation Society expected the National Park Service to plan for its management responsibilities by budgeting for and securing the required funds to cover the station's operating and maintenance costs. Between 1989 and 1992, the Society paid approximately $100,000 for the salaries of rangers assigned to staff the station. In 1993 the National Park Service assured the Society that in the future sufficient funds will be made available for staffing and maintenance.

On December 19, 1996, the Society signed a privatization agreement with the National Park Service to take over the maintenance and operation of the lighthouse and keepers' quarters.

The Society's intention is to increase visitor services and programs for school and other interested groups on a national and international basis. The Board of Directors is determined to keep the doors of this national historic site open for education and preservation of our maritime heritage.

Contributions and supporting memberships to carry out the Society's educational programs are always needed.

KEEPERS' QUARTERS OPEN.

April Thru June (except Easter Sunday): Weekends and holidays 9:30 a.m. to 5 p.m.

July 1 through Labor Day: Daily 9:30 a.m. to 5 p.m.

Labor Day through mid-December: Lighthouse open weekends and holidays 9:30 a.m. to 4 p.m.

January through March: Officially closed - Unofficially open weekends and holidays based upon volunteer availability and weather permitting.

Call (631) 661-4876 to check on winter openings.

TOWER OPEN. Lighthouse tower tours at 10 a.m., 11 a.m., 1 p.m., 2 p.m. and 3 p.m. Reservations are required; call 631-661-4876. Wear flat footwear; children must be 42" tall.

ADMISSION FEES. Nominal charges for Keepers' Quarters' exhibit area only or for a combination exhibit visit/tower tour. Discounts for society members, seniors 65+ and children 5-11.

- Fire Island Lighthouse Preservation Society, 4640 Captree Island, Captree Island, NY 11702-4601.

Phone (631) 321-7028. School and scout programs, and group tours: (631) 661-4876.

Website: http://www.fireislandlighthouse.com

Fire Island National Seashore website: http://www.nps.gov/fiis/

FIRE ISLAND LIGHTHOUSE (WINKING WOMAN).
CHARACTERISTIC: Flashing white 7.5s
HAW: 167' **RANGE**: 24 nm

The first lighthouse on Fire Island was built in 1825-26 for about $10,000. The 85-foot octagonal granite lighthouse had a soapstone deck for the lantern. This round stone decking with its bored access hole can be found in several New England lighthouses, such as Maine's Pemaquid Point and Franklin Island. The lighting apparatus was again one of Winslow Lewis' Argand-styled chandeliers with 14 lamps and 21-inch reflectors. Fifth Auditor Pleasonton reported in 1838 that the optic revolved, producing a flash characteristic by moving the chandelier in back of a fixed eclipser. The beacon's focal plane was 89 feet above the water.

On March 3, 1857, with Congress not satisfied with its effectiveness as an aid to navigation, an appropriation of $40,000 was approved for the construction of a new light tower.

The second tower is the one standing today. It is located about 200 yards northeast of the site of the first lighthouse. The unusual flaring of the tower's base gives the slender 168-foot tower added strength. The tower's double walls are constructed of curved handmade bricks. There are 182 cast-iron steps winding up to the watchroom gallery and 10 more to the lantern. Arched windows appear at landings spaced at 26 step intervals.

During the building of the station's foundation the keepers and their families remained in the station's original stone and wooden house. Everything went smoothly until the masons ran out of stones for the terracing that surrounds the station. The shortage forced the construction engineer to move the keepers' families into an unfinished brick oil house being built next to the tower while he tore down both the old inactive tower and the original keepers' dwelling, a decision not favorably accepted by both keepers. When you visit the lighthouse you will find that the tower's stones form the sloping north side of the foundation. The south facade and the foundation's buttresses were built with brick left over after the tower was completed. The circular remains of the old tower's foundation can be seen west of the lighthouse.

The tower was coated with a thick layer of cement in 1871 and in 1891 received its distinctive black (tar coating) and painted white bands.

In 1896 in anticipation of the optic being electrified, a coal-fired, steam-operated power plant was built next to the lighthouse. Further, it was anticipated that the old 1826 tower's circular foundation would be remade into a cistern to hold water for the engine. At the same time, a tram rail line was laid to a dock where coal shipments were to be unloaded and moved to the power station. Before any more construction took place the plan was dropped. The plant was later dismantled. Today a boathouse stands on the concrete slab and some of the tram's rails have been uncovered.

The station's original first-order Fresnel optic (drum design) was powered by a whale oil lamp. Its flashing white light was first shown on November 1, 1858.

In 1932 the lens' pedestal was placed in a trough of mercury that permitted the "floating" lens to revolve effortlessly. The mercury float was transferred from the Shinnecock Lighthouse. In 1939 the light was electrified via an underwater cable from the mainland. Fire Island's original first-order lens was shipped off to be exhibited in Philadelphia's Franklin Institute after being replaced by a fourth-order lens. In 1952 the fourth-order lens was removed and replaced by an optic that is now on display in the museum's main hallway.

In 1974, after the lighthouse was decommissioned and abandoned, the optic was removed.

OWNER. Dwelling and grounds deeded to the National Park Service in 1983; lighthouse in 1985. Leased to Fire Island Lighthouse Preservation Society in 1996.

PRESERVATION. Listed (1983) in the National Register of Historic Places as part of the Fire Island National Seashore.

Back in 1912 the tower's exterior, badly eroded by water seepage, was wrapped in a steel mesh fastened by bands and coated with cement. Over the years wind, salt and water caused the mesh to rust, the bands to expand and the cement coating to crumble. At midnight on December 31, 1974, the light was discontinued.

FIRE ISLAND

For years the lighthouse stood unattended, neglected and decaying. In 1981 the tower was declared to be "unsafe and beyond repair." With no funds available for its restoration, Fire Island was slated for demolition. In 1982 the Fire Island Lighthouse Preservation Society was incorporated to raise funds for the restoration of the light station. In 1986 after over $1.2 million had been raised, the Society completed the first restoration (Phase I) of the keepers' quarters. On May 25th, Fire Island was relighted (modern plastic lens) and the Visitors Information and Exhibit Center dedicated and opened to the public for the first time. In 1987 after another $500,000 was raised, the deteriorated exterior stucco was replaced by a pressurized and reinforced cement and then waterproofed. That job completed the restoration project (Phase II). The Society also established an endowment (Phase III) to insure preservation of the lighthouse in perpetuity. In 1989 the tower was opened to the public for the first time. In 1992 Congress appropriated $545,000 to restore the stone terrace surrounding the dwelling, the connecting tunnel between the tower and the keeper's quarters, to stabilize the site of the 1824 lighthouse, to furnish new handrails and exterior safety lighting and to repair to the dwelling's interior. Additionally, a ramp and a new entrance for the handicapped were built on the west side of the Keepers' Quarters. The projects were completed early in 1994. On May 15th the Society marked the completion of Fire Island's restoration with a grand opening celebration.

The lighthouse received a new coast of paint in 1997. Cost was shared by the National Park Service and the Society.

LIGHTHOUSE SAFARIS This tour company provides exceptional opportunities to view Long Island lighthouses. The company was started by Gayle Haines, a Past President of the Fire Island Lighthouse Preservation Society and a Board Member for the National Lighthouse Center and Museum.

On each safari you will visit at least one Long Island lighthouse, up to as many as 16 lighthouses, and a side attraction. You can choose a standard tour or your group (40-100 people) can arrange a customized tour.

There are several tours scheduled from spring through fall, from one to four days. All tours include two professional guides, lunch, museum and program fees, snacks, taxes, gratuities, video entertainment aboard a deluxe motorcoach, and a complimetary map pack.

SCHEDULE. Call or check website for the latest schedule.

FARES. No discounts. Reservations required.

- Lighthouse Safaris, Inc., 4636 Captree Island, Captree Island, NY 11702-4601

Phone (631) 422-4213.

Website: http://www.lighthousesafaris.com/   Email: gayle@lighthousesafaris.com

Fire Island Lighthouse

MONTAUK POINT

SHINNECOCK BAY LIGHTHOUSE (demolished).

Enroute to Montauk Lighthouse you will pass the location of this former aid to navigation.

The 170-foot tall brick lighthouse (tower 150 feet) was erected on Ponquogue Point in 1857-58. Its optic consisted of a whale oil lamp inside a fixed first-order Fresnel lens.

MONTAUK POINT STATE PARK

On January 1, 1858, Shinnecock was activated showing a fixed white light, the same warning that was Montauk Point's before its new first-order Fresnel was assigned a fixed white with a flash every two minutes. Unfortunately, there was little time allowed between the announcement to mariners and the change. As a result, a full-rigged ship returning from San Francisco mistook the Shinnecock warning for Montauk's old characteristic and slammed into the rocks west of the point. None of the crew survived.

The lighthouse was darkened in 1931 and destroyed in 1948. As bricks around the base of the tower were removed, shoring timbers were tucked into the gaps between the tower's foundation and the penetrated walls. On December 23, 1948, after fires had been strategically set among the timbers, the historic structure slowly tilted and then gracefully toppled over.

EAST TO MONTAUK. Follow NY 27 (Sunrise and Montauk Highways) to the entrance to the Montauk Point State Park. Enter the park (free) and follow the one way loop road past the lighthouse to the main parking lot. There is a short walk across the park road to the entrance to the lighthouse grounds and ticket kiosk. Expect some exertion in walking uphill (pavement, no steps) to the lighthouse.

OPEN. All year, daily 8 to 4.

PARKING FEE. Vehicle only Memorial Day to Labor Day. Other times free.

MONTAUK POINT LIGHTHOUSE MUSEUM

The museum in the renovated keeper's quarters was opened in May 1987. Among its displays are lighthouse drawings (one drawn in 1797), old photographs and scaled dioramas that show the light-house's four development stages (1796, 1860, 1903 & 1943). There is also a videotape presentation for visitors.

Of particular interest is the museum's excellent display of Fresnel and modern lenses and some rarely seen lighthouse lamps, including one adapted from a locomotive headlamp. When you reach the room at the base of the tower, look for these lenses: Montauk Point's Henri LePaute 3 1/2-order bivalve (1904-1987), a rotating fourth-order Fresnel, a sixth-order range Fresnel and a red 375mm lantern.

MUSEUM OPEN.

The museum is open all year, with very limited hours in winter. Check the museum's website or call (631) 668-2544 for the latest schedule.

TOWER TOURS. Under the supervision of Society members, visitors may climb the tower's 137 spiraling cast-iron steps where the modern optic can be seen in the lantern room. Children under 41 inches tall not permitted to take tour.

ADMISSION FEES. Discount for seniors and children 6-11.
- Montauk Point Lighthouse Museum, RFD 2, Box 112, Montauk, NY 11954.
Phone: (631) 668-2544 or 888-Mtk-Point (outside 631 Area Code)
Website: http://www.montauklighthouse.com
Email: keeper@montauklighthouse.com

MONTAUK POINT

MONTAUK POINT LIGHTHOUSE.
CHARACTERISTIC: Flashing white 5s
HAW: 168' **RANGE**: 24 nm

The lighthouse stands on Turtle Hill, some 68 feet above the sea, where the British during the American Revolution lit signal fires to guide their ships around the point. In 1792 Congress provided $255 to buy the land to build the first Montauk Point Lighthouse. President George Washington issued the order in 1795 to erect the tower using a congressional appropriation of $22,300. Construction of the tower was completed by the famous lighthouse builder John McComb in 1796. Although the lighthouse was finished in 1796, the oil did not arrive until 1797. The beacon was first lighted on November 5, 1797.

The 78-foot tall octagonal tower is made of Connecticut sandstone blocks shaped in Chatham, New York. Its base rests on a foundation laid to a depth of 13 feet. It measures 28 feet across and the tower's walls are six feet thick, tapering to a thickness of three feet at the watchroom deck. The station also received three keepers' houses.

Montauk Point was rebuilt in 1860 to allow the installation of a Henri LePaute first-order Fresnel lens, measuring 12 feet in height and six feet in diameter. Alterations to the tower involved adding 14 feet to the top of the tower (to 92 feet) and adding a service room and a new 10-foot tall octagonal cast-iron lantern manufactured by Ira Winn of Portland, Maine. The lantern was topped with a large bulbous copper ventilator whose exhaust vent was kept pointing leeward by an equally large vane. The station also received a new colonial duplex, an oil house attached to the tower. The fog signal house was added in 1897.

The original 1838 keeper's house located below the lighthouse was converted into a barn in 1860 and into a garage in 1937. Another oil house (1904) north of the tower stored fuel for generators of a naval radio station. The tower attached to the east side of the fog signal house was built in 1942. During World War II it was used as an artillery observation post to adjust the fires of Fort Hero's 16-inch coastal guns located west of the lighthouse.

The first lighting apparatus was a spider device that held 13 whale oil-fed lamps with reflectors on two tiers. By 1838 the lighthouse had been equipped with a new two-tiered Argand-type device containing 18 lamps and 14.5-inch reflectors (10 lamps on the upper cast-iron table, eight on the lower ring). This light had a focal plane of 160 feet above the water and an estimated range of 19 nautical miles. In attempts to gain greater intensity and range, fewer lamps with larger reflectors were installed in 1842 and again in 1850. In 1904, when the first-order lens' clockwork mechanism failed to properly rotate the black glass eclipsing panel, it was decided to replace the huge lens with a smaller and newer Fresnel 3 1/2-order bivalve lens with two flash panels that produced a brighter flashing white light every 15 seconds. The lens was removed in 1987 when the presently active modern optic was installed and automated. The Coast Guard watch crew departed on April 1, 1987.

In the 1800s and early 1900s, when Europe's "tired and poor" emigrees arrived in America, the Montauk Point Lighthouse (not the Fire Island Lighthouse or the Statue of Liberty) was the first landmark to greet them. Montauk Point was again a proud welcoming beacon in 1981, when the former Iranian-held hostages returning to America were greeted by a hearty "WELCOME HOME" printed across a huge yellow ribbon tied around the tower.

OWNER. U.S. Coast Guard. Keepers' Dwelling leased to the Montauk Historical Society on April 1, 1987. Lighthouse leased to the Society in 1997.

PRESERVATION. Listed in the National Register of Historic Places.
During the 1990-96 following restorative tasks were undertaken:
Watchroom's balcony, lantern's supporting black drum, the lantern, its service gallery and the copper-clad roof were restored. The lantern's cast-iron members were cleaned and painted and new bronze window frames glazed with single panes of glass were installed. The cells between the stairway and the interior wall's facing were vented to release moisture that accumulated in the upper tower.

A $500,000 overhaul of the tower's exterior took place in 1998 and 1999. The work performed by International Chimney Corporation included restoring the deck and supports and repointing the cracked sandstone blocks in the tower with lime rich mortar. The exterior paint was then removed by blasting with baking soda (gentler than sandblasting), and the tower was power washed and painted with two coats of Modac paint. The brown band on the tower was restored to its historically correct reddish brown color.

Interior work completed by International Chimney included the restoration of the tower's windows and portholes, as well as repointing the cracks visible in the interior.

EROSION. Back in 1795, although the 101.5-foot tall lighthouse was about 300 feet from the cliff's edge, the contractor had to build dams across gullies and fill the space behind the dams with stones in the earliest attempt to prevent erosion. Today, as is the case with so many other American lighthouses, Montauk Point is seriously threatened by land erosion. The tower is but 57 feet from the edge of the bluff.

Much effort has gone into trying to save the tower, including 15 years of vegetation terracing by Giorgina Reid, a remarkable ecologist who developed, patented and proved successful an anti-erosion plant and grass technique called "Reed Trench Terracing." In this process a low toe wall is constructed using large boulders of basalt to give stability to the work to be done above. The slope is reworked to a shallower pitch and terrace steps are then notched across the slope from bottom to top (much like oriental rice paddies). After that is done, revetment boxes made from wooden timbers are emplaced to hold an acrylic filter cloth (first used were withered reed stems called phragmites). The cloth holds and helps nurture the growth of planted quick-growing vegetation with tenacious root systems, such as Rosa Rugosa. The process halts soil erosion. In commemoration of Reid's work the oil house now houses an erosion stabilization exhibit.

Gregory J. Donohue, a former volunteer with Mrs. Reid, has now taken control of the erosion-control effort. Mr. Donohue has adapted the terrace system. The good news is that the bluff now appears to be stabilized.

EAST & NORTHEAST FACES. After the Federal Government emplaced rock revetments in 1971 and with the subsequent success in its terracing, erosion was halted on the cliff's east and northeast faces. Over the years, storms have dislodged some of the revetments' stones and torn up patches of the terracing. In late 1991, Hurricane Bob and its piggyback Halloween eve storm caused a tremendous amount of damage on the northeast side. Several hundred feet of the wickerwork (gabion) and terrace were washed away. The bluff's rim was pushed inland another 30 feet, creating a sheer cliff that will make further protective work difficult to accomplish. In March 1993 the Coast Guard completed the construction of a 770-foot long protective seawall along the east side below the lighthouse. The rock base consists of huge 10-ton boulders selectively placed well below sea level then piled to a height of 25 feet above the low tide line. One-ton stones were placed on top of the riprap base and fused with poured concrete. In 1994 a similarly protective 300 foot long seawall was completed on the northeast side, flanking the middle east wall. Its construction involved digging a trench below sea level at the bluff's base, lining it with an acrylic filter cloth to prevent sediment from washing away and the laying some 5,500 tons of 10-ton boulders.

SOUTH & SOUTHEAST FACES. Meanwhile, the untouched south bluff also has been seriously eroded. The 1991 storms also ripped away some 50 feet of concrete debris and terrace on the southeast face. A 200-foot long, similarly constructed seawall along the south face completed the erosion control project. All these projects required the expenditure of vast sums of money, all paid out of funds acquired from contributions, the Coast Guard, the U.S. Army's Corps of Engineers, state grants and two special benefit concerts by neighbor Paul Simon.

CEDAR ISLAND

NORTH OR SOUTH ON NY 114. The Cedar Island Lighthouse stands at the end of a sand spit jutting out from below the bluff overlook in the Cedar Point State Park. Stephan Hands Path is about 1.8 miles northeast of NY 27 in East Hampton and 4.7 miles southwest of Sag Harbor. "Stephan Hands Path 1,000'" signs are posted on both sides of the intersection. The map with arrows shows the zig-zag route to follow and the distances between each change in direction.

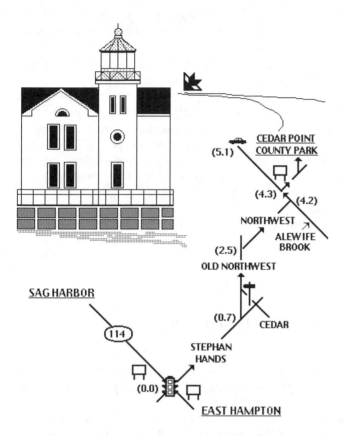

CEDAR POINT COUNTY PARK. Enter the park, check in at the supervisor's office and continue straight ahead on the main road to a parking area (on the left) and food stand. Walk across the level grass lawn to view the lighthouse.

OPEN. All year, daily 8 to 10.

ADMISSION FEES. Park access is by Tourist Registration or Tourist Access Key Cards issued by the county. The access card is available for those not interested in using the reservation system for golf and camping. The cards are good for the year issued. Requests must be mailed with a check or money order for $5.00 per access card made out to the Suffolk County Department of Parks.

The lighthouse can be reached by walking out onto the spit of land. The use of a four-wheel drive vehicle permitted only with the possession a registration card. The only time of the year visiting the lighthouse is not permitted is October through December, when from Wednesday through Sunday duck hunting takes priority. That leaves Mondays and Tuesdays for lighthouse visitors.

APPLICATION. Call the Parks Administrative Office at (631) 854-4961 for key card applications and further information.

- Suffolk County Department of Parks, PO Box 144, West Sayville, NY 11796-0144.

CEDAR ISLAND LIGHTHOUSE (CEDAR POINT).

The first lighthouse on Cedar Island was built in 1839 to guide shipping and whalers into Northwest Bay and the port of Sag Harbor. It was a 35-foot tall wood frame tower that, in 1858, was reported to be in poor condition.

The present lighthouse, completed in 1868, is a massive structure built of solid (Boston style) granite blocks. It shows the same Victorian-Gothic architectural borrowings seen in the Hudson River's Roundout (1867), Stuyvesant (1868) and Coxsackie (1868) Lighthouses. Granite for the 2 1/2-story house and 40-foot tall tower came from quarries in Fall River, Massachusetts. A 65-foot walkway encircles the dwelling.

When active, Cedar Island's lantern held the 1839 tower's sixth-order classical optic 44 feet above the water.

OWNER. Because of high maintenance costs, the light was discontinued in 1934, declared to be surplus government property. In 1937 it was sold to lawyer Phelan Beale for $2,000. The new owner's plan to convert the structure into a hunting lodge for his nearby game preserve did not materialize. In 1943, after Mr. Beale's demise, his widow, Edith, an aunt of Jacqueline Onassis, sold the lighthouse to Isabel (Isabelle) Bradley, who converted the lighthouse into a vacation "cottage." Prior to that resale, 1938's devastating September hurricane created the present sand-filled connection between the island and the mainland. Suffolk County bought the property in 1967. It is managed by the Department of Parks.

PRESERVATION. Not listed in the National Register of Historic Places.   [1]

Seven years after the county acquired the lighthouse, the abandoned structure was gutted by fire. Although the county replaced the roof and sealed the windows with brick while leaving the charred interior untouched, nothing has been done to preserve this historic place. Over the years the subject of lighthouse restoration has been bandied about from one group to another with no results.

In February 1993, Suffolk County's Department of Parks, Recreation and Conservation stated that the "...county has been unable to restore it due to lack of fund [s] for historic projects. Other efforts, combing the county with museums and private enterprise to begin restoration have been unsuccessful."

Some concerned Long Islanders have started the the Cedar Island Lighthouse Committee of the Long Island Chapter of the U.S. Lighthouse Society and hope to launch a new, more fruitful preservation effort.

The stated goals of the group are:

To assess and document the current condition of the Cedar Island lighthouse; to identify stabilization and preservation priorities; to research the history of this light as fully as possible; to document every detail of this light's past and present; to have the light placed on the National Register of Historic Places; to promote the awareness of the past, present and possible futures of the Cedar Island light station; to seek out others who may be interested in helping to find a way to save the lighthouse; to provide a "support group" for the frustrated fans of this wonderful structure; and to establish effective, working lines of communication between everyone involved.

The group is looking for donations, information and volunteers.

- Cedar Island Lighthouse Committee of the Long Island Chapter of the U.S. Lighthouse Society

c/o Long Island Chapter, USLHS

P.O. Box 21

Greenport, NY 11944

Website: http://www.longislandlighthouses.com/FOCIL/

TO THE SHELTER ISLAND FERRY. Follow NY 114 through Sag Harbor to North Haven.

GARDINERS ISLAND LIGHTHOUSE (destroyed).

Gardiners Island lies in Gardiners Bay south of Plum Island and northeast of Long Island's Cedar Point. Originally the light station was connected to Gardiners Island by a long narrow spit of sandy beach. Today the old station's ruins rest on a rocky shoal.

The light station was not at all like other Long Island lighthouses. As a matter of fact, it had its own design personality. The brick dwelling was a square 1 1/2-story structure, whose water cisterns and the shed-sized bathroom were outdoors. The cylindrical brick tower was capped with the usual cast-iron lantern; but, because of its small interior diameter, the sixth-order Fresnel optic had to be reached via an outside spiraling wooden staircase and ladder. Plagued by the constant erosion of the sand beach and the encroaching sea, the aid was discontinued in 1894 and its keeper removed. Since then the sea has claimed the station.

---

1. That fire, by the way, uncovered information about a former keeper who wore a peg leg. During the many years he served the station, he would go about the countryside visiting widows' stable sales to buy wooden legs. No one thought much about his purchases until fire inspectors found a cache of partially burned wooden legs in the lighthouse attic. Some say that the old keeper's stockpiling was because he feared he might not have a leg to stand on, so to speak.

LONG BEACH BAR

NORTH ON NY 114 OR EAST ON NY 25. The Long Beach Bar Lighthouse is located in Gardiners Bay east of Greenport and northeast of Shelter Island. It can be seen with binoculars from three locales:
- Shelter Island via NY 114.
- NY 25 along Orient Harbor's shoreline.
- The village of Orient off NY 25.

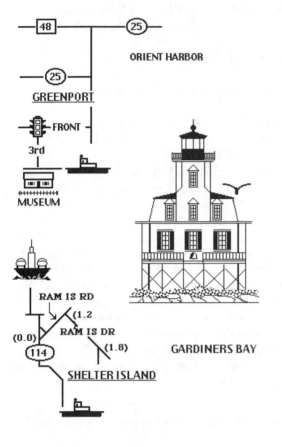

SHELTER ISLAND FERRY SCHEDULE.

North Haven to Shelter Island. Crossing time is three minutes. Continuous daily service every 20 minutes 6:00 am to 11:45 pm.

Shelter Island to Greenport. Crossing time is 10 minutes. Continuous daily service 5:40 am to midnight.

Greenport to Shelter Island.
Continuous daily service 6 to 11:45.

FARES. One way and same day round trip for vehicle/ driver + passengers. Under 8 free.
North Ferry Co. Inc.
Phone (631) 749-0139.
Website: http://www.pagelinx.com/sinferry/index.htm

While on the island take a few minutes to drive out on Ram Island Road and Ram Island Drive for a view of the lighthouse. The NY 114 & Ram Island Road triangular intersection is about 1.2 miles north of the North Haven ferry's dock and 0.6 mile south of the Greenport ferry's landing.

EAST END SEAPORT MUSEUM. This comprehensive and well organized nautical museum is located in the old Long Island Railroad station on the waterfront at the foot of 3rd Street in the Village of Greenport. The facility's centerpiece is Little Gull Island's nine-foot tall second-order Fresnel lens. There is a chart showing all of eastern Long Island's lighthouses with button-controlled interactive backlight photographs.

Other featured subjects include an exhibiting history of the famous American Cup J-Boat racers, a special depiction about Tall Ships, yacht racing trophies, a model marine railway and a "Women in the Maritime" exhibit.

OPEN.
Late May to Labor Day, daily 10 to 5.
Rest of May / rest of September and October, weekends only 10 to 5.
ADMISSION FEES. Discounts for members and children.
- East End Seaport Museum and Marine Foundation, PO Box 624 (One Bootleg Alley), Greenport, NY 11944.
Phone (631) 477-2121.
Website: http://www.eastendlighthouses.org/
Email: lighthouse@peconic.net

VISITING THE LIGHTHOUSE. Visits to the lighthouse are restricted not only because of its difficult access, but also the need to keep unauthorized people off the unattended federally-sanctioned aid. Arrangements can be made for groups, who have their own casualty insurance, to visit the lighthouse. An overnight stay will cost a whopping $1,000 for two. That "donation" provides membership in the foundation, round trip transportation, a catered dinner with wine and breakfast the following morning.

151

EAST ON NY 25. Where NY 25 (Main Road) crosses a causeway as it hugs the shore along Orient Harbor, there is (on the right) a large upright granite stone with a bronze plaque. The monument honors those who made the construction of the lighthouse possible. The lighthouse can be seen from this vantage point.

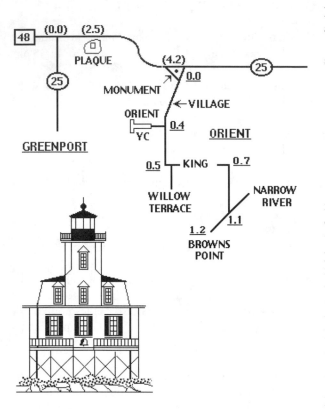

From the roadside plaque motor east on NY 25 past the East Marion-Orient Park (on the left) to a monument at the triangular entrance to the Town of Orient's Village Road.

There are three places from which the lighthouse can be seen:

- At the end of Orient Yacht Club's pier.
- From the high ground on Willow Terrace Lane.
- From the terminus of Narrow River Road.

LONG BEACH BAR LIGHTHOUSE (BUG LIGHT).
CHARACTERISTIC: Flashing white 4s
HAW: 63' **RANGE**: 8 nm

This aid was erected in 1870 on a screw pile platform, much like the utilitarian styled lighthouses built in the sounds of North Carolina, throughout the Chesapeake Bay and in Delaware Bay. But there the similarity ceases, because atop this platform was a handsome two-story wood frame keeper's dwelling surmounted by a four-sided tower with beveled edges. The 60-foot structure's design followed that of the Second Empire style with its mansard roof, protruding roof windows and their treatments. Unfortunately the structural design of the spindle-legged platform was not the wisest of decisions, because during almost every winter the lighthouse was damaged when flood tides would heap ice against the pilings. In 1924 the station's superstructure was placed on a concrete foundation and further protected by a skirt of riprap.

The manned beacon remained active until 1945. The property was sold to Orient Point's Historical Society in 1955 and burned to its foundation on July 4, 1963.

REPLICATION.[1] The first step in rebuilding the lighthouse was to place an additional 60 tons of riprap around the deteriorated and cracked foundation. This was followed by the pouring of a major bond beam (reinforced with iron construction bars) to insure adequate support for the lighthouse. The placement of the concrete was solved by loading a concrete pump and cement mixer trucks onto the Shelter Island ferry and transporting them next to the construction site. The concrete was then pumped during high tide into forms in a matter of hours.

A fundraising campaign was started in January 1990 and, by July 4, 1990, $140,000 was available to begin the building process at the Greenport Yacht and Shipbuilding Company. The replication was based on original archival drawings, calling for the lighthouse to be a 2 1/2-story Victorian structure with side decks 34 feet on each side. The installed light was to be 63 feet above the water and visible for 12 to 14 nautical miles.

By September 2, 1990, the lighthouse was basically finished and ready for its relocation to the readied foundation. The completed lighthouse was loaded aboard a marine railway and with much fanfare moved down the loading dock, much like the launching of a ship. At the dock, the superstructure was taken apart in three sections and loaded aboard barges.

---

1. Courtesy of Merlon E. Wiggin, PhD., M.E., founder and chairman of the East End Seaport and Marine Foundation.

LONG BEACH BAR

On September 5, 1990, only 60 days after the start of the construction project, the loaded barges were towed to the site, where a large crane lifted the first story onto the foundation. Following that transfer, the second story and its mansard roof were moved, followed by the tower with its service gallery, lantern and modern beacon. The erection of the structure was completed and its modern beacon established as a private aid only hours on the day after it left Greenport in sections.

According to Dr. Wiggin there is an East Ender story about a sport fisherman from Connecticut who sailed by the old lighthouse's empty foundation on construction day. When he returned later that same afternoon the fisherman had doubts regarding his vision and sanity upon seeing the completed lighthouse.

In 1993, thanks to community support, along with that of commercial fishermen who depend upon the light, the Coast Guard reestablished the beacon as a federal aid to navigation. Under the certification agreement the Foundation is responsible for the maintenance of the structure and the approaches to it; the Coast Guard maintains the optic.

And after all that good work, in July 1991 two shotgun blasts peppered the house and broke or damaged siding and two windows. That act of vandalism required another $2,000 to repair the windows and siding.

PRESERVATION. "Bug Light" took some nasty bashings during 1996. Three hurricanes and two severe Nor'easters clip the little station. Since then Bug's volunteers have replaced the battered entrance door, security alarm and handrails and sealed the exterior walls against water seepage. Critical repairs to the washed out concrete foundation were completed in 1998. Contributions are needed to meet repair and routine maintenance expenses.

In 2000 the East End Seaport & Marine Foundation is planning a celebration of the Long Beach Bar Lighthouse's 10th birthday. Call for more information (see page 151 for contact information).

LIGHTHOUSE SIGHTSEEING CRUISE. Each year on the first Saturday in June, the East End Seaport and Marine Foundation sponsors a lighthouse cruise of Long Island Sound. Departure is from the Museum Dock at 9 AM. Call the museum for more information (see page 151 for contact information).

The motor vessel attempts to get as close to shore (no landings) as possible for the best views of and optimum spots for photographing the lighthouses. There is usually a noontime anchoring stop with lunch and beverages provided. A guest lecturer is usually aboard to comment on lighthouse history and architecture of these lighthouses:

- Cedar Point, Gardiners Island (ruins), Little Gull Island, Long Beach Bar, North Dumpling, Orient Point, Plum Island, Race Rock. Exact itinerary may vary.

This is a fabulous opportunity to see the Long Island Sound lighthouses up close. To insure getting aboard, place your reservations with the Foundation early in the year.

FARES. Discount for members.

- East End Seaport Museum and Marine Foundation, PO Box 624 (One Bootleg Alley), Greenport, NY 11944.
Phone (631) 477-2121. Fax (631) 477-0198.
Website: http://www.eastendlighthouses.org/
Email: lighthouse@peconic.net

ORIENT POINT
PLUM ISLAND - LITTLE GULL ISLAND

EAST ON NY 25. At the end of NY 25 (Main and Old Roads) turn right and drive to the entrance of an unpaved parking area and turn left. The ferry loading lanes are straight ahead. Walk out onto the stony beach or out onto the ferry terminal's loading apron. The Orient Point Lighthouse is offshore towards the east. Plum Island can be seen farther out to the left of Orient Point.

For another binocular sighting of Plum Island return to NY 25 and a short distance from the ferry terminal entrance turn right into Lands End Road. For a less zig-zag course follow Lands End right, left and left again to a "Dead End" sign. Turn right and drive to the water's edge. Plum Island is located off to the east northeast about 1.5 miles off Orient Point on the east side of Plum Gut.

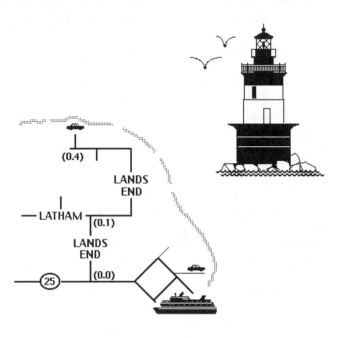

ORIENT POINT LIGHTHOUSE (COFFEE POT).

CHARACTERISTIC: Flashing white 5s
HAW: 64' **RANGE**: 17 nm

The Orient Point Lighthouse is located at the end of Oyster Pond Reef, a rocky outcropping that juts out into Plum Gut.

The high construction and maintenance cost for the architecturally fascinating lighthouses of Long Island, Fishers Island and Block Island Sounds, resulted in the emergence of the no-frills, cast-iron light-house.

Completed and lighted on November 10, 1899, this circular, conical tower was constructed of overlapping and bolted prefabricated boiler plates. The conical tower stands on a circular pier, a cast-iron caisson foundation formed by cast-iron plates filled with concrete. The pier, which sits on the rocky reef, has a 25-foot diameter and is 32 feet tall.

Orient Point's brick-lined superstructure is 24 feet tall with a 21-foot diameter base, tapering to 18 feet at the top. The 45-foot tall lighthouse has six interior decks.

A few years after its completion, rust holes and cracks in the foundation's plates were patched with more plating, and the resulting weight imbalance has caused the tower to tilt about five degrees out of plumb.

The light was automated in 1954. The lantern's fifth-order Fresnel lens (1899) was retired in 1988 when the present modern optic was installed. The aid is controlled from New London.

OWNER. U.S. Coast Guard.

PRESERVATION. Not listed in the National Register of Historic Places.

In 1970 the Coast Guard announced that Orient Point was to be hauled off to the scrap heap. Mariners and other Long Islanders objected and launched a campaign to save Old Coffee Pot. As a result of that outcry, the Coast Guard stayed Orient Point's dismantling in 1973, after determining that despite the tower's list, the lighthouse was worth saving. The Coast Guard, after sandblasting Orient Point's rusted exterior, applied an undercoating and an epoxy finish.

In 1988, with the lighthouse again in need of a paint job, the Coast Guard assigned a 24-man cutter crew the task of sandblasting and repainting the tower's exterior. At the same time, certain repairs were made to better secure the lighthouse from intruders and the effects of weather.

A Coast Guard renovation in 2000 included rebuilding the destroyed boat ramp, removal of the emergency generator, removal of fuel oil, cleaning of the cisterns and modernization/solarization of the Aids to Navigation equipment.

In 1999, the 100th anniversary of this lighthouse, Merlon Wiggin wrote and published a booklet on its history. You can write to him at PO Box 672, Greenport, NY, 11944.

CROSS SOUND FERRY. This ferry offers both an auto/passenger and a high speed (hydrofoil) passenger service between Orient Point and New London, Connecticut. The location the Ferry Street dock is shown in the map on page 192 in the NEW LONDON HARBOR chapter.

- Orient Point (75 yards), Plum Island (one mile), Little Gull Island (1.5 miles), New London Ledge (1.5 miles) and New London Harbor (200 yards).

AUTO-PASSENGER SCHEDULE. All year. Schedule seasonally adjusted. Up to 15 daily sailings (usually on the hour) from both ports. Crossing time 80 minutes.

FARES. Vehicle/driver + passengers. Discount for children under 12, under 2 free. Reservations required. Prepaid vehicle/driver reservation deposit required and credited to total ticket charge. Credit cards accepted. Drivers must pick up boarding tickets no less than 30 minutes before sailngs. Space permitting, those without reservations board on a first come, first served basis.

HIGH SPEED SCHEDULE. All year service. Schedule seasonally adjusted; call or check website for the current schedule. Usually 4-6 sailings daily. Crossing time 40 minutes.

FARES. One way and round trip. Discount for children under 12; under 2 free.

- Cross Sound Ferry, PO Box 33 (2 Ferry Street), New London, CT 06320.

Phone: 24-Hour automated information line: From LI: (631) 323-2525; From CT: (860) 443-5281. Auto reservations and general information (860) 443-5281.

Website: http://www.longislandferry.com/

PLUM ISLAND LIGHTHOUSE (PLUM GUT).

Plum Island's first aid was a 30-foot tall rough stone tower completed in 1827 for $4,000. After deciding that the old tower's structural faults were too severe to remedy and after having received congressional appropriations in 1867 and 1869, the Lighthouse Board built the present granite dwelling with its integrated tower. The overall height of the house and tower is 55 feet.

The first light was established in 1827 using a revolving Lewis-designed device with 10 lamps each backed by a 13-inch reflector. That optic was replaced in 1856 by a fourth-order Fresnel lens manufactured by the Parisian firm of Barrier, Bernard and Turrene. The second light was established in 1870, using the 1856 Fresnel lens.

The original lens was replaced with another fourth-order Fresnel manufactured in 1897. It is the latter lens that is on display, along with its operating clockwork mechanism, in the East End Seaport and Marine Museum in Greenport, NY.

In 1978 the Coast Guard, having decided that it could not afford to spend any more money on maintaining the lighthouse, closed it down. Its replacement is a lighted aid on a 14-foot tall brick shed. Although the Coast Guard announced in 1990 its intention to reestablish the Plum Island beacon the following year, the light has not been moved from the brick building.

During World War II, Plum Island's Fort Terry, a coast artillery post built in the 1890's, was used as a training base for U.S. Army recruits until its closure in 1956. Two years earlier the island had been transferred to the U.S. Department of Agriculture and is now the site of the Plum Island Animal Disease Center, a restricted research laboratory and experimental station.

OWNER. U.S. Department of Agriculture.

PRESERVATION. Not listed in the National Register of Historic Places.

The lighthouse is threatened by neglect and erosion of the bluff upon which it stands, and its future is uncertain.

The Long Island Chapter of the US Lighthouse Society has begun a restoration effort. Their goal is to have the lighthouse, related artifacts, and surrounding property preserved in accordance with the National Historic Preservation Act.

The stabilization of the bluff is a main priority. The Chapter has procured a free source of rocks for bluff stabilization, saving the public an estimated $500,000. In response to pressure from the public, the USDA has nominated the lighthouse for the National Register of Historic Places. The lighthouse's history is being researched, and the support of lighthouse lovers everywhere is being sought.

The East End Seaport and Marine Foundation has also ben involved in the effort to restore this lighthouse. Their annual regional lighthouse cruise (page 153) also contributes to the restoration kitty. Call the East End Seaport Marine Foundation at (631) 477-2121 or email them at lighthouse@peconic.net.

- Long Island Chapter of the U.S. Lighthouse Society, PO Box 21, Greenport, NY 11944.

Phone: (631) 477-4121 / (631) 645-5230

Website: http://www.longislandlighthouses.com/uslhs/saveplumisland.htm

Email: LILighthouses@aol.com

LITTLE GULL ISLAND

LITTLE GULL ISLAND LIGHTHOUSE.
CHARACTERISTIC: Group flashing white 15s
HAW: 91' **RANGE**: 18 nm

About seven miles northeast of Orient Point is Little Gull Island Lighthouse, a small outcropping located between Long Island Sound to the west and Block Island Sound to the east. Between the two bodies of water is The Race, a channel with swift tidal currents and challenging rip tides (surface water flowing away from the shore) and eddies (caused by wind blowing against the current). The Race Rock Lighthouse is located about 3.5 miles to the northeast off the west end of Fisher's Island.

Little Gull Island's first beacon was placed atop a 53-foot tower built of coursed freestone in 1805. Its light was established the following year. The station, including a wood framed keeper's house, was protected by an 11-foot high (300 feet in diameter) circular stone perimeter wall that exists today. The aid's first optic was a whale oil-fed multi-lamp/reflector device that did not have the brightness to fulfill its warning responsibilities. It was removed by the British in 1813, during the War of 1812, and replaced after the war. In 1837 the Lighthouse Service, in one of its many similar efforts to remedy Winslow Lewis' "40 watt" apparatuses, installed another two-tiered optic that had more lamps and larger reflectors. This arrangement together with the relatively low 66-foot high focal plane also proved inadequate.

The Lighthouse Board decided in 1867 to erect the present 81-foot tall gray granite lighthouse. It has a 19-foot diameter granite base, closing to 12 feet at the top. Lined with brick, its walls are five feet thick at ground level. When finished in 1869, the light station consisted of the tower attached to a three-story granite and wooden keeper's house, whose mansard roof and arched window pediments were architecturally of the Second Empire genre.

This lighthouse has had two fixed Fresnel lenses, a third-order installed in 1858 and a second-order introduced in 1869. Over the years their illuminants have been changed from whale oil to lard oil (1883) to kerosene (1885) to incandescent kerosene oil vapor (1907). The Fresnel optic was electrified in 1939 and automated in 1978. The second-order lens was removed in 1995.

Storms and a fire greatly altered the physical appearance of Little Gull Island's light station. That terrible hurricane of September 1938 swept many of the outbuildings into the sound.

In April 1944, a paint locker fire got out of hand and spread through the keeper's house and up the tower into the lantern. Although the valuable lens was saved and the tower refurbished, the keeper's residence was dismantled, leaving only its first floor to be turned into an equipment building. After the light was automated in May 1978, the Coast Guard tore down all structures except the tower and the one-story building.

OWNER. U.S. Coast Guard.
PRESERVATION. Eligible for listing in the National Register of Historic Places.

HORTON POINT

WEST ON NY CR 48. From Orient Point take NY 25 and NY CR 48 to Southold. At the eastern outskirts of Southold and just past Hashamomuck Beach, bear right into Sound View Avenue. The turn is marked with a "Horton Point Lighthouse Nautical Museum" sign. Continue on Sound View past another directional sign and turn right (sign) at Lighthouse Road.

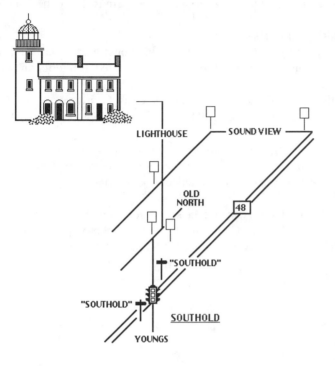

EAST ON NY CR 48. From Setauket follow NY 25A and NY 25 to CR 48 (North Road). In Southold at a "Southold" sign and traffic signal turn left into Youngs Avenue. Then:

    -> Right at Old North Road,

    -> Left at Lighthouse Road to the station property (park).

OPEN. All year, daily 7 to 10.

FREE ADMISSION AND PARKING.

LIGHTHOUSE AND NAUTICAL MUSEUM. This three-room museum on the first floor of the keeper's dwelling features all facets of Eastern Long Island's sea heritage. Early artifacts include work benches, furniture, wrought iron tools, utensils and log books used by the families of former keepers. There are also ship's logs, whaling tools, models, scrimshaw and family souvenirs brought home by ship captains from distant lands.

The Admiral Bauman Room in the finished basement displays the building's early masonry and water cisterns. The room is also used for video programs conducted for children and special groups.

OPEN. Memorial Day to Columbus Day, weekends 11:30 to 4.

FREE ADMISSION. A suggested nominal adult donation for access to the museum and tower helps defray costs of the lighthouse's restoration and upkeep. Children 12 and under free.

- Southold Historical Society, PO Box 1 (54325 Main Road), Southold, NY 11971.

Phone: (631) 765-5500.

Website: http://www.longislandlighthouses.com/hortonpoint/

Email: epb_cjb@yahoo.com

HORTON POINT LIGHTHOUSE.

CHARACTERISTIC: Flashing green 10s

HAW: 103' **RANGE:** 14 nm

In February 1756, George Washington, then 25 years old, traveled by horseback from Virginia to Boston. Heeding the advice of a Dr. Alexander Hamilton of Baltimore, Mr. Washington rode the length of Long Island to Greenport to embark on a boat bound for Boston. In Southold he became acquainted with a future Revolutionary patriot, Ezra L'Hommedieu. Both gentlemen agreed that both Horton Point and Montauk Point possessed the high elevation required for the establishment of effective navigation beacons. It was Mr. L'Hommedieu, who as the representative of the Chamber of Commerce, chose in 1792, Turtle Hill as the site of the Montauk Point Lighthouse.

Although the Horton Point Lighthouse was commissioned to be built by President Washington in 1790, the acreage needed for the light station was not made available until eight acres were offered to the Federal Government in 1855 for $550.

The light station, completed in 1857 for $7,500, consisted of the 55-foot tall square tower and a detached keeper's residence. Both are constructed of New England granite and cut stone and locally acquired brick, timbers and lumber. The dormitory over the connecting annex between the tower and house was added later, as was the oil house.

Horton Point's original optic was a third-order Fresnel lens and a single whale oil-fed lamp. It showed a fixed white light. Horton Point was first established as a federal aid to navigation on October 4, 1857.

In 1907 the lens was powered by an incandescent oil vapor lamp. In June 1932, Horton Point's warning responsibility was transferred to an airport-type optic placed atop a cliffside skeletal steel tower. The Fresnel lens was removed to storage. The presently active modern optic was installed in 1990.

OWNER. Purchased by the Southold Parks District in 1937 for $1.00. Managed cooperatively by the Southold Parks District and the Southold Historical Society.

PRESERVATION. Listed (1994) in the National Register of Historic Places.

Between 1941 and 1950 the light was transferred to a nearby steel tower, while the lighthouse was used as an observation post by Army, Coast Guard and Civil Defense contingents. During the 1960s vandals wrecked its interior and there were efforts by some Southolders to raze the lighthouse.

Since early 1990, the Southold Historical Society, the Southold Parks District and the Coast Guard have cleaned and repainted the light tower, installed new lantern glass, made electrical repairs, developed a new shop area, opened a hallway and built a new stairway to the restored basement.

On June 9, 1990, after the skeletal tower was removed, the lighthouse was recommissioned and relighted.

In 1993 a new service gallery and ladder to the outside of the watchroom and lantern were fabricated and installed. The dwelling's front porch was also replaced. In 1995 the watchroom door to the ladder was restored.

PORT JEFFERSON - BRIDGEPORT FERRY. Stratford Shoal can only be seen distantly with the use of binoculars. The ferry passes close to Tongue Point Lighthouse in Bridgeport, Connecticut (excellent photo opportunity), and provides a frontal view of the Old Field Point Lighthouse. For ferry information see the STRAFORD SHOAL chapter.

OLD FIELD POINT

Unfortunately, the grounds at Old Field Point Lighthouse are not presently open to the public, and parking in the area by outsiders is definitely frowned upon. Hopefully the lighthouse will be open to the public in the future.

For now the best way to see the lighthouse is from the water. The Bridgeport-Port Jefferson ferry (see page 180) offers a fairly distant frontal view.

OLD FIELD POINT LIGHTHOUSE.

Old Field Point's first lighthouse was completed in 1823 after Congress came up with $4,500 to purchase the land and to construct a light station. It consisted of a 30-foot stone and roughcast (plastered) tower and a separate 1 1/2-story stone keeper's dwelling. This earlier keeper's dwelling can be seen on the east side of the newer lighthouse. Established in 1824, the Lewis multi-lamp optic (nine lamps and 13.3-inch reflectors) at 67.5 feet above the water displayed a fixed white beam that could be seen for 13 nautical miles.

The second lighthouse, the existing two-story granite 74-foot tall structure, was completed in 1868. Its walls are two feet thick. The wooden square tower with beveled corners is 28 feet tall. Old Field Point's dwelling-cum-tower design closely resembles the Victorian-Gothic Revival architectural styling seen in Atlantic Coast lighthouses built in 1867-68. Examples exist on Rhode Island's Block Island North, on Connecticut's Morgan Point, Sheffield Island and Great Captain Islands and on Long Island's Plum Island.

The light was discontinued in 1933 and its 1855 fourth-order Fresnel lens removed to storage.

OWNER. The Village of Old Field since 1935. The 1824 keeper's dwelling now houses the Clerk's Office, and the 1868 lighthouse is the home of the village's Chief Constable. The Coast Guard maintains the light.

PRESERVATION. Not listed in the National Register of Historic Places.

Old Field Point Lighthouse

159

EATONS NECK

A visit to the Eatons Neck Light Station requires the permission of the station commander. In your written request include the desired date and time of your visit.

- Commanding Officer, Coast Guard Station Eatons Neck, Northport, NY 11768.

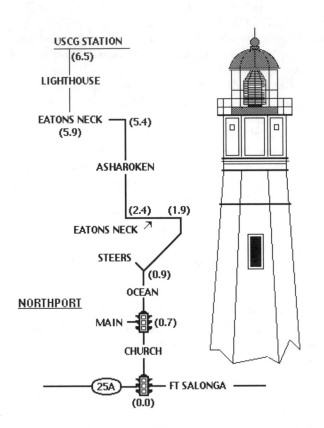

WEST ON NY 25A. Main Street is four miles west of Fort Salonga and just past the intersection of Waterside Road (right) & Vernon Valley Road (left). Not shown on map.

EAST ON NY 25A. Church Street is 1.5 miles east of Centerport and the third street after Reservoir Avenue (left). Lighthouse Road is the station's access road through a private estate. It is heavily posted with no trespassing signs. It would be prudent for you to carry with you the Coast Guard's written permission to visit the station.

EATONS NECK LIGHTHOUSE.
CHARACTERISTIC: Fixed white
HAW: 144' **RANGE**: 18 nm

Eatons Neck is one of America's first lighthouses to be erected during the Colonial Revival design period (1790-1852). John McComb, Jr. built the light station on 10 acres ceded to the new Federal Government in 1798 for $500. When completed in 1799, the 50-foot tall lighthouse cost $9,500.

It is located on a high bluff 144 feet above the sound and warns ships off the rocky shoal that has seen more shipwrecks than any other shoal, rocky outcropping or cape on Long Island's northern shore. For example, during one storm in December 1811, 60 ships and most of their crews were lost on the reef.

In the late 1790s a disastrous shipwreck caused residents to petition Congress to raise the height of the original freestone lighthouse to 73 feet. The tower was lined with brick in 1868. There remains under the dome and above the lens the original copper funnel used to dissipate upwards into the ventilator ball the heat generated by the huge lens. The little vents below the lantern are copper ventilators that allow an intake of a cooling flow of air up and through the lens.

The original lighting apparatus, probably a multi-wicked spider lamp, was replaced in 1838 with another one of Lewis' Argand-styled devices, consisting of 12 lamps with 13-inch reflectors. In order to increase the light's nominal range, different lamp/reflector combinations were tried in 1842 and 1850. In 1858, after the tower had been altered and strengthened (1856-57) to accept a larger lantern, the lighthouse was reequipped with a single whale-oil lamp and a Henri LePaute third-order Fresnel lens. The electrically powered lens continues to generate its light, just as it has for almost 100 years of service.

In 1988 one of Eatons Neck's two foghorns, installed in 1871 and replaced in the 1940s, was found on the beach below the bluff. Apparently it toppled off the eroding cliff from its resting site. The fog horn was to be restored and displayed on station. Not so -- the station does not have it.

OWNER. U.S. Coast Guard.
PRESERVATION. Listed (May 9, 1973) in the National Register of Historic Places.
The only major repair work done on the tower until recently occurred in 1868, when it received a new cast-iron staircase and had its interior walls strengthened with a lining of brick.

EATONS NECK

Eatons Neck was scheduled to be demolished in 1969. It was saved four years later after the Northport Historical Society submitted the historical and survey data required to have Eatons Neck placed in the National Register of Historic Places.

Edges of cliffs are unhealthy spots for lighthouses. Yup, add another lighthouse to the endangered list. In 1996 the Coast Guard announced its concern for the safety of Eatons Neck. Hurricane Bob of October 1992 bit off some 40 feet of the bluff. Since then the edge has crept closer to the lighthouse at a rate of about two feet per year. The erosion has created geologic strains underneath the light tower and cracks have begun appearing in the walls of the nearby brick building and in the concrete retaining walls around the base of lighthouse. The station's complement repaired the cracks in 1997. More renovations were made in 1999 when windows and cornices were repaired and the masonry was patched.

Even the residential area along the bluff is showing signs of underground stress with foundations cracking and cast-iron sewer pipes breaking. The Coast Guard is faced with spending an estimated $10 million to stabilize the bluff and save the station or walk away and let the whole works slide into the sound.

Eatons Neck Lighthouse

HUNTINGTON HARBOR

WEST OR EAST ON NY 25A. The Huntington Lighthouse can be viewed from two places. One is from a dead end turnaround at the end of Southdown Road.

The other spot is located at a roadside clearing near the end of Lloyd Harbor Road. Between the clearing and the water is East Beach, which extends from East Point southwest into Lloyd Harbor. At the tip of East Beach lie the ruins of the harbor's original lighthouse.

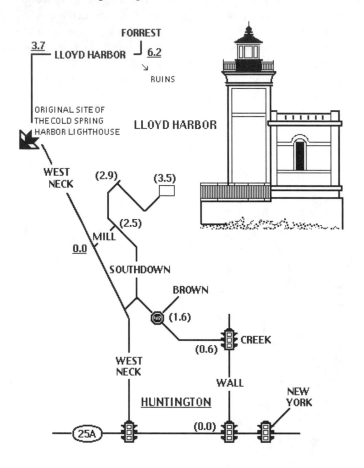

HUNTINGTON HARBOR LIGHTHOUSE
(LLOYD HARBOR; HUNTINGTON ; THE CASTLE).

CHARACTERISTIC: Equal interval white 6s
HAW: 42' **RANGE**: 9 nm

The first harbor lighthouse was a two-story wood framed keeper's house built in 1857 on a brick foundation with a square masonry tower attached to its rear. The lantern was reached via a second story window and ladder.

While the people of Huntington and Lloyd Harbor have developed a rekindled spirit to save the present lighthouse, such a cooperative attitude did not prevail in the 1920s. Then, after the lighthouse had been abandoned (1924), the four-acre station turned over to the state (1926) and then transferred to Huntington (1928), the town of Lloyd Harbor also claimed an interest. At the height of the squabbling, a former lady keeper, who had served for 35 years, resigned her caretaker post because no one could reach a decision on the care and upkeep of the lighthouse. Upon her departure, vandals took over.

After the neglected lighthouse was destroyed by fire on November 12, 1947, the Reverend E. J. Humeston (Huntington's town historian) wrote in the November 20, 1947 issue of the Long Islander "... the fire had put a period to its long sentence to shameful and shameless neglect. Better the pyre than ignominious disuse."

The present Huntington Lighthouse was completed in 1912. It is a one-story dwelling with basement and an attached square tower, whose styling has been described as belonging to the Venetian Renaissance or Islamic temple genres and designed by a Beaux Arts or Art Deco architect. The basement contains a water cistern and two fuel storage rooms. The lighthouse's foundation, a round reinforced concrete caisson, was cast ashore and then barged to the site. Once in place additional concrete was poured around the cistern and room forms to produce a solid base. It is the oldest reinforced concrete lighthouse on the East Coast. Point Arena in California is America's oldest.

The fourth-order Fresnel optic, first lighted on November 15,1857, did not have a sufficient elevation for eastbound ships to pick up its fixed white light. In 1883 the kerosene-fed lens' characteristic was changed to show a fixed red light of greater intensity. By the early 1900s, both the public and politicians were clamoring for a new lighthouse at the entrance to Lloyd Harbor. With the completion of the new light station, the old Lloyd Harbor beacon was discontinued on June 16, 1912.

The new lighthouse's fourth-order optic, transferred from the older tower, was fully automated in 1949. The Fresnel lens was removed in 1967.

OWNER. U.S. Coast Guard. Leased to the Save Huntington's Lighthouse.
PRESERVATION. Listed in the National Register of Historic Places as Lloyd Harbor.

HUNTINGTON HARBOR

Over the years, The Castle has not been able to withstand the effects of salt, erosion, neglect, a leaking roof and vandalism. In 1983, without the funds for its upkeep, the Coast Guard announced plans to abandon the lighthouse and transfer its aid responsibility to a buoy.

Without public support the lighthouse was doomed to demolition or total ruin. Fortunately, a group of citizens, organized as the nonprofit Save Huntington's Lighthouse on October 4, 1985, took on the preservation task. Funds have been and are being collected to restore its structural integrity and exterior appearance and to renovate the interior.

Here is what the organization has accomplished:

1987. Obtained Coast Guard approval to restore the lighthouse by 1998. Arranged for the Coast Guard to remove the collapsed roof and clean the interior of bird droppings. Retained an architect specializing in historic preservation.

1988. Replaced floor timbers, installed a new floor, roof beams and weatherproofed a new roof. Negotiated a 30-year rent-free lease.

1989. Formed a construction committee among contractors, engineers and volunteers, including the Seabees Veterans of Long Island. Seabees repaired the docks and landing ramps and installed gauges over concrete crack to detect and measure any widening of existing cracks. Arranged for the lighthouse to be listed in the National Register of Historic Places. Arranged to have the Coast Guard accept "Huntington Harbor" as the name of the lighthouse.

1990. Called for restoration bids. All bids rejected as submitted for exceeding budget and resources. Windows installed, painted and protected with lexan panels.

1991. Plans for building a dock delayed due to need to obtain various permits from six local, state and federal agencies. Iron railing removed and taken ashore for restoration.

1992. Iron railing, with some new sections fabricated, sanded, primed and painted. Lighthouse roof primed.

1993-94. Finished window and door replacements. Completed railing fabrication. Rewired the interior. Repaired damaged cause by 1991's Hurricane Bob. Completed restoration of concrete base.

1995. Docking facility design completed. Specification written for concrete repair of upper sections of the lighthouse. Purchased lumber for dock.

1996. Dock and ramps repaired.

1997-1999. Work on the exterior has been completed. But, despite the expenditure of over $150,000, the required restoration of the lighthouse's interior has not been completed. And Huntington's benefactors still need at least $100,000 to finish the project.

Contributions welcomed.
- Save Huntington's Lighthouse, Inc., PO Box 2454, Halesite, NY 11743.
Phone (631) 421-1238. Fax (631) 425-1662.
Website: http://www.longislandlighthouses.com/savehuntingtonslighthouse/
Email: PSetchell@aol.com

COLD SPRING HARBOR

COLD SPRING HARBOR LIGHTHOUSE. See the map on page 162.

This wooden light tower was erected offshore west of Lloyd Harbor Village Park in 1890 to mark Plum Point and the shoal off Rocky Point.

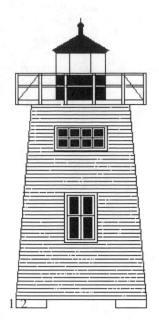

The lighthouse rested on a concrete-filled caisson. Its light was produced by a kerosene-powered fourth-order Fresnel lens. The square pyramidal tower was presumably trashed when its light was deactivated.

In 1990 Elliott Tayman announced that he had found the structure (less lens) standing within an estate on Center Island.

According to Sandra Shanklin, who interviewed the owner, the well preserved lighthouse was purchased and shipped by barge in 1965. The light tower did not reach land, however, until a year later, after the water level rose high enough to refloat the barge off a sandbar.[1]

PRESERVATION. Not listed in the National Register of Historic Places.

1. Shanklin, Sandra, "Cold Spring Harbor ???", *Lighthouse Digest,* November 1995. *Lighthouse Digest* is the best monthly publication for a wide range of lighthouse information. Its editor is Timothy Harrison. Lighthouse Digest, Inc., PO Box 1690, Wells, ME 04090. Website: www.lhdigest.com. Phone (800) 668-7737.

SANDS POINT
EXECUTION ROCKS - STEPPING STONES

Sands Point is the headland for a wide stretch of exclusive shoreline estates. As such, an uncluttered view of the Sands Point and Execution Rocks Lighthouses is hard to find. In the FIRE ISLAND chapter on page 145 note the opportunity to see all three lighthouses while aboard a lighthouse sightseeing cruise vessel.

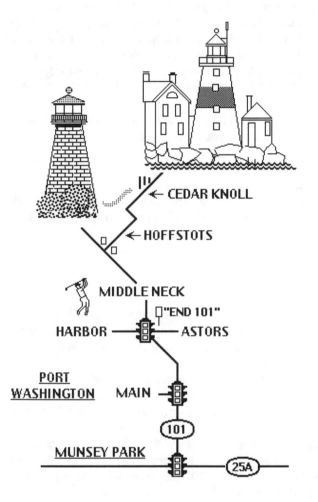

WEST OR EAST ON NY 25A. In Munsey Park turn north into NY 101 (Port Washington Boulevard) (start 0.0 mile). The intersection is msarked with a "Port Washington 2 - Sands Point 3" sign.

Then:

    -> Continue through the Main & Astor's intersection into connecting Middle Neck Road (3.5 miles),

    -> Pass the entrance to the Sands Point Golf Club (4.8 miles),

    -> Right (marked by white brick walls) at Hoffstots Lane (5.9 miles),

    -> Follow Hoffstots into Cedar Knoll Drive.

Please do not park on Hoffstots or on Cedar Knoll. If you do, you could be cited for illegal parking. Instead, park somewhere off Middle Neck Road and walk the 0.25 mile on Hoffstots and along Cedar Knoll's planted windbreak to a three-post opening to the beach. Step through the opening and look to the northwest for a view of that portion of the Sands Point tower that appears above the tree line. Execution Rocks, easily identifiable with its mid-sectional brown band, lies about one-half mile offshore.

SANDS POINT LIGHTHOUSE.

With a little help from its U.S. Senator in 1806, New York received congressional approval and a $6,000 appropriation for a lighthouse on Sands Point. In July 1808, the State purchased the land for $514 and ceded it to the U.S. Government.

With another $9,400 from Congress the construction project was completed. Noah Mason, a Revolutionary War hero from New London, Connecticut, became the aid's first keeper.

The coursed freestone (brownstone) tower is octagonal and conical in shape and is 40 feet tall. During the 1868-69 period, the tower's exterior walls were repaired and cast-iron window frames and a cast-iron access stairway installed. At the same time a new Colonial brick keeper's dwelling was built, along with a connecting passageway to the tower.

The Sands Point 65-foot tall lighthouse was first equipped with a Winslow Lewis Argand-styled lighting device that had 11 lamps and nine-inch reflectors in two tiers. In 1842 the Lighthouse Service once again tried to increase the brightness of a Lewis beacon by fooling around with an outdated and ineffective optic. At that time the service installed 14-inch reflectors. In 1856, after the Lighthouse Board came into the management scene, it replaced the old optic with a new single-lamp fourth-order classical lens showing a flashing white light.

Meanwhile, the Sands Point beacon steadily lost is effectiveness (briefly discontinued in 1894) and was claimed to be of little use to mariners. On December 15, 1922, Sands Point's warning responsibility was transferred to an unattended skeletal steel tower offshore at the end of the rocky reef that juts out from Sands Point.

OWNERS. In 1917 a wealthy New York socialite bought several acres next to the light station and promptly built a huge, beautiful and costly mansion. In 1922 Mrs. Belmont convinced the Bureau of Lighthouses to inform the keeper that he was not to entertain his friends on summer weekends, so as not to interfere with her galas and outdoor activities. As a result of this interference, Mrs. Belmont was considered by many to have been instrumental in having the 1809 beacon discontinued.

With its inactivation, the light station was placed on the auction block. Although the State of New York attempted to acquire the property for a park, Mrs. Belmont blocked those plans on January 31, 1924 by purchasing the station for $100,000. In 1927 Mrs. B, having tired of the costs of taxes, servants, upkeep and opulent living, sold the mansion and lighthouse to William Randolph Hearst for $400,000. At first the Hearsts lived in the keeper's house and used the mansion for guests. Later his prolonged sojourns in his estate at San Simeon, California, contributed to Mrs. Hearst's departure from Sands Point. The mansion complex and lighthouse were offered for sale but there were no buyers. Finally they surrendered the property to a New York bank to satisfy a $93,000 mortgage.

In 1941, when it could not find a buyer, the bank first stripped and sold off parts of the mansion and then demolished it. The property and lighthouse were finally sold to a realtor who divided the grounds into one-acre lots and turned the property into the present residential enclave.

PRESERVATION. Not listed in the National Register of Historic Places.

Over the years, the light station has been subject to erosion by the sea and damage by gales. Many protective works were built, destroyed and rebuilt in efforts to protect the station. Fortunately the original light tower and keeper's residence have been nicely preserved by its private owners.

EXECUTION ROCKS LIGHTHOUSE.
CHARACTERISTIC: Flashing white 10s
HAW: 62' **RANGE**: 16 nm

Execution Rocks, located less than one mile offshore, is so named, say some historians, because the outcropping was used by the British to execute colonial prisoners by chaining them to rocks at low tide. A more plausible reason for its appellation is the fact that the reef upon which the light stands was a notorious ripper of keels as ships strayed across its rocky shallows.

Beset with delays caused by the inexperience of the contractor, the 42-foot granite tower was finally completed in May 1849 and its beacon established on June 15, 1850. This low profile tower's strength and stability derives from the carefully fitted granite blocks rising from its 26-foot diameter base. Prior to the construction of the attached 2 1/2-story granite house in 1867, keepers and their wives resided in tower.

The tower was rebuilt in 1868. In 1878 the foundation was given added protection with the building of a perimeter rock embankment. In 1918 a fire destroyed or extensively damaged the engine house, oil house, the tower's exterior walls and windows, and the interior of the house. A new concrete oil house was added in 1910. The last major work on the station was in 1920, when the foundation was rebuilt and a stone fog signal house added.

Over the years Execution Rocks has had several lighting devices:
1850. 15-lamp optic with 21-inch reflectors.
1856. Fourth-order Fresnel optic.
1912 Incandescent kerosene lamp.
1979. Fresnel replaced by a FA-251 lens and the watch removed.
1988. DCB-10 lens.

OWNER. U.S. Coast Guard.
PRESERVATION. Eligible for listing in the National Register of Historic Places.

SANDS POINT, EXECUTION ROCKS & STEPPING STONES

WEST ON NY 25A. In Thomaston Middle Neck Road is about 0.1 mile west of Shore Road. There is a large water tower in the northeast quadrant of the intersection. An office building faced with reflective glass is on the southeast corner.

EAST ON NY 25A. About 1.3 miles east of the Belt Parkway in Thomaston bear left into Great Neck Road. If you miss Great Neck, continue east for 0.5 mile to Middle Neck Road.

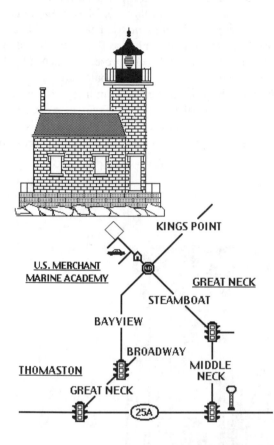

U.S. MERCHANT MARINE ACADEMY. With the gate guard's approval, drive straight ahead to the first stop sign, turn left and then right into a parking lot for visitors located opposite O'Hara Hall. Walk the short distance down to a concrete pier. The lighthouse is located about one mile to the northeast.

OPEN. All year, daily 9 to 4:30. Closed July and national holidays.

FREE ADMISSION.

AMERICAN MERCHANT MARINE MUSEUM. This museum features the Academy's history with model ships, maritime artifacts and paintings. Stepping Stone's original fifth-order Fresnel lens is also displayed.

OPEN. All year.

Tuesdays and Wednesdays 11 to 3; weekends 1 to 4:30.
Closed on national holidays and July.

FREE ADMISSION.

- American Merchant Marine Museum, U.S. Merchant Marine Academy, Kings Point, NY 11024-1699.

Phone (516) 773-5515. Academy (516) 773-5000.
Website: http://www.usmma.edu/museum/

STEPPING STONES LIGHTHOUSE.
CHARACTERISTIC: Occulting green 4s
HAW: 46' **RANGE:** 8 nm

In 1866 Congress appropriated $6,600 to build a lighthouse on Hart Island, about 1.5 miles north of Kings Point. Unable to secure land on the island, the Lighthouse Board decided to build the aid on Stepping Stones Reef. With some $56,000 in construction funds, work on the lighthouse began in 1875. The first task was to build a foundation with randomly placed boulders. The 1 1/2-story, red brick house with its attached tower stands on a 30-foot diameter concrete-filled hat box with carefully laid granite-block retainer walls. The overall height of the lighthouse is 38 feet. The light was established on March 1, 1877. Stepping Stones exhibits an architectural resemblance to the Second Empire styling found in five other Atlantic Coast lighthouses, as well as the Hudson River's Hudson City (1874) Lighthouse, whose construction designs were finally abandoned in favor of the less costly cast-iron light tower.

In 1932 the aid's original fifth-order Fresnel lens (fixed red) was replaced by a brighter incandescent oil vapor-powered fourth-order Fresnel (fixed green). The light was automated in 1967. In 1986 the classical lens was removed when the presently active modern lens was installed.

OWNER. U.S. Coast Guard.
PRESERVATION. Not listed in the National Register of Historic Places.

THROGS NECK (dismantled).

The Throgs Neck light station was located in the Bronx's Fort Schuyler. The fort is passed over while traveling on I-295's Throgs Neck Bridge.

Construction of the first light tower on land that was to become the fort was completed in 1827. The new light station consisted of a three-story wood framed and clapboard tower and a two-story gable-roofed dwelling. Both were demolished when construction of Fort Schuyler began in 1835. Another wooden tower was built closer to the southeast seawall and the earlier tower's multi-lamp and reflector Lewis optic was transferred to it. In 1855 the Lighthouse Board purchased and installed a new sixth-order Fresnel lens. By the late 1880s, both the tower and dwelling had been severely weakened by dry rot. The keeper's dwelling was replaced in 1883. In 1890 the station received a new tower, a steel tubular structure almost identical in design to the Coney Island Lighthouse. The 70-foot structure did not set well with military commanders because it stood in the line of fire from the fort's coast artillery. The tower was dismantled in 1905. In its stead, the Lighthouse Board constructed a 35-foot brick tower farther away from the line of artillery fire to the southwest. This tower endured until 1934, when it was replaced with a simple skeleton steel tower. Only the 1883 keeper's dwelling remains on what is now the campus of the New York State Maritime College.

Great Captain Island Lighthouse

CONNECTICUT
GREAT CAPTAIN ISLAND

The Great Captain Lighthouse is located about 1.3 miles off-shore from Greenwich's Field Point. Ferry service to the island is restricted to Greenwich residents, and the lighthouse cannot be seen from the mainland. Some sails of the three-masted schooner *SoundWaters* may pass fairly close to Great Captain Island; see page 171 for details.

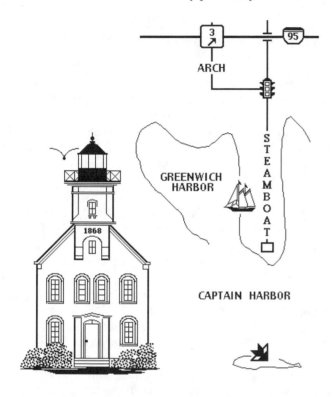

GREAT CAPTAIN ISLAND LIGHTHOUSE.

Congress in 1829 appropriated the funds to build a lighthouse in Captain Harbor. Its construction was delayed from indecision as to where it was to be built. After the Lighthouse Service had both sites surveyed Great Captain was chosen. Using approximately $3,000 of the available funds, the Lighthouse Service purchased three of the island's 17 acres and built a simple 30-foot tall rough stone lighthouse and a small keeper's dwelling on the island's southeast end. [1]

With the old tower about to topple because of its disintegrating mortar and weakened walls, the present granite house and its integrated tower were completed in 1868. The 51-foot tall lighthouse is a 2 1/2-story structure, whose Victorian styling closely resembles Connecticut's Sheffield Island, New York's Old Field Point and Plum Island and Block Island's North Lighthouses.

The first light tower was outfitted with a Winslow Lewis lamp/reflector lighting device. In 1858 it received a whale oil-powered fourth-order Fresnel lens. That lens was transferred to the extant lighthouse in 1868.

PRESERVATION. Listed in the National Register of Historic Places.

In January 30, 1970 the Coast Guard deactivated and abandoned the lighthouse. For the following three years the structure was rather badly vandalized. The light station became the property of the Town of Greenwich in June 1973 and is now incorporated into the 14 recreational acres the municipality bought in 1966. Greenwich now sponsors a resident caretaker to watch over the island.

In 1998 the Greenwich Chamber of Commerce started a campaign to relight the Great Captain Island Lighthouse, called Let There Be Lights, Inc. The Indian Harbor Yacht Club is helping the Chamber raise $50,000 to renovate the lighthouse. The roof and some windows need replacing; the heating and wiring systems need work and the interior needs painting.

1. During prohibition days Great Captain Island was a favorite spot for bootleggers to dilute smuggled foreign liquors before moving their rebottled goods to mainland. The island also had a series of clubs and a casino. By 1966 most of the island, then owned by a private company, had been transformed into a recreation area for its employees.

STAMFORD HARBOR

NORTH OR SOUTH ON I-9. In Stamford take I-95's Exit 8 to Elm Street. Then:
-> Right at Jefferson Street,
-> Left at Magee Avenue to its end at the Harbor & Shippan intersection,
-> Straight ahead on Shippan,
-> Right at Ocean Drive (0.4 mile from Wallace Street),
-> Right at Fairview Avenue,
-> Drive the one block to a dead end. Parking is permitted along Fairview but not at the dead end's turnaround.

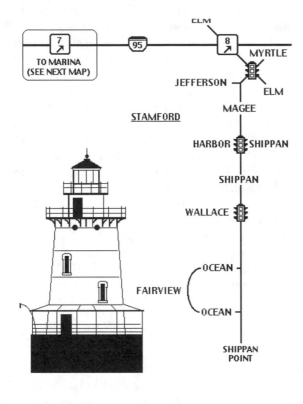

Step through the seawall's opening and walk out onto the beach. The lighthouse stands at the entrance to Stamford Harbor seaward of the far right West Breakwater.

The lighthouse can also be seen from Shippan Point off to the west (right). The Sheffield Island Lighthouse is visible due east. The view is a fairly distant one, so bring your binoculars.

STAMFORD HARBOR LIGHTHOUSE (STAMFORD HARBOR LEDGE OBSTRUCTION; CHATHAM ROCK).
CHARACTERISTIC: Flashing white 4s
HAW: 80'

Although Forked Rock (just west of Shippan Point) was the popular choice for a beacon, in 1881 Congress approved the construction of a lighthouse on Chatham Rock, an outcropping on the southwest end of Harbor Ledge on the west side of the harbor's entrance.

The tower's foundation was formed with rocks and concrete. The red 28-foot tall pier is a cylindrical, cast-iron caisson filled with concrete. As in most piers of this construction design, rooms were built into the pier to function as storage bins for water and fuel. The conical cast-iron tower has five decks with the lantern's elevation some 50 feet above the pier. The lighthouse is 60 feet tall.

The light was established in 1882, using a kerosene-fed fourth-order Fresnel lens.

In August 1931, Keeper Raymond Bliven, a Rhode Island native, was missing for three days before it was noticed that the lighthouse had gone dark. The keeper's body was discovered floating a short distance away, and his boat was also recovered. It was generally believed that the keeper's boat had overturned, but cuts on his head led some to suspect that he had been pushed from the lighthouse.

In 1953 upon the beacon's deactivation as an official aid to navigation, the optic was changed over to a modern lens.

In 1955 the U.S. Government auctioned off the lighthouse for $1.00 to Thomas F. Quigley, former mayor of Stamford, who hoped his gift to the City of Stamford would result in the tower's refurbishment and preservation. Nothing happened. So in 1964, the government retrieved the lighthouse and three years later sold it to an electric utility company.

The new owner wanted to use the tower as a collection and discharge point for the slurry goop that was to flow from a planned mainland generating plant. Fortunately, some engineer's pipe dream never got off the ground. By 1983 the abandoned lighthouse had been passed from the first to a second and finally to a third utility company. Northeast Utilities finally auctioned it off to a New York banker for $230,000.

At the time of the sale the tower had no heat, no water, no electricity (the light is battery operated) and thick deposits from hundreds of roosting seabirds. Of note is the fact that when it was sold, the only way to visit the lighthouse was to approach it by boat at high tide, hook a line over the 12-foot high landing platform's railing and climb up.

STAMFORD HARBOR

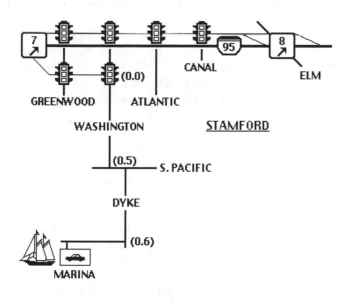

In 1996, the lighthouse, reportedly nicely renovated as a living quarters, was again up for sale -- asking $1.1 million, but will take $860,000. As of early 2000 the lighthouse is still unsold.

OWNER. Privately owned since December 1984.

PRESERVATION. Listed in the National Register of Historic Places.

LONG ISLAND SOUND CRUISES. The public sails of the *SoundWaters*, an 80-foot, steel-hulled, three-masted sharpie, are adventures of ecological discovery with the added possibility of seeing Stamford Harbor Light and possibly one or more of the following: Great Captain Island, Sheffield Island and Greens Ledge. The exact route varies, so there is no guarantee of coming close to the lighthouses.

The schooner's decks are wide and comfortable and can accommodate wheelchair passengers. The sailing experience is not suitable for infants and toddlers.

TO BREWERS YACHT HAVEN MARINA.

If northbound on I-95, take Exit 7's frontage road across Greenwood Avenue to Washington Boulevard and turn right. Then:

-> Left at South Pacific Street,

-> Right at Dyke Lane,

-> Right at the entrance to marina parking. Free parking at the marina.

If southbound on I-95, take Exit 8's frontage road (State Street) across Elm, Canal and Atlantic Streets to Washington Boulevard and turn left. Follow the above directions to the marina.

SCHEDULE. Usually two to three-hour public cruises. For upcoming year's public sails write for the annual calendar. Here is an abbreviated schedule:

June, five sails.

July, three sails.

August to October, two sails each month.

FARES. Reservations required. Prepayment required for public sails. Discounts for children 12 and under and must be accompanied by an adult

- SoundWaters, Brewers Yacht Haven Marina, Washington Boulevard, Stamford, CT 06902.
Phone (203) 323-1978. Fax (203) 967-8306.
Website: http://www.soundwaters.org/

GREENS LEDGE

NORTH ON I-95 TO NORWALK'S CRESCENT BEACH. Take Exit 12 to CT 136 (Tokeneke Road). Then:

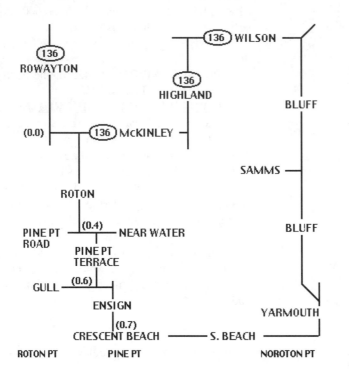

-> East on CT 136 (Tokeneke Road),
-> South on CT 136 (Rowayton Avenue),
-> Left on CT 136 at McKinley Street,
-> Right at Roton Avenue,
-> Leave Roton by bearing left into connecting Pine Point Road,
-> Right at Pine Point Terrace,
-> Left at Gull Road,
-> Right at Ensign Road,
-> Left at Crescent Beach Road and continue into connecting South Beach Drive.

The lighthouse will be seen offshore as you drive along the beach.

SOUTH FROM HOPE DOCK.
Head south on CT 136 (South Main Street and Wilson Avenue). Then:
-> Bear left into Bluff Avenue,
-> Continue south on Bluff, Westmere Avenue and Yarmouth Drive,
-> Left at South Beach Drive.

The lighthouse can also be seen distantly from the ferry from Hope Dock in Norwalk to Sheffield Island (see next page).

GREENS LEDGE LIGHTHOUSE.
CHARACTERISTIC: Alternating white and red 24s
HAW: 62' **RANGES**: White 17; red 14 nm
This lighthouse, located on a rocky reef southwest of Sheffield Island, is another one of those cast-iron structures built in the late 1800s and early 1900s. Its construction and equipment cost $60,000.

The 52-foot tall lighthouse rests on a cast-iron caisson pier. It has an exterior of bolted cast-iron plates and an interior lined with brick. The tower has four interior decks and is surmounted by a gallery-equipped watchroom and lantern.

Its original light characteristic (flashing red), produced by a fifth-order Fresnel lens installed in February 1901, proved to be a poor warning beacon. As a result the lantern received a fourth-order Fresnel lens in May 1902. The light's characteristic was then changed to a combination of fixed white and flashing red. Today the lantern contains a modern rotating optic, installed and automated in 1972.

OWNER. U.S. Coast Guard.
PRESERVATION. Listed in the National Register of Historic Places.
This white (upper half) and brown (lower half) tower leans a bit due to having been clobbered in September 1938 by a tremendously destructive hurricane. In 1971 public concern saved the old iron tower from being dismantled. Today the lighthouse is unmanned and boarded up. The Coast Guard has expressed interest in finding a group or community willing to take responsibility for the structure.

SHEFFIELD ISLAND

NORTH ON I-95 TO HOPE DOCK. Take Exit 14N (South Norwalk/Maritime Aquarium) and follow Fairfield Avenue and Reed Street to West Avenue.

NORTH FROM CRESCENT BEACH. See also the GREENS LEDGE chapter map. Return to CT 130 via Yarmouth Drive, Westmere Avenue and Bluff Avenue. Then:

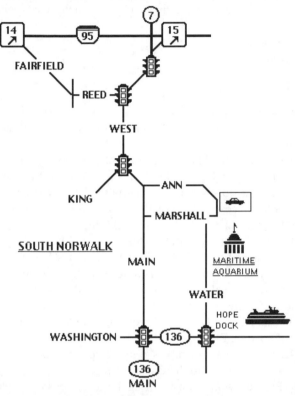

-> Continue north on CT 136 (Wilson Avenue and South Main Street),

-> Right on CT 136 at Washington Street,

-> Left (before bridge) at North Water Street.

Hope Dock is on the northeast corner of Washington and North Water.

SOUTH ON I-95. Take Exit 15S (CT 7 - Norwalk - Danbury - Maritime Aquarium) and bear right at the fork. Then:

-> At the bottom of the ramp turn left at West Avenue and continue south under I-95,

-> At the West - M. L. King - North Main intersection bear left into North Main Street,

-> Left at Ann Street,

-> Continue on Ann to North Water Street and a municipal parking lot, where all-day parking (fee) is available. Parking tickets are validated only by the Maritime Aquarium. Metered parking at Hope Dock is limited to two hours.

VISITING THE LIGHTHOUSE. The Norwalk Seaport Association sponsors narrated excursions to Sheffield Island. Fare includes a round trip cruise on the 44-passenger *Seaport Islander* and a visit to and tour of the lighthouse's four levels and ten rooms. The entire trip takes about two hours, of which one hour is spent on the island. Picnicking permitted.

SCHEDULE.

Full schedule (three trips on weekends, two on weekdays) mid-June to Labor Day. Weekends only May to mid-June and September. Call for the latest schedule.

The *Seaport Islander* is operated by Sound Navigation. For more information:

- Sound Navigation

Phone: (203) 854-4656 or (888) LI SOUND

Website: http://www.soundnavigation.com

Email: soundnav@home.com

FARES. No reservations; passengers accommodated on first come, first served basis. Discounts for seniors and children under 12 and Norwalk Seaport Association members.

- Norwalk Seaport Association, 132 Water Street, South Norwalk, CT 06854.

Phone (203) 838-9444. Reservations (203) 852-6241.

Website: http://www.seaport.org

SHEFFIELD ISLAND LIGHTHOUSE (NORWALK ISLAND; NORWALK; SMITH ISLAND).

In 1804 Captain Robert Sheffield bought the island and before his death sold it to his son-in-law, Gershom Smith, who maintained the island's first lighthouse, a simple wooden structure built by the U.S. Government in 1826. Smith's residence, a 1 1/2-story story granite block house, still stands on the northeast side of the present lighthouse. Upon Smith's death in 1852, his son Theodore bought his 11 brothers' and sisters' shares of the island. Captain Theodore Smith, who had served as acting head of the Lighthouse Board for several years, built the present Sheffield Island Lighthouse in 1868.

Captain Smith's association with the Lighthouse Board no doubt influenced the selection of the lighthouse's architectural design, since it is strikingly similar to those magnificently styled structures on Long Island, Connecticut's Great Captain Island and Morgan Point and Rhode Island's Block Island North.

The lighthouse consists of a 2 1/2-story dwelling and a tower that protrudes from the west gable end and rises to a height of 46 feet. The structure's walls are constructed with rough finished gray, brown and pink granite-like (gneiss) stone. The tower is built with bolted cast-iron plates.

Over the years the lighthouses were fitted with these optics:

1828. 10 lamps each backed with a 14-inch reflector.
1855. Six lamps with 21-inch reflectors.
1857. Fourth-order Fresnel lens.

OWNER. Deeded to the Norwalk Seaport Association on December 30, 1986.

PRESERVATION. Listed (January 19, 1989) in the National Register of Historic Places as Norwalk Island.

For many, many years Sheffield Island was subjected to foolish ventures, failed enterprises, fires, neglect, decay and rampant vandalism. In 1986 the abandoned and neglected lighthouse (1868), the stone keeper's cottage (1826), a wooden cottage (1927) and almost four acres of land became the property of the Norwalk Seaport Association. The cost was $700,000. The U.S. Fish and Wildlife Service manages the remaining 59 acres of the island as the Stewart B. McKinney National Wildlife Refuge.

The Association organized a Sheffield Island Lighthouse Committee to raise funds and plan for the lighthouse's restoration. Through Charter Lighthouse membership fees and donations from local citizens, companies and foundations, the first $235,000 was raised to start the restoration. The State of Connecticut Historical Commission granted $18,000 to restore the keeper's cottage and place the lighthouse on the National Register of Historic Places.

In late May 1992, more than 200 members of the Telephone Pioneers of America (retirees of phone companies) rallied to the cause. Bringing along their own tools, materials and chef, the Pioneers worked on repairing the generator shed, replacing the landscaping, rehabilitating the cottage's kitchen and living quarters, removing debris from along the beach and from inside and around the lighthouse and installing an underground cable between the generator and the cottage. After all that good work a December 1992 storm clobbered the island so badly it has taken thousands of hours and over $100,000 to put the light station back together.

A year later the lighthouse was repaired and again opened to the public. Since then the exterior masonry walls have been sandblasted and the light tower restored. All rooms except the kitchen have been refurbished, and all cast-iron parts painted. The cost for the exterior repairs: $1 million. Next on the restoration agenda is the completion of renovation of the lighthouse's interior.

In 1995 the Association faced financial difficulties with the downsizing corporate market and economic downturn in the state. With a significant deficit, funds were not available to maintain mortgage payments and foreclosure proceedings were started.

In 1997 work was done to slow the erosion near the lighthouse. Gabions were installed and beach grass and roses were planted.

On September 11, 2000 the Norwalk Seaport Association's four-year campaign to retire the $540,000 mortage on the lighthouse culminated in a Mortage Burning Ceremony. Following the ceremony, NSA Executive Director Bill Kissam announced that the Seaport Association had received aprroximately $7,500 in pledges for Phase II of the Capital Campaign, which will support expansion and development of programming on Sheffield Island.

Additional funds are still desperately needed. Persons interested in helping to save the lighthouse can make tax-deductible contributions. Please make checks payable to the "Sheffield Island Lighthouse Capital Campaign" and mail to:
- Norwalk Seaport Association, 132 Water Street, South Norwalk, CT 06854.

PECK LEDGE

HOPE DOCK TO CALF PASTURE PARK. Follow CT 136 (Washington Street -> Van Zandt Street -> Cemetery Boulevard) to Gregory Boulevard. Note the one way travel around the cemetery. Then:

-> Continue south on Gregory through a curve to the left (around a monument) to the Fifth Street & Calf Pasture Beach Road intersection,

-> Right into Calf Pasture Beach and continue to Calf Pasture Park. At the entrance on the left is a large parking area from which the lighthouse (white with brown midsection) can be clearly seen.

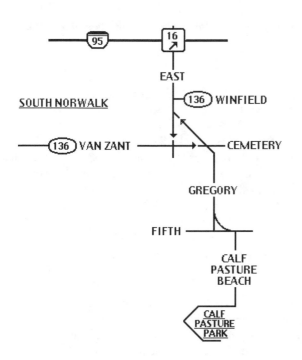

OPEN. All year, daily sunrise to sunset.

PARKING FEE. Memorial Day to Labor Day. Free at other times.

SOUTH FROM I-95. See map.

Peck Ledge Lighthouse can also be seen distantly from the ferry from Norwalk to Sheffield Island. See the previous chapter.

PECK LEDGE LIGHTHOUSE.

CHARACTERISTIC: Flashing white 4s

HAW: 61' **RANGE**: 7 nm

Although Congress approved the construction of this lighthouse in 1901, its completion was delayed until 1906. It is the last lighthouse to be built in Long Island Sound.

Peck Ledge is another one of those generic cast-iron aids built atop a concrete filled cast-iron caisson. The truncated, boiler-plated tower is brick lined and has been assembled in three stages. The three levels contained living space for two keepers and storage areas. The tower is topped with a circular watchroom supporting the lantern. The lantern still has its original curved and diamond shaped storm panes displaying a criss-cross pattern.

The 54-foot tall lighthouse, first equipped with a flashing fourth-order Fresnel lens, was activated on July 10, 1906. Peck Ledge's optics have been changed several times. In 1932, after incandescent oil vapor replaced kerosene as its illuminant, its luminous intensity was rated as 37,000 candlepower. In 1939 the classical lens was removed and replaced by an acetylene-powered aerobeacon, lowering its intensity to 210 candlepower. In 1989 its candlepower was further reduced by the installation of a 375 mm lens. That lamp, by the way, was mounted on top of the lantern's roof. In May 1988 the roof mounted beacon was replaced by a smaller 250 mm lens installed inside the lantern.

OWNER. U.S. Coast Guard.

PRESERVATION. Listed in the National Register of Historic Places.

Unmanned when automated in 1933, the boarded up lighthouse is gradually succumbing to the effects of the weather and vandalism. No organization or group has expressed concern for or interest in saving this historic structure.

PENFIELD REEF

NORTH ON I-95. In Fairfield take I-95's Exit 22 to Round Hill Road and turn right. Follow Round Hill across US 1 (Boston Post Road) into Beach Road. Follow Beach to Fairfield Beach Road and turn right. Then:

-> Follow Fairfield Beach south through the zig-zag Reef Road intersection,

-> A short distance from the intersection on the left there is a narrow lane. It is across the street from College Place. The lane is marked with "Lighthouse Pt." and "Penfield Reef Right Of Way" signs. Walk down the lane to the beach. The lighthouse lies about 1.3 miles off to the southwest.

Parking is not allowed on Fairfield Beach Road near the entrance to the public right-of-way. Parking on Reef Road or other side streets, however, is unrestricted and free.

SOUTH FROM GROVER HILL. Take Fairfield Avenue and Old Post Road or US 1/Boston Post Road to Beach Road. Turn left at Beach and right into Fairfield Beach Road.

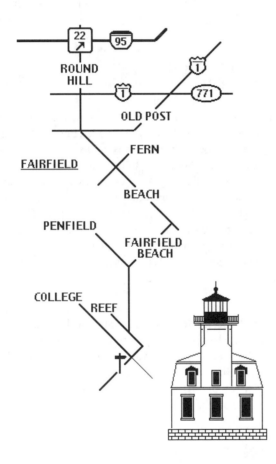

PENFIELD REEF LIGHTHOUSE.
CHARACTERISTIC: Flashing red 6s
HAW: 51' **RANGE**: 18 nm

Penfield Reef is a snakelike promontory with a head of sawtooth rocks. Two hundred years ago the peninsula was once a lush pasture and supported sheep and a dairy herd. Because of this association the rocks are known locally as "cows" or "calves." After the cattle and sheep had stripped away the vegetation and ballast hunters carried away the protective riprap, the peninsula underwent geological changes. First it formed as an island, then a sand bar and finally a reef.

With an appropriation of $55,000, construction of the rock-strewn foundation and the cylindrical granite pier began in March 1871. Two years later both were completed and ready for the lighthouse superstructure.

The pier's center is filled with concrete above the base level of the riprap to allow for the addition of a basement and cisterns. The top of the pier, originally covered with granite slabs, is now surfaced with concrete.

The 35-foot tall lighthouse shows the influence of Second Empire styling with its square plan, quoins, foot-scrolled window surrounds and mansard roof. The square dwelling's first story walls are brick faced with rough granite ashlar with slightly protruding corners (quoins). The base of the structure is outlined in larger granite blocks. The wood framed second story is contained within the mansard roof. The square tower rises from the second deck and at the third level becomes a four-sided structure with beveled corners.

When occupied, the first deck held a parlor, galley and supply room. The second deck contained four bedrooms and the third level was the watchroom. Although the structure's interior lacks any ornamental detailing, it contains a spiraling stairway that begins at the first floor entry and ascends as an oval to the third floor's watchroom.

The reef's first optic was a standard fourth-order Fresnel lens powered by a kerosene lamp. It was placed in operation on January 16, 1874. By 1899 the lantern had a fourth-order Fresnel bullseye lens rotated by a weighted clockwork mechanism manufactured in the Lighthouse Service's Thompkinsville (NY) depot.

The Fresnel optic has been replaced by modern equipment.

PENFIELD REEF

The light marks Penfield Reef which extends into Long Island Sound from Shoal Point. To complicate navigation, this light has often been mistaken for the Stratford Shoal beacon, located midway between Long Island and Connecticut. Only trouble here is that while the Stratford Shoal Lighthouse can be passed on either side, the Penfield Reef Lighthouse is passed only on the Long Island side. This restricted passage and some really violent storms have caused a significant number of shipwrecks.

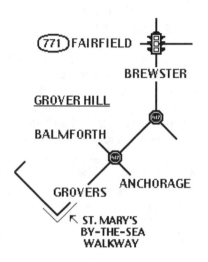

One shipwreck story concerns the lifesaving prowess of the lightkeepers. On one nasty weekend a pleasure boat with 27 passengers and crew aboard plowed into the reef. The keepers worked all night collecting people from the treacherous waters and, by daybreak, all aboard had been brought ashore. To reward them for their heroism the keepers were each handed one dollar! The rescuers refused the generous offer.

A shipwreck also gave the reef the sobriquet "Blue Line Graveyard" when on one stormy night in 1916, a long string of the Blue Line Company's barges heaved up onto the reef.

One of the saddest and best known episodes in the history of Penfield Reef Light occurred on December 22, 1916. The sea was rough when Keeper Frederick A. Jordan left in a dory for the mainland intending to join his family for Christmas. Assistant Keeper Rudolph Iten recorded what happened next in the station's log:

"Keeper left station at 12:20 PM and when about 150 yards NW of the light, his boat capsized, but he managed to cling to the overturned boat. He motioned to me to lower the sailboat, but on account of the heavy seas running from the NE, it was impossible to launch the boat alone. At 1:00 PM the wind died down a bit and shifted to the south."

"I then lowered the boat safely and started off after the keeper who had by this time drifted about one and one half miles to the SW. When about a one half miles from the light, the wind shifted to the SW making a headwind and an outgoing tide which proved too much for me to pull with the heavy boat. I had to give up and returned to the station with the wind now blowing a gale from the WSW. Sent distress signals to several ships but none answered. Lost tract [sic] of the keeper at 3:00 PM. He is probably lost."

The body of Keeper Jordan was soon recovered. In his pocket was a note he had meant to leave for Assistant Keeper Iten instructing him to finish the day's entries in the log. Iten was absolved of any blame for the keeper's death, and in fact became the next keeper at Penfield Reef.

OWNER. U.S. Coast Guard.

PRESERVATION. Listed in the National Register of Historic Places.

In 1969 the Coast Guard raised the hackles of local mariners when it announced that the lighthouse was to be replaced by a skeletal tower. The new light would be automated and, with the removal of its personnel, the old structure was to be demolished. A swell of civic outcry squashed that idea. Several months later the Coast Guard reconsidered and temporarily returned the crew. Best of all, the lighthouse was saved. After the light was automated in December 1971, the Coast Guard withdrew its keepers.

Not much work has been done to preserve this boarded up lighthouse; and as far as can be determined, no governmental or private organization has expressed any interest in preserving this historic structure.

NORTH TO GROVER HILL. Both the Black Rock Harbor and Penfield Reef Lighthouses can be clearly seen from along Grover Hill's Street's Mary's By-The-Sea Walkway.

Return to US 1 and at the US 1 & CT 771 intersection turn right into Fairfield Avenue. Continue to Brewster Street (sixth street after the Ash Creek bridge), turn right at Grovers Avenue and continue to the walkway. Parking on Grovers is by permit only. One can avoid this restriction by parking on one of the side streets and strolling the short distance to the walkway.

BLACK ROCK HARBOR

NORTH FROM FAIRFIELD. Take Fairfield Avenue east and northeast through the I-95 and railroad underpasses. Then:

     -> Right at Iranistan Avenue,

     -> Right at Sound View Drive (one way) into P.T. Barnum Boulevard (one way) to a free parking area and fishing pier. The pathway (sand spit) to the lighthouse begins just off the parking area.

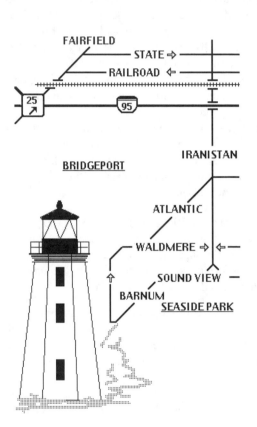

Black Rock Harbor Lighthouse stands about 0.5 mile south of the parking area. Penfield Reef Lighthouse lies offshore about 2.3 miles to the south southwest.

There is no charge for travelers who enter the park for visits of short duration. If you intend to spend some time in the park, be aware that a vehicle parked for an extended period must show a "Parks Permit." The out-of-state fee is twice that charged nonresidents of Bridgeport.

If you walk out to the lighthouse, it is suggested that you either post a note on the vehicle's windshield informing the park police who and where you are and what you are doing or leave behind a driver. Best way is to avoid summer weekends and holidays. The park is not only crowded, but checks for permits are more frequently and more closely made. If your timing is wrong and/or a sense of caution prevails, the lighthouse can be clearly seen and enjoyed from Grover Hill's seaside walkway (see directions below).

BLACK ROCK HARBOR LIGHTHOUSE
(FAYERWEATHER; FAIRWEATHER ISLAND).

The first beacon on the southeast end of Fayerweather Island was placed in a small wooden tower built in 1808. The light was established the following year. The tower endured until a gale toppled it in 1821.

The present 41-foot tall rubble stone lighthouse took its place. The tower's double walls show an unusual construction technique. The builder, either in an attempt to economize in the use of stone or to reinforce the space between the walls, filled the 8-inch space with wooden planks placed horizontally between layers of sand and small rubble stones.

The first lighting device was a whale-oil spider lamp. When rebuilt in 1823 the lantern received a Lewis optic, consisting of eight lamps and 14-inch reflectors. Before the light's deactivation in March 1933, it displayed a fixed white light intensified by a Fresnel-designed fifth-order lens installed in 1854.

The most remarkable personality in the long history of Black Rock Harbor Lighthouse was Catherine Moore. The daughter of the lighthouse's third keeper, Stephen Moore, Kate learned to trim the wicks and care for the light when she was 12 years old.

Keeper Stephen Moore became disabled after an accident in 1819 and Kate took over full duties at the lighthouse. Her father remained official keeper until 1871, when he died at the age of 100. Kate was then officially appointed keeper at the age of 66. She remained at the station for seven more years, resigning in 1878. Kate Moore lived to the age of 105.

Kate Moore was credited with 21 lives saved during her 62 years at Fayerweather Island. There were frequently vessels wrecked nearby in storms, and many times Kate Moore managed to pull survivors to safety in the keeper's house.

BLACK ROCK HARBOR (FAYERWEATHER ISLAND)

OWNER. Licensed to the City of Bridgeport since 1933. Managed by the Black Rock Community Council.

PRESERVATION. Listed in the National Register of Historic Places as part of the Seaside Park National Register District.

Although a ward of the City of Bridgeport, this pretty little lighthouse stood abandoned for more than 48 years. Neglected, it became yet another victim of vandalism. In 1980 the Bridgeport Environmental Protection Commission decided that the lighthouse had taken enough abuse and took charge of the property. In 1983 the Commission, with the assistance of the Friends of Seaside Park, completely restored the lighthouse, cleared the island of debris, established walk paths and hiking trails and landscaped the nine-acre island. The lighthouse again became a popular target for vandalism, and by the 1990s the interior was gutted and the outside was covered by graffiti.

New hope arrived with a preservation effort initiated by two local residents. Black Rock artist David Grant Grimshaw and caterer Patricia Roche often wondered what could be done to save the lighthouse. As a result of their concern, a lighthouse fund was established and the group began raising money in 1993. A Preservation Ball was initiated in 1994 by Grimshaw and became an annual event. The yearly party, which is open to the public, includes a silent auction. The group, in association with the Black Rock Community Council, raised $25,000 in cash and in-kind services, and the City of Bridgeport's Board of Park Commissioners matched the amount by granting $25,000.

The Black Rock Seaport Foundation, affiliated with the Black Rock Community ouncil, oversaw a 1998 restoration. By the end of the year the masonry was repaired, a coat of graffiti-resistant paint was applied, the lantern room was reglazed, rust on the railings was removed and new doors and windows were installed. The new windows have vandal-proof steel panes, which from the water have the appearance of glass. A protective stone seawall was also reconstructed, affording better protection for the foundation of the lighthouse.

The renovation was complete, except for one thing — the group felt the landmark should be visible at night. Two power companies, United Illuminating and Bridgeport Energy, stepped in to help. The companies donated solar panels and lighting equipment. Workers and materials were transported to the island by Captain's Cove Seaport and the Fayerweather Yacht Club, and the panels were installed in the top of the lighthouse away from public view. The lights illuminate the tower but aren't meant to serve as a navigational aid.

To find out more or to donate to the continued preservation of the lighthouse, contact:

- Black Rock Community Council, 20 Quinlan Ave., Bridgeport, CT 06605.

SOUTH TO GROVER HILL. See the maps on pages 177 & 178.

Take Barnum Boulevard and Waldemere Avenue (one way east). Then:

-> Left at Iranistan Avenue,

-> Left at Railroad Avenue (one way),

-> Left at Fairfield Avenue,

-> Left at Brewster Street (fifth street on left after Ellsworth Street),

-> Right at Grovers Avenue to the walkway.

Parking on Grovers is by permit only. You can avoid this restriction by parking on one of the side streets and strolling the short distance to the walkway.

VIEWING TONGUE POINT LIGHTHOUSE. See the map on page 180.

If you can find a parking spot off Sound View Drive, you can see the lighthouse after walking across the lawn out to the water's edge and looking to the northeast. The observation area is on the right as Sound View Drive curves left into connecting South Main Street.

BRIDGEPORT HARBOR LIGHTHOUSE (destroyed).

Built in 1851, this lighthouse was a two-story, rectangular house attached to a light tower. The styling was that of the mansard roof genre with two dormers on one side and one window on each end. The structure and tower sat on a simple platform supported by driven pilings.

One interesting item concerning this lighthouse is the story that a battery of four 10-inch guns (or possibly mortars) were installed on the platform in 1898 as a precaution against possible naval attacks during the Spanish-American War. When one looks at a photograph of the structure there is little space on the catwalk surrounding the house to emplace four hefty 10-inchers. If the battery could have been accommodated and fired salvos, it appears that the frail wooden structure would have suffered more damage than any ship entering the harbor. Perhaps someone will come up with the historical correctness of the "gun" story.

In 1952 the light was taken out of service and sold to a private citizen, who wanted to move the lighthouse onto the mainland. Unable to get official approval for the relocation, the owner decided to dismantle it. Before he could do so the structure caught fire and was destroyed.

STRATFORD SHOAL

NORTH FROM THE BLACK ROCK HARBOR LIGHTHOUSE. From Seaside Park follow the Barnum loop into Waldemere Avenue (one way east). Then:

-> Left at Iranistan Avenue and through the I-95 and railroad underpasses,
-> Right at State Street (one way),
-> Right at Water Street,
-> Left through the railroad underpass to Union Square Dock.

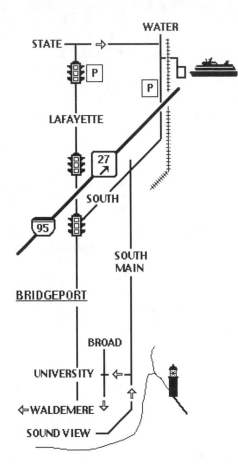

WEST ON I-95. At the western end of the Pequonnock River Bridge take Exit 27 (Lafayette Boulevard - Downtown - L.I. Ferry) to Lafayette Boulevard and turn left. Then:

-> Left at Frontage Road and connecting Silliman Street,
-> Left at Water Street,
-> Right through the railroad underpass to the dock.

PARKING. For a same day, round trip crossing (three+ hours) of Long Island Sound you can park your vehicle in a municipal garage (nominal fee) off Lafayette Boulevard or in a hotel parking garage (slightly higher fee) located off Water Street just south of the underpass entrance to the dock.

BRIDGEPORT - PORT JEFFERSON FERRY. Stratford Shoal can only be seen distantly with the use of binoculars. The ferry passes close to Tongue Point (excellent photo opportunity) and provides a frontal (fairly distant) view of the Old Field Point Lighthouse. The auto/passenger ferry carries 90 cars. Crossing time is 1 1/2 hours. Advance vehicle reservations are recommended.

SCHEDULE. Call or check website for current schedule.

FARES. Vehicle/driver + each passenger + Bridgeport Port Authority tax on each ticket. Monday through Friday noon "Off-Peak" rates are about 15% less than "Peak" tickets.

Discount for children 6-12; under 6 free. Foot passenger tickets available. Credit cards accepted; no checks.

- Bridgeport & Port Jefferson Steamboat Company, 102 West Broadway, Port Jefferson, Long Island, NY 11777.

Phone: Bridgeport (203) 367-3043. Port Jefferson (516) 473-0286. Schedule information (203) 335-2040.

Website: http://www.bpjferry.com/

STRATFORD SHOAL LIGHTHOUSE (MIDDLE GROUND).
CHARACTERISTIC: Flashing white 5s
HAW: 60' **RANGE**: 13 nm

This light, which marks a dangerous rock and gravel shoal, lies seven miles south of Bridgeport about midway between Stratford Point and Long Island's Old Field Point.

As early as 1831, Congress appropriated $1,000 for a beacon to be established on the shoal. Instead of building a lighthouse, the Lighthouse Service ordered a lightship on station in 1837. The ship was removed in 1866 and replaced by a newer vessel the following year. Since the lightship had problems remaining at its mooring and because of the excessive swinging of the light in heavy weather, a decision was made in 1873 to build a lighthouse. The light was established on December 15, 1878.

Stratford Shoal was to have had a piling-type foundation similar to the screwpile structures usually built in bays and sounds. In recognition of the fragility of the spindle-legged platform in ice filled waters, the design was tabled. Instead the Lighthouse Board built (1874-76) Stratford Shoal's foundation with huge undressed blocks of granite attached to each other by thick cast-iron staples set in lead. The pier's diameters range from 55 feet at its underwater footing to 46 feet at the tower's base. It rises almost 19 feet and is filled with concrete. Inside the pier is a basement lined with brick above two storage cisterns.

STRATFORD SHOAL

Although Stratford Shoal and Race Rock share a basic similarity, they differ in stone finishes, window arches and roof shapes. Both lighthouses are beautiful examples of the granite workmanship which first appeared in lighthouses built along the Hudson River in the 1860s. Their massiveness, roof treatments and pointed windows show some Gothic Revival styling.

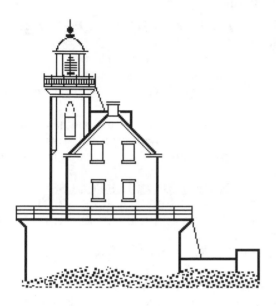

The 28-foot square dwelling and its attached gray conical tower are both constructed of granite ashlar with Victorian styled rough hammered facings. The three-story tower projects outwardly from the south side of the dwelling. Its first story is square in shape; above the second story the tower is octagonal. The tower is further strengthened with a lining wall of bricks laid in header form. The tower has five windows, one off each of three levels on the south wall and one on each of the east and west sides off the third deck. Inside, on each side of the three south windows, there is a vertical chute built into the brick lining. The chutes or tubes were used to channel the clockwork's weights as they dropped through the watchroom's deck. On the first level's east wall there is a small alcove below a load bearing granite lintel that was used to store oil containers. There is one stylish addition to the border (cornice) between the top of the lantern and the roof's eaves -- a cast-iron ornamental frieze with alternating panels of embossed leaves and repeated circles and double lines. Centered above each leaf panel is a projecting border (boss) which covers a molded horizontal cornice that joins the frieze to the roof.

Some keepers at isolated lighthouses developed severe psychological problems. This seems to have happened at Stratford Shoal.

In 1904 Julius Koster of New York City was assigned to Stratford Shoal as second assistant keeper. In May 1905 the keeper went ashore and left Assistant Keeper Morrell Hulse and Second Assistant Koster in charge. The next night Koster suddenly went into a rage and locked himself in the lantern room. He threatened to destroy the light and actually stopped its rotation for a while. Koster finally emerged, then tried to take his own life. The suicide was prevented by Hulse. A few days later Koster was fired from the Lighthouse Service.

In 1894 the lighthouse was refitted with a new kerosene-powered Fresnel optic. In 1978 the power source was converted to wet batteries. The lighthouse's fourth-order classical lens, installed in 1905, has been removed. Stratford Shoal's modern aerobeacon is now powered by solar charged batteries. Unoccupied since its automation in 1970, the lighthouse has been stripped of much of its interior detailing.

OWNER. U.S. Coast Guard.

PRESERVATION. Listed in the National Register of Historic Places.

TONGUE POINT

Tongue Point Lighthouse is located within the confines of United Illuminating's Bridgeport Harbor Station. The station is not open to the public. The Bridgeport-Port Jefferson Ferry (see the previous chapter) passes close to the lighthouse, and it can also be viewed from two places on shore. One is from Sound View Park. It is discussed in the BLACK ROCK HARBOR chapter. If dodging traffic across Sound View Drive and a walk across a grass lawn does not appeal to you, then another viewing place is from the fishing pier on Pleasure Beach.

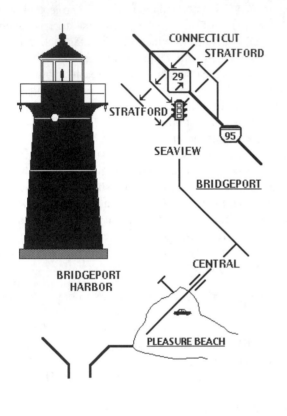

NORTH OR SOUTH ON I-95 Take Exit 29 to Seaview Avenue. Then:
   -> South and southeast on Seaview,
   -> Right at Central Avenue,
   -> Across the Lewis Gut Bridge to Pleasure Beach's fishing pier.

There are no entrance, parking or pier fees. Walk out onto the pier for an unobstructed view of the lighthouse off to the northwest across Bridgeport Harbor.

TONGUE POINT LIGHTHOUSE
(INNER HARBOR; WELLS POINT; LITTLE BUG; LITTLE BLACKIE; BRIDGEPORT BREAKWATER).
CHARACTERISTIC: Flashing green 4s
HAW: 31' **RANGE**: 5 nm
Tongue Point was first built in 1891 at the end of a long breakwater pier. After years of complaints from commercial shipping companies that the sharp turn around the breakwater was a hazard to navigation, it was decided to do away with the pier. In 1919, after 350 feet of the inner breakwater had been torn down and added to the outer breakwater, the lighthouse was dismantled and moved 275 feet inland to its present location. The inner surfaces of the tower's cast-iron wall and deck plates and brass fittings still show the painted numbers that facilitated the reassembly of the structure.

The 21-foot tall lighthouse rests on a 10-foot tall concrete pier, marking the east end of Tongue (Wells) Point, on the west shore of Bridgeport Harbor. The rings around the unlined and unadorned tower are formed by the overlapping of the tower's bolted sections. Because of its low profile there are but two decks.

With no onsite living quarters, the keeper had to row out to the breakwater to service the light. And to make his task a bit more difficult there was, for the first five years, no structure upon which the keeper could land his boat. Although there were government proposals for the construction of a keeper's house at the end of a plank walk built in 1900 between the tower and the breakwater, the project never materialized. In 1906 the keeper, although having been supplied with a landing dock in 1896, built a shack on the breakwater to facilitate his tending the light.

During the tower's construction, it received a single kerosene lamp and a sixth-order Fresnel. The light was established in March 1895 and automated in 1954. Although the classical lens was removed when a modern lens was installed in 1988, the Coast Guard did not remove the 1881 fog bell nor its striking mechanism.

OWNER. U.S. Coast Guard.

PRESERVATION. Not listed in the National Register of Historic Places.

Although The Bug was scheduled for deactivation in 1967, public protests persuaded the Coast Guard to retain the beacon as an active aid to navigation.

STRATFORD POINT

NORTH ON I-95. Take Exit 30 and follow CT 113 (Lordship) past the Bridgeport Municipal Airport into Lordship. Then:

-> Left at Oak Bluff Avenue southwest corner of the fenced airport property,

-> Continue on Oak Bluff through a traffic rotary and straight ahead into Prospect Drive.

SOUTH ON I-95. Take Exit 32. Then:

-> Left on frontage road to CT 113,

-> Continue south on CT 113 (Short Beach Drive) past the airport into Lordship,

-> At a 5-way intersection turn left into Prospect Drive.

Visitors may view the lighthouse station from the outside the fence but are not allowed to enter the station grounds. The keeper's house is now home to a Coast Guard family.

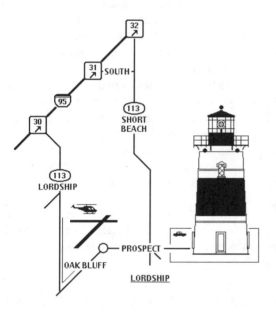

STRATFORD POINT LIGHTHOUSE.
CHARACTERISTIC: Group flashing white 20s
HAW: 52' **RANGE:** 16 nm

A 28-foot tall wood framed and shingled tower was erected in 1821 on the west side of the dangerous mouth of the Housatonic River. The station also included a small wooden keeper's dwelling. The revolving light consisted of 10 lamps and reflectors on two tables of five lamps each.

Stratford Point Light had a female keeper, Amy Buddington, for several years beginning in 1853.

In 1871 Benedict Lillingston was keeper and son Frederick was assistant. In October, the keeper's granddaughter Lottie was visiting the lighthouse when the keepers had to go to the aid of a vessel in distress. Twelve-year old Lottie, left alone, noticed that the light had gone out. Lottie decided to put her knowledge gained from watching her uncle and grandfather into action.

Climbing to the lantern room by herself for the first time, Lottie lit a backup safety lamp and suspended it in place of the primary lamps. The captain of the steamer *Elm City* noticed the dim light showing as he passed the lighthouse.

In July and August 1880, the Lighthouse Board approved a common design for eight lighthouses. One of those is the present Stratford Point light tower. Like its cast-iron contemporaries, Stratford Point's tower consists of five rows of curved cast-iron plates bolted together through flanges cast at the plates' inner edges. Like that of Saybrook Breakwater, this unadorned tower's only feature of architectural interest is the conservative cast-iron styling of its molded window surrounds, which are embellished with projecting shallow peaked lintels, recessed spandrels with cornices and flanking consoles.

Stratford Point's first lighthouse held a multi-lamp fixed optic that was 44 feet above the water and could be seen out to 12 nautical miles. In 1822 the tower was reequipped with a Lewis 10-lamp Argand device that was given a flashing characteristic by a revolving clockwork-powered metal eclipser. The mechanism was manufactured by Simon Willard, a master clockmaker. During the mid-1850s the old tower received a fifth-order Fresnel lens. When the present bricklined tower was built in 1881, it was fitted with a Henri LePaute third-order Fresnel lens and a kerosene-powered constant level lamp, both rotated by a clockwork mechanism. In 1906 the lantern was equipped with a new fourth-order Fresnel lens that revolved in a trough of mercury. In 1932 the classical lens was reequipped with an incandescent lamp.

Today the light station contains the 35-foot tall lighthouse, a 1 1/2-story, wood framed Gothic Revival keeper's dwelling built in 1881 and a brick fog signal building added in 1911.

OWNER. U.S. Coast Guard.

PRESERVATION. Listed in the National Register of Historic Places. The tower's original lantern was removed in 1969 to facilitate the installation of oversized automated rotating aerobeacons. It was found, donated and ceremoniously returned to the refurbished tower along with a modern lens on July 14, 1990.

FIVE MILE POINT
SOUTHWEST LEDGE

NORTH OR SOUTH ON I-95. Take Exit 50N or Exit 51S to Townsend Avenue. Follow Townsend and "Lighthouse Park" signs south to Lighthouse Road and turn right to the entrance to Lighthouse Point Park. The 82-acre park has swimming, natural history displays, nature trails, a picnic grove, bird sanctuary and an antique carousel.

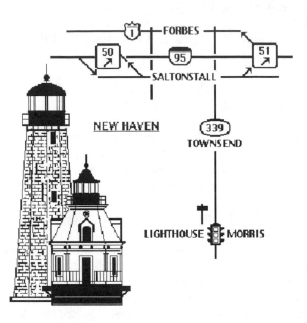

OPEN. All year, daily from 6 AM to sunset.

PARKING FEE. Memorial Day weekend to Labor Day. Weekday fees are slightly less than those charged on weekends. No parking fee at other times of the year. Grounds are handicapped accessible.

- Department of Parks, Recreation and Trees, 720 Edgewood Avenue, New Haven, CT 06515.

Phone: (203) 787-8020. Park (203) 946-8005.

Website: http://www.newhavenparks.org/lighthouse_point.htm

The Five Mile (five miles from downtown New Haven) Point Lighthouse is located on shore at the water's edge. The tower is not open on a regular basis. The Lighthouse Point Park Rangers offer a historical program that includes a climb of the lighthouse. The program is available to groups upon request. For more information, contact the Lighthouse Point Park Rangers at (203) 946-8790.

The Southwest Ledge Lighthouse is located 1.1 miles offshore on the west end of the East Breakwater. It marks the reef on the east side of New Haven Harbor.

FIVE MILE POINT LIGHTHOUSE (OLD NEW HAVEN; NEW HAVEN HARBOR).

In 1805 a 30-foot tall wooden tower and keeper's house were erected on Lighthouse Point. A 2 1/2-story brick keeper's residence was added in 1835.

The light was not high enough for mariners approaching New Haven Harbor and with a weakening of the tower's wooden frame, so it was replaced in 1840 by the existing 70-foot tall lighthouse. The octagonal structure's inner brick lining and its outer stone wall have been bonded or tied together by shaped freestone (Connecticut brownstone) blocks placed at regular intervals around the tower. The Colonial Revival tower shows no ornamentation. Its three rectangular windows have been sealed. The empty round lantern is built of bolted cast-iron plates.

Access to the watchroom is by means of a decidedly unique staircase, consisting of a series of steps (no landings) formed by wedge-shaped granite slabs chiseled into a helical form. The slabs' inside lobes are stacked around a center post. Their outer edges are inserted into the brick lining.

Five Mile Point's first optic consisted of a simple wheel fitted with eight whale oil lamps, each with a reflector. In order to increase the beacon's brightness, the lamps were increased to 12, each backed by a 21-inch reflector. The light at 50 feet above the water could be seen out to six nautical miles.

In 1845, five years after the new tower's completion and after the construction of an attached keeper's house, the second light was activated. It was a fourth-order classical lens with a focal plane some 97 feet above the harbor. It was discontinued in 1877 when the Southwest Ledge light was commissioned.

OWNER. City of New Haven has owned the lighthouse and the 1835 dwelling since 1949.

PRESERVATION. Listed in the National Register of Historic Places.

The tower is well preserved, having received a complete cleaning and refurbishing as recently as 1986.

FIVE MILE POINT & SOUTHWEST LEDGE

SOUTHWEST LEDGE LIGHTHOUSE (NEW HAVEN BREAKWATER).
CHARACTERISTIC: Flashing red 5s
HAW: 57' **RANGE**: 13 nm

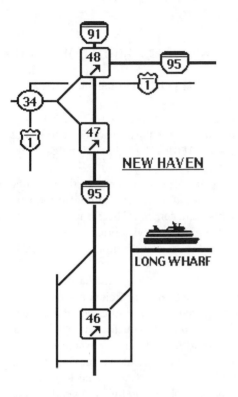

In June 1875, Ramsay and Carte of Baltimore began the fabrication of two cast-iron superstructures, one for New Haven and the other for Delaware Bay's Ship John Shoal. With its manufacturing schedule ahead of Delaware's, the Lighthouse Board decided that the Southwest Ledge Lighthouse would be displayed at Philadelphia's 1876 Centennial Exposition before being shipped to New Haven.

Meanwhile, the contractor in New Haven finished building the caisson pier ahead of schedule, resulting in a second decision to send the Delaware lighthouse to New Haven and, after the exhibition, reassemble the second structure on Ship John Shoal. The New Haven aid was activated on January 1, 1877.

The 45-foot tall lighthouse rests on a cylindrical cast-iron, concrete filled caisson with a brick-lined basement and cisterns. The cast-iron superstructure has been built in three stages. Surmounting the pier is a square one-story cast-iron house with beveled corners (often referred to as being octagonal). The second stage is the mansard roof. Atop the roof is an octagonal lantern.

The structure's architectural style is that of the French Second Empire. According to Connecticut's Nomination Form for the lighthouse's entry into the National Register of Historic Places, this styling is quite apparent in the structure's first story pilasters which support an encircling entablature, consisting of a "stepped and molded architrave beam that rests directly on columns, bracketed frieze and molded cornice." The resemblance continues in the mansard roof with its gabled dormers, each with "round-arched window openings within a surround featuring a keystone, incised detail, rosettes, a peaked, molded cornice, and footscrolls above the projecting sills."

When constructed, the lighthouse was fitted with a fourth-order Fresnel lens. That lens was removed in 1988 when it was replaced by an automated electric modern lens.

OWNER. U.S. Coast Guard.
PRESERVATION. Listed in the National Register of Historic Places.
Since 1988 the unmanned Southwest Ledge Lighthouse is a ghostlike structure. Its doors and windows have been sealed with steel, plywood and sheet metal ventilators. In 2000 the Coast Guard performed some maintenance and gave the tower a new coat of paint.

FAULKNER'S ISLAND

NORTH OR SOUTH ON I-95. Take the interstate's Exit 58 and follow CT 77 (Church Street) into Guilford center.
VIEWING THE LIGHTHOUSE. Faulkner's Island lies between Old Saybrook and New Haven and about five miles south of Guilford center. The lighthouse, which stands in the middle of the island, can be seen from these locations:
- South southeast from Guilford's marina (free parking).
- South southwest from the end of Mulberry Point Road.
- Southeast from Sachems Head's Prospect Avenue.
- From Chaffinch Island (town park) at the end of Chaffinch Island Road.

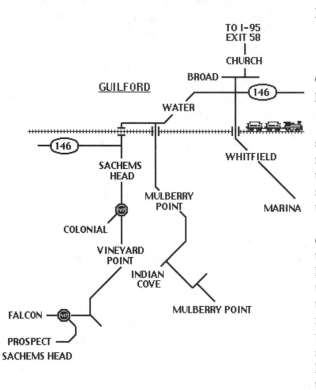

FAULKNER'S ISLAND LIGHTHOUSE (FALKNER ISLAND).

CHARACTERISTIC: Flashing white 10s
HAW: 94' **RANGE:** 13 nm

After Congress appropriated $6,000 and the Federal Government purchased the land, the State of Connecticut ceded the property on July 23, 1801. The light station was completed in 1802.

The 40-foot tall octagonal freestone (brownstone) tower stands on a capped, uncoursed foundation formed with rubblestone (schist) and cement. There is no exterior ornamentation. The interior is lined with brick. The lantern deck is supported by a corbel of coursed brick. The overall height of the lighthouse is 46 feet.

The light tower was built by Abisha Woodward, considered in his day to have been a proficient mason. He also built the New London Harbor (1801) and Lynde Point (1838) lighthouses. Mr. Woodward's techniques used in laying and coating the structure are worthy of mention. For example, to add strength to walls he used the chinking method of mixing stone chips and mortar for filling masonry crevices. And to give the tower's walls a homogeneous look, he carefully prepared his mortar with sand pulverized from brownstone castoffs so that the color of his plastering would blend in with the purple-brown color of the primary stones.

Its first optic was a spider lamp, which was replaced by a Winslow Lewis apparatus consisting of 12 lamps and reflectors with eight of the lamps fitted with his rather inefficient plano convex lenses. The optic rotated on two circular tables. In 1840, after enlarging the lantern, Lewis introduced a device consisting of nine lamps each backed by 16-inch reflectors.

The tower's outside spiral cast-iron stairway was added in 1871 because the lantern was not large enough to hold a Fresnel optic while allowing enough deck space for the usual trap door access from the watchroom below. Two years later, the lantern was equipped with an L. Sautter fourth-order Fresnel lens.

The beacon was automated in 1978. In 1988 the Coast Guard replaced the fourth-order Fresnel lens with a plastic lens and transferred its radiobeacon to Horton Point on Long Island. The light is now solar-powered. The solar cells of the two photo-voltaire panels positioned on the southside of the gallery railing charge three batteries located inside the lantern.

In March 1976 a fire broke out in the keeper's quarters while two Coast Guardsmen were on duty. Fire fighters couldn't arrive in time, and when the smoke cleared the 1871 keeper's house was gone and the tower was scorched.

The station's bell tower, original boathouse, workshed and oil house have all disappeared. Today the station consists of the lighthouse, a stuccoed and terra cotta tiled fog signal building (c. 1922) south of the tower, a boathouse (1940) and a wooden observation tower erected seasonally and used by naturalists.

OWNER. U.S. Coast Guard (lighthouse only). The island has been owned by the U.S. Fish and Wildlife Service since July 1985 as part of the Stewart B. McKinney Wildlife Refuge.

PRESERVATION. Listed (1990) in the National Register of Historic Places.

FAULKNER'S ISLAND

After the March 1976 fire, vandals did further damage to the lighthouse. In 1978 the Coast Guard repaired the tower (sandblasting, repointing and painting), bricked in the windows, added a steel door and automated the light.

Although mariners who sail in Long Island Sound and depend on the beacon had expressed their concern for the threatened tower, Faulkner's Island Lighthouse remained a lonely, neglected and vandalized structure for nearly 20 years. Explanations for its "orphaned" status ranged from its isolation to the glamorization of the plights of the more accessible Atlantic Coast lighthouses.

In January 1991, the Guilford Preservation Alliance formed, as one of its special committees, the Faulkner's Light Brigade, a private, nonprofit organization dedicated to save the lighthouse. Assisted by another group to perform land and erosion surveys, the Brigade acts as a catalyst and adviser in the preservation of this famous beacon. The group now has about 1,000 members.

On February 6, 1997, the Town of Guilford approved the signing of a five-year license with the U.S. Coast Guard for the municipality to maintain the light station.

As a result of the Brigade's effort and the cooperation among political leaders, other shoreline communities, yacht clubs, commercial marine interests and its membership, much has been accomplished. The Town of Guilford received a grant of $250,000 from the State's Department of Transportation (ConnDOT) for the restoration of the lighthouse and the wharf. The town pledged matching in kind services.

Walter Sedovic Architects of Irvington, New York, were chosen to oversee the restoration project, and International Chimney Corporation of Buffalo, New York was chosen to implement the restoration of the lighthouse. The restoration project was completed in 1999.

The lighthouse is threatened by an embankment erosion that has progressed on one face at a rate of up to six inches annually. A major problem facing the Brigade was to determine just how close erosion could progress without toppling the structure. George Gdovin, an environmental biologist affiliated with Little Harbor Laboratory, donated his services to make an initial study as to at what distance from the edge of the eroding cliff would the tower's subbase begin to weaken, resulting in structural cracks, underground stress faults and eventually the collapse of the light tower. They found that the safe distance between embankment and tower ranges between 22 feet and 13 feet. Based on other engineering data, Gdovin concluded that the tower must have a supportive subbase averaging 18 feet in all directions. In 1997 the embankment was 35 feet from the tower.

Erosion control measures were implemented by the Army Corps of Engineers beginning in September 2000. An armada of heavy construction equipment arrived on the island under the direction of Zenone, Inc., of Franklin, Massachusetts. The contract demanded that work could not take place during the nesting cycle of the roseate tern, which runs from May through August. As work progressed in early October, high winds and seas battered the floating wharf installed by Zenone. Weeks were lost while the landing barges were moved to make them less vulnerable to westerly winds. On December 12 a southwesterly storm again ripped into the barges. Icy gale-force winds of over 60 miles per hour, combined with seven-foot waves to throw both barges onto the island's shore. One of the barges was severely damaged and the roadway access was washed out. Jim Zenone, president of Zenone Inc., said the weather made it very hard on the crews. But despite the setbacks, Phase 1 of the erosion control work was finished in early 2001, providing protection from the island's north tip to a point 250 feet south of the lighthouse.

A massive stone wall nearly 20 feet high and 50 feet wide was installed along the east embankment, with an outer armor layer consisting of stones weighing as much as three tons each. The upper face of the embankment was cut back to a slope of about 30-40 degrees, and hardy vegetation was planted to help buffer wind and rain. Next to the lighthouse for 300 feet, additional stability was created by the placement of six-inch high "geo cells," a system of plastic fabric with holes, covered with earth and planted with vegetation. In all, 600 linear feet of the east embankment were stabilized under Phase 1 of the erosion control project.

Phase 2 of the project will include the construction of another 600-foot revetment "wrapping" the south end of the island. Between phases there will be an evaluation of the impact on the tern colony. The Brigade hopes to finish the anti-erosion project and to develop other subprojects to improve the island, in cooperation with the U.S. Fish and Wildlife Service. They also plan to establish a middle school curriculum using the island as a focus for various studies, and to increase their membership. An annual "open house" on the Faulkner's Island refuge / light station is typically staged at the end of summer, just after Labor Day.

- Faulkner's Light Brigade, PO Box 199, Guilford, CT 06437. Phone (203) 453-8400.
    Website: http://lighthouse.cc/FLB/

187

Faulkner's Island Lighthouse just after the 1976 fire destroyed the keeper's house
(U.S. Coast Guard photo)

Lynde Point Lighthouse

LYNDE POINT
SAYBROOK BREAKWATER

NORTH ON I-95. Take Exit 67 to Elm Street and turn right. Then:
-> Cross US 1 to CT 154 (Main Street),
-> Left at CT 154 to Saybrook Point.
SOUTH ON I-95. Take Exit 69 to US 1. Then:
-> Continue into Old Saybrook center on US 1/CT 154,
-> Bear left and follow CT 154 (Main Street) to Saybrook Point.

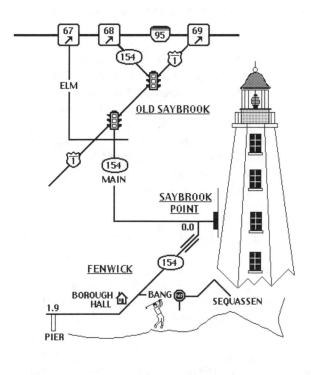

VIEWING THE LIGHTHOUSES. Both lighthouses are located in Fenwick on the Connecticut River. Both can be seen from a public access dock at Saybrook Point. The Lynde Point beacon marks the mouth of the river. The Saybrook Breakwater light warns mariners of two sand bars lying on the west and east sides of the river's entrance.

Entry into the Lynde Point station is prohibited.

Here are mileages from the CT 154 turn in Saybrook Point (start 0.0 mile)
-> Lynde Point can be seen from the South Cove bridge and causeway (0.5 mile).
-> Divided entrance to North Bang Avenue, golf course and road (Sequassen) to the Lynde Point Lighthouse (0.8 mile).
-> Both lighthouses can be seen from CT 154 (1.2 to 1.4 miles).
-> Both lighthouses can be seen from the Knollwood Beach Pier (1.9 miles).

LYNDE POINT LIGHTHOUSE
(SAYBROOK; INNER LIGHT).
CHARACTERISTIC: Fixed white
HAW: 71' **RANGE**: 14 nm

The first Lynde Point beacon, established in 1803, was housed in a 35-foot octagonal wooden tower, originally equipped with whale oil-burning lamps.

The present 65-foot tower was completed in 1838. It has a 25-foot diameter base. The tower's walls are five feet thick at the bottom and two feet at the top. It is constructed of carefully dressed brownstone blocks laid in octagonal courses in an alternating stretcher (length) and header (end) pattern. The walls were laid with lime mortar and the joints pointed in hydraulic cement. There are six levels with the top deck supporting the watchroom. Atop the watchroom and surmounting the brownstone service gallery deck is a cylindrical cast-iron lantern. Access to the watchroom is by a set of wooden steps (1868) cantilevered up and around a wooden centerpost. The lantern is reached by a ladder that rises through a hole bored in the solid stone.

The keepers' residence seen today is the third dwelling to have been built on the station. The first, a small wooden structure, was replaced in 1858 by a larger gambrel roofed house showing some Gothic detailing. The house was originally attached to the tower, as evidenced by the roof outline showing on the tower's west side. The residence was demolished and replaced by the present masonry duplex in 1966.

Although the 1803 tower was reported in 1835 to be in poor shape, it was fitted with a Lewis lighting device consisting of 10 lamps and 9-inch reflectors. With a focal plane of 44 feet above mean high water the beacon had a range of 12 nautical miles. That optic was transferred to the 1838 light tower.

189

In 1852 Lynde Point was equipped with a fourth-order Fresnel lens. In 1890 a fifth-order Fresnel, manufactured by Barbier & Fenestre of Paris in 1881, replaced the fourth-order. Kerosene replaced whale oil in 1879. Although electric power reached Fenwick in 1915, Lynde Point was not electrified for another 40 years. The 1890 fifth-order classical lens was automated in 1978.

OWNER. U.S. Coast Guard.

PRESERVATION. Listed in the National Register of Historic Places.

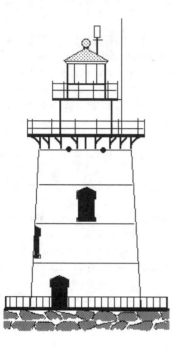

SAYBROOK BREAKWATER LIGHTHOUSE (OUTER LIGHT).

CHARACTERISTIC: Flashing green 6s

HAW: 58' **RANGE**: 11 nm

Although authorized and funded in 1883, the tower's completion was delayed until the west breakwater (started in 1875) and the parallel east jetty were completed.

The 49-foot tall lighthouse rests on a 32-foot tall pier constructed of bolted cast-iron plates and filled with concrete. The walls of the tower's first three levels are insulated and strengthened with a brick lining. The fourth deck, which holds the cylindrical cast-iron watchroom, is not lined.

An interesting architectural feature of this otherwise plain tower is its window treatments which, like those of the Stratford Point Lighthouse, show a conservative cast-iron styling in its molded window surrounds embellished with projecting shallow-peaked lintels, recessed spandrels with cornices, and flanking consoles.

The light was established on June 15, 1886. Originally equipped with a whale oil-powered fifth-order Fresnel optic, the tower was refitted with a fourth-order Fresnel lens in 1890. In 1917 the oil lamps were replaced by an incandescent oil vapor lamp. In 1958 the light was operated by remote control by Coast Guard personnel living in the Lynde Point residence. Until its automation in 1959, the optic had been powered by more than 50 wet batteries. The lantern now holds a modern lens.

OWNER. U.S. Coast Guard.

PRESERVATION. Listed in the National Register of Historic Places.

In 1996 this lighthouse underwent a $64,000 major inside-and-out refurbishing, funded by the Coast Guard. The restoration included its first new coat of paint since 1982.

LIGHTHOUSE SIGHTSEEING CRUISES.

FROM SAYBROOK POINT. The M/V *Aunt Polly* (two decks; bottom enclosed) departs from the Saybrook Point dock and sails down the Connecticut River and out into Long Island Sound.

The Duck Island Cruise and the Lighthouse Cruise pass close by the Lynde Point and Old Saybrook Lighthouses. The former excursion (two hours) continues out into Long Island Sound to Duck Island; the latter (one hour) turns around just outside the mouth of the river.

SCHEDULE. Phone or check website for the latest cruise schedule.

FARES. Moneywise, lighthouse seekers should take the Lighthouse Cruise. No discounts.

- Deep River Navigation Company, PO Box 382, Deep River, CT 06417. Phone (860) 526-4954.

Website: http://www.deeprivernavigation.com/

Email: deep.river.navgtng@snet.net

FROM HADDAM. To reach Haddam from I-95 take Exit 69 to CT 9. Continue north and take Exit 7 off CT 9. Then:

    -> At the end of the ramp (approximately one mile) turn left into CT 154,

    -> At the first traffic signal (1/4 mile) turn right into CT 82,

    -> Just before the bridge across the Connecticut River to East Haddam, turn tight into Marine Park.

LYNDE POINT & SAYBROOK BREAKWATER

During the **Sag Harbor Cruise** or the **Greenport Village Cruise**, the M/V *Camelot* sails down the Connecticut River, across Long Island Sound to either of the ports.

- Cedar Island (-> Sag Harbor), Long Beach Bar (-> Greenport), Lynde Point, Saybrook Breakwater and Orient Point (-> Sag Harbor).

SCHEDULE. Phone or check website for the latest schedule.

FARES. Discounts for children 5-11. Under 5 and bicycles free.

- Camelot Cruises, 1 Marine Park, Haddam, CT 06438.

Phone (860) 345-8591.

Website: http://www.camelotcruises.com/

Email: cruises@camelotcruises.com

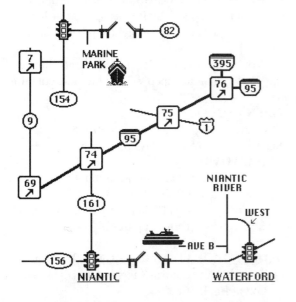

FROM WATERFORD.

To reach Capt. John's Sport Fishing Center take I-95's Exit 74 and follow CT 161 south to CT 156. Then:

    -> Continue on CT 156 across the Niantic River Bridge,

    -> Left at the first traffic signal after the bridge,

    -> At a stop sign turn left,

    -> Right at Avenue B and continue on to the center.

Although Captain John N. Wadsworth offers a variety of cruises, his Lighthouse Cruise is one that should not be missed. Each cruise is narrated by Captain Benjamin Rathbun, author and historian. Lighthouses viewed on these cruises include Latimer Reef, Little Gull Island, Lynde Point, New London Harbor, Saybrook Breakwater, Orient Point, Plum Island and Race Rock.

SCHEDULE. Phone or check website for the latest schedule.

FARES. Discounts for seniors 62+ and children 12 and under. Also group rates.

- Sunbeam Fleet, Capt. John's Sport Fishing Center, 15 First Street, Waterford, CT 06385.

Phone (860) 443-7259. FAX (860) 437-3699.

Website: http://www.sunbeamfleet.com

Email: sunbeamfleet@snet.net

NEW LONDON HARBOR

TO THE ACADEMY FROM I-95. If eastbound, take Exit 82A's frontage road to Briggs Street. If westbound, take Exit 83 to Briggs. Then:

   -> North at Briggs,

   -> Right at Monhegan Avenue to the academy's main gate.

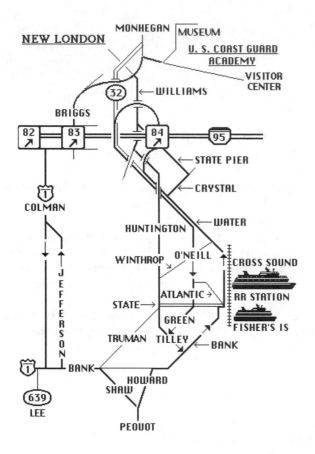

U.S. COAST GUARD ACADEMY MUSEUM. The museum is located in one large room renovated in 1994) in Waesche Hall. It contains several glass cases with copies of historical documents, some Coast Guard gear and a few Fresnel lenses. At the entrance to the one room exhibit stands a first-order lens (from Thacher Island, Massachusetts) with two upper panels missing. A fourth-order and a fifth-order Fresnel and two lightship lenses are also on display.

Parking permitted only in "Visitors" spaces. Waesche Hall is handicapped accessible and contains restrooms.

OPEN. All year.

Mondays through Fridays 9 to 4:30.

Saturdays 10 to 5. Sundays noon to 5.

FREE ADMISSION.

- U.S. Coast Guard Academy Museum, 15 Monhegan Avenue, New London, CT 06320-4195.

Phone (860) 444-8511. Academy (860) 444-8444. Website: http://www.uscg.mil/hq/uscga/

TO THE LIGHTHOUSE FROM I-95. If northbound, take Exit 82A to Colman Street and turn right. Then:

   -> Left at Bank Street,

   -> Right at Shaw Street into connecting Pequot Avenue.

If southbound, take Exit 82B into Colman Street and follow the above northbound directions. This route avoids congested downtown New London.

TO THE LIGHTHOUSE FROM THE ACADEMY. One suggested route is to depart the academy and turn left into Monhegan Avenue. Then:

   -> Left at Williams Street and under I-95,

   -> Left at Huntington Avenue,

   -> Continue south on Huntington,

   -> Bear left into connecting Tilley Street (one way),

   -> Right at Bank Street,

   -> Left at Howard Street into Pequot Avenue to the lighthouse.

The lighthouse keeper's house is a private home and visitors are not allowed to enter the property. Trees may block the view in summer, but otherwise a vew of the lighthouse is possible from the sidewalk.

NEW LONDON HARBOR LIGHTHOUSE (NEW LONDON; PEQUOT).

CHARACTERISTIC: Equal interval white 6 (red sector)

HAW: 89' **RANGES**: White 17; red 14 nm

As early as 1750 there was a beacon at this location. In 1760 the first New London lighthouse was completed. This light was the fourth to be built in the Colonies. The lottery-funded tower, was built of hammer-dressed stone. It had a base diameter of 24 feet and was 62 feet tall. Prior to the Revolutionary War the lighthouse was maintained by state grants. After the Revolution and until the Federal Government assumed control of America's lighthouses, the tower was maintained with funds derived from ship tonnage taxes.

NEW LONDON HARBOR

In 1800, with a 10-foot crack in its wall and in total disrepair, Congress appropriated $15,700 for the repair, alteration and upgrading of the light station. The new station, consisting of the tower, keeper's dwelling and storage vault for oil, was completed in 1800 at a cost of $16,500. Although 1801 is often accepted as the year the light was established, the Lighthouse Service reported in 1838 that the beacon was placed in operation in 1800.

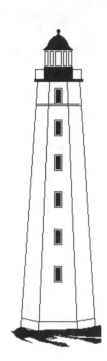

The tapered octagonal tower's base rests on a foundation consisting of a mix of brownstone, granite and native stone. The 9-inch thick brick-lined exterior walls are constructed of freestone (brownstone) laid in cylindrical courses. The tower is 80 feet tall. Supporting the 12-sided cast-iron lantern and its service gallery is an octagonal brownstone corbel that was added in 1833 when the lighthouse underwent extensive repairs. The upper halves of the lantern's twelve faces consist of glass storm panes; the lower halves have cast-iron plates. One interesting item is the tower's lantern gallery-to-ground lightning arrester, consisting of a series of wrought iron strips fastened to the northside wall with large iron staples.

The first dwelling fell into disrepair and was replaced in 1818 with a wooden house erected some distance to the west of the tower. The present 2 1/2-story brick keeper's residence was built in 1863. In 1900 the shed-roofed dormers were added to the third floor to provide space for an assistant keeper's apartment.

The original lighting device was a Lewis Argand-styled optic consisting of 11 lamps, each backed by a 13-inch reflector. The lantern now holds the Henri LePaute fourth-order Fresnel lens installed in 1857. It was electrically powered and automated in 1912.

OWNER. U.S. Coast Guard (lighthouse). The dwelling and grounds have been privately owned since 1928.

PRESERVATION. Listed in the National Register of Historic Places.

Over the years repair work done on the tower involved recovering the lantern's roof with copper sheeting, a new lantern with copper dome, repointing of the exterior walls with hydraulic cement, adding new wooden stairs and applying an external coating of whitewash. All of the station's outbuildings added after 1903 (oil house, brick fog signal building, barn and workshop) have been razed.

New London Harbor Lighthouse

NORTH DUMPLING

There are two ferry trips out of New London that enable passengers to view several lighthouses in Fisher's Island Sound and Long Island Sound. Refer to the New London map on page 192.

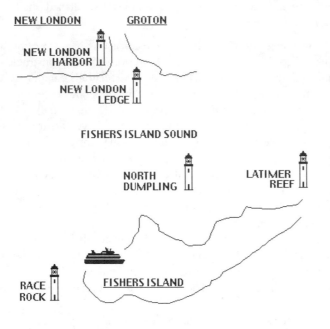

TO THE FERRY DOCKS FROM I-95.

If northbound, take Exit 83's frontage road to Huntington Street. Then:

   -> Turn right and continue south on Huntington,

   -> Bear left into connecting Tilley Street (one way),

   -> Left at Bank Street,

   -> Opposite State Street (monument) turn right across railroad tracks to the Fisher's Island Ferry dock on New London Pier.

   -> Continue north on Bank Street (one way) through a zig-zag intersection into connecting Water Street (one way),

   -> Pass the Amtrak railroad station,

   -> Right across railroad tracks to the Cross Sound Ferry dock. If southbound, take Exit 84's ramp to Williams Street Then:

   -> Turn right and motor under I-95,

   -> Left at Huntington Street,

   -> Bear left into connecting Tilley Street (one way),

   -> Left at Bank Street (one way) to the docks.

Parking (fee) is available in the municipal Water Street Parking Garage on Atlantic Street. Access to Atlantic is via Water Street (one way north) or O'Neill Drive (one way south).

CROSS SOUND FERRY. See the ORIENT POINT, PLUM ISLAND & LITTLE GULL ISLAND chapter (page 155).

FISHER'S ISLAND FERRY. Four lighthouses can be seen as the ferry passes New London Harbor (within 600 yards), New London Ledge (200 yards), North Dumpling (1.5 miles) and Race Rock (0.5 mile).

This auto/passenger ferry provides year round daily service, except December 25. Ferry capacities are 24 and 34 cars. Crossing time is 45 minutes.

As you pass the New London Ledge Lighthouse off your port side note the markings painted on the pier's southwest elevation. These markings are used by submarine crews to calibrate gun and missile guidance systems and sighting instruments. See the NEW LONDON LEDGE chapter's sketch.

VEHICLE RESERVATIONS. Boarding the ferry to Fisher's Island is on a first come, first served basis. Upon reaching the island a reservation for return to New London can be made at the Ferry's Annex Office. If no reservation is available, then reboarding is again on a first come, first served basis. Return reservations may be made in person or by mail with payment and added surcharge. Thus, because the problem of coordinating a one day auto trip to the island, it is recommended that travelers take the ferry as foot passengers. Taxi service is available on the island.

SCHEDULE. Phone or check website for current schedules.

FARES. Vehicle + each passenger one-way tickets. No vehicle reservations from New London. November to April foot passenger round trip fares are almost one-half the same fares charged during the rest of the year. Discount for children 5-11.

- Fisher's Island Ferry District, Box H, Fisher's Island, NY 06390.

Phone: Fisher's Island main office (631) 788-7463. Annex Office (631) 788-7744. New London terminal (860) 442-0165. Recorded schedule information (860) 443-6851.

Website (schedule only): http://www.benkard.com/ferry

NORTH DUMPLING, RACE ROCK & LATIMER REEF

North Dumpling Light, Race Rock Light and Latimer Reef Light can also be seen from the lighthouse cruises offered by Capt. John's Sport Fishing Center in Waterford, Connecticut. See the Lynde Point / Saybrook Breakwater chapter (page 191) for details.

NORTH DUMPLING LIGHTHOUSE.

CHARACTERISTIC: Fixed white (red sector)

HAW: 94' **RANGES**: White 9; red 7 nm

Massachusetts' Governor Winthrop acquired the island from its Indian owners in 1639. It remained in the Winthrop family until 1847. The new owner first built the house and added the light tower two years later.

North Dumpling with its Second Empire mansard roof and attached tower once resembled several other lighthouses, including Connecticut's Penfield Reef. The 60-foot tall octagonal, brick lighthouse is sheathed in shingles.

North Dumpling's first optic was probably a whale oil-fed multi-lamp/reflector device. The lighthouse was restructured in 1871 to facilitate the installation of a fifth-order Fresnel lens.

In 1959, after the beacon was moved to a nearby steel tower and automated, the property was sold to a New York financier for $18,000. His absences and vandalism took a heavy toll of the deactivated light station. After it was sold in 1980 for $95,000, the new owner remodeled the keeper's dwelling. Despite that bit of architectural heresy, he did manage to have the optic returned to the 31-foot tall lighthouse and its former steel tower removed.

In 1987 the island was again on the real estate market for the handsome asking price of $2.5 million. It was purchased by a company president for much less. Shortly after the new owner took control of the property, the news media filed a spate of "lighthouse" items that proved to have been nothing more than a public relations ploy that had the following story line.

The story reportedly began after the owner was unsuccessful in getting Suffolk County's (NY) permission to erect a windmill to power his electric generator. Fed up with bureaucratic red tape, he bestowed upon himself the title of "Lord Dumpling II" and summarily declared his island the "North Dumpling Republic." The new sovereign "nation" was to have its own currency based on the republic's "Dumpling," a national anthem and, purportedly, a nonaggression pact with the great State of Connecticut. The owner and his "Dumpling Republic" lighthouse were even filmed for "Lifestyle of the Rich and Famous" and featured on NBC's "Today Show." Along with all the reported tommyrot was the encouraging statement by the owner that he planned to open his lighthouse to the public. It hasn't happened.

PRESERVATION. Not listed in the National Register of Historic Places.

RACE ROCK LIGHTHOUSE.

CHARACTERISTIC: Flashing red 10s

HAW: 67' **RANGE**: 19 nm

In 1838, after eight ships in the same number of years had been lost in the area and despite Congress' $3,000 appropriation to erect a light tower, there was no effort to build the lighthouse. In 1852 the Lighthouse Board reported on its inability to mark the reef with buoys. In 1871, with a total of $261,000 appropriated, $96,000 had been spent on the construction of the foundation. By 1878 additional surveys and construction delays raised the cost of the project to $270,000.

Although historical accounts indicate a great deal of bureaucratic waste and indecision, the building of the aid's foundation pier was indeed a tough engineering task. The underwater ledge was small and had to be enlarged. The strong tidal currents around the reef made the widening task extremely difficult. The reef was finally enlarged and raised by dumping thousands of tons of up to 4-ton granite boulders.

Atop the artificially created island rests a 9-foot tall concrete foundation pier, laid from bottom to top in decreasing concentric tiers with diameters ranging from 19 feet at the base to 12 feet at the surface. The round 30-foot pier placed on top of the foundation pier has granite block walls filled in with concrete.

The granite tower of Gothic Revival styling is attached to the side of the 1 1/2-story keeper's residence. The 45-foot tall lighthouse, similar in design to the Stratford Shoal Lighthouse, took seven long years to complete.

The light was automated in 1978. The following year a rotating modern lens replaced the 1879 fourth-order Fresnel.

PRESERVATION. Eligible for listing in the National Register of Historic Places.

LATIMER REEF LIGHTHOUSE (LATIMERS REEF).
CHARACTERISTIC: Flashing white 6s
HAW: 55' **RANGE**: 9 nm

Latimer Reef light marks a rocky shoal lying about one mile north of Fishers Island's East Point and 2.3 miles southwest of Stonington. It can be seen from East Point on the north shore of eastern Fisher's Island.

This cast-iron lighthouse is 49 feet tall and rests on a concrete-filled, cast-iron shell. It is painted white with a brown band around its midsection.

When established on July 1, 1884, the tower's optic was a kerosene-powered fifth-order Fresnel lens that replaced a lightship first placed on station in 1849. The light was automated in 1974.

The aid's 1899 fourth-order Fresnel lens was removed in 1983. That lens has been reported to have been reinstalled in Delaware Bay's Elbow of Cross Ledge Lighthouse. Today Latimer Reef's modern optic is powered by an improved version of the successful solar system first used in the Florida Keys.

PRESERVATION. Not listed in the National Register of Historic Places.

The light tower was repainted in 1966 and refurbished with a new coat of paint in 1997.

TO THE U.S. COAST GUARD ACADEMY MUSEUM.
North on Water Street (one way). Then:
-> Right at Crystal Avenue,
-> Left at State Pier Road,
-> Right at Williams Street,
-> Right at Monhegan Avenue to the academy's main entrance.

TO THE NEW LONDON HARBOR LIGHTHOUSE. North on Water Street (one way). Then:
-> Left at Governor Winthrop Boulevard (one way),
-> Left at O'Neill Drive (one way),
-> Across State Street's Captain Walk into Green Street (one way),
-> Left at Tilley Street (one way),
-> Right at Bank Street (two way),
-> Left at Howard Street,
-> Continue on connecting Pequot Avenue to the lighthouse.

Race Rock Lighthouse

New London Ledge Lighthouse

NEW LONDON LEDGE

NORTH OR SOUTH ON I-95. If northbound, take Exit 86 (US 1) to CT 349 (Defense Highway). If southbound, take Exit 87 to CT 349. Then:

    -> Left at Rainville Avenue,

    -> Left at Benham Road,

    -> Left into Eastern Point Road,

    -> At Eastern Point's end at Shennecossett Road turn right into Beach Pond Road,

    -> Bear left into Rita Santa Croce Drive and the entrance to Eastern Point Park.

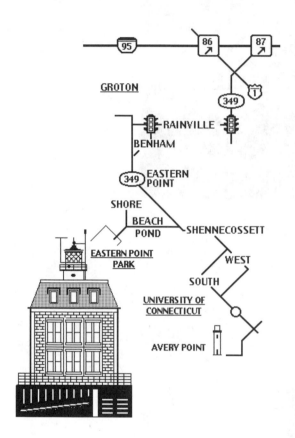

OPEN.

June to Labor Day only to Groton residents. No restrictions at other times of the year.

From June to Labor Day a gate attendant is on duty. You may be allowed in if you put on your best smile and try the "lighthouse only" request. If denied entry, drive the short distance north on Shore Avenue to a small beach on the left. One hour parking (free) is permitted on the west side of Shore. New London Harbor Light can also be seen from this location.

New London Ledge Light can also be viewed from the Cross Sound and Fishers Island ferries out of New London. See the North Dumpling / Race Rock / Latimer Reef chapter (page 194) for details.

TO AVERY POINT. Return to Eastern Point Road and turn right. Then:

    -> Bear left through the curve into Shinnecossett Road,

    -> At the entrance to the University of Connecticut's Avery Point Campus turn right into West Street and follow the small blue signs to the Project Oceanology building. Free parking in front of the building. If you do not take the cruise, it is but a short downhill walk from the Project Oceanology building to the boat landing and the Avery Point tower.

VISITING THE NEW LONDON LEDGE LIGHT-HOUSE.

Project Oceanology and the New London Lighthouse Foundation sponsor boat trips to the ledge. Visitors are permitted to take a walking tour of the lighthouse. The 55-foot research vessel *EnvironLab* departs the campus' boat landing. Reservations are strongly recommended.

SCHEDULE.

Mid-June to early September. Tuesdays, Thursdays, Saturdays and Sundays at 4. Returns at 6.

FARES. Payment required in advance. Call Project Oceanology between 9 and 4.

Visa and Mastercard accepted. Discount for children 6-12.

- Project Oceanology, Avery Point, 1084 Shennecossett Road, Groton, CT 06340-6097.

Phone (860) 445-9007. In USA (outside CT) toll-free (800) 364-8472.

Website: http://www.oceanology.org/

Email: info@oceanology.org

NEW LONDON LEDGE LIGHTHOUSE.

CHARACTERISTIC: Group flashing white and red 30s

HAW: 58' **RANGES**: White 17; red 14 nm

This 58-foot tall brick and granite lighthouse and its foundation were constructed at a cost of $95,000. Its light was established on November 10, 1909.

NEW LONDON LEDGE

The 50-foot square concrete-filled pier stands on a 50-foot square (52-foot square before the original timber cribbing was removed in 1938) concrete and stone foundation, rising some 18 feet above low water and containing a basement with two cisterns. Atop the pier is the 35-foot tall square house. The upper roof supports the octagonal brick watchroom and the smallish cast-iron lantern. The three-story, 14-room lighthouse is an architectural hybrid, evolving from both its Colonial Revival (sometimes referred to as Georgian) and French Second Empire stylings. It has red brick and white trim, prominent groins, small rectangular windows, pedimented dormers and hip joints derived from its sloping or mansard-styled roof. The structure's decks were built with cinder concrete supported by steel I-beams, an early use of this technology in the United States.

The original optic consisted of a Henri LePaute fourth-order Fresnel lens and a kerosene lamp. The beacon was rotated by a weighted clockwork that had to be rewound every six to eight hours. In 1913 the power source was an incandescent kerosene vapor lamp. After the laying of an underwater cable, the lens was electrified. The fourth-order Fresnel lens was removed in 1984 prior to the installation of an automated modern beacon.

Citing the high costs to both operate and staff the light, the Coast Guard withdrew its personnel and closed the light station on May 1, 1987. New London Ledge was Long Island Sound's last occupied lighthouse. When withdrawn from duty on the "rock," one disenchanted member of the crew noted in the station's log that the lighthouse was "Ernie's domain." "Ernie" is the spirit of a former lightkeeper who, after learning that his wife ran off with a boat captain, jumped off the roof. His spectre has been held responsible for a number of strange nighttime events, such as opening and closing the heavy entrance door, cleaning and swabbing the decks and switching the fog signal and light on and off.

OWNER. U.S. Coast Guard. Leased to the New London Ledge Lighthouse Foundation.

PRESERVATION. Listed in the National Register of Historic Places.

In April 1987, after the closing of the light station, a small group of concerned citizens decided to invest their time and effort in preserving the lighthouse, establishing an educational center and museum and opening the station to the public. The first item of business for the private New London Ledge Lighthouse Foundation was to cosign with the Coast Guard a long-term management lease. With this accomplished, the Foundation next secured a State grant of $100,000 to build a new sewage treatment plant and a desalinization plant. Those projects were completed in 1992. Using funds from private contributions, the Foundation completed the refurbishing of the lighthouse's interior in 1994. In 1994 the City of New London applied for a $2 million grant to link the area's marine attractions and establish boat transportation to the lighthouse. New London Ledge, now a museum and educational facility, will eventually become a part of southeastern Connecticut's maritime park system. There is discussion of making rooms available at the lighthouse for overnight stays.

- New London Ledge Lighthouse Foundation, PO Box 855, New London, CT 06320.
Phone (860) 442-2222.

AVERY POINT TOWER. This octagonal concrete tower was built to be a memorial tower. The builder, hoping to add a little glamour to his project, tried to establish a privately maintained light in the tower. Since the light would interfere with New London Ledge's mission, his request was denied. While not an established aid to navigation, the tower once held an active beacon. In 1944, with Avery Point having been acquired for use as a U.S. Coast Guard Training Center, a multi-lamp, low candlepower optic was installed in the tower. The light, a symbolic representation of the Coast Guard's lightkeeping responsibilities, was never officially proclaimed an aid to navigation. When the Coast Guard closed the Center in 1967, the beacon was discontinued. Since then, lack of maintenance has caused significant deterioration to the lighthouse.

The Avery Point Lighthouse Society was formed in February 2000 with the goal of saving, restoring and relighting the Avery Point Lighthouse. You can send your tax deductible donation to:

- Avery Point Lighthouse Society, P.O. Box 1552, Groton, CT 06340
Phone: (860) 445-5417
Website: http://apls.tripod.com
Email: APLS1941@aol.com

MORGAN POINT

The privately owned Morgan Point Lighthouse is barely visible from the entrance to its residential enclave. For those interested in viewing the lighthouse there is a cruise that takes passengers down the Mystic River past Morgan Point (about 100 yards) and a short distance into Fisher's Island Sound before returning to port.

Morgan Point Light can also be seen from the lighthouse cruises offered by Capt. John's Sport Fishing Center in Waterford, Connecticut. See the Lynde Point / Saybrook Breakwater chapter (page 191) for details.

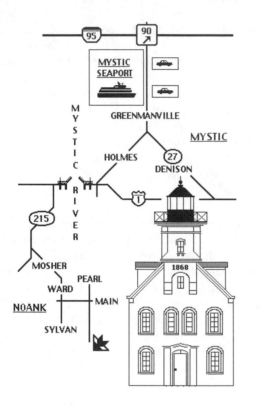

MYSTIC SEAPORT MUSEUM. This complex is easily reached from both I-95 (Exit 90) and US 1. There is ample free parking in both the south and north lots off Greenmanville Avenue.

The Seaport is a nationally acclaimed living history museum with authentically structured buildings representative of the 19th and early 20th Century maritime trades and domestic life. Exhibits include ships, shops, craft demonstrations, a planetarium and the last of the wooden whaling ships.

The lighthouse at the tip of the Seaport's Adams Shipyard Point is an authentic replica of Nantucket Island's Brant Point Lighthouse. The tower contains a fourth-order Fresnel lens.

OPEN. Daily all year. Closed December 25.
January through March 10 to 4.
April and May 9 to 5.
June through August 9 to 6.
September and October 9 to 5.
November and December 9 to 4.

ADMISSION FEES. Discounts for the handicapped and children 6-15. Under 5 free.

- Mystic Seaport Museum, PO Box 6000 (75 Greenmanville Avenue), Mystic, CT 06355.
Phone (860) 572-5315. Reservations (860) 572-0711. Website: http://www.mysticseaport.org

RIVER CRUISE. To reach the cruise dock enter the Seaport's main entrance opposite the south parking lot. The dock is straight ahead, where the fishing schooner *L. A Dunton* is berthed. The ticket booth, a small gray building, is at the head of the dock.

The 1 1/2-hour narrated cruise is aboard the Seaport's preserved coal-fired steamboat, *Sabino* (two decks; lower with cabin).

While aboard the *Sabino*, you will be given a first hand look at her steamplant. The old passenger steamer, built in 1908, sailed on Maine's Damariscotta River as the *Tourist*. Sunk in 1918, she was salvaged, refitted, given a new name and transferred to Maine's Casco Bay. There she carried passengers until 1958. After a period of private ownership and another several years working out of Newburyport, Massachusetts, she was donated in 1973 to the Mystic Seaport. The Seaport's Preservation Shipyard restored the steamboat to her present bristol condition. While aboard, listen to the rarely heard chug of her 75-horsepower compound engine.

SCHEDULE. Call or check the website for the current schedule. Be sure to call ahead to confirm, since the *Sabino* is sometimes booked for private charters.

FARES. The purchase of a museum admission ticket is not required to take the evening cruise. Discount for children 6-12; under 5 free.

MORGAN POINT LIGHTHOUSE.

The first lighthouse on Morgan Point was erected on the present lighthouse grounds in 1831. The 25-foot tower, located some 80 feet from the stone keeper's house, was a circular granite structure equipped with a Lewis lighting apparatus. In 1868 the tower and house were torn down to make way for the a new lighthouse erected the following year.

This 52-foot tall lighthouse, a 2 1/2-story dwelling with an integrated tower, is built of solid Rhode Island granite blocks (Boston style) with walls that are two feet thick. The structure resembles the Great Captain Island Lighthouse off Greenwich and Block Island's North Lighthouse.

The 1831 lighthouse was first equipped with a multi-lamp/reflector apparatus. In 1855, the power source was changed over to a lard oil-fed single lamp intensified by a sixth-order Fresnel lens of either French or English manufacture, but known to have been purchased in Germany. The light's focal plane was 61 feet above mean high water and had a range of 12 nautical miles. That classical lens was lost when the September 1938 hurricane tore the lantern off its deck.

Morgan Point was deactivated in 1919 (as recorded by the lighthouse's first private owners) and its responsibility transferred to a minor beacon at the entrance to the Mystic River.

Hard work and meager salaries were the usual lot of the keepers and their families. Bravery and devotion to their assigned tasks far exceeded any remuneration the government could have offered them. One difficult job involved the handling and preparation of lard oil. It was a lightkeeper's nightmare. The fuel came in blocks, or butts, and before they could be used the semisoft blocks had to be heated to avoid congealing before being poured into the lamp's reservoir. This process was usually accomplished twice each day to insure proper burning. In the cold of winter with preheating at ground level, the lard oil container had to be wrapped in blankets or cloths to get the oil up the stairway to the service deck and into the lamp's reservoir before it hardened. Fortunately for all lighthouse keepers, Pennsylvania's crude oil find and the subsequent introduction of kerosene, or mineral oil, ended these up-the-stairs-down replenishment tasks.

PRESERVATION. Listed in the National Register of Historic Places as part of the Noank Historic District.

The lighthouse, keeper's residence and grounds were declared surplus government property and sold at auction on June 25, 1922 for the grand sum of $8,625.

Having remained in the possession of one family for over 70 years, the old light station was placed on the real estate market in 1989 for $1,950,000. Sale of the station property in 1991 (reportedly for $1.3 million) was made to a Californian, Jason Pilalas, who gutted the interior of the 1868 lighthouse to make way for its complete remodeling. In 1993 Mr. Pilalas topped the watchroom with a new aluminum lantern and roof, authentically fabricated using old Lighthouse Service blueprints.

NOANK HISTORICAL SOCIETY MUSEUM.

This museum displays maritime artifacts, local memorabilia, early 20th century art and the photographs of the original interior of the Morgan Point Lighthouse. The Society's Latham-Chester Store Museum is at 108 Main Street.

OPEN.
Summer months, Wednesdays and weekends 2 to 5.
Fall months, Wednesdays 2 to 5.
FREE ADMISSION.

- Noank Historical Society, PO Box 9454 (17 Sylvan Street), Noank, CT 06340.
Phone (860) 536-7026 or (860) 536-3021.

STONINGTON HARBOR

NORTH OR SOUTH ON US 1. Take US 1A into Stonington center via Water Street. Free parking is available across the street from the lighthouse and farther south on Water Street.

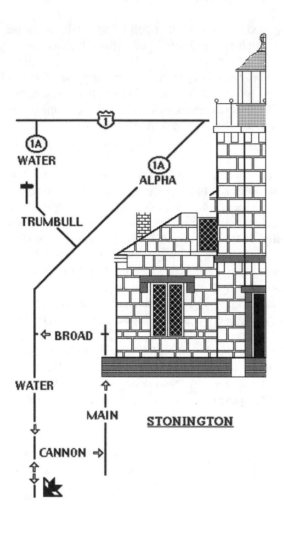

STONINGTON

OLD LIGHTHOUSE MUSEUM. This museum contains six rooms of artifacts representing Stonington's history from pre-1649 days. Display subjects include seal hunting, whaling, the China trade, salt, glazed pottery, wooden farm and kitchen tools and ice harvesting. A childrens' room is filled with a doll house, dolls and toys from earlier years. The aid's original 1855 sixth-order Fresnel lens is also on display along with lighthouse photographs. A short climb up the granite stairway to the lantern affords a panoramic view of Long Island Sound.

OPEN.

May to October, every day except Monday 11 to 5.

ADMISSION FEES. Discount for children 6-12. Under 6 free.

- Stonington Historical Society / Old Lighthouse Museum, 7 Water Street, Stonington, CT 06378.

Phone (860) 535-1440.

Website: http://www.stoningtonhistsoc.org

STONINGTON HARBOR LIGHTHOUSE. This lighthouse was first erected in 1823 at Windmill Point, on the west side of Stonington Harbor. The station, consisting of a 30-foot cylindrical stone tower and a 1 1/2-story attached house, was funded by an 1822 congressional appropriation of $3,500. The original multi-lamp Lewis optic (10 lamps with 13-inch reflectors), showed a fixed white light some 47 feet above mean high water. It was first established in 1824 with range of 12 nautical miles.

In 1838 the Lighthouse Service reported that the sea had reached to within 30 feet of the lighthouse's base. Because of the ensuing erosion, the structure was dismantled in 1840 and moved to its present site on the harbor's east side. When rebuilt the granite tower was given an octagonal shape and raised in height to 33 feet. The relocated (extant) lighthouse held a Lewis lighting device, consisting of eight lamps and 16-inch reflectors. Since the rebuilt lighthouse had a higher base elevation, its optic's focal plane was 62 feet above the water. The Lewis lighting apparatus was replaced in 1855 with a sixth-order Fresnel optic.

OWNER. The unattended Stonington Harbor lighthouse and grounds were sold at auction to a private party, who transferred them to the Stonington Historical Society in 1925.

PRESERVATION. Listed in the National Register of Historic Places.

STONINGTON BREAKWATER LIGHTHOUSE (dismantled).

In 1899 two major changes were made to Stonington Harbor's aids to navigation. The harbor light was discontinued and its warning responsibility transferred to the Stonington Inner Breakwater beacon placed atop a steel tower. The second change was the completion of the Stonington Breakwater Lighthouse, a 25-foot tall conical stone tower surmounting an octagonal foundation that was anchored to the breakwater that extends southward from the harbor's west side. Adjoining the tower was a small family dwelling no larger than an equipment shed. The lantern was fitted with a fourth-order Fresnel lens that showed a fixed red characteristic. The breakwater light was discontinued in 1926 and its tower was later dismantled.

RHODE ISLAND
WATCH HILL

NORTH OR SOUTH ON RI SCENIC 1A. The Watch Hill Lighthouse is located on a bluff on the north side of the east entrance to Fishers Island Sound. In Avondale on RI Scenic 1A turn south into Watch Hill Road. Then:

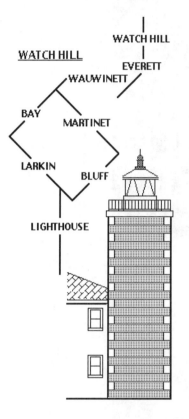

-> Continue south on Watch Hill Road and Everett Avenue,
-> Bear right into Wauwinett Road,
-> Bear left into connecting Bay Street,
-> Left at Larkin Road,
-> Just before Bluff Road on the right is Lighthouse Road, a paved lane that heads downhill to the station's main gate and then up to the fenced visitors' section. Seniors (64+) and the handicapped are permitted to drive to the lighthouse. All others must park outside of Lighthouse Road and walk to the lighthouse.

LIGHTHOUSE MUSEUM. While the keeper's house and the tower are closed to visitors, the oil house, located to the left of the station's gate, has been restored and converted into a small maritime museum. Its main attraction is the lighthouse's original fourth-order Fresnel lens and its intricate clockwork mechanism.

VISITORS' SECTION OPEN. All year, daily 8 to 8. No pets.
MUSEUM OPEN. July and August, Tuesdays & Thursdays 1 to 3.

FREE ADMISSION. Donations for upkeep welcomed.
- Watch Hill Lighthouse Keepers Association, 14 Lighthouse Road, Watch Hill, RI 02891.
WATCH HILL LIGHTHOUSE.
CHARACTERISTIC: Alternating white and red 5s
HAW: 61' **RANGES**: White 16; red 14 nm
During King George's War (1744-48) the colonists erected a maritime observation tower on Watch Hill's "point." It is not known if the tower held a beacon. It is recorded, however, that the structure was destroyed in 1781 during a storm.

By 1793 the U.S. Senate became interested in establishing a permanent beacon on Watch Hill "point." In 1806, after Congress had appropriated the funds, President Jefferson commissioned the building of a new lighthouse. The 35-foot tall wood framed and weatherboard tower was equipped with a revolving multi-lamp optic that became operational in 1808. The present granite lighthouse, erected in 1856-57, stands about 50 feet northwest of the earlier tower. It is a 45-foot tall (10-foot square) brick-lined structure. The attached keeper's residence is a two-story brick house. The tower's architectural styling is very similar to Rhode Island's Beavertail light tower. The station also contains a fog signal building built in 1986.

The Coast Guard removed its personnel and the 1857 fourth-order Fresnel lens after the light was automated in August 1986.

OWNER. U.S. Coast Guard. Leased to Watch Hill Lighthouse Keepers Association since August 1986.

PRESERVATION. Listed in the National Register of Historic Places as part of the Watch Hill Historic District.

In 1986 upon the leasing of the keeper's dwelling, oil house and acreage, the Association secured the station by hiring a resident caretaker. Since then the organization, through contributions and grants, has raised sufficient funds for the initial restoration work and to establish an endowment fund for the station's preservation. The old oil house has been refurbished and is now the station's museum.

In 1992, in addition to storm repairs that both slowed work and siphoned funds earmarked for the restoration project, the station's buildings were repainted and screening and storm windows replaced on two sides of the keeper's dwelling.

The Association intends to proceed with its plan to restore the dwelling's interior. The lighthouse caretaker is restoring the apartment on the second floor. During the renovation original architectural designs and details have been uncovered.

Watch Hill Lighthouse

Point Judith Lighthouse

POINT JUDITH

NORTH OR SOUTH ON US 1. In Wakefield depart US 1 and follow RI 108 (Old Point Judith Road) south to its Point Judith terminus at a four way stop. Turn right and follow Ocean Road to the light station. Although the Coast Guard closed its station in 1995, present tenants permit visitors to enter to view and photograph the lighthouse.

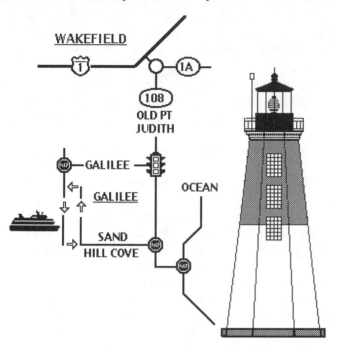

POINT JUDITH LIGHTHOUSE.

CHARACTERISTIC: Group occulting white 15s

HAW: 65' **RANGE**: 16 nm

Although a beacon may have been established in the late 1700s, the first light tower was established in 1810 after the Federal Government purchased its parcel of land for $700. The octagonal wooden tower was equipped with a spider lamp containing 15 whale oil-burning wicks. The light had a flashing characteristic that was produced by a platformed rotating eclipser that blocked out the light every 2.5 minutes. The tower collapsed in September 1815 during a hurricane.

Point Judith Lighthouse was reestablished on December 14, 1816, using one of Winslow Lewis' optics, consisting of 10 whale oil-fueled lamps fitted with 8.5-inch reflectors and green plano-convex lenses.

The old tower's eclipser mechanism was repaired and placed in the new lantern. Interestingly, in 1818 Rhode Island's lighthouse superintendent wrote that lighting apparatuses taken by the British from America's lighthouses were unloaded in Bermuda, purchased by American privateers and sold to none other than Winslow Lewis, who reinstalled at least two of them in the lighthouses at Point Judith and Massachusetts' Gay Head.

The present tower was built in 1857. It is octagonal and conical in shape and is constructed of rough granite stone blocks and beveled Connecticut freestone. The exterior walls are coated with cement. It has a 20-foot diameter base with walls tapering to a 9-foot diameter at the lantern deck.

A stone fog signal building was added in 1923. The brick oil house was erected in 1917. The present light station's administrative and support buildings were constructed by the Coast Guard in 1937. The property, by the way, was first occupied by a lifesaving station that burned down in 1938. The old keeper's quarters was demolished in 1954.

The presently active 1857 fourth-order Fresnel optic was automated in 1954.

Incidentally, the origin of Point Judith's name is disputed. Some say it was after the wife or mother-in-law of merchant John Hull, others say it was named for the Tribe of Judah in the Bible. The most colorful explanation concerns a Nantucket sea captain who was lost in the fog off the point. The captain's daughter shouted that she spotted land. The captain, unable to discern anything in the fog, exhorted his daughter to "Point, Judy, point!"

OWNER. U.S. Coast Guard.

PRESERVATION. Listed in the National Register of Historic Places.

In the summer of 2000 Point Judith Lighthouse underwent a major restoration. Coast Guard architect Marsha Levy did the design work and oversaw the restoration by Campbell Construction of Beverly, Massachusetts. The lens was removed to the Coast Guard Aids to Navigation Team in Bristol, Rhode Island, and the lantern went to Campbell Construction for refurbishing. Some of the lantern's panels were replaced, and a repainting left it in pristine condition.

The refurbished lantern was returned to the lighthouse on July 13, 2000. New galvanized steel windows with six panes of safety glass were installed, similar to the tower's original wrought iron windows.

Some of the original brownstone, which "weathers horribly" according to Levy, had to be replaced. Brownstone is hard to come by these days, but a quarry was found in Cheshire, Connecticut. The new stones were dyed to match the old ones. The project also utilized special mortar from Holland, which is custom formulated to match any stone. Cracks were patched on the interior and exterior of the tower. Rather than paint the upper half of the tower brown, Levy decided to leave it the natural brownstone color, with a dye making it slightly darker.

According to Marsha Levy, the restoration should leave the tower in excellent condition for at least 100 years.

BLOCK ISLAND SOUTHEAST
BLOCK ISLAND NORTH

FERRY FROM GALILEE. The Galilee ferry landing can be reached via Galilee Road from RI 108 or via Sandhill Cove Road from the Point Judith Lighthouse. A parking lot (fee) is located across the street from the pier. Motels and restaurants are located along the waterfront. The ferry operates all year, except December 25. Vehicle reservations required. Foot passengers and bicyclists do not require prior scheduling. Crossing takes about 70 minutes.

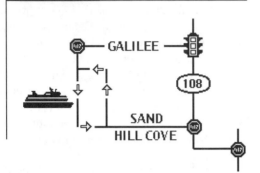

SCHEDULE. Call or check website for the latest schedule.

FARES. Same day round trip vehicle (two one way tickets) and driver each passenger (one round trip ticket). Discount for seniors 65+ and children under 12.

- Interstate Navigation Company, PO Box 482, New London, CT 06320.

Phone: New London (860) 442-7891 or (860) 442-9553. For vehicle reservations from Galilee (401) 783-4613.

Website: http://www.blockislandferry.com/

Note also the very popular Providence - Block Island cruise in the CONIMICUT - POMHAM ROCK - NAYATT POINT chapter

BLOCK ISLAND. With a landscape that compares favorably with that of Ireland and Scotland and delightful summer and fall weather, Block Island has become a vacation mecca for artists, mainland residents and tourists. Transportation is available for a delightful tour of the island and visits to its lighthouses. Taxis can be hired by the hour. A one hour taxi ride costs less than a rented car's four hour minimum rate. There are also mopeds and bicycles for rent by the hour or by the day. The lighthouses are no more than four miles from the ferry dock. Since shops, inns and restaurants are clustered around Old Harbor, transportation is not required to browse and dine.

CONTINUE ON. The Southeast Lighthouse is located on Mohegan Bluffs. Leave Old Harbor via Water Street and at a small rotary (with statuary) drive or walk straight ahead. Follow Spring Street and Southeast Light Road to the lighthouse.

BLOCK ISLAND SOUTHEAST INTERPRETIVE CENTER. This visitor and educational center reopened in 1995 in the relocated lighthouse. It holds exhibits and photographs depicting the history of the aid and its original 1875 first-order Fresnel beehive lens.

OPEN.

July to Labor Day, daily 10 to 4.

September to Columbus Day, Saturdays and Sundays 10 to 4.

LIGHTHOUSE TOURS. When the center is open 10:15 to 4.

ADMISSION FEES. Discounts for seniors and children.

- Block Island Southeast Lighthouse Foundation, PO Box 949, Block Island, RI 02807.

Phone (401) 466-5009.

BLOCK ISLAND SOUTHEAST LIGHTHOUSE.

CHARACTERISTIC: Fixed green 5s

HAW: 261' **RANGE**: 20 nm

By 1854 Congress decided that the Mohegan Bluffs required a beacon, and on August 18, 1856, it appropriated $9,000 for the lighthouse. The Lighthouse Board, however, spent the money to rebuild the Block Island North Lighthouse on a site farther inland on Sandy Point. In May 1858, the *Palmetto* was lost on the reef below the bluffs and many urged the immediate installation of a fog whistle and a lighted aid. President Grant signed the congressional appropriation bill in 1872, and later, during his presidency, visited the station.

The 52-foot tall octagonal tower and its attached 2 1/2-story dwelling are constructed of red brick and rest on a foundation of dressed granite blocks. The structure's design shows a Victorian-influenced Gothic Revival styling. The lighthouse tapers from a 25-foot diameter at the base to 15 feet at the lantern deck. The cast-iron lantern has inside dimensions of 10 feet by 12 feet, ample space for its original first-order Fresnel lens. Note that the lantern has 16 rather than the more common octagonal or decagonal shapes. A spiral stairway to the lantern is also made of cast iron. The completed lighthouse and its steam-operated fog signal system cost $80,000.

BLOCK ISLAND SOUTHEAST & NORTH

When first lighted on February 1, 1875, the optic consisted of a Henri Lepaute first-order lens and a lamp with a series of four circular wicks. All four wicks dropped through the tower to its base, where they rested in a barrel of whale oil. The lamp consumed 900 gallons of oil annually and used 1/2 inch of the wicks daily.

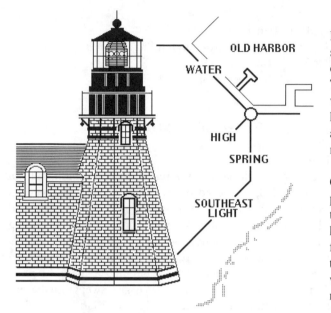

In 1880 the optic was changed to a single kerosene-fed lamp inside a newly installed modified LePaute first-order classical lens, consisting of eight bullseye (no catadioptric or dioptric prisms) panels fitted to a 1 1/2 inch solid brass frame.[1] The lens rotated on a bath of mercury and was driven by a weight powered clockwork that had to be rewound every four hours. On July 7, 1990, the Coast Guard deactivated the light and transferred its warning mission to a beacon placed on a nearby steel tower.

RELOCATION. In an amendment to the U.S. Army's Corps of Engineers' 1990-91 budget, Congress gave its approval to move the lighthouse away from the cliff to a site near the steel tower. The nonprofit Block Island Southeast Lighthouse Foundation announced in October 1991 that it had the funds needed to complete the relocation project. The relocation, completed on August 13, 1993 at a cost of $1.9 million, was accomplished by first bracing the windows, doors, chimneys and the massive Fresnel lens.

The real work began with the reinforcing the rubblestone foundation with gunite, the formation of a concrete compression ring within the tower and the application of a strengthening steel jacket outside. After those preparatory projects a network of steel beams was laid underneath the 2,000-ton structure, using diamond wire saw to cut the insertion holes in the foundation. With the support beams in place the structure was slowly and evenly raised two feet by 38 hydraulic lifting jacks. It was then pushed over rollers placed between the jacks and supporting roller beams. To avoid disturbing the coursed brickwork, the lighthouse had to be displaced at right angles with the 245-foot move back from the bluff accomplished in three moves. The relocation was completed on August 24, 1993.

Since the hybrid first-order lens rested on a potentially toxic mercury float, it was replaced by Cape Lookout's original first-order Fresnel lens that had been displayed at the Coast Guard's Support Center in Portsmouth, Virginia. The new stationary optic was lighted on August 27, 1994.

OWNER. U.S. Coast Guard. Tower, dwelling and grounds leased to the Block Island Southeast Lighthouse Foundation.

PRESERVATION. Listed in the National Register of Historic Places. Given National Historic Landmark designation in 1997.

In the summer of 1999 the Block Island Southeast Lighthouse Foundation received a $475,000 grant from the National Transportation Enhancement Program for restoration of the lighthouse. The foundation estimates that it will cost about $1 million to fully renovate the structure. In 2000 the foundation received another $300,000 in federal funds from the America's Treasures grant program.

There are plans to enlarge the museum and possibly convert some of the dwelling into overnight accommodations.

CONTINUE ON. The Block Island North Lighthouse stands on Sandy Point some four miles from Old Harbor. Leave Old Harbor via Water and Dodge Streets. At Corn Neck Road (post office is on the corner) turn right and continue to the road's end. Parking (free) is permitted at the end of Corn Neck. There is a 0.5 mile beach walk out to the lighthouse.

Handicapped visitors may call one day in advance of visit for transportation to the lighthouse.

---

1. The 1880 date for the installation of the hybrid first-order Fresnel lens was provided in a paper entitled "Southeast Light" by Coast Guard keeper R.C. Niesel in May 1985. A Historic American Building Survey (HABS) of 1988 states the lens was installed in 1929. The 1929 date may be the valid one, because it is known that the optic was electrified in 1928 and its characteristic changed to flashing green 3.7s on April 16, 1929.

NORTH LIGHT INTERPRETIVE CENTER. This center with its galleries and rest room is housed on the first floor of the restored lighthouse. Exhibits cover the lighthouse's history, Block Island's lifesaving service, and the island's flora and fauna. Also on display is Block Island North's original fourth-order Fresnel lens. The building is handicapped accessible.

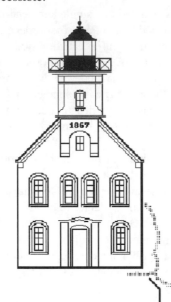

OPEN.
Mid-June to Labor Day, daily 10 to 4.
Rest of September to Columbus Day, Fridays through Sundays 10 to 4.
ADMISSION FEE. Nominal. Under 12 free.
- North Light Fund, PO Box 1183, Block Island, RI 02807.
Phone (401) 466-2982.

BLOCK ISLAND NORTH LIGHTHOUSE (SANDY POINT).
CHARACTERISTIC: Flashing white 5s
HAW: 58' **RANGE**: 13 nm

Four lighthouses have been built on Sandy Point. The first station, built in 1829 with an appropriation of $5,000, is believed to have been a wood framed keeper's house sandwiched between two 45-foot tall wooden towers. The structure was washed away a few years later. In 1837 another lighthouse, consisting of a granite building flanked on each end by a light tower, was built about 0.25 mile inland of the 1829 site. The optic, consisting of 17 whale oil lamps, was 25 feet above mean high water. Although they merged a short distance from the lighthouse, the fixed white lights were visible for 12 nautical miles. The structure was also swept into the sea. The third aid was a 50-foot tall granite tower completed in 1857 farther inland on the spit of land. It was destroyed by fire. The $9,000, appropriated in 1854 for an aid on Mohegan Bluffs, was diverted to rebuild the 1857 lighthouse. The foundations of both the 1837 and 1857 lighthouses can be seen farther out on the point.

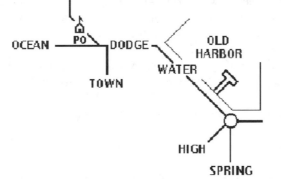

The present 52-foot tall lighthouse was constructed in 1867 using Connecticut granite. Its base, only two feet above mean high water, is about 700 yards from the tip of Sandy Point. The 2 1/2-story structure's architectural styling shows the influence of the Victorian-Gothic Revival genre.

In 1953, after the fourth-order Fresnel lens had been removed and donated to the Block Island Historical Society, the light was transferred to a nearby skeletal steel tower.

OWNER. Lighthouse and surrounding 2.4 acres were deeded to the Town of New Shoreham in 1984.
PRESERVATION. Listed in the National Register of Historic Places.

After its deactivation in 1973, the U.S. Fish and Wildlife Service acquired the lighthouse and surrounding acreage for use as a national wildlife refuge. At the same time and in anticipation of its future role in preserving the lighthouse, the Town of New Shoreham established the North Light Restoration Commission. After several years of negotiation, New Shoreham and the Fish and Wildlife Service concluded an exchange agreement that gave the Service 20 acres as a conservation easement, and the town received the deteriorated and vandalized lighthouse. By 1989 the town and commission with support from the Block Island Historical Society had succeeded in securing $500,000 in government grants and donations for the restoration of the lighthouse. Restoration of the tower began immediately. The lighthouse was reactivated on August 5, 1989, using a modern plastic lens.

The last restoration project is the finishing of the tower and upper floors. That task will require an estimated $300,000 to complete. To raise funds the Commission is selling commemorative (donor's name inscribed) bricks to be laid in building an apron around the lighthouse. The donation is tax-free.

Block Island Southeast Lighthouse

Block Island North Lighthouse

DUTCH ISLAND

This lighthouse stands on an island in Narragansett Bay's West Passage off Conanicut Island. A good place from which to view the lighthouse is Jamestown's Fort Getty Recreation Area. See also the CONANICUT POINT & PLUM BEACH chapter's map.

This lighthouse and several others can also be viewed from the special lighthouse cruises offered by Bay Queen Cruises of Warren, RI. See the Bristol Ferry Light chapter (page 225) for details.

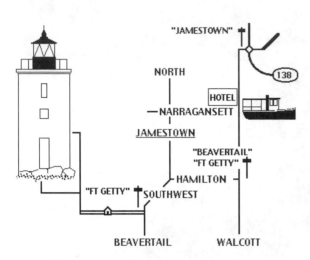

TO JAMESTOWN. If eastbound on RI 138, cross over the Jamestown Bridge (free) and continue across the island to an exit just west of the Newport Bridge. The exit is marked with a "Jamestown" sign.

If westbound, cross over the Newport Bridge (toll westbound only) to the exit. Then:

-> Follow Walcott Avenue south past a large hotel and marina to Hamilton Avenue,

-> Right at Hamilton,

-> Left at Southwest Avenue to the entrance to Fort Getty Recreation Area. The entrance to the park is marked with a small "Fort Getty" sign tacked on a pole. After checking at the entrance gate, follow the outer perimeter road as it loops north then west around the park and up onto the high ground by the bay.

OPEN. Late May to early October, daily 7 AM to 10 PM.

ADMISSION FEES. Varying fees are charged for camping, overnight stays for recreation vehicles and day parking.

According to the Jamestown Recreation Office the gatekeeper is permitted to allow lighthouse seekers into the park without paying the entrance fee. When requesting free entry, emphasize to the gate keeper that you wish to view and photograph the Dutch Island Lighthouse and that your stay will be one of short duration.

- Jamestown Town Offices, 44 Southwest Avenue, Jamestown, RI 02835.

Phone (401) 423-7211. Gate (401) 423-7264.

DUTCH ISLAND LIGHTHOUSE.

In 1825 the southern tip of the island was ceded by Rhode Island to the Federal Government for the construction of a 30-foot tall lighthouse. The tower, which was connected to a keeper's dwelling, was completed in 1826. Its beacon was established the following year. In 1838 the Lighthouse Service reported that the dwelling had been built with slate and stone found on the island. In 1844 an inspection report called the tower and keeper's dwelling the State's worst example of lighthouse construction. Over the years, requests to Washington to upgrade the light, tower and support buildings were largely ignored.

Finally, in 1857, funds were available to rebuild the tower in the Federal Design style and renovate the dwelling. The existing square, 42-foot tall lighthouse is constructed of brick and rests on the island's surface rock. In 1960 the keeper's house was razed, leaving only the tower and a concrete storage building standing.

The first lighthouse's lantern held a Winslow Lewis lamp-reflector optic which, at an elevation of 56 feet above the bay, showed a fixed white light with a range of 13 nautical miles. When the lighthouse was rebuilt, it received a fourth-order Fresnel lens. In 1924 its characteristic was changed to occulting red. In 1939 the lens was fitted with an incandescent oil vapor lamp. The beacon was discontinued in 1979 due to vandalism.

OWNER. U.S. Coast Guard lease to American Lighthouse Foundation. The island is managed by the Rhode Island Department of Environmental Management.

- **American Lighthouse Foundation** , PO Box 889, Wells, Maine 04090.

Phone: (207) 646-0515.

Website: http://www.lighthousefoundation.org

PRESERVATION. The Dutch Island Lighthouse is an abandoned and decaying structure; it has been open to the elements and nesting birds for years. There is new hope, however, since the lighthouse was leased by the Coast Guard to the American Lighthouse Foundation in early 2000. A chapter of the foundation called the Dutch Island Lighthouse Society has been established to restore the lighthouse.

DUTCH ISLAND, WHALE ROCK

The Dutch Island Lighthouse Society plans to renovate the structure inside and out. A full restoration of the lighthouse has been estimated at about $106,000. Unfortunately, as of the summer of 2001 the Rhode Island Department of Environmental Management has officially closed Dutch Island to visitors because of hidden holes related to the old military installation on the island. It is hoped that these issues can be worked out so that tours of the restored lighthouse can eventually be offered.

Regardless of the access issues, the Dutch Island Lighthouse Society is dedicated to saving the lighthouse and hopes to reactivate it as an aid to navigation.

- Dutch Island Lighthouse Society, PO Box 40151, Providence, Rhode Island 02940
Website: http://www.dutchislandlighthouse.org
Email: dlomba@loa.com

Dutch Island Lighthouse

TO BEAVERTAIL POINT. Return to Beavertail Road and turn right. As you enter Beavertail State Park (free) pull into parking lot #2 on the right. The foundation of the former Whale Rock Lighthouse is located offshore to the southwest.

WHALE ROCK LIGHTHOUSE (destroyed).

The outcropping once supported the Whale Rock Lighthouse, a truncated cast-iron tower placed atop a cylindrical, concrete filled ring of cast-iron plates. The combined lighthouse and foundation had an exceptional high-rise appearance during periods of low water. The structure had five working levels: a storage basement formed in the foundation, a galley on the main deck, three more bedroom levels and the watchroom. Whale Rock's beacon came on station on October 1, 1882.

Walter Barge Eberle, assistant keeper at Whale Rock Light in 1938, was the father of six children. On September 21, 1938, Keeper Eberle saw that the seas were growing rough around Whale Rock. Because of the conditions, he left the mainland earlier than had been scheduled to relieve Keeper Dan Sullivan at the lighthouse. With practically no advance warning, a devastating hurricane was bearing down on New England's south facing coast. The waves grew higher and higher as the Hurricane of '38 battered the tower.

Over 700 people died in the hurricane across New England, including five people at the lighthouse station on Rhode Island's Prudence Island. Many days passed before the seas calmed down enough to get a boat out to Whale Rock. The lighthouse was completely gone, and to this day the tower and the body of Walter Eberle have not been found. Eberle was 40 years old and had been in the Lighthouse Service for one year.

The remains of the structure were removed in 1939 and an automatic light on a steel tower was erected. The spot is now marked by a lighted buoy. There are memorials elsewhere to lighthouse keepers who have made the ultimate sacrifice, but so far no organization has erected a memorial to Rhode Island's Keeper Walter Eberle.

BEAVERTAIL

BEAVERTAIL STATE PARK. From parking lot #2 follow the loop road to free parking on the east side of the light station. There are two spaces for the handicapped (HP on map) on the west side. Across the road in front of the station are the remains of the foundation for the 1754 tower. This forgotten ruin was uncovered after the September 1938 hurricane demolished a fog signal shed that had been built on it in 1856. The walk around the lighthouse provides spectacular views of lower Narragansett Bay.

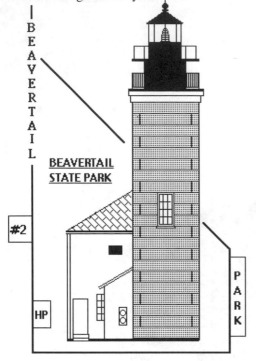

BEAVERTAIL LIGHTHOUSE MUSEUM. After leasing the 1898 assistant keeper's dwelling, the Rhode Island Parks Association, a private nonprofit organization, renovated the structure and converted it into a maritime natural history museum with displays of photographs, charts and historic memorabilia commemorating Rhode Island's lighthouses and their keepers.

The museum also displays Beavertail's original fourth-order Fresnel lens. In 1994 the museum received 33 wooden models of Rhode Island's lighthouses handcrafted by Robert Dennis. This exhibit was previously displayed at the Naval War College and Fort Adams' Museum of Yachting.

On certain days park naturalists offer history and nature talks and walks.

In 1994 the Champlain Foundation of Rhode Island donated $13,500 to the museum for the replacement of the dwelling's original roof with a red one and to prepare a room for displaying the lighthouse models. The museum is now managed by a nonprofit group of lighthouse preservationists.

OPEN. Weekends and Memorial Day, beginning May 24 through mid-June, noon to 3 p.m. Open daily, June 21 through Labor Day, 10 a.m. to 4 p.m. Labor Day through Columbus Day, open weekends, noon to 3 p.m.

FREE ADMISSION. Donations welcomed.

- Beavertail Lighthouse Museum Association, PO Box 83, Jamestown, RI 02835.
Phone (401) 423-3270.
Website: http://www.beavertaillight.org

This lighthouse and several others can also be viewed from the special lighthouse cruises offered by Bay Queen Cruises of Warren, RI. See the Bristol Ferry Light chapter (page 225) for details.

BEAVERTAIL LIGHTHOUSE (BEAVER TAIL; NEWPORT).
CHARACTERISTIC: Flashing white 6s
HAW: 64' **RANGE**: 15 nm

THE 1749 TOWER. Rhode Island's first Beavertail Lighthouse was the third lighthouse to be built in Colonial America. A request for a lighthouse on the point occurred in 1712. Funds to build the aid began in 1731 by taxing ships' cargoes through the port of Newport. Delayed by the war between France and England, the lighthouse was finally completed in 1749. The 58-foot tall wooden tower had a 24-foot diameter at its base with walls tapering to a 13-foot diameter at the lantern deck. The lantern was eight feet in diameter and 11 feet tall. With the tower's base 12 feet above the bay, the light had a focal plane height of 70 feet. Presumably, the lantern held a whale oil-powered spider lamp.

THE 1754 TOWER. The tower burned to the ground on July 23, 1753 and was replaced the following year with a 58-foot tall brick and rubble stone tower. The new lantern was equipped with a two-tiered spider lamp consisting of 15 whale oil-burning wicks each fitted with a 9-inch reflector.

BEAVERTAIL

After 1647, as Rhode Island grew both in population and industry, the colonists developed a strong sense of independence. In 1772, three years before the opening skirmishes of the Revolutionary War at Concord and Lexington in Massachusetts, Rhode Islanders burned the British revenue ship *Gaspee* in Warwick Harbor. On May 4, 1776, they withdrew their allegiance to the British throne. During the war, Rhode Island was neutralized as a participating colony, while the British occupied Newport and effectively blockaded Narragansett Bay. That sense of independence emerged again in 1790 when the state belatedly ratified the Constitution and again in May 1793, when Rhode Island finally ceded its historic lighthouse to the U.S. Government with the proviso that, if the lighthouse were not kept as an active aid to navigation and in a good state of repair, the state would take it back.

In October 1779 during their withdrawal, the British set fire to the Beavertail Lighthouse and reportedly removed the optic. Although the heat of the fire warped the masonry walls, repairs were made quickly, including the possible raising the height of the tower. The aid was back in service in 1783.

In 1827 a contract was let for the lowering the height of the tower to its original 68 feet where the top of the tower was 15 feet in diameter. The lantern was refitted with a two-tiered Winslow Lewis optic with seven lamps on the upper table and eight on the lower platform. Each lamp was backed by a 9-inch reflector. The beacon was reported in 1838 to be 90 feet above mean high water and showing a range of 16 nautical miles.

EXPERIMENTS. The Beavertail Lighthouse has been used as an experimental station for fog signal equipment. In 1817 a new illuminant entered America's lighthouse history books. Then a local inventor, David Melville, was permitted to try out his new coal gas process. Melville generated a gas by burning a mixture of distilled bituminous coal and tree resin, and piped it through copper tubing to a chandelier in the lantern room. This design was not unlike earlier residential natural gas ceiling fixtures. Although cheaply manufactured on the premises and producing a brighter and cleaner white light, Melville's work ended abruptly less than a year later, after the whaling industry (or more pointedly the purveyors of whale oil) lobbied the Lighthouse Service to abandon the experiment.

Another unusual test of 1851-52 involved a foghorn powered by compressed air. The air was pumped into a holding tank by a horse tethered to a revolving walker.

THE 1856 TOWER. After the present granite block Beavertail tower and the brick and stucco keeper's residence were completed in 1856, the old keeper's dwelling (1816) and all but the 1754 tower's foundation were razed. The main keeper's residence was built in 1859.

The new aid showed a fixed white light generated by a whale oil-powered third-order Fresnel lens. By 1899 a smaller fourth-order classical optic was in place. After its automation in 1972 the Coast Guard keepers were withdrawn. The fourth-order classical lens was retired in 1991. Today, the 52-foot tall Beavertail Lighthouse is equipped with a modern plastic lens and a radiobeacon broadcasting a Morse "N."

Note the lantern's green storm panes. The original clear glass panes were covered with green plexiglass when the light was electrified in 1931. On the lower right section of the keeper's house next to the tower is a strobe device. When the two strobe lights detect fog within a distance of two miles they automatically turn on the fog signal.

OWNER. U.S. Coast Guard. Assistant keeper's dwelling leased to the Rhode Island Parks Association in 1989. Project managed by the Parks Association and the State's Department of Environmental Management.

PRESERVATION. Listed in the National Register of Historic Places.

TO WETHERILL STATE PARK. On the way to the Conanicut Point Lighthouse and before reaching Jamestown center, the Castle Hill Lighthouse can be seen across Narragansett Bay's East Passage from this park. To reach the park return north on Beavertail Road. Then:

-> Bear right into connecting Southwest Avenue,

-> Right again at Hamilton Street,

-> Right at Walcott Avenue,

-> Bear left at a "Fort Wetherill State Park" sign,

-> Right at the park's entrance,

-> Left after entering the park,

-> Right at the first triangular intersection and follow the loop road to an overlook with ample free parking. The short white Castle Hill tower can be seen off to the east on the far shore.

OPEN. All year, daily 6 to 11.

FREE ADMISSION.

FERRY TO NEWPORT AND ROSE ISLAND. In Jamestown center on Walcott Avenue and opposite a large hotel is the Conanicut Marina North Pier at East Ferry. There passengers can board Captain Bill Sprague's *Edgartug* (open seating under canvas) for an exhilarating trip across Narragansett Bay to Bannister's Wharf in Newport, passing Rose Island and to the Viking Tours dock on Goat Island. The ferry accepts "on demand" stops at Rose Island.

Free parking at marina restricted to two hours. Free unlimited parking in front of hotel and south on Walcott. Call or check website for the latest ferry schedule.

- Jamestown and Newport Ferry Service.
Phone (401) 423-9900.
Website: http://www.jamestownri.com/meetings/ferry.html-ssi

Beavertail Lighthouse

CONANICUT POINT
PLUM BEACH

TO CONANICUT POINT. From Jamestown center return to RI 138 and cross it into East Shore Road. At the northern tip of the island where East Shore turns west, turn right into a dirt road. The Conanicut Point Lighthouse is on the left about 0.1 mile from the turn, largely hidden by trees.

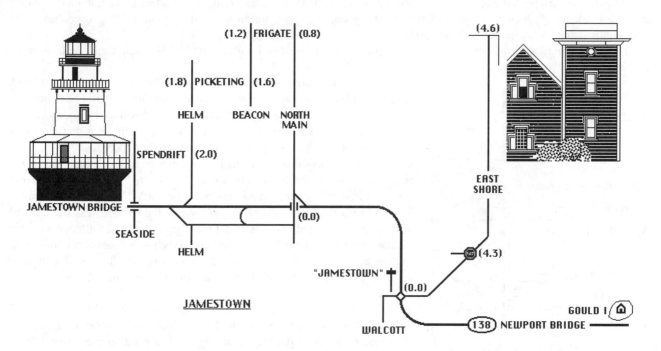

CONANICUT POINT LIGHTHOUSE (NORTH LIGHT).

This aid was activated on April 1, 1886. It is a square wood framed house with attached tower. The two-story dwelling's eaves are fringed with delicate gingerbread trim and its window surrounds are scrolled. Both touches are fine examples of the American adaptation of the Victorian architectural style. Of particular interest is the lighthouse's plain frame construction, a design that differs greatly from Rhode Island's other lighthouses.

Its fifth-order Fresnel optic, installed in 1891, was discontinued and removed in 1933.

OWNER. Privately owned since 1934.

PRESERVATION. Listed in the National Register of Historic Places.

The tower, although well preserved, stands empty and has been stripped of its lantern. Also still standing on the property are a barn raised in 1897, the old station's brick oil house built in 1901 and a fog signal building constructed in 1907.

TO THE PLUM BEACH LIGHTHOUSE. Return to East Shore Road and RI 138, motor west on RI 138 and exit at North Main Street. Continue north on North Main. Then:

-> Left at Frigate Street,
-> Left at Beacon Street,
-> Right at Picketing Street,
-> Left at Helm Street,
-> Right at Spendrift Street.

The lighthouse can be seen at the end of Spendrift and south along Seaside Street. This lighthouse and several others can also be viewed from the special lighthouse cruises offered by Bay Queen Cruises of Warren, RI. See the Bristol Ferry Light chapter (page 225) for details.

215

PLUM BEACH LIGHTHOUSE.

Shortly after the construction of this cast-iron tower began in the summer of 1896, the bedrock bottom was found to be deeper than first estimated. As a result the project ran out of funds before the foundation could be securely anchored. Work was halted on January 31, 1897 and the foundation, then just barely above mean high water, was covered with timbers. A red lantern placed atop the obstruction was serviced by an attendant living in Saunderstown. Later a temporary fog bell was added. With an additional congressional appropriation, construction resumed in late 1898, paused during the winter and was finally completed in May 1899.

Earlier submerged cast-iron caissons were formed after timber-lined cofferdams had been built and sunk onto the seabed.

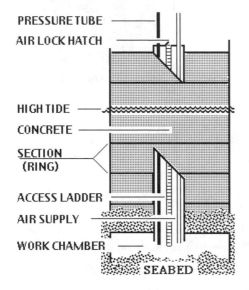

Those enclosures were not only subject to being breached due to depth pressure and wave action, but also had to be continuously pumped to provide a sufficiently water-free space for workers to dig down to the bedrock.

Plum Beach's cast-iron foundation is unique in that it is one of 13 that were built using an emerging pneumatic construction technique. In this process a multi-sectioned caisson was put together on a large barge. Before it was transported to the construction site, it was fitted with a central access pipe that housed air supply and pressure tubes, a ladder and a conveyance system to lift the muck and sand. At the site the caisson was righted and allowed to sink onto the soft seabed. Once the caisson had settled, water was pumped out of the empty bottom section. At the same time the sections from high mean water to the top of the bottom section were filled with concrete. As they cleared out the debris, the caisson settled some 30 feet onto the bedrock.

When the light was activated on June 1, 1898, its light was produced by a kerosene-powered fourth-order Fresnel lens that revolved on a mercury float and produced a flashing white light. The rotation was created by a clockwork mechanism that was activated by weights that dropped through a central tube.

PRESERVATION. The first Jamestown Bridge, completed in July 1940, rendered Plum Beach an unnecessary aid. The light was discontinued in January 1941 and a few years later abandoned. Since then the 54-foot tall coffee pot has deteriorated badly. Windows and doors no longer exist, the exterior paint has long disappeared, its cast-iron body is rusted and its decks are covered with bird droppings. For years the Coast Guard and the State of Rhode Island squabbled over the structure's ownership. In 1988 the O'Connell Development Company tried to purchase the lighthouse and move it to a Quincy, Massachusetts condominium complex, where it would have been converted into a museum devoted to lighthouse history. Once the proposed dismantling became known, one concerned woman, Shirley Silvia, began a campaign to save the Plum Beach Lighthouse. Unfortunately, the Friends of Plum Beach Lighthouse, Inc., faced the same ownership problem.

To complicate matters, in the early 1970s a health hazard lawsuit was filed against the state. The litigant, James Osborn, claimed to have become severely ill and suffered permanently blurred vison after working inside the guano-saturated structure. The lawsuit was shuttled between Rhode Island's Superior and Supreme Courts for over 20 years. In June 1998 a Superior Court ruled that the state "owned and controlled Plum Beach Lighthouse" at the times relevant to Osborn's suit. Three months later the suit was finally settled as the state awarded Osborn $42,000.

The settlement of the ownership issue cleared the way for the Friends of Plum Beach Lighthouse to acquire the lighthouse. In October 1999 the Rhode Island Department of Environmental Management transferred the deed for the 100-year old structure to the nonprofit organization.

The Friends of Plum Beach Lighthouse, Inc. have received $500,000 from the federal government under the Transportation Act for the 21st Century, known as TEA-21. The money was first used for an engineering study, leading to an estimate of $900,000 for a complete restoration. The group is now working to secure another grant so the work can begin.

- Friends of Plum Beach Lighthouse, Inc. PO Box 451, Portsmouth, RI 02871.

POPLAR POINT

GOULD ISLAND (destroyed) This former lighthouse island can be clearly seen while crossing the Newport Bridge from east to west. Its brick oil house can be seen almost under the bridge.

Only a glimpse of the lantern and a top portion of the Poplar Point tower can be seen at its Wickford location at the end of Poplar Avenue. The best view is from the Wickford Harbor breakwater off Sauga Point.

NORTH OR SOUTH ON US 1. Camp Avenue is about 0.5 mile north of Oakdale Road and the same distance south of the RI 433 and Davisville Road underpass.

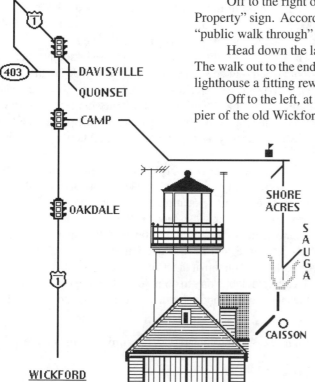

Although prohibited on both sides of Shore Acres through the Sauga Avenue turn, permissible and free parking is available farther north on Shore Acres and northeast on Sauga Avenue.

Off to the right of the curve is a pathway that may be marked with a "Private Property" sign. According to the North Kingstown Police Department, the path is a "public walk through" and visitors may use the lane to reach the beach.

Head down the lane to the beach steps and walk westward to the breakwater. The walk out to the end of the breakwater is an easy one with the ensuing view of the lighthouse a fitting reward for your effort.

Off to the left, at the channel entrance to Wickford Harbor, lies the foundation pier of the old Wickford Harbor Lighthouse.

POPLAR POINT LIGHTHOUSE.

Two aids to navigation have marked the entrance to Wickford Harbor. The first, Poplar Point, was built in 1831. The octagonal wooden tower is attached to the one-story wood framed and shingled keeper's dwelling. Among Rhode Island's lighthouses, Poplar Point is the oldest unrebuilt tower still standing on its original foundation.

In 1855 Winslow Lewis' multi-lamp/reflector optic (eight lamps and 14.5-inch reflectors) was replaced by a lard oil-powered fifth-order Fresnel lens, showing a fixed white light 48 feet above the water. The light was discontinued in 1882. Today, although its lantern is empty, both tower and Cape house are well preserved.

OWNER. A private residence since 1892.
PRESERVATION. Listed in the National Register of Historic Places.

WICKFORD HARBOR LIGHTHOUSE (WICKFORD) (dismantled) .

The other harbor aid, the Wickford Harbor Lighthouse, supplanted the older Poplar Point in 1882. The lighthouse consisted of a concrete-filled caisson supporting a wood framed dwelling with an attached 51-foot tall tower. The aid was discontinued and torn down in 1930.

WARWICK

NORTH ON US 1. In Apponaug turn right into RI 117 (West Shore Road), right again at Warwick Neck Avenue and continue south to the light station.

SOUTH FROM SHAWOMET. Follow RI 117 (West Shore) 1.1 miles south to Warwick Neck, turn left and park near the gate to the station. The station grounds are closed to the public, but the lighthouse can be seen from the gate.

This lighthouse and several others can also be viewed from the special lighthouse cruises offered by Bay Queen Cruises of Warren, RI. See the Bristol Ferry Light chapter (page 225) for details.

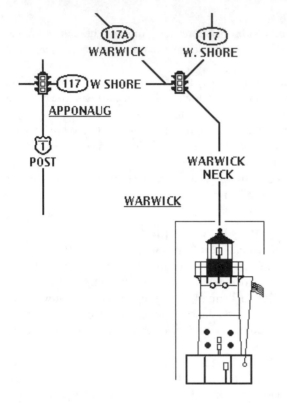

WARWICK LIGHTHOUSE
(WARWICK NECK; WARWICK POINT).
CHARACTERISTIC: Occulting green 4s
HAW: 66' **RANGE**: 12 nm

Construction of the first light station on Warwick Neck was completed in 1826 and consisted of a stubby 30-foot tall wooden tower attached to a small (120 square feet) stone house.

The light was established in 1827. In 1833 a somewhat larger three-room wood framed keeper's dwelling was added to the smaller building. In 1835 the exteriors of the structures were roughcast with a lime and pebble covering. In 1888 the smaller structure was moved and converted into a barn. A year later the present keeper's residence, a 1 1/2-story Victorian wood framed house, was built.

By 1932 the tower was in danger of toppling into the bay. Erosion of surrounding sand and rock due to wave action and storms foretold of its eventual relocation away from the shoreline. The hurricane of September 1938 tore up the shore and the resulting erosion placed the 51-foot tall light tower at the water's edge. As a result, the structure was moved the following year to its present location and placed on top of the 8-foot tall octagonal concrete base. The relocation took one day to complete, allowing the 1856 fourth-order Fresnel optic to continue to show its fixed green light without interruption.

In 1985 Warwick Neck was the last of Rhode Island's lights to be automated. At that time the Fresnel lens was replaced by a modern lens.

OWNER. U.S. Coast Guard. The station is the residence of a Coast Guard family.
PRESERVATION. Listed in the National Register of Historic Places.

CONIMICUT
POMHAM ROCKS - NAYATT POINT

NORTH FROM WARWICK TO THE CONIMICUT LIGHTHOUSE. Follow RI 117 (West Shore Road) northeast. Then:

-> At the point where RI 117 turns toward the north (left) turn right into Terrace Avenue,

-> A very short distance after the turn into Terrace, turn left again into Symonds Avenue,

-> Right at Point Avenue to the entrance to Conimicut Point Park.

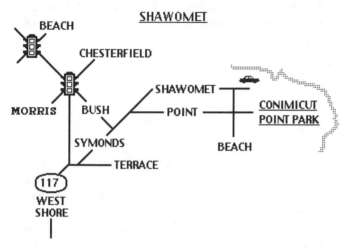

VIA I-95 (NORTH OR SOUTH).

Take Exit 13 to Airport Access Road. Then east to US 1 (Post Road). Turn left (north) at US 1 then right (east) at Airport Road. Follow Airport Road across RI 117A (Warwick Avenue) into RI 117 (West Shore Road). Then:

-> About 0.5 mile from the Beach Avenue (traffic signal) continue straight ahead on Bush Avenue through the next intersection,

-> Left at Symonds Avenue,

-> Right at Point Avenue to the park.

Conimicut Lighthouse is located in the middle of the Providence River Approach. Its light marks Conimicut Shoal, a sand bar that extends from the point to the lighthouse. Across the river stands the Nayatt Point Lighthouse.

OPEN. All year, sunrise to sunset.

ADMISSION FEE. July to Labor Day vehicle fee. Other times free.

If you do not wish to pay the fee and still view the lighthouse, take Beach Street a short distance north to Shawomet Avenue and turn right. At the end of Shawomet there is an unimproved parking area (free). Walk to the water's edge to view the lighthouse.

Conimicut Light and several others can also be viewed from the special lighthouse cruises offered by Bay Queen Cruises of Warren, RI. See the Bristol Ferry Light chapter (page 225) for details. It can also be seen from the Providence-Block Island Ferry; see details on the next page.

CONIMICUT LIGHTHOUSE (CONIMICUT SHOAL).

CHARACTERISTIC: Flashing white 2.5s (red sector)

HAW: 58' **RANGES**: White 15; red 13 nm

The first lighthouse on the ledge was a granite stone tower equipped with a fourth-order Fresnel optic showing a fixed white light. The beacon was established on November 1, 1868. A small wood framed keeper's house, built in 1873 on a pier on the north side of the tower, was demolished two years later by a massive ice floe. After the dwelling's destruction, the keeper moved his residence to Nayatt Point.

In 1883, after the deteriorated granite tower had been razed, the present caisson-type lighthouse and landing pier were completed. The three-stage lighthouse is 58 feet tall.

The original 1868 fourth-order Fresnel remains inside the lantern. In 1960 this cast-iron tower was the last of America's lighthouses to be converted from acetylene gas to electricity. The beacon was automated in 1966.

OWNER. U.S. Coast Guard.

PRESERVATION. Listed in the National Register of Historic Places.

PROVIDENCE - BLOCK ISLAND FERRY.

From Interstate 95 North or 95 South take 195E to the Wickendon Street exit (exit 3). Follow the signs to the ferry at India Point. Parking is available on India (metered) and a nearby parking lot (fee).

Even if you plan to visit Block Island via the ferry out of Galilee, this one day cruise down the Providence River and Narragansett Bay should not be missed. It is a postcard adventure with superb sightings of the lighthouses located in Narragansett Bay's east passage.

Crossing time is four hours from Providence, two hours from Newport's Fort Adams.

SCHEDULE. Late June to early September, daily at 8:30 AM. There is an outbound stop at Newport's Fort Adams at 10:30 AM and an inbound stop at 5:30 PM. With a Block Island departure at 3:45 PM, there should be enough hours on the island to visit the lighthouses, browse and have lunch on the waterfront.

FARES. Same day round trip. Discount for children.

- Interstate Navigation Company, 304 Great Island Rd., Galilee State Pier, Point Judith, RI 02882

Phone: (401) 783-4613.

Website: http://blockislandferry.com/

FULLER ROCK LIGHTHOUSE (destroyed).
SASSAFRAS POINT LIGHTHOUSE (dismantled).

These offshore lighthouses, both wooden octagonal towers standing on granite foundations, marked the swift-running reach between Providence Harbor (north) and the Providence River (south). The area is just west of Kettle Point Road off RI 103 (South Broadway and Veterans Highway) in East Providence, Rhode Island. Both towers had sixth-order Fresnel lenses with Fuller Rock showing a fixed white light and Sassafras Point a fixed red.

Both optics were tended by a mainland keeper who had to sail his boat to Fuller Rock and then across the hazardous channel to Sassafras Point. Although Congress wanted to upgrade Fuller Rock and accommodate the lightkeeper by building him a house, that plan never materialized. In 1912 after the widening of the channel had been completed, Sassafras Point was dismantled. In 1923 the Fuller Rock's acetylene tanks blew up and destroyed the tower. Strange as it may seem one of the sites is still marked on some road maps as the "Fuller Rock Lighthouse."

SABIN POINT LIGHTHOUSE (dismantled).

Sabin Point is located between the Fuller Rock and Pomham Rocks Lighthouses. The lighthouse once stood offshore from what is now the Metacomet Golf Club. The lighthouse was built in 1872 for $43,000. Its architectural styling was of the Second Empire Revival genre, mimicking the Pomham Rocks Lighthouse. Sabin Point was also hit by the 1938 hurricane's surge that carried away practically every object both inside and outside the structure. Although it survived the onslaught because of its sturdy granite construction, the state demolished it in 1969 to facilitate the widening of the Providence River channel.

CONTINUE EAST ON I-195 TO THE EAST BAY BIKE PATH / POMHAM ROCKS LIGHTHOUSE.

Finished in 1992, the East Bay Bike path is 14.5 miles long and 10 feet wide. The path extends from Providence to Bristol along the abandoned railroad line, and for most of its length it passes near the shore of the Providence River and the Narragansett Bay.

Take I-195 Exit 4 Riverside / Veteran's Memorial Parkway (Rte 103). Continue about five miles to the Bullocks Point Road parking area for the East Bay Bike Path. The Pomham Rocks Lighthouse can be viewed via a short pleasant walk (or bike ride) to the north on the path. When walking on the path remember to keep your eyes open; cyclists always have the right of way. Alternative access to the path can be gained at any one of 49 intersections from Providence to Bristol.

OPEN Year round, sunrise to sunset.

FEES None.

- East Bay Bike Path. Colt State Park, Bristol, Rhode Island 02809-1710.

Phone: (401) 253-7482. Fax (401) 253-6766.

POMHAM ROCKS LIGHTHOUSE (POMHAM ROCK; PUMHAM ROCKS).

The keeper's residence with its integrated tower is almost a twin of Rhode Island's dismantled Sabin Point as well as Vermont's Colchester Reef. Here, we see a square, wood framed two-story building with its upper story enclosed within its Second Empire mansard roof and supporting the emerging tower and lantern. The upper half of the tower, although appearing to be of hexagonal shape, actually has beveled corners which flare out to form the square lower half. Note the roof window frames with their Victorian-influenced foot-scrolled edgings.

The little stone building served as the station's oil storage house.

When Pomham Rocks became operational on December 1, 1871 it held a sixth-order Fresnel (fixed red) optic 69 feet above the water. When the 40-foot tall lighthouse was retired in 1974, its fourth-order classical lens (installed in 1939) was removed and later donated to the Custom House Maritime Museum in Newburyport, Massachusetts.

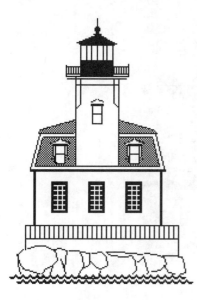

OWNER. Mobil Oil Company since 1980. Although resident caretakers have lived at this historic property in the past, there is no caretaker at present. Mobil Oil is still caring for the property.

PRESERVATION. Listed in the National Register of Historic Places.

BULLOCK POINT LIGHTHOUSE (dismantled).

This lighthouse once stood offshore at the end of Bullocks Point Road. The point's first aid to navigation was an unlighted daymark erected in 1860. In 1870 the daymark was retired in favor of a movable lighted beacon placed on a granite stele. Finally Congress appropriated $16,000 for a new lighthouse. The architects came up with a beautifully styled structure resembling the Federal Design genre. It had a centered gable with vergeboards along the roof's projections and pronounced window hoods and sills. The square tower sat above the gable and had a wide balustraded service gallery. The lantern was octagonal in shape and topped with an ogee dome. The aid's sixth-order Fresnel showed a fixed red light some 26 feet above the water. That violent hurricane of September 1938 severely damaged both the lighthouse and its granite foundation. The light was discontinued in 1939 and the structure was torn down in the early 1940s.

TO BARRINGTON TOWN BEACH

The Nayatt Point Lighthouse can be viewed via an approximately two-mile walk from Barrington Town Beach. During the summer the municipal beach is restricted to town residents who have paid a permit fee. The beach is open to anyone in the off season.

Take RI 103/114 into Barrington. At a triangular intersection with a blinking caution light turn left into Rumstick Road. Continue south to Nayatt Road and turn right. Continue to Bay Road and turn left. Continue to the beach parking area. Walk west on the beach toward Nayatt Point. The Conimicut Lighthouse can be seen offshore from Nayatt Point.

Nayatt Point Light and several others can also be viewed from the special lighthouse cruises offered by Bay Queen Cruises of Warren, RI. See the Bristol Ferry Light chapter (page 225) for details.

NAYATT POINT LIGHTHOUSE

Nayatt Point's first lighthouse, built in 1828, consisted of the present brick house with an attached stone tower. It was equipped with a multi-lamp and reflector optic (fixed white).

In 1856 the tower was rebuilt in the form of the Federal Design style. The two-story brick keeper's residence, which has never been altered or rebuilt, is Rhode Island's oldest standing lighthouse dwelling. The lighthouse is 25 feet tall.

Because the 1863 fourth-order Fresnel optic's focal plane was only 31 feet above the river, it was decided that a beacon on the shoal off Conimicut Point would not only better serve shipping entering the Providence River, but would also assist mariners in skirting the point. In 1868 the Conimicut Lighthouse became operational using Nayatt Point's transferred lens.

OWNER. Nayatt Point's keeper's house was the family residence (except for 1873-74) of the Conimicut lightkeeper until the lighthouse and grounds were sold in 1890 to a private party for $4,500. In 1997 the 14-room residence and tower with 450 feet of water frontage were put on the real estate market for a cool $1,275,000.

PRESERVATION. Listed in the National Register of Historic Places.

Over the last one hundred years its owners have taken excellent care of this historic light station.

Pomham Rocks Lighthouse

Prudence Island Lighthouse

PRUDENCE ISLAND

NORTH OR SOUTH ON RI 114. In Bristol take any cross street to Thames Street and the Church Street Wharf. A parking lot (fee) is located on Thames south of Church Street.

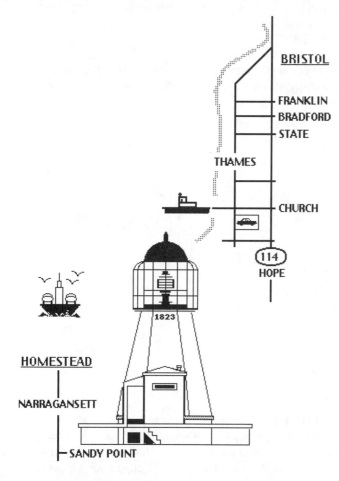

FERRY TO PRUDENCE ISLAND. This auto/ passenger ferry services Bristol, Hog Island and Homestead on Prudence Island. It carries 12 cars. Crossing time is 20 minutes. Vehicle reservations required.

SCHEDULE. Located at the end of this chapter.

FARES. Vehicle/driver (round trip) + passenger (one way) fares. Discount for children.

- Prudence Ferry, Church Street Wharf, Bristol, RI 02809.

Phone (401) 253-9808.

In Homestead head south on Narragansett Avenue for about one mile. Take the first left to the Sandy Point Dock (former passenger ferry landing) and the lighthouse.

There is a small convenience store and public restrooms in Homestead, but no restaurants, no picnic groves and no tourist attractions. It is suggested that you take along box lunches or some munchies. The walk to and from the lighthouse is about 2.5 miles. The island is infested with deer ticks that carry lyme disease. Spray for ticks and carefully avoid underbrush and bushes.

Prudence Island Light can also be viewed from the lighthouse cruises offered by Bay Queen Cruises in Warren, RI. See page 225 for details.

PRUDENCE ISLAND LIGHTHOUSE
(SANDY POINT).
CHARACTERISTIC: Flashing green 6s
HAW: 28' **RANGE**: 6 nm

This 30-foot tall octagonal granite structure is Rhode Island's oldest lighthouse, having been built in 1823 on the southern end of Newport's Goat Island. In 1851 the tower and lantern were dismantled, moved to Sandy Point, reassembled and placed in operation on January 17, 1852.

A new fifth-order Fresnel lens (fixed white) replaced its antiquated Winslow Lewis lighting apparatus in 1857. In 1924 the optic's characteristic was changed to a flashing mode with the addition of a weight-activated rotating mechanism. The lighthouse's presently active fourth-order Fresnel optic was installed and electrified in 1939 and automated in 1961. Note the "bird cage" lantern treatment.

The worst hurricane in the recorded history of New England hit the coast in September 1938, doing tremendous damage at Prudence Island. The wife and son of Keeper George Gustavas, a former keeper named Martin Thompson, and a visiting married couple were all swept to their deaths. Keeper Gustavas escaped death when he was swept back to the beach and was pulled to safety by an 18-year old island resident.

Here is a very interesting bit of history concerning this lighthouse. Mr. Steve Johnson, a craftsman of brass Christmas ornaments featuring lighthouses, located an old deed to the light station wherein the property was specifically donated to President Millard Fillmore. Furthermore the deed stipulates that ownership of the lighthouse is to be handed down to each succeeding President of the United States. ("Bill Clinton's Lighthouse," *Lighthouse Digest*, February 1995.)

PRUDENCE ISLAND, BRISTOL FERRY

A new grouping of so-called "presidential" lighthouses? We could begin with the favorite vacation places of these presidents: Coolidge's and Hoover's Sapelo Island, Roosevelt's East Quoddy (Campobello), Truman's Key West, Kennedy's Hyannis (Hyannisport), Nixon's Cape Florida (Key Biscayne) and Bush's Goat Island (Kennebunkport). Any others?

OWNER. U.S. Coast Guard, leased to Prudence Conservancy.

- Prudence Conservancy, P.O. Box 115, Prudence Island, RI 02872.

PRESERVATION. Listed in the National Register of Historic Places.

PRUDENCE FERRY SCHEDULE. Homestead departures are 1/2 hour after the departure from Bristol. Example: depart Bristol at 6; leave Homestead at 6:30. Dates change annually. Phone (401) 253-9808 to confirm the schedule.

	BRISTOL ->
Late April to Late June	
Mondays, Tuesdays & Thursdays	6, 8, 3:30, 5:30
Wednesdays	6, 8, 3:30, 5:30
Fridays	6, 8, 10, 3:30
Saturdays	8, 10, 3:30
Sundays & holidays	10, 3:30, 5:30
Late June to Early September	
Mondays through Thursdays	6, 8, 10
Fridays	6, 8, 10, 3:30, 6, 7:45
Saturdays	8, 10, 3:30, 5:30
Sundays & holidays	8, 10, 3:30, 4:40, 6:30
Early September to Mid-October	
Mondays, Tuesdays & Thursdays	6, 8, 10*, 3:30, 5:30
Fridays	6, 8, 3:30, 6, 7:30
Saturdays	8, 10, 3:30
Sundays & holidays	10, 3:30, 5:30
* September 9-15 only	

TO BRISTOL FERRY LIGHT - **NORTH OR SOUTH ON RI 114.** This lighthouse is located in Bristol under the Mount Hope River Bridge (vehicle toll). On the northern end of the bridge, just past its toll booth turn east into Ferry Road and continue downhill to a large turnaround. Since parking is not permitted in the turnaround (old ferry landing area) park along Ferry Road or in the visitors parking lot on the campus of Roger Williams University. Keep in mind that the lighthouse is a private residence; be sure to respect the privacy of the owners.

TO BAY QUEEN CRUISES (BLOUNT MARINE SHIPYARD, Gate #4 Water Street, Warren, RI).

Bristol Ferry Light can also be viewed from the lighthouse cruises offered by Bay Queen Cruises of Warren, RI. Other lighthouses seen on this cruise aboard the *Vista Jubilee* include Hog Island Shoal, Prudence Island, Rose Island, Newport Harbor, Ida Lewis Rock, Castle Hill, Beavertail, Dutch Island, Plum Beach, Conanicut Point, Warwick, Nayatt Point and Conimicut. Some views may be distant and the route may very according to conditions. These cruises are scheduled several times each year and last five hours (11:00 to 4:00). Phone or check website for current schedule and fares (special children's and group rates).

From I-95 Providence: Take I-195 East to Exit 7, Rt. 114. Stay on Rt. 114 through Barrington Shopping Center. Go over two small bridges to Warren. At the first light, bear right at fork on Water Street. One mile down is the Blount Shipyard.

From Rt. 24, Rt. 138 & Rt. 114 (Aquidneck Island): Take the Mount Hope Bridge, bear right after Roger Williams University to Rt. 136, Metacom Avenue for about 3 1/2 miles. After the Ocean State Plaza, make a left just after a Pro Muffler Store to Vernon Street. Go to the end, turn right onto Main Street in Warren. Go 1/4 of a mile, just after a Super Mart Store, at light, turn left onto Campbell Street. Go to end.

From I-195 (Fall River) take Exit 4A onto Rt. 103 Take Rt. 103 West into Warren, past Rt. 136 to Rt. 114, Main Street, Warren. Turn right, then left at light on Miller Street. Take Miller to Water Street, turn left to Blount Shipyard.

- Bay Queen Cruises, 461 Water Street, Gate #4, P.O. Box 368, Warren, RI 02885-0368
 Phone: (401) 245-1350. Toll-Free: (800) 439-1350. Fax: (401) 245-6630.
 Website: http://www.bayqueen.com/   Email: vjcruise@aol.com

BRISTOL FERRY

BRISTOL FERRY LIGHTHOUSE.

The first lighthouse at the confluence of the Mount Hope River and Narragansett Bay was a short wooden tower built in 1846 and operated as a private aid. Faced with a narrow channel between two rock outcroppings, Hog Island Shoal to the southwest and Musselbed Shoals across the river, mariners complained that the Bristol Ferry beacon did not have the desired elevation nor the intensity to help them navigate the channel. In 1854 Congress approved the construction of the present lighthouse.

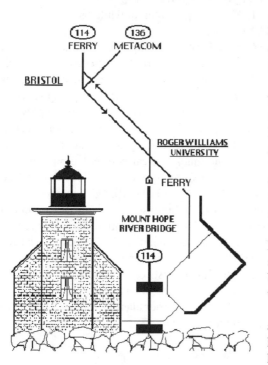

Built in 1854-55, the lighthouse is a brick house with an attached 28-foot tall brick tower capped with a wooden deck and lantern. The tower was raised six feet to its present height in 1916 to accommodate a cast-iron lantern removed from the old Roundout Lighthouse on the Hudson River.

As seen in Rhode Island's Dutch Island and Nayatt Point lighthouses, Bristol Ferry's brick house and attached square brick tower reflect the cubic styling influence of the Federal Design genre. The lighthouse closely resembles the Sand Point Lighthouse in Escanaba, Michigan, constructed in 1868.

The light was established on October 4, 1855, using a fixed sixth-order classical lens and a whale oil lamp. This optic was replaced in 1902 with an electrified fifth-order Fresnel. When active, the optic showed a fixed white light that was some 35 feet above the river.

In 1927, before the completion of the Mount Hope River bridge, Bristol Ferry was retired and its warning responsibility transferred to a skeletal steel tower. That beacon was discontinued in 1930 after the bridge was completed. The lighthouse (less lantern and optic) was sold to a Bristol resident for $2,000.

The Lundin family, who purchased the lighthouse in 1991, installed a new lantern room containing an automatic light that comes on for two hours each evening, making Bristol Ferry Light look like a real lighthouse again.

They also renovated the interior, even adding a sleeping area with bunk beds in the lighthouse tower.

OWNER. In 2000 the lighthouse was sold to another private party for more than $400,000.

PRESERVATION. Listed in the National Register of Historic Places.

MUSSELBED SHOALS LIGHTHOUSE (dismantled).

Musselbed Shoals lies offshore just southwest of the Mount Hope Bridge. The first lighthouse was a wooden keeper's dwelling with a light tower standing in front of the house. Its sixth-order Fresnel (probably powered with a lard oil-fed lamp) showed a fixed red beam. The optic was first established on August 1, 1873. The lighthouse was continuously subjected to damage by ice moving through the narrow and swift channel connecting Narragansett Bay with Mount Hope Bay. In 1875 an ice jam actually moved the aid's stone foundation several feet. In 1877 the lighthouse was temporarily moved onto the mainland while a new granite pier was constructed. In July 1938 the authorities decided to deactivate the light. The September 1938 hurricane further damaged the weakened lighthouse and put it out of commission. It was torn down a few months later.

ANOTHER VIEW OF THE BRISTOL FERRY LIGHTHOUSE. If southbound on RI 114, note the presence of the Hog Island Shoal Lighthouse at two o'clock (right front) while crossing the Mount Hope River Bridge (vehicle toll). Then:

-> Just after leaving the bridge turn right into a cloverleaf interchange,
-> Circle around to Bristol Ferry Road and turn left,
-> Cross a set of railroad tracks and just before making a right turn, drive straight ahead to the old ferry wharf.

The turn is marked with a "Bristol Ferry Wharf" sign. The Bristol Ferry Lighthouse can be clearly seen across the river. If northbound on RI 114 and at the intersection before the bridge approach, drive straight ahead on Bristol Ferry Road.

HOG ISLAND SHOAL

VIEWING HOG ISLAND SHOAL LIGHTHOUSE. This lighthouse can be seen from the end of Miller Street, located about 0.3 mile south of the RI 114 (Bristol Ferry Road) and Boyd Lane junction or about 0.9 mile north of the intersection where RI 114's West Main Road connects with Bristol Ferry Road.

This lighthouse can also be viewed from the lighthouse cruises offered by Bay Queen Cruises of Warren, RI. See page 224 for details.

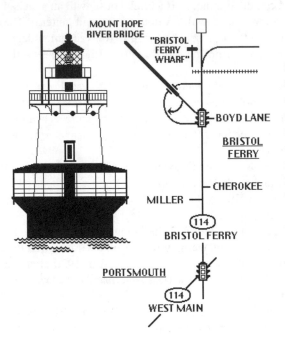

HOG ISLAND SHOAL LIGHTHOUSE.
CHARACTERISTIC: Equal interval white 6s
HAW: 54' **RANGE**: 12 nm

This caisson-supported tower is similar in design to many cast-iron aids built during the 1871-1915 period. The construction technique used to build Hog Island Shoal's and Plum Beach's caissons differed from earlier similar foundations. Instead of pumping water out of the caisson's bottom excavation area, engineers employed a new pneumatic technique that entailed pressurizing the bottom stage (or ring) to provide workers a relatively dry work chamber. As they removed the seabed's silt and muck, the caisson settled onto the bedrock. For a more detailed discussion, refer to Plum Beach's construction in the CONANICUT POINT & PLUM BEACH chapter.

This 60-foot tall cast-iron lighthouse, erected in 1901, replaced the *Hog Island*, a lightship that had been on station since 1886. It has five decks. When manned, a galley occupied the first level. The second and third decks held the crew's living quarters; the fourth a workshop and storage area. The lantern rests on the last deck.

Originally equipped with a fifth-order Fresnel lens, the tower was refitted, in 1903, with a fourth-order classical optic. The lantern now holds an automated modern lens.

OWNER. U.S. Coast Guard.
PRESERVATION. Listed in the National Register of Historic Places.

NEWPORT HARBOR
ROSE ISLAND - IDA LEWIS ROCK

SOUTH ON RI 114. At One Mile Corner in Newport turn right at Admiral Kalbfus Road. Then:
-> Left at Third Street,
-> Right at Sycamore Street (one way),
-> Left at Washington Street (both Newport Harbor Light and Rose Island Light can be seen while passing Battery Park),
-> Right at Goat Island Connector.

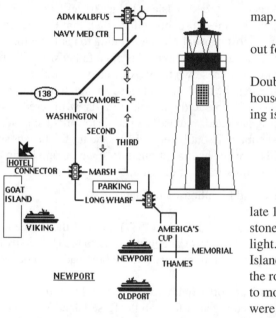

NORTH FROM CASTLE HILL. See the CASTLE HILL chapter's map.

Just before crossing over the connector road, pull into a short turn-out for an excellent view of and opportunity to photograph the lighthouse.

The grounds of the Newport Harbor Lighthouse, adjacent to the Doubletree Islander Hotel, are open to the public. The Rose Island Lighthouse can be seen from the seawall on the west side of Goat Island. Parking is free.

NEWPORT HARBOR LIGHTHOUSE (GOAT ISLAND).
CHARACTERISTIC: Flashing green
HAW: 33' **RANGE**: 11 nm
Construction of the first lighthouse on Goat Island was completed in late 1823 and its light established on January 1, 1824. It was a 20-foot tall stone tower fitted with a multi-lamp/reflector optic showing a fixed white light. Unfortunately, the location of this beacon on the south end of Goat Island confused mariners, with the result that many vessels ended up on the rocks at the northern tip of the island. In 1837 the decision was made to move the aid to the north end. The breakwater and the new light station were completed in 1838. The original 1823 tower was moved to Prudence Island in 1851.

During 1864-65, the 1838 tower was removed to make way for the present lighthouse. Newport Harbor's exterior masonry walls are made of rough hewn granite stone. Its interior is constructed of hammered stone. The lantern is reached via a spiralling stone staircase. The 1864 keeper's dwelling, badly damaged when an American submarine rammed the pier in 1922, has been removed.

When rebuilt the lighthouse was fitted with a fourth-order Fresnel lens. In 1923 the tower was refurbished, the personnel were withdrawn and the light was electrified. The beacon was refitted with a fifth-order classical lens in 1963 and automated.

OWNER. Leased to the American Lighthouse Foundation in January 2000. The beacon will still be maintained by the U.S. Coast Guard.
- American Lighthouse Foundation , PO Box 889, Wells, Maine 04090.
Phone: (207) 646-0515.
Website: http://www.lighthousefoundation.org
PRESERVATION. Listed in the National Register of Historic Places. In 1989 the Coast Guard completely renovated the 35-foot tall lighthouse.

ROSE ISLAND LIGHTHOUSE.
CHARACTERISTIC: Flashing white 6s
HAW: 48'
During the 18th century, Rose Island was considered strategically important in the defense of Narragansett Bay. The island's Fort Hamilton, under construction from 1798 to 1800, was never finished. It was later used during World Wars I and II for storage of explosives used by the U.S. Navy's torpedo manufacturing plant in Newport.

The present wood framed lighthouse was built in 1869 on Fort Hamilton's South Battery (Rose Island's southwestern point) for $7,500. When activated on January 20, 1870, it replaced a light maintained by the Bristol Steam Boat Company.

Rose Island's mansard roof (second floor) and integrated 35-foot tall tower reflects, as does the Pomham Rocks Lighthouse, the influence of the French Second Empire Revival. There is a touch of Victorian ornamentation in the scrolling on the window surrounds. The station's brick oil house was added in 1912.

Its original optic was a sixth-order Fresnel displaying a fixed red light with a range of six nautical miles. From 1870 to 1971 the beacon marked the island in Narragansett Bay's east passage. On August 7, 1993, after its restoration, the beacon was reactivated as a private aid.

While family life aboard many light stations had its moments of danger and sorrow, there are many stories about how keepers tried, within their austere means, to feed and clothe their families. Two longtime keepers of the Rose Island light, Charles Curtis (1887-1918) and Jesse Orton (1921-1936), had bovines to supply milk to their families. Keeper Orton's cow arrived on Rose Island in a most unusual way. According to Paul Stedman, a grandson of Jesse and a summer vacationer at the lighthouse, his grandfather went ashore, purchased a cow and loaded her aboard the Jamestown ferry. All went well until the ferry captain tried to maneuver the ferry through the shallows and close enough to the shore to drop a gangplank to offload the animal. Unable to do that, the ferry crew lowered Elsie into the water, gave her an encouraging push and watched her paddle towards land. With all hands shouting encouragement she made it, but barely. When she hit the beach, she collapsed. It took another 24 hours before she had the strength to stand up and begin to graze. Amazingly, she was able to give milk the next day, too!

OWNER. City of Newport since 1985. Managed by the Rose Island Lighthouse Foundation.

PRESERVATION. Listed in the National Register of Historic Places.

With the completion of the Newport Bridge in 1969, both Gould Island Lighthouse (1887) north of the bridge and Rose Island lost their value as aids to navigation. Rose Island was deactivated in 1971 and turned over to the University of Rhode Island for marine research in 1976. Unable to maintain the property, the university returned the badly vandalized station to the federal government for disposal.

It was offered to the City of Newport at no cost. Realizing that Newport would have difficulty budgeting for the restoration of the derelict lighthouse, a group of concerned citizens banded together to form the Rose Island Lighthouse Foundation. The nonprofit organization, with public contributions plus grants from the Alletta Morris McBean Charitable Trust, American Express Foundation, Rhode Island Foundation and the National Park Service, has completely restored the historic lighthouse.

The refurbishing of the structure's exterior was completed in 1990, along with the installation of a septic field, a cistern to hold rain water for purification and construction of a landing dock. The interior received new insulation, new plaster walls, plumbing and new wiring and an in-floor radiant heat system that maintains the inside temperature at 65 degrees (F), while using a minimum of fuel and electricity.

During a final "Light the Light" campaign in 1993, the Foundation raised $100,000 to pay the last of the restoration bills and to install a new 24-volt "solar" battery bank and a windmill for electricity so the beacon could be operated without using fossil fuels. After all was said and done, the restoration cost approximately $1.25 million, with over 60% of those costs being provided by volunteer laborers, plus donated "in-kind" materials and supplies.

On June 25, 1999, the Rose Island Lighthouse Foundation purchased the 17+ acre balance of Rose Island that had been used as a magazine through the end of World War II. The purchase ended a 15-year effort by members of the Foundation to protect the environmentally and historically significant Island from commercial development. Funding for the purchase price of $629,750 was provided largely by the State Department of Environmental Management ("DEM") from an open space grant which requires the property to be protected as a Wildlife Refuge. The Alletta Morris McBean Charitable Trust and the Prince Charitable Trusts also provided funding for the purchase.

VISITING ROSE ISLAND. In 1992 the Foundation opened the lighthouse's first floor and basement to the public. Between April 1 and July 15, because of nesting birds, access to Rose Island is allowed by appointment only. Between July 16 and Labor Day, visitors may arrive by private boat, by ferry or take the Foundation's boat to the island, picnic, stroll the grounds and visit the lighthouse (nominal fee). The first floor has been restored to the 1918-21 period, complete with a pitcher pump at the pantry sink and a player piano in the music room.

OPEN: 10 a.m. to 4 p.m. daily by appointment. Back on the charts, the Rose Island Light Station operates year-round. Access is not allowed to the private keeper's quarters or the lantern room.

NEWPORT HARBOR, ROSE ISLAND & IDA LEWIS ROCK

PUBLIC TOURS. 10 AM to 4 PM from mid-July to Labor Day, then weekends to Columbus Day. At other times by appointment. Visitors are advised to wear walking shoes for the uphill climb to the lighthouse.

TRANSPORTATION. Rose Island is serviced by ferry that runs between Jamestown and Newport during the summer only. For details see the BEAVERTAIL chapter, page 214.

ADMISSION FEES. $1 landing fee per person. Members free.

OVERNIGHT STAYS. Also available are overnight stays after the lighthouse is closed to visitors. All household necessities and bottled water are supplied; guests bring their own food. Cistern rain water is pumped by hand in the shared "WC/pantry." The bedrooms have wash bowls; an outdoor two-gallon solar shower is available during the summer months. Continental breakfast. No smoking, no pets. Guests also serve as "keepers" during their stay, recording weather data and performing some basic maintenance. Seasonally adjusted double and single rates for weekdays and weekends. Additional charge for children to age 12. Transportation fares extra.

- Rose Island Lighthouse Foundation, PO Box 1419 (365 Thames Street), Newport, RI 02840.

Phone (401) 847-4242 (between 9:00-1:00, M-F) Fax: (401) 849-3540.

Website: http://www.roseislandlighthouse.org

HARBOR CRUISES. Rose Island Light can be viewed from the lighthouse cruises offered by Bay Queen Cruises of Warren, RI; see page 225 for details. In addition, three companies offer sightseeing tours of Newport Harbor, passing the Ida Lewis Rock (close), Rose Island (about 0.5 mile), Beavertail (1.0 mile) and Castle Hill (close) Lighthouses. The tours are narrated and operate mid-May to mid-October with several daily departures. Parking is available at the municipal Gateway Center Parking (fee) and at dockside on Goat Island (free).

- **Amazing Grace** (open upper and open/closed lower decks) sails from the Oldport Marina (past the Newport Harbor Hotel and next to the Mooring Restaurant) at the Newport Yacht Center on America's Cup Avenue. Discounts for seniors 55+ and children 4-11. Minimum ten passengers per sailing.

- Oldport Marine Services, PO Box 141, Newport, RI 02840. Phone (401) 847-9109 or (401) 849-2111.

- **Spirit of Newport** (two decks; lower glass enclosed) sails from the Newport Harbor Hotel & Marina at 49 America's Cup Avenue. Discounts for seniors 64+ and children 12-16 and under 12.

- Newport Navigation, PO Box 3316, Newport, RI 02840. Phone (401) 849-3575.

- **Viking Queen** (two decks; lower enclosed) departs from the Goat Island Marina next to the Newport Doubletree Hotel. Discount for children 4-11.

- Viking Tours, PO Box 330, Newport, RI 02840. Phone (401) 847-6921.

IDA LEWIS ROCK LIGHTHOUSE (LIME ROCK).

See the map on page 231.

On the way to and from the Castle Hill Lighthouse and off Wellington Avenue, at the end of a long boardwalk, is the old Lime Rock Light Station now occupied by the private Ida Lewis Yacht Club. Since the yacht club acquired the property it has added to the original keeper's dwelling and its small square tower. As a result of this expansion, the station and its aid, now located in the northwest corner of the clubhouse, barely resembles its original form.

The lighthouse is also seen from the deck of the Providence-Block Island ferry. See page 220. It can also be viewed from the lighthouse cruises offered by Bay Queen Cruises of Warren RI; see page 225.

The lighthouse was built in 1854 on Lime Rock about 200 yards offshore. That distance is now traversed by the boardwalk leading to the club's premises. In 1856 a two-story, brick and granite Greek Revival-styled keeper's dwelling was built on the rock and connected to a 13-foot tall brick tower.

In 1927 the light was automated and transferred to a steel tower located in front of the dwelling; that beacon was discontinued in 1963. At the time of the transfer the aid's 1854 sixth-order classical lens was placed in storage in Staten Island. In 1932 it was returned to the Ida Lewis Yacht Club and later transferred to and exhibited in the Newport Historical Society's Museum (82 Truro Street). It is no longer displayed. The museum's Ida Lewis exhibit has also been discontinued.

Although originally named after its offshore rocky location, this lighthouse derives its fame from its lady keeper, Idawalley (Ida) Zorada Lewis, whose father was assigned as keeper in 1854. Shortly after his arrival, Keeper Lewis had a stroke and his wife had to take over. Ida assisted her mother and eventually became keeper of the lighthouse. She handled the demanding keeper's chores and also managed over the years to rescue at least 18 persons from the cold, and sometimes treacherous, waters off Lime Rock. Unofficially the number of saved souls ran into the dozens.

Many of the rescued were soldiers returning to Fort Adams after a night of sipping libations in Newport. As a result of her long service and lifesaving feats, Ida Lewis entertained President Grant in 1875. In 1880 she was the first female recipient of the Carnegie Foundation's gold medal for heroism. In tribute to Ida Lewis her beacon remains lighted as a private aid mid-May to mid-October.

OWNER. Ida Lewis Yacht Club since 1928.

PRESERVATION. Listed in the National Register of Historic Places.

Rose Island Lighthouse

CASTLE HILL

SOUTH IN NEWPORT. Take America's Cup Avenue and Thames Street (one way) to Wellington Avenue and turn right. Then:

-> Left at Halidon Avenue,
-> Right at Harrison Avenue,
-> Right at Castle Hill Road,
-> Left into Ocean Drive,
-> Right into a paved road, possibly marked with a small "Inn at Castle Hill" sign.

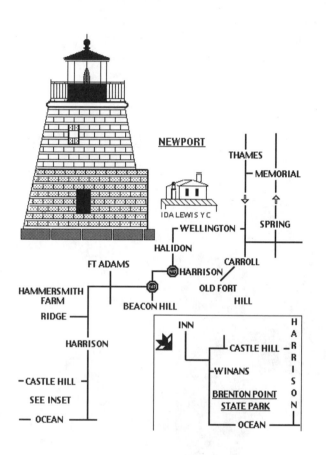

NORTH ON OCEAN DRIVE. Pass the entrance to Brenton Point State Park and Winan Avenue. Just before Ocean Drive makes a right turn into Castle Hill Road, turn left into the "Inn at Castle Hill" road. The paved road leads past Collins Beach (on the left), the Castle Hill Cove Marina (right) and up to the inn. Parking at the inn is for guests only. Turn right into the marina. Parking is free.

The lighthouse can be reached via a trail that begins opposite the marina entrance and leads straight up and over the hill to the concrete steps down to the tower. The distance from road to lighthouse is about 0.25 mile. The view from the lighthouse's vantage point is a spectacular one, especially when Newport's sailing "fleet" is returning to port.

CASTLE HILL LIGHTHOUSE (RAMS HEAD).

CHARACTERISTIC: Equal interval red 6s
HAW: 40' **RANGE**: 12 nm

This granite lighthouse was built in 1890, after a series (1875-89) of congressional appropriations totaling $40,000 were authorized.

When completed and its light established on May 1, 1890, the light station consisted of the 34-foot tall lighthouse, a 1,300-pound fog bell and a keeper's residence. The dwelling, destroyed in the September 1938 hurricane, was located back away from the tower at Castle Hill Cove, where the Coast Guard now maintains a boathouse.

OWNER. U.S. Coast Guard.

PRESERVATION. Listed in the National Register of Historic Places. This solidly built lighthouse has required but routine care and maintenance. The old wooden stairway was replaced by the present concrete steps in 1992.

NORTH TO DOWNTOWN NEWPORT. To reach Newport's waterfront and the Newport Harbor and Rose Island Lighthouses, return to Ocean Drive and turn left. Then:

-> Right at Castle Hill Road,
-> Left at Harrison Avenue,
-> Left at Carroll Avenue,
-> Left at Spring Street (one way),
-> Left at Memorial Boulevard,
-> Right at America's Cup Avenue,
-> Left at Long Wharf and right into Washington Street,
-> Left at Goat Island Connector.
A more scenic, but slightly longer route:
-> East on Ocean Drive,

-> Left at Bellevue Avenue and its fabulous mansions,
-> Left at Memorial Boulevard,
-> Right at America's Cup Avenue.

EAST TO SAKONNET POINT. A suggested route:
-> East on Ocean Drive,
-> North on Bellevue Avenue,
-> In Newport northeast on RI 138A (Memorial Boulevard),
-> In Middletown north on RI 138A (Aquidneck Avenue),
-> North on RI 138 (East Main Road) through Portsmouth,
-> East on RI 177 to Tiverton,
-> South on RI 77 to Sakonnet Point.

Castle Hill Lighthouse

SAKONNET POINT

SOUTH ON RI 77. In Tiverton take RI 77 south to its terminus near the beach in the town of Sakonnet. Just before the beach parking area (free), turn left into a narrow paved lane and continue to its end at a walled beach overlook. During the summer months the overlook may have a posted security guard. His presence does not preclude the public's use of the lane or the overlook to view the lighthouse standing about 0.6 mile offshore.

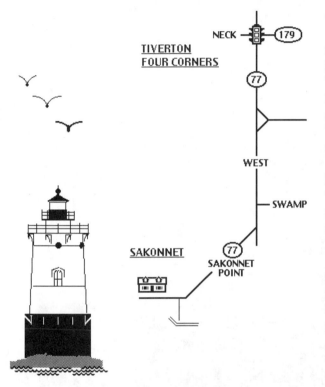

SAKONNET POINT LIGHTHOUSE.
CHARACTERISTIC: Flashing white 6s (red sector)
HAW: 58' **RANGES**: White 7; red 5 nm

Approval for a lighthouse off Sakonnet Point was provided in a congressional funding of $20,000 in August 1882.

Construction began in early 1883 and by November the tower's pier was ready for its superstructure. Harsh weather, however, delayed renewal of the project until spring of 1884. The beacon was first lighted on October 1, 1884. Sakonnet Point is a cast-iron, brick-lined conical tower resting on a standard cast-iron and cement-filled caisson. There are three decks. Two were used for living quarters and storage; the third held the former watchroom.

Equipped with a fourth-order Fresnel lens, Sakonnet Light exhibited a flashing white light 70 feet above sea level. The brick-lined iron tower held two rooms on the first level and two on the second. From the lantern room the keepers could see the mansions of Newport and as far away as Martha's Vineyard.

The lens' rotation was controlled by a clockwork whose weights descended the tower through a central tube. In 1891 the Lighthouse Board replaced the fourth-order lens with another fourth-order Fresnel equipped with a kerosene lamp. The new beacon retained its previously assigned characteristic. In 1939, after having been damaged by the September 1938 hurricane, the lighthouse's new owner, the Coast Guard, installed a kerosene-fed incandescent vapor lamp and a foghorn.

After Sakonnet Point was again damaged by Hurricane Carol in 1954, the Coast Guard decided to forego a large and unbudgeted repair cost and discontinued the light in 1955. The structure was sold to Carl and Carolyn Haffenreffer in 1961 for $1,300.

OWNER. Friends of Sakonnet Point Lighthouse since 1987.

PRESERVATION. Listed in the National Register of Historic Places.

In 1985 the owners offered to deed the lighthouse to a nonprofit organization if the group could raise the estimated $75,000 required to restore the lighthouse. In 1984 the Friends of Sakonnet Point Lighthouse accepted the challenge and in a little more than one year raised $100,000. Although the lighthouse has been nicely restored at a cost of over $80,000, it is not open to the public.

In early 1994 the Rhode Island Foundation provided $2,000 for further restorative work.

For years the Coast Guard had been willing to reactivate the light provided the Friends would purchase liability insurance to cover any maritime mishap if the light malfunctioned. The Friends' membership was unable to accept the culpability proviso and the high cost of liability insurance. In 1996 Senator John Chaffee was responsible for the inclusion in the U.S. Coast Guard's 1997 appropriation bill a clause absolving the Friends of all liability.

On March 22, 1997, Sakonnet Light was relighted after 43 years in darkness. A band played on the beach and hundreds arrived for the event in cars and buses. The .77 amp bulb produces a flash every six seconds, visible for seven nautical miles.

- Friends of Sakonnet Point Lighthouse, Inc., PO Box 154, Little Compton, RI 02837.

TO THE CASTLE HILL LIGHTHOUSE. Return to Tiverton and take RI 177 west to RI 138. A suggested route:
-> South on RI 138 (East Main Road) through Portsmouth,
-> In Middletown, south on RI 138A (Aquidneck Avenue),
-> In Newport, southwest on RI 138A (Memorial Boulevard),
-> South on Bellevue Avenue past its fabled mansions,
-> West and north on Ocean Drive to the lighthouse.

Sakonnet Point Lighthouse

MASSACHUSETTS
BORDEN FLATS

NORTH FROM TIVERTON. Enter Fall River on MA 138 (Broadway). Turn left at Bradford Avenue (one way) and right at Almond Street. Drive to Almond's dead end at Park Street and turn left into the Borden Light Marina (free).

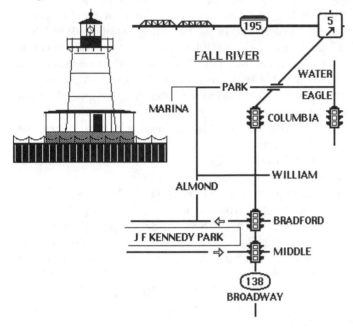

SOUTH ON I-195. Take Exit 5 (Taunton - North Tiverton) to MA 138 (Broadway), motor southwest to Bradford Avenue and turn right.

The lighthouse, west of the marina, sits on an oversize caisson that has been submerged atop an 8.8-acre ledge at the mouth of the Taunton River.

BORDEN FLATS LIGHTHOUSE.
CHARACTERISTIC: Flashing white 2.5s
HAW: 47' **RANGE**: 11 nm

For a number of years before the Borden Flats Lighthouse was built there was an unlighted day beacon in the area. The 1872 Annual Report of the Lighthouse Board described a "stone beacon, with iron column and day-mark." The present tower was built in 1881 at a cost of $24,000.

The 48-foot tall lighthouse is constructed of bolted cast-iron plates. It was originally supported by an unprotected concrete foundation that was badly damaged during the September 1938 hurricane.

The present pier is a cylindrical caisson that was placed around the old foundation, sunk onto the reef and filled with concrete. Inside the pier and below the main deck are fuel and water tanks. Water was collected on the roof and delivered through gutters to the cistern.

There are five decks; the top four are accessible by circular cast-iron stairs. The first deck, used to store equipment and supplies, has access to the service gallery that circles the base of the superstructure. The second and third levels provided living quarters for the crew; the fourth deck served as the watchroom. The last deck, reached by ladder, holds the 10-sided lantern. A 4-foot wide service balcony, which circles the lantern, supported the tower's automated fog bell.

When first established, the optic was a kerosene-fed fourth-order Fresnel lens. After the light station was automated in 1963 the Coast Guard removed its station personnel. In 1977 the lantern's classical lens was replaced by a modern plastic lens. Today the tower is almost in the shadow of the Braga Bridge, named for one of the first men from Fall River to die in World War II.

While in Fall River be sure to visit Battleship Cove, home port to the Battleship *Massachusetts*. The excellent Fall River Marine Museum is also nearby, featuring an extensive exhibit on the *Titanic*.

OWNER. U.S. Coast Guard.
PRESERVATION. Listed in the National Register of Historic Places.

PALMER ISLAND, BUTLER FLATS & CLARKS POINT

<u>**NORTH ON I-195**</u>. In New Bedford take Exit 15 and follow MA 18 (Downtown Connector) south. Then:
-> Take the "Downtown" exit into Water Street,
-> Left at Union Street (one way) and cross divided MA 1 (Kennedy Highway),
-> Right at Frontage Road (Front Street),
-> Where Frontage turns right turn left into Twins Pier.

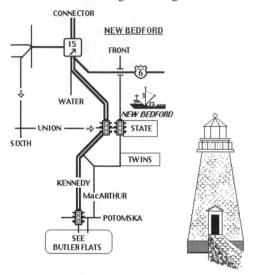

<u>**SOUTH ON US 6**</u>. Turn south into Sixth Street. The turn occurs at the end (eastbound) or the beginning (westbound) of US 6's divided lanes (see map). Then follow the Union -> Frontage (Front) route to Twins Pier and turn left. The lighthouse can be seen to the southeast in front of New Bedford's storm barricade. Although there is no scheduled transportation to the lighthouse, the grounds around the tower are open to the sailing public.

The ferry from New Bedford to Cuttyhunk Island passes close by Palmer Island Light.
- Cuttyhunk Boat Lines, Inc., Pier 3 / Fisherman's Wharf, New Bedford, MA 02740. Phone: (508) 992-1432
  Website: http://www.cuttyhunk.com/
  Email: Alert2@Cuttyhunk.com

The Whaling City Launch Service offers water taxi service from the New Bedford waterfront and a 50-minute harbor tour on the motor launch *Acushnet* that includes views of Palmer Island Lighthouse. Discount for children under 12.
- Whale City Launch Service, Phone (508) 269-5815.

<u>**PALMER ISLAND LIGHTHOUSE**</u> (PALMER'S ISLAND).
CHARACTERISTIC: Flashing white 4s
HAW: 42' **RANGE**: 5 nm

This conical stone lighthouse is a fine example of Colonial Revival styling. It was built in 1849 for less than $2,000. The 3-foot deep foundation slab and the tower are constructed of rough quarry stone (rubble stone). The conical tower's walls are three feet thick at its base, tapering to 18 inches at the top. The interior is not cylindrical in shape, but tapers from its brick flooring on the first deck (18-foot diameter) to the top (10-foot diameter).

The present nonagonal lantern with its larger storm panes replaced the original octagonal lantern in 1863. Over the years new construction on the station included a small keeper's house (pre-1900), a covered walkway (1902), a fog signal building and a wooden bell tower (c.1929).

From 1888 to 1891 a red light on the nearby Fairhaven Bridge served as a range light with Palmer Island Light. This arrangement helped mariners past Butlers Flats before the lighthouse was established there. Later for a time a light on the Wamsutta Mill served as a range light with Palmer Island Light.

The house and walkway were destroyed during the September 1938 hurricane. Mabel Small, wife of Keeper Arthur Small, died in the hurricane while trying to come to the aid of her husband, who was injured but survived.

Palmer Island Light was automated in 1941. After the construction of a massive hurricane wall in New Bedford Harbor in the early 1960s, Palmer Island Light was deemed useless. In 1966 arsonists torched the structure. The fire and heat vaporized the old wooden bell tower and gutted the tower's interior, destroying its door and windows, warping the cast-iron lantern frame, destroying the roof and ventilator and crumbling the rubble stone foundation.

In 1978 ownership of Palmer Island went from Norlantic Diesel to the City of New Bedford, and local resident Dr. John O'Toole mounted a preservation effort. New Bedford youngsters picked up 20 tons of trash and debris from the island which they converted into $300 for the lighthouse fund. A new fiberglass lantern was constructed to replace the badly burned one, and a 500-pound steel door was installed. The New Bedford Fire Department contributed a new iron spiral staircase.

After another restoration in 1989, the lighthouse soon fell victim to more vandalism. Through the 1990s the lighthouse was an empty shell and the lantern was empty. Led by Tourism and Marketing Director Arthur B. Motta, Jr., concerned people in New Bedford worked to restore Palmer Island Light for its 150th birthday. The lantern was lifted off and refurbished, and the lighthouse was relighted on August 30, 1999. There is discussion of establishing a human presence once again on Palmer Island in an effort to prevent vandalism.

PALMER ISLAND, BUTLER FLATS & CLARKS POINT

OWNER. City of New Bedford.

PRESERVATION. Listed in the National Register of Historic Places.

TO BUTLER FLATS. Leave Twins Pier on Frontage/Front to MacArthur Drive and turn left. Then:

-> Right at Potomska Street,

-> Left at Front Street,

-> Cross Gifford Street into Norton Court,

-> Left at Cove Road,

-> Into East Rodney French Boulevard.

Enroute on East Rodney French is Billy Woods Wharf, terminal for the passenger ferry to Martha's Vineyard Island.

Motor south on East Rodney French alongside New Bedford's harbor. The best spot for viewing the lighthouse is from the seawall just south of Ricketson Street. There are seasonal parking restrictions along East Rodney French, but none on the boulevard's side streets. Three municipal parking lots (free) are located a few short blocks south between Portland Street and the entrance to Fort Rodman.

For an excellent closeup view, the ferry from New Bedford to Martha's Vineyard passes very near Butler Flats Light. See page 247 for details.

- Cape Island Express Lines, Inc., PO Box 4095, New Bedford, MA 02741.

Phone: (508) 997-1688.

BUTLER FLATS LIGHTHOUSE.

CHARACTERISTIC: Flashing white 4s   **HAW**: 53'

The first beacon in the area was established in 1804 at Clarks Point. The present lighthouse rests on a concrete-filled cast-iron caisson located in the New Bedford Channel at the entrance to New Bedford Harbor. It was erected in 1898.

Instead of using the design popular in the late 1890s, the Lighthouse Board erected a brick tower festooned with brick window sills and fancy arches and raised brick below the watchroom deck. Italianated cast-iron brackets support the lantern gallery. Even the service balcony's balustrade does not resemble other New England lighthouses. Above the basement storage area are four decks. When inhabited by watch personnel, the levels were utilized for office space, living quarters, a galley, and the watchroom.

The 53-foot tall lighthouse's beacon, first established on April 30, 1898 using a kerosene-powered fifth-order Fresnel lens, replaced the Clarks Point light.

In 1975 a new automatic light and fog signal were placed on New Bedford's hurricane barrier. The Coast Guard deemed the lighthouse unnecessary and it came under the control of the City of New Bedford in 1978. It was automated and became one of the first solar-powered lighthouses.

OWNER. City of New Bedford.

PRESERVATION. Listed in the National Register of Historic Places.

 In 1992 vandals got into the tower and broke windows, battered the walls, and damaged the battery-operated light. In 1993 the lighthouse was fitted with a new optic, and it was made more secure by the addition of an exterior lighting system. The tower was also made more difficult to enter.

In September 1997 inmates from the Bristol County House of Correction went to work at Butler Flats Light. The project was a joint venture of Bristol County Sheriff Thomas Hodgson and New Bedford Mayor Rosemary S. Tierney. The inmates rewired the electrical system and did work on the tower's walls, ceilings, floors and stairway.

On April 30, 1998, more than 600 people attended a celebration of Butler Flats Light's 100th birthday. A new, brighter optic, powered by a cable from the shore, was installed by Hugh Murray, the retired New Bedford wire inspector who in recent years has headed up the preservation efforts.

Butler Flats Light is currently the only lighthouse in the U.S. flying a lighted American flag 24 hours a day.

THE FORTS AT CLARKS POINT. After the British landed at Clarks Cove in 1778 and marched inland to burn New Bedford, Clarks Point became a key site in the planning for the defense of New Bedford and its harbor. During the War of 1812 local citizens threw up earthworks on the point and established a battery of muzzle-loaded cannon, but Clarks Point would not be integrated into the nation's coastal defense system until 1840! By 1846 Major Richard Delafield and Captain Robert E. Lee had completed the plans for a granite "Fort at Clarks Point." The land was purchased in 1858 and site preparations began in 1859. With the delivery of cranes and the first shipment of granite blocks, construction of the vertical and angled redan commenced in early 1861, continued through out the Civil War and terminated in 1871 with only two of the proposed three tiers completed.

At the outbreak of the Civil War in 1861 the fort had not yet received its artillery pieces. To bolster the defense of the harbor, the mayor of New Bedford, Isaac Taber, ordered the construction and the equipping of an earthwork artillery battery. Although the defensive position remained untested, the mayor's initiative gave his name to the fort. By 1866 Fort Taber was a formidable arsenal holding twenty 10-inch long-range Rodman cannons, fourteen 8-inch "Rods," four 10-pound repeating (parrot) guns and two flanking 24-inch howitzers.

CLARKS POINT LIGHTHOUSE.

A small patch of land on Clarks Point was deeded to the United States in 1800 for the construction of a 42-foot tall stone light tower. The lighthouse, completed in 1804, was equipped with one of Winslow Lewis' lamp-reflector optics whose focal plane was 50 feet above the harbor. The keepers dwelling, a small wood framed structure, was built by the light's first keeper.

In 1863 the keeper's house was moved and completely refurbished in order to provide a larger work area for the project's stone cutters. A year later the engineers built a privacy wall around the small light station. As the fort rose in height it increasingly masked the light, so in 1869 Army Engineers moved the beacon to the fort. Choosing the fort's northerly square staircase tower for the construction of the new aid, engineers laid a wooden floor across its granite walls, raised a one-story wood framed dwelling and then added a hipped roof covered with sheet metal. A circular wooden gallery placed atop the square two-room dwelling formed the deck for the lantern. Clarks Point light was reestablished in its new home on June 15, 1869. Twenty-nine years later, when the Butler Flats light became operational, Clarks Point was discontinued. The old stone tower was demolished in 1906.

Fort Taber, staffed only by the lighthouse keeper (caretaker) and a gunnery sergeant, remained an inactive Army post until its donation to the City of New Bedford in 1892. During the Spanish-American War, Washington retrieved the land, renamed it Fort Rodman and proceeded to build five low-profile, reinforced concrete artillery batteries. The fort was reactivated during both World Wars and retained thereafter for reserve training purposes. Although Fort Rodman was declared an obsolete and surplus military post in 1947, the Pentagon held on to the property until 1970 when the General Services Administration leased or deeded most of Fort Rodman's 60 acres to the City of New Bedford to be used for "historical, educational and recreational purposes."

OWNER. City of New Bedford.

PRESERVATION. Listed in the National Register of Historic Places as part of the Fort Taber (Historic) District.

With deed in hand, the city turned its administration over to the Fort Taber Historical Association. In turn, the nonprofit association prepared the fort for visitors, erected a building in front of the structure, established therein a museum with donated historic displays and, best of all, completely restored the Clarks Point tower.

Unfortunately, Clarks Point became New Bedford's role model for vandals. After a few years all that remained of the lantern were its rusting mullions. The keeper's dwelling was ransacked and the exterior was marred with graffiti. Fort Taber's guns could not have done a more destructive job. But there is much happier recent news.

Fort Rodman has been upgraded with the elimination of some of the old military structures and the screening from public view the nearby new wastewater treatment plant. The area has been converted into a park with planted trees, shrubs and grass lawns. City officials also decided to fully restore and relight the historic beacon on the fort. Restoration of the lantern was carried out during the winter months of 2000-2001 inside the city's wastewater treatment plant's welding facility, and the wood frame upper portion of the lighthouse was rebuilt by city crews. The lighthouse restoration was funded in part by a grant from NStar.

On Friday evening, June 15, 2001, more than 3,000 people braved foggy, chilly weather to gather for a relighting event. Mayor Frederick M. Kalisz addressed the crowd, saying "Tonight we bring light back to the historical lighthouse," he said. "Join me in being proud of our city. Be proud of where we're going. Leave here with a renewed spirit. The light was turned on at 9 p.m., followed by cannons blasting, fireworks bursting in air and the playing of the *1812 Overture.*

---

1. The "First System Fortifications," the national coastal defense plan calling for the construction of harbor defenses all along the Atlantic seaboard, was initiated in 1794.

Palmer Island Lighthouse

Butler Flats Lighthouse

TARPAULIN COVE
DUMPLING ROCKS

Tarpaulin Cove Lighthouse's location is on Naushon Island's south central shore on the west side of Tarpaulin Cove. Tarpaulin Cove Lighthouse cannot be seen from the mainland, and unfortunately there are no public cruises that pass the lighthouse. The New Bedford - Martha's Vineyard ferry passes between the Elizabeth Islands and Nobska Point on Cape Cod, but the lighthouse is not visible from the ferry. At the present time the best ways to view this lighthouse are by private (or charter) boat or plane.

TARPAULIN COVE LIGHTHOUSE
CHARACTERISTIC: Flashing white 6s
HAW: 78' **RANGE**: 9 nm

An early beacon was erected privately on Naushon Island by tavern keeper Zaccheus Lumbert in 1759, for the "public good of Whalemen and Coasters." Lumbert paid for the upkeep of the light himself, except for whale oil he obtained from the people of Nantucket. This beacon, one of the earliest on the continent, was maintained by tavern keepers for 58 years.

The first government application for a lighthouse at Tarpaulin Cove was made in 1807. The federal government bought property for the building of a lighthouse on Naushon Island in 1817.

A 38-foot rubblestone lighthouse tower was built , exhibiting a fixed light about 71 feet above sea level. The lantern held a system of 10 lamps and reflectors. John Hayden was the first keeper of the light and remained at Tarpaulin Cove for at least 25 years.

In 1842 Keeper Hayden complained that the tower was leaky "from top to bottom" and filled with ice in the winter. Hayden stated, "I consider the establishment was not faithfully built in the first instance," and added that the dwelling was "cold and uncomfortable." Inspector I. W. P. Lewis recommended a new tower, saying the "whole establishment (was) in a dilapidated state." Nothing was done for decades except for the installation of a fifth order Fresnel lens from Paris in 1856.

In 1888 the old stone house was replaced, and in 1891 a new 28-foot brick lighthouse tower was built, with an iron lantern and a new fourth order lens. A 1,200 pound fog bell in a tower with striking machinery was also installed. The bell tower was destroyed in the Hurricane of '38.

After the light was automated in 1941, the house and other buildings fell into disrepair and were torn down in 1962. The Fresnel lens was replaced by a modern optic.
OWNER. U.S. Coast Guard.
PRESERVATION. Listed in the National Register of Historic Places.

DUMPLING ROCKS LIGHTHOUSE (destroyed).
In 1828 Congress appropriated $4,000 to build a lighthouse on Dumpling Rocks, a barren rocky outcropping whose highest elevation is but a few feet above the sea. The keeper's dwelling and its integrated tower were first lighted on October 19, 1828. The tower's multi-lamp Winslow Lewis optic had a focal plane height of 43 feet.

In 1890 the old stone house was torn down and a new combination dwelling and tower was erected on the old foundation. The house was a two-story, gabled and wood framed structure with a square wooden tower attached to its front elevation. The lantern was of the standard hexagonal cast-iron design and equipped with a fourth-order Fresnel lens. Because the sea continued to menace the station, an elaborate U-shaped bulkhead, some 90 feet long, was constructed out of pine timbers and bolted securely to the reef. To add additional strength, the bulkhead was reinforced on the seaward side with a wall built with the stones from the dismantled keeper's house.

When that monstrous September 1938 hurricane swept over the rock, it almost totally destroyed the light station. During the storm there was a thunderous crash and a violent shaking of the house. Keeper Octave Ponsart and Assistant Keeper Henry Fontineau found the first floor flooded almost to the ceiling. A huge piece of Dumpling Rock itself had been torn away and crashed through the living room wall. The boulder stayed in place partly inside the house, anchoring the dwelling to the rock. This lucky accident may have saved the lives of the keepers and their families as the house remained anchored throughout the storm.

Attempts made to repair the damage were unsuccessful. The light was discontinued in 1940 and the property abandoned. Its replacement is a skeletal steel tower surmounted by an automated beacon.

CUTTYHUNK ISLAND

CUTTYHUNK ISLAND LIGHTHOUSE (demolished).

Tucked away unseen in the southwestern corner of Cuttyhunk Island stands an old stone oil house (sans door and vent), the last remnant of a light station established in 1823. The station also had a 25-foot tall stone conical tower attached to a stone keeper's dwelling.

A Lighthouse Service report of 1838 complained of the tower's poor condition, citing the fact that twice it had to be strengthened with an exterior sheathing of coursed brick. In 1860, with the tower in terrible shape, a second story was added on top of the keeper's residence and the beacon moved into a square tower placed at mid-roof. Finally a permanent 45-foot tower was built in 1891. The oil house was added in 1903.

The Hurricane of 1944 hit Cuttyhunk directly, changing the shape of the island. Coast Guard Keeper Octave Ponsart and his daughter, Seamond, weathered the storm and managed to keep the light going.

In 1947 both the light tower and house were demolished and the warning beacon placed on a steel tower.

A ferry from New Bedford will take you to Cuttyhunk, providing a close view of Palmer Island Light on the way out of New Bedford Harbor. The island, which has a year-round population of under 100 people, is no longer worth visiting as a lighthouse destination, but is a fascinating place in its own right. There are good views of Martha's Vineyard's Gay Head cliffs from Cuttyhunk.

- Cuttyhunk Boat Lines, Inc., Pier 3 / Fisherman's Wharf, New Bedford, MA 02740.

Phone: (508) 992-1432

Website: http://www.cuttyhunk.com/

Email: Alert2@Cuttyhunk.com

Ned Point Lighthouse

NED POINT

NORTH ON US 6. In Mattapoisett Center at the town's first traffic signal, turn right into Main Street. There is a "Town Hall" sign on the intersection's northwest corner. Follow Main, Water and Beacon Streets for about one mile and bear right into Ned's Point Road. Continue south on Ned's Point for about 0.6 mile to the lighthouse.

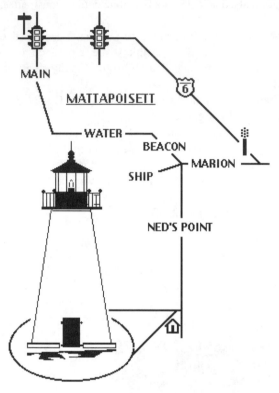

SOUTH ON US 6. About 1.5 miles from an "Entering Mattapoisett" sign and where US 6 leaves Marion Road and curves to the right as County Road, continue straight ahead on Marion Road. There is a blinking yellow caution light at the intersection. Follow Marion for another 0.5 mile to Ned's Point Road, turn left and continue to the lighthouse.

NED POINT LIGHTHOUSE (NED'S POINT).
CHARACTERISTIC: Equal interval white 6s
HAW: 41' **RANGE**: 12 nm

On four acres of land purchased in 1837 for $240, the Lighthouse Service built the Ned Point light station, consisting of a 35-foot tall rubble stone tower, a wooden keeper's dwelling, an oil house (located at the park's entrance) and a barn. Ned Point's multi-lamp/reflector optic displayed a fixed white light. The station cost $4,500.

In 1888 the conical tower was rebuilt to a height of 39 feet and provided an octagonal lantern equipped with a new fifth-order lens powered by a single kerosene lamp.

A new wood framed residence, also built in 1888, is no longer on Ned Point, but at Pocasset's Wings Neck Lighthouse on Cape Cod, where it was moved in 1930.

The beacon was decommissioned in 1952. The Coast Guard reactivated the lighthouse in 1961, using a dome-shaped acrylic optic. The beacon was automated in 1977.

OWNER. U.S. Coast Guard (lighthouse). The grounds and a right-of-way easement were sold to the Town of Mattapoisett in 1961. The land is now the Veterans of Mattapoisett Park.

PRESERVATION. Listed in the National Register of Historic Places.

In 1993 Ned Point became the first lighthouse in the United States to be adopted by a U.S. Coast Guard Auxiliary Flotilla. In early 1994, Mattapoisett was invaded by spray can wielding vandals bent on covering every structure in town. Yes, the lighthouse was also covered with graffiti. Mr. Clayton Hagy, a Flotilla member, painted over the graffiti. Mr. Hagy served as the lighthouse's "keeper" for a number of years.

In July 1995 Auxiliary members and Coast Guard personnel completely rehabilitated the tower's exterior. The restoration work included the removing of the lantern's plexiglass panes and replacing them with safety plate glass. A new optic and bulb changer were installed, increasing the light's visibility to 12 nautical miles. During the project, bronze astragals and vent plates were discovered under layers of old paint. They were removed, cleaned, refurbished and reinstalled.

VISITING THE LIGHTHOUSE. Good news for lighthouse seekers! The lighthouse has been open during July and August, Thursdays, 10 a.m. to noon. There are 32 granite steps to the gallery where there is a spectacular view of Buzzards Bay. On a clear day Martha's Vineyard Island can be seen to the south. For tour information.
- U.S. Coast Guard Auxiliary Flotilla 1N67, PO Box 421, Marion, MA 02738.
Email: aucoot@cgaux1nr.org

BIRD ISLAND

NORTH ON US 6. About 1.3 miles northeast of the US 6 & MA 105 junction in Marion center turn right off US 6 into Butler Point Road. Continue down Butler Point across Sippican Neck to its dead end at a golf course. The lighthouse can be seen from along a roadside seawall.

SOUTH ON US 6. The turn into Butler Point Road is about 0.6 mile from a "Marion" town limit sign.

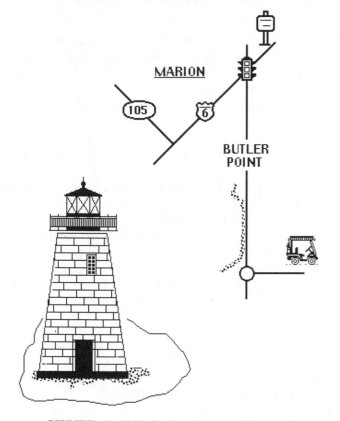

BIRD ISLAND LIGHTHOUSE.

After purchasing the two-acre island for $200 and having the property ceded by Massachusetts, the Federal Government built the extant tower and an attached stone keeper's quarters in 1819. The 25-foot tall conical, rubblestone light tower is capped with the standard cast-iron lantern and roof. Its original multi-lamp optic revolved, showing a white light 30 feet above mean high water.

The lantern's service gallery projects beyond the tower without coving or support brackets. The tower's stairway has granite steps. Note the window astragals.

In 1856 a fourth-order Fresnel lens was installed at Bird Island Light. In 1889 the dwelling was rebuilt.

Bird Island Light was taken out of service on June 15, 1933. The building of the Cape Cod Canal had led to more traffic in Buzzards Bay, but lighted buoys close to the main shipping channels eliminated the need for Bird Island Light. Nevertheless, the lighthouse endured until a 16-foot hurricane surge swept over the island on September 21, 1938, damaging the 37-foot tall lighthouse and destroying all of the station's outbuildings. In 1939 the light was decommissioned, its classical lens removed and declared to be surplus government property. The station's fog signal building was also dismantled.

OWNER. In 1940 the island was sold at auction to a private party. Since 1966 the property has been owned by the town of Marion. The island is under the care of the Audubon Society. Bird Island is now considered an important nesting site for common terns and endangered roseate terns. The small light station is managed by the Marion Conservation Commission and cooperatively cared for by the Sippican Historical Society and the Bird Island Lighthouse Preservation Society.

PRESERVATION. Listed in the National Register of Historic Places.

In the early 1970s the Town of Marion and the Sippican Historical Society raised $13,000 from local contributors to repair the tower. On July 9, 1976, the restored tower, sporting new coats of paint, a new ventilator ball and lightning rod, and an automatic optic, was reactivated as a private aid. In 1981 vandals caused $1,000 of damage to the structure, lantern and optic. Although the repair bill was paid by the Sippican Historical Society, the beacon was not relighted.

In 1994 the Massachusetts Conservation Commission granted the Society permission to restore the lighthouse. The Society raised funds privately and secured a federal grant. Since 1994 the organization has raised $120,000. The lighthouse tower has been restored by International Chimney Corporation.

On June 27, 1997, the Marion Board of Selectmen asked Charles Bradley of the Bird Island Preservation Society if his group had the funds for a new optic to be installed in the tower. Bradley replied that they didn't, so the selectmen decided to provide $3,000 for a new solar-powered flashing light and its installation. At 9:00 PM on July 4, 1997, with 3,000 people gathered onshore, Bird Island Light was relighted as a private aid to navigation.

- Bird Island Lighthouse Preservation Society, Attn: Charles Bradley, 64 Front Street, Marion, MA 02738.
Phone: (508) 748-0550. Information also available from the Marion Town House (508) 748-3500.
Website: http://by-the-sea.com/birdislandlight/
Email: JPKEO@banet.net

WINGS NECK
CLEVELAND EAST LEDGE

<u>SOUTH ON MA 28.</u> The tour around Cape Cod is presented as a counterclockwise loop beginning with these lighthouses.

To reach Pocasset from either Buzzards Bay or Sagamore follow US 6 to the Bourne traffic rotary. Then:

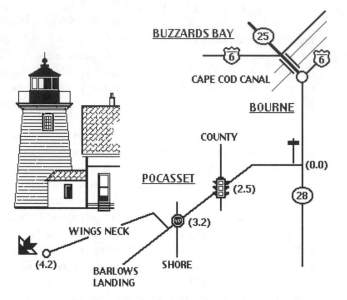

-> Pick up MA 28 and continue south to Pocasset,

-> Right at Barlow's Landing Road marked with a "Pocasset 1 - Barlows Landing - Wings Neck 3" sign on the southwest corner,

-> A short distance from Shore Road (stop sign) turn right into Wings Neck Road,

-> Along the way Wings Neck divides. Take either artery and continue to the road's end at a small cul-de-sac.

There are parking and trespassing restrictions posted on both sides of Wings Neck and beyond the public road's dead end. The Wings Neck Lighthouse can be viewed from the cul-de-sac. Cleveland East Ledge can be seen to the south southwest about 3.8 miles offshore.

WINGS NECK LIGHTHOUSE.

The first lighthouse on Wings Neck was built in 1849 on about 12 acres of swamp land purchased for $330.

The first Wings Neck Light, built in 1848, was a Cape Cod style structure with a wooden lantern room on top of a stone keeper's house. Total cost of the station was $4,500. In the 1870s it was reported that the weight of the lantern was crushing the roof of the dwelling. In 1878 the tower was destroyed by a fire that started in the lantern's ventilator. The stone dwelling survived and served as a temporary beacon until it was replaced in 1889 with a 1 1/2-story wood framed keeper's dwelling with a wooden tower. The walkway connecting the house and tower was added in 1899.

The extant octagonal tower rests on a fieldstone foundation and is sheathed in oak shingles. There are three decks, with the top deck supporting a cast-iron lantern topped with the usual ventilator ball and lightning rod.

When first established, Wings Neck's oil-burning lamps had a focal plane of 50 feet above mean high water and showed a fixed white light that could be seen for 14 nautical miles. Although Wings Neck's records are not complete, it is possible that a Fresnel lens was installed in the tower built in 1889. The optic's illuminant was changed from kerosene liquid to kerosene vapor in 1914.

With the building of Cleveland East Ledge Light, Wing's Neck Light was considered expendable. The station was discontinued in 1945 and went up for sale in 1947. It was bought by Frank and Irene Flanagan of Boston for $13,738. The von Trapp family singers of *Sound of Music* fame were among the summer guests of the Flanagans at the lighthouse. Irene Flanagan lived at the lighthouse for many years and was known as the "Lady in the Lighthouse."

A structural survey made in 1981 revealed the existence in the tower of two unique Lighthouse Service items. One is a fine brass framed slot imbedded in the landing near the lantern deck through which passed the weighted chains of the tower's 1,000-pound fog bell striking mechanism. The other item is an unusual air vent. To operate it one must grab hold of a leather strap and then pull a cylindrical copper fitting out of its housing. The partially withdrawn copper can has large round perforations that allowed air to flow into the lantern.

The inactive light station consists of the keeper's residence and oil house, a wooden dwelling and light tower (1889), the former Ned Point's keeper's house (1880s) that was floated to Wings Neck in 1930 and a boathouse that has been converted into a dwelling.

OWNER. The station has been privately owned since 1947.

PRESERVATION. Listed in the National Register of Historic Places.

TO OLD SILVER BEACH.

There is another spot that offers a distant view of the Cleveland East Ledge tower. Although it will be a bit closer than from Wings Neck, the structure is still about 2.7 miles away. Be sure to bring your binoculars.

Head south on MA 28 to a clover leaf exit at MA 151. Then:

-> Right (west) off MA 28 to MA 28A,

-> Left at MA 28A through North Falmouth,

-> Right at Wild Harbor Road to Old Silver Beach.

OPEN. All year, daily 9 to 8.

PARKING FEE. Daily Memorial Day weekend to Labor Day. Double cost on weekends. Free at other times of the year.

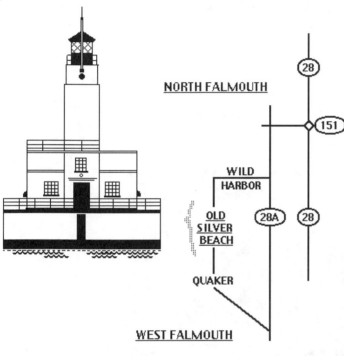

To return to MA 28 continue south on Quaker Road and Nashaweena Street and in West Falmouth take Old Deck Road east to MA 28.

CLEVELAND EAST LEDGE LIGHTHOUSE (CLEVELAND LEDGE).

CHARACTERISTIC: Flashing white 10s

HAW: 74' **RANGE**: 17 nm

This light marks the east side of the southern channel approaching the Cape Cod Canal. Its rock-filled caisson pier is 52 feet tall and stands in 21 feet of water on a rocky outcropping. Originally a State funded project started in 1940, the unfinished lighthouse with its temporary light was transferred to the Federal Government on September 18, 1941. The steel and reinforced concrete lighthouse was completed in 1943.

Cleveland East Ledge, a two-story structure with an integrated tower, has sometimes been classified as being Art Noveau, a genre that does not quite fit the design of this structure. The lighthouse resembles the Art Deco style.[1] Instead of the listless curves of the former, Art Deco shows very sharp, angular geometric forms and stylized natural designs.

The design of the main deck is rather unusual, having been described in a 1981 survey as resembling the bridge of a 1930 luxury ocean liner. Above the caisson deck there are two levels. The round lower level has square rooms with two-story high ceilings. It is enclosed by eight exterior walls that alternatingly contain wide and narrow windows in their lower sections. The upper level is in the shape of a cross that has been laid across the round lower level. The windows of this level are located at the four ends of the cross and immediately above the windows of the lower level. The 50-foot tall tower, resting on the center of the cross, contains a portholed watchroom and is topped by the usual cast-iron lantern.

As late as 1958 the kerosene-powered fourth-order Fresnel lens displayed a fixed white light. The Coast Guard automated the aid in 1978 after an underwater electric power cable had been laid to the structure, and replaced its classical lens with a modern plastic one. At the same time the crew was withdrawn and all wall openings sealed.

OWNER. U.S. Coast Guard.

PRESERVATION. Listed in the National Register of Historic Places.

In 1944 the 70-foot tall lighthouse almost lost its watch personnel during a raging storm that tore out one of the exterior walls and allowed the sea to roll through the structure. Fortunately the crew managed to erect a temporary barrier that saved both themselves and their charge.

In 1990 Cleveland East Ledge received a much needed refurbishing. A Coast Guard cutter crew, working 12 hours each day, finished the job in three weeks. They replaced the roof, rebuilt cisterns, cleaned the interior and, after sealing its cracks and seams, sandblasted and repainted the exterior.

---

1. The term "Art Deco" was coined by the historian Bevis Hillier in 1968 to describe the modern design emanating from the 1925 Exposition des Arts Decoratifs et Industriels Modernes in Paris. The art form is known by many names: Art Moderne, Streamline, Zig Zag, Jazz Age and Skyscraper.

LIGHTHOUSE SIGHTSEEING CRUISE. See the Falmouth Ferry map on page 247.

The Woods Hole Historical Collection, on behalf of the Woods Hole Historical Museum, sponsors a Sunset Lighthouse Cruise on the *Patriotoo* into Vineyard Sound and Buzzards Bay. The views of some of the lighthouses are distant, and since the cruise takes place mostly after sunset, photographic opportunities are limited. The cruise departs from the Island Commuter Corporation's ferry dock in Falmouth. See the map on page 247.

Lighthouses included are Cleveland East Ledge, East Chop, Gay Head, Nobska Point, Tarpaulin Cove and West Chop. Nobska Point Lighthouse, being the first on the tour, is likely to be the only one that will be visible in complete daylight.

SCHEDULE. Two days, usually in May.

FARES. Payment in advance required. No discounts.

- Woods Hole Historical Museum, PO Box 185, Woods Hole, MA 02543.

Phone (508) 548-7270.

Cleveland East Ledge Lighthouse

MARTHA'S VINEYARD LIGHTHOUSES
EAST CHOP - WEST CHOP - GAY HEAD
EDGARTOWN HARBOR - CAPE POGE

FERRY TRANSPORTATION. Ferries to Martha's Vineyard Island depart from New Bedford, Woods Hole, Falmouth, Hyannis and New London, Connecticut.

FROM NEW BEDFORD. The New Bedford run (90 minutes) to Vineyard Haven takes 15 minutes less than the Hyannis crossing. It takes passengers only — no cars. It provides a close view of Butler Flats Lighthouse, and medium-distance views of Nobska Point Lighthouse and West Chop Lighthouse. This is an excellent cruise for lighthouse enthusiasts.

From Route 1-195 take Downtown Exit 15 (Route 18 South). Continue on Route 18 to 4th set of lights, turn left and follow signs to the day and overnight parking lot, across the street from the Schamonchi Dock and Billy Wood's Wharf. Follow the signs to the Ferry.

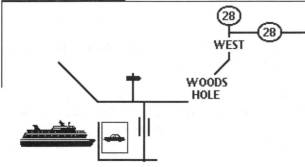

WOODS HOLE FERRY

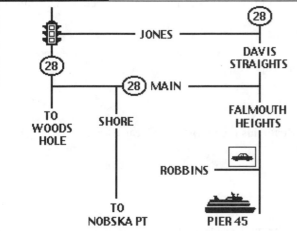

FALMOUTH FERRY

SCHEDULE.

Spring (May to mid-June) and fall (early September to mid-October) schedule:

Leaves New Bedford 9 AM every day; Friday 1 PM

Leaves Vineyard Haven Mon. through Thurs. 3 PM; Friday 11 AM, 3 PM & 8:45 PM; Saturday & Sunday 11 AM, 3 PM & 6:45 PM

Summer schedule (mid-June to early September):

Leaves New Bedford 9 AM, 1 PM and 5 PM every day; 9 PM Friday only.

Leaves Vineyard Haven 11 AM, 3 PM, 6:45 PM every day; 10:45 PM Fri. only.

Call or check website to confirm schedule.

FARES. Adult and child same day round trip or one way fares. Fee for bicycles. Group rates available.

- Cape Island Express Lines, Inc., P.O. Box 4095, New Bedford, MA 02741

Phone: (508) 997-1688

Website: http://www.mvferry.com/

CONTINUE TO WOODS HOLE. In Falmouth turn left off MA 28 (Palmer Avenue) at West Street and follow this route into Woods Hole Road. Then:

-> South on Woods Hole to a "Martha's Vineyard" sign at a bridge intersection,

-> Left and cross over the bridge,

-> Right at the next "Martha's Vineyard" sign into Juniper Street to the Steamship Authority's ferry terminal.

Company-operated parking lots (calendar day fees) are available at or within walking distance of the ferry terminals. Two Woods Hole lots off MA 28 are serviced by a free shuttle bus. Parking reservations can be made when ordering tickets. For parking information tune radio to 1610 AM as you approach Falmouth.

There are also a number of auto rental companies located near the ferry docks.

SCHEDULE. The Steamship Authority's ferries operate all year to Vineyard Haven and Oak Bluffs. Crossing time 45 minutes. The Woods Hole ferry schedule calls for more months of operation and more frequent sailings than provided by the Falmouth ferry. The Woods Hole terminals are equipped with ramps for the handicapped; the Eagle, Nantucket and Martha's Vineyard ferries are equipped with elevators.

It is suggested that the traveler avoid the same day round trip from Woods Hole to Vineyard Haven to Nantucket and return. It does not provide sufficient time ashore to visit both island's lighthouses.

Phone or check website for current departure times.

FARES. Same day passenger one way vehicle, passenger and bicycle fares. Discount for children 5-12. Vehicle reservations are often made months and up to a year in advance. During the summer months a same day round trip fare for an automobile has been about $140 for a family of four and a very iffy chance of obtaining a car ticket. It is recommended that you plan to visit the island without your vehicle and arrange for island-based transportation. Credit cards accepted.

- Reservation Bureau, Pine Tree Place, 509 Falmouth Road, Suite 1C, Mashpee, MA 02649.

Phone: Information and advance vehicle reservations (508) 477-8600 or (508) 693-9130.

Day of sailing information only (vehicle reservations not accepted at this number): (508) 548-3788.

To request a brochure / schedule (508) 477-8600 or (508) 693-9130.

- Woods Hole, Martha's Vineyard & Nantucket Steamship Authority, PO Box 284 (Railroad Avenue), Woods Hole, MA 02543.

Phone (508) 548-3788.

Website: http://www.islandferry.com/

OR TO FALMOUTH. One route to the Falmouth ferry is via MA 28:

-> Left off MA 28 at Jones Road,

-> Continue for 1.0 mile to MA 28 (Davis Straights) and turn right,

-> At the intersection where MA 28 turns to the right (west), continue straight ahead into Falmouth Heights Road. The ferry dock is located about 0.25 mile down Falmouth Heights south of Robbins Road.

A second way to reach the ferry dock:

-> Follow MA 28 (Main Street) through downtown Falmouth,

-> At the intersection where MA 28 turns north (left), turn right into Falmouth Heights Road. Continue on to the pier. Parking lot about 100 yards from the pier. Baggage drop off allowed. There is a daily parking fee.

SCHEDULE. Daily service late May to Columbus Day. Crossing time to Oak Bluffs 45 minutes. Phone or check website for current departure times.

FARES. Passenger and bicycle fares are comparable to those charged by the Woods Hole ferry. Discount for children under 13; under 3 free. July and August, Mondays through Fridays children under 5 ride free on the company's Family Plan Special.

- Island Queen, 297 Dillingham Avenue, Falmouth, MA 02540.

Phone (508) 548-4800.

Website: http://www.islandqueen.com/   Email: islqueen@cape.com

OR TO HYANNIS From Upper Cape Area (Falmouth):

-> Take Route 28 into Hyannis,

-> At Airport Rotary take your first right onto Barnstable Road; this road turns into Ocean Street,

-> Hy-Line's ferry terminal is 1-1/4 miles from the rotary.

From Lower Cape Area (Provincetown):

-> Take Route 6 to Exit 7,

-> At the end of off-ramp, take a left onto Willow Street,

-> At traffic lights go straight until you reach stop sign,

->Take right onto Main Street; at second set of lights take left onto Ocean Street,

-> After you have crossed South Street, Hy-Line's ferry terminal is approximately 1/4 mile on the left.

SCHEDULE. Early May to late October. Crossing time from Hyannis to Oak Bluffs is one hour 45 minutes. Phone or check website for current schedule.

FARES. Adult and child one way or round trip fares; fee for bicycle.

Hy-Line Cruises also operates an inter-island ferry to Nantucket, departing Oak Bluffs daily in season.

Hy-Line Cruises, Ocean Street Dock, Hyannis, MA 02601.

Phone: (508) 778-2600. Fax: (508) 775-2662.

Website: http://www.hy-linecruises.com/

FROM NEW LONDON, CONNECTICUT: From 95N:

-> Take exit 83,

-> Left onto Williams St.,

-> First right onto State Pier Rd., straight to State Pier parking lot.

MARTHA'S VINEYARD ISLAND LIGHTHOUSES

From 95S:

-> Take exit 84S,

-> Stay in left lane, this will put you on Eugene O'Neil Dr.,

-> Turn left at first light. At next light turn right. Follow road to State Pier parking lot.

SCHEDULE: Summer through Columbus Day, departing New London once daily Thursday through Sunday. Crossing time from New London to Vineyard Haven on the high-speed TriCat is two hours. Phone or check website for current schedule.

FARES. "Admiral class" and "Clipper class" round trip fares.

Fox Navigation, Phone (888)-SAILFOX for information and tickets.

Website: http://www.foxnavigation.com

MARTHA'S VINEYARD ISLAND. Mid-May to mid-October ferry arrivals at Vineyard Haven and Oak Bluffs connect with narrated two hour bus tours that take visitors through "down island" Oak Bluffs and its quaint gingerbread village, through Edgartown, a fashionable harborside community of narrow streets fringed by stately old captains' homes, and out to enjoy the panoramic views of the "up island" rural villages of Chilmark and West Tisbury. Tickets for the bus tours are available at ferry ticket offices or on board the ferries. Auto, jeep, dune buggy and moped rentals are available at docksides or short walking distances from the terminals. While the bus is an economical, easy and quick way to see the island, the more inquisitive visitors, especially lighthouse seekers, will want to do their own exploring. A rented auto or a taxi is the best means to enjoy the island's sights and sounds. There is also a company, KOTL Ventures, that offers tours of every lighthouse on the island for groups of five or more. KOTL Ventures also offers other New England lighthouse and historic tours.

- KOTL Ventures, P.O. Box 1104, Marlboro, MA, 01752-1104

Phone (508) 494-4241 Fax (419) 781-1580.

Website: http://maxpages.com/kotl   Email: light1104@yahoo.com

THE VINEYARD MUSEUM. This museum of the Martha's Vineyard Historical Society, located at 59 School Street in Edgartown, includes the Thomas Cooke House (1765), Native American Gallery, the Childrens' Gallery and the Captain Francis Pease House. The museum also includes the Luce House Gallery and Studio Art School in Vineyard Haven.

The Society's Gale Huntington Library of History and the Francis Foster Museum are located on Cooke Street. The latter contains displays of whaling material, scrimshaw, fishing gear and navigation aids. There are outdoor exhibits, including a replica of a tryworks with two 250-gallon whaleship cauldrons (used to boil whale blubber), a carriage shed, an herb garden and a replica of the old 1856 Gay Head tower with its original revolving first-order Fresnel lens, now electrified.

OPEN.

Mid-June to mid-October, Tuesdays through Saturdays 10 to 5.

Rest of year, Thursdays and Fridays 1 to 4. Saturdays 10 to 4, one Sunday per month.

ADMISSION FEES. Discounts for children 6-13. Members and children under 6 free.

- Martha's Vineyard Historical Society, Box 827, Edgartown, MA 02539.

Phone (508) 627-4441. Fax (508) 627-4436.

Website: http://www.vineyard.net/org/mvhs/

VISITING THE LIGHTHOUSES. West Chop is the first lighthouse a Martha's Vineyard visitor sees as the ferry approaches Vineyard Haven, East Chop (see next sketch) and West Chop if heading for Oak Bluffs. Once ashore and with transportation to move you around the island, the choice of direction is all yours. Martha's Vineyard lighthouses except West Chop (a residence) are open to the public on a very limited basis.

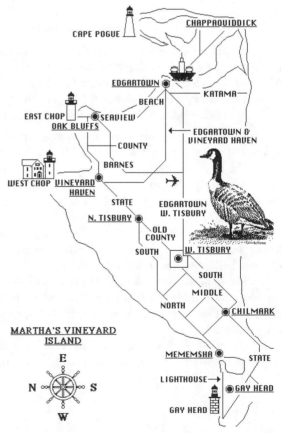

MARTHA'S VINEYARD ISLAND

EAST CHOP. Mid-June to August, Sunday evenings only around sunset.

GAY HEAD. Mid-June to August, Friday though Sunday, hour before to 1/2 hour after sunset.

ADMISSION FEE. A nominal donation is requested. Children free.

Phone (508) 627-4441.

VINEYARD ENVIRONMENTAL RESEARCH INSTITUTE. The VERI story concerns the determination and untiring work of one ecologically oriented person, William E. Marks, who founded VERI in 1984 to conduct scientific research relative to acid rain, water quality and coastal erosion. It soon became apparent to Bill Marks that access to the island's lighthouse properties was a requirement for the placement and protection of VERI's scientific equipment. In their discussions with the Coast Guard about the placing of equipment on waterfront property, the group's scientists decided to go for broke, namely the taking over responsibility of caring for the island's lighthouses and their properties.

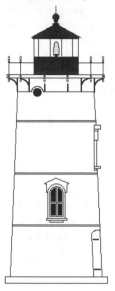

In 1985, when that decision became VERI doctrine, the nonprofit organization embarked on its effort to secure light station leases. In 1986, after numerous negotiations and testimony before a subcommittee of the U.S. House of Representatives, VERI signed a 35-year lease for the East Chop, Gay Head and Edgartown Harbor Lighthouses. It is important to note that, while VERI maintained the lighthouses, it was also very much involved in the preservation of the ecological well being of each light station.

In late 1993, VERI worked closely with the Coast Guard and the Dukes County (now the Martha's Vineyard) Historical Society in transferring VERI's license to the society.

Although supported by fundraising campaigns and private donations, the Society will be in need of funds to maintain its caretaker properties. The Society's annual membership fee (partially tax deductible) includes newsletters, the quarterly *The Dukes County Intelligencer* and lighthouse tour discounts.

EAST CHOP LIGHTHOUSE (TELEGRAPH HILL; CHOCOLATE LIGHTHOUSE).
CHARACTERISTIC: Equal interval green 6s
HAW: 79' **RANGE**: 9 nm

The East Chop Lighthouse stands at the edge of the East Chop cliffs ("the marlin's fin") above Oak Bluffs. Its light marks the east side of the entrance to Vineyard Haven Harbor.

Between 1828 and 1853 East Chop, then called Telegraph Hill, had a wooden signal tower, one of a string of semaphore signaling stations that stretched from Boston's Central Wharf, across Cape Cod, to Edgartown and Oak Bluffs on Martha's Vineyard and to New Bedford on the Massachusetts south shore. The stations were responsible for notifying ship owners when ships were sighted off Martha's Vineyard. In 1853 East Chop was recorded as being a lighthouse.

In 1869 a ship captain decided that ships rounding Oak Bluffs should be warned by a beacon.

So, with $1,700 collected from shipping companies, marine insurance firms, island residents and merchants, a wooden tower was erected and a beacon established. The structure was destroyed by fire in 1871.

The next tower, a wooden structure, went up in 1872. A year later, because of the tower's deterioration, the Lighthouse Board decided to purchase the light station for $6,000. After a major rebuilding in 1875 the new beacon was reestablished in 1876 as a federal aid to navigation.

The 40-foot tall tower is unremarkable in its style and design. It is a standard truncated cast-iron structure with the usual Italianate flame finials, fluting, acanthus leaves and window moldings. Its cast-iron lantern is 10-sided. The new light station also received a Gothic Revival-styled, 1 1/2-story wood framed keeper's dwelling and a brick oil house. Both of these buildings were removed in 1934.

The light was automated in 1934. Until 1984 when the presently active optic was introduced, East Chop's light was produced by a single lamp, burning whale oil and later kerosene, and a Fresnel lens. The new optic consists of a trapezoidal plastic lens that is powered by six electric bulbs, each with a burn life of 500 hours. When a bulb burns out, it is automatically replaced by a fresh one.

OWNER. U.S. Coast Guard (lighthouse). Grounds owned by the Town of Oak Bluffs since the 1940s. Lighthouse leased to the Martha's Vineyard Historical Society in 1993.

PRESERVATION. Listed in the National Register of Historic Places.

In 1962, because of a mixup in the paint shipment, the lighthouse was painted not the intended red color, but a reddish brown. Then in 1984 the Coast Guard, during a $40,000 renovation project, repainted the tower not reddish brown but with an expensive paint that "lightened [the tower] one shade." Thus the "chocolate" nickname.

Since 1989 VERI repaired by sandblasting or priming and repainting (1) the tower's exterior (the chocolate coat caused the interior to overheat) service gallery and balustrade, (2) the lantern's wainscot, floor, lens pedestal and brass air hole fittings and (3) the interior staircase. Also repaired were broken lantern glass, a ground level window and the perimeter fence. A turnstile was added at the main entrance to prevent mopeds and motorcycles from entering and tearing up the grounds.

WEST CHOP LIGHTHOUSE.
CHARACTERISTIC: Occulting white 4s (red sector)
HAW: 84' **RANGES**: White 15; red 11 nm

The West Chop Lighthouse, on the west side of the entrance to Vineyard Haven (Holmes Hole) Harbor, is located off West Chop Road (take Main Street out of Vineyard Haven) between Quinsigamond Avenue on the north and Minnesota Street on the south. Although visitors are not permitted inside the station (a residence for search and rescue personnel), the lighthouse is clearly visible from West Chop Road. In 1816 the citizens of Holmes Hole, then the busiest harbor on the island, petitioned for a lighthouse. They were turned down so that what funds were available could be spent on the construction of a lighthouse at Tarpaulin Cove on Naushon Island in the Elizabeth Islands. Nevertheless, the citizenry convinced Congress to appropriate the $4,900 to build the West Chop Lighthouse. This first light station, completed in 1817, consisted of a cylindrical 25-foot tall stone tower and two 2 1/2-story rubble stone keeper houses. The cast-iron lantern was octagonal in shape and held a two-tiered multi-lamp Lewis apparatus. The light had a focal plane of 60 feet above sea level.

The station was threatened by erosion and the second lighthouse, built of brick in 1846, was erected farther away from the eroding cliffs.

By 1891 West Chop had become a summer resort and the proliferation of large houses in the area began to obscure the light. A 17-foot mast with the light on top was added to the tower, then the 1846 tower was replaced by a new 45-foot brick tower, painted red. The new West Chop Light was painted white in 1896.

The cylindrical brick tower with its attached entry house lacks ornamentation. The watchroom is reached via a spiral stairway with four levels. Windows appearing at the upper three levels have granite sills and lintels.

Today the station also includes two Victorian residences and an 1882 fog signal house (all remodeled in 1891) and a brick oil house (built in 1895 and now used as a paint shed).

The decagonal lantern retains its original (1857) fourth-order Fresnel lens. The light was automated in 1976.
OWNER. U.S. Coast Guard.
PRESERVATION. Listed in the National Register of Historic Places.

In 1992 VERI received a lease extension of 35 years for the two station outbuildings it used for its offices. VERI also agreed to take care of the station grounds as part of the extended building lease. Accomplishments: (1) removed derelict unregistered vehicles from the two-acre site, (2) removed all debris and garbage, (3) landscaped and manicured the yard, (4) repaired the beach stairs, front picket fence and entry gate and (5) refurbished the old fog signal building and paint shed.

GAY HEAD LIGHTHOUSE (AQUINNAH). The people of Gay Head (named by settlers after the area's colored
cliffs) recently voted to change the name of their town to "Aquinnah," a Native American word for "Land Under The Sun." Aquinnah is home to the Wampanoag Tribe, the only federally recognized Native American tribe in Massachusetts.
CHARACTERISTIC: Alternating white and red 15s
HAW: 170' **RANGES**: White 24; red 20 nm

The Gay Head Lighthouse, standing on the edge of red clay cliffs, marks the offshore Devil's Bridge rocks, a ridge of stones and sand that extends towards the Elizabeth Islands from the base of the cliffs. It is located north of the intersection of Lighthouse and State Roads in Gay Head Lighthouse Park.

In 1798 Congress appropriated $5,750 and in December of that year Massachusetts ceded the land for the construction of a 47-foot tall light tower. A change in contractors delayed its completion until November 1799. That cliffside octagonal wooden lighthouse, although only 54 feet tall, held a light that was some 160 feet above the water.

By 1837 the upper portion of the tower was officially reported to be in a decaying state. With extensive repair work completed in 1838, the tower was given a new lantern. In 1844 the lighthouse was moved inland.

Construction of the extant 51-foot tall lighthouse cost $30,000. The height of the brick tower is 45.5 feet. Its outside diameter is 17.5 feet. The thicknesses of the masonry walls range from three feet at door level to two feet at the watchroom deck. The tower has a waist band consisting of four projecting rows of brownstone blocks, then a flat band above the projection, two quarter round (twice one ovolo) cornice brackets and finally the flat lower gallery. In a design similar to the Highland Lighthouse, an outside ladder provides access to the lantern gallery from the lower balcony. Inside the tower, cast-iron steps wind around the tower's centerpost with a landing at a lower window, one at the middle gallery and the last at the watchroom's deck.

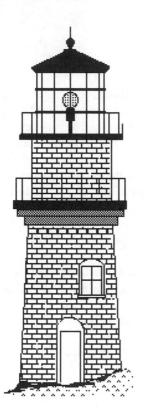

Gay Head's first optic was a whale oil-burning spider lamp, consisting of five concentric wicks. Later, the lighthouse was one of the first of America's lighthouses to receive Winslow Lewis' lighting system. In this case the apparatus was a revolving group of 10 reflector-equipped lamps.

In 1856 Gay Head was refitted with a new $16,000 first-order Fresnel lens powered by a single whale oil-fed lamp. The beacon was lighted on December 1, 1856. Before its installation the lens had been exhibited at the World's Fair in Paris.

The LePaute lamp, a modified Argand, consisted of a cylindrical reservoir base topped with a standpipe leading vertically up to four concentric wicks. During its operation, a heavy gravity-fed piston within the reservoir forced oil up through the standpipe to the wicks. The piston had to be cranked to its starting position every 1 1/2 hours. The light's flashing characteristic was created by an 8-foot high and 4.5-foot wide eclipser that rotated around the lens.

In 1912 the illuminant was changed to kerosene. In 1952 the Coast Guard installed a new high-intensity optic. The Coast Guard's watch crew was removed when the beacon was automated in 1956.

OWNER. U.S. Coast Guard. Leased to the Martha's Vineyard Historical Society in 1993.

PRESERVATION. Listed in the National Register of Historic Places.

In 1902 the damp and mildewed brick keeper's dwelling (1856) was torn down and replaced by a wood framed house. All of the station's buildings, constructed between 1856 and 1906, have been dismantled or destroyed. Only the tower remains.

During 1988-89, VERI established the Gay Head Lighthouse Park and at the urging of the Gay Head Selectmen, Conservation Commission, Police Department and the Wampanoag Tribe, installed a post and rail fence around the park. The fence was sorely needed to halt the destruction of the fragile Gay Head cliffs by thrill seekers and climbers going to the popular Gay Head beach. VERI also restored the lantern with new storm panes. In 1990 the lighthouse was opened to the public for the first time in 35 years.

Then in 1991-92, VERI (1) sanded, primed and repainted the tower's three landing decks, ceilings, stairs, center tube and two exit doors, (2) repaired the electrical lighting system, (3) repointed and painted the exterior brick masonry and (4) installed a telephone.

EDGARTOWN HARBOR LIGHTHOUSE.

CHARACTERISTIC: Flashing red 6s

HAW: 45' **RANGE**: 5 nm

The first lighthouse in Edgartown is believed to have been established as early as 1816. The second Edgartown Harbor Lighthouse, completed in 1828 and lighted on October 25, 1828, was a 2 1/2-story wooden building with an integrated tower. The entire structure sat on a wooden platform located 0.25 mile offshore. The 10-sided cast-iron lantern rested on an octagonal base. The land and construction cost about $4,480. A year later the lighthouse was connected to the shore by a wooden walkway ($2,500), which in 1847 was replaced by a stone breakwater. The old wooden walkway was known in those days as the "bridge of sighs," where young men, about to depart on long whaling voyages, would walk with their girlfriends.

The house and tower, although remodeled in the late 1800s, finally deteriorated to the point of collapse. The lighthouse was severely damaged in the September 1938 hurricane. In 1939, the cylindrical cast-iron Essex range light tower, located on Crane Beach in Ipswich, Massachusetts, was dismantled and barged to Edgartown as a replacement.

MARTHA'S VINEYARD ISLAND LIGHTHOUSES

OWNER. U.S. Coast Guard. Leased to the Martha's Vineyard Historical Society in 1993.

PRESERVATION. Listed in the National Register of Historic Places.

Since 1986 when VERI signed a 35-year maintenance lease, the group removed all graffiti, repaired broken lantern glass, sanded and repainted the service gallery, window trim and, in cooperation with Edgartown's Conservation Commission, Board of Selectmen and the Highway Department, repaired the causeway and culvert system.

In 1991 the lighthouse was badly vandalized by partying beer guzzlers. After three break-ins, all of the tower's windows were smashed. VERI installed heavy locks, cleaned up the broken beer bottles and glass on the beach and around the tower and on one window facing the town added a fake window painted on a sheet of plywood.

In 1992 the Edgartown Harbor Lighthouse underwent a complete refurbishing: (1) broken windows replaced, (2) anti-vandalism (rock throwing) wire mesh built around lantern, (3) the remaining two vandalized windows (one facing the Chappaquiddick ferry landing and the other facing Vineyard Sound) replaced with painted plywood, (4) door lock hasps (broken and jimmied several times) replaced with heavy cast-iron hasps and (5) the tower's exterior, gallery's balusters and roof repaired and sanded, primed and painted.

In 1995 the Martha's Vineyard Historical Society made more improvements to the lighthouse.

There are plans to further renovate the tower and to open it to the public at times. There is also a new memorial at the base of the lighthouse. The Martha's Vineyard Children's Lighthouse Memorial consists of stones engraved with the names of children who have died, along with part of a poem by Tomas Napolean called "Remembrance of an Unforgotten Vineyard Summer." As of mid-July 2001 he foundation bears the names of 100 children. "These kids are bright lights that shine on forever," says Roberta Hoffman, who bought a stone for her son Aaron, who died in 1994 at age 18 after a five-year battle with cancer. "What better way to commemorate them than with a lighthouse meant to stay lit eternally." For information or to donate to the Martha's Vineyard Children's Lighthouse Memorial, write to:

- M.V.H.S. Children's Memorial, P.O. Box 827, Edgartown, MA 02539

Website: http://www.childrenslighthousememorial.org

An engraved cobblestone with the name of a child is $175.

TO THE CAPE POGE LIGHTHOUSE. The Cape Poge Lighthouse is located within the Cape Pogue Reservation on East Beach at the northeast point of Chappaquiddick Island. The island is reached via the three-car, 49-passenger "on time" Chappy Ferry that departs from Edgartown's Dagget Street landing. Crossing time five minutes.

Getting to the lighthouse is possible with a four-wheel drive vehicle. After leaving the Edgartown ferry, head east on Chappaquiddick Road into Dyke Road and the Dyke (Dike) Bridge. Once across the bridge, let some air out of the vehicle's tires and head north on either the west side's Cape Pogue Pond road or the Atlantic beach route to the lighthouse. The former route winds along a scallop pond past hammocks and scrub pine.

SCHEDULE.

Mid-May to mid-October, daily 7 to midnight.

At other times of the year service available 7:30 to noon and 1 to 6.

FARES. Round-trip vehicle/driver + passenger fares.

- Edgartown Ferry, Inc., RFD 32 B, Edgartown, MA 02539.

Phone (508) 627-9427.

TRUSTEES OF RESERVATIONS TOUR The Trustees of Reservations offer a 1 1/4 hour narrated tour to the Cape Poge Lighthouse.

SCHEDULE. The tour leaves Dike Bridge on Chappaquiddick at 10 AM and 1 PM daily Monday - Friday in the summer.

FARES. Discount for children under 15.

Phone for reservations: (508) 627-3599.

Website: http://www.vineyard.net/org/trustees/Nantucket.htm

Email: Email: capepoge@ttor.org

CAPE POGE LIGHTHOUSE (CAPE POGUE).
CHARACTERISTIC: Flashing white 6s
HAW: 65' **RANGE**: 9 nm

Cape Poge was Martha's Vineyard's second lighthouse. Although there is one reference to an earlier aid (probably an unlighted daymark) on the cape, it was not until Congress appropriated $2,000 in January 1801 that a beacon was officially established. The 35-foot tall tower was a shingled wooden structure that had a base diameter of 19 feet and seven feet at its top.

The Cape Poge aid has been moved or reconstructed no less than nine times. The original tower was moved in 1838; an octagonal wooden tower was erected on a rubble stone foundation in 1844; another wooden tower was built in 1880. With the old 1880 tower in disrepair and threatened by erosion, the fourth and present tower was erected in 1893. It is a 55-foot tall wood framed tower that rests on a platform tied to outboard anchors. When the tower was ready to be topped off, its optic and cast-iron housing were manhandled and slid inch-by-inch over a temporary wooden skid. After 5 1/2 hours of huffing and puffing, the beacon was installed and turned on at sunset. The present tower has been moved four times.

OWNER. U.S. Coast Guard.
PRESERVATION. Listed in the National Register of Historic Places.

In January 1987 the lighthouse was moved about 500 feet inland. A U.S. Army heavy-lift helicopter accomplished the job in three flights: (1) removal of the 2.5-ton lantern, (2) transfer of the 7-ton clapboard and stucco tower onto its new foundation and (3) replacement of the lantern. After the move inland, the Coast Guard stretched new stabilizing guylines, scraped and repainted the exterior, replaced broken windows and cleaned the interior of bird deposits.

In October 1997 the lantern was removed from the tower by helicopter. It was taken to Falmouth and then trucked to New Bedford, where it was sandblasted and repainted, and broken panes of glass were replaced.

Cape Poge Lighthouse

NOBSKA POINT

FROM WOODS HOLE. Return to Woods Hole Road and about 0.3 mile east of the bridge intersection turn right into Locust Street. At Church Street bear left and continue on Church and Nobska Roads to the lighthouse. There is free parking in front of the light station. The grounds are open to the public until dusk every day.

FROM FALMOUTH. Return to MA 28 (Main Street), turn left at Shore Road and follow Shore, Surf and Beach Roads to the lighthouse.

The Martha's Vineyard-New Bedford ferry offers good views of Nobska Point Light; see page 247. It can also be viewed from the lighthouse cruises offered by the Woods Hole Historical Society; see page 246.

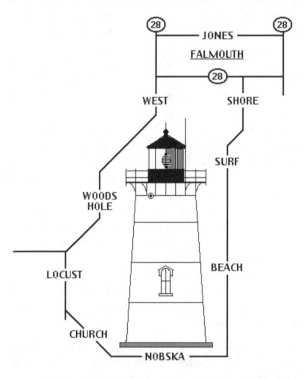

NOBSKA POINT LIGHTHOUSE (NOBSQUE POINT).

CHARACTERISTIC: Flashing white 6s (red sector)

HAW: 87' **RANGES**: White 16; red 12 nm

The first lighthouse on Nobska Point was a small stone cottage with a tower on its roof. The 1829 beacon consisted of a whale oil-fed multi-lamp and reflector device. By the early 1870s, the lighthouse, although having been rebuilt in 1849, was in general disrepair. It was replaced by the present lighthouse in 1876.

The tower's iron plates were cast in Chelsea, Massachusetts and transported to Cape Cod in three sections. The cylindrical structure is lined with red brick to provide added strength and some insulation. The tower, a 1 1/2-story wood framed Victorian residence, a brick oil house and two paint lockers cost about $60,000 to build.

The 40-foot tall lighthouse has four ringed panels of cast-iron plating. There are the typical Italianate windows at the first three levels and four portholes at level four. The lantern is a standard 10-sided one with its red sector created by a pane of red glass installed over one of the storm panes.

A delicate addition to the service gallery's balustrade is the series of miniature brass lighthouses set atop each baluster.[1]

This treatment was used on only two other Atlantic Coast lighthouses - Maine's Cape Neddick and Lubec Channel. The optic is the original fourth-order Fresnel lens with a 1,000-watt electric lamp installed. It was automated in 1985. One lens panel has been removed to eliminate the high intensity beam on the mainland side of the lighthouse.

The station consists of the light tower, the 1876 keeper's dwelling (now the family residence of the Commander of Coast Guard Group Woods Hole), a brick oil house (1876), a paint locker (1876), a garage (1931) and a radio beacon building (1937). A covered walkway (1899) that connected the tower to the main house (1876) and an assistant keeper's quarters (1900) have been removed.

OWNER. U.S. Coast Guard.
PRESERVATION. Listed in the National Register of Historic Places.

---

1. Lubec Channel's supporting poles for its main deck gallery's canopy were topped with little brass lighthouses. They disappeared many years ago when the Coast Guard removed the framework and awning.

HYANNIS

EAST ON MA 28. At the rotary intersection of MA 28 and MA 132, turn right into Barnstable Road and continue south into Ocean Street. At Gosnold Street turn right, pass Old Colony Road on the right and turn left into Harbor Road. The lighthouse is located at the end of Harbor.

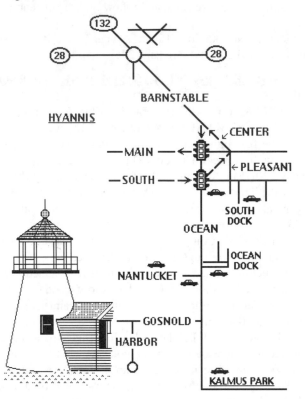

HYANNIS (RANGE REAR) LIGHTHOUSE
(HYANNIS PORT; SOUTH HYANNIS).

The first South Hyannis Light was a privately built shack on the beach with a lamp that hung in a window. It was erected by Daniel Snow Hallett. He was assisted in his lightkeeping duties by his son, Daniel, who often spent the night in the shack with his dog for company.

Congress authorized the building of a lighthouse at South Hyannis in 1848. A small tower was built for $2,000, and Daniel Hallett was appropriately appointed first keeper. The light was fixed white with a red sector warning mariners away from dangerous Southwest Shoal. It was first equipped with a Lewis-designed multi-lamp and reflector device. The brick lighthouse was attached to the 1 1/2-story wood framed Cape Cod keeper's residence by a covered walkway.

In 1856 a larger lantern room was installed to make room for a Fresnel lens. In 1885 a range light was added on the nearby Old Colony Railroad Wharf, a simple lamp hoisted to the top of a 20-foot tower.

The beacon was decommissioned in 1929 and replaced by the presently active Hyannis Breakwater light.

Shortly after having been deactivated, the lantern, roof and optic were removed.

PRESERVATION. In 1985 antique dealers Alan Granby and Janet Hyland purchased the 136-year old property and spent more than $600,000 on its restoration. By late 1987, the owners had added a circular steel stairway leading to the tower's fabricated lantern. The old Hyannis station is superbly restored and maintained. Unfortunately, as a result of the government's dismantling of the structure, the lighthouse has been denied a nomination for entry into the National Register of Historic Places. On the property next door is the station's brick oil storage house (1902), which holds the station's 1,000-pound bell set in gimbals.

HARBOR CRUISE. Hy-Line Cruises offers a narrated, one hour boat tour of Lewis Bay and Hyannis Harbor. The cruise skirts the shores of Hyannis and Hyannisport and offers an excellent frontal view of the Hyannis light station.

The "lighthouse" seen off the starboard side while clearing Hyannis' inner harbor is a privately built replica of Nantucket's Brant Point Lighthouse. Also, the Point Gammon Lighthouse discussed in the NANTUCKET ISLAND LIGHTHOUSES chapter can be seen while aboard the harbor cruise boat, from the end of Ocean Street and from the decks of Nantucket Island ferries.

SCHEDULE. Five cruises daily in summer. Check website or call for current schedule.

FARES. Discount for children. Children with parents ride free on the summer schedule's excursions.

- Hy-Line Cruises, Ocean Street Dock (36 Ocean Street), Hyannis, MA 02601.

Phone: Information (508) 778-2600. Reservations (508) 790-0696.

Website: http://www.hy-linecruises.com/

CATBOAT RIDES. Captain Marcus Sherman offers day sails on the 34-foot catboat *Eventide*. Depending on wind, this cruise may offer views of Hyannis Lighthouse and more distant views of Point Gammon Lighthouse.

Phone (508) 775-0222

Website: http://www.capecod.net/catboat

E-mail: shermanm@capecod.net

NANTUCKET ISLAND LIGHTHOUSES
BRANT POINT - BRANT POINT RANGE - SANKATY HEAD - GREAT POINT

HY-LINE CRUISES FERRIES. This company now offers passenger only service on its large motor vessels (crossing time one hour and 50 minutes) as well as a high speed water jet catamaran (70 minutes).

Parking (fee) is available at the dock and in private lots within walking distances from the dock.

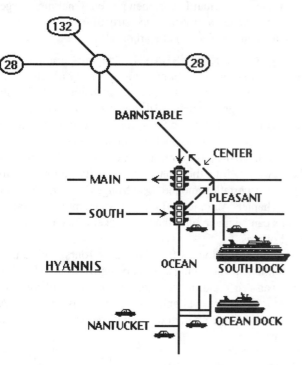

Passenger reservations (none allowed on the day of departure) are strongly recommended. Without reservations, passengers are requested to arrive at least one hour prior to departure time and place their names on the standby list. Hy-Line reports that its weekend cruises are the least crowded.

There are two passenger classes on the larger vessels: regular class (R) and first class (F). The latter is available only on the *Great Point*, offering a comfortable lounge with tables and upholstered seating arrangements.

FARES. Round trip passenger and bicycle fares. First class tickets (F) are almost twice the cost of regular class. No discounts for first class. No pets. Regular class (R) offers a discount for children under 12. Caged or leashed pets ride free.

SCHEDULE. Phone or check website for current schedule.

- Hy-Line Cruises, Ocean Street Dock (36 Ocean Street), Hyannis, MA 02601-4036.

Phone: Information (508) 778-2600 or (800) 492-8082 (MA only). Advance sales and parking: (508) 778-2602.

Website: http://www.hy-linecruises.com/

HIGH SPEED SERVICE. Year round service. For a same day round trip the motor vessel departs Hyannis at 6:30, 9:10 and noon. From Nantucket at 4:35, 7:25. and 10:05. Fares are higher with discounts for children 12 and under.

Phone (508) 778-0404. USA toll-free (800) 492-8082.

STEAMSHIP AUTHORITY FERRY. This company operates an auto/passenger ferry to Nantucket. Transporting one's vehicle to Nantucket Island is not recommended nor needed to enjoy a same day trip. Crossing time is two hours and 15 minutes.

The ferry terminal is located off South Street just past Pleasant Street. Parking (fee) is available in the company's area on South Street and private lots.

SCHEDULE. All ferries on the Nantucket run are handicapped accessible with elevators. Phone or check website for current schedule.

FARES. Round trip passenger and one way bicycle fares. Discount for children 5-12; under 5 free.

Up to five transactions (one way or round trip) can be made per phone call or fax request.

- Steamship Authority, Reservation Bureau, Pine Tree Place, 509 Falmouth Road, Suite 1C, Mashpee, MA 02649.

Phone: Information and advance vehicle reservations (508) 477-8600. TTY/TDD (for hearing-impaired customers) (508) 540-1394. Hyannis ticket office (508) 771-4000. Fax number for vehicle reservations: (508) 477-9225.

Website: http://www.islandferry.com/

That "lighthouse" off the ferry's starboard side while leaving the port area is a privately built replica of Nantucket's Brant Point Lighthouse.

POINT GAMMON LIGHTHOUSE (GAMMON POINT).

After the ferry clears Hyannis Harbor and heads south, look to the east (portside) for a distant look at this inactive lighthouse located on the southern end of Great Island.

The lighthouse, a conical stone tower topped by a shingled, wood framed lantern room, was built in 1816. The tower's lantern (probably rebuilt after 1878) has narrow windows with an unusually wide expanse of wall between each window. The aid was discontinued in 1858 (replaced by Bishop and Clerks Lighthouse) and was sold in 1878 to a private party after years of neglect and deterioration.

BISHOPS AND CLERKS LIGHTHOUSE (destroyed).

Out in Nantucket Sound about seven miles south of Hyannis lies a group of rocks that received a magnificently built lighthouse, an architectural twin of the Minot's Ledge Lighthouse. Its light was first established on October 1, 1858, using a whale oil-powered fifth-order Fresnel. The 68-foot tall granite tower, badly damaged in 1935 during a violent storm, was eventually abandoned. On September 11, 1952, under orders from the Coast Guard, workmen placed dynamite charges in holes bored into the tower's base and within minutes destroyed the weakened and vandalized structure.

The ferry passes within 50 yards of Brant Point Lighthouse as it enters Nantucket Harbor.

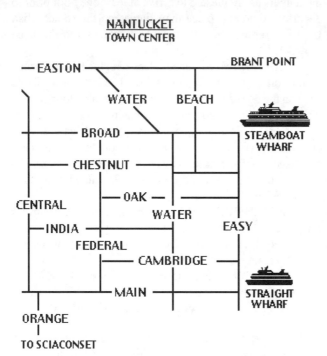

NANTUCKET ISLAND. During summer months scheduled tour buses meet morning and early afternoon arrivals and offer visitors 90-minute narrated tours of the island. Tour service is greatly reduced during the spring and fall months. Tickets (adult and children fares) for the bus tours are available aboard the ferries and at dockside ticket offices.

Frankly, the bus tour is a poor way to see the lighthouses. The answer? Tour the island and visit its lighthouses using rented transportation and the "beach buggy" tour discussed later in this chapter. Auto, jeep, dune buggy and moped rental reservations can be made with the ferry ticket office or at dockside rental offices.

Another option is offered by Ara's Tours. This tour travels 30 miles of the island with personalized guided commentary in an air conditioned van, and includes all three lighthouses. Tours are available on a daily basis from mid-April through mid-November, and Ara will pick up at your hotel if you wish.

- Ara's Tours.

Phone (508) 228-1951.

Website http://www.nantucket.net/members/ara/

Email: ara@nantucket.net

NANTUCKET WHALING MUSEUM. With the historical importance of Nantucket's whaling industry, it is fitting to have this museum housed in a spermaceti candle factory built in 1849. The museum contains every imaginable artifact from the island's whaling days, such as scrimshaw, tools, ship's logs, a whale skeleton, ship models, and Sankaty Head's large second-order Fresnel lenses. The museum is located on Broad Street at the head of Steamboat Wharf.

OPEN. June to September, daily 10 to 5. Limited hours during rest of year. Closed December 25.

ADMISSION FEES. Discount for children 5-14. One visitor pass is good for admissions to 12 historic places built between 1686 and 1904. A walking tour takes from 2 1/2 to 3 1/2 hours. A printed tour guide and free information brochure are available.

- Nantucket Historical Association, PO Box 1016, Nantucket, MA 02554. Phone (508) 228-1894. Museum (509) 228-1736.

BRANT POINT LIGHTHOUSE.

CHARACTERISTIC: Occulting red 4s

HAW: 26' **RANGE**: 10 nm

Since 1746 Brant Point has had no less than seven lighthouses:

1746. Construction of the original tower was funded by residents of the Village of Sherburne (now Nantucket) with the understanding that the town would pay for the tower's upkeep while its operation (especially the supply of whale oil) would be financed from taxes collected from ships of 15 tons or more that used the harbor. The tower was funded and built, but the town fathers reneged on the maintenance part of the agreement. Regardless, the light remained in operation until the structure burned to the ground in 1758.

1758. The second tower was destroyed in 1774 by what was described in local newspapers as a violent gust of wind lasting no more than one minute.

1774. Nantucket's citizens immediately decided that the town government would build a third tower and maintain it with tonnage dues paid by captains of vessels of more than 15 tons. Mariners, especially those from other ports, objected all the way to the Massachusetts General Court. They lost the case and Nantucket lost its lighthouse when the tower burned down in 1783.

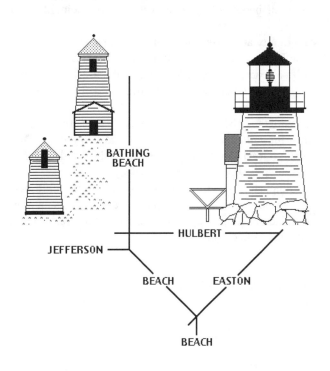

1783. The next aid was not a light tower but rather a cheap wooden platform fitted with a dimly lighted lamp enclosed in a glass globe. Mariners and the locals labeled it the "Bug Light."

1786. A wooden structure built in 1786 was washed out to sea during a 1788 storm.

1788. The fourth lighthouse on the point was ceded to the Federal Government on June 23.

1795. The Grant of the Commonwealth of Massachusetts stated, "The United States derives its title to the Light House situated on Brant Point at the entrance to the Harbor of Nantucket, together with the land and tenements..." In that year, the Town of Sherburne changed its name to Nantucket. In 1825 the tower was torn down.

1826. A small wooden tower was built on top of the 1788 keeper's house at a cost of $1,600. The light had eight oil-burning lamps each backed by a 12.5-inch reflector.

1856. The tower-on-house structure rotted away, so the sixth tower was erected at a cost of $15,000. The lighthouse, the one still standing (sans lantern) within the Brant Point Light Station, rests on a concrete foundation with a 12-foot high base of granite and 2-foot thick walls. The 47-foot tall brick tower once held a 12-sided cast-iron lantern that was fitted with a fourth-order Fresnel optic.

1900. Because of shifts in the channel, the Brant Point light was discontinued and a fixed red light was placed on a pole located about 600 yards in front of the tower.

1901. A new shingled wood framed tower was constructed. This is the lighthouse seen today. The watchroom at the top of the conical structure is reached by a circular wood staircase. The original fifth-order Fresnel optic has been electrified and is in use today.

OWNER. U.S. Coast Guard.

PRESERVATION. Listed in the National Register of Historic Places as part of the Brant Point Light Station.

The entire Brant Point Light Station, which includes the 1856 lighthouse and attached brick keeper's dwelling, was thoroughly renovated in 1983. The older light tower is now used as a Coast Guard communications station.

BRANT POINT RANGE LIGHT TOWERS (CLIFF RANGE LIGHTS).

Although on private property, both towers can be seen from Bathing Beach Road, a street leading to The Jetties Beach. There are two convenient routes to view the light towers.

Note that as an aid to visual identification the towers on the Brant Point map are reversed from their original orientation.

From the Brant Point Light Station return to Easton Street. Then:
-> Right at Hulbert Avenue,
-> Right at Bathing Beach. The towers will appear on the left as you approach the public beach's parking lot.
From Nantucket's Steamboat Wharf take South Beach Street north. Then:
-> Cross Easton Street into North Beach Street,
-> Right at Bathing Beach.

The towers are of wood framed construction with wood siding and circular pitched roofs. In each tower at the top of its winding stairs and at the aperture is a cabinet that housed the optic. The construction design used for these structures is quite similar to the range towers on Maine's Kennebec River.

On August 12, 1911, Nantucket's *Inquirer and Mirror* reported that the lighthouse keeper had resigned, claiming that without an assistant he could not take adequate care of the Brant Point light, the front and rear range beacons and the channel entrance's two jetty lights. Soon after his resignation, the newly appointed Bureau of Lighthouses decided to do away with the two range beacons. In July 1912, after their decommissioning, the towers were sold to a private party for $1,840. Reportedly, their relocation off Brant Point station was accomplished by placing the structures on their sides and with a team of mules rolling them away.

OWNER. In 1921 the towers were purchased by the Gilbreth family and moved to their present sites.

PRESERVATION. Listed in the National Register of Historic Places as part of the Brant Point Light Station.

NANTUCKET LIFE SAVING MUSEUM. Located on Polpis Road at Folger's Marsh and about 2.7 miles from Nantucket's rotary or 2.4 miles from the junction of Polpis and 'Sconset Road ('Sconset runs into Main Street in the village of Siasconset).

This museum is a veritable storehouse for all things associated with the U.S. Lifesaving Service. There are sailboats, a horse-drawn boat carriage, relics, artifacts, photographs, Lyle and Hunt guns, a Francis Life Car and two lenses. Displayed are Brant Point's original fourth-order (1856) and Nantucket's (Great Point) fully operational third-order (1857) Fresnel lenses.

After the hurricane destroyed the Nantucket (Great Point) Lighthouse in 1984, the founder of the museum, Robert Caldwell, hauled the dome out of the sea and stored it next to the museum. Due to the efforts of the museum's curator, Maurice Gibbs, enough funds were raised to repair the dome and place it atop a replicated lantern which rests on an abbreviated version of the Great Point tower. Inside the lantern is the magnificent third-order lens.

OPEN. Mid-June to Columbus Day, daily 9:30 to 4.

ADMISSION FEES. Discount for children; under 5 free.

- Nantucket Life Saving Museum, 158 Polpis Road, Nantucket, MA 02554-2320.

Phone (508) 228-1885.

Brant Point Lighthouse

NANTUCKET ISLAND LIGHTHOUSES

SANKATY HEAD LIGHTHOUSE.
CHARACTERISTIC: Flashing white 7.5s
HAW: 158' **RANGE**: 24 nm

Baxter Road, called "The Path," extends from Siasconset ('Sconset) Village along the top of the 100-foot high cliffs to the Sankaty (sanc' ity) Head Lighthouse. The grounds are open to the public. There is free parking outside the light station.

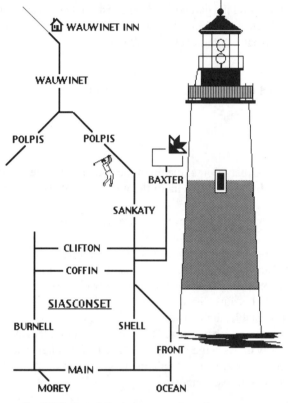

Construction of the tower and a 1 1/2-story brick keeper's house with connecting walkway was completed in December 1849. The light was established on February 1, 1850, using a whale oil lamp. The new station cost about $22,000.

The tower is unique in that it is constructed of brick from the bottom of its 5-foot deep foundation to a height 54 feet above ground level. On top of this shaft, the builder added another six feet of coursed granite blocks. The lantern room is nine feet tall. Including the lantern's roof and its ventilator, the overall height of the lighthouse is 70 feet.

Sankaty Head was the first lighthouse in Massachusetts to receive a Fresnel lens. The second-order optic was rotated by a brass clockwork mechanism enclosed in a glass case. The clock was wound by weights that descended by cable. In 1875 the lens received a new English-made single wick lamp that burned lard oil and needed to be trimmed but once each night. Its beam could be seen out to 25 nautical miles.

During 1887-88 the old brick house was demolished and a new dwelling was constructed, the tower received a new lantern and service gallery and the light's energy source was changed over to kerosene. When the optic was electrified in 1938, which increased the light's candlepower seven-fold, the brass clockwork mechanism was disconnected and removed.

In 1970 the aid's lantern and optic were removed to make room for the installation of a large aerobeacon. The disfigurement did not set right either with mariners or islanders. In response to public pressure the Coast Guard reinstalled an aluminum lantern and a smaller modern optic.

OWNER. U.S. Coast Guard.
PRESERVATION. Listed in the National Register of Historic Places.

Sankaty Head is doomed to topple into the sea if it is not moved away from the bluff. In October 1991 a hurricane followed by a severe storm tore away eight feet of land from the bluff. During the 1993-94 winter season, marked by two nasty Nor'easters, another 30 feet washed away. At that time, two endangered assistant keeper's houses were removed and donated to the Nantucket Housing Authority. With a tearing away of about five feet each year, there isn't much time left before the cliff gives up enough of the remaining 95 feet to deny the use of heavy relocation equipment.

In 1991 a group of concerned Siasconset citizens formed the nonprofit Save Our Sankaty organization under the auspices and guidance of the Nantucket Historical Association, and began the campaign to move, at an estimated cost of $2 million, the 600-ton lighthouse some 200 feet away from the bluff to a new site adjacent to the fifth fairway of the Sankaty Head Golf Club.

In 1992, the Coast Guard asked the Nantucket Historical Association to assume ownership of the light station so that the Save Our Sankaty group or any other interested party could make plans to raise funds, relocate the lighthouse and see to its maintenance and preservation. In 1993 the Nantucket Historical Association backed away from the agreement, forcing Save Our Sankaty to look elsewhere in the community for guidance and support. The group turned to the 'Sconset Trust, Inc., a nonprofit organization that holds for conservation 62 acres of land in and around the village of Siasconset.

VISITING THE GREAT POINT (NANTUCKET) LIGHTHOUSE. The Trustees of Reservations, an organization dedicated to preserving properties of exceptional scenic, historic and ecological value, governs the 1,100-acre windswept Coskata-Coatue Wildlife Refuge. From May to October the Foundation offers three hour guided Great Point Natural History Tours. Reservations are required. The point of departure is the Wauwinet Inn, where lodging and meals are available. Call for schedule and reservations.

The Refuge is accessible only by foot or by oversand vbehicles beyond the gatehouse. No pedestrian fee. Please note: Oversand-vehicle permits are required; access is subject to occasional closure during shorebird nesting season.

- Coskata-Coatue Wildlife Refuge, PO Box 172 (118 Eel Point Road), Nantucket, MA 02554.

Call for tour reservation: (508) 228-6799.

Website: http://www.vineyard.net/org/trustees/Nantucket.htm

Great Point and the lighthouse can be viewed on the trips offered by Ara's Tours. See page 258 for details.

GREAT POINT LIGHTHOUSE (NANTUCKET LIGHTHOUSE)
CHARACTERISTIC: Flashing white 5s (red sector)
HAW: 71' **RANGES**: White 14; red 12 nm

As early as 1769, a "Nantucket Beacon" had been established on Great Point at the tip of the island's "Whale's Tail." The first lighthouse on the point was constructed in 1784 and ceded by Massachusetts to the newly established Federal Government in 1790.

In 1816 the first Great Point Light was destroyed by fire. Winslow Lewis believed the fire was deliberately set but nothing was proved. A new 60-foot stone tower was finished in 1818 at a cost of about $7,400.

In 1842 I. W .P. Lewis inspected the tower and found it leaky, the lantern corroded and the reflectors worn out. In 1857 Great Point Light was fitted with a third-order Fresnel lens. That same year the tower was lined with brick and an assistant keeper's house was built. Despite the improved light, shipwrecks continued in the area. Between 1863 and 1890 there were 43 wrecks near the lighthouse. Many of the wrecks occurred because Great Point Light had been confused with the Cross Rip Lightship. To eliminate the confusion a red sector was established in 1889.

Great Point Light was automated in the 1950s. In 1966 the keeper's house was razed by a suspicious fire, leaving the old stone tower alone at Great Point. Erosion brought the sea perilously close to the lighthouse. The Coast Guard rejected Nantucket Islanders' pleas to move the lighthouse inland. Some of the local residents planned to build an artificial reef around Great Point to protect the lighthouse. Unfortunately, they never had the chance.

REPLICATION. On March 30, 1984 a devastating storm swept New England. As the storm moved off the coast of Massachusetts, the 166-year old tower virtually disappeared. The storm also broke through the barrier beach near Great Point, temporarily turning the Point into an island. This break occurred again in October 1991, when Great Point was cut off for four months.

With the help of Massachusetts Senator Edward M. Kennedy, $2 million in federal money was set aside for the building of a new Great Point Light. A replica, 300 yards west of the site of the old tower, was finished by Hydro-Dredge, a New Bedford construction company, in 1986 at a cost of over a million dollars. This was more than 200 times the cost of the tower in 1818. The surplus funds were used for the rehabilitation of Cape Poge Light and Monomoy Point Light.

The tower is built on a 5-foot thick concrete slab which rests on a 30-foot deep caisson (cofferdam). The inner cylindrical access tube, which also reinforces the outer stone walls, is concrete and waterproofed with a plastic coating. The new solar powered light is visible for 12 miles.

Great Point Light's original Fresnel lens is on display at the Nantucket Lifesaving Museum (see page 260 for details).

OWNER. U.S. Coast Guard.
PRESERVATION. Not listed in the National Register of Historic Places.

Sankaty Head Lighthouse

Great Point Lighthouse

WEST DENNIS [1]

TO THE LIGHTHOUSE INN. In West Dennis, a short distance east of the Bass River Bridge on MA 28, turn right at School Street. Bear left at Main Street and then right at Lighthouse Road. Drive 0.5 mile to Lighthouse Inn Road and turn left. Continue on to the inn's parking lot (free). On the east side of the inn there is a paved path that leads to a seawall.

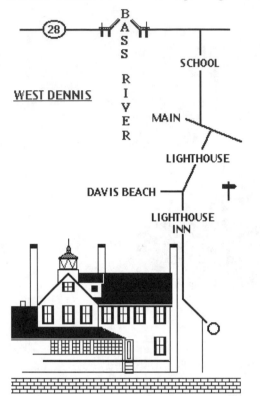

The expansive inn hides the original outline of the keeper's dwelling. But, if you stand out on the seawall and eliminate the wide addition (front), the three-story addition (right) and the one-story building (left), you will be able to discern the outline of the old lighthouse underneath its short white tower, lantern and painted red roof.

WEST DENNIS LIGHTHOUSE (BASS RIVER)
CHARACTERISTIC: Flashing white 6s
HAW: 44'
In 1850 $4,000 was appropriated by Congress for a lighthouse to be built on the Bass River breakwater. The site inspector reported that, in his opinion, a lighthouse was not needed. The area's ship captains, who had been donating 25 cents a month to buy oil for a lantern placed in the window of a house on West Dennis' Wrinkle Point, on the east side entrance to the Bass River, appealed the inspection report. As a result the Lighthouse Board decided to build the "Bass River" Lighthouse.

Beginning in early 1854, materials were hauled by ox carts over the marshes and dunes to the construction site and work began. The light station, completed in early 1855, consisted of the extant 2 1/2-story Victorian (modified) and Gothic Revival-styled keeper's residence and a roof top cast-iron lantern resting on the short wooden tower. The overall height of the lighthouse is 44 feet.

The beacon was activated on April 30, 1855.

In 1880, after the Stage Harbor light was established, Bass River Lighthouse was discontinued, but not for long. In response to mariners' objections the beacon was back in service the following year. The 1855 fourth-order Fresnel lens was removed in 1914 when the beacon was taken out of service.

On August 7, 1989, a modern optic was placed in service as a private aid to navigation. The light is in operation May to October and only when the inn is open.

PRESERVATION. Not listed in the National Register of Historic Places.
In 1914, with the completion of the Cape Cod Canal and with fewer ships taking the longer route around the Cape, the Bass River Lighthouse was deactivated and the property sold at auction. The third private owner expanded the keeper's dwelling, built a lodge, converted the stable into a guest house and added two garages and a caretaker's house. In 1938 State Senator Everett Stone of Auburn, Massachusetts, bought the estate and eventually developed the property into what is now known as The Lighthouse Inn. The Stone family still operates this super vacation resort on Nantucket Sound.
- The Lighthouse Inn, P.O. Box 128, 1 Lighthouse Inn Road, West Dennis, MA 02670
Phone: (508) 398-2244. Fax: (508) 398-5658.
Website: http://www.lighthouseinn.com
Email: General Information: inquire@lighthouseinn.com
Wedding Information: shoe@lighthouseinn.com
Group Sales & Conference Information: nelson@lighthouseinn.com

1. The U.S. Coast Guard's Light List does not recognize this aid's traditional name - BASS RIVER.

STAGE HARBOR

TO HARDING BEACH. Turn right off MA 28 at Barn Hill Road. Bear right into Harding Beach Road and continue to the beach's parking lot. There is about a one mile walk over a sandy trail to the Stage Harbor Lighthouse. Alternatively, it is possible to walk along the water's edge to the lighthouse.

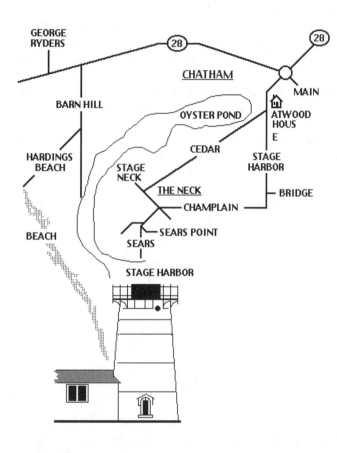

OLD ATWOOD HOUSE & MUSEUM. At Chatham's rotary, turn right into Stage Harbor Road. Set the trip odometer at 0.0 for mileage check enroute to Sears Point.

This Chatham Historical Society museum displays antiques from as early as 1635 and an excellent shell collection.

Chatham Lighthouse's original cast-iron lantern and its fourth-order Fresnel bullseye lens (with rotating mechanism) is sheltered in an enclosed gazebo in the museum's garden.

OPEN. Mid-June to September, Tuesdays through Fridays 1 to 4.

ADMISSION FEES. Discounts for students; children free. Lens exhibit is free.

- Old Atwood House & Museum, 347 Stage Harbor Road, Chatham, MA 02633.

Phone (508) 945-2493.

Website: http://www.atwoodhouse.org/

Email: chs@capecod.net

CONTINUE TO SEARS POINT. From the rotary (0.0 mile) motor south on Stage Harbor into Champlain Road. Then:

-> A short distance past the Champlain & Battlefield intersection bear left into Sears Road (1.7 miles from the rotary),

-> Left at Sears Point Road and continue to a public boat landing (2.1 miles).

The tower and keeper's dwelling can be seen straight ahead across Stage Harbor on Harding Beach. Monomoy Point Lighthouse is farther out to the southeast.

STAGE HARBOR LIGHTHOUSE.

This 1880 lighthouse, before losing its lantern room, stood 48 feet tall. The light tower is another generically designed cast-iron structure that is attached to the two-story wood framed keeper's dwelling by a covered walkway.

According to Admont G. Clark's *Lighthouses of Cape Cod,* the floor under the covered walkway between the house and tower became a hiding place for liquor for a time during prohibition. An inspector on a surprise visit noticed the loose floorboards, but much to the keeper's relief he merely told him to nail them down more securely.

Its flashing white light, produced by a kerosene-powered fifth-order Fresnel lens, was replaced by an automated light on a skeleton tower in 1933. The government removed the lantern and capped the tower, and Stage Harbor Light passed into private hands.

OWNER. Privately owned since 1934.

PRESERVATION. Not listed in the National Register of Historic Places.

Based on the observations of persons who were permitted to visit the station during a sponsored Cape Cod Lighthouse weekend, the property is well maintained. The inside of the house, however, is as markedly simple as when it served as the family home of the lighthouse keepers. There are no electrical appliances or fixtures and no plumbing, except a water pump in the kitchen. Despite the lack of modern comforts, the house has served as a family summer home for generations.

MONOMOY POINT

VISITING THE LIGHTHOUSE. The Cape Cod Museum of Natural History sponsors both a naturalist-guided one day trip to South Monomoy Island and an overnight stay, when visitors sleep in the keeper's dwelling with kitchen and toilet on site. Quarters are rustic but comfortable. Dinner and breakfast are provided.

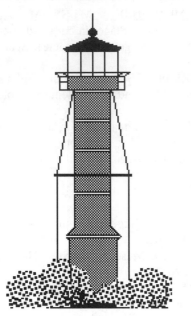

SCHEDULES. Phone or check website for current schedule. Below is the schedule for the summer of 1999.

DAY. June to September, Wednesdays 9 to 3. Minimum age 12.

OVERNIGHT. June to September, Tuesday, Thursday and Saturdays. Saturdays Sept. 11 - Oct. 1. Two day trip lasts from 9:30 first day to 1:00 second day. Minimum age 12.

FEES. Member and nonmember. Four person minimum required for tour. Preregistration and prepayment by check or credit card required.

The visitor should be prepared to get wet to the ankles debarking from the boat. Wear boots or sneakers and long, light-colored pants (poison ivy and ticks). Bring a light jacket, sweatshirt or sweater and hat. Also carry a lunch, your optical and photographic equipment and insect repellant. The island tour is a leisurely walk of four miles.

- The Cape Cod Museum of Natural History, Route 6A, PO Box 1710, Brewster 02631.

Phone (508) 896-3867. Fax (508) 896-8844.

Website: http://www.ccmnh.org/

Email: ccmnh@capecod.net

Cape Cod's fifth lighthouse was built for $3,000 in 1823 at Monomoy Point, also called Sandy Point, eight miles from Chatham near the southern end of the peninsula. Like many early lighthouses in the area, it was a Cape Cod style light with a wooden tower and iron lantern room on the roof of a brick keeper's house. The lantern held eight lamps with 13-inch reflectors.

The station was rebuilt in 1849. A contract assigned to Pelham Bonney provided for the building of a separate two-story wood framed keeper's house. Another contract, also signed in 1849 with Cyrus Alger, called for the construction of a cast-iron tower.

An 1850 inspection referw to a new iron lighthouse at Monomoy. Monomoy Point's cast-iron tower was among the first. There were, however, cast-iron lighthouses similar in style to Monomoy's erected on Boston Harbor's Long Island Head in 1844 and Lake Champlain's Juniper Island in 1846.

Monomoy Point's stove pipe-styled light tower is constructed of curved cast-iron plates bolted together to form a cylindrical tube. Its interior is lined with brick. To further strengthen the tower, two exterior cables were installed from top of the tower across a midsection tension spar to its foundation.

In 1882 the tower received its last official furbishing, when it was given a fresh coat of red paint. During that same year, the "surfmen" were withdrawn and their stations closed.

James P. Smith, a native of Copenhagen, became keeper in 1899. His wife died early in his stay at Monomoy, but Keeper Smith had three daughters who assisted him in his duties. The oldest daughter, Annie, acted as housekeeper and tended the light when her father was away.

In later years one resourceful keeper converted his Model T Ford into an early dune buggy, making the trip by land to Chatham much faster.

With the opening of the Cape Cod Canal in 1914 and an increase in the power of Chatham Light, Monomoy Light was considered expendable. The light was discontinued in 1923 and the property passed into private hands.

The first private owner was George Bearse. When he came to visit the property he was surprised to find that Navy planes had been using it for machine-gunning target practice. One bullet had come through a wall of the keeper's house and knocked out a rung on a rocking chair; another had lodged itself in a four by four beam.

MONOMOY POINT

The tower, by the way, stands on the original dune line, which is about one-half mile from the sea.

    OWNER. After the 2,750-acre island's designation as a National Wilderness area by Congress in 1970, the Massachusetts Audubon Society was instrumental in having the island and its properties transferred to the U.S. Fish and Wildlife Service as the Monomoy National Wildlife Refuge in 1977.
    PRESERVATION. Listed (1978) in the National Register of Historic Places.
    In 1964 the Massachusetts Audubon Society restored the lighthouse and keeper's house. In 1988 Massachusetts Senator Edward M. Kennedy helped secure a federal grant for further refurbishing, a project initiated by the Lighthouse Preservation Society.

Chatham Lighthouse

CHATHAM

EAST ON MA 28. At MA 28's Chatham rotary bear right into Main Street and continue to the lighthouse. If traveling on Bridge Street, turn left at Main. Parking across the street is free, but restricted to 30 minutes from 9 to 5.

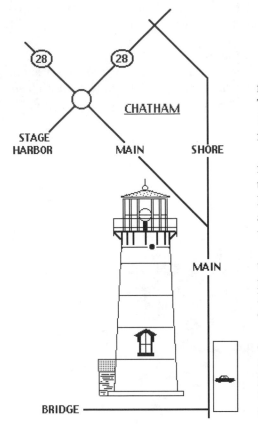

CHATHAM LIGHTHOUSE.
CHARACTERISTIC: Group flashing white 10s
HAW: 80' **RANGE**: 24 nm

In 1806, because of the difficulty in identifying one fixed white light from another, the Federal Government decided to erect two at Chatham. The twin towers were completed in 1807 and their lights established in 1808. They were sturdy octagonal, pyramidal wood structures built on a foundation of heavy oak timbers.

One tower was a stationary structure. The other was built on skids to facilitate realignments as the shape of the harbor changed. The 40-foot tall towers were 22 feet in diameter at their bases, tapering to eight feet at their lanterns' decks. The lanterns were equipped with spider-type lamps. Later, after Winslow Lewis arrived on the lighthouse scene, his Argand-style lamps with reflectors were installed.

By 1841 Chatham's twins were badly deteriorated and threatened by the eroding cliffs. The Lighthouse Service, hoping to avoid the erosion problem, erected two 40-foot tall brick towers inland of the original towers. Each of the larger lanterns placed atop the new towers was fitted with another one of Lewis' multi-lamp systems.

During the early days of the Lighthouse Service, lightkeepers were commissioned by none other than the President of the United States. The system produced some weird maneuvering among state authorities and applicants. In Chatham, for example, one of the keepers died leaving a destitute widow. Experienced in keeping the light burning, as were most keepers' wives, the widow was appointed to the position.

A former keeper who wanted the job wrote to Washington complaining about the appointment. That one missive soon grew into a Chatham-Boston-Washington chain letter fiasco that had to be resolved by the president. Fortunately the widow stayed on as Chatham's keeper.

On December 15, 1879, the south tower fell off the bluff, followed in 1881, by both the north tower and the keeper's house. The fixed fourth-order Fresnel lenses, installed in 1857, were removed prior to the towers' destruction.

In early 1877, with the old light station doomed, authorities constructed farther inland twin cast-iron towers (100 yards apart), two wood framed keepers' houses and a brick oil house. Each of the 48-foot tall lighthouses was bolted together in five boilerplate sections with five staircase levels, one at each sectional seam. Windows with Italianated arches circle the tower at levels two through four. The fifth level has five portholes. Inside there is a spiral cast-iron stairway that is fastened to the brick lining.

The rescued fixed fourth-order Fresnel lenses were installed in the new light towers in September 1877 and converted from lard oil to kerosene the following year. In 1923 the northern tower was dismantled and shipped to Eastham where it became the present Nauset Lighthouse. The remaining south tower was refitted with an incandescent oil vapor lamp and a revolving fourth-order Fresnel optic.

In 1969 the Fresnel lens and the entire lantern room were removed from Chatham Light. Modern aerobeacons producing a rotating 2.8 million candlepower light were installed, and a new, larger lantern room was built to accommodate the larger optics. The new light could be seen for 25 miles. The new lantern room left Chatham Light almost, but not quite, looking like a traditional lighthouse. The old lantern room and lens are now on the grounds of the Old Atwood House and Museum, operated by the Chatham Historical Society (see page 265).

In August 1993, the two aerobeacons installed in 1969 were replaced by a smaller, but equally brilliant, modern lens. Unable to remove the older beacons through the lantern's glass panes, the Coast Guard accomplished the task by using a crane to lift the roof off the aluminum lantern frame and installing temporary lighting devices. Two weeks later the new light was in operation.

CHATHAM

The monument standing near the foundation of the old north light was erected in memory of seven members of the crew of the Monomoy Life Saving Station who died attempting to save the crew of a coal barge in 1902.

OWNER. U.S. Coast Guard.

PRESERVATION. Listed in the Register of Historic Places.

The erosion of James Bluff in front of the lighthouse has continued through the years. A few years ago another erosion problem arose. East of the lighthouse lies North Beach, a barrier island of sand. In 1978 a northeaster cut through North Beach in several places. Fortunately, all the gaps were filled in by subsequent tides. Then, two storms in October 1991, Hurricane Bob and a following northeaster, created a break that today is a swift-running channel two miles wide and 25 feet deep. Additionally, the cut has closed the harbor's southern exit, leaving fishermen to fight their ways through the channel's swells. Another danger lies in further erosion of James Bluff, since the storms undermined the parking lot.

In an effort to save the lighthouse the Town of Chatham has dumped tons of scree to form a seawall that slopes up to a narrower parking lot. Along the top of the wall beach roses have been planted to help stop surface erosion. In 1994 the Town of Chatham received a state grant of $13,700 to pay for signs, bicycle stands, park benches and a public telephone at the overlook.

Nauset Lighthouse

NAUSET
THREE SISTERS OF NAUSET

NORTH ON MA 6. In Eastham, at the "Cape Cod National Seashore" sign, turn right off US 6 onto Nauset Road. The Salt Pond Visitor Center on the right is the Cape Cod National Seashore's orientation center. It is a resource center with a museum, films, bookstore, exhibits and seasonal talks by rangers. Nauset Lighthouse's original fourth-order Fresnel lens is displayed in the museum.

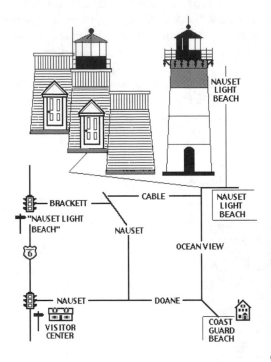

OPEN. 9 to 4:30 daily. Extended hours in the summer. Subject to reduced hours in winter. Closed December 25.
FREE ADMISSION.
- Salt Pond Visitor Center, Route 6, Eastham, MA 02642
Phone (508) 255-3421.
PARKING FEE. End of June to Labor Day.
TO THE LIGHTHOUSES. Motor east on Nauset and Doane oads to Ocean View Drive, turn left and continue north to the Nauset ight Beach parking area.

Alternate directions from Route 6: Take Route 6 to Bracket Road hird traffic signal from Eastham/Orleans rotary). Right onto Bracket oad. Go to end and take left onto Nauset Road. Take first right onto able Road. At end of Cable Road, take left onto Ocean View Drive to arking lot.

Nauset Light is located on a treed hill west of Nauset Light Beach oad. Nauset Lighthouse and the keeper's house can be clearly seen om the parking lot. The Nauset Light Preservation Society, in conjunc- on with the 1996 relocation project, completed some major renovations f the tower: new lantern room windows, railing system, repairs to the oof and deck and a fresh coat of paint.

VISITING NAUSET LIGHTHOUSE.

Open houses are held on a number of dates spring through fall. Call Nauset Light Preservation Society at (508) 240-2612 or check their website at http://www.nausetlight.org for the current schedule.

NAUSET LIGHTHOUSE
CHARACTERISTIC: Alternating white and red 5s
HAW: 114' **RANGES**: White 23; red 19 nm

The present Nauset Lighthouse was established when one of the two Chatham cast-iron towers was moved to Eastham in 1923. The tower's architectural and construction characteristics match its Chatham twin. The keeper's house, a 1 1/2 story wood frame Victorian house, was built in 1875. A brick oil house was added to the original Three Sisters light station in 1892. A detached garage was built on the site in 1926.

Nauset Light's first optic was a kerosene-powered fourth-order Fresnel lens removed from The Beacon lighthouse (see the next page). That lens was removed in 1952 when its modern lens replacement was electrified and automated.

OWNER. The tower (1877), brick oil house (1892) and the dwelling (1875) are now the property of the National Park Service.

PRESERVATION. Listed in the National Register of Historic Places.

The Nauset Beach cliffs are eroding rapidly. In July 1996 the edge of the cliff was but 35 feet from the base of the lighthouse.

In 1993 the Coast Guard announced that the light was to be decommissioned and that they had no funds available to move the tower. The Nauset Light Preservation Society, a nonprofit volunteer organization, was formed on November 10, 1993. It undertook the challenge of raising the funds needed to relocate the lighthouse away from the cliff. The Society, through memberships, donations and gift shop sales, raised $140,000 for the project. A $300,000 federal transportation grant plus $30,000 from the Society paid for the relocation and restoration. Over the weekend of November 15, 1996 the lighthouse and oil house were moved to safety. On May 10, 1997, the relocated lighthouse became the property of the National Park Service and was reactivated as a private aid to navigation.

NAUSET & THREE SISTERS OF NAUSET

Mary Daubenspeck, owner of the keeper's dwelling, donated the house to the National Park Service in return for a use and occupancy permit for 25 years. A second federal transportation grant of $200,000 was awarded to the National Park Service and the Nauset Light Preservation Society. One hundred thousand dollars of this money funded the October 17, 1998 move of the keeper's house to the new site beside the lighthouse.

In early 1999 the Nauset Light Preservation Society received a grant of $4,000 from the Cape Cod Chamber of Commerce. The funds were the result of sales of a Cape Cod and Islands license plate featuring Nauset Light and the keeper's house. The grant money was used for the production of a ten minute educational tape on the history and move of Nauset Light and equipment to run it. Donations are still needed to finish the tower's renovation and to landscape the new site. Other goals of the Nauset Light Preservation Society include restoration of the oil house and the establishment of an endowment fund.

- Nauset Light Preservation Society, PO Box 941, Eastham, MA 02642.

Phone (508) 240-2612.

Website: http://www.nausetlight.org

Email: ssabin@capecod.net

TO THE THREE SISTERS. Across Ocean View Drive and north of Cable Road there is the marked entrance and paved walk that leads to the restored Three Sisters of Nauset Lighthouses, so named because their offshore silhouettes looked like three ladies in white dresses wearing black hats.

TOURS. Rangers conduct one hour narrated tours (free) of the restored lighthouses. Each tour involves a leisurely one-quarter mile walk along a paved path through the woods from the parking lot to the towers. This is the only time that the towers are opened to visitors.

May to mid-October.

Contact the Salt Pond Visitor Center at (508) 255-3421 to confirm tour dates and times.

THREE SISTERS OF NAUSET.

In 1836 the citizens of Eastham requested the government to build a lighthouse to warn mariners off the shoals and swift currents located east of the Nauset cliffs. Two years later the Lighthouse Service constructed three towers at Nauset to differentiate the signal from the one at Highland Light and the two at Chatham. The brick towers were only 15 feet tall and stood 150 feet apart. The station included a keeper's dwelling and cost just under $7,000.

To keep within his contract's specifications, Winslow Lewis chose to build the towers on a level elevation close to the cliffs. He completed the job in less than seven weeks, leaving poorly coursed brick walls and a cockeyed lantern room. Boston's Custom Office inspector refused to certify the job. Lewis rushed to Washington ahead of the Customs Office report and convinced his friend and mentor, Stephen Pleasonton, that he had produced three well-built light towers.

The three beacons were designed to keep ships on course well offshore and parallel to the shoreline as they sailed between the Highland and Chatham lights. Their optics burned a lot of costly whale oil, but the original Lewis Argand-type lamps were not replaced until 1858, when the Lighthouse Board approved the installation of sixth-order Fresnel optics. These lenses were replaced in 1870 with larger and brighter fourth-order Fresnels.

In 1892 the brick towers were close to the edge of the eroding 60-foot cliff. They were replaced by three 22-foot tall conical towers erected 30 feet inland. A wood-frame construction was selected so that, if erosion threatened them, they could more readily be moved inland. The wooden lighthouses were located on a north-south line east of the keeper's house. One lighthouse stood south of the dwelling; the other two stood north of it.

In 1911 erosion once again threatened the towers. The Bureau of Lighthouses decided to do away with two of the lighthouses and discontinued use of the north and south beacons. The center tower, which became known as the Beacon, was moved and attached to the keeper's house by a covered walkway. The tower's fixed fourth-order lens was converted to a revolving optic flashing three times every ten seconds. The Beacon was discontinued in 1923 to make room for the transferred Chatham tower.

OWNER. The two earlier retired towers (sans lanterns) were sold in 1918 to a private party. In 1920 they were relocated to Cable Road where they were attached to either side of a small beach house.

In 1923 the Beacon was moved to the area which is now the Nauset Light Beach parking lot, where it was attached to a one-story cottage.

Preliminary to their eventual restoration, the National Park Service purchased the three towers in 1975. In 1983 the Beacon was moved and stored next to the other two lighthouses, then located a few yards west of their present location.

PRESERVATION. Listed in the National Register of Historic Places.

By the time restoration work on the three structures commenced in December 1988, they were in rather sad shape. Their shingled exteriors were riddled with holes made by woodpeckers, rodents had chewed chunks out of the interior woodwork and their frames and floors had been practically destroyed by beetles. Despite their deteriorated conditions, the towers were gingerly moved onto their new foundations and restored. The $510,000 project was completed on September 7, 1989.

Highland Lighthouse after its 1996 move

HIGHLAND

NORTH ON US 6. In North Truro on US 6 and at a "Cape Cod Light" sign, turn right into Highland Road. At the next T-head intersection turn right into South Highland Road. At another "Cape Cod Light" sign turn left into Lighthouse Road.

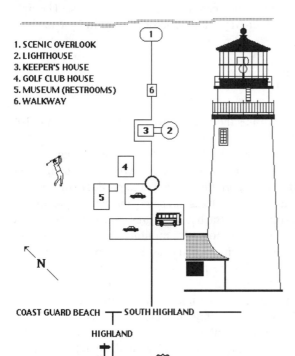

1. SCENIC OVERLOOK
2. LIGHTHOUSE
3. KEEPER'S HOUSE
4. GOLF CLUB HOUSE
5. MUSEUM (RESTROOMS)
6. WALKWAY

N

COAST GUARD BEACH — SOUTH HIGHLAND

HIGHLAND

6

MUSEUM OF THE TRURO HISTORICAL SOCIETY.
This fine little museum features a shipwreck room, whaling artifacts, firearms and exhibits depicting the history of Truro, the lighthouse and maritime subjects.

OPEN. Memorial Day to September, daily 10 to 5.

Phone (508) 487-3397.

Website: http://www.capecod.net/ths

HIGHLAND LIGHTHOUSE INTERPRETIVE CENTER.
The Truro Historical Society has converted the keeper's dwelling into an interpretive center and gift shop. The tower is open for tours in the summer (visitors to the lighthouse tower must be at least 51 inches tall).

There are public restrooms and ample parking. Handicapped-licensed vehicles are permitted to drive directly to the light station. A scenic overlook is located near the old site.

OPEN. May 1 to October 31, daily. Open 10 until sunset in the summer; closes earlier in spring and fall.

ADMISSION FEES. There are separate admission fees for the museum and the lighthouse; a combination ticket is available. Discounts for groups and children.

- Highland Museum and Lighthouse, Inc., PO Box 486, Truro, MA 02666.

Phone (508) 487-1121.

HIGHLAND LIGHTHOUSE (CAPE COD; TRURO).
CHARACTERISTIC: Flashing white 5s
HAW: 173' **RANGE**: 23 nm

The 10 acres of land for Cape Cod's first lighthouse were purchased in 1796. A year later, a 45-foot tall wooden tower and a keeper's house were constructed on Truro Clay Pound at the edge of the 125-foot bluff. The lighthouse was the 20th in the United States.

When first lighted in 1797, the lantern contained a two-tiered, whale oil-fueled optic, consisting of 15 lamps (8 upper; 7 lower) each backed with a 15-inch reflector. In 1800 the beacon's characteristic was changed to a flashing light with the addition of a clockwork-operated circular screen that revolved around the lamp at the rate of one revolution every eight minutes. Unfortunately, the eclipser reduced the light's intensity. It was removed in 1811, changing the optic's characteristic to a fixed light. In 1839 the Lighthouse Service decided that the lamps should have 21-inch reflectors to increase the optic's brilliance.

There is some controversy as to whether the tower was replaced or rebuilt in 1832-33. Recorded history suggests a refitting, since an 1839 government report states that the tower had received a new lantern and a different lighting apparatus.

With the old tower in danger of falling into the sea, a new lighthouse was constructed in 1857. The light station included the present 66-foot tall conical brick lighthouse equipped with a Fresnel lens, a Queen Anne-styled, wood framed and shingled keeper's house with attached walkway, an oil house and a boathouse. After its completion, the old tower and house were dismantled. The new station cost $15,000.

In 1860 the light's illuminant was changed to lard oil. In 1899 the fixed kerosene-powered optic was declared obsolete. It was replaced two years later with a newer revolving first-order Fresnel lens that did not have the upper tier of catadioptric prisms nor the centrally located bullseyes. In an arrangement similar to the first-order lens installed in the Block Island Southeast Lighthouse, Cape Cod's lens contained only dioptric prisms. The lens rested on a mercury float. Its rotation around a wheeled rail was accomplished by a clockwork mechanism powered by gravity fed weights. The light was electrified in 1932, and in 1945 the Fresnel lens was replaced by two (four-way) electric aerobeacons. In 1986 the light was changed to an electric single (two-way) beacon and automated.

OWNER. National Park Service. The Coast Guard maintains the beacon.
PRESERVATION. Listed in the National Register of Historic Places.

In 1797 the tower was 510 feet from the cliff's edge. By the early 1990s the distance was not much more than 100 feet. In October 1991, back-to-back storms tore eight feet off the cliff.

In 1990 a group of committed Truro Historical Society members formed a Lighthouse Committee to undertake the tasks of locating experienced lighthouse movers, designing access roads, parking areas and service buildings to allow the relocation of the 430-ton light tower and collecting contributions and acquiring grants. In 1992 the president of Spencer, White and Prentice, a New York engineering firm experienced in moving large structures, prepared and gave to the Society his personal estimate of $1,169,000 to move only the light tower and its two small attached structures. Site preparations, the dwelling's relocation, road repair and electrical work would bring the total bill to about $1.5 million. That estimate was an accurate one. In March 1996 Lighthouse Committee Chairman Gordon Russell announced that "all the money is in place." The contract was awarded for moving the lighthouse and the building of public restrooms, parking areas and the scenic overlook. The $1.5 million contract went to the International Chimney Corporation of Buffalo, New York.

Between July 12 and August 5, 1996, the move was accomplished in much the same manner as used to relocate the Block Island Southeast Lighthouse. The tower's foundation was first reinforced with gunite. To protect the tower during the move a concrete compression ring was formed within the tower and a strengthening steel jacket placed around the outside. After those preparations, a network of steel beams was laid underneath the structure, using diamond wire saw to cut the insertion holes in the foundation. With the support beams in place the structure was slowly and evenly raised by hydraulic lifting jacks and then pushed over rollers placed between the jacks and supporting roller beams.

During the move workers placed quarters on the beams. The coins, flattened by the lighthouse, were later auctioned off for as high as $57 with the money going to the Truro Historical Society.

The cost of the 450-foot relocation was allocated among the Truro Historical Society, the Commonwealth of Massachusetts, the Coast Guard and the National Park Service. In addition, the Town of Truro and the Truro Golf Commission donated the location site and approved the building of an access road.

On Sunday, November 3, 1996, Highland Light was relighted in its new location. Over 200 people toured the tower's interior before the relighting ceremony. The Highland Light Bagpipe Band performed in full regalia, and Congressman Gerry Studds, an important proponent of the move, spoke to the assembled crowd. "While this light may not save lives," said Studds, "it will inspire lives for a long time to come."

Officials of the Cape Cod National Seashore and the Truro Historical Society had planned for visitors to be able to go to the top of the relocated tower. The Coast Guard at first objected to this plan because the light is designated to operate 24 hours a day. This problem was solved by the installation of a smaller optic high up in the lantern room, above the heads of visitors.

The relocated lighthouse stands close to the seventh fairway of the Highland Golf Links, prompting some to declare it the world's first lifesized miniature golf course. After an errant golf ball broke a pane in the lantern room, new unbreakable panes were installed.

In August 1999 a one-ton stone bearing a bronze plaque was installed to mark the location of the ligthouse before the 1996 move.

LONG POINT
WOOD END - RACE POINT

PROVINCETOWN. The Long Point Lighthouse can be seen from MacMillan Wharf. Wood End is best viewed from the Pilgrim's Landing Plaque at the end of one way Commercial Street and opposite the breakwater that extends out to the lighthouse. The breakwater can be crossed at low tide. One locale for viewing Race Point Lighthouse is Herring Cove Beach (all day parking fee during the summer months). The lighthouse is a two-mile beach hike from the parking lot.

In addition, Long Point is accessible via a water shuttle offered by a company called Flyer's located in Provincetown's West End adjacent to the Coast Guard pier. Operates May 15 to October 15, weather permitting. The shuttle runs hourly from 10 to 6, and Flyer's will take groups of up to 14 persons as a private charter. They also offer a variety of vessels for rent.

- Flyer's, 131A Commercial Street, PO Box 561, Provincetown, MA 02657.
Phone (508) 487-0898 or (800) 750-0898.
Website: http://www.sailnortheast.com/flyers/
Email: flyers@capecod.net

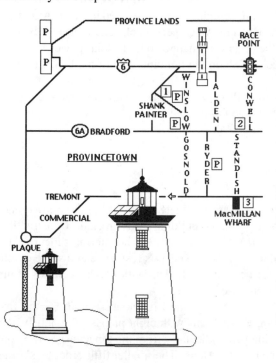

WHALE WATCH CRUISES. These popular trips are high seas adventures to the Stellwagen Bank, one of the richer feeding grounds in the world teeming with humpbacks, rights and finbacks along with dolphins, seabirds and other marine life. Of particular interest to the lighthouse seeker is that the cruise vessels heading to the bank some six miles north of Provincetown sail within 50 feet of Long Point and also pass the Wood End and Race Point Lighthouses. The Highland Lighthouse can be seen at a distance of about five miles.

All cruises take from 2 1/2 to 3 1/2 hours and are scheduled April or May to October, daily with morning, afternoon and sunset trips. Call ahead to confirm the day's departure times. Reservations are required. Warm clothing, sunglasses and rubber soled shoes are recommended.

PARKING. See corresponding numbers on map.
[1] Portuguese Princess main ticket office at 70 Shank Painter Road. Ticket holders park free.
[2] Duarte Motors Parking on Bradford Street near Standish Street. A 3-minute walk to the wharf. Ticket holders park free.
[3] MacMillan Wharf (fee)
[P] Other public lots (fees).

- **Dolphin Fleet of Provincetown**, PO Box 243, Provincetown, MA 02657.
Phone (508) 349-1900. In USA toll-free 800/826-9300.
Website: http://www.whalewatch.com/   Email: aavellar@capecod.net
FARES. Seasonally priced. Discounts for seniors and children 7-12. Under age 7 free with family. Tickets are sold in the Chamber of Commerce building on Commercial Street at the head of the wharf.

- **Portuguese Princess**, PO Box 1469, 309 Commercial St., Provincetown, MA 02567.
Phone (508) 487-2651. In USA toll-free (800) 442-3188.
Website: http://www.princesswhalewatch.com/   Email: whales@princesswhalewatch.com
FARES. Seasonally priced. Discounts for families, seniors 60+, students and children 7-12. Tickets are sold in the company's main office at 70 Shank Painter Road and in the Whale Watcher's General Store at 309 Commercial Street (opposite the wharf).

- **Provincetown Whale Watch, Inc.**, PO Box 129 (132 Bradford Street), Provincetown, MA 02657.
Phone (508) 487-3322. In USA toll-free (800) 992-9333. Fax (508) 487-7388.
FARES. Seasonally priced. Discount for seniors 62+. Children under 10 free with parents. Tickets can be purchased at the red ticket booth on the wharf.

275

LONG POINT LIGHTHOUSE (PROVINCETOWN HARBOR).
CHARACTERISTIC: Quick green
HAW: 36' **RANGE**: 8 nm

Four acres of land at the very tip of Cape Cod's "arm" were purchased in 1826 for the construction of Long Point's first lighthouse. The light station, which consisted of a small house surmounted by a tower and a storage shed, cost $16,000. The light was established in 1827. In 1838 the Lighthouse Service reported that the lighthouse was equipped with a two-tiered Lewis optic.

The next, and present, lighthouse to be placed on Long Point was constructed in 1875. It is architecturally classified as belonging to the Federal Design genre. While the 1827 tower was razed, the station's original keeper's house was retained. The square brick tower is 38 feet tall. Its watchroom deck is on the cast-iron staircase's fifth landing. The nearly 3-foot square glass storm panes are about four feet above the metal deck. Interestingly, the condenser disk and ventilator ball are missing, leaving an open hole above the optic.

The station now consists of the tower and a brick oil house (1875). The remains of the two Civil War forts can be seen in the shape of small hills. The keeper's dwelling (1827) and a fog signal building were destroyed in 1980. After the fourth-order Fresnel (1875) was automated in 1952, the Coast Guard removed its watch personnel. The Fresnel was replaced in 1952 by a modern lens when the light was automated. In 1982 the optic was changed over to solar power.

OWNER. The American Lighthouse Foundation obtained a lease on the lighthouse from the U.S. Coast Guard in 1998. The light itself is still maintained by the Coast Guard.

PRESERVATION. Listed in the National Register of Historic Places. The Coast Guard restored the lighthouse in 1981. The American Lighthouse Foundation renovated the tower in the fall of 1999.

- American Lighthouse Foundation, PO Box 1690, Wells, ME 04090.
Website: http://www.lighthousefoundation.org

WOOD END LIGHTHOUSE.
CHARACTERISTIC: Flashing red 10s
HAW: 45' **RANGE**: 13 nm

The first lighthouse on Wood End, a pyramidal wooden tower, was built in 1864. That lighthouse may have been damaged or destroyed by 1872, when records show that a temporary "signal building" was erected. Construction of the present 39-foot tall brick lighthouse (another Federal Design structure) followed in 1873. The interior is identical to that of the Long Point Lighthouse, except for the latter's missing ventilating parts. A keeper's residence and some outbuildings were added in 1896. The stone breakwater to Wood End was constructed in 1911. The station today consists of the tower and a brick oil house. The original dwelling and a storage shed were razed in 1961.

The originally installed optic was a fourth-order Fresnel lens. In 1916 the Lighthouse Board, for the first time, installed an incandescent oil vapor lamp in a fifth-order revolving Fresnel lens with eight panels. Previously, the vapor lamp was used only in the larger fourth-order lens where heat, rising perpendicularly from the top and spreading out into a 10 to 15-degree cone, could be more readily dissipated through the top of the lens. The smaller fifth-order lens' installation was made possible by placing a metal heat deflector atop the lens to protect it from cracking. The lens was removed in 1960 when an automated modern rotating optic was installed. The beacon was converted to solar power in 1981.

OWNER. The American Lighthouse Foundation obtained a lease on the lighthouse from the U.S. Coast Guard in 1998. The light itself is still maintained by the Coast Guard.

PRESERVATION. Listed in the National Register of Historic Places. The Coast Guard restored the lighthouse in 1981. The American Lighthouse Foundation renovated the tower in the fall of 1999.

- American Lighthouse Foundation, PO Box 1690, Wells, ME 04090.
Website: http://www.lighthousefoundation.org

RACE POINT LIGHTHOUSE.
CHARACTERISTIC: Flashing white 10s
HAW: 41' **RANGE**: 16 nm

Race Point's first tower was a 20-foot tall rubble stone structure built in 1816. The lighting apparatus was probably a spider lamp because ship captains, faced with an ever increasing number of shipwrecks on the point, complained bitterly about the light's low intensity. In 1838 the tower received one of Winslow Lewis' systems, a rotating device consisting of 10 lamps and 13-inch reflectors. A fog bell was in place by 1852. In 1863 the tower's rubblestone walls were lined with brick, shingles added to its exterior and a new lantern installed. Two keepers' houses were also constructed. One, a Victorian-Gothic Revival duplex for assistant keepers, was razed in 1960. A steam-operated foghorn (whistle) was in place by 1874.

LONG POINT, WOOD END & RACE POINT

The present cast-iron lighthouse is 40 feet tall and lined with brick. It was built in 1876 for about $28,000. For an additional $8,000 two oil houses and a garage were added.

RACE POINT BEACH

USCG STA

RACE POINT

PROVINCE LANDS

HERRING
COVE
BEACH

6

SHANK
PAINTER

W
I
N
S
L
O
W

C
O
N
W
E
L
L

PROVINCETOWN

6A BRADFORD

Three keepers and their families lived at the lighthouse in the two separate keeper's houses. The children had to walk two and a half miles across soft sand to school each day. In the 1930s a keeper named James Hinckley made the trip much quicker by customizing a Ford into an early dune buggy. The trip that took 75 minutes on horseback was shortened to 30 minutes.

When constructed, the lantern was fitted with a fixed fourth-order optic. The light was electrified in 1957 and automated and un-manned in 1978. Note the column of solar panels.

OWNER. U.S. Coast Guard (lighthouse). Station properties leased to the American Lighthouse Foundation in 1995. Grounds belong to the Cape Cod National Seashore.

PRESERVATION. Listed in the National Register of Historic Places. In 1995 the entire Race Point Light station looked like a western ghost town. The tower was badly rusted and the keepers dwelling, abandoned and boarded up for 20 long years, was a rotting mess.

In 1995 the surrounding property, including the keeper's house and oil house, was leased to the American Lighthouse Foundation. International Chimney Corporation, the same company that has moved three New England lighthouses, repaired the roof of the keeper's house and rebuilt the chimney. Contractor Richard Davidson of Onset also did a great deal of work on the interior and exterior.

Volunteers have finished renovating the interior, and the five-bedroom keeper's house is now open for overnight stays. The building now has space heaters, hot water, flush toilets, refrigeration and a gas stove. Guests must bring their own bedding and the kitchen is shared with other guests. For information on overnight stays:
- Race Point Lighthouse, (508) 487-9930. Email: racepointlighthouse@mediaone.net

The Center for Coastal Studies, a marine mammal research and educational group, has leased the 1876 fog signal building. After a $45,000 renovation, their new field station was dedicated in June 1999. The station will be used as a laboratory for Center for Coastal Studies research, the National Seashore and the Cape Cod Museum of Natural History.

There is also an artists' residency program for the month of October. For information on the artists' residency program, contact the Fine Arts Work Center, (508) 487-9960.

If you'd like to donate to the ongoing restoration of the buildings at Race Point Light Station, contact:
- American Lighthouse Foundation , PO Box 889, Wells, Maine 04090.
Phone: (207) 646-0515.
Website: http://www.lighthousefoundation.org

PILGRIM MONUMENT. From Route 6: Take Shankpainter Road exit, then take the first left, the next right and follow the signs. This edifice is America's tallest (252 feet) granite monument and museum. Among the museum's many and varied exhibits are a whaling ship captain's quarters, a captain's parlor ashore, objects washed up from shipwrecks and The Pilgrim Room that displays a scaled model diorama of the merchant ship *Mayflower*. From the observation deck (60 ramps and 116 steps) you can see the entire Cape, including the Provincetown lighthouses, and across Cape Cod Bay to Plymouth.

OPEN. April 1 to November 30, daily 9 to 5, except July and August daily 9 to 7. Last admission is 45 minutes before closing. Call for winter hours.

ADMISSION FEES. Admission includes monument and museum. Discount for children 4-12; under 4 free.
- The Pilgrim Monument & Provincetown Museum, PO Box 1125 (High Pole Hill Road), Provincetown, MA 02657.
Phone (508) 487-1310. In USA toll-free (800) 247-1620.
Website: http://pilgrim-monument.org/

SANDY NECK
MAYO BEACH - BILLINGSGATE

SOUTH ON US 6. The Mayo Beach Light Station's original keeper's dwelling still stands in Wellfleet. To reach it, turn right at a traffic signal on MA 6 into Main Street (start 0.0 mile). The intersection is marked with a "Wellfleet Ctr & Harbor" sign.

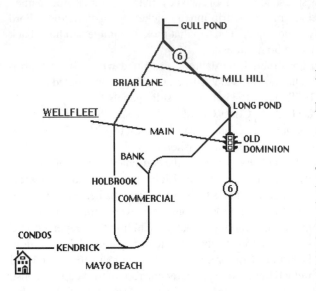

Then:
-> Left at East Commercial Road (0.3 mile),
-> Pass Bank Road (0.5 mile),
-> Continue through a right curve into connecting Kendrick Road,
-> Continue past Mayo Beach's parking lots to the restored house located opposite "The Billingsgate Condos" (1.2 miles).

MAYO BEACH LIGHTHOUSE (dismantled).
In 1838 a Navy inspector reported to the Secretary of the Treasury that the lighthouse was not needed and recommended that its construction be halted. He wrote that it was his opinion that if there must be a beacon at the head of Wellfleet Harbor, it should be a minor harbor light. Unfortunately he filed his report on November 1, 1838, after the lighthouse had been finished and its multi-lamp and reflector optic placed in operation. The lighthouse was a 1 1/2- story brick house that supported a mid-roof wooden tower and cast-iron lantern.

In 1881 the original lighthouse gave way to a new cast-iron tower and an L-shaped two-story, clapboard keeper's dwelling. The tower's optic was a sixth-order Fresnel. In 1919 the optic was powered by a kerosene acetylene vapor lamp. The light was discontinued in 1922 and the station sold to a private party the following year. The owner dismantled the tower in 1939. Today the house and the 1907 oil house remain, kept in pristine condition by the present owners. There is a circle on the ground next to the house that marks the former site of the lighthouse.

BILLINGSGATE LIGHTHOUSE (destroyed).
Billingsgate Island's first lighthouse, a wood frame keeper's house topped by a short tower and lantern, was built in 1822. The beacon, located on a small island on the western end of Billingsgate some 15 miles northeast of Barnstable's Sandy Neck Lighthouse, marked the entrance to Wellfleet Bay and Harbor. The lighthouse was equipped with a multi-lamp and reflector Lewis optic. The light had a focal plane 40 feet above sea level. Despite ever threatening erosion problems, the Lighthouse Board decided in 1854 to build a new light station, consisting of a 1 1/2-story brick dwelling and an attached square brick Federal Revival tower. In 1915 with the tower atilt and about to collapse into the sea, the decision was made to discontinue the station. After the tower had been secured with ropes, the lens was removed. Shortly thereafter the light tower toppled into the sea. The station was closed and sold to a private party. By 1922 the keeper's dwelling and the land beneath it had disappeared.

CONTINUE SOUTH ON MA 6A. See the following map.
In Barnstable center at the Hyannis Road & Mill Way intersection, turn north into Millway. There is a "Barnstable Harbor" sign on the northeast corner. Follow Millway straight ahead past the Millway Marina into a waterside parking area.

The Sandy Neck Lighthouse is off to the right on the tip of Sandy Neck Beach, a seven-mile narrow strip of land that protects Barnstable Harbor.

Sandy Neck Lighthouse may also be viewed from a whale watch cruise leaving Millway Marina in Barnstable Harbor April through October.

- Hyannis Whale Watcher Cruises, PO Box 254, Barnstable, MA 02630.
Phone : (800) 287-0374 or (508) 362-6088.
Website: http://www.whales.net/
Email: whales@whales.net

SANDY NECK

SANDY NECK LIGHTHOUSE.

Captain Henry Baxter was the light keeper between 1833 and 1844. His logs record his charge as being the BEACH POINT, SANDY POINT light. Also referred to in government documents as the BARNSTABLE light.

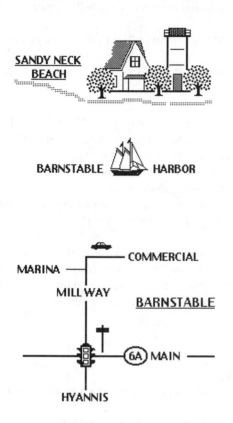

With a $3,500 congressional appropriation, the Beach Point light station was built in 1827. The first lighthouse was a typical Cape Cod style structure with a wooden lantern on the roof of a brick keeper's house. In July 1838, the Lighthouse Service's Fifth Auditor reported that the "Barnstable" light was equipped with a Lewis-designed multi-lamp optic arranged in two tiers, producing a fixed white light. The report also recommended that the upper tier of lamps be suppressed, because ship captains were mistaking Plymouth's twin beacons with the equally bright "Beach Point" light some 23 miles to the southeast of Plymouth.

This lighthouse was replaced in 1857 by the brick one that still stands. In 1880, the present 1 1/2-story Victorian-Gothic keeper's residence replaced the older house.

In 1887 the brick tower was badly cracked and was strengthened with two iron hoops and six staves. This addition, still in place, gives the tower a distinctive look.

In 1931, after a storm altered Beach Point, the government deactivated Sandy Neck Lighthouse and transferred its warning responsibility to a beacon atop an automated skeletal steel tower built on the tip of the Sandy Neck strand. This tower was discontinued in 1952.

OWNER. Shortly after having been taken out of service, Sandy Neck's lantern and classical lens were removed. The property was sold to a private party in 1953.

PRESERVATION. Listed in the National Register of Historic Places as part of the Sandy Neck Cultural Resources District.

PLYMOUTH
DUXBURY PIER

NORTH OR SOUTH ON MA 3 OR MA 3A. The Plymouth Lighthouse is located at the entrance to Plymouth Bay on the Gurnet, a sandy peninsula stretching southeast from Duxbury Beach. Access to the lighthouse site is limited, since the land on Gurnet Point and its access roads are private. Project Gurnet & Bug Lights held an open house at the lighthouse in May 2001 as part of Duxbury's "Opening of the Bay" festival; it's possible that the open house will become an annual event.

The Duxbury Pier Light, which marks the north side of the main channel into Plymouth Harbor, is located about two miles northeast of Plymouth's inner harbor.

If traveling on MA 3, depart the highway via Exit 6 (MA 44/Samoset Street). MA 3A's north-to-south trace in Plymouth follows Court, Main and Sandwich Streets.

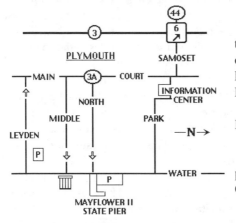

HARBOR CRUISE.

One way to view both lighthouses is the narrated 75-minute harbor tour that departs from the Mayflower II State Pier on Water Street. The cruise offers medium distance viewing of Duxbury Pier Light and a distant view of Plymouth Light. Parking is available in the harbor area at a lot between Middle and Leyden Streets and along Water Street.

A trolley (fare) takes visitors from downtown parking lots to the pier. Board at the sign of "The Trolley." Phone (508) 747-3419.

SCHEDULE.

The *Plymouth Belle* operates from May through November, weather permitting. Harbor cruises depart every 90 minutes, from 9:30 am to sunset. Charter obligations may alter the schedule, so it's a good idea to call ahead.

FARES. Discounts for seniors 62+ and children under 12.

- Capt. John Boats, 117 Standish Avenue, Plymouth, MA 02360.
Phone (508) 746-2400. In USA toll free (800) 242-2469.
Website: http://www.captjohn.com/
Email: info@captjohn.com

Another way to see Plymouth Light is from a special cruise offered periodically (once or twice a year) by the Friends of the Boston Harbor Islands, Inc. Call for current event schedule.

- Friends of the Boston Harbor Islands, Inc. 349 Lincoln Street, Bldg. 45, Hingham, MA 02043-1601
Phone (781) 740-4290.
Website: http://www.fbhi.org

PLYMOUTH LIGHTHOUSE (THE GURNET).
CHARACTERISTIC: Group flashing white 30s (red sector)
HAW: 102' **RANGES**: White 16; red 14 nm

The first beacon on the Gurnet may have been lighted as early as 1746. Officially, the first light was established in 1769. It was basically a single family house sandwiched between two attached towers, each equipped with two oil-burning fixed lamps. The twin lights had an elevation of 20 feet above the sea.

During the American Revolution, the towns of Duxbury, Kingston and Plymouth constructed a fort on the Gurnet. Later, when the British frigate *Niger* ran aground nearby on Browns Bank, the fort and the frigate became involved in a cannon duel. One of the frigate's firings was a "Maggie's drawers" shot that hit the lighthouse.

John Thomas, later a general in the Revolution, became the first keeper of the light, and after his death his wife, Hannah Thomas, became America's first woman lighthouse keeper. Hannah Thomas was still keeper at a salary of $200 per year when the lighthouse was ceded to the federal government in 1790. Her son, John, did much of the work as his mother grew older, and John was officially appointed keeper later that year. He remained until 1812.

The lighthouse burned to the ground in 1801 and a temporary beacon, funded by Plymouth merchants, took its place.

In 1802 a Congressional appropriation gave $270 to the merchants for the establishment of the temporary beacon and $2,500 to be used to construct a new lighthouse. Twin 22-foot tall light towers, 30 feet apart, were completed in 1803.

The 1803 towers were equipped with a wheel-shaped optic, consisting of six oil lamps with reflectors. The beacons stood 70 feet above the water and had a range of 19 nautical miles.

A U.S. Navy inspection report of 1838 (by the same inspector mentioned in the SANDY NECK chapter) adjudged the lights to be too close together, horizontal instead of vertical and often mistaken for the Sandy Neck light off Barnstable. Because of dry rot and other wear, the lighthouses were rebuilt in 1843 as octagonal, pyramidal wooden towers.

PLYMOUTH & DUXBURY PIER

The 1843 lanterns held fourth-order Fresnel optics whose focal planes were 102 feet above the sea.

Beginning in 1890 and extending into the early 1900s, Plymouth's number of port calls by international shipping companies declined drastically. In turn, the Plymouth Lighthouse's value as a coastal beacon waned.

Following the opening of the Cape Cod Canal in 1914, the lighthouse on the Gurnet again became an important navigation aid. In 1924 the northeast tower was discontinued and dismantled.

The southern 39-foot tall lighthouse remains active with its revolving 1,000-watt flashing optic. The red sector covers the dangerous Mary Ann Rocks, located to the north northwest. In 1994 the Coast Guard converted the optic to solar power.

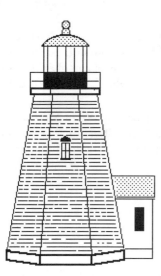

OWNER. The lighthouse, a modern ranch-type keeper's quarters and 4.5 acres had been leased to the U.S. Lighthouse Society. With the disbandment of the Society's Massachusetts chapter in 1996, the license was terminated. Project Bug & Gurnet Lights has now has leased the lighthouse from the Coast Guard. The Coast Guard still maintains the beacon.

- Project Bug & Gurnet Lights, PO Box 2167, Duxbury, MA 02331.
Website: http://www.buglight.org
Email: cindyr0713@mediaone.net

PRESERVATION. Listed in the National Register of Historic Places. This lighthouse was about 35 feet from toppling into the briny, and the cliff was eroding at about one foot per year. An earlier attempt to halt the erosion by planting beach grass, rugosa and crinkled rose bushes had no effect in halting the slope erosion along the 45-foot cliff. As a result, the Coast Guard decided in 1997 to move the nation's oldest free-standing wooden lighthouse inland. In December 1998, D & K Building Movers of Scituate, Massachusetts, subcontracted by Northern Construction Service, LLC, of Hingham, Massachusetts, moved the lighthouse about 140 feet to safer ground. The move was managed by the Coast Guard's Civil Engineering Unit in Providence, Rhode Island.

DUXBURY PIER LIGHTHOUSE (BUG LIGHT).
CHARACTERISTIC: Group flashing red 5s
HAW: 35' **RANGE**: 6 nm

Duxbury Pier is the first coffee pot-shaped, cast-iron lighthouse to have been built in the United States. It is a 47-foot tall tower that rests on a tall concrete-filled caisson. The superstructure's three decks support the vacant main operations area, the former crew's living quarters and the empty watchroom. The main deck and lantern, with its fourth-order classical lens, can be serviced from wraparound galleries.

The Pilgrim Society's library holds an interesting item concerning the building of the lighthouse. It is a biographical history writtten by William W. Burgess, Jr. He briefly describes his and his father's involvement as follows:

"Along in April, '71 ... they decided to build an iron lighthouse near the Duxbury pier on the flats close to the edge of the Channel, and my father contracted with the Government Inspector to build it. It was built of iron plates, 10 ft. long with flanges on each to bolt them together and form a circle 28 ft. in diameter at the bottom. This section was put together in North Dock and a cofferdam built inside of it to float it, and one Sunday we towed it down with the government Schr [schooner] and our sloop Rose Wood, placed it in position then broke in the coffer-dam and sunk it. I got $3.00 for my part of the job, which was looking on."

And to further confirm its construction in 1871, a letter to the editor published on December 26, 1872 in Plymouth's newspaper, The *Old Colony Memorial*, cites the need to dredge Plymouth Harbor and to build brush and stone groins around the "Bug Light."

OWNER. U.S. Coast Guard. Lighthouse is leased to Project Gurnet & Bug Lights.

PRESERVATION. In 1983 Duxbury Pier Light was slated by the Coast Guard to be replaced by a fiberglass tower much like the one that had replaced Boston Harbor's old Deer Island Lighthouse. A group of concerned local residents formed Project Bug Light.

Project Bug Light convinced the Coast Guard to grant it a five-year lease. In turn, the group raised $20,000 in contributions and used the money to make temporary repairs to the upper catwalk and roof. At the same time solar power replaced the older battery system. The fog signal was also converted to solar power. Unfortunately, the group disbanded at the end of the lease period.

In 1993 Dr. Donald Muirhead organized a second effort to save the lighthouse. Since then, a small army of volunteers from Project Bug & Gurnet Lights, a nonprofit organization, have put in many, many hours of labor cleaning the inside of the tower, weatherproofing the roof and installing a distress signal device to keep cormorants and other birds from resting and roosting in the lighthouse.

In 1996 an Aids to Navigation Team (1) repaired a popped seam and re-painted the caisson, (2) replaced two rusted floorings with heavy steel gratings, (3) installed a new ladder on the east side, (4) repainted (white) the interior of one level and (5) hand scrubbed and scraped the old paint off the tower's exterior. Project Bug & Gurnet Lights has also made temporary repairs to the lantern roof by laying down a sand-type covering. At this writing it looks like a complete renovation is imminent. The tower's deteriorating seams will be repaired along with the roof.

Our hats off to the Coast Guard and Project Bug & Gurnet Lights for their cooperative endeavors to save this historic structure. The president of Project Bug & Gurnet Lights at this writing is Dorothy Bicknell, daughter of the late historian and "Flying Santa" Edward Rowe Snow.

Although Project Bug & Gurnet Lights has raised funds from contributions from private foundations, businesses and individuals, more funds will be required for the upkeep of the lighthouse. If you are interested in Duxbury Pier Lighthouse's future, send your contributions to:

- Project Bug & Gurnet Lights, PO Box 2167, Duxbury, MA 02331.
Website: http://www.buglight.org
Email: cindyr0713@mediaone.net

Duxbury Pier Lighthouse

SCITUATE

NORTH OR SOUTH ON MA 3A. If northbound, in Greenbush at the MA 123 (Main Street) & Country Way intersection turn right and follow Country Way into Scituate Center. Turn right at First Parish Road. The intersection is marked with a "Scituate Harbor" sign.

If enroute north or south on MA 3A turn east into First Parish Road and at a "Scituate Center" sign turn right. Continue east on First Parish across Country Way.

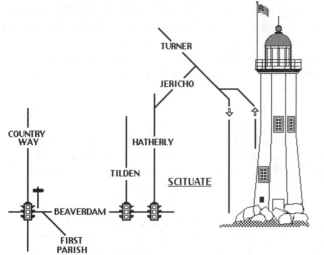

SOUTH ON COUNTRY WAY. In Scituate Center at a "Scituate Harbor" sign turn left into First Parish Road.

CONTINUE ON. At another "Scituate Harbor" sign, where First Parish bears right to the southeast, continue straight ahead on connecting Beaverdam Road. Then:

-> Follow Beaverdam past Tilden Road,

-> Left at Hatherly Road,

-> Bear right into Jericho Road,

-> At the Jericho - Turner - Lighthouse intersection turn right into Lighthouse Road,

-> Continue on Lighthouse (one-way south) to the light station's free parking lot. Rebecca Road (one way north) returns to the Jericho - Turner - Lighthouse intersection.

VISITING THE LIGHTHOUSE. The Scituate Historical Society holds tours of light station, usually four times a year on dates announced in the local newspapers.

- Scituate Historical Society, PO Box 276, Scituate MA 02066.
Website: http://www.scituate-history.org
Phone (781) 545-1083.

A local organizations runs occasional lighthouse cruises featuring good views of Scituate Lighthouse. Call for the latest schedules.

- Friends of the Boston Harbor Islands, Inc. 349 Lincoln Street, Bldg. 45, Hingham, MA 02043-1601
Phone (781) 740-4290.
Website: http://www.fbhi.org

SCITUATE LIGHTHOUSE (OLD SCITUATE).
CHARACTERISTIC: Flashing white 15s
HAW: 70'

In May 1810 the Federal Government allocated $4,000 for the construction of a lighthouse on Cedar Point. Squabbling over the tower's location delayed construction for a few months. When completed in 1811, the light station contained the light tower, a wood framed keeper's dwelling, an oil house and a well. The new beacon was activated on September 19, 1811.

In September 1814 (during the War of 1812), a British naval ship entered Scituate Harbor with plans to burn the town to the ground. As a British landing party approached the town, the absent keeper's two teenaged daughters, Rebecca and Abigail Bates, extinguished the light. The girls then proceeded to play a fife and a drum in the woods nearby, hoping to convey to the incoming British marines the impression that either federal troops were arriving or that militiamen were mustering to save the town. The ruse worked and the British withdrew. The girls have since been immortalized as "The American Army of Two."

The 25-foot tall octagonal tower is built of split granite blocks and lined with rubble stone. The tower has an 18-foot diameter at its base tapering to 10 feet at the top.

Scituate's first lighting device was a pan (reservoir) with multiple whale oil-burning wicks whose focal plane was 35 feet above the water. Its fixed white beam could be seen for six nautical miles.

In 1827 the tower's height was raised 15 feet with brick and four granite post and lintel window bays were built into its walls. Two lanterns were added. The upper one (atop the tower) held an eight-lamp and reflector optic; the lower one (imbedded in the tower) housed a seven-lamp and reflector device.

The top signal's characteristic was fixed white, the bottom fixed red. This arrangement proved to be ineffective as the white and the dimmer red beams merged a short distance offshore.

In an attempt to improve upon this new concept, Winslow Lewis was awarded a contract in 1841 to rebuild the tower's walls, the lantern's roof and ventilator ball. At the same time Mr. Lewis was assigned the task to further separate the lights and increase their intensity. He decided that his patented lamps would do just that. In they went and, while they were brighter, the lights still merged into one. Nothing else was done to improve upon the situation until around 1852, when the lower optic was removed and the wall bricked up. The outline of this masonry patchwork can still be seen. Finally, the top beacon was removed in 1855, when a Fresnel lens and new lamp were installed.

The Scituate beacon was darkened on the morning of November 15, 1860. That night the rebuilt Minot's Ledge Lighthouse entered the lighthouse service, eliminating the need for an aid at Scituate. The classical lens was removed soon after.

OWNER. In 1913 the Town of Scituate began work on acquiring the light station. On June 17, 1917, the town paid the federal government $1,000 for the 50-foot tall lighthouse and another $1,500 for the land southeast of the tower. The deed specifies that the town must maintain the property "as an historic landmark." The Scituate Historical Society, responsible for the station's upkeep since 1968, has taken excellent care of this historic structure. Resident caretakers live in the keeper's dwelling.

PRESERVATION. Listed in the National Register of Historic Places. Although a small blue light was installed in 1966 during the tower's renovation, Scituate remained dark until July 6, 1991. On that date, in recognition of the aid's historic past, the light was reactivated as a privately maintained beacon seen only from the mainland side of the lantern. Another addition was a new 30-inch diameter copper ventilator ball fashioned out of the ball that once belonged to Nantucket Island's Sankaty Head Lighthouse.

In 1994 Scituate was certified as a private aid to navigation. Its new modern lens was activated on the 5th of August.

Scituate Lighthouse

MINOT'S LEDGE

NORTH FROM SCITUATE. Motor north on Country Way through North Scituate into Cohasset Center. Then:
-> Right at Highland Extension. A "Robert E. Jason Road" sign is on the northeast corner,
-> Left into Highland Avenue,
-> Right at Beach (Beech) Street,
-> Continue to Beach's end at Atlantic Avenue and turn left. About 0.5 mile north on Atlantic is a large parking area owned by the Sandy Beach Association. If the parking lot is closed to visitors, there is an unobstructed view of the lighthouse from along the sandy beach just north of the lot.

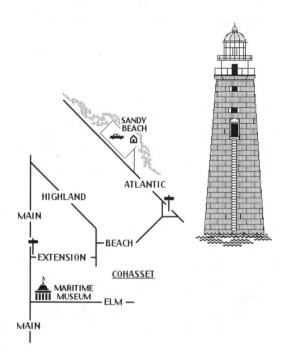

SOUTH FROM NANTASKET. See also the BOSTON, GRAVES & LONG ISLAND HEAD chapter's map.

Take Atlantic Avenue (start 0.0 mile) to its juncture with Forest Avenue Extension (1.3 miles). Turn left and continue on Atlantic past Jerusalem Road (2.1 miles) to the parking lot (2.8 miles). The lighthouse first comes into view between 2.2 and 2.4 miles.

Two local organizations run occasional lighthouse cruises featuring good views of Minot's Ledge Lighthouse. Call for the latest schedules.

- Friends of the Boston Harbor Islands, Inc. 349 Lincoln Street, Bldg. 45, Hingham, MA 02043-1601
Phone (781) 740-4290.
Website: http://www.fbhi.org
- Boston Harbor Explorers, P.O. Box 744, Quincy, MA 02269.
Phone: (617) 479-1871

MINOT'S LEDGE LIGHTHOUSE. (MINOT LEDGE)
CHARACTERISTIC: Group flashing white 45s
HAW: 85' **RANGE**: 10 nm

The Cohasset Rocks group of rocks and ledges, has had a long history as a destroyer of many ships and lives. The story of the construction of the first tower (1847-50), is one of determination, toil and failure. The tower had to be built on a rocky outcropping no wider than 20 feet.

The top of the rock was but 3.5 feet above the water at low tide, which allowed only three hours to work on the rock during each low tide. In early 1847 work commenced on building the skeletal tower. Nine holes, each 12 inches in diameter and five feet deep were drilled into the rock. The workers first erected a 75-foot tall iron scaffolding on Outer Minot Ledge, one of two outcroppings comprising Minot's Ledge. Work progressed, but only on calm days. Meanwhile, they ate and slept on a schooner anchored nearby. If a storm threatened, they returned to Cohasset.

Then, two sections of cast-iron pilings (each 10 inches in diameter at its base, tapering to five inches at its top) were cemented into the holes. The submerged sections ranged from 35 feet to 38 feet to compensate the varying depths of the ledge. All of the upper sections were 25 feet long. The sections were joined by 3-foot tall gunmetal sockets, each weighing 800 pounds. When in place the eight legs formed a cross-braced (to 38 feet) octagon with an underwater diameter of 25 feet, tapering to 14 feet at the top. The ninth piling was centered within the octagonal framework. Topping the skeleton was a 5-ton cast-iron spider that joined and firmly held together the 60-foot tall tower. Atop the spider a two-story, octagonal and wooden living space was erected. The first floor served as a bedroom and storeroom; the second deck held the watchroom and galley. A 16-sided lantern topped quarters. At that stage a storm swept the scaffolding into the sea and by the winter of 1847, work had stopped. The optic, consisting of 15 whale oil-fueled lamps and reflectors, was officially lighted on January 1, 1850.

Storms took their toll. The crossarm braces often had to be taken to the mainland to be repaired and reinforced. In March 1851, a terrific storm caused the tower to sway so violently that the keeper and his assistant had difficulty climbing the ladder to service the light. On April 16, 1851, while the keeper was on the mainland, another hurricane-strength storm hit the area. Although the two assistant lightkeepers were able to keep the bell ringing and the lamps burning, the gale in all its fury tore the tower apart piece by piece. The first to go was the center support, leaving the heavy top of the tower resting on the outer pilings. Then the pilings snapped and the entire tower slid into the sea. By the morning of April 17th, the tower had disappeared. Both assistant keepers perished trying to reach the mainland.

AMERICA'S ATLANTIC COAST LIGHTHOUSES - MASSACHUSETTS

The 114-foot tall lighthouse we see today on Minot's Ledge is indeed an engineering triumph. Started in 1855, it took one day less than five years to complete. After construction of a cofferdam, seven large granite blocks were cut to a finite tightness, anchored to the new pilings by 2-inch wrought iron bolts and cemented together two feet below low tide. In July 1858, the first granite block for the tower was laid. Each of the 29 blocks in the second course, above the seven-block foundation, weighs two tons. The blocks were locked together by dovetailing. It is said that during storms the pressure created by wind and sea strengthens the tower by forcing the wedge-shaped blocks inward. The strongest gale has caused but minor vibration, and there have been times when waves sweep over the top of the lighthouse.

A total of 3,514 tons of Quincy granite were shaped into 1,079 blocks weighing 2,307 tons. The first 40 feet consists of solid granite blocks. The next 40 feet of the tower contains a storeroom, living quarters and work spaces. The watchroom and lantern take up the final 17 feet.

With the tower completed and equipped with a new catadioptric second-order Fresnel lens, the light was tested for the first time on August 23, 1860 and officially reestablished on November 15, 1860.

While the reconstruction project was underway, the lightship *Minot's Ledge* temporarily covered for the darkened tower. The ship was positioned 0.8 mile at 360 degrees from the ledge. The lightship was withdrawn after Minot's Ledge Lighthouse came back on station.

In May 1894, a new optic was installed with a group flashing 1 + 4 + 3 characteristic. With a local "I Love You" interpretation, the beacon has become known as the "Lover's Light" or the "I-Love-You Lighthouse."

Minot's Ledge was automated in 1947 and its Fresnel lens removed. The lens' replacement was converted to solar power in 1983.

OWNER. U.S. Coast Guard (lighthouse). Town of Cohasset (mainland duplex).

PRESERVATION. Listed in the Register of Historic Places.

Not having been worked on for many years and having received some damage during a 1978 storm, the beacon was extinguished by the Coast Guard, who spent almost $500,000 on a renovation project that required the use of a helicopter to complete. The first task was to remove the lantern to Government Island, where it was disassembled and refinished. With the lantern off the tower, the top courses of granite blocks were removed. The blocks were so well dovetailed and fastened together with iron pins (not previously known to have been used) that the last stone had to be located and the blocks removed in reverse order. The blocks were also airlifted to Government Island, where they were numbered and measured for the shaping of new blocks mined from the original New Hampshire quarry. The beacon was reactivated on August 20, 1989.

GOVERNMENT ISLAND. See the following map. To build the 26-foot tall Minot's Ledge Monument the Cohasset Historical Commission acquired the watchroom blocks taken from the tower and had them reassembled into a 7.5 tall circular foundation to hold a fabricated lantern and Minot's Ledge's original lens pedestal. The mini-tower's 2.5-ton steel-ribbed lantern was made with donated materials by a steel company in Quincy. Two local artisans roofed the 5-ton bronze-ribbed lantern with $3,300 worth of copper sheeting and topped it with a handcrafted copper ventilator ball. In 1997 Minot Ledge's 1,500-pound second-order Fresnel lens, on loan from the Coast Guard to the Town of Cohasset, was placed in the lantern. The multimillion dollar relic has been insured for $175,000. It is not the complete lens; when first removed from the lighthouse's lantern, it was stored in a lower level where it was heavily damaged by vandals.

Government Island was used by the tower's masons to shape Minot's Ledge's original granite blocks. On the grounds are the temporary ground templates used by the masons to preassemble each dovetailed course of granite blocks.

During 1992-93, a group of citizens raised $200,000 to restore the keepers' two-story wood framed duplex (two seven-room units) built in 1858. The first floor has been converted into meeting rooms and the second floor into two apartments. The grounds have been landscaped with walks and picnic tables.

After its automation, there was an attempt to steal (in broad daylight) Minot's Ledge's 1,500-pound fog bell. The heist was spotted by a fisherman, who alerted the Coast Guard. Later, the Cohasset Historical Society acquired the bell for display on Government Island.[1] After the expenditure of much elbow grease, cans of polish and buckets of epoxy, Herb Jason beautifully restored the bell. It was rung in June 1994 for the first time in almost 50 years.

---

1. Shore Village Newsletter No. 1-96, April 11, 1996. The bell story was relayed to the Shore Village Museum's director Ken Black by Bob Fraser, noted lighthouse historian. Ken Black's quarterly newsletter is always full of varied and mighty interesting lighthouse information. It's free for the asking, although a donation to the museum is not unwelcomed. Send request to: Shore Village Museum, 104 Limerock Street, Rockland, ME 04841. Website: http://www.lighthouse.cc/shorevillage

MINOT'S LEDGE
NARROWS

In 1997 a group of local residents began a campaign to erect a granite memorial to Joseph Antoine and Joseph Wilson, the young assistant keepers who lost their lives in 1851. The monument will be installed on Government Island near the replica of the top of the present Minot's Ledge Lighthouse. At this writing it is scheduled to be dedicated in May of 2000.

- Cohasset Lightkeepers Corporation, PO Box 514, Cohasset, MA 02025.
Phone (617) 383-0505.

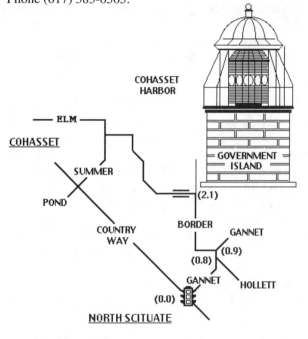

COHASSET MARITIME MUSEUM. The Cohasset Historical Society's Maritime Museum located at 4 Elm Street, originally a ship chandlery and the headquarters for a fishing fleet, contains a magnificent collection of maritime artifacts. The museum, using documents, drawings and photographs, presents a comprehensive historical account of the construction of the lighthouse.

OPEN. June to September, Tuesdays through Sundays 1:30 to 4:30. Saturdays 10 to 4:30.

FREE ADMISSION. Donations welcomed.

- Cohasset Historical Society, 14 Summer Street, MA 02025.

Phone (617) 383-6930.

THE NARROWS (destroyed).

This old screw pile lighthouse, nicknamed Bug Light, was built in 1856 on Boston Harbor's Brewster Spit (northeast of George Island) at the southeast entrance to The Narrows that runs between Lovell's and Gallop's Islands. Its optic was a whale oil-powered fifth-order Fresnel with a focal plane some 35 feet above high mean water. The lighthouse was destroyed by fire on June 7, 1929, when the keeper chose a windy day to remove paint from the lighthouse's exterior using a blowtorch. A spark ignited the roof and Keeper Tom Small barely escaped with his life. An automatic beacon still marks the spot.

BOSTON
GRAVES - LONG ISLAND HEAD

NORTH FROM COHASSET. Take Beach Street to Atlantic Avenue and turn left. Then:
-> Right at the Atlantic & Forest Avenue Extension intersection and continue on Atlantic,
-> Right at Nantasket Avenue and continue north to Hull.

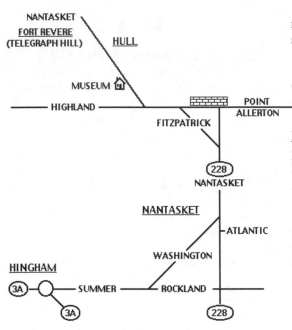

SOUTH FROM BOSTON. Take MA 3 through the Hingham rotary to Summer Street. The route is marked with a "Nantasket 3" sign. Then:
-> Left into Washington Boulevard,
-> Bear left into merging Nantasket Avenue and continue north to Hull.

FORT REVERE - FORT INDEPENDENCE HISTORIC PARK. There are excellent views of the lighthouses from the fort's parapets and the observation deck of its water tower on Telegraph Hill, where American artillery pieces were positioned during the American Revolution, the War of 1812 and World War II.
PARK OPEN. Daily all year, daytime.
TOWER OPEN. Memorial Day to Labor Day, daily 1 to 5. On weekends a French marine and a World War I doughboy (volunteers of the Fort Revere Park and Preservation Society) relate stories of the Revolutionary fort, its strategic importance during later years and its telegraph stations.
FREE ADMISSION.
Phone: Information (781) 925-1778.

HULL LIFESAVING MUSEUM. The lighthouses also can be seen quite clearly from this museum's watch tower.
The museum, located in the old Point Allerton Lifesaving Station, is fully furnished and equipped as if its 19th century surfmen had just run for their lifesaving boats. The station was first captained by Joshua James, world renowned lifesaver.
After an introductory video, there are exhibits in the Galley about surfmen, a surfboat in the Boat Room, and the story of the Great Storm of 1888 in the Mess Room. There is an extensive collection of books by popular maritime historian Edward Rowe Snow in the Edward Rowe Snow Room and an old telegraph set and crank phone in the Radio Room. Of particular interest to lighthouse buffs are Plymouth Lighthouse's fourth-order Fresnel and a model of the Minot's Ledge Lighthouse.
OPEN.
July and August, Wednesdays through Sundays noon to 5.
Rest of year, weekends and Monday holidays noon to 5.
Closed January 1, Thanksgiving Day and December 25.
ADMISSION FEES. Discount for seniors and children 5-17. Members and under 5 free.
- Hull Lifesaving Museum, PO Box 221 (1117 Nantasket Avenue), Hull, MA 02405.
Phone (781) 925-5433.
Website: http://www.nantasket.com/lifesaving.html

BOSTON LIGHTHOUSE (BOSTON HARBOR).
CHARACTERISTIC: Flashing white 10s
HAW: 102' **RANGE**: 27 nm
First, let us go back in time to when Little Brewster Island (named after the 1621 *Mayflower* Brewsters) was deeded to the Town of Hull. That was in the year 1641. Then:
1679. A Dutch traveler noted in his diary that the ship he was aboard passed a beacon in outer Boston Harbor. That beacon could have been a bonfire, a torch set on a pole or, as commonly used in Europe since 1624, a coal-fired brazier hoisted on a pole.

1713. A Bostonian petitioned the Massachusetts Colony's General Court to replace the beacon with a lighthouse. After several surveys by selectmen, ship captains and merchants, it was decided to place the new lighthouse on Little Brewster Island. Little Brewster was sometimes called "Lighthouse Island" or "Beacon Island," and it was also sometimes considered part of Great Brewster because the two islands were joined by a sand bar.

1715. After having received England's approval, the Colony authorized on the 23rd of July the construction of a lighthouse.

1716. Construction of Boston's first lighthouse on Little Brewster was completed. The light was established on the 14th of September. The tower was a hewn granite block structure that initially burned candles. A short time later it was fitted with an oil-burning candelabra. The lighthouse's upkeep was paid out of tonnage taxes collected from ships entering Boston harbor. The lighthouse keepers in those early years also served as harbor pilots.

1718. The first lightkeeper, George Worthylake, and his family accidentally drowned. Benjamin Franklin, then only 13 years old, penned a ballad about the Worthylakes' demise, entitled "The Lighthouse Tragedy."

1719. Keeper John Hayes requested and was granted an observation deck seaward of the tower and a fog cannon to be used as America's first fog signal. A drawing made in 1729 shows the cannon near the tower with the date "1700" engraved on it. In 1963 the cannon was removed to the U.S. Coast Guard Academy in New London, Connecticut. In May 1993, after having a new mount made and the cannon cleaned, a Coast Guard helicopter airlifted the old artillery piece back to Little Brewster Island. Visitors will see it inside the museum at the base of the tower.

1751. A fire destroyed the tower's wooden interior, creating cracks in the walls.

1775. After the British blockaded the harbor, an American raiding party burned the house, support buildings and some of the tower's wooden interior.

Before the British could make repairs to the damaged structure, a 300-man assault team tried unsuccessfully to capture the island. Upon withdrawing, the American party was intercepted and taken under fire by British marines approaching the island in whaleboats. Fortunately, a direct hit on one of the boats by an American field piece located on Hull's Nantasket Hill (now Telegraph Hill) caused the British to withdraw to their ships.

1776. When the British sailed out of Boston Harbor some of their ships received extensive damage from cannon fire from Nantasket Hill and Quincy's Long Island. Before leaving, however, the British planted a delayed explosive charge which completely destroyed the tower. The remains of the cast-iron lantern and dome were melted down to manufacture ladles for cannons.

1783. Massachusetts provided the funds to rebuild the tower. This is basically the structure you see today on Little Brewster Island. The walls are 7.5 feet thick at its base, tapering to 2.5 feet at the top. Although tightening bands were first added in 1783 to strengthen the cracked walls, the steel bands you see today date from 1973.

1790. The lighthouse was ceded to the new Federal Government.

This 89-foot tall lighthouse has witnessed many terrible shipwrecks on nearby islands and shoals, as well as the birth of a nation. For instance, during the naval engagement fought under its lantern in 1813 between the American naval ship *Chesapeake* and the British *Shannon*, it was the American Captain Lawrence who told his crew as he lay dying, "Don't give up the ship." Unfortunately, the *Shannon's* complement surrendered minutes later.

Then there is the story of one entrepreneur who ferried young ladies to the island to manufacture cigars he sold to Bostonians as imported Cuban cheroots. The lightkeeper was charged with fraud and summarily dismissed.

In 1859, because of the poor workmanship of the 1783 tower, the structure underwent a major overhaul. The tower was lined with brick and weakened portions of the outer stone wall removed and patched with brick. At the same time the height of the lighthouse was raised 15 feet with coursed brick and topped with a new lantern large enough to accommodate the 1851 second-order Fresnel lens in use today. Its light source is a 1,000 watt electric bulb.

OWNER. U.S. Coast Guard.

PRESERVATION. Listed in the National Register of Historic Places.

On September 14, 1991, after having been extinguished for repairs and the replacement of its carriage wheels, Boston's classical lens was relighted on the lighthouse's 275th birthday.

Boston Lighthouse is also threatened by the sea. In this case it is not the erosion of cliffs or bluffs, but the peeling away of the layered granite ledge that supports and surrounds Little Brewster Island. With each storm, hunks of the island's base are torn off. The light station's very existence was severely tested at the end of October 1991 by Hurricane Bob and the "No Name" Halloween eve storm. The pair caused serious damage to the island's property. The damage assessment ($400,000) read like a war zone report: pier damaged with many parts missing; boathouse doors blown off; roofs of the keepers' dwelling and outbuildings torn away; buildings' walls cracked, broken or caved in; damaged and inoperative fresh water system. Storms of December 1992 and March 1993 inflicted additional damage.

During 1993-94 the Coast Guard made these improvements to the light station: (1) removed two damaged 2,000-gallon fuel tanks and installed a new 4,000 gallon underground tank, (2) repaired the rain-water retention building, (3) built a new 200' long concrete and granite transit pier, (4) laid wider sidewalks, (5) placed heavy wire gabions filled with stone along the shoreline to control erosion, (6) renovated the 1885 keeper's residence, (7) constructed reinforced trenches to protect underground oil and utility lines and (8) landscaped the grounds.

VISITING THE BOSTON LIGHTHOUSE. Little Brewster Island and Boston Light are now part of the Boston Harbor Islands National Recreation Area. While the Coast Guard continues to staff the Atlantic Coast's last attended light station, the National Park Service is responsible for the island's care. Meanwhile, a funded Preservation and Stewardship Plan is supporting ongoing restorative work that will include interpretive exhibits and improved public access.

- Boston Harbor National Recreation Area, National Park Service, Office of the Project Manager, 408 Atlantic Avenue, Boston MA 02210-3350.

Phone: Visitor Information: (617) 223-8666.

Website: http://www.nps.gov/boha/index.htm

The Friends of Boston Harbor Islands (FBHI) offer a visit to Boston Lighthouse. This tour is very popular, so call early in the year for the current year's schedule and make your reservations pronto. FBHI member (annual dues) receive the organization's quarterly newsletter *Tidings* and discounts on trips and tours. All trips sail rain or shine. Landing is at the captain's discretion. If tides and swells are too dangerous, passengers will be taken to another island instead.

SCHEDULE. June to September, usually one trip per month. Round trip lasts about four or five hours. Departs from either Long Wharf or Rowes Wharf in Boston. See the map on page 293.

FARES. Phone reservations can be made in advance. Tickets sold at dockside on trip day. Discounts for members, seniors and children 5-12. Under 5 free.

- Friends of Boston Harbor Islands, 349 Lincoln Street, Building 45, Hingham, MA 02043.

Phone (781) 740-4290. Website: http://www.fbhi.org

There are now trips leaving Boston for Boston Light, run by the Boston Harbor Islands Partnership.

SCHEDULE. Mid-May through mid-October. Friday, Saturday, Sunday. Times: 10 a.m. to 2 p.m. and 2 p.m. to 6 p.m. The trip lasts 2 1/2 hours, with over an hour spent on Little Brewster Island.

FARES. Discounts for children.

- Boston Light trip. Phone: (617) 223-8666.

Boston Light can also be viewed from various cruises offered by Boston Harbor Cruises, leaving from Boston Harbor's Long Wharf.

- Boston Harbor Cruises, One Long Wharf, Boston, MA, 02110.

Phone: (617) 227-4321. Website: http://www.bostonharborcruises.com/

BOSTON, GRAVES & LONG ISLAND HEAD

GRAVES LIGHTHOUSE.
CHARACTERISTIC: Group flashing white 12s
HAW: 98" **RANGE**: 24 nm

Besides the previously mentioned vantage points, Graves Light can be viewed from some of the cruises offered by the Friends of the Boston Harbor Islands, the Boston Harbor Explorers, and Boston Harbor Cruises. Call for current schedules (see the preceding page).

The Graves' construction project began in early 1903 with the cutting of the tower's granite blocks on Cape Ann, Massachusetts. During the following two years the foundation was laid, the granite blocks taken by barge to the work site and the top masonry work completed. The light was activated on September 1, 1905.

The 113-foot tall Graves Lighthouse resembles the Ram Island Ledge Lighthouse south of Portland, Maine. Forty feet above its 30-foot diameter base is the tower's first deck. Below the deck is a water cistern that is 35 feet deep. The holding tank had a capacity to provide water for two keepers for six months. On the second deck is the engine room with two generators, one to operate the foghorn and the other for standby emergency power. The third deck holds the crew's quarters, the fourth the galley and the fifth a library and the watchroom. The sixth deck, which in height is the equivalent of two lower decks, supports the extra large lantern. Once filled with an equally large first-order Fresnel lens, the lantern now holds a modern lens that was automated in 1976. The original lens sits in storage at the Smithsonian Institution in Washington, D.C.

OWNER. U.S. Coast Guard.
PRESERVATION. Listed in the National Register of Historic Places.

The October 1991 hurricane and storm also did considerable damage to the lighthouse. The attached entry way was separated from the tower, most of the landing platforms (remnants of a 90-foot connecting walkway built in 1905) and its fog signal house were washed away and the submarine electric power cable severed. The granite oil house was not damaged. The landing platform and additional damage done by vandals were repaired in 1993.

LONG ISLAND HEAD LIGHTHOUSE (INNER HARBOR).
CHARACTERISTIC: Flashing white 2.5s
HAW: 120' **RANGE**: 6 nm

Long Island Head Lighthouse is located in Boston Harbor on the tip of Long Island northeast of Quincy. It marks President Roads at the north entrance (Nubble Channel) to Nantasket Roads. Because there is a former prison hospital (now a homeless shelter) located astride the road leading to it, the lighthouse is not open to the public. Many of Boston's scheduled commercial cruises or inter-island ferries pass the lighthouse. It can be viewed from some of the cruises offered by the Friends of the Boston Harbor Islands, The Boston Harbor Explorers, and Boston Harbor Cruises (see the previous page for contact information). Massachusetts Bay Lines, leaving from Boston's Rowes Wharf, also offers cruises with views of Long Island Head Light.

- Massachusetts Bay Lines, 60 Rowes Wharf, Boston, MA 02110.

Phone: (617) 542-8000. Website: http://www.massbaylines.com/

A 23-foot rubblestone and granite lighthouse tower was built on the hill on Long Island Head and lighted in October 1819. Long Island Head Light, sometimes called the Inner Harbor Light, was 109 feet above the water. It was a fixed light with nine lamps and reflectors.

In 1844 Long Island Head Light received a new cast-iron lighthouse, one of the first in the nation. The island's fortification, Fort Strong, was enlarged around 1900. A 52-foot brick lighthouse, the third at Long island Head, was built in a new location to make room for the military installation. The act signed by the Secretary of the Treasury stated that the lighthouse would be relocated to a site that would "not be exposed to injury by the firing of guns in the new sea coast battery."

The present tower is a simple structure, cylindrical in shape with four windows, each with a coursed brick arch and framed with granite posts, a lintel and sill. Between the brick entry floor and the lantern deck there are 54 steps, with an intermediate landing at the 27th step level. Except for the balcony, the only decorative touch to the tower is a brick corbel (four courses) circling the shaft below the lantern deck. The light, automated in 1918, is now produced by a modern optic.

OWNER. U.S. Coast Guard.
PRESERVATION. Listed in the National Register of Historic Places.

In 1982, after a Coast Guard survey of the badly deteriorated tower, the beacon was discontinued. In 1985, after having been repaired, repainted and its lantern equipped with a solar-powered optic, the lighthouse was returned to active service. In 1994 the Coast Guard sandblasted and repainted the tower's cast-iron stairway. The tower again received a major renovation in the summer of 1998. The tower and lantern were repainted, and some of the original brick, mortar, and iron work were replaced.

DEER ISLAND LIGHTHOUSE (dismantled).

A 51-foot tall cast-iron lighthouse marked Presidents Roads Channel south of the town of Winthrop. It was built in 1890. The structure was torn down in 1982 and was replaced by a fiberglass tower. It rests on the original cast-iron caisson. The latter structure, by the way, looks like an elongated dumbbell with a bulbous base, a slender cylindrical body and an equally bulging top that houses equipment and supports a lantern that is roofed but not glass-enclosed. There are three of these English-designed towers on the Atlantic coast. The other two are Block Island's Great Salt Pond and Massachusetts' Cape Cod Canal Breakwater. This design (although admittedly better looking than skeletal towers) was proposed (and rejected) as a replacement for the destroyed Nantucket Lighthouse on Great Point, Nantucket Island. In fact, the Deer Island tower was originally built to be installed at Great Point.

TO ROWES AND LONG WHARVES. See the following map. Keep in mind that at this writing (early 2000) Boston is in the midst of the "Big Dig," a rerouting of the Central Artery (I-93). If possible, it is best to take public transportation into the city. Long and Rowes Wharves, the departure points for most cruises, are near the Aquarium stop on the MBTA's Blue Line (subway).

NORTH ON I-93. Stay on the right lane through the tunnel. Take Exit 22 "Atlantic Ave. - Northern Ave." to Atlantic Avenue" (one way). Then:

-> Right at Northern Avenue and cross over the bridge to on-street parking east of Sleeper Street (look for signs).

-> Walk back on Northern and right on Atlantic to Rowes Wharf.

-> There are public parking garages (fee) on Atlantic in the Long Wharf vicinity.

SOUTH ON I-93. Take Exit 23 "High St. - Congress St." to High Street. Then:

-> Left at High,

-> Left at Congress and pass over the end of I-93's tunnel,

-> Left at Atlantic Avenue (one way),

-> Right at Northern and cross over the bridge to on-street parking.

-> Walk back on Northern and right on Atlantic to Rowes Wharf.

-> There are public parking garages (fee) in the Long Wharf vicinity.

LIGHTHOUSE SIGHTSEEING CRUISES FROM BOSTON

- Friends of Boston Harbor Islands Annual Fall Foliage Lighthouse & Extravaganza Cruise: Usually includes Baker's Island, Boston, Cape Ann (Thacher Island), Deer Island, Eastern Point and Gloucester Breakwater, Fort Pickering, Hospital Point, Long Island Head, Marblehead, Straitsmouth, Ten Pound Island and The Graves. Exact itinerary may vary. The boat company and departure point also varies.

SCHEDULE. Once yearly in late September or early October. Round trip about six hours.

FARES. Prepaid; no refunds. Discounts for Friends of Boston Harbor Islands members, seniors and children 3-12. Under 3 free. Added discount for early reservations. No refunds.

- Friends of Boston Harbor Islands Boston to Plymouth Lighthouse Expedition Cruise via a Boston Harbor Cruises motor vessel. Includes a two-hour visit ashore in Plymouth. Usually includes viewings of the following lighthouses: Boston, Duxbury Pier, Minot's Ledge, Plymouth, Scituate and The Graves.

SCHEDULE. Usually once a year in May. Round trip about eight hours.

FARES. Prepaid with no refunds. Discounts for members, seniors and children 3-12. Under 3 free.

- **Friends of Boston Harbor Islands**, 349 Lincoln Street, Building 45, Hingham, MA 02043.

Phone: (781) 740-4290.

Website: http://www.fbhi.org

- Boston Harbor Explorers' Lighthouse Cruise Extravaganza.

Usually includes Baker's Island, Boston, Cape Ann (Thacher Island), Deer Island, Eastern Point and Gloucester Breakwater, Fort Pickering, Hospital Point, Long Island Head, Marblehead, Minot's Ledge, Ten Pound Island and The Graves. Exact itinerary may vary. The boat company and departure point also varies.

SCHEDULE. Twice a year, usually in July and August. Sails at 10. Returns about 4.

FARES. Discounts for seniors 55+ and children under 12.

- Boston Harbor Explorers, Inc., PO Box 744, Quincy, MA 02669-0744.

Phone: (617) 479-1871.

BOSTON, GRAVES & LONG ISLAND HEAD

FROM HINGHAM. Also see map on page 288.

- Friends of Flying Santa Lighthouse Cruise leaves the Massachusetts Bay Lines commuter terminal off MA 3A in Hingham. Free and secured parking at the terminal.

Usually includes Baker's Island, Boston, Eastern Point, Hospital Point, Long Island Head, Marblehead, Minot's Ledge and The Graves.

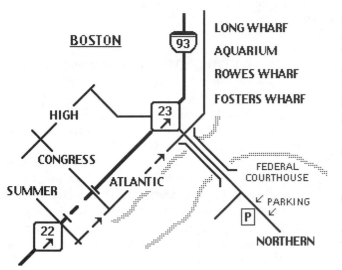

This cruise is a benefit for the Friends of Flying Santa, a non-profit organization which carries on the tradition of delivering Christmas gifts to people living at lighthouses. The tradition was started in 1927 by pilot Bill Wincapaw and was continued for over 40 years by author Edward Rowe Snow. It has brought much public attention to lighthouses and the important role of lighthouse keepers and their families.

SCHEDULE. Once a year, usually in June. Departs at noon. Returns around 5.

FARES. No discounts.

- Friends of Flying Santa, PO Box 791, Hull, MA 02045-0791.

Phone: (781) 925-0783. Fax (781) 925-2322.
Website: http://www.gis.net/~santa
Email: santa@gis.net

Besides lighthouses, the islands offer hiking, camping, swimming, and fascinating historic sites like George's Island's Fort Warren. For additional information on the Boston Harbor Islands, check the Boston Harbor Islands Visitor Guide website at http://www.bostonislands.com/ or call the visitor information line at (617) 223-8666.

Boston Lighthouse

MARBLEHEAD

NORTH ON MA 129. In Marblehead, turn right into Ocean Avenue (start 0.0 mile) and cross a causeway to a fork in the road (0.8 mile). Then:
-> Bear left into Harbor Avenue,
-> Continue on connecting Ocean Avenue (1.7 miles),
-> At Ocean's terminus turn left into Follett Street (one way),
-> Straight ahead into Chandler Hovey Park (free admission, free parking).
The Baker's Island Lighthouse can be seen far offshore to the east.

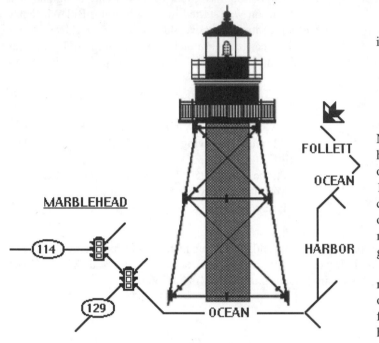

SOUTH ON MA 114. The Ocean Avenue turn is marked with a "129 Lynn-Boston" sign.

MARBLEHEAD LIGHTHOUSE
CHARACTERISTIC: Fixed green
HAW: 130' **RANGE**: 7 nm
The first lighthouse in the part of Marblehead Neck known as Point O'Neck, at the entrance to the harbor, was a white tower 20 feet high built near an old fort at a cost of $4,500, first lighted on October 10, 1835. The lighthouse was attached to the keeper's cottage by a covered walkway. The lamp burned lard or whale oil and its white light could be seen for 12 miles. The first keeper was Ezekiel Darling, a former gunner on "Old Ironsides," the *U.S.S. Constitution.*

By 1880 the light had become masked by surrounding cottages. In 1883 a light was put at the top of a 100-foot mast near the lighthouse. This sufficed for a while, but soon it was decided that a new lighthouse was in order.

The present 105-foot tall cast-iron lighthouse, completed in 1895, is the only skeletal lighthouse built in New England. The tower consists of eight 84-foot tall pilings placed 12 feet apart at the ground level and anchored to concrete foundations. Diagonal crossbracing with tie rods and turnbuckles stabilize the structure. Access to the watchroom is via a spiral 105-step stairway in the central cast-iron tube. Landings are located between each set of 21 steps. All of the former sash windows have been filled in with glass blocks.

When built, a distinctive triangular molded frieze was welded above the door frame. Its Greco-Second Empire motif was similar to the period's architectural trim found on the West Executive Building in Washington, D.C. Unfortunately, the frieze has been either torn or chiseled off the frame.

It is believed that the optic, when first established, consisted of a Fresnel lens (fourth or fifth-order) powered by a kerosene lamp. The lantern now holds a modern plastic lens automated in 1960.

OWNER. U.S. Coast Guard (lighthouse). Marblehead Neck resident Chandler Hovey purchased the land around the lighthouse and the brick oil house. In 1948 he donated it to the town.

PRESERVATION. Listed in the National Register of Historic Places.

In 1993 the tower was sandblasted and repainted. Although the cost was not disclosed, the same job cost $100,000 in 1980. Not long after the task was completed, vandals broke in and caused considerable damage that cost several hundred dollars to repair.

DERBY WHARF

Salem is about 15 miles north of Boston, and can be reached by commuter rail and bus. The Newburyport/Rockport Commuter Line (train) from Boston's North Station is about a 30-minute ride to Salem. For information phone (617) 222-3200. Website: http://www.mbta.com/

There are also two ferries from Boston to Salem. One, operated by A.C. Cruise Line, travels between Boston's Northern Avenue (in the Seaport District, next to Jimmy's Harborside restaurant) and Salem Willows Park. This trip gives you over four hours ashore in Salem. Call (617) 261-6633. Website: http://accruiseline.home.mindspring.com

The other is operated by Boston Harbor Cruises and operates between Boston's Long Wharf and Blaney Street Ferry Terminal in Salem, four blocks north of Pickering Wharf on Derby Street.. This trip is approximately an hour and a half each way. Operates daily from Late June to Labor Day with a reduced schedule through October. Call Boston Harbor Cruises at (617) 227-4321 for reservations. Website: http://www.bostonharborcruises.com/

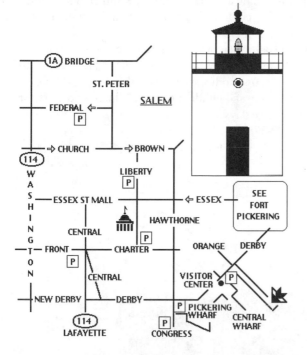

NORTH ON MA 114. Take MA 114 (Lafayette Street) into Salem. Where MA 114 turns west into New Derby Street turn right into Derby Street.

FROM WINTER ISLAND. Return to Fort Avenue. Then:

    -> Southwest on Fort Avenue,

    -> Bear right into Webb Street,

    -> Left at Essex Avenue (one-way),

    -> Left at Hawthorne Boulevard to Derby St.

A motorized trolley (fare) connects Winter Island Park with downtown Salem.

Website: http://www.salemweb.com/trolley.htm

For tourists Salem is a park and walk city. On-street parking is difficult to find. If you do drive to Salem, it is best to park in a lot or garage and walk or ride the trolley. Parking facilities (fees) are shown as [P] on the map; some are free on weekends.

SALEM MARITIME NATIONAL HISTORIC SITE. This historic area is a waterfront collection of restored 17th through 19th century wharves and buildings. Derby Wharf is the long earth and rock pier at the end of which stands the Derby Wharf Lighthouse.

It was funded through private donations. Between 1806 and 1808, the wharf was extended another 100 yards. Today Derby Wharf stretches about 0.5 mile out into the South River. The National Park Service's Orientation Center is located on Central Wharf. Salem Maritime also operates a major regional Visitor Center in downtown Salem.

SITE AND CENTER OPEN.

All year, daily 9 to 6. Closed January 1, Thanksgiving Day and December 25.

TOURS.

July and August, daily 9 to 6. Rest of year, daily 9 to 5.

FREE ADMISSION. Fees for guided tours, including the lighthouse. Discounts for seniors (62 and older) and children 6-16. No charge under 6. Reservations required.

- Salem Maritime National Historic Site, 174 Derby Street, Salem. MA 01970.

Phone (978) 740-1650. Fax (978) 740-1655.

Central Wharf Orientation Center (978) 740-1660. Website: http://www.nps.gov/sama/

DERBY WHARF LIGHTHOUSE.

CHARACTERISTIC: Flashing red 6s

HAW: 25' **RANGE**: 4 nm

In 1870 Congress appropriated $3,000 to build several aids to navigation within Salem's inner harbor. For Salem's waterfront the end of Derby Wharf was chosen and 103 square feet of land was purchased by the Federal Government. The first beacon, a temporary one, was an oil-burning lamp hung on a pole.

The present 12-foot square brick tower (painted white in 1922) was completed in 1870 and its light activated in January 1871. The entire lighthouse package cost a little over $3,000.

OWNER. National Park Service. Beacon maintained by the U.S. Coast Guard.
PRESERVATION. Listed in the National Register of Historic Places.

The light was deactivated in 1977. Two years later the property was transferred to the National Park Service. For years the lighthouse was subjected to deterioration by the weather, neglect and vandalism. After considerable effort on the part of The Friends of Salem Maritime, a nonprofit organization, a modern solar powered beacon was installed and, in 1983, relighted as a private aid to navigation.

PEABODY ESSEX MUSEUM. This famous museum is located west of Liberty Street and between Essex Street (pedestrian) Mall and Charter Street. The museum exhibits a bit of everything associated with New England's predominant role in the shipping trade to and from the Orient. While in the museum be sure to visit the Derby Wharf Lighthouse exhibit, an historical presentation of the times and activities of the wharf and its lighthouse.

OPEN. Open seven days a week from Memorial Day through Halloween: Monday through Saturday 10 to 5. Sunday noon to 5. Summer Weekend Hours: 9 am to 6 pm (through October). Closed Thanksgiving, Christmas, and New Year's Day, and Mondays from November 1 until Memorial Day. For shop and library hours call (978) 745-9500.

ADMISSION FEES. Discounts for families, seniors 61+, students and children 6-16. Children under six, Salem residents and members free. Rates include admission for two consecutive days.

- Peabody Essex Museum, East India Square, Salem, MA 01970-3783.

Phone: (978) 745-1876. Recorded information (978) 745-9500. In USA toll-free (800) 745-4054.

Website: http://www.pem.org/

Email: pem@pem.org

Derby Wharf Lighthouse

FORT PICKERING

NORTH FROM DOWNTOWN SALEM. Follow Derby Street and Fort Avenue northeast to an intersection marked with a large "Winter Island Marine Recreation Area" sign. Turn right into Winter Island Road and continue through the park's entrance, staying on the left side of the parking apron.

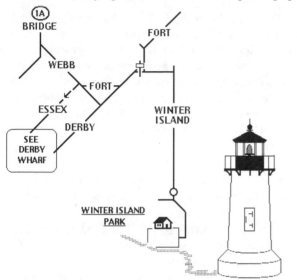

SOUTH FROM BEVERLY. Take MA 1A across the bridge into Salem. Then:
    -> Left into Webb Street (0.7 mile from mid-span),
    -> Left into Fort Avenue,
    -> Right at Winter Island Road.

WINTER ISLAND MARITIME PARK.
Baker's Island Lighthouse can also be seen (distantly) from the park.
OPEN. All year, daily 8 to 10.

PARKING FEES. Resident and non-resident, two hour and all day, May to Labor Day, daily.
September and October, weekends.
Two hours free parking with food purchase and validation from the park's Winter Island Grill.

- Winter Island Maritime Park, 50 Winter Island Road, Salem, MA 01970.
Phone (978) 745-9430.

FORT PICKERING LIGHTHOUSE.
CHARACTERISTIC: Flashing white 4s
HAW: 28'
The lighthouse at Fort Pickering on Winter Island was authorized in 1869, at the same time as lighthouses at Hospital Point in Beverly and Derby Wharf Light in Salem. Fort Pickering's light tower and keeper's dwelling were built in 1871 and the beacon was placed in service in 1872. The conical tower is constructed of coursed brick covered by a cast-iron sheath painted white.

The walkway connecting the tower to the mainland had to be rebuilt in 1879 and again in 1904, after it had been destroyed by ice. The walkway, keeper's house and other outbuildings, including a barn, no longer exist.

A Coast Guard airplane hangar was put on Winter Island in 1934. The Coast Guardsmen lived temporarily in the old lighthouse keeper's house until new quarters could be built. In January 1934, a blizzard imprisoned 30 men in the house until a plow could get through. Their heating fuel had just about run out with temperatures dipping to 12 below zero.

With the decline of Salem as an international shipping port, the inner harbor's beacons' maintenance and repair costs outstripped their importance as aids to navigation. Both Fort Pickering and Derby Wharf were considered no longer necessary for navigation. Fort Pickering Light was discontinued in 1969.

The infamous Blizzard of 1978 took the door right off the tower and it remained underwater for several years.

OWNER. U.S. Coast Guard. Managed by the City of Salem.
PRESERVATION. Listed in the National Register of Historic Places.
A group of concerned citizens and businesses formed the Fort Pickering Light Association in the early 1980s. They fished the door out of the harbor and put it back on the tower. The lighthouse was refurbished, and Fort Pickering Light was relighted in 1983 as a private aid to navigation.

The lighthouse went dark for a few months in early 1995 when conduit erosion cut off the power supply from shore. It was converted to solar power in April 1995, with a white flash of four-tenths of a second every four seconds. The $2,300 cost of the new light was split by the City of Salem and the Fort Pickering Light Association.

Fort Pickering Light received another facelift in the spring of 1999, thanks to a community development block grant. The American Steeple Corporation of Salem, which had previously restored Boston's Old North Church and Quincy's Church of the Presidents, completed $13,800 worth of iron work repairs, painting and lantern glass replacement.

HOSPITAL POINT

Hospital Point (Range Front) Lighthouse can be viewed from some of the lighthouse cruises offered by Boston Harbor Cruises, the Friends of the Boston Harbor Islands, and the Boston Harbor Explorers. See page 290 for details. Also, the lighthouse can be seen clearly from Salem Willows Park in Salem, and an excursion boat leaving from Salem Willows Park affords water views.

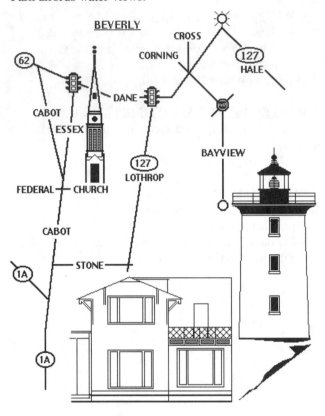

TO SALEM WILLOWS PARK FROM WINTER ISLAND. Follow Fort Avenue northeast to the park. Free parking. Salem Willows Park is an old amusement park offering picnic grounds, arcades, a carousel and several food stands. The park is also accessible via a ferry from Boston; see page 295 for details. Hospital Point (Range Front) Lighthouse can be seen clearly from Salem Willows Pier. The ticket booth for Sun Line Cruises is right next to the pier.

- Sun Line Cruises, Ltd., 123 Bay View Avenue, Salem, MA 01970.

Phone: (978) 741-1900. Fax (617) 631-3452 Website: http://www.salemweb.com/biz/sunlinecruises/

NORTH TO THE FIRST BAPTIST CHURCH. In Salem take MA 1A into Beverly. Continue northeast on Cabot Street. Turn right at Church Street. The First Baptist Church is located on the northeast corner of the five-street intersection. The range rear optic is positioned behind the small square aperture above the spire's round window.

NORTH TO HOSPITAL POINT. Follow Essex Street north to Dane Street. Then:

-> Right at Dane (MA 62),

-> Straight ahead into MA127 (Hale Street),

-> Right at Corning Street (about 0.4 mile northeast of the MA 62 & MA 127 junction),

-> Right at Beverly to the lighthouse.

SOUTH TO HOSPITAL POINT. Enroute on MA 127 and 0.5 mile southeast of the sharp left turn (marked with a blinking amber light) turn left at East Corning Street and right into Bayview Avenue.

SOUTH TO THE CHURCH. Take MA 127 (Hale Street) south. Then:

-> Right at MA 62 (Dane Street),

-> Left at Essex Street,

-> Left at Church Street.

HOSPITAL POINT (RANGE FRONT) LIGHTHOUSE.

CHARACTERISTIC: Fixed white

HAW: 70'   **RANGE**: Visible 360 degrees. Higher intensity on rangeline.

As early as 1711 there was a maritime observation or watch tower on Paul's Point, a rocky promontory on the west side of Beverly Cove on the main channel to Salem Harbor. In 1755 a pre-Revolutionary earthen fort, in the shape of a "J," was constructed on the upper level to the rear of the house. Its outline is still discernible. The area acquired its present name after a smallpox hospital was built there in 1801. During the War of 1812 the hospital was used as a barracks. In 1849 the hospital was destroyed by fire.

In 1871 the Town of Beverly transferred ownership of almost two acres to the U.S. Government for the purpose of constructing a permanent lighthouse. The first tower was a temporary wooden structure that was replaced when the present brick light tower, a wood framed keeper's house and a brick oil house were completed in 1872. The tapered Federal Design-styled tower has five wooden windows that have granite sills and lintels.

The dwelling is a two-story Queen Anne Revival with elaborate trim, a cross gable with large supporting brackets and double windows. The original structure had two wide balconies on its seaward side. They were probably removed when major alterations were made in 1968. During World War II, the house was again used as a military barracks. The station retains a brick oil house (1871) and an equipment building (1875).

HOSPITAL POINT

Its 3 1/2-order Fresnel optic has a condensing panel (vertical magnifying glass) offset from the main lens. It is a 24-inch tall convex lens with three prisms on each side. The condensing panel concentrates the horizontal beam on the centerline of the channel. A mariner will notice the light diminish in intensity if he drifts off the center line. The lighthouse was once the residence of retired Rear Admiral Bauman when he commanded the First Coast Guard District. Admiral Bauman had this to say about the panel, "I have climbed well over 600 lighthouses in this country and have never seen another condensing panel like it."

OWNER. With the light's automation in 1947, the station became the family quarters for the Commander of the First Coast Guard District.

PRESERVATION. Listed in the National Register of Historic Places.

HOSPITAL POINT RANGE REAR LIGHT.
CHARACTERISTIC: Fixed white
HAW: 183'
RANGE: Visible two degrees each side of the rangeline formed with the range front light.

On May 1, 1927, a new light was established in the spire of the First Baptist Church (1801). The church is almost a perfect nautical mile (2,050 yards) west northwest of the Hospital Point Range Front Light. The spire for years had been used by day as a range with the Hospital Point tower. For it to be above all other obstructions, it was necessary to place the light at an elevation of 127 feet. At that height there was little space available in the spire to install the optic.

To solve the problem, two 300 mm reflector lenses, discarded lightship optics, were installed and a 94-watt headlight-type electric lamp added. The light is automated, using a clock that turns it on at sunset and off at sunrise. The clock is wound each day by a small electric motor.

This beacon, known as "the church with the harbor light," is not the first church to have been utilized as an aid to navigation. The St. Phillips Episcopal Church in Charleston, South Carolina was similarly used before and during the Civil War. After an 1865 survey of Charleston Harbor revealed that old channels had been closed and new ones opened, the harbor's aids to navigation were relocated and the church range light discontinued.

Hospital Point (Range Front) Lighthouse

BAKER'S ISLAND

NORTH ON MA 127. The viewing locations for this lighthouse are on West Manchester-by-the-Sea's Boardman Avenue / Harbor Street loop, a route that dips down to Black Cove beach. Boardman Avenue is east of Beverly and about 0.3 mile from Highland Avenue (on the left).

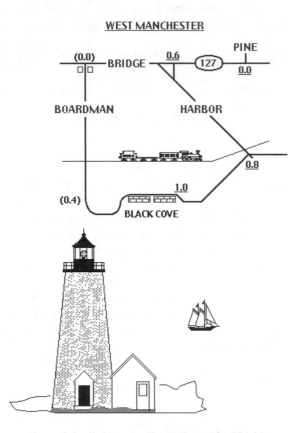

SOUTH ON MA 127. Harbor Street is west of Manchester-by-the-Sea and about 0.6 mile from Pine Street. The lighthouse lies due south of Black Cove. The higher elevation viewing spots are on Boardman at (0.4) mile and on Harbor at 1.0 mile. Another observation point is on the beach, accessible through a break in the seawall. Parking is permitted (free) west on Boardman at the top of the hill and east on Harbor before reaching the seawall.

Baker's Island Lighthouse can also be seen from some of the cruises offered by Boston Harbor Cruises, the Friends of the Boston Harbor Islands, and the Boston Harbor Association. See page 295 for details. It can also be seen distantly from Salem Willows Park and from some of the cruises offered by Sun Line Cruises; see page 298 for details.

BAKER'S ISLAND LIGHTHOUSE.
CHARACTERISTIC: Alternating white and red 20s
HAW: 111' **RANGES**: White 16; red 13 nm

Baker's Island, named in 1630 by Governor Winthrop, is 60 acres of massive rock outcroppings. In 1660 the island was deeded to the Town of Salem. In 1731 it was sold to a private party. By 1791 a daymark had been erected on the island. Finally, in 1796, after much lobbying by Salem's ship captains and merchants, Congress authorized the construction of two towers located on top of a two-story keeper's house, about 40 feet apart at either end of the building.. Both beacons were lighted on January 3, 1798.

One of the lights was discontinued in 1816 because of the deteriorated condition of its tower. Mariners claimed this made it difficult to distinguish the light from Boston Light, a fact that was proven by an increased number of wrecks. As a result, in 1820 the Federal Government initiated plans for two new towers and temporarily reestablished the twin lights. Completed in 1821, the two granite stone and concrete towers apparently were the models for the construction, six years later, of Matinicus Rock's two light towers. The Baker's Island towers, however, were not "twins," since one was taller than the other. For the two lights to show a dual signal (equal focal plane elevations above the water), one of the towers had to be shortened to compensate for the construction site's sloping terrain. Because of their size differences the structures became known locally as the "Mr. and Mrs." lighthouses.

The smaller lighthouse was discontinued on June 30, 1926, and subsequently torn down. The main light station consists of the larger 59-foot tall lighthouse, two Victorian wood framed keepers' residences (1878), a brick oil house (1855) and a fog signal building (1907). Baker's Island's first optic was a Lewis multi-lamp and reflector device. It was reequipped with a fourth-order Fresnel lens in 1855. In 1916 the classical lens was replaced by a single acetylene-powered lamp. The lantern now houses an electrified modern rotating optic with alternating red and white bullseyes. It was automated in 1972.

OWNER. U.S. Coast Guard (lighthouse and fog signal building). Grounds and oil house leased to the Baker's Island Association.

PRESERVATION. Listed in the National Register of Historic Places.

In 1993 the Coast Guard repaired the roof to the generator building and repainted the lantern. In 1996 the Coast Guard contracted for the complete overhaul of the tower's deteriorating walls. Contractor Martin Nally and crew replaced granite blocks that had fallen to the ground, repointed the exterior masonry and applied a protective coat of stucco. They also restored some of the cast iron and removed all lead paint from the structure. The job cost $250,000.

TEN POUND ISLAND

TO GLOUCESTER. Four recommended stops in Gloucester: (1) Pavilion Beach Park, (2) the Cape Ann Historical Museum, (3) Harbor Loop and (4) Rose's Wharf.

Pavilion Beach Park is on MA 127 (Main Street) just east of the Annisquam River drawbridge and about 1.0 mile west of the Washington and Commercial intersection. On-street parking is permitted and free on Main along the park. Eastern Point Lighthouse, located farther out at the harbor's entrance, can be seen to the right of Ten Pound Island. To the right of Eastern Point is the Gloucester Breakwater beacon.

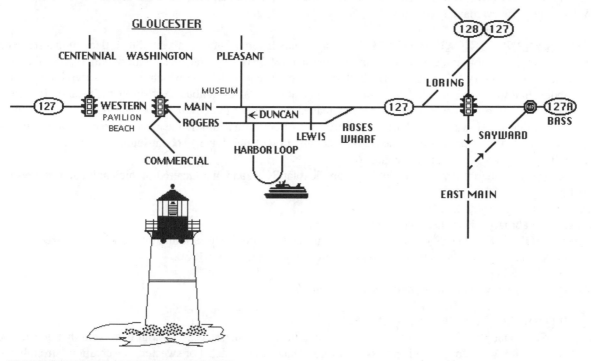

TEN POUND ISLAND LIGHTHOUSE
CHARACTERISTIC: Equal interval 6s
HAW: 57'   **RANGE**: 5 nm

In 1820 the Commonwealth of Massachusetts and the Town of Gloucester ceded approximately 1.7 island acres to the U.S. Government for the erection of an inner harbor lighthouse. By 1821 a 40-foot stone tower, a covered passageway, a wood framed house, a stone and slate oil house and a storage shed had been built. Cost: $24,200. The stone tower was replaced by the present cast-iron structure in 1881. The brick-lined tower is 30 feet tall. A decorative touch not usually seen on other light towers is the presence of acanthus leaves and flutes surrounding the ventilator hole. The cast-iron service gallery is supported by curved, triangular cast-iron brackets; its balustrade shows the characteristic Italianate influence.

When the light was discontinued in 1956, the keeper's dwelling and oil house were in ruins with only their foundations and portions of the walls standing. A fishery, first established on the southwest end of the island in 1887 and abandoned in 1954, had also been reduced to ruins.

n 1925 a Coast Guard air station was put on the island, with one small scout plane. Later two amphibious vehicles were added to the station. The initial purpose of the operation was to catch rum runners in the area during Prohibition.

When the lighthouse was taken out of service in 1956, the fifth-order classical lens was removed and its warning responsiblity transferred to a modern lens atop the station's conical bell tower. In 1966 the beacon, a 375 mm lens, was transferred to a skeletal steel tower. In 1976 a newer plastic 250 mm condensing lens, lamp changer and flasher were introduced. That optic is now active in the restored lighthouse.

OWNER. City of Gloucester. Beacon is maintained by the U.S. Coast Guard.

PRESERVATION. In 1988 the Lighthouse Preservation Society, seeking federal funds for the tower, requested the Massachusetts Historical Commission to nominate the station for entry in the National Register of Historic Places, which the commission did that same year. Consequently the Society, on behalf of the City of Gloucester, matched a $17,000 federal grant from the Lighthouse Bicentennial Fund with a grant from the Bank of New England. That financial support enabled the city to make sufficient repairs to the tower. With the Coast Guard's help, the lighthouse was relighted on August 7, 1989.

In 1995 the Lighthouse Preservation Society again matched leftover Lighthouse Bicentennial Funds to restore, at a cost of $11,000, one of America's older oil houses. It was built in 1821. Commemorative plaques have been placed on the island and in Pavilion Park.

For further information about the lighthouse contact:

- The Lighthouse Preservation Society, 4 Middle Street, Suite 226/225, Newburyport, MA 01950.

Phone: (978) 499-0011. In USA toll-free (800) 727-BEAM (2326). Fax (978) 499-0026.

Website: http://www.mayday.com/lps/

CAPE ANN HISTORICAL MUSEUM. The Cape Ann Historical Museum's exhibits reflect Gloucester's role in the fishing industry, maritime trade and the arts. "Gloucester 1892" is a special focus gallery which gives the visitor a unique look at a 19th century fishing port. The gallery's centerpiece is a diorama which includes surviving building and schooner models that were exhibited in Gloucester's pavilion at the 1892 Columbus Exposition in Chicago. Eastern Point Lighthouse's old fourth-order Fresnel lens is also displayed, as well as the *Great Republic*, a Gloucester sloop which legendary Gloucesterman Howard Blackburn sailed across the Atlantic. In addition, the museum boasts a wonderful collection of paintings including a number by famed Gloucester artist Fitz Hugh Lane. The museum's research library includes approximately 2,500 titles supporting the collections.

Parking is available in the museum's lot (free) on Pleasant Street and in a metered municipal lot across the street.

OPEN.

Tuesdays through Saturdays 10 to 5.

Closed all February and on national holidays.

ADMISSION FEES. Discounts for seniors, students and children. Museum members and under 6 free.

- Cape Ann Historical Association, 27 Pleasant Street, Gloucester, MA 01930.

Phone (978) 283-0455.

Website: http://www.cape-ann.com/historical-museum/

LIGHTHOUSE SIGHTSEEING CRUISE.

Captain Steve Douglas' Cape Ann Lighthouse Cruise aboard is a narrated 2 1/2-hour excursion that departs from a wharf on Harbor Loop. Wear comfortable non-skid shoes and take along a jacket or sweater. Reservations strongly recommended.

The itinerary and lighthouse sightings:

1. Through Gloucester's inner harbor and Ten Pound Island Light.
2. Up the Annisquam River into Ipswich Bay and Annisquam Harbor Light.
3. Around Halibut Point to Rockport and Straitsmouth Island Light.
4. South past Thacher Island Twin Lights.
5. Around Eastern Point Light and Gloucester Breakwater Light.

SCHEDULE. Call ahead to confirm cruise is on schedule. June, weekends only at 2:30.

July through Labor Day, daily at 2:30.

FARES. Discounts for seniors 60+ and children 12 and under.

- Harbor Tours, Inc., PO Box 345 (19 Harbor Loop), Gloucester, MA 01930.

Phone: (978) 283-1979.

Another way to see Ten Pound Island Light is the popular Moby Duck amphibious sightseeing tour. Ticket sales and boarding at the "Duck Stop" on the Harbor Loop, on Rogers Street in Downtown Gloucester. The tour passes many attractions on land and water including the famed Gloucester Fisherman statue and the schooner *Adventure*.

- Moby Duck amphibious sightseeing tour.

Phone: (978) 281-DUCK (3825).

Website: http://www.salemweb.com/biz/mobyduck/gloucester.htm

Other sightseeing cruises and whale watches in Gloucester may pass Ten Pound Island; contact the Chamber of Commerce, 33 Commercial Street, Gloucester, MA 01930. Phone: (800) 321-0133 or (978) 283-1601.

Website: http://www.cape-ann.com/cacc/   Email: cacc@shore.net

Ten Pound Island Lighthouse

Eastern Point Lighthouse

EASTERN POINT

NORTH ON MA 127A. See the map of Gloucester on page 301. Follow East Main Street and Eastern Point Road to Eastern Point's eastern extension into Farrington Avenue.

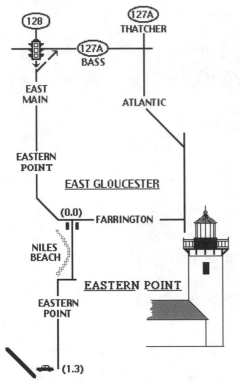

SOUTH ON MA 127A. South of Good Harbor Beach where MA 127A (Thatcher Road) turns right into Bass Avenue, drive straight ahead into Atlantic Road. Follow Atlantic south and Farrington west to Eastern Point Boulevard (West).

TO EASTERN POINT. Eastern Point Boulevard (West) is the main thorofare to the lighthouse. The entrance is marked by two pillars.

Although Eastern Point Boulevard (West) traverses an exclusive residential neighborhood with posted "Residents Only" and privacy signs, the road is a public right-of-way. Should a guard, sometimes posted at the entrance, halt your progress, inform him that you only want to view and photograph the lighthouse. According to Gloucester's town clerk, the guard is not authorized to prevent persons wishing to view the lighthouse, but you must drive directly to and from the light station.

The station is used for Coast Guard housing and, although the gate may be open, entry is prohibited. There is an excellent view of the lighthouse from outside the entrance gate and from the granite breakwater.

The Eastern Point Lighthouse stands on a rocky promontory at the east side entrance to Gloucester Harbor. Its light marks Dog Bar Reef (Bar), a troublesome shoal at the entrance to Gloucester Harbor. Look towards downtown Gloucester and you will see the Ten Pound Island Lighthouse.

At the end of the nearby 2,250-foot breakwater, a $300,000 project that took eight years (1894-1904) to complete, is the Gloucester Breakwater light, a beacon (occulting red) that rests atop a tower that surmounts a small white building. The keeper of Eastern Point Light also had the duty of keeping this light, a dangerous task when ice covered the stone breakwater. Today the breakwater is a favorite spot for walking and fishing. The automatic sensor that activates the electronic fog signal was recently moved to the end of the breakwater.

The Cape Ann Lighthouse Cruise offered by Harbor Tours, Inc., of Gloucester, offers views of Eastern Point Light; see page 302 for details. Occasional cruises offered by the Friends of the Boston Harbor Islands and the Boston Harbor Explorers may also offer views; see page 292 for details. Also see page 306 for information on lighthouse cruises offered by the Thacher Island Association of Rockport.

EASTERN POINT LIGHTHOUSE.
CHARACTERISTIC: Flashing white 5s
HAW: 57' **RANGE**: 24 nm

Before the first lighthouse at Eastern Point, a grove of oak trees served as a landmark. In 1829 the Federal Government purchased one acre of land on Eastern Point and a two-mile road easement around the cove to the site, and a day marker was placed at Eastern Point. The first stone lighthouse was completed three years later. Its fixed white light emanated from 10 whale oil lamps with 12-inch parabolic reflectors. The old structure was torn down after a second 34-foot tall tower was completed in 1848.

In 1890 the present Federal Design-styled lighthouse was erected on the 1832 tower's foundation. It is 36 feet tall, cylindrical in shape, constructed of brick and painted white. There is but one ornamental touch to an otherwise plain tower and that is a decorative masonry corbel upon which rests the service gallery's triangular support brackets. A 40-step cast-iron staircase circles the interior to the watchroom.

In 1886 the Lighthouse Board reported an operating bullseye fourth-order Fresnel lens, manufactured by the Parisian firm of Barrier, Bernard and Turene. That lens was removed in 1946. The octagonal lantern now holds a rotating aerobeacon lens installed in 1919. In 1986 the beacon was automated and the keepers removed.

In addition to the tower and the red and white checkerboard walkway (painted to serve as a daymark) the station consists of the following structures.

EASTERN POINT

1879.   Two-story, wood framed keeper's duplex architecturally classified as a variation on both the typical Gothic Revival and Queen Anne styles.

1894.   Brick oil house.

1947.   One-story, wooden building that is now used as a garage. The garage stands on the site of the former assistant keeper's house (1908) that was sold to a private party and moved off station.

1951.   Fog signal building.

OWNER. U.S. Coast Guard.

PRESERVATION. Listed in the National Register of Historic Places.

In 1991 the Coast Guard, short of manpower and unable get Congress to appropriate the estimated $500,000 required to upgrade the light station, announced that Eastern Point was for sale or lease. The Lighthouse Preservation Society became engaged in negotiations with the Coast Guard, state officials and even members of Congress to acquire the light station, renovate the keeper's house and light tower and turn them into a museum. In 1994, however, after the Society spent almost three years creating a feasibility study, developing a museum plan, gathering community support and raising over $100,000 in dedicated funds, the Coast Guard decided that it would keep the station for housing purposes. Two Coast Guard families currently reside at the station.

The twin towers of Thacher Island

CAPE ANN (THACHER ISLAND TWIN LIGHTS)

NORTH OR SOUTH ON MA 127A. If northbound, Penzance Road is about 1.6 miles north of an "Entering Rockport" sign (on the left). Enroute look for the towers as MA 127A skirts along the top of the cliffs.

If southbound, Penzance Road is 1.1 miles south of Rockport's Marmion Way.

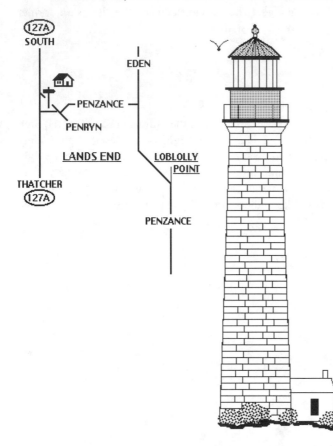

CONTINUE ON. The turn into Penzance (start 0.0 mile) is marked with a "South Street - Thatcher Road" sign in the triangle. A motor inn is located on the northeast corner.

A short distance from MA 127A (no more than 0.1 mile), Penzance Road turns left. Its eastward extension is Penryn Lane. Follow Penzance to a T-head intersection (0.3 mile) and turn left into Eden Road, a shore road that may be a bit rough due to storm damage, but passable with caution. The first good viewing spot on Eden is at a roadside boulder about 0.1 mile from Penzance. There offshore stand the majestic Twin Towers of Thacher Island. What a view!

THACHER ISLAND ASSOCIATION LIGHT-HOUSE CRUISE

The Thacher Island Association runs lighthouse cruises once or twice yearly. The cruises usually circumnavigate Cape Ann, offering views of the Thacher Island, Straitsmouth Island, Eastern Point, Ten Pound Island and Annisquam Lighthouses. Call or write for more information.

- Thacher Island Association, PO Box 36, Rockport, MA 01966.

Phone (978) 546-7697.

Website: http://www1.shore.net/~gfisher/tia/

In addition, the Cape Ann Lighthouse Cruise offered by Harbor Tours, Inc., of Gloucester, offers views of Thacher Island; see page 302 for details. Occasional cruises offered by the Friends of the Boston Harbor Islands and the Boston Harbor Explorers may also offer views; see page 292 for details.

CAPE ANN LIGHT STATION (TWIN LIGHTS; ANN'S EYES).

THACHER ISLAND SOUTH LIGHTHOUSE
CHARACTERISTIC: Flashing red 5s
HAW: 166' **RANGE**: 19 nm

THACHER ISLAND NORTH LIGHTHOUSE.
CHARACTERISTIC: Fixed yellow

In 1771 the Massachusetts Bay Colony authorized and built the twin granite stone lighthouses on Thacher (Thatcher) Island, a 52-acre pile of rocks with little soil or vegetation. The lights were established on December 21, 1771.

The first lightkeeper, a Tory, was removed and the lights extinguished during the early days of the American Revolution. In 1790 the 45-foot tall towers, some 298 yards apart, were turned over to the fledgling Federal Government. The Cape Ann towers were one of eight sets of twin or dual Atlantic Coast lighthouses built between 1768 and 1839, namely, Baker's Island, Cape Elizabeth, Chatham, Highlands, Matinicus Rock, Newburyport Harbor and Plymouth.

CAPE ANN

During 1860-61, both light towers were rebuilt with granite stone to raise their overall heights to 124 feet. A small entry house was attached to each tower. Small windows were added to provide light for the climb up the circular stairway. There are two service galleries. One circles the watchroom; the other the lantern.

One touching episode concerns the wife of a Cape Ann keeper who, close to Christmas in 1864, while her husband was on the mainland, kept the lamps burning during a nasty New England storm. Maria Bray braved fierce winds and snow to tend both lights during her husband's absence. This was one small, but laudatory example of the dedication prevalent among the wives and daughters of America's lightkeepers. The U.S. Coast Guard launched a new 157-foot Coast Guard Cutter, the *Maria Bray,* on August 28, 1998, in recognition of her valiant actions.

The two 1860-61 towers were originally equipped with fixed first-order Fresnel optics. They have since been removed; a first-order lens from the station is now on display at the U.S. Coast Guard Academy Museum in New London, Connecticut. In 1932, after a submarine cable was laid from the mainland, the north light was discontinued. The south tower was then equipped with a 250-watt incandescent lamp and an electronic flasher that produced a group of five white flashes every 20 seconds. The station also received an emergency five-kilowatt generator. Since then, the optic's characteristic has been changed to a flashing red light.

OWNER. The Town of Rockport's Thacher Island Committee in partnership with the Thacher Island Association now maintains and operates the island. The U.S. Fish and Wildlife Service owns the northern section of the island.

PRESERVATION. Listed in the National Register of Historic Places as part of the Twin Lights Historic District. The Thacher Island Association submitted an application for National Historic Landmark status in September 1999.

In 1983 the Thacher Island Association was formed as a nonprofit organization to support and encourage historic preservation and restoration of the structures on the Island. The association financed the design and construction of a custom made aluminum mini-landing craft to provide access to the island. In 1988 $75,000 from a $2 million state grant raised by the Lighthouse Preservation Society was used to restore the north tower. The U.S. Fish & Wildlife Service handled the contract and was responsible for the completion of the task. The base-to-roof refurbishing involved the complete restoration of the entry house (a mere shell when work started), filling granite cracks with epoxy, repointing the tower's granite exterior and installing new handrails on both service balconies. Interior work included the filling of stress cracks, repointing the coursed brick lining, cleaning the cast-iron staircase and all other interior ironwork and patching holes in the lantern's roof.

In 1989 the north light was restored and opened to visitors, offering a panoramic view of the area. The north light has since been relighted as a private aid to navigation. Its amber light once again makes Thacher Island the only operating twin light station in the United States. The fluorescent light in the north tower shines 24 hours a day. The south light is now solar powered and is maintained by the Coast Guard.

For several years the Thacher Island Association ran a boat to the island from T Wharf in Rockport, and rooms in the keeper's house were made available to overnight visitors. In the harsh winter of 1995, the boat ramp was washed out, making landing at the island difficult. The north tower was still checked frequently by former caretakers George and Dorothy Carroll of the Thacher Island Association. How? By rowing an inflated rubber raft to the island and taking their chances on having a decent landing ashore.

In 1998 United States Representative John F. Tierney secured $250,000 for a new boat ramp as part of a spending bill passed by Congress. This funding, combined with money raised by the Thacher Island Asociation and the Rockport Town Committee's revenue sharing funds, meant that a new ramp could be rebuilt. Work on the 120-foot ramp was completed in the fall of 2000. Caretakers were again living on the island for the summer of 2001.

On January 3, 2001, Interior Secretary Bruce Babbitt designated Cape Ann Light Station on Thacher Island a National Historic Landmark, making it the ninth lighthouse station, and one of less than 2,500 sites nationwide, to receive this designation.

The Rockport Board of Selectmen accepted the southern end of the island from the Coast Guard officially on July 24, 2001. The Town of Rockport now owns about 28 acres, including the south tower, two keepers' houses, the boathouse and ramp, cistern, utility house, oil house, and fog signal house. The Town has taken over responsibility for the maintenance of the south tower as well as the continued maintenance of the north tower.

- Thacher Island Association, P.O. Box 73, Rockport, MA 01966
Website: www.thacherisland.org

STRAITSMOUTH

NORTH ON MA 127A. Enter Rockport center and continue straight ahead to Bearskin Neck. The lighthouse is located at the entrance to Rockport Harbor. It can be seen from along Black Beach and from the end of Bearskin Neck, a narrow, pedestrian filled thoroughfare lined with shops.

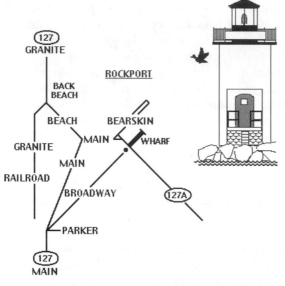

SOUTH ON MA 127. There are two routes to Bearskin Neck:

1. Granite -> Railroad -> Broadway -> Mt. Pleasant.

2. Beach -> Main (one-way south) -> Broadway -> Mt. Pleasant.

Finding a parking space during the summer months can be a frustrating experience. Your options:

1. Find an on-street parking space perhaps blocks away and walk to and out on Bearskin Neck.

2. Drive carefully (slowly is the only pace possible) out to Bearskin Neck's small turnaround and hope there is a empty space in the small parking area that contains one free handicapped and ten metered (two-hour limit) spaces.

3. Try to capture a space on Rockport's Town Wharf, where public metered parking is available only on the right (south) side of the wharf with one free handicapped space at the foot (west end) of the pier.

4. Rockport can be reached by commuter rail from Boston. The Newburyport/Rockport Commuter Line (train) runs from Boston's North Station. For information phone (617) 222-3200. Website: http://www.mbta.com/

Straitsmouth Island Lighthouse can also be seen from the lighthouse cruises offered by the Thacher Island Association (see page 306) and by Harbor Tours, Inc. in Gloucester (see page 302).

STRAITSMOUTH LIGHTHOUSE (STRAITSMOUTH ISLAND).
CHARACTERISTIC: Flashing green 6s
HAW: 46' **RANGE**: 6 nm

Rockport's vital granite business began in the 1820s, joining the fishing industry to put the town on the map. A 19-foot brick lighthouse tower, along with a brick keeper's dwelling, was built on Straitsmouth Island in 1835 to help guide mariners into the harbor at nearby Pigeon Cove.

Several vessels were lost in storms in the 1830s and '40s in the vicinity of Straitsmouth Island, and a severe gale in October 1844 destroyed practically every boat at Pigeon Cove. As an added safety measure a warning buoy was placed near Avery's Rock, not far from Straitsmouth Island.

A new 1 1/2 story Gothic Revival-styled, wood framed keeper's house was built in 1878. The present 37-foot brick tower replaced the old one in 1896. The cylindrical tower's 8-foot tall base consists of five rows of coursed granite blocks.

When first established the tower held a multi-lamp and reflector optic. Sometime in the 1850s the Lewis device was replaced with a Fresnel lens. In 1932 the light was converted from white to green. In 1967 the Fresnel gave way to a modern plastic lens with an electric flasher. The optic was converted to solar power in 1985 (note panel in sketch).

OWNER. U.S. Coast Guard (lighthouse). In 1941 the island and light station, less light tower, were sold to a private party for $3,050. In the 1960s, the Massachusetts Audubon Society acquired the island, the 1 1/2-story keeper's residence and oil house. The island became part of the Ipswich River Wildlife Sanctuary.

PRESERVATION. Listed in the National Register of Historic Places.

The tower was painted and new windows and a door were installed in 1982. The "No-Name" storm of October 1991 destroyed the old entryway to the tower. It was replaced in 1992 with the entry shown in the accompanying sketch.

The keeper's house still stands but is currently boarded up and in disrepair. At this writing in July 2001, there are plans underway for Rockport officials to visit Straitsmouth Island for an inspection of the house. Where this will lead is far from certain, but hopefully something positive will result. There has also been a plan introduced by the Lighthouse Preservation Society to move the house to the city of Newburyport, but that plan was not well received by the Rockport Selectmen.

ANNISQUAM HARBOR

<u>**NORTH OR SOUTH ON MA 127.**</u> The turn off MA 127 (Washington Street) into Lane Road is possibly marked by the presence of a white church on the southwest corner and a "Leonard" sign posted on a telephone pole on the northwest corner.

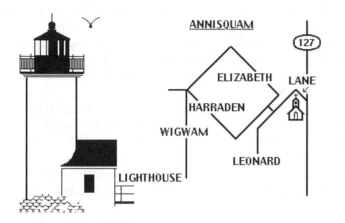

If traveling on MA 127 from Rockport, Lane Road is about 1.0 mile from Plum Beach Cove Beach (look for a large park sign on the right). If entering Annisquam via MA 128/127, Lane Road is 3.0 miles north of Grant Circle. Lane Road, a very short distance from MA 127, runs into Dennis Court and at that juncture meets Leonard Street (start 0.0 mile). Then:

    -> Right into Elizabeth Road at a "Norwood Heights" sign (0.3 mile),

    -> Just after entering the residential area Elizabeth Road turns right (one way),

    -> Circle across Ocean Avenue to its connection with Harraden Circle,

-> Right towards the harbor (0.5 mile),

-> A short distance past the Elizabeth & Harraden intersection, turn left off Elizabeth into Wigwam Road,

-> Follow Wigwam to its right turn connection with Lighthouse Road (0.6 mile). The lighthouse is at the end of Lighthouse Road (0.7 mile).

The old keeper's dwelling serves as the residence of a Coast Guard family. Please do not disturb the occupants. There are limited, short term visitors' parking spaces at the station, but the lighthouse is close enough to Lighthouse Road to be adequately viewed and photographed. For fantastic views of the lighthouse take the lighthouse cruise out of Gloucester (see page 302) or visit Wingaersheek Beach (see below). Occasional lighthouse cruises offered by the Thacher Island Association also provide views of Annisquam Harbor Light; see page 306.

ANNISQUAM HARBOR LIGHTHOUSE.
CHARACTERISTIC: Flashing white 7.5s (red sector)
HAW: 45' **RANGES**: White 14; red 11 nm

In 1800 Congress authorized the construction of a lighthouse on Wigwam Point (named because it was a gathering place for local Native Americans). The Commonwealth of Massachusetts ceded the station's 6.5 acres for $140. A wooden tower and the present wood framed keeper's dwelling were erected in 1801. The walkway was added in 1814. By the 1820s the tower was so weakened by dry rot that it had to be propped up with long poles. It was completely rebuilt in 1851.

The second wooden tower was 40 feet tall, octagonal in shape, but the range of the light was only four nautical miles. In 1856 the height of the tower was lowered and a fifth-order Fresnel lens installed. The lens was rotated by a clockwork powered by descending weights.

The present 41-foot tall brick tower and the existing brick oil house were built in 1897. The lighthouse is architecturally classified as belonging to the Federal Design genre. The cylindrical tower's walls are four feet thick. Inside, 33 iron steps ascend along the wall. At the top of the stairway is a half deck that holds the watchroom. A cast-iron ladder extends upward into the octagonal cast-iron lantern. Two blackened storm panes mask the light on the Annisquam side of the lantern. The service gallery is supported by a corbel of coursed brick.

In 1919 the kerosene-powered fifth-order Fresnel optic was reported to have a range of eight nautical miles. In 1922 the older lens was removed and an electrified fourth-order classical lens installed.

To illustrate the efficacy of the larger Fresnel lens, the optic's first light source was an ordinary 100-watt bulb that had a luminous intensity rating of 1,300 candlepower. In 1965 the lens was fitted with a 1,000-watt bulb that increased the intensity of its flashing white light to 250,000 candlepower.

The beacon was fully automated in 1974. A controversy erupted that year when the Coast Guard removed the fog signal. Local boaters and fishermen complained, and one collected thousands of signatures on a petition to save the fog signal. In response to the pressure the signal was reinstalled. In 1975 a switch to activate the fog signal was installed at the local police station. Today the electronic fog signal is automated, activated by a sensor.

    OWNER. U.S. Coast Guard.

PRESERVATION. Listed in the National Register of Historic Places.

Over the years, the light station has been well maintained. A protective seawall was built before 1900. A fog signal added in 1965 on the seawall on the north side of the 1 1/2-story, shingled wood framed keeper's dwelling was moved in 1993. The original storm-damaged walkway was replaced in 1978. In 1985 the tower was repaired, repointed and re-painted. In 1993 the tower underwent minor repairs and the keeper's house (renovated in 1980) received new storm windows.

In the late 1990s it was found that iron beams in the tower, installed to support a landing below the lantern level, had badly rusted and deteriorated, causing the upper part of the tower to lift more than three inches. Daylight could actually be seen from inside the tower through the resulting crack. It was decided that the beams needed to be replaced, along with about five to six feet of brickwork all the way around the tower.

Coast Guard architect Marsha Levy, from Civil Engineering Unit Providence, did the design work for the restoration of the lighthouse. Campbell Construction Group of Beverly, Massachusetts, was the contractor. The company has restored more lighthouses than anyone in New England. According to Marty Nally, mason and vice president of Campbell Construction Group, the lighthouse was very well built by the original masons. They couldn't have foreseen the problem with the rusting beams, he says, and they didn't have the advantage of today's rust resistant metals. Nally and his crew removed and replaced about 3,000 bricks in the tower during the restoration. They also removed the old glass block windows and replaced them with new ones.

As part of the restoration project, the dwelling's roof was replaced, using durable, wind resistant shingles. Some windows were replaced and the dwelling was painted as well.

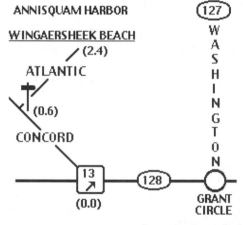

WINGAERSHEEK BEACH There is an excellent frontal view of the lighthouse from across the mouth of the Annisquam River on this beach, a recreational area for Gloucester residents. Between Memorial Day weekend and Labor Day non-residents may use the beach after paying a parking fee. There is no parking fee in the offseason. At low tide it's possible to walk a good part of the way toward Annisquam Harbor Light.

Annisquam Harbor Lighthouse

NEWBURYPORT HARBOR (PLUM ISLAND)

This lighthouse is located within the headquarters compound of the Parker River National Wildlife Refuge on the northern end of Plum Island. It is reached via the Plum Island Turnpike and the island's Northern Boulevard. Entry and parking are free.

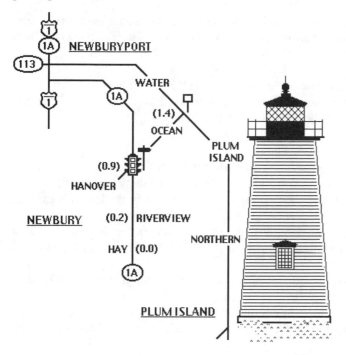

NORTH ON MA 1A. About 2.7 miles north of the Parker River bridge and 0.7 mile north of Riverview Drive (on the right) you will come to Newbury's first traffic signal. Then:

-> Right at Ocean Avenue marked with a (possibly partially hidden in foliage) "Plum Island" sign on the southeast corner,

-> Right at Plum Island Turnpike marked with a "Plum Island - Parker River Refuge" sign.

-> Left on Northern Boulevard (second left after crossing the bridge to Plum Island); continue to the lighthouse.

SOUTH FROM NEWBURYPORT. Follow Water Street into connecting Plum Island Turnpike. Left on Northern Boulevard (second left after crossing the bridge to Plum Island); continue to the lighthouse.

FRIENDS OF PLUM ISLAND LIGHT CRUISES
The Friends of Plum Island Light offer occasional lighthouse cruises from Plum Island.

In recent years these cruises have gone as far south as Boston Harbor and as far north as Maine's Cape Neddick Lighthouse. Contact the group for the latest cruise schedule.
- The Friends of Plum Island Light, Inc., PO Box 381, Newburyport, MA 01950.

NEWBURYPORT HARBOR LIGHTHOUSE (PLUM ISLAND).
CHARACTERISTIC: Group occulting green 15s
HAW: 50' **RANGE**: 10 nm
Newburyport, on the Merrimack River, was an important port by the late 18th century, but the entrance to the harbor was dangerous with shifting channels at the mouth of the river near the northern end of Plum Island. To aid shipping entering the river, local mariners at first built fires on the beach and erected poles holding torches. This proved inadequate, and the General Court of Massachusetts authorized the building of "two small wooden lighthouses on the north end of Plumb Island" in 1787. They were finished the following year.

The original two towers were built on movable foundations so their positions could be changed easily as the sand bars around Plum Island shifted. The two towers served as range lights; mariners knew if they lined up the lights that they were following the best channel into the harbor. A signal tower was also erected, used by the lightkeeper to signal with flags that a pilot was needed or a vessel was in trouble. A cannon was placed at the station to help the keeper summon aid in an emergency. Keepers at Plum Island frequently were involved in the rescue of shipwreck victims.

The building of the lighthouses was paid for by local merchants. In 1790 they were ceded to the federal government.

In 1838 the lighthouses were replaced by a new pair of octagonal towers, again built on moveable foundations.

In 1855 a strange looking small tower called the "Bug Light" was added, and the following year one of the lighthouses was destroyed by fire. It was decided not to rebuild, and the surviving lighthouse received a fourth order Fresnel lens. The shifting sands left the remaining tower and the "Bug" too far inland; they were moved several times between 1870 and 1882. In 1898 a new 45-foot wooden tower was built next to the old one. The lens was transferred to the new lighthouse. The present Plum Island Lighthouse was first lighted on September 20, 1898.

The wood framed and shingled tower has a wooden staircase with 30 steps. A polished hand-carved railing ascends the wall to the watch room. A ladder must be climbed to reach the octagonal cast-iron lantern.

Note the unusual and historic glass treatment in the 45-foot tall lighthouse's curved triangular and diamond-shaped storm panes. Several of the lighthouse's panes can be seen in the Shore Village Lighthouse Museum in Rockland, Maine.

The two-story Victorian keeper's house (1898) now serves as a headquarters building for the Parker River National Wildlife Refuge.

The beacon was automated in 1951. In 1981 a microwave system (relay disc and camera) was attached to the lantern, which allowed Coast Guard Merrimack River Station to monitor maritime activity in the channel. That equipment has been removed. The 1856 fourth-order Fresnel lens remains in place.

OWNER. The Coast Guard retains custody of the lighthouse and the surrounding 0.3 acre of land.

In 1951 the U.S. Coast Guard transferred the keeper's residence, oil house, garage and 2.2+ acres to the U.S. Fish & Wildlife Service. In 1996 the Coast Guard leased the lighthouse to the Friends of Plum Island Light.

PRESERVATION. Listed in the National Register of Historic Places.

In 1990 this historic structure received some much needed restorative care when the tower's walls were repaired and painted and a new ventilator ball added. In 1992-93, the Coast Guard did a superb job in refurbishing the tower's interior, hinging the main entrance with an authentically crafted oak door and setting new glass panes in the lantern's existing diamond-shaped frames.

In 1994 the Friends of Plum Island Light was formed to prepare for the eventual leasing of the light station. That event occurred in 1996. The Friends of Plum Island Light reshingled the tower in 1997. In 1999 they replaced the tower's windows, and they are planning to restore the tower's interior.

On August 1, 1998, the Friends of Plum Island Light celebrated the lighthouse's 100th birthday. About 1,000 people attended the festivities, which included live music and lighthouse tours.

The Friends of Plum Island Light are selling commemorative bricks that are being incorporated into the landscape design as a walkway in front of the lighthouse. Bricks are now available for $50.00 each; funds will be used for the continued restoration and upkeep of the station.

The lighthouse is sometimes open to the public on summer weekends.

- The Friends of Plum Island Light, Inc., PO Box 381, Newburyport, MA 01950.

Newburyport Harbor (Plum Island) Lighthouse

NEWBURYPORT HARBOR RANGE

TO NEWBURYPORT. Three main routes lead into Newburyport center:

1. North from Plum Island via Water Street.
2. East from I-95 on MA 133.
3. South from New Hampshire on US 1/NH 1A. The range rear light tower is located on Water between Fair and Fruit Streets. The range front tower stands inside the Coast Guard Merrimack River Station located off Water between Federal and Tremont Streets.

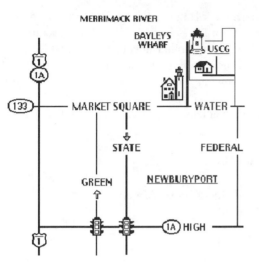

Visitors to the station are required to report their presence to the station's duty officer, located inside the headquarters' front entrance. Free parking is available behind the headquarters building. If the station is closed, the range front tower can be viewed from the street behind the range rear lighthouse.

NEWBURYPORT HARBOR TOUR

One of the best ways to see the Newburyport Harbor Range Lights, and to learn about Newburyport's history, is to take a harbor cruise with Captain Bill Taplin aboard his vessel *Yankee Clipper*. The cruises leave from the boardwalk along the city's Waterfront Park.

SCHEDULE Hourly departures from 11:00 to 6:00 in season (spring to fall). Cruises are approximately 45 minutes. There is also a daily 1 1/2 hour sunset cruise in the summer.

FEES Discounts for children.

- Yankee Clipper, Captain Bill Taplin, 1 Merrimac Landing #26, Newburyport, MA 01950

Phone (978) 462-9316

Website: http://www.harbortours.com/

Email: captbill@harbortours.com

NEWBURYPORT HARBOR FRONT RANGE.

In the 18th and 19th centuries Newburyport, which is about two miles from the mouth of the Merrimack River, was a center for shipbuilding and maritime trade. In 1873 the original owner of old Bayley's Wharf sold two parcels of land to the U.S. Government for the purpose of establishing two range lights to help mariners entering Newburyport Harbor from the Merrimack. The towers were built that same year. There may have been some form of privately maintained range lights in the vicinity as far back as 1790.

The front range light tower was constructed on Bayley's wharf about 350 feet forward of the present location of the rear range tower. The cylindrical 15-foot tower is constructed of cast-iron plates and is lined with coursed brick. The Front Range Light was altered in the 1950s. A 20-foot shingled wooden lantern was installed on top of the 15-foot cast-iron tower, making it similar in appearance to the Doubling Point Range Lights on the Kennebec River in Maine. Three years after the beacon was discontinued (1961), the tower was moved from Bayley's Wharf to its present location within the Coast Guard station. In 1990 it was changed back to a more traditional appearance with an iron lantern room.

PRESERVATION. Listed in the National Register of Historic Places. The Lighthouse Preservation Society, based in Newburyport, has been working for the restoration of the tower under an agreement with the Coast Guard.

- Lighthouse Preservation Society, 4 Middle Street, Newburyport, MA 01950.

Phone: (508) 499-0011 or toll-free (800) 727-BEAM.

NEWBURYPORT HARBOR REAR RANGE.

This tower is a square one with a slight tapering from base to its midsection. It is constructed of brick, cast iron and wood. The 53-foot tall structure has a spiral cast-iron staircase that ascends every six steps to a small landing. There is no watchroom. The octagonal lantern's frame, deck and roof are all made of cast iron. Four of its storm panes have been blackened; the other four facing the river are clear. The lantern has a square cast-iron service balcony. This beacon was discontinued in 1961 and sold to the owner of the Range Lights Marina, located on the former Bayley's Wharf.

PRESERVATION. Listed in the National Register of Historic Places. In 1999 the Lighthouse Preservation Society, based in Newburyport, initiated the restoration of the Newburyport Harbor Range Lights. The group hopes to raise $65,000 to renovate the front range light, while developer David Hall plans to spend $20,000 to $25,000 to renovate the rear range tower, which he owns. Both towers will have exterior renovations; the rear range light will have its masonry repointed and its lantern painted black. The front range light will have extensive work done on the interior. It is hoped that both light-houses will eventually be opened to the public on a limited basis.

- The Lighthouse Preservation Society , 4 Middle Street, Newburyport, MA 01950.
Phone: (978) 499-0011 or (800) 727-BEAM.   Fax: (978) 499-0026
Website: http://www.mayday.com/lps/

CUSTOM HOUSE MARITIME MUSEUM. The Newburyport Marine Society's museum is located at 25 Water Street just west of Federal Street. It contains exhibitions depicting Newburyport's 300-year history as a major shipbuilding community and seaport.

There are excellent displays commemorating the Society's and the Merrimack Humane Society's efforts to aid victims of shipwrecks, including a model of the shelter huts placed on Plum Island from 1787 into the 1800s. The museum also honors the U.S. Coast Guard with historical accounts, such as the George Washington - John Hancock meeting on October 24, 1789 in Newburyport that resulted in the building of America's first revenue cutter and the accomplishments of the Revenue Marine, taproot of our Coast Guard establishment. There is also an interesting 15-minute audiovisual presentation on the history of Newburyport.

Of particular interest to lighthouse buffs is the museum's fourth-order Fresnel lens, last active in the Pomham Rocks Lighthouse located in the Providence River in Rhode Island.

OPEN.
April to mid-December, Mondays through Saturdays 10 to 4. Sundays 1 to 4.
Closed December 25 to March.
ADMISSION FEES. Discounts for groups, seniors 59+, children 7 and older. Under 7 free.
- Custom House Maritime Museum, PO Box 306, Newburyport, MA 01950.
Phone (978) 462-8681.

Newburyport Harbor Range Lighthouses

NEW HAMPSHIRE
ISLES OF SHOALS (WHITE ISLAND)

NORTH ON NH 1A TO RYE. Leave Newburyport on US 1/NH 1A. In Hampton take NH 27 east to NH 1A. Continue north to the Rye Harbor State Marina located north of Rye Beach.

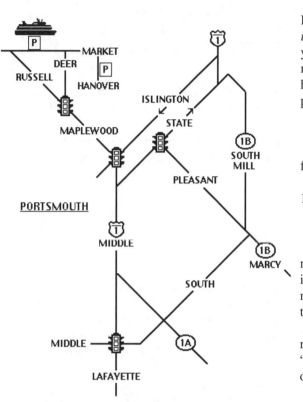

ISLES OF SHOALS CRUISE. On Captain Leo Axtin's Isles of Shoals Sunset Fireworks Cruise, his 150-passenger *Granite State* (two decks; lower with enclosed cabin) sails within 100 yards of the lighthouse on White Island. The marina is about 5.5 miles from the island group, shaving the narrated round trip to 2 hours. The excursion includes the sea tour and a fireworks display at Hampton Beach. Free parking at the marina for passengers

SCHEDULE. Call for the latest schedule.
FARES. Discounts for seniors and children 5-12. Under 5 free.
- New Hampshire Seacoast Cruises Inc., PO Box 232 (Route 1A - Ocean Boulevard), Rye, NH 03870.
Phone (603) 964-5545. In USA toll-free (800) 964-5545.

NORTH TO PORTSMOUTH ON US 1. Since there are no interchanges on I-95 between Hampton and south Portsmouth, it is suggested that the motorist return to US 1, continue into Portsmouth and follow the Maplewood -> Russell -> Market connection to the Ceres Street Dock and Barker Wharf.

Ceres Street (actually a small alley) is (1) located on the north side (towards the river) of Market Street, (2) marked by "Private Way" and "Olde Harbour District" signs and (3) lies west of Barker Wharf.

The location of Barker Wharf is shown on the map at left.

NORTH ON I-95 (TOLL). If bypassing Rye Beach, take Exit 7 and Market Street Extension east to the wharf and dock.

SOUTH ON US 1. Enter downtown Portsmouth on Islington (one way) and follow the Maple-wood -> Russell -> Market route to the cruise docks.

HARBOR CRUISE. This excursion aboard the 49-passenger *Heritage* (one deck with enclosed cabin) takes about 1 1/2 hours and passes the Portsmouth Harbor and Whaleback Lighthouses while circling the harbor.
SCHEDULE. - Call or check website for the latest schedule.
FARES. Discounts for seniors and children. Family discount on the 10 a.m. trip.
- Portsmouth Harbor Cruises, Inc., One Harbour Place, Suite 10, Portsmouth, NH 03801.
Phone (603) 436-8084. In USA toll-free (800) 776-0915.
Website: http://www.portsmouthharbor.com
PARKING.
- Free at Barker Wharf for Isles of Shoals Steamship ticket holders.
- Fee per hour in the municipal garage on Hanover Street off Market.
- Free on-street only on Sundays.

ISLES OF SHOALS CRUISE. The Historic Isles of Shoals and Portsmouth Harbor Cruise is a narrated sightseeing tour of Portsmouth Harbor and the island group, including excellent views of the Portsmouth Harbor, Whaleback and the Isles of Shoals Lighthouses. On very clear days the light seeker will see Cape Neddick and Boon Island Lighthouses, some eight to ten miles to the north. If it is an especially clear day, one can see the two Cape Ann towers 20 miles to the south. The *Thomas Laighton* (three decks, enclosures on the lower two) is steered right up to White Island just below the high cliff on the east side, which places the traveler inside 100 yards of the lighthouse and its old keeper's cottage. There is no safe way to disembark passengers due to the shallow waters in close and exposure to the sea.

SCHEDULE. Usually three cruises daily in season, fewer in the spring and fall. Call or check website for the latest schedule.

FARES. Discounts for seniors 65+ and children 3-11. Under 3 free. Tickets are held 1/2 hour before departure time.

- Isles of Shoals Steamship Company, Box 311 (315 Market Street), Portsmouth, NH 03802.
Phone (603) 431-5500. In USA toll-free (800) 441-4620.
Website: http://www.islesofshoals.com/ Email: info@islesofshoals.com

LIGHTHOUSE SIGHTSEEING CRUISE.

The Isles of Shoals Steamship Company's 2000 schedule includes a weekly lighthouse cruise on the *Oceanic*. This four hour tour is fully narrated and allows the viewer a close-up view of five lighthouses. Offers views of Boon Island, Cape Neddick, Isles of Shoals, Portsmouth Harbor and Whaleback.

The Friends of Flying Santa's narrated Columbus Day Lighthouse Cruise is also aboard the *Oceanic*. Departs from Barker Wharf at 10. Returns around 2. Offers views of Boon Island, Cape Neddick, Isles of Shoals, Portsmouth Harbor and Whaleback Lighthouses.

Proceeds go to the Friends' Endowment Fund.

SCHEDULE. Usually on Columbus Day in October.

FARES. Discount for seniors 60+.

- Friends of Flying Santa, PO Box 791, Hull, MA 02045.
Phone (617) 925-0782.

THE ISLES.

See the following map. The Isles of Shoals, some nine miles east of the mouth of Portsmouth's Piscataqua River, are nine rocky, windswept islands. They were frequented by European fishermen for many years before they were explored in 1614 by Captain John Smith. The island grouping was first known as the Smythe Isles until fishermen renamed them for the plentiful "shools," of fish harvested among the islands. The profitable fishing industry led investors to divide the islands down the center between two states. As a result, the southern four islands now belong to New Hampshire; the remainder to Maine. They are from north to south:

Duck (ME). Owned by Star Island Corporation and used as a wildlife refuge.

Appledore (Hog) (ME) is the largest (four acres) of the islands with an elevation of 75 feet. The first settlers on Appledore came from Wales. In 1676 a young sailor named Pepperell arrived and discovered a new curing treatment for the cod being caught in local waters. Using the profits he made, William Pepperell set up a fishing industry and, with the venture, began amassing a financial fortune. His son, William, founded the Pepperell Knitting Mills in Biddeford, Maine. Today, the island is the site of the Shoals Laboratory of Cornell University. The Shoals' first summer resort hotel, the Appledore House, was built in 1848. Appledore is the site of poet Celia Thaxter's cottage and garden.

Malaga (ME) is connected to Smuttynose by a breakwater built around 1800 by Captain Samuel Haley with the proceeds from selling four bars of silver he reportedly found on the island.

Smuttynose (Haleys) (ME) has the Haley Cottage, one of Maine's older houses. In the 1800s, the small hamlet that grew up around the Haley family's land included a windmill to power a grist mill, salt collection ponds, bakery, blacksmith shop and wooden cask repair works.

Cedar (ME) is connected to both Smuttynose and Star Islands by breakwaters constructed in 1821.

Star (NH) was incorporated in 1641 as a town. Maine's first church was built on Star Island. Pirate captains Dixey Bull, Kidd, Blackbeard, Scott and Quelch allegedly frequented Star and other islands. Captain Kidd is reported to have been especially fond of Star, where he rested his crews and supposedly buried some of his ill-gotten loot. Islanders say that the ghost of Kidd's wife, abandoned by him in 1723 when he hastily fled to escape capture, haunts the Shoals. Gosport, now a tourist stop, was once the center of a prosperous fishing industry. The community's Oceanic Hotel built in 1873, as the successor to Appledore House, is now a religious conference center.

Lunging (NH) was previously known as Londoners Island.

White (NH) is a picturesque little island that supports the Isles of Shoals Light Station.

Seaveys (NH) is an island only at low tide. It is linked to White Island by a narrow strip of land.

ISLES OF SHOALS (WHITE ISLAND)

ISLES OF SHOALS LIGHTHOUSE (WHITE ISLAND).
CHARACTERISTIC: Flashing white 15s
HAW: 82' **RANGE**: 21 nm

Although a warning beacon was established in 1790, the first Isles of Shoals Lighthouse was an 87-foot tall stone tower. Its light, some 90 feet above the sea, was established in 1821, one year after Maine became a state.

Thomas Laighton, who became the beacon's keeper in 1839, was not the ordinary Lighthouse Service employee. Before becoming the light's keeper, he ran for the office of governor and lost. He then applied for the lightkeeper's job and by calling in a few political IOUs, he received the appointment. Mr. Laighton actually took on the keeper's job to be closer to the property he had purchased in 1814 from Captain Haley, namely, the islands of Appledore, Malaga, Smuttynose and Cedar. After his appointment, Mr. Laighton turned over his duties to an assistant keeper and reentered New Hampshire politics. He was elected to the New Hampshire legislature in 1841 and to the Portsmouth Board of Selectmen in 1843. In 1846 he built the resort hotel, Ocean House, and retired from the Lighthouse Service the following year. Laighton's daughter, Celia, later gained widespread fame as Celia Thaxter, poet and author.

The second lighthouse on White Island, the one standing today, was erected in 1859. Its design is of the Federal Design genre. It is 58 feet tall, cylindrical in shape and constructed of coursed granite blocks and red brick (now painted white) with walls two feet thick. The four wrought-iron reinforcing bands around the tower's exterior were added in 1865. Some sources claim a new duplex keeper's house was built in 1859, others say 1877. The most recent keeper's house no longer stands, while an earlier dwelling remains.

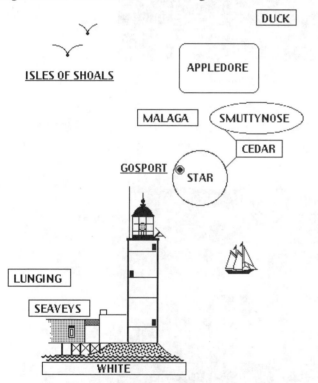

The 1859 optic, a second-order Fresnel lens, was removed in 1987 to allow the installation of an automated modern plastic lens. The light is now solar powered.

OWNER. Station deeded to the State of New Hampshire on December 17, 1993. Managed by the Department of Parks and Recreation. Coast Guard maintains the light.

PRESERVATION. The light station is listed in the National Register of Historic Places as part of the Isles of Shoals.

Hurricane Bob in combination with a severe nor'easter hit the island in October 1991. The combined power of the storms gave the light station a mighty raking. The fog signal tower, covered walkways, fuel tanks, generator sheds, boathouse and boat ramp were all washed into the sea. Luckily, the lighthouse, the keepers' triplex and the old oil house held firm against the raging storms.

With the necessary storm damage repairs having been completed, the State hopes to resurrect its plan to convert the property station into a retreat for writers, poets and artists. Captain Bob Whittaker of the Isles of Shoals Steamship Company, by the way, was supposed to be the first writer in residence until that piggybacked storm system hit the island.

In the summer of 1998 a diving school opened on White Island. Don Stevens of Aquatic Aqua Sport signed a 10-year contract with the Department of Parks and Recreation to operate the school in exchange for maintaining the keeper's house. Divers are ferried to the island from Rye Harbor for snorkeling tours around the island, and they also get lectures on the island's history and marine life.

For information on the diving school, contact:
- Aquatic Aqua Sport, (603) 436-4443.

Isles of Shoals (White Island) Lighthouse

Portsmouth Harbor Lighthouse

PORTSMOUTH HARBOR

EAST ON NH 1B. This lighthouse is located in Newcastle adjacent to Fort Constitution. There are three main ways to reach NH 1B (Newcastle Avenue) from Portsmouth's US 1. See also the Portsmouth map on page 315.
1. Northeast via South Street to NH 1B (Marcy Street).
2. Southeast via Pleasant Street to NH 1B (Marcy Street).
3. East and south via NH 1B (South Mill Street) to Marcy.

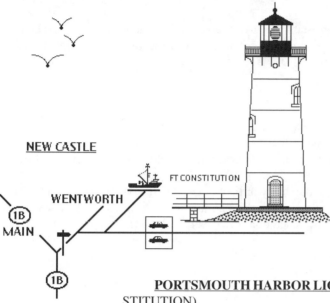

IN NEWCASTLE. About 0.1 mile past Main Street's post office on the right, turn left into Wentworth Road, marked by "U.S. C.G. Sta." and "Ft. Constitution Historic Site" signs. At the next fork bear right and continue to either of two large parking lots (free). Parking is not permitted on the tarmac inside the station. Both the lighthouse and the entrance to Fort Constitution are but a short level walk across the station's paved area. At present visitors are not allowed into the area near the lighthouse, so close views are impossible. There is an excellent view of the Whaleback Lighthouse from the fort. The Friends of Portsmouth Harbor Lighthouse hold occasional open houses at the lighthouse; check their website or call (603) 431-9155 for the current schedule.

For water views, see the listings for cruises leaving Portsmouth on pages 315 and 316.

PORTSMOUTH HARBOR LIGHTHOUSE (NEWCASTLE; FORT POINT; FORT CONSTITUTION).
CHARACTERISTIC: Fixed green
HAW: 52' **RANGE**: 12 nm

The first beacon on the point (1771) was a lantern strung on a pole located on a parapet of Fort William and Mary (now Fort Constitution). The first Portsmouth Harbor Lighthouse, built and commissioned during the years 1782-84, was one of America's twelve colonial lighthouses. The 80-foot tall octagonal and wood framed structure was turned over to the new Federal Government in 1791.

From its beginning, the light station has had a number of distinguished visitors. George Washington inspected the tower in 1789. General Lafayette visited in 1782. Daniel Webster, from 1807 until he moved from Portsmouth nine years later, was a frequent visitor.

President Washington's inspection visit was not all protocol and roses. While in Portsmouth, he and friends went fishing on the Piscataqua River. During their trip the wind picked up and tossed their boat about causing many in the party to become seasick. The president's line snagged in a bunch of rocks and, when he yanked on the line to free it, he lost his balance, got hit in the eye by the corner of a fellow fisherman's tricorner hat and unceremoniously fell down onto a bait bucket. According to the source of this tidbit, the fishing party returned to port with "two small fish, seven sick band musicians and the president of the United States holding a handkerchief over his battered eye."

In 1804 the earlier tower, then in a state of decay and fractured by blasts from cannon fire, was torn down and replaced by a new octagonal wooden tower.

The station received a 1 1/2-story wood framed keeper's dwelling in 1872. In 1877 the second tower was replaced by the present 48-foot tall lighthouse. It is constructed of curved and bolted cast-iron plates that rest on the 1804 tower's foundation.

The 1804 lighthouse held a two-tiered spider-type lighting apparatus that held 13 whale oil-fed lamps and their 14-inch parabolic reflectors 80 feet above the water.

The optic installed in 1877 consisted of a kerosene lamp and a fourth-order Fresnel lens, which, although now electrified and automated (1960), remains an active lighted aid to navigation.

Note that the lens is protected by a green domed acrylic cylinder. Other Atlantic Coast lighthouses with these protective shields are Edgartown Harbor on Martha's Vineyard Island and Whitlocks Mill near Calais, Maine.

319

---

1. Fowler, Carl Delano, "But Nobody Drowned," The New England Sampler, *Yankee*, November 1994.

OWNER. Leased to the American Lighthouse Foundation in January 2000. The beacon is still maintained by the U.S. Coast Guard.
- American Lighthouse Foundation , PO Box 889, Wells, Maine 04090.
Phone: (207) 646-0515.
Website: http://www.lighthousefoundation.org

The Friends of Portsmouth Harbor Lighthouse has been established as a chapter of the American Lighthouse Foundation. The group has been holding monthly open houses in summer and working for the preservation of the lighthouse.
- Friends of Portsmouth Harbor Lighthouse, P.O. Box 5092, Portsmouth, NH 03802-5092 Website: http://www.portsmouthharborlighthouse.org
Email: keeper@lighthouse.cc

PRESERVATION. Listed in the National Register of Historic Places as part of Fort Constitution.
In 1998 the lighthouse was made "environmentally friendly" at a cost of over $73,000. The Coast Guard had all the lead paint removed from the exterior and interior of the tower, and it was then repainted. The work was done by Seacoast Diversified Inc., a contractor from Dover, NH.
What is often overlooked in lighthouse chronicles is the durability of the truncated cast-iron light tower. The Portsmouth Harbor Lighthouse has required but routine maintenance. It is indeed a monument dedicated to America's lighthouse engineers, the period's artisans and the TLC provided by generations of keepers and the U.S. Coast Guard.

Whaleback Lighthouse

MAINE
WHALEBACK

TO FORT FOSTER NORTH ON US 1. In Kittery turn right into ME 103 (Walker Street). Stay on ME 103. Then:
-> Left at Wentworth Avenue,
-> Right at Whipple Road and past the Portsmouth Naval Shipyard,
-> Into connecting Pepperell Road and past the Fort McClary State Memorial,
-> Into Tenney Hill Road,
-> About 0.2 mile past ME 103's intersection with Haley and Hoyts Island Roads (post office on the northeast corner), bear right into Chauncy Creek Road,
-> Right at Gerrish Island Lane and cross over a concrete bridge,
-> Bear right at Pocahontas Road to the Fort Foster Park entrance.

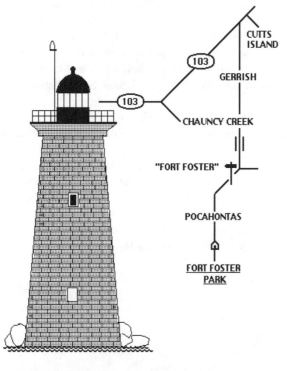

OR SOUTH ON ME 103. In York Harbor on US 1A take ME 103 south. Then:.
-> About 4.0 miles from US 1A pass Cutts Island Lane,
-> Continue 0.1 mile and turn left into Gerrish Island Lane,
-> Continue across the bridge to Pocahontas Road and continue to Fort Foster.

OPEN. All year, daily 10 to 8.

ADMISSION FEES. Vehicle and each passenger. Collection times:

Memorial Day to mid-June, weekends only.
Mid-June to mid-September, daily.
Mid-September to mid-October, weekends only.
No collection at other times of the year.

Continue straight ahead into the recreational area and to the harborside parking area. The Whaleback Lighthouse lies to the south on the northeast side of Portsmouth Harbor at the entrance to the Piscataqua River. To the northwest and across the harbor stands the Portsmouth Harbor Lighthouse.

Whaleback Light can also be viewed from many of the cruises leaving Pormouth Harbor. See pages 315-316 for details.

WHALEBACK LIGHTHOUSE (WHALE BACK LEDGE; TEA KETTLE).
CHARACTERISTIC: Group flashing white 10s
HAW: 59' **RANGE:** 24 nm

The first beacon on this rocky outcropping was erected in 1820. It was damaged beyond repair by a series of winter storms.

Construction of the second lighthouse began in 1829; it was completed a year later and commissioned in early 1831. This tower had construction faults that should have led to its destruction in any violent storm. Its major deficiencies were that the tower's granite block foundation was irregularly laid and not properly bolted to the bedrock and the tower's mortar had been so poorly mixed that, during heavy rains, water would seep into and soak the interior. With a little bit of luck and some strengthening measures, such as being sheathed in cast-iron tightening buckles and the widening of its foundation to protect the tower from crashing waves, the wobbly structure remained in service for almost 40 years.

In 1868 a storm bashed the tower, snapping the bands, splitting the walls and knocking granite blocks out of line. That did it. After having spent $42,000 to shore up the old tower, Congress was finally moved to appropriate $70,000 for a new lighthouse.

The 75-foot tall lighthouse we see today was completed in 1872. By using the bottom portion of the old structure and granite blocks from its upper part, the tower was rebuilt on the design of England's Eddystone Lighthouse. It was designed by famed Boston architect and engineer Alexander Parris. In this case, the tower's foundation was first secured to the ledge with iron bolts. Then, the conical tower was erected on a base of stone and timber, using dovetailed granite ashlar.

From Fort Foster a projection of the old foundation (still showing some of its red paint) can be seen at the base of the tower. It once supported a very large cylindrical fog signal. The windows above the main entrance were sealed in 1886 after storm waves smashed them and drenched the tower's interior.

In 1855 the lantern, which was first fitted with a Lewis multi-lamp and reflector lighting device, was given a revolving fourth-order Fresnel optic. Whaleback was automated in 1963. Its lantern now holds a modern lens.

In 1991 the Coast Guard lowered the volume of Whaleback's fog signal because its sound vibrations were causing structural damage (premature aging and erosion) to the tower's walls.

OWNER. U.S. Coast Guard.

PRESERVATION. Listed in the National Register of Historic Places.

In 1996 the Coast Guard made minor repairs to the tower.

WOOD ISLAND (PORTSMOUTH HARBOR) LIFESAVING STATION. That forlorn and boarded up building with tower on Wood Island seen to the right of Whaleback (if still standing) is the remnant of the old Jerrys Lifesaving Station first established, in 1887, at Fort Stark south of Newcastle. The station was deactivated in 1906 to make way for the installation of additional coast artillery. In 1907 the outfit was reactivated, renamed the Portsmouth Harbor Lifesaving Station and moved into new quarters on Wood Island. The structure's construction design, developed by George Tolman and called the Great Lakes or Duluth styling, is the same as used in most stations built in the United States between 1894 and 1907.

Other preserved lifesaving stations on the Atlantic seaboard that are open to the public are Little Kinnakeet (Avon, NC), Chicamacomico (Rodanthe, NC), Sandy Hook (Highlands, NJ), Fletchers Neck (Biddeford Pool, ME) and Hunnewell Beach (Popham Beach, ME).

In 1992 the station's owner, the Town of Kittery, announced that the dilapidated structure, on the National Register of Historic Places since 1987, would be torn down. That was a mistake, since the register's places cannot be arbitrarily destroyed. Since then the only act of preservation has been the repair of the sea wall on the island's south side. Funds for that project were obtained from a grant by the Federal Emergency Management Administration.

A new preservation group, the Wood Island Preservation Group, now plans to restore this landmark and establish the Wood Island Life Saving Museum. Such a museum could certainly be a jewel of Portsmouth Harbor.

- Wood Island Preservation Group
Website: http://www.woodisland.org
Email: info@WoodIsland.org

CAPE NEDDICK
BOON ISLAND

NORTH OR SOUTH ON US 1A. The Cape Neddick Lighthouse, one of the most photographed on the east coast, stands on Nubble Island, or just "The Nubble," located some 200 yards off Cape Neddick Point. The turn off US 1A into Nubble Road is marked with a small "Nubble Light" sign. Follow Nubble Road and more signs east and north to Sohier Park Road and turn right. Drive to the road's end and overlook with ample free parking, a welcome station, gift shop, picnic area and public restrooms.

On a clear day you can see the Isles of Shoals to the southwest and Boon Island Lighthouse about seven miles to the south.

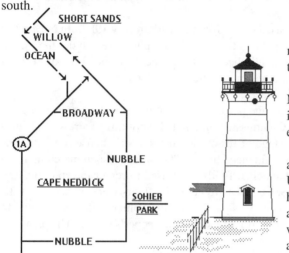

OPEN. Memorial Day to Labor Day, daily 10 to 7.

Although at low tide one can walk and wade across the channel, don't try it. Beside being a safety risk, any crossing is in violation of a York ordinance.

CRUISES. Besides being easily viewed from Sohier Park, Cape Neddick Light can be seen from occasional lighthouse cruises leaving Portsmouth, New Hampshire (see pages 315-316) as well as an excursion boat leaving Perkins Cove in Ogunquit.

Finestkind Cruises, located at Perkins Cove in Ogunquit, offers a 90-minute Nubble Light cruise up to four times daily in season. On US Route 1, go north to Ogunquit. Watch for the Ogunquit Playhouse, a large white building on the right. Make the first right turn after the Playhouse, Bourne Lane. At the end of Bourne Lane you will come to Shore Road. Turn right on Shore Road. Go 1/2 mile to a fork in the road; stay left. Finestkind Cruises is approximately 300 yards down on the right, just past Barnacle Billy's restaurant.

- Finestkind Scenic Cruises. PO Box 1828, Ogunquit, ME 03907
Phone: (207) 646-5227. Fax: (207) 646-4513.
Website: http://www.finestkindcruises.com   Email: info@finestkindcruises.com

CAPE NEDDICK LIGHTHOUSE (NUBBLE LIGHT; THE NUBBLE).
CHARACTERISTIC: Equal interval red 6s
HAW: 88' **RANGE**: 13 nm
Placing a lighthouse on the Nubble had been recommended by many local mariners since 1807. An 1837 proposal was rejected on the grounds that there were already three lights in the vicinity: Boon Island, Whaleback, and Portsmouth Harbor Light. The 41-foot tall lighthouse we see today was completed and its light established on July 1, 1879. The tower has a cast-iron sheathing with an inner double lining of brick. There are 33 cast-iron steps to the watchroom (portholes); seven more steps lead to the lantern. The lantern is enclosed with two sets of glass panes. The outside panes are glazed with clear glass and the inside red. The station, including the light tower, the Victorian keeper's dwelling, outbuildings and a bell tower, cost $15,000.

The bell tower was a pyramidal wooden tower that contained the weights that powered a clock-work mechanism that rang the station's 1,200-pound bronze fog bell. Although the tower and fog signal system have been removed, the station retains its bell and horn. An oil house was added to the station in 1902.

Look closely and you will see an artistic touch seen only on Cape Cod's Nobska Point Lighthouse.[1] The tops of the service gallery's balusters are adorned with tiny cast-iron lighthouses. Also, note that the house is built in the form of a cross with the building's ells facing north, east, south and west.

In 1912 the light's keeper reportedly went into the business of ferrying picnickers to and from the island for ten cents a head. His wife also was into the tourist trade. For five cents she would provide an escorted tour of the keeper's home. The daily accommodation of hundreds of visitors resulted in a neglected light and the keeper losing his job.

Early newspaper articles variously reported on the popularity of Nubble Island. Visitors flocked to the island not only to visit the lighthouse, but to catch a glimpse of the keeper's amazing 19-pound cat, Sambo Tonkus. Mr. T, reportedly the best mouse snatcher on the York coast, swam the channel several times a day to visit his mainland friends and to catch and sup on his favorite entree.

---

1. Lubec Channel's supporting poles for its main deck gallery's canopy were topped with little brass lighthouses. They disappeared many years ago when the Coast Guard removed the framework and awning.

In 1938 the station saw two important improvements. The beacon's incandescent kerosene vapor lamp was converted to electricity and the keeper's residence received indoor plumbing.

The great Blizzard of February 1978 washed out the Nubble's boathouse, which was replaced by the present structure.

Cape Neddick Light was automated in 1987. Its present optic consists of a 1,000-watt lamp and its original fourth-order Fresnel lens.

In 1977, when NASA sent Voyager II into space with artifacts designed to teach extraterrestrial civilizations about our planet, one of the images it carried was a picture of the Nubble Light along with the Grand Canyon and the Great Wall of China.

OWNER. The island, keeper's house and the oil house were leased to the Town of York in July 1987. In November 1997 the people of York voted overwhelmingly to allow the town's selectmen to "adopt" the lighthouse. Under the Maine Lights Program coordinated by the Island Institute, the lighthouse officially became the property of the Town of York on December 15, 1997. Managed by York's Parks and Recreation Committee and the Sohier Park Committee.

PRESERVATION. Listed in the National Register of Historic Places.

York's Selectmen established the Sohier Park Enterprise Fund for the perpetual care of the island property. In 1988 York matched a $12,500 grant from the Maine Historic Preservation Commission and in its first of three work stages, used the funds to repair the roof of the keeper's dwelling. In the second stage of restoration the keeper's house received new siding and refurbished molding and gingerbread trim. This project was financed by $54,000 in federal and matching town funds. In the third stage another $24,000 in matching federal and municipal funds were used to repair the station's fuel storage building and tool shed. In the final stage, completed by a U.S. Coast Guard crew, the floors were sanded, all walls repaired, and the dwelling's electrical wiring replaced. It cost $7,000 and was paid for by the Sohier Park Committee. In late 1998 the York Parks and Recreation Department announced plans to further renovate the keeper's house. The plan is to find sponsors to help pay for the work.

- Friends of Nubble Light, PO Box 9, York, ME 03909.

Phone (207) 363-1040.

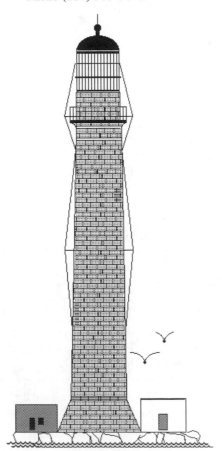

BOON ISLAND LIGHTHOUSE.

CHARACTERISTIC: Flashing white 5s

HAW: 137' **RANGE**: 19 nm

This lighthouse, about six miles off the Maine coast south southeast of York Village, stands on a rocky, barren islet about 400 yards square.

Note in the ISLES OF SHOALS chapter the lighthouse cruise out of Portsmouth (page 315).

The first lighthouse on this storm-swept heap of granite boulders was built in 1799. Its light was established in 1800. It was an unstable and cheaply built 50-foot wood framed and shingled tower. Destroyed in a storm in 1804, it was replaced in the same year by a stone tower. The second lighthouse was replaced in 1811 by another masonry structure that cost a bit over $2,500. It was destroyed during an 1831 storm. It was rebuilt again the following year.

In 1852 the Lighthouse Board decided that Boon Island should have a sturdier and more reliable aid to navigation. With an appropriation of $25,000, the board went to work on the project. The lighthouse was lighted on January 1, 1855, using a whale oil-fed second-order Fresnel lens.

The 133-foot tall lighthouse (base diameter 25 feet, tower top 12 feet) is constructed of gray granite blocks, all hewn and dressed by hand. A narrow circular staircase with 130 steps leads to the watchroom. The lantern room is reached by an inside ladder. In 1885 six iron tie rods, designed to strengthen the top of the structure, were strung from top to bottom along the tower's exterior, tightened and bolted to the foundation.

The lighthouse is subject to tremendous beatings during Atlantic storms. As a matter of fact, the island received its name from the packaged food and clothing (boon) placed on the island by mainland fishermen for shipwrecked personnel lucky enough to have been swept up onto the rocks.

BOON ISLAND

In 1932 the station experienced a storm that washed the island clean, tore out the submarine telephone cable and threw 70-foot waves at the house and tower. In February 1978, Boon Island took another bashing. While the crew sought safety in the tower, one of the century's worst blizzards tossed the giant granite boulders about, destroying the 1899 keeper's dwelling, fuel tanks, support buildings, launching ways and part of the helicopter landing pad. The island was inundated with water five feet deep. The next day a helicopter flew in, landed, hauled aboard the two keepers and took off between surging waves. After the storm the Coast Guard automated the light and removed its personnel. In late October 1991, a combination hurricane and storm piled numerous 100-pound granite boulders against the entry door.

BOON ISLAND LENS. In 1993 as part of the aid's conversion to solar power and the installation of a modern plastic optic, Boon Island's 1855 second-order lens was removed by the Coast Guard and sent to South Portland, Maine. The lens, which is eight feet tall and five feet wide, is now on display at the Kittery Historical and Naval Museum. There had been a dispute between the towns of York and Kittery over the disposition of the lens before the Coast Guard decided the Kittery location was the most suitable one because of the town's historical ties to the light station; many of the light's keepers were from Kittery.

The station's old fog bell is located in the Shore Baptist Church in Hingham, Massachusetts.

OWNER. U.S. Coast Guard, leased in 2000 to the American Lighthouse Foundation.
- American Lighthouse Foundation , PO Box 889, Wells, Maine 04090.
Phone: (207) 646-0515.
Website: http://www.lighthousefoundation.org

PRESERVATION. Listed in the National Register of Historic Places.

Boon Island Lighthouse

GOAT ISLAND

NORTH OR SOUTH ON ME 9. In Cape Porpoise Center, where the highway makes a 90 degree turn, bear right (northbound) or turn left (southbound) into Pier Road. Continue for 0.6 mile to its end at the town wharf. Parking (free) is available next to the wharf. The view of Goat Island Light from the wharf is fairly distant, but at low tide it is possible to walk (in mud) part of the way to the island.

A sightseeing cruise company in Kennebunkport offers a closer view of the lighthouse. Second Chance's Lighthouse Folklore Cruise leaves daily at 7 PM in season.

- First Chance Whale Watch / Second Chance Scenic Lobster Cruise. 4A Western Ave, Lower Village, Kennebunk, Maine 04043.

Phone: (800) 767-BOAT or (207) 967-5507.

Website: http://www.FirstChanceWhaleWatch.com/

Email: lobsters@nh.ultranet.com

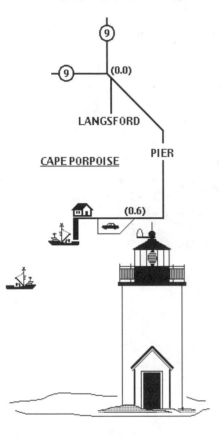

GOAT ISLAND LIGHTHOUSE.

CHARACTERISTIC: Flashing white 6s

HAW: 38' **RANGE**: 12 nm

In 1834 Congress appropriated $6,000 for a light station on Goat Island. The 20-foot tall tower and rubble stone keeper's dwelling were completed the following year. Both structures were rebuilt in 1859-60. According to the Maine Historic Preservation Commission, the present 25-foot brick Goat island Lighthouse was built in the 1880s; the exact date is not known.

The station consisted of the presently active brick tower, a gabled colonial cape cottage (1860), and a covered walkway connecting the tower and house. The boathouse was built in 1905 and the brick oil house in 1907. The walkway was destroyed by a storm in February 1978.

The lighthouse is an excellent architectural example of Federal Design lighthouse architecture, a midsized, masonry tower with a protruding entry, a simple octagonal lantern and no stylistic ornamentation.

Goat Island's first lighting apparatus was a Lewis multi lamp device. Its 1859 fourth-order Fresnel lens was replaced in 1990 by an automated modern lens.

OWNER. In 1976 the Coast Guard declared the station's 3.5 acres surplus property and offered it to the Town of Kennebunkport and the City of Biddeford for use as a recreation area. Both municipalities declined, because they considered the lighthouse keeper essential to the safety of the harbor. As a result the Coast Guard decided to keep the station manned. In the summer of 1990 the Coast Guard finally withdrew the last of Maine's lightkeepers. Boatswain Mate Brad Culp and his family climbed into their outboard motorboat and headed for a mainland assignment.

In 1992 after several years of negotiations, the Coast Guard leased the light station to the Kennebunkport Conservation Trust, a nonprofit environmental organization. In December 1997, under the Maine Lights Program, the lighthouse officially became the property of the trust, which since its founding in 1969 has protected 560 acres of town land from development. The trust plans to rebuild the covered walkway from the house to the tower and the station's bell tower.

PRESERVATION. Listed in the National Register of Historic Places. Since the station had been used as a security post for former President Bush when he was at his Walker Point residence, the property was turned over in good condition. The interior of the keeper's house was modernized during the years it was used by the Secret Service. The Kennebunkport Conservation Trust has provided caretakers who have lived the past few summers on Goat Island.

Although the Trust does not operate a ferry service to the island, visitors by private boat are welcomed. The station will also be used for educational purposes, such as docent seminars in the area's history and environment and field trips for students. Preservation of the lighthouse is made possible through private contributions to the Trust. Fundraising functions are held throughout the year in order to raise money to maintain and protect the island.

- Kennebunkport Conservation Trust, PO Box 7028, Cape Porpoise, ME 04014.

Phone (207) 967-3939.

WOOD ISLAND

NORTH OR SOUTH ON ME 9. Between Cape Porpoise and Biddeford turn off ME 9 into ME 208 (Bridge Road). Then:

-> At a T-head intersection turn left,

-> Continue on ME 208 through Biddeford,

-> Just before the road turns right into Ocean Avenue and skirts the shoreline, there is a closed vehicular gate (on the left) with an opening for pedestrian entry onto a pathway. Off-road parking is permitted at the gate and westward along the road's northern shoulder. The walk to the inlet's shoreline is about 0.3 mile. The first third of the stone-strewn path heads slightly uphill past a golf course and then levels off for an easy walk to the inlet. The view of the lighthouse from the path is fairly distant, so bring your binoculars.

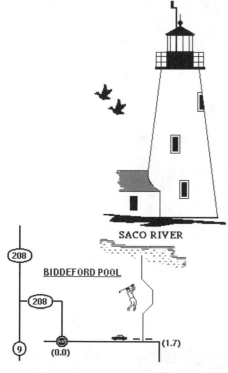

WOOD ISLAND LIGHTHOUSE.

CHARACTERISTIC: Alternating white and green 10s

HAW: 71' **RANGES**: White 16; green 14 nm

This aid is a conical rubble stone (granite structure) erected in 1808. It is Maine's last remaining light tower to retain its original form.

In 1858 the station received a new keeper's dwelling. It was a one-story, three-bay wooden structure sheathed in clapboards and attached to the tower. Also added to the station was a pyramidal wooden fog bell tower. The oil house was added in 1903. During the 1960s the fog bell's support frame was destroyed during a storm and the bell fell into the sea. In 1976 the bell was recovered and donated to the Biddeford Historical Society. It now rests on the grounds of the Union Church. In 1966 the house was reconfigured to a Dutch colonial styling with the raising of the gambrel roof to create a two-story house.

Wood Island Light has had a historic succession of lighting devices. When first established the lantern held a multi-wick spider lamp. Then in the 1820s it received a Lewis Argand-styled optic. In 1858 it was fitted with a weight powered clockwork that turned a new fourth-order Fresnel lens on its characteristic for 6 1/2 hours.

During World War II the Army sometimes used the island for target practice. A flare nearly burned down the bell tower, and while in the lighthouse tower Keeper Earle Benson saw tracer bullets flying by him. He phoned the Army and asked them to stop shooting at the lighthouse. They denied that they ever had.

The tower was disfigured in 1972 when its lantern was removed to facilitate the installation of a large rotating aerobeacon. Fortunately public concern convinced the Coast Guard to return the 10-sided lantern and equip it with a smaller modern lens. The light was automated in 1986.

OWNER. U.S. Coast Guard. Since 1976, 28 of the island's 36 acres have been managed by the Maine Audubon Society. The lighthouse is leased to the Wood Island Lighthouse Society.

PRESERVATION. Listed in the National Register of Historic Places.

In 1992 the Coast Guard completed a structural survey of the light station's tower and buildings. The survey was taken to establish repair requirements and their cost bases for negotiating a long term lease with either an organization or a private party. Although offered to the Biddeford Pool Improvement Association (and others), the lack of funds delayed this historic station's rehabilitation. In 1993 the Coast Guard made some repairs to the tower's roof and then contracted for a general refurbishing of the tower (stucco and paint) and keeper's house (roof and paint), the rebuilding of the boat landing and the boardwalk to the house. The project was completed during the 1994-95 period.

FLETCHERS NECK LIFESAVING STATION. This privately owned and restored real estate is located on the beach on Ocean Road (around the curve from the pedestrian entry). There are two buildings. The one nearest the ocean was built in 1915. The second structure is be-hind the larger building and is believed to have been built and occupied by U.S. Lifesaving Service personnel on December 1, 1874. The newer building is similar in design to other Atlantic seaboard and Great Lake stations built between 1874 and 1907, such as New Jersey's Spermaceti Lifesaving Station reviewed in the SANDY HOOK chapter. The Fletchers Neck station, after having been on the real estate resale market in 1993 for $450,000, was purchased in January 1994. The new owners have renovated the older house, which is now listed in the National Register of Historic Places.

Cape Elizabeth - the east tower after the keeper's house was remodeled

Cape Elizabeth - the west tower

CAPE ELIZABETH

NORTH ON US 1. In Oak Hill take ME 207 (Black Point Road) southeast to ME 77. Follow ME 77 (Spurwink and Bowery Beach Roads) northeast for about 5.5 miles to a triangular intersection marked with a "Two Lights State Park" sign. Turn right into Two Lights Road.

SOUTH FROM PORTLAND HEAD. From Fort Williams Park (start 0.0 mile):

-> Take Shore Road to its juncture with ME 77 in Pond Cove (2.3 miles),

-> Continue south on ME 77 (Ocean House Road) to the triangular intersection (3.9 miles),

-> Bear left into Two Lights Road.

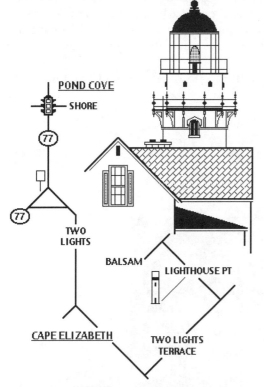

CONTINUE ON. About 1.4 miles from the intersection turn left at Two Lights Terrace. The lighthouse stands on a knoll at the end of Two Lights Terrace. The keeper's dwelling and grounds are privately owned.

For another view of the tower motor to the end of Balsam Street.

CAPE ELIZABETH LIGHTHOUSE (TWO LIGHTS).
CHARACTERISTIC: Group flashing white 15s
HAW: 129' **RANGE**: 15 nm

In 1811 a 50-foot tall tower was erected on Cape Elizabeth as a memorial to a wrecked ship. The octagonal structure was built of rubble stone and lime mortar and painted black (upper half) and white (lower half). The memorial also served as an unlighted daymark, but was demolished after the first light towers were built.

The first lighthouses on the cape were twin undressed stone towers completed in 1828 for $4,250. A fog bell was added to the station in 1852. Although both 65-foot tall lighthouses were upgraded with the installation of Fresnel optics in 1854, the Lighthouse Board discontinued the west beacon on August 1, 1855. That did not sit well with local fishermen and lobstermen, so the Board relented and reestablished the light on April 1, 1856. In 1865 the towers were repainted. The west tower was decorated with vertical red bands, the east tower with four horizontal red bands.

EAST TOWER. In 1874 twin 67-foot tall cast-iron lighthouses replaced the weatherworn older towers. The active east lighthouse is a leading candidate to win the blue ribbon for being Maine's most beautiful lighthouse. Although the shaft (six stages) is unremarkable in design, note the extremely fine Italianate influence in the gabled pediments above the windows at the tower's first, third and fifth stages. Italianate detail is also represented in the handsome circular watchroom service gallery (sixth stage) with its ornamented support brackets and delicately turned balusters.

WEST TOWER. The west tower, slated for decommissioning in 1882 and saved by protesting mariners and an influential Maine congressman, was finally discontinued, partially dismantled (lantern and optic) and abandoned in 1924, when all coastal twin lighthouses were reduced to a single beacon.

During World War II civil defense authorities constructed the tall cylindrical steel turret that still rests atop the tower. This double decked observation room had small window slots on its east side, so designed to protect wary watch personnel from possible small arms fire from submarine-launched infiltrators.

In 1971 actor Gary Merrill (Bette Davis' ex-husband) purchased at auction the 54-foot tall (without lantern) tower and the surrounding 10.5 acres for $28,000. Interestingly, one of the bidders for the property was Bruce D. Woollett, who is the builder of Maine's newest lighthouse, Rockland Harbor Southwest. Mr. Merrill, who later purchased lighthouse property in Canada, intended to convert the tower's six decks into living quarters with the old observation turret serving as his master bedroom. He never completed the project. Instead, he sold it to another private party in 1983 for $80,000. One year later the light tower was again sold for $90,000 to a contractor, who also owned a house on Two Lights Terrace.

Both light towers were fitted with second-order classical lenses. The presently active east tower first exhibited a flashing white beam; its twin 300 yards to the west showed a fixed white light. In 1994 the lighthouse's beautiful second-order lens was removed and is now on display in Cape Elizabeth's Town Hall at 320 Ocean House Road. The light is now produced by an automated modern lens.

By the way, some of Edward Hopper's (1882-1967) many paintings capture the beauty of Cape Elizabeth's east tower and the Portland Head Lighthouse. One of Hopper's paintings of Cape Elizabeth Lighthouse was portrayed on a United States postage stamp issued on July 9, 1970 in commemoration of the 150th anniversary of Maine's admission into the Union.

OWNER. U.S. Coast Guard (lighthouse). The two bedroom Victorian-styled residence of 1878 was largely remodeled in 1979. It was placed on the real estate market in late 1994 for $465,000 and purchased by Mr. William Kourakos, Jr., of Connecticut. Despite protests from area residents and lighthouse preservationists, Mr. Kourakos demolished much of the keeper's house and converted it into a larger residence. Since the Town of Cape Elizabeth had no laws dealing with preservation of historic property, and because the keeper's house was not on the National Register of Historic Places, nothing could be done to halt the remodeling. The house today is far different from the dwelling immortalized by Edward Hopper.

PRESERVATION. The east tower is listed in the National Register of Historic Places as part of Two Lights.

Portland Head Lighthouse

PORTLAND HEAD
RAM ISLAND LEDGE

NORTH OR SOUTH ON ME 77. From 295 in Portland take Route 77 south to South Portland. Go left on Broadway, then right on Cottage Road. Cottage Road becomes Shore Road at the Cape Elizabeth town line. Approaching from the south, take Route 1 north to Oak Hill in Scarborough. Go right on Route 207, then left on Route 77 north to Cape Elizabeth. Turn right at the blinking light on to Shore Road. Portland Head Light is located in Fort Williams Park, 1000 Shore Road. There is ample free parking. Also note that the lighthouse can be seen from some cruises leaving Portland; see page 337.

CAPE COTTAGE

SHORE

FORT
WILLIAMS
PARK

Fort Williams, an important military asset during World War II, was deactivated in 1963. Today, Fort Williams Park welcomes almost one million visitors a year.

The Portland Head Lighthouse marks the south side entrance to Portland Harbor. The Ram Island Ledge Lighthouse stands about 0.25 mile offshore and marks the north side of the harbor's entrance.

OPEN. All year, sunrise to sunset.

FREE ADMISSION.

To reserve the picnic shelter or other areas of the park for group gatherings, call Community Services, (207) 799-2868.

Website: http://www.capeelizabeth.com/tFort.html

MUSEUM AT PORTLAND HEAD LIGHT. This museum was dedicated on September 20, 1992. It has multimedia educational displays covering the histories of the light station, other aids to navigation and Fort Williams. The tower is not open to the public. There is also a gift shop featuring lighthouse and Maine-related gifts.

When Portland Head's original second-order Fresnel lens was removed in 1946, the classical optic was first sent to Boston for storage and then transferred to the Mystic Seaport in Connecticut, where it remained uncrated. With a desire to display this masterpiece at Portland Head, committee members traced the lens to Mystic. Although the lens was thought to be in "excellent" condition, it was discovered that, when the crates were opened in 1992, one panel was damaged and the entire framework (vertical brackets that hold the prisms) was missing, necessitating the fabrication of new prism supports. Because of the missing parts and the lack of sufficient space to accommodate the entire lens, only one half of the huge bivalve lens is on display. The museum also exhibits, courtesy of the Coast Guard, Squirrel Point Lighthouse's fourth-order lens.

OPEN.

Mid-April to Memorial Day, weekends 10 to 4.

Late May (Memorial Day) to October (the Friday following Columbus Day), daily 10 to 4.

Mid-October to late December (just before Christmas), weekends 10 to 4.

Closed late December to mid-April.

ADMISSION FEES. Discount for children 6-18.

- The Museum at Portland Head Lighthouse, PO Box 6260 (1000 Shore Road), Cape Elizabeth, ME 04107.

Phone (207) 799-2661. Recorded information when office is closed. Website: http://www.portlandheadlight.com

PORTLAND HEAD LIGHTHOUSE.

CHARACTERISTIC: Flashing white 4s

HAW: 101' **RANGE:** 24 nm

In 1787 John Hancock, then Governor of the Massachusetts Bay Colony, authorized the Colony's Maine District to build the Portland Head Lighthouse. Lacking the funds to erect a granite tower, masons were instructed to search the area for construction materials. At the same time, the artisans were given two years to complete the project. In 1789, when the new Federal Government took over the management of America's lighthouses, Portland Head was still an unfinished tower. At the urging of Alexander Hamilton, Secretary of the Treasury and lighthouse overseer, Congress granted $1,500 to continue the project. The lighthouse was ceded to the Federal Government in 1790 and dedicated by General Lafayette on January 10, 1791.

Portland Head Light has undergone several alterations. Here are the major ones:

1813: The original 72-foot tall tower received a new wooden and copper covered deck and a new octagonal cast-iron lantern was installed. The 15-foot tall lantern, reportedly, was glazed with the best double glass storm panes then available. It is believed that the contractor, Winslow Lewis, also installed one of his systems of multi-lamp and reflector optics.

1821: The lantern received a new optic consisting of 15 lamps with 15-inch reflectors.

1850: Optic changed again to 13 lamps with 21-inch reflectors.

1855: After having received a new, larger lantern in 1851, the tower was lined with brick, given a cast-iron stairway and equipped with a fourth-order Fresnel lens. At the same time the station received its first fog bell.

1865: Tower was raised eight feet and a new and larger lantern was installed in order to accommodate an improved second-order classical lens. The new optic was chosen to provide increased range and an earlier warning of the rocks and shoals at the entrance to Portland Harbor.

1883: The second-order lens was removed, the tower lowered 20 feet and the size of the lantern reduced for the reinstallation of the old fourth-order lens.

1885: Tower's height again raised 20 feet and a second-order lens was again installed.

1900: Tower extensively renovated. Many of the rubble stones were replaced when its exterior walls were repointed.

1989. Portland Head's fourth-order Fresnel replaced by an automated modern lens.

PORTLAND HEAD LIGHT AND STORMS. During an 1869 storm, the fog bell and its tower were knocked into a ravine, nearly killing Keeper Joshua Strout. A 1962 storm cracked the engine room walls. Ten years later, a storm wave broke a window that was 25 feet above the sea. In 1975 a mighty blow took out the fog signals and darkened the light. Another storm in early 1977 disrupted electrical power and put the light and fog horn out of service for 18 hours. The keepers and their families had to seek shelter in a nearby motel.

PORTLAND HEAD AND THE ARTS. Portland Head has had many friends from the world of literature and the arts. Visitors have included Harriet Beecher Stowe, Elizah Kellogg (author of boys' books), Henry Wadsworth Longfellow, who described his friend as "... a pillar of fire by night, a cloud by day," and Edna St. Vincent Millay, who resided on nearby Ragged Island. On station is a marked boulder upon which it is believed poet laureate Longfellow rested and was inspired to pen his poem, "The Lighthouse." One of the more famous of George M. Hathaway's seascapes, Portland Head Light, can be seen in the Portland Museum of Art. In addition to his stay at Massachusetts' Eastern Point Lighthouse, Winslow Homer also visited Portland Head while composing his magnificent portraits of the sea, ships and shores. Edward Hopper's paintings of both Portland Head and Cape Elizabeth capture the architectural beauty of both lighthouses.

PORTLAND HEAD AND FORT WILLIAMS. Arthur Cameron[1] claims that the storms at Portland Head were "Magnificent sights - wonderful to see but terrifying to hear." He also comments on the deafening roar and the shaking of ground, house and tower when the Army rolled out the fort's coast artillery and commenced the annual battery-by-battery firing exercise. Once he saw the kitchen's heavy coal stove "jump right off the floor." At another time during individual rifle training, an errant (but accurate) Army marksman shot a knob off the lower balcony railing.

OWNER. U.S. Coast Guard (lighthouse and fog signal). On August 7, 1989, Portland Head became an automated light. With the removal of the Coast Guard's watch personnel, the keepers' residence, oil house (1881), fog signal building (replicated in 1975) and grounds were leased to the Town of Cape Elizabeth. In 1992 the property was deeded to the town, largely through the efforts of United States Senator George Mitchell.

PRESERVATION. Listed in the National Register of Historic Places.

The Cape Elizabeth Town Council, with an initial donation of $10,000 from the Unum Mutual Life Insurance Company, took out a 10-year bond for $280,000. With the funds, work on the renovation of the keepers' duplex began. Thereafter, Cape Elizabeth's citizens, through contributions and matching funds, raised $600,000 to restore the keepers' residence. The first floor restoration is superbly done; the dwelling's second floor was converted to an apartment . It is now used for storage and other purposes by the Museum at Portland Head Light. The museum and accompanying gift shop now generate enough income to make the operation totally self-sustaining.

---

1. Cameron, Arthur H., "Boyhood Days at Portland Head Light," *Down East*, September 1978.

RAM ISLAND LEDGE

RAM ISLAND LEDGE LIGHTHOUSE.
CHARACTERISTIC: Group flashing white 6s
HAW: 77' **RANGE**: 12 nm

The first aid on Ram Island Ledge was a daymark, a cast-iron spindle embedded in the rock in 1855. In 1873 a 55-foot tall wooden tripod beacon replaced the daymark. Although planning for a new lighthouse to replace the often destroyed tripod began in 1902 with an appropriation of $83,000, the required purchase of the outcropping from private parties delayed construction until May 1903.

The tower's granite blocks were cut, numbered for ease of assembly and shipped from quarries on Maine's Vinalhaven Island. The first four-ton blocks were laid in circular fashion with 20 stones to each course. When the masonry work on the tower was completed, 700 blocks equaling 2,800 tons of granite had been laid in 16 courses to a height of 32 feet. By mid-1904, the 13-ton cast-iron lantern arrived from Atlanta, Georgia.

The 72-foot tall lighthouse's third-order Fresnel optic was first lighted on April 10, 1905. In 1959, after the Fresnel lens was replaced by an automated plastic lens and its control passed to Portland Head, the Coast Guard keepers were removed. The lighthouse was included in the Maine Lights Program but no organization applied for the property.

OWNER. U.S. Coast Guard.
PRESERVATION. Listed in the National Register of Historic Places.

Ram Island Ledge Lighthouse

SPRING POINT LEDGE
PORTLAND BREAKWATER

NORTH FROM PORTLAND HEAD. Take Shore Road and motor 0.4 mile to Preble Street. Then:
-> Turn right at Preble (0.0 mile),
-> Continue through the Preble & Davis Street intersection (0.5 mile),
-> Right at Fort Street (0.7 mile).
-> Continue past the campus of the Southern Maine Vocational Training Institute and downhill to the waterfront. On-street parking (free) is permitted. The public may walk out to the lighthouse.

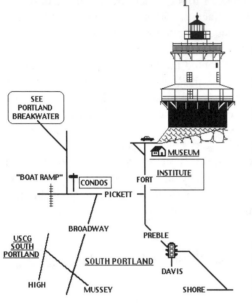

SOUTH FROM PORTLAND.
-> Cross over the Casco Bay Bridge (Rt. 77) to South Portland.
-> Pass through the second set of lights. This will put you on Broadway.
-> Proceed 1.7 miles to the end of Broadway and turn right onto Pickett Street.
-> At the end of Pickett St. turn left onto Fort Road and follow it over Fort Hill to Spring Point.
-> The Portland Harbor Museum exhibit hall and Spring Point Ledge Lighthouse are located at the end of the road to your right.

SPRING POINT LEDGE LIGHTHOUSE.
CHARACTERISTIC: Flashing white 6s (2 red sectors)
HAW: 54 ' **RANGES:** White 12; red 9 nm
Spring Point Ledge is a dangerous obstruction on the west side of the main shipping channel into Portland Harbor. Many vessels ran aground before requests from seven steamship companies in 1891 convinced the government to build a lighthouse on the ledge. The steamship companies had carried more than 500,000 passengers through the area during the previous year.

Congress initially appropriated $20,000, but setbacks in construction, including storms and poor quality cement, ran the cost of the tower to $45,000. Construction of the superstructure's offshore pier began in August 1896. The following month a storm badly damaged the caisson's cast-iron plates, requiring another contract for the fabrication of new plates. Work on the pier resumed and by October the concrete-filled caisson had been constructed above the waterline. The pier contains a basement storeroom and cisterns for fuel and water

The 54-foot tall cylindrical brick lighthouse is built in four levels. The first deck housed the galley. The next level, where the large glass block windows are located, was the keeper's office and living quarters. The third level was reserved for the assistant keeper. The next deck above that was the watchroom.

In 1951, after the present granite breakwater was completed, the lighthouse was dismantled and moved to its present location.

The lantern was fitted with a fifth-order Fresnel lens rotated by a hand-wound, weight-powered clockwork. The light was activated on May 24, 1897. The original kerosene-fueled optic was replaced with an automated modern lens in 1934.

Keepers at Spring Point Ledge had to be creative in their means of exercise. Somebody figured that it took 56 jogs around the tower's main deck to make one mile. One keeper was running laps in this fashion and forgot to close a trap door. He slipped through the opening and only a ladder prevented him from falling 17 feet to a rock ledge and swirling waves.

OWNER. U.S. Coast Guard. Under the Maine Lights Program coordinated by the Island Institute of Rockland, Spring Point Ledge Light was scheduled to be transferred from the Coast Guard to some other group. The city of South Portland had applied to co-own the property with Southern Maine Technical College, but in October 1997 the City Council voted to withdraw the application after 90 minutes of debate. A handicapped-rights activist had threatened to take the city to court if the lighthouse wasn't made handicapped accessible, which would cost approximately $250,000. In March 1998 the Spring Point Museum (now the Portland Harbor Museum) was allowed to make a late application to the Maine Lights Selection Committee. On April 28, 1998, the Maine Lights Selection Committee announced the transfer of Spring Point Ledge Light to the Spring Point Ledge Lighthouse Trust, made up of the Portland Harbor Museum and other local businesses and organizations. The Trust will maintain and showcase the structure, while the Coast Guard will retain responsibility for its navigation beacon. The museum has pledged $2,500 per year to the trust fund.

SPRING POINT LEDGE & PORTLAND BREAKWATER

Since the summer of 1999 the lighthouse has been opened for occasional public tours, with a small admission fee. Contact the Portland Harbor Museum for the schedule of open houses.

The Portland Harbor Museum is located on the grounds of Fort Preble overlooking Casco Bay, a short distance from the lighthouse. Its exhibit of 19th century shipbuilding includes sections of the South Portland built clipper ship, *Snow Squall.*

- Portland Harbor Museum, Fort Road, South Portland, ME 04106.

Phone: (207) 799-6337.

Website: http://www.portlandharbormuseum.org/

Email: info@portlandharbormuseum.org

PRESERVATION. Listed in the Register of Historic Places.

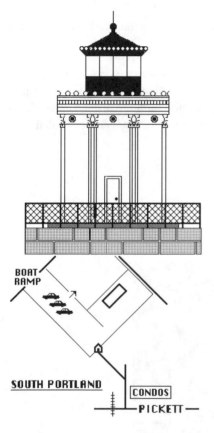

CONTINUE ON. Return to Pickett Street, drive west past Broadway and at the next major intersection and before a railroad crossing turn right. Continue on this road, bearing left towards the entrance to the parking area for Bug Light Park. Entrance to the parking area is free.

PORTLAND BREAKWATER LIGHTHOUSE (BUG LIGHT; PORTLAND HARBOR).

After a disastrous storm tore up Portland Harbor's facilities and moored ships in 1831, authorities began to plan for a 2,500-foot long storm barrier to protect the inner harbor. In 1833 work began on a breakwater that by 1837 extended one-half mile into the harbor. Although providing the required protection, the breakwater was short of its planned length, unfinished and according to mariners both an eyesore and a navigational hazard.

In 1854 the Portland Breakwater Lighthouse was authorized. The lighthouse, completed within four months in 1855, was an octagonal, pyramidal wooden tower built on a double-coursed foundation of ashlar stone formed atop the breakwater.

The first wooden tower was equipped with a sixth-order Fresnel optic whose focal plane was 25 feet above mean high water. The light became operational on March 19, 1855.

There was no keeper's house built initially, so the keeper had to walk over the breakwater to the light. This often became a battle against waves, wind and ice. Keepers sometimes had to crawl 1,800 feet to the lighthouse on their hands and knees.

The controversy over the breakwater continued. In 1866 the U.S. Army's Corps of Engineers, without formal approval of Congress, decided to cap the breakwater. That job was completed in 1867. The extension of the terminal pier had to wait until 1872, when Washington finally gave its approval. Although that phase of the breakwater project was completed in 1873, the pier remained unfinished until 1886, when all of its 1,990 feet had been capped with coursed granite blocks.

The wooden tower created all sorts of maintenance problems. Standing but two feet above high tide, it was constantly washed by high waves. Dampness rotted the tower's exterior wood sheathing, requiring several recoverings. The lantern and other cast-iron parts rusted. A new and imaginatively designed tower, constructed for $6,000, replaced the original tower in 1875. The old structure, less its cast-iron lantern, was moved to Little Diamond Island. There, after having been topped with a windowed observation turret, it served as a lookout tower for buoy tenders.

The present lighthouse was modeled after the Greek Choragic Monument of Lysicrates, built in the fourth century B.C. as a gift to the gods by a choragus (leader) for having won a Greek dramatic choral contest. It is petite and neatly dressed with six fluted Corinthian columns. The 13-foot tall cast-iron tower is lined with brick for added strength. The cylinder's diameter measures almost 12 feet. Its base is a concrete slab bolted to the granite pier head.

The second beacon's fixed red sixth-order Fresnel optic was established in June 1875. Its characteristic was changed to flashing red three years later.

In 1889 a keeper's dwelling was built next to the tower. Two more rooms and an attic were added in 1903. The structure was removed in 1934. In 1897 a 400-pound fog bell was relocated from the nearby Stanford Ledge Buoy to the breakwater. In 1903 a 1,000 pound bell was installed at the base of the tower.

In 1934 the beacon was electrified via an underwater cable and its control was transferred to the Spring Point Ledge Lighthouse. In 1939 the Fresnel lens was removed and placed in storage in the Coast Guard Station South Portland.

OWNER. World War II signaled the end of the lighthouse, after shipyards were expanded across and out over the breakwater to meet America's and England's ship repair and construction requirements. No longer an effective harbor aid, the light was extinguished in June 1942. The next year it was declared surplus government property and abandoned. It is now owned by the City of South Portland.

In 1996 the City of South Portland purchased eight acres of land on Breakwater Point. The land has become a public park encompassing the adjacent lighthouse.

PRESERVATION. Listed in the National Register of Historic Places.

After so many years standing idle and unattended, this unique lighthouse acquired new benefactors. In 1989, with half of a total of $26,000 provided by the National Park Service's Bicentennial Lighthouse Fund and the other half donated by the South Portland and Cape Elizabeth Rotary Club, Bug Light received substantial structural repairs and a new coat of paint. The restoration project was administered by Maine's Historic Preservation Commission in cooperation with the City of South Portland.

Portland Breakwater Lighthouse

HALFWAY ROCK

IN PORTLAND. There are three lighthouse viewing adventures in Portland. One is the opportunity to select from three harbor cruises that pass the Portland Breakwater Lighthouse, Spring Point Ledge, Portland Head and Ram Island Ledge. All cruises depart from Commercial Street's (US 1A) wharves. There is metered parking on Commercial Street. Parking (hourly rate) is available in the following lots. See corresponding map numbers:

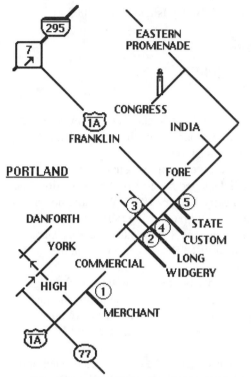

(1) Merchants Wharf opposite Center Street.
(2) Between Long and Widgery Wharves.
(3) One block north of Long Wharf on Fore Street.
(4) DiMillo's Restaurant opposite Moulton Street.
(5) State Pier garage.

The second lighthouse activity is a boat cruise across Casco Bay. Halfway Rock Lighthouse and Little Mark Island Monument can be seen on a clear day as the motor vessel sails from the waterfront's State Pier to Bailey Island.

The third event is a climb up 102 steps to the Portland Observatory's observation deck (104 feet above sea level). On a clear day one can see Cape Elizabeth Light to the south and Halfway Rock Light at the eastern approach into Casco Bay. The observatory is located on Monjoy Hill at 138 Congress Street.

PORTLAND HARBOR CRUISES.

- **Portland Head Light Cruise / Seals.** Narrated one hour cruise aboard the *Fish Hawk* (one open deck). Departs Long Wharf.
SCHEDULE.
Late June to Columbus Day, daily at 4:45.
FARES. Discounts for seniors, students and children 5-9.
- Eagle Tours, 19 Pilot Point Road, Cape Elizabeth, ME 04107.
Phone (207) 774-6498.

- The **Casco Bay/ Portland Head Light /Seal Watch Cruise** is a 1 1/2-hour narrated cruise aboard the *Bay View Lady* (two decks; lower enclosed). Departs from Fisherman's Wharf opposite Dana Street.
SCHEDULE.
June to September; call or check website for the latest schedule.
FARES. Discounts for seniors 65+ and children under 12.
- Bay View Cruises, 184 Commercial Street (Fisherman's Wharf), Portland, ME 04101.
Phone (207) 761-0496.
Website: http://www.cascobaybiz.com/bayview/home.html

- **Portland Head Light / Lobster Cruise.** An 80 to 90 minute narrated cruise that features a close look at Portland Head Light as well as a glimpse into the daily routines of a Maine lobsterman.
- Lucky Catch Lobstering, 170 Commercial St., Portland, ME 04101.
Phone: (207) 233-2026.
Website: http://www.luckycatch.com/home.html

CASCO BAY CRUISE.

The **Bailey Island Cruise** covers the full length of Casco Bay in separate routes to and from Bailey Island. Although the cruise does not feature lighthouses, it is a relaxing trip with beautiful scenery, a passing view of Little Mark Island Monument and, if it is a clear day, a distant sighting of the Halfway Rock Lighthouse. The Bailey Island layover allows 1 3/4 hours ashore for sightseeing or lunch. The round trip takes 5 hours and 45 minutes. **SCHEDULE.**
Late June to Labor Day, daily (except Saturdays) at 10.
FARES. Round trip fares. Discounts for seniors 65+ and children 5-9. Under 5 free.
- Casco Bay Lines, Casco Bay Ferry Terminal, Commercial & Franklin Streets, Portland, ME 04101.
Phone (207) 774-7871.

HALFWAY ROCK CHARTER CRUISE

There is also an opportunity for the lighthouse seeker to get a closeup view of Halfway Rock Light. Les McNelly operates the 23-foot Wellcraft sportfishing boat *Sea Escape* out of Bailey Island and offers two hour sunset, island and seal watch cruises in the Casco Bay, and also fishing trips and charters to area lighthouses. If the sea conditions are right you might get a look at Ram Island Ledge Light as well as Halfway Rock.

- **Sea Escape Cottages and Charters**, Donna & Les McNelly, P.O. Box 7, Bailey Island, ME 04003

Phone (207) 833-5531.

Website: http://www.seascapecottages.com/   Email: seaesc@mail.gwi.net

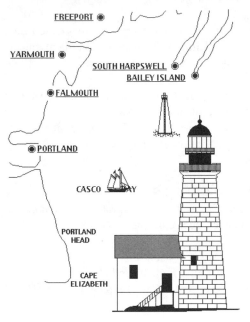

HALFWAY ROCK LIGHTHOUSE.

CHARACTERISTIC: Flashing red 5s

HAW: 77' **RANGE**: 19 nm

Halfway Rock, lying some 11 miles from Portland and midway between Cape Elizabeth and Cape Small, is a barren bunch of rocks that is barely an area of one acre during the calmest low tide.

Construction of the lighthouse received congressional approval in 1869, and $50,000 was appropriated. Delayed by storms, the foundation was laid and ready for the tower in early January 1870. Work did not proceed due to more weather interruptions and purchasing mistakes that required unspent funds to be returned, at the year's end, to the Treasury Department. With $10,000 funded in early 1871, work resumed on the lighthouse.

This 76-foot tall lighthouse is solidly built in the architectural design of Massachusetts' Minot's Ledge Lighthouse. The foundation and lower sections of the tower were put together with hand hewn dovetailed granite blocks. The tower has base and top diameters of 22 feet and 17 feet, respectively.

After its completion, the lighthouse received a third-order Fresnel optic. The light was established on August 15, 1871. In 1883 the optic's lard oil illuminant was changed over to kerosene. Halfway Rock's modern plastic lens was automated in 1975.

The first keepers lived in rooms inside the tower, much like the arrangement at Minot's Ledge Light. Subsequent light station improvements have included a 43-foot tall bell tower (1887), a boathouse constructed next to the tower with loft quarters for the keepers (1888), a new wooden oil house (1890), and a powerful Daboll trumpet (1905).

A new modern house was built for the Coast Guard keepers in 1960. A new boathouse was also added, and the following year a helicopter landing pad was put in. In a February 1972 storm the crew had to be removed by helicopter and the station's buildings were badly damaged.

OWNER. U.S. Coast Guard. Leased in 2000 to the American Lighthouse Foundation.

- American Lighthouse Foundation , PO Box 889, Wells, Maine 04090.

Phone: (207) 646-0515.

Website: http://www.lighthousefoundation.org

PRESERVATION. Listed in the National Register of Historic Places.

The station was badly damaged in storms of 1962, 1972 and 1991. The 1972 nor'easter shook the tower violently and tore up the station's boathouse, catwalk, fuel tanks and generator. The 1991 storm washed away the station's marine railway.

Today all that is left of the light station is the tower with its attached entry and the 'copter pad. Although the lighthouse's masonry appears to be in sound condition, not much restrengthening work has been done on the tower since 1960.

LITTLE MARK ISLAND MONUMENT.

CHARACTERISTIC: Flashing white 4s

HAW: 74' **RANGE**: 5 nm

Little Mark Island lies at the entrance to Casco Bay, about 3.5 miles inside the Halfway Rock Lighthouse and on the ferry route to Cook's Landing on Bailey Island.

HALFWAY ROCK

The monument, built in 1827, is a 65-foot tall obelisk (black and white) built of rubblestone collected on the island. The tower has an 18-foot square base and walls that are three feet thick. The only interior space in the monument is a ground level 12-foot square room. It now contains storage batteries. The top of the obelisk, normally pointed, is chopped off to allow for a four foot square platform to hold the beacon. The optic is reached via a cast-iron ladder fastened to the outside of the tower.

PORTLAND OBSERVATORY. The observatory, an octagonal, brown-shingled and white-capped structure, looks very much like a lighthouse. It is located at 138 Congress Street. Built in 1807, this 84-foot tall building is the last remaining signal tower on the Atlantic Coast. It once served as an unlighted daymark and observation platform for ship owners, mariners and those awaiting the return of their seafaring friends and relatives.

In 1995 the observatory was closed to visitors in order to prepare for major repairs to beetle (not termite) damage. The restoration has entailed the dismantling of the tower, piece by piece, so that each board, beam and post can be inspected for rot. A June 2000 grand reopening ceremony is planned.

OPEN. Past schedule follows.

July and August, Wednesdays, Thursdays and Sundays 1 to 5. Fridays and Saturdays 10 to 5.

June and September to October, Fridays through Sundays 1 to 5.

ADMISSION FEES. Discount for children under 12.

Phone (207) 774-5561.

NORTHBOUND. In addition to land visits, there are several sightseeing boat cruises that offer excellent on board viewings of many lighthouses between Pemaquid Point and the Kennebec River below Bath. Before proceeding farther north, check out the cruises available in Boothbay Harbor as described in the BURNT ISLAND chapter.

Halfway Rock Lighthouse

SQUIRREL POINT
PERKINS ISLAND - POND ISLAND - SEGUIN ISLAND

NORTH ON ROUTE I-95 AND US 1. Take I-95 to Exit 22. Follow Route 1 North through Brunswick to Bath. Take the "Historic Bath" exit down the hill to a traffic light. Turn right on to Washington Street. Go South for 1.6 miles past the Bath Iron Works complex to Maine Maritime Museum and the free parking area.

SOUTH ON US 1. Take Route 1 South across Kennebec River. Exit off bridge at "Front St./Bath/Phippsburg" sign, bearing left down hill. At the traffic light, turn left under the bridge on to Washington Street. Go South for 1.6 miles past the Bath Iron Works complex to Maine Maritime Museum.

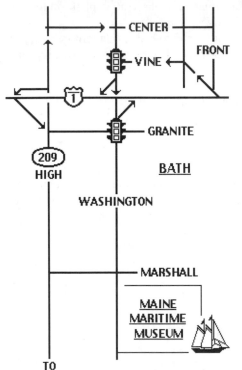

MAINE MARITIME MUSEUM. This complex is the major repository for the preservation of Maine's maritime artifacts and archives, with rich collections and exhibits interpreting the role of ships and sailors since 1607. The visitor may explore the restored turn-of-the-century shipyard buildings, go aboard a Grand Banks fishing schooner (when in port), and browse through a mansion filled with ship portraits and models, dioramas, scrimshaw and seafaring memorabilia.

There also is an indoor "wharf" of the lobstering industry and a film presentation inside a boat-shaped mini-theater. A new exhibit features artifacts from and restorations of wrecked ships, including the Revolutionary War's privateer *Defence*, two Wiscasset-built schooners and a clipper ship, the *Snow Squall*. The latter's restoration was done in the conservation facilities of the Portland Harbor Museum next to the Spring Point Ledge Lighthouse in South Portland. During the summer months the museum plays host to tall ships.

OPEN.
All year, daily 9:30 to 5.
Closed January 1, Thanksgiving Day and December 25.

ADMISSION FEES. Discounts for families, seniors 65+ and children 6-17.

- Maine Maritime Museum, 243 Washington Street, Bath, ME 04530. Phone (207) 443-1316.
Website: http://www.bathmaine.com/
Email: maritime@bathmaine.com

LIGHTHOUSE SIGHTSEEING CRUISES. The museum offers a full schedule of cruises. All cruises depart from the museum dock. Call the museum or check their website for the current cruise schedule.

FARES FOR ALL CRUISES. Discounts for members of the Maine Maritime Museum on all above cruises. Discount for members of the Friends of Seguin Island on the island's cruise.

- **Daily Kennebec River excursion trips**: Memorial Day to Columbus Day. These 50-minute trips highlight the shipbuilding heritage of the Kennebec River. Aboard the *Chippewa*, a 1923 ferry, visitors get a unique opportunity to explore the beautiful Kennebec River and the Bath Iron Works, where vessels are built for the U.S. Navy. This excursion also features a trip around Doubling Point Light (see page 345).

- **Mid-Coast Lighthouse Cruise** sails down the Kennebec River, across Sheepscot Bay, north towards Boothbay Harbor and east into Fisherman Island Passage. Departs at 9 and returns about 4. Typically there is one departure in June, September and October, three in August and four in July. This cruise provides view of at least five lighthouses and seven other navigational lights in Midcoast Maine. Depending on sea conditions, the lighthouses seen may include Burnt Island, Doubling Point, Doubling Point Range, Perkins Island, Pond Island, Ram Island, Seguin Island, Squirrel Point and the Cuckolds. Depending on weather and tide the trip includes a landing at Ram Island, Burnt Island <u>or</u> Seguin Island.

- **Night Lights on the Coast of Maine.** Same itinerary as the midcoast excursion. One trip in August. Departs at 4 and returns at 9.

- **Boothbay Harbor Cruise** traverses the Sasanoa River, Hockamock Bay, Lower Hell Gates, Sheepscot River, Townsend Gut to Boothbay Harbor. July, one trip 9 to 3. This cruise provides sightings of Burnt Island Light and Hendricks Head Light.

SQUIRREL POINT, PERKINS ISLAND, POND ISLAND & SEGUIN ISLAND

- **Foliage Cruise**. Depending on sea conditions and foliage, this cruise may travel to Merrymeeting Bay, Boothbay Harbor or the Sheepscot River, with sightings of several lighthouses possible.

- **Seguin, The Island Sentinel** cruise sails down the Kennebec River and out to the island. June and July, one trip each month 9 to 3. Provides sightings of Squirrel Point, Doubling Point, Doubling Point Range, Perkins Island and Pond Island.

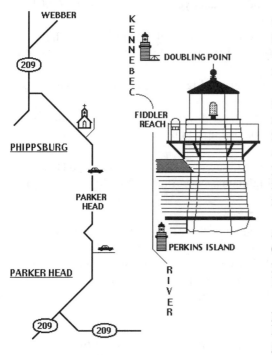

There's enough time ashore to climb to the top of the island and take the guided tour of the lighthouse and keeper's house. From the island's 145 foot summit you can see the White Mountains 90 miles away, while the Maine coast from Cape Elizabeth to Matinicus Island reaches majestically towards the horizon.

Expect moderate to strenuous physical exertion climbing the "Tortoise." Debarking and boarding the launch is not an easy task. There is no dock or pier landing. Passengers are loaded into a skiff for the transfer to the beach. The climb to the summit is a steep, and for some, an arduous one. If the island is enshrouded in fog (as it is for 1/3 of each year) and the fog signal has not been silenced, take along ear plugs. The island's electric foghorn is a powerful one whose blasts can be a shattering experience for the unprepared visitor.

TO PHIPPSBURG. From the museum take Washington Street and connecting Webber Avenue south to ME 209 and turn left. About 0.6 mile south of the intersection and while crossing a causeway, look to your left front and you will see the Doubling Point Lighthouse across the Kennebec River.

About 4.7 miles south of the intersection in Phippsburg and just past the post office and the library (on the right) turn left into Parker Head Road. About 0.4 mile from the turn and past the Phippsburg Congregational Church, is a small, well worn off-road parking area. The Squirrel Point Lighthouse can be seen directly across the river.

It is also possible to walk to Squirrel Point Light. Take Route 127 off Route 1 in Woolwich. After 4.2 miles bear right onto Bald Head Road. Follow the road another 2.3 miles to its end. At the end of the road there is a well defined path that leads to the lighthouse. Although the walk is most beautiful in the early fall, be sure to use insect repellant in any season.

SQUIRREL POINT LIGHTHOUSE.
CHARACTERISTIC: Equal interval red 6s (white sector)
HAW: 25' **RANGES**: White 9; red 7 nm

Squirrel Point is one of three similar light towers built on the Kennebec River in 1898. It is a 25 foot tall, octagonal wood framed and shingle structure. The station's 1 1/2-story wood framed keeper's dwelling is Victorian in design. The garage and barn seen on station were also built in 1898. The brick oil house and boathouse were added in 1901.

The light was automated in 1979. The following year Squirrel Point's original fifth-order Fresnel lens was removed and replaced by a plastic lens. The lens is displayed in the Museum at Portland Head Light.

OWNER. Mike Trenholm, a semi-retired real estate dealer from Yarmouth, Maine, first saw Squirrel Point Light while birdwatching on the Kennebec River in 1993. Three years later he formed a nonprofit organization, the Squirrel Point Light Associates, Inc., and was granted the five-acre station by the Coast Guard. Mr. Trenholm has made improvements on the property and hopes to establish it as an educational center.

PRESERVATION. Listed in the National Register of Historic Places.

TO PARKER HEAD. Motor south on Parker Head Road for another 2.2 miles and you will pass a large boulder on a narrow curve painted with the words "Parker Head." Continue for another 0.1 mile and turn left downhill into a paved public landing road. Drive the short distance down to the Kennebec River.

The Perkins Island Lighthouse, located directly across the Kennebec River in Georgetown about three miles from the mouth of the Kennebec River, cannot be seen or reached on its side of the river.

PERKINS ISLAND LIGHTHOUSE.
CHARACTERISTIC: Flashing red 2.5s (2 white sectors)
HAW: 41' **RANGES**: White 6: red 5 nm

The station built in 1898 includes the 23-foot tall, octagonal, wood and shingle lighthouse (the bracketed gallery was added in 1899), the two-story wood framed keeper's dwelling and barn. Added in later years are the boathouse (1901), the pyramidal wooden bell tower (1902) and the brick oil house (1906).

Perkins Island's original fifth-order Fresnel was removed in 1979 when the string of Kennebec River lights was automated. Today the lantern holds a modern lens. The station's 1,000-pound fog bell is located on the grounds of the Georgetown High School.

OWNER. U.S. Coast Guard (lighthouse only), leased in 2000 to the American Lighthouse Foundation. The keeper's dwelling is the responsibility of the State of Maine.

PRESERVATION. Listed in the National Register of Historic Places. Except for a 2000 restoration of the fog bell tower, the State of Maine has done little for this station. The dwelling is boarded up and in very poor condition.

TO POPHAM BEACH. See the following map. From Parker Head continue south on Parker Head Road to ME 209 and turn left. The first sightings of the Pond Island and Seguin Island Lighthouses occur along ME 209 as the highway reaches and skirts the shoreline and passes Popham Beach State Park.

HUNNEWELLS BEACH LIFESAVING STATION. Enroute you will pass this beautifully restored historic structure built in 1883. It is now a lodging facility whose architectural styling closely resembles the yet to be restored Portsmouth Harbor Lifesaving Station off Maine's Kittery Point (WHALEBACK chapter) and the restored and open Sandy Hook (Spermaceti Visitor Center) in the Gateway National Recreation Center in Highlands, NJ (SANDY HOOK chapter).

- Popham Beach Bed & Breakfast, HC31, Box 430, Popham Beach, Phippsburg, ME 04562. Phone (207) 389-2409.

FORT POPHAM STATE HISTORIC SITE. This semi-lunette granite and brick coast artillery fortification, begun in 1861, was built to protect Bath from marauding Confederate ships. The warships never arrived and the unfinished fort was abandoned. Of architectural interest are the undisturbed circular granite staircases. Note also the partially shaped granite blocks strewn about the grounds. There is a splendid panoramic view from the fort's parapets.

OPEN. Memorial Day to September, daily 9 to sunset.
FREE ADMISSION. Ample free parking.
Phone (207) 389-1335.

Pond Island is the closer of the two lighthouse islands. Its light marks the east side entrance to the Kennebec River. Seguin Island light, which marks the river's west side entrance, lies about two miles offshore to the south southeast. Although the public is permitted on Pond Island, except during the nesting season in the spring and early summer, there are no scheduled excursions to the island.

POND ISLAND LIGHTHOUSE.
CHARACTERISTIC: Equal interval white 6s
HAW: 52 ' **RANGE**: 9 nm

Pond Island is the first of the Kennebec River beacons mariners pass bound for Bath. A white conical stone tower was first built in 1821. In 1855 the lighthouse was completely rebuilt as a cylindrical brick tower in the Federal Design architectural style.

The 20-foot tall lighthouse's original optic was a whale oil-fed lamp and a fifth-order Fresnel lens.

A ferocious storm that caused widespread damage on September 8, 1869, did not spare Pond Island. The fog bell tower was destroyed along with the striking mechanism, but the bell survived.

After the light was automated and the Coast Guard keepers departed in 1963, the keeper's dwelling, oil house, fog signal building and boathouse were dismantled. The Fresnel lens was replaced by a modern lens.

OWNER. U.S. Coast Guard. The 10-acre island is a migratory bird refuge under the care of the U.S. Fish and Wildlife Service.

PRESERVATION. Not listed in the National Register of Historic Places.

SQUIRREL POINT, PERKINS ISLAND, POND ISLAND & SEGUIN ISLAND

SEGUIN ISLAND LIGHTHOUSE.
CHARACTERISTIC: Fixed white
HAW: 180' **RANGE**: 18 nm

The first lighthouse on Seguin Island was Maine's second; it was built by order of President George Washington. It was a 38-foot tall wooden tower built on a stone foundation and completed in 1795. Its light was established in 1796 for about $6,300.

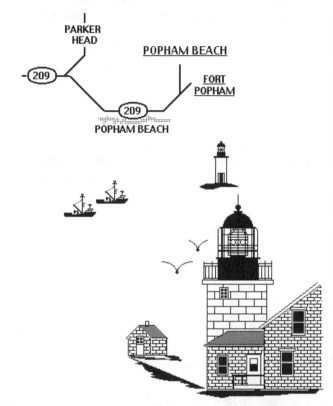

Seguin Island's first keeper was a French Alsatian who emigrated to Maine, fought in the American Revolution and was discharged with the rank of Major. For his war services, John Polereczky was given the keeper's job and a special congressional stipend of $150 to clear some acreage for farming purposes. He endured six years of want and hardship. Denied a decent salary and forced to pay for his family's upkeep, new buildings and boats out of his own pocket, the neglected and often marooned keeper left the island in 1802 and returned to his hometown of Dresden, Maine.

Seguin Island's second lighthouse was a granite stone tower erected in 1819. It replaced the original tower that was toppled by a storm.

Construction of the present 53-foot tall granite block lighthouse was necessary to permit the installation of Maine's only first-order Fresnel lens. The tower's design is of the Federal Design genre.

Seguin Island's classical optic, first lighted in 1857, remains in the lantern and is protected by bulletproof storm panes.

In 1857 the station also received the present keepers' house, a 1 1/2-story dormered duplex cape. The brick oil house was added in 1892 and a fog signal tower in 1889. The station's original fog bell can be seen on the grounds of the Boothbay Harbor Coast Guard Station.

Seguin Island also has Maine's only remaining tramway, a donkey house with diesel engine that pulled the tram on rails from the landing wharf to near the top of the bluff. The tramway was used to bring supplies to the lighthouse.

In 1985 the light was automated and the keepers were removed. A Coast Guard crew arrived to remove the giant Fresnel lens, only to be told by local lobsterman Pat Moffatt that an act of Congress was needed to dismantle the lens. The men checked and found out it was true.

OWNER. U.S. Coast Guard (lighthouse). After automation the future of Seguin Island Light was uncertain. Some concerned local citizens founded the Friends of Seguin Island in 1986. The Friends of Seguin Island received a ten-year lease on the property from the Coast Guard in 1989. In February 1998, under the Maine Lights Program, the property was transferred to the group.

PRESERVATION. Listed in the National Register of Historic Places.

In June 1990, with contributions received from the public and a generous grant from the U.S. Congress through the National Park Service, the Maine Historic Preservation Commission plus other matching funds programs, the Friends of Seguin Island announced they had restored the dormered duplex cape sufficiently and installed, repaired or reactivated enough household facilities (well and pump, hot water heater, furnace, septic tank, plumbing and tramway) to hire summertime caretakers. Large materials for the renovation project were airlifted by a helicopter donated by a Cape Cod Coast Guard unit. Smaller items were landed (often in rough seas) by the contractor's 21-foot utility boat. The occupation of the keepers' dwelling was made on one rare clear June day, when the Maine Air National Guard's 112th Medical Company helicopters provided the airlift to move furniture and supplies onto the island.

As the restoration progressed through 1992, it was discovered that damage to the interior walls and ceilings from water leaking through the old roof was more extensive than originally estimated. After removing the walls and ceilings on the first floor, it was decided a refinishing job was not necessary. Instead of false interiors, the old keeper's dwelling now shows its original and authentic inner brick walls and wide natural beamed ceiling.

SQUIRREL POINT, PERKINS ISLAND, POND ISLAND & SEGUIN ISLAND

On August 31, 1993, despite sea swells that prevented many travelers from reaching the island, the Friends opened their small museum in the lower two rooms on the north side of the keepers' quarters. The museum supplements the guided tour of the station with its displays containing historical memorabilia from Seguin Island's past.

In February 1998 the Coast Guard announced plans to replace Seguin's first-order Fresnel lens with a modern solar powered plastic optic, with the intention of doing away with the submarine cable providing power to the optic. The Friends of Seguin Island want the lens to remain in the lighthouse under their care. The lens is the last operating first-order Fresnel lens in Maine. The Coast Guard has announced that they will put off any solarization plans until 2003. The disposition of the lens is still under discussion in early 2000.

You can help support the continuing preservation of this historic place by becoming a "Friend" of the lighthouse. To do so, contact:

\- Friends of Seguin Island, PO Box 866, Bath, ME 04530.

Phone (207) 443-4808.

__A 'HIGH ON A WINDY HILL' ADVENTURE.__ Recruiting caretakers is a year-round task. The Friends are always looking for two hale and hardy people (or family) to take care of Seguin Island, its keepers' quarters and the historic lighthouse. The job entails yard care, house maintenance work, greeting visitors and conducting tours. If you are interested and feel you are able and ready for few adventurous months from the Memorial Day weekend through Labor Day, contact the Friends at the above address.

Seguin Island Lighthouse

DOUBLING POINT RANGE
DOUBLING POINT

SOUTH ON ME 127. In Woolwich, at the east end of the Kennebec River's Carlton Bridge (sometime in 2000 this Bridge will be replaced by a new, as yet unnamed, bridge), turn south off US 1 onto ME 127 (start 0.0 mile). Then:

-> Right into unpaved Whitmore's Landing Road (1.7 miles). It is marked with a "Whitmore's Landing Rd.- To Doubling Pt. Rd." sign,

-> At a "T" in the route, turn left into Doubling Point Road (2.2 miles).

-> To visit the Doubling Point Range Light Station, take a small dirt road on your left about one-tenth mile after the "T" beginning Doubling Point Road.

-> Continue on Doubling Point Road to the Doubling Point Lighthouse (2.7 miles). There is free parking for two cars at the end of the lane.

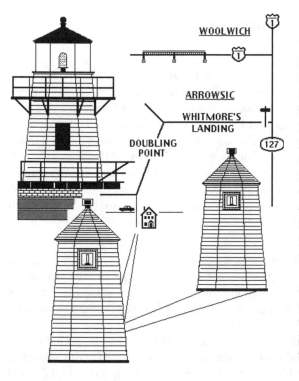

KENNEBEC RIVER LIGHT STATION.

Back in 1938, the Federal Government began a long range Kennebec River retrenchment program by selling the Doubling Point keeper's house and grounds to a private party and transferring responsibility for the light to the keeper of the Doubling Point Range Lights. In 1979, when the Doubling Point range beacons were automated and the station closed, responsibility for those aids and the Doubling Point light was transferred to the keeper of the Squirrel Point Lighthouse. It happened again in 1981. Citing hardship reasons, especially the boating of the keeper's children across the swift flowing Kennebec River to go to school in Phippsburg, the Coast Guard moved the Squirrel Point lightkeeper and family up to the closed Doubling Point Range Light Station. With this last move, the Coast Guard had to install new radio equipment to control the fog signals at Squirrel Point and Doubling Point and, at the same time, monitor all four lights.

The Kennebec River Light Station came into being in 1982 in an effort to control the once watched but now automated lights strung along the river from Doubling Point below Bath to Perkins Island at Georgetown. In that year also, the station was designated a single family assignment and Boatswain Mate Karen McLean became the Coast Guard's first woman lighthouse keeper.

Following the end of her tour of duty, her husband, BM1 Daniel W. McLean, assumed the keeper's position. With the station's complete automation in 1990, Bos'n McLean became the last keeper of the Kennebec River beacons.

DOUBLING POINT RANGE FRONT & RANGE REAR LIGHT TOWERS.

CHARACTERISTICS: Front continuous quick flashing white; rear equal interval white 6s

HAW: Front 18'; rear 33'

Prior to 1898, the Kennebec River's navigational aids were privately maintained by shipping companies. In 1892 the Lighthouse Board decided to establish its own beacons. With $17,000 in appropriations, the Board constructed the above mentioned four light stations.

The Doubling Point range lighthouses are octagonal, wood and shingle structures, 235 yards apart with a connecting wooden walkway. The front tower is 21 feet tall, the rear one 13 feet tall. The station's keepers' residence, also built in 1898, is a wood framed Victorian dwelling. Other station properties include a fuel shed (1898), a boathouse (1901) and an oil house (1902).

When built, both towers were equipped with fifth-order Fresnel optics. The optics were automated in 1979, removed and replaced by modern plastic lenses. Today one of the Fresnel lenses is active in the Rockland Harbor Southwest Lighthouse.

The Doubling Point aids are the only active range lights in Maine. They guide mariners through the river's navigable channel. To do so, captains and pilots align the lights as they approach Fiddler Reach, the river's sharp double bend at Doubling Point.

OWNER. Under terms of the Maine Lights Program the station was turned over to the Range Light Keepers, a nonprofit group. The Range Lights Keepers focus will be to preserve the historic scene on the river as it has been viewed for over 100 years. The organizations has made a partnership with the Maine Maritime Museum and it is hoped that some of the museum's cruises may be able to land at the Range Lights in the future. The U.S. Coast Guard maintains the active optics.

- Range Light Keepers, c/o Michael Kreindler, HC 33 Box 79, Arrowsic, ME 04530.
Phone (207) 442-7443
Website: http://www.rlk.org/

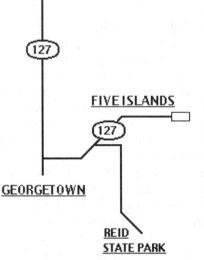

PRESERVATION. Listed in the National Register of Historic Places as part of the Kennebec River Light Station.

DOUBLING POINT LIGHTHOUSE.
CHARACTERISTIC: Quick white
HAW: 18'

This 35-foot tall shingled wood framed lighthouse, with its concrete pier and distinctive walkway, was constructed at the same time as Kennebec River's other aids. The octagonal tower, which no longer holds a fifth-order Fresnel lens, is located at the upper end of Fiddler Reach where the Kennebec River straightens out and leads northward to Bath. The lens supported optic was automated in the mid-1970s and the lantern was refitted with a modern lens. The Fresnel lens is now on display at the Shore Village Museum in Rockland. The station complex includes the light tower, an L-shaped wood framed house (1898), a bell tower (1898), an oil house (1906) and an outbuilding (1898). In August 1980 the bell was removed by the Coast Guard; its location is unknown.

OWNER. Dwelling, support buildings and grounds are privately owned. Under the Maine Lights Program the lighthouse property was transferred to the Friends of Doubling Point Light in April 1998. The group had been working to save the lighthouse since 1996. The Friends of Doubling Point Light plan to improve access to the lighthouse. Officials from the Maine Maritime Museum in Bath have said they plan to offer boat and van tours to the lighthouse and keeper's house in the future. The still-active light is maintained by the U.S. Coast Guard.

PRESERVATION. Listed in the National Register of Historic Places. In 1985 the old walkway to the lighthouse was replaced by a new walkway made of unpainted, pressure-treated wood. Over the decades ice floes in the Kennebec damaged and shifted Doubling Point Light's foundation of granite blocks. The Friends of Doubling Point Light raised $24,000 and received a matching grant of $25,000 to save the historic landmark. In December 1999 the lighthouse was lifted from its foundation by a crane on a barge. The tower was carried on the barge to temporary storage in Woolwich while repairs were done to the foundation. A temporary light on a pole served as an aid to navigation until the repairs were completed a few weeks later, and the lighthouse was returned to its home.

- Friends of Doubling Point Light, c/o Betsy Skillings-Coleman, HCR 33 Box 61B, Arrowsic, ME 04530.
Website: http://www.doublingpoint.org

FIDDLER'S REACH FOG BELL TOWER

The Fiddler's Reach Fog Signal, the bell tower standing at the water's edge between the range lights and Doubling Point, has been in terrible shape for many years. The structure is one of very few towers left along the Atlantic seaboard. In 1999 a crew led by Bob Stevens of West Point stabilized the tower, replacing underpinnings and sills, and replacing a badly damaged window. Downeast Energy & Building Supply of Brunswick donated building materials needed for this project. The Range Light Keepers now have the responsibility of restoring and maintaining the fog signal. Help is welcomed.

TO FIVE ISLANDS.
Before leaving the area, you might want to take a look at a view of the Hendricks Head Lighthouse. To do so, continue south on ME 127 to Georgetown, then northeast on ME 127 past its juncture with the Reid State Park road and into the village of Five Islands. Drive straight ahead to the Georgetown Fisherman's Co-op's wharf. Parking is free. Walk out onto the wharf. Hendricks Head Lighthouse can be seen about one mile away (binoculare help), directly across the Sheepscot River. Before you leave, try the co-op's fresh and reasonably priced lobster roll.

HENDRICKS HEAD
THE CUCKOLDS

On US 1 five miles southwest of Newcastle (or 2 miles east of Wiscasset) take ME 27 through Boothbay Harbor to West Southport. About 2 miles south of the ME 27 and ME 238 junction in West Southport bear right around a triangular intersection (statue and flagpole) and past the Southport Island General Store. The turn is also marked with a small "Beach Rd" sign. Where the road dips downhill into Dogfish Head Road, bear left into Beach Road and continue for 0.5 mile to a public beach and free parking. The view of the lighthouse is somewhat blocked by the keeper's dwelling from this location. The lighthouse can also be seen from Five Islands (see the previous page) and from cruises leaving Boothbay Harbor (see page 349) and the Maine Maritime Museum in Bath (see page 340).

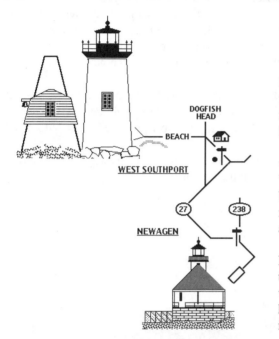

HENDRICKS HEAD LIGHTHOUSE.
CHARACTERISTIC: Fixed white (red sector)
HAW: 43' **RANGES**: White 9; red 7 nm

The first light station on the point was built in 1829. The lighthouse was a rubblestone house surmounted by a short tower and lantern. Its whale oil-powered multi-lamp and reflector optic produced a fixed white light some 39 feet above the water. The station was rebuilt in 1875.

Today the complex includes the 39-foot tall brick Federal Revival lighthouse connected to the two-story wood framed house with Victorian styling by an elevated wooden walkway, a pyramidal wooden bell tower (1890) and a brick oil house (1895) that is connected to the main walkway by an open catwalk. Both walkways had to be rebuilt after a 1978 storm washed the boathouse into the Sheepscot River.

The light station was discontinued in 1933 and sold to William Prichard Browne two years later for less than $5,000. Unfortunately, the keeper's house lacked the essentials for comfortable living. There was no electricity, no plumbing and no telephone. The heating system had been removed and water had to be collected by rain gutters and sent into basement cisterns via downspouts.

In 1951, after Mr. Browne had brought electrical power to his residence and with an increase in river traffic, the Coast Guard returned the optic. In 1979 the Fresnel lens was replaced by an automated plastic lens.

OWNER. After having remained in the same family for two generations, this historic Maine landmark was placed on the real estate market in June 1987 for $1,450,000. In 1988 at $1.2 million asked, the owners, Gil and Mary Browne Charbonneau reportedly turned down an offer from a developer who wanted to buy the lighthouse to build expensive houses on the station property. The U.S. Coast Guard maintains the beacon.

PRESERVATION. Listed in the National Register of Historic Places.

In February 1991, the five-acre station was sold to Benjamin and Luanne Russell of Alexander, Alabama for around $850,000. The new owners have completely restored all of the structures to near perfect condition. To return the property to its original appearance, the station's buildings have been given red roofs and all, except the brick oil house, have been painted white. The Russells intend to maintain the property's integrity while using the station as their personal summer retreat. Although the station is not open to the public, it is sufficiently exposed to be able to see their outstanding restorative accomplishments.

For more information:
Ben Russell, 2544 Willow Point Road, Alexander City, AL 35010
Website: http://www.benrussell.com/HH-home.htm
Email: benr@webshoppe.net

TO NEWAGEN. Return to ME 27 and motor south for 2.8 miles to Newagen center. At the town's post office and ME 27's 90-degree turn north into ME 238, bear southeast into a paved road. There is a small "Town Landing" sign at the corner. Continue for about 0.2 mile to a small parking area (free) at the foot of a public pier. The Cuckolds Lighthouse lies 1,000 yards off Cape Newagen on a barren outcropping. The lighthouse can also be seen from some of the cruises leaving Boothbay Harbor (see page 349) and the Maine Maritime Museum in Bath (see page 340).

THE CUCKOLDS LIGHTHOUSE (CUCKOLDS).
CHARACTERISTIC: Group flashing white 6s
HAW: 59' **RANGE**: 12 nm

The first aid to navigation on this ledge was a wooden tripod-shaped daybeacon that was established as early as 1802. In 1892 a companion round stone fog signal house was built at a cost of close to $25,000. The original signal was a steam-powered trumpet.

Then in 1907, after a two-story, square wood framed keeper's salt box had been attached to the original signal house, the present octagonal lighthouse tower was placed atop the complex between both structure's sloping roofs.

The structure was not well built, and to add to the keepers' miseries the station's low elevation caused it to be inundated during windy high tides and storms. In January 1933 a storm swept over the Cuckolds and destroyed the belongings of Keeper Harold Seavey, who was reimbursed in full by the Department of Commerce. Another keeper's wife said she was sewing near a second story window one August day when a "freak wave" poured through the window, damaging much of the furniture.

When the light was automated in 1975, the property was boarded up and abandoned. At the same time, the 48-foot tall lighthouse's fourth-order Fresnel lens, manufactured by the McBeth Glass Company of Pittsburgh, Pennsylvania, was removed. The lens is on display at the Shore Village Museum in Rockland. The light is now produced by an automated modern lens.

The dwelling, helicopter pad, boat launchway and support buildings were subsequently washed away in 1978 during a winter storm. After the blizzard cleared, the house could be seen floating in the harbor.

OWNER. U.S. Coast Guard.
PRESERVATION. Not listed in the National Register of Historic Places.

The Cuckolds Lighthouse

BURNT ISLAND

IN BOOTHBAY HARBOR. The cruise dock are located on Commercial Street. At ME 27's Oak - Townsend - Todd intersection turn right into Wharf Street (one way) and right again into Commercial (one way). Parking in downtown Boothbay is available in several private and municipal lots. See maps.

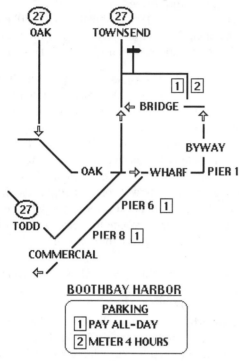

BOOTHBAY HARBOR

PARKING
1 PAY ALL-DAY
2 METER 4 HOURS

By all means don't pass up the opportunity to visit Monhegan Island and its lighthouse and museum. But before you jump aboard a boat departing Boothbay Harbor, check out your options as presented in the MONHEGAN ISLAND chapter.

Also note that Burnt Island Light can be seen from some of the cruises leaving the Maine Maritime Museum in Bath (see page 340). Depending on sea conditions, some of the trips allow visitors to disembark at Burnt Island.

REGIONAL LIGHTHOUSE CRUISES. Although Boothbay Harbor offers a variety of sightseeing cruises, Captain Bob Fish's excursions are varied and well presented. His *Island Lady* and the *Pink Lady* (both have enclosed decks) depart from Pier 1. Reservations are recommended. Keep in mind that occasional charters may preempt scheduled cruises.

- The **Spectacular Kennebec River - Bath Cruise** is a 44-mile trip from Boothbay Harbor to the Sheepscot Bay, the Kennebec River and the Sasanoa River, through Lower Hell Gates to Hockamock Bay, then to the Sheepscot River, Townsend Gut and returning to Boothbay Harbor.

Passes Burnt Island, Doubling Point, Doubling Point Range, Perkins Island, [Pond Island and Seguin Island distant viewings], Squirrel Point and the Cuckolds.

SCHEDULE. A three hour trip.
July to September, Tuesdays at 9:30. Weekends at 1.

- The **Pemaquid Point Lighthouse cruise** takes two hours. Passes Burnt Island, Ram Island and Pemaquid Point.
SCHEDULE. June to August, Mondays at 1 and Thursdays at 10.

- The **Little Bit O' Maine** cruise takes two hours. Passes Burnt Island, Hendricks Head and the Cuckolds.
SCHEDULE.
June to September, Mondays and Fridays at 10. Tuesdays at 1.
Early June and October, Sundays only at 1.

FARES FOR ALL CRUISES. Discounts for seniors (Mondays) and daily for children under 12.
- R. N. Fish & Son, PO Box 660 (65 Atlantic Avenue), Boothbay Harbor, ME 04538-0660.
Phone (207) 633-3244 or 633-2626. In USA toll-free (800) 636-3244.
Website: http://www.capnfishmotel.com/boattrips.htm

VIEWING THE BURNT ISLAND LIGHTHOUSE. See the following map. This lighthouse can be seen from along the road to Spruce Point.
TO SPRUCE POINT. Follow ME 27 (Townsend) north to Union Street and turn right. Then;
-> Right at Atlantic Avenue (start 0.0 mile),
-> Continue on Atlantic past Lobster Cove Road (0.4 mile) and Roads End Road (0.7 mile) into Grand View Road. There are several places along Grand View that afford glimpses of the lighthouse. Probably the best place to view the lighthouse is 0.7 mile south of the Roads End intersection.

BURNT ISLAND LIGHTHOUSE.
CHARACTERISTIC: Flashing red 6s (2 white sectors)
HAW: 61' **RANGES:** Red 12; white 15 nm

AMERICA'S ATLANTIC COAST LIGHTHOUSES - MAINE

This 30-foot tall fieldstone and brick tower and a wooden keeper's house (torn down in 1857) were constructed in 1821. In 1857, after the tower's lantern was enlarged to accommodate a Fresnel lens, the rebuilt lantern's service gallery was propped up by angled wooden struts anchored at the structure's midriff, giving the tower the appearance of a Dutch windmill. The supports were removed in 1921, when the tower underwent another refurbishing.

The station includes a 1 1/2-story keeper's cottage and connecting covered walkway (1857), a boathouse (1880) and a brick and slate oil house (1899). A fuel building added in 1886 has been dismantled. When first established, Burnt Island held a Lewis multi-lamp/reflector optic. In 1857 the lighthouse was refitted with a Barrier, Bernard and Turrene fourth-order Fresnel lens.

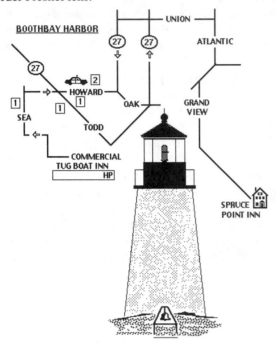

Because it interfered with the Cuckolds' warning beam, Burnt Island's fixed white light was altered in 1888 to show a dark sector (dead angle). This change allowed ships to be guided first by the Cuckolds' beacon. Then, once past the ledges around the Cuckolds, the Burnt Island light took over for the passage into Boothbay Harbor. In 1890 the light's characteristic was changed to fixed red with two white sectors, eliminating the need for the dead angle. Finally in 1892, the light was again changed to show its present characteristics.

In April 1962, Burnt Island Light became the last lighthouse in New England to be converted from kerosene to electricity, then in 1989 it became one of the last Maine lights to be automated, when an automated modern lens was installed.

OWNER. The beacon is maintained by the U. S. Coast Guard. The station was leased to and managed by the Burnt Island Lighthouse Society from 1980 to 1998. In February 1998, as part of the Maine Lights Program, the Maine Lighthouse Selection Committee approved the transfer of Burnt Island Light to the Maine Department of Marine Resources. The DMR intends to use the property for educational purposes. The Burnt Island Educational Facility will provide maritime history programs as well as programs in navigation, ecosystems, fisheries, art, literature and music.

- Maine Department of Marine Resources, Boothbay Headquarters,
Phone (207) 633-9500.
Website: http://janus.state.me.us/dmr/
PRESERVATION. Listed in the National Register of Historic Places.

Burnt Island Lighthouse

MONHEGAN ISLAND
FRANKLIN ISLAND

Monhegan Island can be reached from Boothbay Harbor, New Harbor and Port Clyde. Travelers should review the following transportation offerings before planning a trip to the island. The Boothbay Harbor cruise may be the most popular one, but it covers the longest sailing distance. It does offer a special predeparture boat ride around the island. Port Clyde's round trip fares are a few dollars less than the New Harbor and Boothbay Harbor ferries. Passenger space on the Port Clyde ferry is the most difficult to secure, since it serves the island's postal, commercial and tourist transportation needs.

If either disembarkation or embarkation occurs at low tide, the walk down or up the gangway may be a fairly steep one.

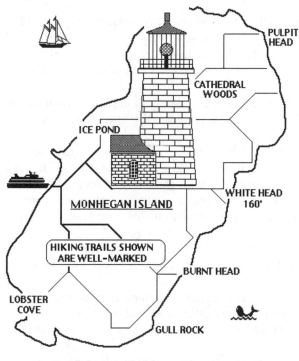

FROM BOOTHBAY HARBOR. See the Boothbay Harbor map on page 349. Captains Bob and Bill Campbell's *Balmy Days II* (two decks, lower enclosed) is docked at Pier 8 on Commercial Street. Parking (all day fee) is available on Chimney Pier next to Pier 7 and in other all day downtown lots. Reservations (recommended) are held until 9:15. Crossing time one hour and 25 minutes.

SCHEDULE. All departures at 9:30. Arrives Monhegan Island at 11, allowing plenty of time to take the one-half mile walk up to Lighthouse Hill to visit the lighthouse and its museum.

Departs at 2:45. For a small additional fee passengers may take a one-half hour jaunt around the island. The cruise begins at 2 and returns to pick up passengers for the 2:45 departure. Recommended for its fascinating views of Monhegan Island.

May and first three weekends in October, weekends only. First week in June to September, daily at 9:30.

FARES. Round trip fare. Discount for children under 12.

- Captains Bob and Bill Campbell, PO Box 535, Boothbay Harbor, ME 04538.

Phone (207) 633-2284. In USA toll free (800) 298-2284.

FROM NEW HARBOR. See the map on page 356.

Stacie Davidson and Captain Al Crocetti's 60-passenger *Hardy III* (two decks, lower enclosed) departs New Harbor's Shaw's Fish and Lobster Wharf in New Harbor. Reservations are held until 20 minutes before departure. Parking (free) is required at the ball field located one-half mile north of the ME 130 and ME 32 intersection or south just beyond Shaw's Restaurant on ME 32.

SCHEDULE. All departures at 9. Departs Monhegan Island at 2:30.

Mid-May to mid-June: Wednesdays, Saturdays and Sundays, and Memorial Day.

Mid-June to late September: daily.

First two weeks in October: Wednesdays, Saturdays, Sundays and Columbus Day.

FARES. Round trip ticket. Discount for children under 12. Reservations required.

- Hardy Boat Cruises, PO Box 326, New Harbor, ME 04554.

Phone: (207) 677-2026. In USA toll free (800) 278-3346.

Website: http://www.hardyboat.com/   Email: hardy@gwi.net

FROM PORT CLYDE. See the map on page 358.

Captain James Barstow operates the cargo and mail boat service to Monhegan Island the year round. Parking (all-day fee) is available at the dock. Reservations are required and will be held until one hour and 15 minutes before each 10:30 departure. A non-refundable deposit is required to hold a reservation until 45 minutes before departure.

Crossing time is 70 minutes for the *Laura B* (one deck, aft cabin); 50 minutes for the newer light freight/passenger *Elizabeth Ann* (two decks, lower enclosed).

SCHEDULE. Daily service most of the year, with limited trips in winter. Dates change yearly. Call or check website for the latest schedule.

FARES. Round trip ticket. Discount for children under 12. Pets permitted for extra fare. Credit cards accepted. Advance reservations are required.

- Monhegan-Thomaston Boat Line, PO Box 238, Port Clyde, ME 04855.

  Phone (207) 372-8848. Fax (207) 372-8547.

  Website: http://www.monheganboat.com/   Email: barstow@monheganboat.com

THE ISLAND. Lying 10 miles off the Maine coast, the island is the site of Maine's first fishing village settled in 1619. Before that Monhegan Island was long used by local Indians who gave it its name, which means "Island of the Sea." Today most of its 100 or so permanent residents are still engaged in the fishing and lobster harvesting industries. The island's beauty has also attracted a good many tourists and vacationing naturalists, writers and such well-known artists as Robert Henri, Jamie Wyeth, Rockwell Kent and George Bellows.

The island is 1.5 miles long and a mere 0.5 mile wide. Rusting shipwrecks line the island's shores. In the center of the island is Cathedral Woods, a thick stand of tall, fragrant balsams. The eastern shore's granite cliffs rise 150 feet above the ocean. The lighthouse is located on the island's highest elevation.

Vehicles are not permitted on the island's unimproved gravel roads. Scenic hiking trails, some rugged, are well marked. Camping is not allowed. Until a few years ago, residents produced their own electricity or did without. In 1986 an enterprising chap bought a generator and is now supplying some island homes with electricity. Don't be surprised, however, if as an overnight guest you must find your way to the bedroom by flashlight, candlelight or a kerosene lamp.

The village has gift shops, art galleries and restaurants. Groceries and trail maps are available at the Monhegan Store in the village center. There are no fancy lodgings, just these bed and breakfast inns and old hotels.

- **Island Inn**. (207) 596-0371. On the harbor. Mid-June to mid-September. Modified American plan.
- **Monhegan House**. (207) 594-7983. Across from the church. Mid-May to mid-October. No electricity. Breakfast only. Guests must be at least 15 years of age.
- **Shining Sails Guest House**. (207) 596-0041. All year. Rooms and efficiencies. Continental breakfast.
- **Hitchcock House**. (207) 594-8137. Top of Horn's Hill. All year. Rooms, efficiencies and one cabin.
- **The Trailing Yew**. (207) 596-0040. On Lobster Cove Road. Mid-May to mid-October. Modified American plan. Controlled pets allowed.
- The Tribler Cottage. (207) 594-2445. On the Meadow (village center). All year. Four housekeeping apartments and one private room.

MONHEGAN ISLAND LIGHTHOUSE.
CHARACTERISTIC: Flashing white 30s
HAW: 178' RANGE: 21 nm

The first lighthouse on Monhegan Island was a short granite block tower. Construction of the light tower and a small wooden keeper's dwelling, costing $3,000, was completed in 1824. Storms so damaged the gray conical lighthouse that it had to be rebuilt during the 1850-51 period, raising its overall height to 48 feet. With its light 178 feet above sea level, Monhegan Island Light is the second-highest light in Maine (after Seguin Island).

The tower's first optic was a Winslow Lewis lighting device consisting of 10 lamps each backed with a 16-inch reflector. The optic produced both flashing red and white signals. In 1856 the 47-foot tall lighthouse was fitted with a second-order Fresnel lens.

The beacon was automated in 1959, using a modern lens powered by an electrical generator housed in a fog signal building located on Manana Island. That change forced the retirement of the classical lens and its kerosene-fed Welsbach mantle and the weight-activated rotating system. At the same time the Coast Guard announced that the station was surplus government property. The aid is operated and maintained by Coast Guard personnel headquartered on Manana Island.

A clockwork powered fog bell installed on Monhegan in 1854 was inaudible in high winds. In 1870 it was replaced by a steam operated Daboll trumpet (whistle) on neighboring Manana Island. The trumpet was not always heard at sea, so a more powerful Daboll was placed in operation on Manana in 1877. The older trumpet was reinstalled at the Portland Head Lighthouse. The 1877 Daboll trumpet was replaced in 1912 with a siren. Today an electronic diaphragm horn punctuates foggy days or nights with two gale-strength blasts every minute.

MONHEGAN ISLAND & FRANKLIN ISLAND

OWNER. U.S. Coast Guard (lighthouse). The two-story Victorian-styled keeper's house (1874), brick oil house (1893), garage, storage building and grounds were sold on June 1, 1962 to the Monhegan Associates, Inc., an historic preservation organization formed in 1954. In 1985 title to the museum was transferred to a new organization, the Monhegan Historical and Cultural Museum Association, incorporated in 1984. Under the Maine Lights Program the lighthouse became the property of the association in December 1997.

PRESERVATION. Listed in the National Register of Historic Places.

After having been transferred to the Monhegan Associates in 1962, the station's properties underwent extensive restorations. That project culminated in the opening of the museum on July 1, 1968. After the station's transfer to the Association in 1985, a major restoration of the buildings was begun. That project, now completed, was made possible by grants from the Maine Preservation Commission and funds from the National Park Service.

In 1995 the Monhegan Museum announced that it would replicate the station's keeper's dwelling that was raised in 1851 and torn down in the 1920s. The Association has reconstructed the house to serve as a museum for their art collection. It is the first time a keeper's house has been reconstructed in Maine. A destroyed outbuilding also will be rebuilt and used as a storage vault.

THE MONHEGAN HISTORICAL AND CULTURAL MUSEUM. The museum, housed in the restored two-story keeper's Victorian residence (1874) and outbuildings, has been open to the public since July 1968. It displays photographs and artifacts pertaining to the island's people, flora, fauna and marine life as well as a collection of paintings and crafts created by visiting and part time resident artists. From the top of the lighthouse one can enjoy a panoramic view of the island, its harbor and Manana Island. The museum has another interesting exhibit. Outside hanging from its stanchion is the original fog bell placed in operation on Manana Island in 1855. In 1969 the old fog signal was declared surplus government property. Without the heavy equipment to handle the inter-island transfer, the bell was doomed to remain on Manana. Fortunately, a solution was found when the Monhegan Water Company hired a helicopter in 1972 to move a new water tower onto the island. Once the water tower was in place, the aircraft flew over to Manana, picked up the bell and lowered it onto its present resting spot. The bell is featured in Jamie Wyeth's painting "Bronze Age."

OPEN. July to mid-September (possibly to end of September), daily 11:30 to 3:30.

FREE ADMISSION. Donations welcomed.

- Monhegan Historical and Cultural Museum Association, Monhegan Island, ME 04852.

VIEWING THE FRANKLIN ISLAND LIGHTHOUSE. Stacy Davidson and Captain Al Crocetti offer this viewing advantage on their Fall Coastal Cruise. This 1 1/2-hour coastal trip passes the isolated and near forgotten historic lighthouse. A rare treat.

SCHEDULE. Early September to early October, daily at 4:30. Limited trips continue until Columbus Day; check for shedule.

FARES. Discount for children under 12.

See contact information for Hardy Boat Cruises on the previous page.

FRANKLIN ISLAND LIGHTHOUSE.

CHARACTERISTIC: Flashing white 6s

HAW: 57 ' **RANGE**: 8 nm

This lighthouse is located on Franklin Island lying west of Port Clyde off Friendship. Although approved for construction in 1803, the unavailability of building materials and foul weather delayed the station's completion until 1807. The light itself was first established in 1805.

The present circular brick tower was constructed in 1855 of undressed stone and capped with a round, solid sandstone deck upon which rests its lantern. Today the tower and its brick oil house (1895) are the only structures on the island. Its companion buildings, the attached keeper's residence and outbuildings, have been demolished.

When first built Franklin Island's optic was a whale oil-fed spider lamp. Later in the 1820s it received a Lewis Argand-styled lighting device. Then in 1855, the 45-foot tall lighthouse was rebuilt and refitted with a fifth-order Fresnel lens. When the beacon was automated in 1967, the classical lens was removed and a plastic lens installed. The Fresnel lens is on display at the Coast Guard's Boothbay Harbor Station.

OWNER. U.S. Coast Guard. Under the Maine Lights Program the light station was slated to be turned over to a community or nonprofit group. There were no applicants, leaving the future of the lighthouse uncertain.

PRESERVATION. Maine's third oldest lighthouse station is not listed in the National Register of Historic Places.

353

Monhegan Island Lighthouse

Ram Island Lighthouse

RAM ISLAND

TO OCEAN POINT.   In Boothbay Harbor take ME 96 east and south to Ocean Point and follow its shoreline extension, a two-mile one way loop road that takes you back to ME 96.   Along the coastal drive there are numerous roadside parking spots to view the lighthouse located across Fisherman Island Passage.   Off to the far right is the Cuckolds Lighthouse.

Note that Ram Island Light can be viewed from cruises leaving Boothbay Harbor (see page 349) and the Maine Maritime Museum in Bath (see page 340).   Some of the Maine Maritime Museum's cruises land at Ram Island.

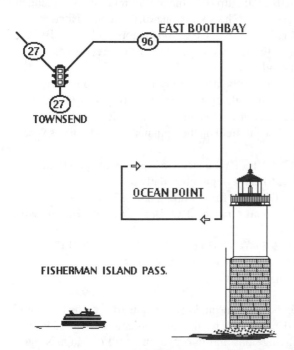

RAM ISLAND LIGHTHOUSE.
CHARACTERISTIC: Equal interval red 6s
HAW: 36 ' **RANGES**: White 11; red 9 nm

The history of aids to navigation on Ram Island begins in the mid-19th century when a fisherman, after narrowly escaping the dangerous rocks near the island, began hanging a lantern for the benefit of local mariners.   The fisherman left the area after a number of years and the lantern was kept by a second keeper, then a third.

The third lantern keeper anchored a dory and rigged the lamp in its bow.   It became the custom for the last fisherman coming into the harbor each day to light the lantern.   This ended when the dory was smashed in a storm.

A fourth fisherman, the lone resident of Fisherman's Island, took over the tending of the light.   Apparently the light he displayed was too weak, causing an increase in wrecks.

In 1883 the dory was replaced by the extant light station.   The lighthouse is composed of a granite ashlar base, surmounted by a brick tower of slightly smaller diameter.   The L-shaped Victorian residence stands inland and to the left of the tower.   The brick oil house to the rear of the dwelling was added in 1898.   The small building on the right was used to store oil drums.   The bell tower built in 1883 has disappeared.

In 1975 its 1881 Fresnel lens was stolen.   Luckily the lens was recovered in Boston and is now at the museum of the Boothbay Region Historical Society.   Ram Island's light is now produced by an automated modern lens.

OWNER.   In 1975 the Coast Guard offered the property on a long term lease to the Town of Boothbay.   Citing the costs of maintenance and an unwillingness to accept the responsibility of preserving the station, the town turned down the offer.   In 1983 the keeper's house was scheduled to be destroyed.   Then, the Grand Banks Schooner Museum Trust (associated with the Boothbay Railway Village) leased the keeper's dwelling, outbuildings and grounds.   Under the Maine Lights Program the property was transferred to the Grand Banks Schooner Museum Trust in February 1998.   The Ram Island Preservation Society, part of the Grand Banks Schooner Museum Trust, now has responsibility for the property.   Caretakers live on the island in summer.   The U.S. Coast Guard maintains the beacon.

PRESERVATION.   Listed in the National Register of Historic Places.

After the light was automated in 1965 the station was all but abandoned.   For the next ten years the keeper's dwelling became a hangout for drifters and vandals.   The bridge from shore to tower rotted away.   In 1977 the Coast Guard, faced with an unwanted and vandalized light station, decided to do some work on the structure.   The 35-foot tall lighthouse was rebuilt with new bricks, painted and its cast-iron lantern refurbished.   The damaged catwalk was removed and an access ladder was attached to the seaward side of the tower.   The keeper's house remained boarded up and untouched.   Since then, the Trust has managed to restore the old station property by repairing all damaged interior and exterior woodwork, repainting exteriors and reroofing (several times thereafter after storms) the keeper's house and outbuildings.   The grounds have also been cleaned of debris and trash.

VISITING RAM ISLAND.   Note the cruise to the island on page 340.   Other visitors should contact:
- Ram Island Preservation Society, Box 123, Boothbay, Maine 04537.
Phone: (207) 882-9721.

Boaters are permitted to land and visit the station.   It is requested that visitors do not litter and obey the prominently posted instructions and restrictions.

PEMAQUID POINT

NORTH ON US 1. In Damariscotta turn right into ME 130/129. Follow ME 130 into Pemaquid Point and Lighthouse Road to Pemaquid Point Lighthouse Park (total 15 miles).

SOUTH ON US 1. In Waldoboro take ME 32 into New Harbor. Then follow ME 130 into Pemaquid Point.

OPEN. All year, daily sunrise to sunset.

PARKING FEES. Collected Memorial Day to Columbus Day. Discount for seniors 54+. Under 12 free.

The lighthouse stands on the tip of Pemaquid Point at the west side of the entrance to Muscongus Bay. The spot is one of the most visited attractions of the Maine coast, receiving about 100,000 visitors each year. Be sure to walk out onto the edge of the sea swept granite bluff where, on a clear day, one can see Monhegan Island.

Hardy Boat Cruises, a tour boat company in New Harbor, offers the chance to see Pemaquid Point Light from the water. To get to Hardy Boat Cruises while heading south toward Pemaquid Point, turn left on Rt. 32. Parking (free) is located at the baseball field on the right just beyond Shaw's Wharf Restaurant.

SCHEDULE. The sunset cruise past Pemaquid Point runs from late June to early September, daily at 7 PM.

FARE. Discount for children under 12.

- **Hardy Boat Cruises**, P.O. Box 326, New Harbor, ME, 04554.

Phone (207) 677-2026 or toll-free 1-800-2-PUFFIN.
Website: http://www.hardyboat.com/
Email: hardy@gwi.net

THE FISHERMEN'S MUSEUM. This museum is dedicated to the maritime and fishing industries of the Pemaquid region. On display in the Navigation Room is Baker Island's fourth-order Fresnel lens, the same order as Pemaquid Point's operating optic. There is also a large wall map showing locations, photographs and information on all of Maine's lighthouses. Step back from the map and behold Maine's expansive lighthouse system. The Fish House Room, with its displays of tools, gear and buoys, is dedicated to Maine's lobstermen. The Net Room features the tools of the harvesters of the sea. Among the many displays there is a scallop dredge, a sink-gill net for pollock, hake and cod, an underline trawl for hake, a purse seine for herring and a variety of eel traps. The Gallery Room exhibits working boat models and photographs covering aspects of the shipbuilding industry.

OPEN. Memorial Day through Columbus Day, Monday through Saturday 10 to 5. Sundays 11 to 5.

FREE ADMISSION. Donations welcomed.

- The Fishermen's Museum, Pemaquid Point Road, New Harbor, ME 04554. Phone (207) 677-2494.

PEMAQUID POINT LIGHTHOUSE
CHARACTERISTIC: Flashing white 6s
HAW: 79' **RANGE**: 14 nm

Pemaquid Point's first lighthouse was built during the 1824-27 period. According to the construction contract's specifications, the conical tower was to be built of undressed stone, tapering from a base diameter of 18 feet to 10 feet at the top. The walls from base to top were to be of graduated thicknesses of from 3 1/2 to 2 feet. The lime mortar was to be mixed with only fresh water. The capping of the tower was done differently from most other Maine lighthouses. This tower had a circular slab of soapstone laid on top, with a hole bored through it to permit passage from the tower into the lantern. A stone keeper's dwelling was also constructed. The new station cost the Federal Government $2,800.

Apparently the masons did not mix their mortar properly, because the tower began to shed its stones. In 1835 it had to be rebuilt. That new tower, the one standing today, is 30 feet tall and at variance with the 1827 specifications, has double walls with the space between them filled with mortar and rubble stone. The overall height of the lighthouse is 38 feet.

In 1857 the old stone keeper's dwelling, having deteriorated in the same fashion as the tower, was demolished and replaced with a wood framed cape cottage. That residence is today's museum.

The lantern's 1856 fourth-order Fresnel optic, automated in 1934 (Maine's first), now is powered by a 250-watt electric bulb.

PEMAQUID POINT

On the station grounds you will see a small red brick building and a tall obelisk-type tower. The building was originally constructed in 1897 to house an automatic bell-striking machine that was powered by weights housed in the tower. The rewinding of the weights to the top of the tower allowed the bell to sound at a set interval for as long as eight hours. The bell was removed in 1934. The tower was badly damaged by a storm in April 1991 and destroyed during Hurricane Bob in October 1992. The tower's reconstruction was completed in 1992. Southeast of the keeper's house and nestled in a small grove of trees is the station's 1896 brick oil house.

OWNER. The station, other than the lighthouse tower itself, was deeded to the Town of Bristol on September 27, 1940. The lighthouse was leased in 2000 to the American Lighthouse Foundation. The U.S. Coast Guard maintains the light.
- American Lighthouse Foundation, P.O. Box 889, Wells, ME 04090.
Phone: (207) 646-0515
Website: http://www.lighthousefoundation.org

PRESERVATION. Listed in the National Register of Historic Places. The tower was refurbished and repainted in 2000. Glass in the lantern was replaced and the entire structure was repainted.

Pemaquid Point Lighthouse

MARSHALL POINT
TENANTS HARBOR - WHITEHEAD

These lighthouses will be found along a route that follows a two-part north-south-north trace:
1. Thomaston (US 1/ ME 131) -> St. George (ME 131) -> Tenants Harbor (US 131) -> Port Clyde, and
2. Port Clyde (ME 131) -> Tenants Harbor (ME 131) -> Sprucehead (ME 73) -> Owls Head (ME 73).

IN PORT CLYDE. Enter Port Clyde and, at the first paved intersection, turn left into Drift Inn Road (0.0 mile). The turn is marked with a "Marshall Point Museum" sign. Continue up the hill past another museum sign to the first intersection and turn right into Marshall Point Road (0.2 mile). Continue straight ahead past a "Dead End" sign 0.6 mile) and a pair of stone pillars to the light station (1.0 mile). Parking is free.

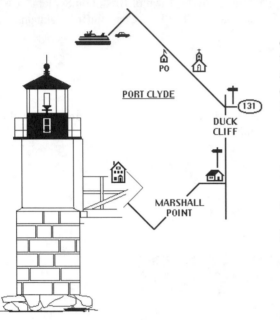

The **MARSHALL POINT LIGHTHOUSE MUSEUM** is dedicated to the preservation and display of memorabilia relating to the histories of St. George and the Marshall Point, Tenants Harbor and Whitehead Lighthouses. It is managed by a separate museum committee and board of directors selected from within the St. George Historical Society.

OPEN.

May and October, weekends only 1 to 5.

June to September, Sundays through Fridays 1 to 5. Saturdays 10 to 5.

FREE ADMISSION. Donations for the museum's upkeep welcomed.

- Marshall Point Lighthouse Museum, PO Box 247, Port Clyde, ME 04855. Phone: (207) 372-6450.

MARSHALL POINT LIGHTHOUSE.
CHARACTERISTIC: Fixed white
HAW: 30' RANGE: 13 nm

The original 1832 light station consisted of a circular tower built with four-foot soapstone blocks and a rubble stone keeper's house. The cast-iron lantern was fitted with seven oil-powered lamps each backed with a 14-inch reflector. The optic was only 20 feet above ground level, indicating that the lighthouse was no more than 30 feet tall. The beacon was first lighted in July 1832.

The present light tower, completed in 1858 at a cost of about $5,000, is built in two 12 foot sections with granite blocks on the lower half and coursed brick on the top half. The 31-foot tall lighthouse resembles Maine's Isle Au Haut and Ram Island Lighthouses. It is connected to the shore by a four-span wooden walkway (originally covered) built on four supporting granite piers.

After the keeper's house was badly damaged by lightning and a resulting fire in June of 1895, the present 1 1/2-story colonial residence was constructed. The granite oil house to the east of the house was built in 1905.

In 1898 an obelisk-type bell tower was added that had a hammer whose handle protruded through its wall and over a 1,000-pound fog bell. The bell tower housed a weight-powered mechanism that caused the hammer to strike the bell every 20 seconds. In 1898 the station became one of the first to be connected by telephone to a local weather station, allowing the lighthouse keeper to display storm warning flags on a specially built tower.

During the 1969-72 period, the Marshall Point Light Station underwent several changes:
1. Transfer of the last keeper and his family.
2. Removal of its fifth-order Fresnel optic to the Coast Guard's Rockland Station. The lens was stolen in 1974 and never recovered.
3. Replacement of its fog bell with a foghorn.
4. Dismantling of the bell tower, barn, storage shed and boathouse.
5. Integration into a LORAN-A radio navigation system.

In 1980 the LORAN-A equipment was removed and Marshall Point was reinstated as an automated light and fog signal station. The keeper's house was boarded up and the station's fog bell sent off to the Southwest Harbor Coast Guard Station and later transferred to a Coast Guard warehouse in Boston.

MARSHALL POINT, TENANTS HARBOR & WHITEHEAD

The current Marshall Point Lighthouse's original optic was a fifth-order Fresnel lens powered by a single whale oil lamp. That lens, with a kerosene lamp as a standby source of power, was electrified in 1935. The aid was automated in 1980 using the presently active modern lens.

OWNER. The U.S. Coast Guard maintains the beacon. The Town of St. George owns the property, including the lighthouse. In 1980 the light station was declared surplus property and nearly auctioned off to become a resort hotel. Fortunately, the auction was delayed long enough for the Town of St. George to secure a three year lease on the dwelling and the station grounds. In 1983 the lease's term was increased to five years. In 1986 the Town of St. George, dismayed with the deterioration of the keeper's house, asked the St. George Historical Society to plan for the dwelling's preservation. In December of that year the Society formed the Marshall Point Restoration Committee. In 1988 the committee negotiated a 30-year term lease for both the grounds and keeper's dwelling and succeeded in having the latter placed in the National Register of Historic Places.

Under the Maine Lights Program the entire station, including the lighthouse, became the property of the Town of St. George in April 1998.

PRESERVATION. Listed in the National Register of Historic Places.

Using over $100,000 from grants from the National Park Service's Bicentennial Lighthouse Fund, matching funds from the Town of St. George and public contributions, the keeper's house has been beautifully restored. The Society opened the first floor museum to the public in June 1990. Tenant caretakers reside in the remodeled second story apartment.

The replication of the summer kitchen that was originally attached to the house was completed in 1995. Future plans for the station include rebuilding the bell tower, barn and outbuildings.

IN TENANTS HARBOR. On ME 1131 between the Jackson Memorial Library (look for a sign in front of the building) and post office, turn south into an unmarked paved road and drive down to the St. George Public Landing. The Tenants Harbor Lighthouse is located on high ground at the east end of Southern Island at the harbor's entrance. The view of the lighthouse from this vantage point is very distant and is largely obscured by trees.

For a better view, try a lighthouse cruise on the *Lively Lady Too* out of Camden, in conjunction with the Elms Bed and Breakfast. There are several trips each season with varying itineraries, see page 376 for details.

- The Elms Bed and Breakfast, 84 Elm Street, Camden, ME 04843.

Phone: (207) 236-6250 or toll-free: (800) 755-ELMS

Website: http://www.midcoast.com/~theelms/ Email: theelms@midcoast.com

Another company offers cruises out of Tenants Harbor, passing close by the lighthouse on Southern Island. Some of the trips offered by Goddess of the Sea Cruises pass other area lighthouses including Two Bush Island, Owls Head and Whitehead.

- Goddess of the Sea Cruises, Tenants Harbor, ME. Phone: (207) 877-7824 or toll-free (888) 724-5010.

Website: http://www.goddesscruise.com

TENANTS HARBOR LIGHTHOUSE (SOUTHERN ISLAND).

Construction of the light station was completed in 1857. The 27-foot tall brick light tower is connected to the 1 1/2 story wooden colonial cape residence by a covered brick passageway. The lantern was fitted with a fourth-order Fresnel lens. The annex on the right of the house was added in 1887. Also on station are a storage shed (1895), a brick oil house (1906) and an owner-built pyramidal bell tower.

OWNER. After the light was discontinued in 1934, the island and station were sold to Isadore Gordon of Rockland. Over the years ownership of the property has been passed to Bostonian Adriel Bird of the LaTouraine Coffee Company, to a local hospital, to Walter Whitehead and then in the late 1970s to Betsy James Wyeth, wife of artist Andrew Wyeth. Betsy and Andrew Wyeth lived on the island until 1990, when they moved to an island off Port Clyde. Upon their departure their son, artist Jamie Wyeth, moved his studio and residence to the island. The pyramidal bell tower, which is not original, serves as Jamie Wyeth's studio.

PRESERVATION. Listed in the National Register of Historic Places.

As a result of the Wyeth family's tireless efforts, the lighthouse and keeper's residence have been beautifully maintained.

TO SPRUCEHEAD ISLAND. From Tenants Harbor continue north on ME 131 and ME 73 to Sprucehead. The right turn into Sprucehead Island Road is about 3.4 miles north of the ME 131 / 73 junction and a very short uphill distance north of ME 73's 90-degree left turn in Sprucehead.

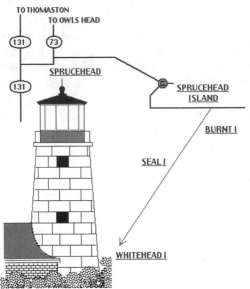

From Owls Head follow ME 73 through South Thomaston. The left turn into Sprucehead Island Road is about 2.6 miles south of the South Thomaston Volunteer Fire Department and 1.8 miles south of Grierson Road (on the right).

ON SPRUCEHEAD ISLAND. Follow Sprucehead Island Road for 1.2 miles to a stop sign, turn right and continue for another 0.3 mile to the road's end. Whitehead can be seen off to the south between Burnt Island (nearest on the left) and Seal Island (more distant on the right). The lighthouse can be seen quite clearly with the use of binoculars.

For a closer view, try a lighthouse cruise on the *Lively Lady Too* out of Camden, in conjunction with the Elms Bed and Breakfast. There are several trips each season with varying itineraries, see page 376 for details.

Goddess of the Sea Cruises out of Tenants Harbor offers some cruises that pass by Whitehead Island. See details on page 359.

WHITEHEAD LIGHTHOUSE.
CHARACTERISTIC: Occulting green 4s
HAW: 75' **RANGE**: 10 nm

Whitehead Light was approved for construction in 1804 and completed in 1807. The present 41-foot tall gray granite lighthouse was built in 1852.

The station's original rubble stone keeper's house was replaced in 1852 with the existing wooden dwelling. Another 1 1/2-story, gabled house (1891) was dismantled sometime after 1986. The station also has a brick fog signal building (1888), a brick oil house, a garage and two storage sheds (all 1891).

Whitehead's third-order Fresnel lens (1857) was removed in 1982 when the presently active modern plastic lens was installed and automated.

The Whitehead light station, from its inception, had its ups and downs. Its first keeper was ignominiously fired for selling the surplus whale oil sent to him on the basis of his overstated usage reports. In 1813 Winslow Lewis inspected the station and found the lighthouse poorly managed.

Since 1820, after West Quoddy Head had been equipped with a fog bell, local mariners had clamored for a fog signal. Arguing that Whitehead Island had as many fog bound days as West Quoddy Head, they got their wish in 1839. The fog signal was a newly engineered contraption that rang a 2,000 pound bell by means of weights mechanically rewound by a pulley-tracked cable tied to a heavy log boom that lifted the weights during tidal stages.

In 1842 I. W. P. Lewis (Winslow's nephew) visited Whitehead and found the "perpetual fog bell" no longer in operation after being damaged in storms. The keeper had tied a line to the bell's clapper and run the line into his bedroom where he sometimes amused himself by sounding the bell from his bed. The bell was eventually replaced by a steam-driven fog whistle in the 1860s.

One item of historical note is that Whitehead became the first Maine light station to have its own one-room schoolhouse and hired teacher.

OWNER. Pine Island Camp owns the property, including the lighthouse. The U.S. Coast Guard maintains the beacon.

In December 1997 the Maine Lighthouse Selection Committee, under the Maine Lights Program, announced that Whitehead Light would be transferred from the Coast Guard to Pine Island Camp, a historic boys' camp situated on Pine Island in Great Pond of the Belgrade Lakes.

The owners of Pine Island Camp, the Swan family, had bought 70 acres of Whitehead Island in 1956, and campers have been visiting the island ever since. Under a work program the campers, who are boys and girls aged 15 and 16, will help restore the lighthouse and keeper's dwelling. The group hopes eventually to establish a museum at the lighthouse.

- Pine Island Camp, phone: (207) 729-7714.
Website: http://www.pineisland.org/
PRESERVATION. Listed in the National Register of Historic Places.

Tenants Harbor Lighthouse

Whitehead Lighthouse

ROCKLAND HARBOR SOUTHWEST
OWLS HEAD - SADDLEBACK LEDGE

NORTH OR SOUTH ON ME 73. Between South Thomaston and Rockland turn right into North Shore Road. The turn is marked by "Owl's Head Light State Park - 3.6 miles" signs.

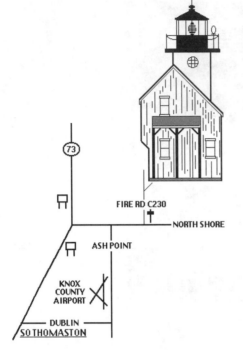

CONTINUE ON. Motor east on North Shore for about 0.6 mile (past Ash Point Road on the right) and turn into a narrow unpaved lane. The turn is marked with a small red "Fire Road #C230" sign. Continue down the lane and bear right into the ample parking area in front of the lighthouse.

While visitors are welcomed to drive onto the grounds to view the lighthouse, the owners and keepers, Bruce and Nancy Woollett, prefer to show their charge only to those visitors with a genuine interest in lighthouses. Please write or call to receive permission to go aboard. Don't knock on their door.

- Rockland Harbor Southwest Lighthouse, Owls Head, ME 04854. Phone (207) 594-2383.

ROCKLAND HARBOR SW LIGHTHOUSE.
CHARACTERISTIC: Flashing yellow 2.5s
HAW: 44'

Dr. Bruce Woollett says that his interest in lighthouses began when he was 12 years old. He spent a considerable amount of his youth at York Beach near Cape Neddick and at Pemaquid Point. Later, after he finished his tour in the U.S. Navy, he tried to buy Cape Elizabeth's old west tower. Actor Gary Merrill outbid him with his offer of $28,000.

During the building of his house in Owls Head, he stayed with his adopted grandparents at the head of the bay. His bedroom faced out to sea and during the nights with no fog, the flashing Rockland Breakwater Light bounced off the foot of his bed and hit the wall above his head. It was at that time that he decided to build his own lighthouse.

From 1981 to 1987 the project took shape. Much of the wood was donated by a local contractor. The tower's lightning protection was provided by an artisan, who had worked on lighthouses in the Rockland area. The equipped lighthouse cost about $14,000. The light was first established on November 11, 1987. It marks Seal Ledge and the shallow water south and southwest of it.

The light station consists of a keeper's house with a tower attached. The house is a wood framed structure with a kitchen, dining area and enough room for a twin-sized bed downstairs. On the second deck is a bedroom, sitting area and bath. The square tower has been built with wood, steel and concrete. The octagonal, 8-foot diameter lantern room, constructed of wood, glass and copper, is 35 feet above the tower's base. The lantern is reached by a ladder located inside the tower.

The 44-foot tall lighthouse's first optic was an electrified 155 mm marine lens. In 1989 following the August grounding of a cruise boat on offshore Seal Ledge, the original optic was moved to the service gallery as a backup light, after having been replaced by an AC-powered, flasher-equipped fifth-order Fresnel lens that had been originally installed in one of the Kennebec River's Doubling Point range light towers in 1908. The present optic uses the same lens, but it now rotates around a high pressure sodium light source, producing the beacon's yellow (amber) characteristic. The color was selected by the Coast Guard so that the light would not interfere with the Rockland Breakwater aid.

In 1994 the Wooletts placed the light station on the real estate market with an asking price of $358,000. They later withdrew the property with the intention to stay at the lighthouse for an undetermined period.

TO OWLS HEAD. Return to North Shore Drive and motor east some 1.9 miles into Owls Head. Then:
-> Left at a triangular intersection ("Owl's Head State Park" sign) into Main Street (start 0.0 mile).
-> Left at Lighthouse Road (0.1 mile),
-> Continue on Lighthouse to the large free parking area (0.7 mile) of the Owl's Head State Park. In 1994 Maine's Department of Conservation resurfaced the gravel access road to the light station, cleared out the park's overgrown bushes, repaired the picnic tables, put up new road signs and added barbecue grills.

Only handicapped-licensed vehicles are permitted to drive farther on to a two vehicle parking space or the one vehicle parking space in front of the station's steel fire gate.

There is a 0.2 mile walk to the lighthouse along a steep cliff overlooking Penobscot Bay. The lighthouse is reached via a sloping ramp, a stairway (eight steps), another ramp to the oil house and then a long (low-riser) stairway to the tower. If the foghorn is in use, be sure to plug your ears before heading up to the tower.

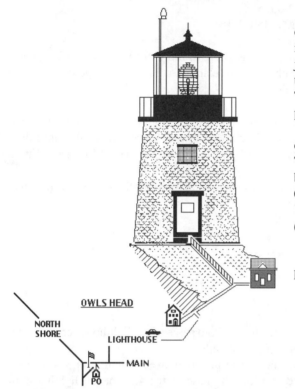

CRUISES NEAR OWLS HEAD. There are a number of cruises in the midcoast area that pass near Owls Head Light. These include the periodic lighthouse cruises out of Camden offered in conjunction with the Elms Bed and Breakfast (see page 376), as well as the Goddess of the Sea Cruises out of Tenants Harbor (see page 359). The ferry from Rockland to Vinalhaven also passes Owls Head (see page 368).

There are also a number of one day or longer schooner sails out of Rockland, Camden and Rockport that pass near Owls Head. The best bet is to check with the Rockland-Thomaston Area Chamber of Commerce or the Camden-Rockport-Lincolnville Chamber of Commerce for the latest cruise possibilities.

- Rockland-Thomaston Area Chamber of Commerce. Phone: (800) 562-2529.

Website: http://www.midcoast.com/~rtacc/

- Camden-Rockport-Lincolnville Chamber of Commerce. Phone: (207) 236-4404 or toll-free (800) 223-5459.

Website: http://www.camdenme.org/

Email: chamber@camdenme.org

OWLS HEAD LIGHTHOUSE.
CHARACTERISTIC: Fixed white
HAW: 100' **RANGE:** 16 nm

The Owls Head Lighthouse was placed in service on September 10, 1826. Although Winslow Lewis' 30-foot lighthouse has never been rebuilt, its brick walls were set with mortar subject to disintegration. As a result of this error, the 20-foot tall tower's exterior shows only slight bulging, probably because of patch work done over the years. The problem occurred in other early masonry structures, such as, Maine's Pemaquid Point and the Boston Lighthouse. Some damaged towers had to be strengthened with encircling wrought-iron bands or sheathed in wood or cast-iron plates to forestall further disappearance of the mortared walls.

The 1 1/2-story keeper's dwelling (1854) is now a Coast Guard residence. The little brick structure below the lighthouse is the oil house built in 1895. The station's boathouse (1894) and bell tower (1906) have been dismantled.

The optic's original fourth-order Fresnel lens is now automated.

There are many, many distinguished, dramatic and amusing stories about life among the wickies. Some concern the deeds of the keepers' dogs. Here is Spot's contribution to lighthouse history.

Spot, who had been taught to pull on the fog bell's rope whenever boats came near the rocks off Owls Head, was asleep in his favorite corner of the house. Outside, the snowfall had turn into a blizzard. Then came a telephone call from the wife of the captain piloting the Matinicus mailboat on its return run to Rockland. She was worried. He was hours overdue. Had the keeper seen or heard his whistle as he rounded the point? If not, would he please call her as soon as he heard the boat clearing the rocks? The keeper roused Spot and sent him outside. A short time later, Spot was scratching on the door. Let in, he went back to his corner. A few minutes later, Spot jumped up, barked, ran to the door and was let out. Once outside, the keeper's little friend ran to the fog bell, but could not find the rope in the snow. He didn't give up. Standing at the cliff's edge, Spot barked into the cold winter night until he heard the boat's whistle acknowledging that she had cleared the rocks and was headed safely into Rockland harbor. Spot is buried on the station's grounds.

OWNER. U.S. Coast Guard. The station is not included in the Maine Lights Program.

PRESERVATION. Listed in the National Register of Historic Places.

LIGHTHOUSE SIGHTSEEING FLIGHTS. Here are two opportunities to get a gull's eye view of a bunch of Maine's lighthouses.

Gray Webster Aviation is an on demand air charter company that is able to provide your own customized flight plan for lighthouse viewing. Using twin engined aircraft, for $2 a statute mile Gray Webster can pick you up anywhere and fly you over any lighthouse(s) of your choice. For a quote call (800) 359-0015.
- Gray Webster Aviation, phone (207) 865-0083, or toll-free (800) 359-0015.
Website: http://www.graywebster.com/   Email: fly@graywebster.com
This company can provide lighthouse flights not only in Maine, but anywhere in the U.S. When you call, specify what state you're interested in and the approximate location of each lighthouse in relation to the nearest large town. Using that information Gray Webster Aviation can provide aircraft nationwide.

Downeast Air of Rockland offers a second lighthouse flight option. Their scenic lighthouse flight features the following itinerary: Take off from Rockland, fly to Owls Head Light, Rockland Breakwater Light, Marshall Point Light, Two Bush Island Light, Whitehead Light, Matinicus Rock Light, Pemaquid Point Light, Browns Head Light and Curtis Island Light.
FARE Flights in single and twin engine aircraft are $170 per hour. A fifteen minute flight for three people is less than $15 per person. A 30 minute flight is $85 for up to three passengers.
- Downeast Air Inc., PO Box 966, Rockland, Maine 04841.
Phone: (207) 594-2171. Toll-free: (888) 594-2171.
Website: http://www.midcoast.com/~dea/   Email: dea@midcoast.com

SADDLEBACK LEDGE LIGHTHOUSE.
CHARACTERISTIC: Flashing white 6s
HAW: 54 ' **RANGE**: 11 nm
Besides the flights described above, Saddleback Ledge Light can be viewed from some of the lighthouse cruises offer in conjunction with the Elms Bed and Breakfast in Camden. See page 376 for details.
Saddleback Ledge, one of the more isolated of Maine's coastal aids, lies midway between Vinalhaven and Isle Au Haut at the south end of Isle Au Haut Bay. When first established in 1839, the base of the 42-foot tall lighthouse of hammered granite stone housed the keeper's quarters and a water cistern. Later, the tower was connected to a 2 1/2-story wood framed equipment building, whose first floor (basement) served as a boathouse. In 1856 the original Lewis multi-lamp/reflector device was replaced by a fourth-order Fresnel lens. In 1883 the lighthouse was refurbished with a new lantern and service gallery and given a kerosene-powered fourth-order Fresnel optic. The light is now produced by an automated modern lens.
One night in 1927 when a storm hit the ledge, birds began to bombard the lighthouse. One bird sailed through the lantern's glass storm pane and flopped around the floor with a broken wing and "his bill telescoped almost through his head," according to the keeper. In came another bird and out went another pane. The process continued until the platform was heaped with an untidy bunch of dead and fluttering fowl. Then, just when the keeper thought it was over, through another pane and into the lens came a 10-pound drake and out went the light.
In 1960 the keeper's residence was destroyed in a training exercise by explosives planted by a special forces team.
OWNER. U.S. Coast Guard.
PRESERVATION. Listed in the National Register of Historic Places.

ROCKLAND BREAKWATER

IN ROCKLAND ON US 1. To reach Jameson Point turn into Waldo Avenue. The turn is about 3 miles north of US 1's intersection with US 1A (Maverick Street) and about 0.4 mile south of the Harbor Plaza shopping center. Look for the Littlefield Memorial Baptist Church on the southeast corner and a "Samoset Resort Hotel" sign. Then:

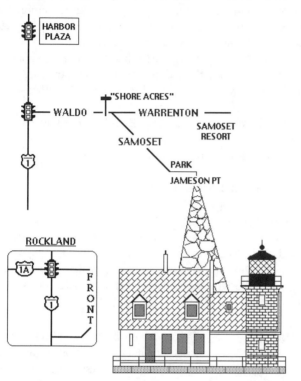

-> Pass the church on Waldo and continue into connecting Warrenton Road,

-> About 0.4 mile from US 1 turn right at Samoset Road. The turn is marked by a "Shore Acres" sign,

-> Continue to its terminus at the Marie H. Reed Breakwater Park. Parking is free. The park is open from sunrise to sunset. Off to the left is a footpath leading down to the breakwater. Visitors are permitted to walk out (use caution) to the lighthouse.

 Other lighthouse viewing possibilities:

- Littlefield Memorial Baptist Church parking lot.
- Samoset Resort located farther east off Warrenton.
- Bluff along the Maverick Street - Front Street loop (see inset).
- Ferries that service North Haven and Vinalhaven Islands (see page 368).
- Cruises offered in conjunction with the Elms Bed and Breakfast in Camden; see page 376 for details.
- Various other cruises leaving Rockland and Camden. For information:
- Rockland-Thomaston Area Chamber of Commerce. Phone: (800) 562-2529.
Website: http://www.midcoast.com/~rtacc/

- Camden-Rockport-Lincolnville Chamber of Commerce. Phone: (207) 236-4404 or toll-free (800) 223-5459. Website: http://www.camdenme.org/
Email: chamber@camdenme.org

ROCKLAND BREAKWATER LIGHTHOUSE.

CHARACTERISTIC: Flashing white 5s

HAW: 39' **RANGE**: 17 nm

The first beacon off Jameson Point was established in 1827. This aid was an oil lamp placed on a pole or wooden tripod. In the mid-1880s, as the volume of shipping (especially lime carriers) entering and leaving Rockland Harbor increased, the lime industry, merchants, ship owners and captains decided that the harbor should be provided better protection from storms. Their voices prevailed and a plan was drawn up to build two breakwaters. One was to extend southward from Jameson Point, the other northward from the peninsula that juts out in front of the ferry terminal on Main Street. This latter area once contained the docks and loading facilities of Rockland's important lime industry. Although Congress agreed with the plan, funds were appropriated piecemeal. Construction of the present breakwater began in April 1881. When funds ran out, work on the pier stopped; when Congress opened its purse, construction continued. Meanwhile, that little tripod beacon moved along with the breakwater, being reestablished on the unfinished end whenever work on the project ceased. The nine section pier was completed in November 1899. Its southern cousin never got off the drawing boards. The breakwater required 700,000 tons of granite boulders. Its exterior trapezoidal dimensions are 43 feet wide at the top, 175 feet wide at the bottom and 65 feet high.

After the breakwater was completed, the present lighthouse was built. The compact station, completed in 1902, consists of the 25-foot tall, square brick tower rising from the roof of a brick fog signal building and the attached gambrel roof, brick keeper's dwelling, all atop a rectangular platform of dressed granite blocks.

A construction oddity is the tower's interior lining of ceramic tile. Unfortunately, moisture collects behind the tiles, causing mildew problems and the loosening of the tiles. The only other Atlantic Coast lighthouse with tiled interior walls is Whitlocks Mill located on the St. Croix River east of Calais, Maine.

Originally equipped with a fourth-order Fresnel optic, the lantern now holds a modern lens.

ROCKLAND BREAKWATER

OWNER. The beacon is maintained by the U.S. Coast Guard. Rockland Breakwater Lighthouse lost its keepers when it was automated in 1964. In that year also the Coast Guard offered to lease it to either the City of Rockland or the Maine League of Historical Societies. The catch, of course, was that the lessee would be responsible for the lighthouse's upkeep. There were no takers. In 1973, three years after the Coast Guard announced that it was about to demolish the lighthouse, the owners of the Samoset Resort entered into an agreement to maintain and preserve the lighthouse. In 1989 the resort, unable to continue to finance the upkeep of the lighthouse, relinquished its licensing agreement.

The Rockland City Council applied for the property in October 1997 under the Maine Lights Program. The goal, said the Rockland City Council, is "to protect and preserve our own history to increase the access to this historic structure for our own citizens and visitors to the history of our region and that of the Breakwater." Rockland Breakwater Lighthouse is on the City of Rockland's emblem and letterhead.

In February 1998, the Maine Lighthouse Selection Committee approved the transfer of Rockland Breakwater Lighthouse to the City of Rockland. With the help of Tim Harrison, President of the American Lighthouse Foundation, the Friends of Rockland Breakwater Lighthouse was established. The Friends are working to restore the interior of the lighthouse and create a living history museum.

- Friends of Rockland Breakwater Lighthouse, P.O. Box 741, Rockland, Maine 04841.

Website: http://www.midcoast.com/~brkwater/

PRESERVATION. Listed in the National Register of Historic Places.

In 1990 the Coast Guard assigned one of its cutter crews the task of refurbishing, scraping and painting the structure inside and out. Repairs to the slate roof and chimneys were done by a private firm.

In the summer of 1999 the exterior of Rockland Breakwater Light was scraped and repainted by volunteers, including sailors from a visiting U.S. Navy Destroyer, the *U.S.S. Stump*. A local Sherwin-Williams paint store donated paint for the refurbishing, and local restaurants provided food for the volunteers.

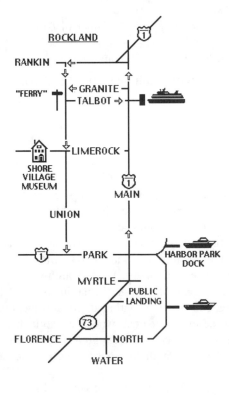

SHORE VILLAGE MUSEUM. "Maine's Lighthouse Museum" is a veritable storehouse of lighthouse history, Fresnel lenses, ships' fittings, lighthouse keeper records, equipment, fog signals and whatever lighthouse service artifacts there are to assemble and display.

The collection is the work of retired Coast Guard Chief Warrant Officer Ken Black, who as Commanding Officer of the Rockland Station began collecting his relics while on active duty and with the approval of his district commander. The first lighthouse and maritime artifacts museum was housed in the Rockland Station's large warehouse headquarters. It was called the First District Marine Exhibit. Ken retired in 1973. Two years later the Coast Guard built a new headquarters building that did not have space for the museum. As a result, the City of Rockland accepted the collection and placed it in its present location.

The new museum was dedicated in 1977 with a hired director. Then in 1980, because it was short on revenues, the city asked Ken to take on the job as the museum's volunteer director. If for no other reason, go to the museum for a look at "Mr. Lighthouse's" assemblage of classical and modern lenses. It is the largest lens exhibit in America. Here are some of the lenses on display:

Petit Manan: second-order; Baker's Island: fourth-order; Doubling Point: fifth-order; Matinicus Rock: third-order; Burnt Island : fourth-order; Isle au Haut fifth-order; Whitehead: third-order; The Cuckolds: fourth-order; Sakonnet Point: fifth-order (1/4 section); Whitlocks Mill: fourth-order; Ten Pound Island: fifth-order.

When you visit the museum, you will be uncontrollably drawn into spending an extended amount of time among the exhibits, looking at the tools of the keeper's trade, foghorns that groan, dolls, housekeeping utensils and furniture, fog bells that clang, lanterns that blink and a host of other maritime gear. All visitors, especially children, are encouraged to explore, touch, ask questions and operate the exhibits.

SHORE VILLAGE MUSEUM

OPEN.
June to mid-October, daily 10 to 5.
At other times only when personnel are in the building or by appointment.
FREE ADMISSION. Donations for operating expenses welcomed.

- Shore Village Museum, 104 Limerock Street, Rockland, ME 04841.
Phone (207) 594-0311.
Website: http://lighthouse.cc/shorevillage/   This is part of author Jeremy D'Entremont's website "New England Lighthouses: A Virtual Guide," at http://lighthouse.cc
Email: kblack@ime.net

Rockland BreakwaterLighthouse

BROWNS HEAD

VINALHAVEN ISLAND. Settled in 1789, Vinalhaven in the 1800s was a famous and busy source of granite for many buildings built in Washington and New York. Abandoned and water-filled quarries abound. Today the granite industry is but a memory, while the island's main industry is lobstering.

Overnight lodging and restaurants are available in the town of Vinalhaven.

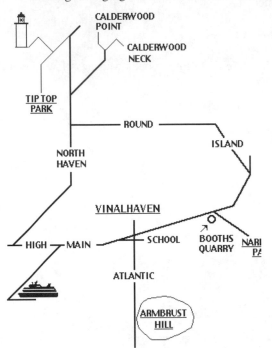

FERRY TO VINALHAVEN ISLAND. See the Rockland city map in the ROCKLAND BREAKWATER chapter.

The Maine State Ferry Service's auto/passenger ferry to Vinalhaven Island departs from the ferry terminal located at 517A Main Street in downtown Rockland. It carries 17 cars and 250 passengers. The 15-mile crossing takes 75 minutes to the ferry landing in Carver's Harbor.

A vehicle reservation (extra nonrefundable fee) is mandatory to obtain a same day, round trip visit to the island. There are only four car and two truck reserve spaces.

FARES. Vehicle plus passenger round trip fares. Discount for children 5-11. Make reservations (extra fee) through the Rockland office. Sunday trips avoid the weekday commercial traffic.

SCHEDULE. Call for the current schedule.
- Vinalhaven Ferry (Maine State Ferry Service).
Phone: In Rockland (207) 596-2203
In Carver's Harbor (207) 863-4421.

TO THE LIGHTHOUSE. Turn right out of the ferry terminal. Then:

-> Follow Main Street to High Street,
-> Left at High,
-> Right into North Haven Road,
-> Continue north for about 6.1 miles to a group of mailboxes and a "Tip-Toe Mtn Town Park" sign,
-> Left into unpaved Crockett River Road (start 0.0 mile),
-> Right at the second dirt road on the right (0.3 mile),
-> Continue past a cemetery on the right to a small free parking area (0.8 mile).

The light station's grounds are open to the public. The keeper's dwelling is a private residence. Both the house and tower are closed to visitors.

Browns Head Light can also be viewed from some of the cruises offered in conjunction with the Elms Bed and Breakfast in Camden; see page 376 for details.

BROWNS HEAD LIGHTHOUSE.
CHARACTERISTIC: Fixed white (2 red sectors)
HAW: 39' **RANGES**: White 14; red 11 nm

This granite rubble stone tower and a house were built in 1832 at a cost of $4,000. In 1857 the tower was repointed and the weather-worn keeper's residence torn down. The present 1 1/2-story, wood framed cottage took the latter's place. Later, the 20-foot tall lighthouse and the new residence were connected by the extant short covered passageway. A pyramidal fog bell tower was also built in 1857. In 1987, the Coast Guard, after having removed its watch crew, torched and destroyed the tower.

The lighthouse's original optic was a whale oil-fed fifth-order Fresnel lens. That lens was replaced in 1902 by the presently active and automated fourth-order Fresnel lens. In 1987 Browns Head Lighthouse became one of the last lighthouses in Maine to be automated.

OWNER. The U.S. Coast Guard maintains the beacon. Under the Maine Lights Program, established by congressional legislation in 1996, the lighthouse buildings were transferred to the town of Vinalhaven in April 1998. The town now spends about $1,200 yearly for the maintenance of Browns Head Lighthouse.

This lighthouse is now the residence of Vinalhaven's Town Manager.

PRESERVATION. Listed in the National Register of Historic Places. Vinalhaven has done an excellent job in maintaining the property.

BROWNS HEAD

RETURN TO VINALHAVEN. One can retrace the route from Vinalhaven or take a sightseeing tour along the island's paved roads. The accompanying route map shows the main road leading across the island. There is no reason to worry about getting lost. Just point your nose, stay out of the water and you will end up back in downtown Vinalhaven.

VINALHAVEN HISTORICAL SOCIETY MUSEUM. This museum, located in Vinalhaven center, displays artifacts from the island's fishing and maritime industries and the tools, equipment and photographs from the granite quarrying years. Browns Head's old 1,000-pound fog bell is in the museum.
OPEN. Mid-June to Labor Day, daily 11 to 3.
FREE ADMISSION. Donations welcomed.
- Vinalhaven Historical Society, PO Box 339, Vinalhaven, ME 04863.
Phone: (207) 863-4318.

VIEWS FROM THE ISLAND. After visiting the museum, you may want to visit the following two observation sites that provide, on clear days, fabulous views of the outlying lighthouse islands. The hiking trails are well maintained.

TO ARMBRUST HILL. Parking is not allowed on Atlantic Avenue. Park your car in the Town Parking Lot on Main Street. Walk east on Main to Water Street (fountain). Turn right at Atlantic Avenue and continue south to a path marked with an "Armbrust Hill Reservation" sign. Follow the path to Armbrust Hill's summit. Look east to southwest for Isle au Haut, Saddleback Ledge, Matinicus Island and Two Bush Island.

TO NARROWS PARK. From downtown's main parking lot continue east and northeast on Main Street for about 2.7 miles to Booth's Quarry. At the quarry turn right and follow the road into Narrows Park. Look northeast to southwest for Deer Island, Mount Desert Island, Swans Island, Isle au Haut and Saddleback Ledge.

HERON NECK
GOOSE ROCKS

LIGHTHOUSE SIGHTSEEING CRUISE. See the map on page 383.

On his Special Excursion Captain Reginald Greenlaw's 49-passenger *Palmer Day IV* (single open deck; forward cabin) sails from Stonington past the Heron Neck Lighthouse enroute to Vinalhaven for a 75-minute stopover. The motor vessel continues on to North Haven, passing the Browns Head Lighthouse. There is a 45-minute layover in North Haven. On the return leg to Stonington the boat passes the Goose Rocks Lighthouse.

SCHEDULE. July to September 1, Thursdays at 8. Returns at 1:30.

FARES. Discount for children under 10.
- Palmer Day IV, PO Box 95, Stonington, ME 04681.
Phone (207) 367-2207.

Heron Neck Light and Goose Rocks Light can also be seen on some of the lighthouse cres offered by the Elms Bed and Breakfast in Camden. See page 376 for details.

HERON NECK LIGHTHOUSE.
CHARACTERISTIC: Fixed red (white sector)
HAW: 92' **RANGES**: Red 10: white 13 nm

Southwest and offshore of Vinalhaven's Carvers Harbor is the Heron Neck Lighthouse built in 1853. It stands on a sharply defined rock ledge on the southern tip of Green Island, marking the east entrance to Hurricane Sound.

Heron Neck was built in 1853 in the style of the Federal Design genre. It is an unadorned, cylindrical brick tower surmounted by a polygonal cast-iron lantern. There are two small stair windows. The tower was attached to the original brick keeper's dwelling by a narrow enclosed passageway. When the second keeper's residence was built, the passageway was retained.

The station's brick oil house (1903) stands on the east side of the lighthouse. North of the tower and house is the station's fog bell tower erected in 1944. The station's old foghorn is displayed in the Shore Village Museum in Rockland.

The 30-foot tall lighthouse's original optic was a fifth-order Fresnel lens. It was replaced by an automated plastic lens in 1982.

OWNER. With the help of Maine's Senator Mitchell ownership of the Heron Island light station and its 10 acres was transferred to the Island Institute of Rockland in November 1994.

PRESERVATION. Listed in the National Register of Historic Places.

In April 1989 the unoccupied L-shaped, wood framed keeper's quarters (1895-96) and the connecting breezeway to the tower were gutted by a fire from an electrical short. Vinalhaven firefighters hauled two sea water pumps to Green Island. Although they battled the blaze throughout the morning, low pressure and the inability to get close to the fire prevented them from saving the structure. Fortunately the tower, protected by Halon fire extinguishers, was not damaged. After the fire, the Coast Guard announced that it had no plans to rebuild the dwelling.

In early 1990 an NBC telecast covering the destruction of the house implied that some of Maine's lighthouses could be leased for one dollar a year. While not exactly true at the time of the broadcast, the story brought forth at least three serious offers to lease the station with commitments to rebuild the dwelling.

In 1992 a Boston developer offered to restore the dwelling at no cost to the government. With the Coast Guard's permission, the developer began planning for the $300,000 restoration project. The Coast Guard then decided to halt the project and destroy the dwelling. That decision, according to the Coast Guard, was based on its interpretation of the restoration rules for structures entered into the National Register of Historic Places. They claimed that the only way the badly damaged structure could be restored to its original architectural design was to start at the foundation and rebuild. That effort, ergo, would constitute a reproduction of the building and not its restoration. In Heron Neck's case, however, the Coast Guard claimed that a structural engineering survey concluded that it was impossible to restore the building to its architectural origins.

Without further explanation the Coast Guard said the engineer report allowed it to circumvent the "no destruction" rule. A second reason for the flip-flop was that real estate negotiations had to be temporarily suspended while a guidance manual, used for the disposal of light station properties, was being rewritten. A third reason was that the Coast Guard thought the lease was to be signed by a nonprofit organization and not a private indvidual.

Later, in a conference between the Coast Guard and lighthouse preservationists the latter received assurances that the keeper's house would not be destroyed while all concerned sought a solution to the problem.

The final solution to the Heron Neck dilemma was the eventual title transfer of the station to the Island Institute of Rockland. In turn the Institute leased the property to a private party who completed a $200,000 restoration of the house. The lessee is also responsible for the maintenance of the active optic. Eventually, the Institute plans to establish an educational center at the station.

It was the Heron Neck Light project that inspired Island Institute Vice President Peter Ralston to initiate the Maine Lights Program, under which almost 30 Maine lighthouses were turned over to communities and organizations.

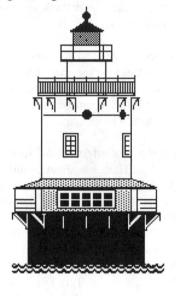

GOOSE ROCKS LIGHTHOUSE.
CHARACTERISTIC: Flashing red 6s (white sector)
HAW: 51' **RANGES**: Red 11; white 12 nm

Located between Vinalhaven Island and North Haven Island and sitting on a ledge in the middle of the Fox Islands Thorofare's eastern approach is the Goose Rocks Lighthouse.

Refer to the map on page 368. Goose Rocks can be seen from Vinalhaven Island, but only after a 1.5-mile hike from Calderwood Neck out to Calderwood Point. In the past the unimproved trail has been deeply rutted in many places and may be overgrown with grass and bushes. It is definitely not recommended for the family car. Unless you are a hardy hiker, take the boat.

This "spark-plug" styled lighthouse was erected in 1890. It is a white cast-iron superstructure resting on a black cylindrical foundation. The tower's interior is divided vertically into three levels that once housed the keepers' quarters (window), storage space and the watchroom (portholes). Its first optic consisted of a kerosene-fed lamp and a fourth-order Fresnel lens. The lantern now holds a solar powered modern plastic lens that was automated in 1963.

OWNER. U.S. Coast Guard. Goose Rocks Light was included in the Maine Lights Program but there were no applicants.

PRESERVATION. Listed in the National Register of Historic Places.

During the 1995-96 period the light tower was repaired and painted by the U.S. Coast Guard.

MATINICUS ROCK
TWO BUSH ISLAND

Matinicus Rock lies some six miles south southeast of Matinicus Island and 25 miles from Rockland. The lighthouse stands on the south side of a 32-acre (at high tide) barren rocky outcropping, halfway between Monhegan Island and Mount Desert Island and 22 miles south of the entrance to Penobscot Bay. Matinicus Rock is a favorite of birdwatchers with its nesting areas for at least ten species of seabirds, including Atlantic puffins, razorback auks, Arctic terns, shearwaters and storm petrels.

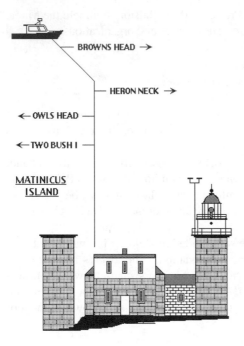

CRUISES TO THE ROCK. Over the years various companies have offered birdwatching cruises to Matinicus Rock. The companies offering this cruise vary from year to year. The best advice is to check with the Rockland-Thomaston Chamber of Commerce at (800) 562-2529.

Website : http://www.midcoast.com/~rtacc/

Cruises to Matinicus Rock sail across open water and sometimes encounter large swells, squalls and brisk winds. Passengers in expectation of sea spray and wet decks should dress warmly and carry or wear rain gear. The use of a seasickness medication and/or wrist sea bands is recommended. Don't forget a lunch or snacks, water or sodas, cameras and binoculars.

- Hardy Boat Cruises in New Harbor sometimes offers special springtime cruises to Matinicus Rock. The trip from New Harbor is about 28 miles.

DIRECTIONS TO HARDY BOAT CRUISES. From the South, from I-95N, take exit 22 (Bath-Brunswick) to Coastal Rt. 1N. Continue through Bath and Wiscasset. At Damariscotta take Business Rt. 1 (to Rts. 129/130). Turn right at the First National Bank on Rt. 129 (watch for the signs). Bear left on Rt. 130 and travel for approximately nine miles. Turn left on Rt. 32. Parking is located at the baseball field on the right.

From the North, Take Coastal Rte. 1S to Waldoboro. Turn left on Rte. 32 at Shop 'n Save. Follow scenic Rte. 32 approximately 19 miles to New Harbor. Parking is located at the baseball field just beyond Shaw's Wharf Restaurant.

- **Hardy Boat Cruises**, P.O. Box 326, New Harbor, ME, 04554.
Phone (207) 677-2026 or toll-free 1-800-2-PUFFIN.
Website: http://www.hardyboat.com/   Email: hardy@gwi.net

- Occasional lighthouse cruises on the *Lively Lady Too* out of Camden, in conjunction with the Elms Bed and Breakfast, also offer views of Matinicus Rock Light. There are several trips each season with varying itineraries. Some offer views of Two Bush Island Light. See page 376 for details.

- **The Elms Bed and Breakfast**, 84 Elm Street, Camden, ME 04843.
Phone: (207) 236-6250 or toll-free: (800) 755-ELMS
Website: http://www.midcoast.com/~theelms/   Email: theelms@midcoast.com

- Captain Bob Bernstein of Atlantic Expeditions in Rockland offers trips to Matinicus Rock by special arrangement. Call him for details.

- **Captain Bob Bernstein, Atlantic Expeditions**, St. George, Maine 04857.
Phone: (207) 372-8621
Website: http://www.midcoast.com/~atlantex/bob.html
Email: atlantex@midcoast.com

TWO BUSH ISLAND LIGHTHOUSE.
CHARACTERISTIC: Flashing white 5s (red sector)
HAW: 65' **RANGES**: White 22; red 18 nm

Two Bush Island Light can be seen from some of the cruises offered by the Elms Bed and Breakfast in Camden. See page 376 for details.

MATINICUS ROCK & TWO BUSH ISLAND

Prior to the establishment of this beacon in 1897, the island was named by local fishermen for the only two tall island pines that were used as daymarks.

The light marks the north end of Two Bush Channel and the east side entrance to Muscle Ridge Channel, a principal sea lane to west Penobscot Bay. The 42-foot tall square and tapered brick Federal Design lighthouse rests on a rubblestone base. It has an entry vestibule on one side and a work house on the other. Two Bush Island's original fifth-order Fresnel lens was removed in 1963 and replaced by an automated modern lens. The aid was unmanned in 1964.

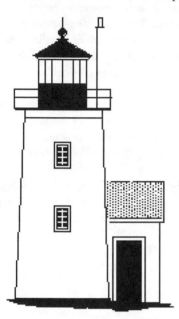

In 1970, with no one willing to move the unwanted and deteriorated keeper's dwelling, the Coast Guard allowed the U.S. Army's Special Forces to destroy the structure with explosives.

OWNER: Under the Maine Lights Program the lighthouse became the property of the U.S. Fish and Wildlife Service in 1997. The Coast Guard still maintains the beacon.

PRESERVATION. Not listed in the National Register of Historic Places.

<u>MATINICUS ROCK LIGHTHOUSE</u> (TWIN TOWERS).
CHARACTERISTIC: Flashing white 10s
HAW: 90' **RANGE**: 20 nm

Matinicus Rock is a desolate, isolated and a crucially essential outpost that gets battered by the most violent of New England's Atlantic storms. The Rock is continuously scoured by waves. There are no trees or grass growing on the surface, for there is no soil. The island's highest elevation is a mere 50 feet. In earlier days to land by boat, keepers had to first catch a breaker on their approach, steer with strength and hope that the boat landed in the boatway, and then haul the boat up as far and fast enough so that the next wave did not pick it up and carry it seaward. Helicopters now service the station.

Over the years Matinicus Rock has seen the following changes:

1827. Twin wooden towers, erected about 40 feet apart with a connecting rubble stone house, were the first aids placed on the rock. Their fixed white lights, each generated by a multilamp and reflector optic and standing 83 feet above the sea, could not be seen at the planned distance of 14 nautical miles. Then too, since the beacons possessed the same elevation, the lights blended together.

1846. A new separate two-story, granite keeper's house built.

1848. In a remodeling task begun in 1847 by Alexander Parris, the original towers were replaced by twin cylindrical gray granite ashlar towers standing about 60 yards apart.

1855. The station's first fog bell was installed. Matinicus Rock is fogbound some 20% of the year.

1857. To prepare the station for new towers, the 1848 towers' silhouettes were lowered by removing their lanterns and the top portions of their walls. Then, two granite block towers were erected about 60 yards apart. Although both lighthouses were supposed to be 48 feet tall, the northern one was five feet taller than its southern counterpart. The difference in heights was necessary to adjust to a sloping terrain, while keeping both lights' focal planes at the same elevation above the sea. The light towers were equipped with new third-order classical lenses. Note that the main keeper's house, also built in 1857, consists of a tall granite basement (the 1846 dwelling) topped with a wood framed living quarters. Attached to each end of the house are the chopped-off shafts of the 1848 granite towers.

1869. The station's 2,000 pound fog bell became the backup signal after the installation of a steam-operated Daboll trumpet housed within a small brick house. The Daboll trumpet was a long megaphone-shaped tube internally fitted with a large reed, similar in design to that of a clarinet. Compressed air passing through the trumpet vibrated the reed to produce the sound of a locomotive whistle. Matinicus Rock's fog whistle and those installed at the Cape Elizabeth and the West Quoddy Head Lighthouses were the first to be placed in operation. The trumpet was swept off the rock in 1883.

1883. The north light was discontinued and the south light's characteristic changed to fixed red.

1888. The single beacon proved unsatisfactory and both towers were brought back into operation and refitted with their former fixed white optics.

1924. The north light was discontinued and its third-order lens removed. The fully operational classical lens can be seen in Rockland's Shore Village Lighthouse Museum. Unfortunately, because of space limitation, only the top of the lens is displayed.

1950. After a great storm, the damaged and unrepairable 1827 keeper's house and the station's accumulation of keeper dwellings, support buildings, sheds and cisterns were removed. Remaining on station today are the 1890 brick oil house, fuel tanks, a heliport and prefabricated equipment modules needed to support the station's automated aids.

1983. The south tower's third-order Fresnel was removed and replaced by an automated plastic lens.

There is a poignant tale about a 17 year-old girl and one of her many experiences on the Matinicus Rock. In January 1856, while the keeper and his only son were absent, a violent storm hit the Rock. With the storm raging all about her, Abbie Burgess assumed her father's responsibilities. First she checked the light. Then, as the storm's surge swept over the ledge, Abbie led her invalid mother and three sisters into the tower. Forty-foot waves thundered over the outcropping, tossing granite boulders about like tenpins. The older keeper's dwelling was washed into the sea; the newer granite house had three feet of water swirling through it. Before closing the tower's door behind her, however, Abbie decided to save her pets. Running back and forth between incoming waves, Abbie was able to scoop up and rescue all but one of her hens. For four weeks without male assistance, Abbie tended the light and cared for her family.

When her father retired, she remained on the station to help orient the new lightkeeper. She stayed a bit longer than first planned, because in 1861 she married the new keeper's son, Isaac Grant, who later became the keeper of the Matinicus Rock Lighthouse. In 1875 Isaac and Abbie and their four children were transferred to the lighthouse on Whitehead Island. Abbie had spent 14 years on Matinicus Rock. The Grants remained at Whitehead for 15 years. Both retired in 1890 with Abbie having lived in a lighthouse for 37 years.

Abbie is buried in the tiny Forest Hill Cemetery off ME 73 between South Thomaston and St. George. In honor of her long service a small metal lighthouse was placed at the foot of her grave by historian Edward Rowe Snow. In 1995 the American Lighthouse Foundation, with contributions from "Friends of Abbie," completely restored the Grants' gravesites.

OWNER. Under the Maine Lights Program the lighthouse became the property of the U.S. Fish and Wildlife Service in 1997. The U.S. Coast Guard still maintains the beacon.

PRESERVATION. Listed in the National Register of Historic Places.

Two Bush Island Lighthouse

INDIAN ISLAND

IN ROCKPORT ON US 1. At the juncture of US 1 and ME 90, turn east into West Street. Then:

-> Continue southeast to Pascals Avenue and turn left,

-> Since a right turn into Andre Street is prohibited, cross over the Goose River bridge to Main Street, make a U-turn and head back on Pascals,

-> Just past the end of the bridge and High Street (on the right), turn left into Andre Street,

-> Motor downhill into Rockport Marine Park. Parking is free.

The lighthouse is located at the entrance to Rockport Harbor. Another sighting of the lighthouse can be made from the Goose River bridge. A third viewing spot is from a small marine park located off Elm Street.

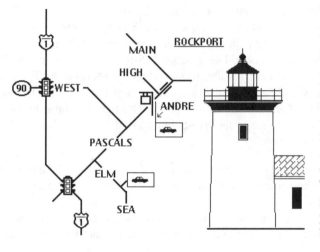

INDIAN ISLAND LIGHTHOUSE (INDIAN NECK; GRAVES LIGHT).

The light station, built in 1850, was restructured in 1874. The main station consists of the brick tower attached to a rather large ground level watchroom, which in turn is connected to another building leading through a breezeway to the brick keeper's dwelling. Indian Island's tapered, square light tower is of the Federal Design styling .

The station also includes a duplex-styled support building (c. 1875), a fuel house (1888) and a stone oil house (1904).

The island's first beacon, established in 1850, consisted of a lantern and optic mounted atop the present front part of the T-shaped residential complex. A fourth-order Fresnel lens was introduced in 1856. The light was inactive for a number of years before 1874, when a special appropriation was granted by the Lighthouse Board to reactivate the aid on January 15, 1875.

Indian Island Light was discontinued in 1934 and replaced by an automatic light on nearby Lowell Rock.

OWNER. Privately owned since the station's deactivation in 1934.

PRESERVATION. Listed in the National Register of Historic Places.

LIGHTHOUSE SIGHTSEEING CRUISE. Captain Rick and Karen Miles' 20-passenger schooner *Timberwind*, in conjunction with *Lighthouse Digest*, sails once each year (usually in mid-September) on a spectacular six-day cruise featuring these lighthouses:

- Burnt Coat Harbor, Curtis Island, Deer Island Thorofare, Dice Head, Indian Island, Isle Au Haut, Owls Head, Rockland Breakwater and Saddleback Ledge. Reservations strongly recommended.

FARE. Deposit required to confirm reservations. Full payment must be received no less than 30 days prior to sailing date. If cancellation within 30 days of sailing, payment refunded if space can be rebooked. Credit cards accepted. Ask about the early bird discount.

- Schooner Timberwind, PO Box 247, Rockport, ME 04856.
Phone (207) 236-0801. In USA toll-free (800) 759-9250.
Website: http://www.schoonertimberwind.com/
Email: info@schoonertimberwind.com

Indian Island Light can also be seen from some of the cruises offered by the Elms Bed and Breakfast in Camden. See page 376 for details.

CURTIS ISLAND

IN CAMDEN ON US 1. Although it is now a municipal park, there is no public transport to the island. There are two mainland locations in Camden from which the Curtis Island Lighthouse can be seen:
- A reasonably close but partially masked view from between houses on Bayview Street.
- A distant but uncluttered view from the Megunticook River Bridge.

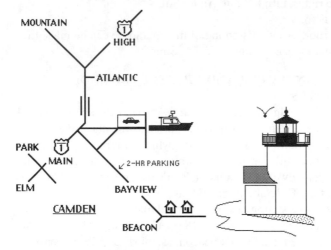

CURTIS ISLAND LIGHTHOUSE.
CHARACTERISTIC: Occulting green
HAW: 52' **RANGE**: 8 nm

This light was first established in a brick tower in 1836. At that time the five-acre island was called Negro Island, reportedly after an African cook who lived on the island. The keeper's dwelling was replaced in 1889 by present 1 1/2-story wood framed residence sheathed in clapboards Then in 1896, the extant Federal Design-styled 25-foot tall, cylindrical brick tower was erected and furnished with a fourth-order Fresnel lens. The station also includes a barn (1889), a boathouse (1889) and an oil house (1895). The light station stands on the south side of the five-acre island; the boat dock is on the northern end.

The name of the island was changed in 1934 in memory of Cyrus H. K. Curtis, publisher of the *Saturday Evening Post* and other publications. Curtis was a longtime summer resident and benefactor of Camden. He gave the town the land and building that became the Camden Yacht Club.

In 1970 word spread that the Coast Guard was planning to auction Curtis Island Light Station, except for the tower. Three Camden residents travelled to Philadelphia for a meeting and managed to convince the Coast Guard that the station should go to the Town of Camden rather than a private party.

In October 1971 the Coast Guard's two keepers were removed. During the following year the beacon was automated and the station's fog bell was replaced by an offshore bell buoy. The Fresnel optic is now solar-powered.

OWNER. Under the Maine Lights Program, created by congressional legislation and coordinated by the Island Institute of Rockland, the lighthouse became the property of the Town of Camden on December 15, 1997. The U.S. Coast Guard maintains the beacon.

PRESERVATION. Listed in the National Register of Historic Places.

The light station is beautifully maintained. In 1989 the town decided that the T-shaped keeper dwelling's green shingles simply were not compatible with the traditional daymark color used for other light stations. As a result the house now sports a red roof.

LIGHTHOUSE SIGHTSEEING CRUISES. Ted Panayotoff, innkeeper of The Elms Bed and Breakfast in Camden, member of the Maine Lights Program and an extremely knowledgable lighthouse historian, offers lighthouse cruises aboard Captain Alan Philbrick's *Lively Lady Too* (single open deck; forward cabin). Cruises depart 8:30 from Sharp's Wharf (see map). A picnic lunch is included.

Five different cruises were offered in the 1999 season between May and September, encompassing the following lighthouses in the various itineraries:
- Curtis Island, Indian Island, Rockland Breakwater, Owls Head, Whitehead, Two Bush Island, Tenants Harbor, Eagle Island, Deer Island Thorofare, Goose Rocks, Browns Head, Heron Neck, Saddleback Ledge, Isle au Haut, Grindle Point, Fort Point, Dice Head, Matinicus Rock.

For more information, contact The Elms or check their website.
- The Elms Bed & Breakfast, 84 Elm Street, Camden, ME 04843.
Phone: (207) 236-6250. In USA toll-free (800) 755-ELMS.
Website: http://www.midcoast.com/~theelms/
Email: theelms@midcoast.com

GRINDLE POINT

CAMDEN HILLS STATE PARK. Halfway between Camden and Lincolnville turn west off US 1 into the entrance to the 5,000-acre park. The paved road leads to the 900-foot summit of Mount Battie where there are expansive panoramic views of Camden Harbor (including Curtis Island) and the Penobscot Bay.

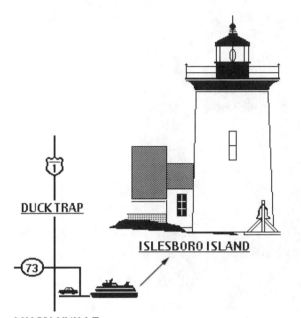

OPEN. May to October, daily from 7 to 7.

ADMISSION FEES. Individual.

FERRY TO ISLESBORO. Islesboro, once known as Long Island, is a 10-mile long, narrow island in the upper Penobscot Bay. The ferry off US 1 between Lincolnville and Islesboro Island operates all year. It carries 30 cars and 226 passengers. The three mile crossing takes 20 minutes. Since the lighthouse and its museum are located next to the ferry landing, it is suggested that you park in the free parking lot and board as a foot passenger. Otherwise make vehicle reservations (extra fee) through the Lincolnville office.

SCHEDULE. Call or check website.

Grindle Point Light can also be viewed from some of the lighthouse cruises offered by the Elms Bed and Breakfast in Camden; see page 376 for details.

SAILOR'S MEMORIAL MUSEUM. This museum is located in the keeper's dwelling. It holds an assortment of maritime and historical exhibits.

OPEN. July to Labor Day, daily (except Mondays) 10 to 4.

FREE ADMISSION.

GRINDLE POINT LIGHTHOUSE (GRINDEL POINT).

CHARACTERISTIC: Flashing green 4s

HAW: 39' **RANGE**: 6 nm

On March 3, 1849, the Lighthouse Service approved the expenditure of $3,500 for the construction of a lighthouse at Islesboro's Gilkey Harbor. The station's three acres were purchased from Francis Grindle for $105. The station with its 28-foot tall brick tower was completed in the summer of 1850. Mr. Grindle not only gave the site its name (albeit misspelled by the government), but, with his appointment as the station's second keeper in April 1853, became the only keeper in the Lighthouse Service to tend his namesake. This early lighthouse and its small keeper's house succumbed to the elements.

In June 1874 the Lighthouse Board decided to rebuild the station. The present 39-foot square brick tower was constructed on the 1850 foundation. Its design is architecturally of the Federal Design genre. The former keeper's house became the connecting passageway to a new 11/2-story, clapboard-sheathed dwelling. The station's boathouse (1881) and oil house (1906) have been removed.

In 1934 the Federal Government deactivated the station, removed the fifth-order Fresnel lens and established a new automated beacon atop a tower erected next to the lighthouse.

While Islesboro maintained the keeper's residence as the Sailor's Memorial Museum, its citizens were determined to return their lighthouse to the U.S. Coast Guard Light List. The town worked long and hard to relight Grindle Point. After 53 years they succeeded. The tower was refitted with a modern lens and converted to solar power. On November 4, 1987, Grindle Point was reactivated. At its recommissioning the station also received a 1,000-pound fog bell manufactured in 1881. The cradle-mounted bell, on loan from Rockland's Shore Village Lighthouse Museum's collection, rests on the south side of the light tower.

OWNER. Purchased in 1934 by the Town of Islesboro for $1,200. The Coast Guard maintains the light.

PRESERVATION. Listed in the National Register of Historic Places.

LINCOLNVILLE TO ISLESBORO FERRY.

FARES. Round trip vehicle + passengers. Discount for children 5-11.

- Maine State Ferry Service, PO Box 214, Lincolnville, ME 04849-0214.

Phone: Lincolnville (207) 734-6935. Islesboro: (207) 734-9714.

Schedule information: (207) 624-7777. Operations update: in Maine toll-free (800) 491-4883.

Website: http://www.midcoast.com/~jcoffin/#Transportation Schedules

Grindle Point Lighthouse

Fort Point Lighthouse

FORT POINT

NORTH ON US 1. In Stockton Springs, just north of a "Ft. Point State Park - 4 1/2 miles" sign and a "Stockton Springs" marker turn right off US 1. Then:

-> Continue for 0.6 mile through the town's small business district and turn right at a "Fort Point State Park" sign into East Cape Road,

-> Continue on East Cape and turn left at Fort Point Road to the park's free parking area.

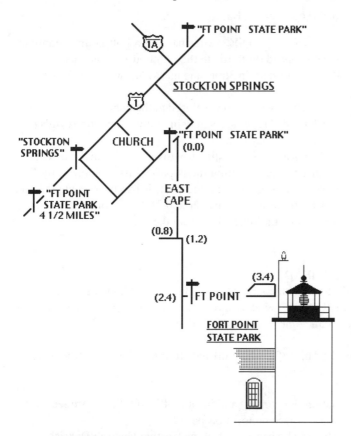

SOUTH ON US 1. The left turn off US 1, also marked with a "Ft. Point State Park" sign, is about 0.7 mile south of the US 1 & US 1A junction. East Cape Road is about 0.3 mile from US 1.

Visitors may stroll about the station. The lighthouse and keeper's dwelling, the family residence of a park ranger, are not open to the public.

FORT POINT STATE PARK. This place was called Wasaumkeag by Native American Indians. It was the site of the British-built Fort Pownall. Completed in 1759, the fort's cannon covered the approach from and to lower Penobscot Bay. The British at that time were equally concerned about a French military push down the Penobscot River from Bangor. The British thought that by denying the French a coastal toehold, they could keep the Gulf of Maine and the Bay of Fundy open to British shipping. The strategy worked. Later, fearing that the American Revolutionaries might seize Fort Pownall, the British destroyed it. The fort's foundations, partially restored, lie near the light station. Open all year, daily 9 to sunset. Free admission.

- Fort Point State Park, Stockton Springs, ME 04981. Phone: (207) 941-4014.

FORT POINT LIGHTHOUSE.
CHARACTERISTIC: Fixed white
HAW: 88' **RANGE**: 15 nm

The first tower, completed in 1836, was a wooden structure that withstood both storm and wear for 20 years. The present keeper's dwelling and attached brick tower were built in 1857. Fort Point's square, slightly tapered light tower is another architectural product of the Federal Design period. The lighthouse is 31 feet tall. Still a part of the light station is the 1890 pyramidal bell tower built in 1890. It no longer holds the striking machinery and its fog bell rests outside the bell tower. This structure, one of the few remaining on the Atlantic Coast, has been placed in the National Register of Historic Places. The barn on station was erected in 1890 and the brick oil house, northeast of the keeper's house, in 1897. The main house's front elevation shows a shed-roofed dormer that was added in 1899.

Fort Point's first light, the product of a multiple lamp and reflector system, was established in 1837. The Coast Guard keeper was removed when the 1857 fourth-order Fresnel lens was automated in October 1988.

OWNER. Under the Maine Lights Program the lighthouse became the property of the Maine Bureau of Parks and Land in Decmber 1997. The U.S. Coast Guard still maintains the beacon.
PRESERVATION. Listed in the National Register of Historic Places.

DICE HEAD

NORTH TO CASTINE. In Orland turn right off US 1 onto ME 175. Follow this route and ME 166 (or 166A) into Castine.

FROM STONINGTON. Take ME 15 to Sargentville. Then:
-> North on ME 175,
-> South on ME 199,
-> South on ME 166 into Castine on Mayflower Hill Road. Then right at Battle Avenue.

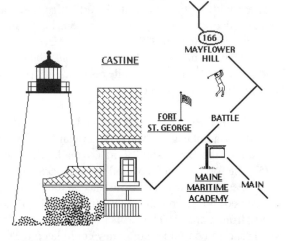

IN CASTINE. After passing a golf course, continue straight ahead on Battle to the lighthouse, a distance of about 0.9 mile from Main Street and its "Maine Maritime Academy" sign.

The tower has been closed to the public until it receives much needed repairs, a safety inspection and the Town's purchase of liability insurance.

CASTINE. Castine is a town whose quiet existence is a far cry from its tumultuous past. First colonized by Plymouth Pilgrims as a trading post, it has been occupied and lost by the French, British and Dutch. Some of Castine's houses and buildings date from the 1700s.

DICE HEAD LIGHTHOUSE. (DYCE HEAD; DYCES HEAD).

This undressed conical granite rubblestone lighthouse is lined with coursed brick. Built in 1828, the light was established the following year using a Lewis lighting device. In 1858 the tower was remodeled into an octagonal shape by encasing it within a clapboard-sheathed wooden frame. At the same time it was connected to the extant 1 1/2-story colonial cape dwelling by a covered passageway.

Some 20 years later the wooden covering was removed. The 1858 whale oil-fed fourth-order Fresnel lens' focal plane was 130 feet above the bay and was visible for 17 nautical miles.

OWNER. After Dice Head's deactivation in 1937, the station (less tower) and its plot of land (100 square feet) were deeded to the Town of Castine. In December 1956 the entire station became town property.

PRESERVATION. Listed in the National Register of Historic Places as part of the Castine Historic District.

For over 40 years the keeper's dwelling was a rental unit and the income was used exclusively to maintain the house. Since 1990, with $18,000 in national and state grants and matching municipal funds, the tower's exterior walls have been repointed and painted and carpentry and structural repairs have been made to the tower's interior and the 1888 barn that serves as a garage.

In 1997 the Lighthouse Preservation Society offered to purchase the property and turn it into a bed and breakfast facility. The proposal came on the heels of a town sponsored study on what to do about the lighthouse. With $132,000 available to repair and maintain the light station, the town's residents rejected all options that would have taken the property out of their hands.

Then, in the spring of 1999 a late night fire burned through the roof of the keeper's house, apparently starting in a faulty chimney. The resident of the house was home but was not injured in the blaze, and the tower wasn't damaged. After some deliberation, the town decided to repair the badly damaged structure rather than completely rebuilding it.

- Municipal Office, Town of Castine, PO Box 204, Castine, ME 04221.
Phone: (207) 326-4502.

PUMPKIN ISLAND
EAGLE ISLAND - DEER ISLAND THOROFARE

FROM CASTINE. Follow ME 166 north -> ME 175 south -> ME 15 south to Sargentville.

FROM ELLSWORTH. Take ME 172 south through Surry and Blue Hill to Sedgewick. Then follow ME 175 to Sargentville.

TO LITTLE DEER ISLE. In Sargentville take ME 15 and cross over the Eggemoggin Reach bridge (free). At the end of the bridge, where ME 15 turns left, bear right through a triangular intersection and turn right into Eggemoggin Road. Continue for 2.7 miles to its end at a fishing pier just past the Eggemoggin Inn. Free parking. Pumpkin Island lies off to the right.

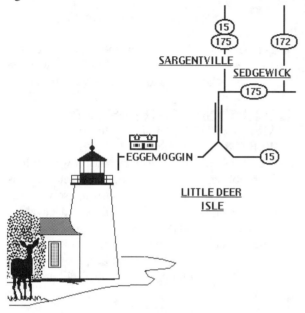

PUMPKIN ISLAND LIGHTHOUSE.

In 1852 Congress approved the building of a light station on what was then known as Tent Island. The island's owner agreed to deed the island to the Federal Government only after the purchase agreement stipulated that he was to be appointed the station's first keeper. The light was commissioned on April 18, 1854. The tower is of double wall, coursed brick construction. The 25-foot tall lighthouse was fitted with a fifth-order Fresnel optic, making it the second station in Maine to receive this lens. The new station consisted of the light tower, a 1 1/2-story wood framed house with an attached kitchen, a brick work shed that connected the house to the tower, a barn and that early American facility, the outdoor privy. While the tower has been neither renovated nor restored, the colonial cape dwelling has undergone numerous alterations and renovations, including a clapboard exterior during the 1880s and the addition of the southeast wing and the northeast dormer in 1902. The station's boathouse was built in 1885 and enlarged in 1906, when a new slip was added. The brick oil house was erected in 1904.

In 1889 the lighthouse received a new lantern which increased its overall height to 28 feet. At the same time, the fifth-order Fresnel was converted to burn mineral oil (kerosene). In 1909 Pumpkin Island received an L. Sautter of Paris fifth-order Fresnel lens that had been removed from another Maine light station and rebuilt by the repair station in South Portland. In 1930 the keeper was removed and the light automated.

OWNER. In 1934, after the light had been decommissioned and the station had been declared surplus government property, the island was sold for the grand sum of $552 to Bar Harbor resident, George Harmon.[1] In 1946 the island was purchased by Alexander Stewart, who with evident pride, said in September 1982 that his "Island of Magic" was the "most photographed lighthouse in Maine." The following year the beautiful two-acre island and its attractive and superbly maintained lighthouse were for sale for $395,000. In 1990 Pumpkin Island was again on the real estate market for $1.2 million.

PRESERVATION. Listed in the National Register of Historic Places.

TO DEER ISLE. Return to ME 15 and continue south into the town of Deer Isle.

The following directions to view the Eagle Island Lighthouse are provided with the request that the traveler not drive down the privately owned lane, but will walk the short distance to the shoreline.

At Deer Isle's post office turn right off ME 15 (0.0 mile). The turn is marked by a "Sunset" sign. Bear right again at Pressey Village Road (0.5 mile). The lane is an extension of Pressey Village at its sharp left turn into Dunham Point Road (2.6 mile).

Park along Pressey Village or Dunham Point and walk down the lane to the shoreline. Eagle Island is located almost due west of Dunham Point.

381

---

1. George Harmon also acquired the Winter Harbor Light Station in 1935. Shortly thereafter, Harmon resold the station to a New Yorker for a handsome profit. He also purchased Frenchman Bay's Crabtree Ledge Lighthouse off Hancock Point. That lighthouse (1890) was one of those generic cast-iron structures built on concrete-filled cast-iron caisson foundations during the late 1890s and early 1900s. Although in poor condition when purchased, Harmon reportedly sold it to Newbold Noyes, editor of the Washington Star. Noyes gave the lighthouse to his three sons as a gift. The sons sold the lighthouse to a friend, and it collapsed into the bay in 1934.

EAGLE ISLAND MAIL BOAT CRUISE. Continue down Dunham Point Road into the village of Sunset. Follow the "Mailboat Parking" signs to Sylvester Cove and the Yacht Club's pier. The two-hour cruise aboard the *Katherine* (single open deck with awning, forward cabin) passes close by the Eagle Island Lighthouse. Although passengers may stretch their legs after the boat docks, the cruise is exclusively a sightseeing tour with little time to walk beyond the landing areas.

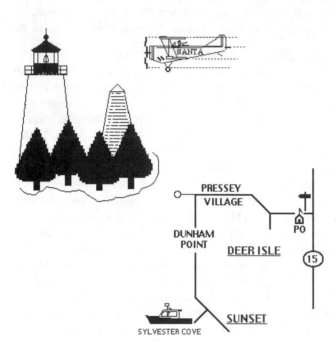

SCHEDULE. Mid-June to mid-September, Mondays through Saturdays at 8:30.

FARES. Reservations required. $15 round trip. No discounts.

- Sunset Bay Company, Eagle Island, Sunset, ME 04683. Phone (207) 348-9316.

For another possible view from the water, check the cruises on the Lively Lady II offered in conjunction with the Elms Bed and Breakfast in Camden. See page 376 for details.

EAGLE ISLAND LIGHTHOUSE.
CHARACTERISTIC: Flashing white 4s
HAW: 106' **RANGE**: 9 nm

The lighthouse on 260-acre Eagle Island was built in 1839. It is a rubblestone tower that originally held a Lewis multiple lamp and reflector optic. The station also was provided a wood framed, four-bedroom dwelling and a pyramidal wooden tower to house the weights for a clockwork mechanism that rang the station's fog bell. An oil house was added in 1895 and a storage shed in 1902. The keepers' residence, by the way, did not have running water until 1947 or indoor plumbing until 1949.

In 1858 the lantern was fitted with a fourth-order Fresnel lens. The Fresnel lens was removed in 1963 and replaced with an automated plastic lens.

In 1963 the Coast Guard crew burned the keeper's house, demolished all other structures except the light and bell towers, and removed all fixtures and equipment. During that destructive binge, the crew attempted to remove the large fog bell. While moving the heavy bell downhill to the shore, it slipped from the handlers' grasps, bounced down the hill and over the cliff into the water. Later, a lobsterman spotted it, retrieved it and sold it to photographer Eliot Porter of neighboring Great Spruce Head Island.

OWNER. In 1972 five of the six acres (one acre retained for the tower), comprising the old light station were declared surplus property and were made available at no cost to the state or for sale to a private party. The property around the lighthouse is now owned by the Howe family. There are no public ways into the one acre plot. Under terms of the Maine Lights Program the lighthouse, bell tower and land were turned over to the Eagle Island Caretakers. The U.S. Coast Guard still maintains the beacon.

PRESERVATION. Not listed in the National Register of Historic Places.

TO STONINGTON. See the following map. Return to ME 15 and motor south into Stonington and west through its waterfront district on ME 15 (Main Street). At Billings Road turn left and cross over the causeway to Moose Island and the Billings Diesel and Marine Services. Enter through the repair yard's open gate and make your courtesy call at the company's main office. Then motor to the right of the main entrance and continue southwest and south past the large repair buildings to the water's edge, an area studded with abandoned boats and a large pile of lumber debris. The Deer Island Thorofare Lighthouse, lying off to the south southwest, stands on the west end of the island at the west entrance of the thorofare.

The lighthouse can also be seen from the higher elevation of ME 15 (West Main Street) about 0.4 mile west of Billings Road.

For a closer view from the water, check the schedule of lighthouse cruises on the *Lively Lady Too* offered in conjunction with the Elms Bed and Breakfast in Camden. See page 376 for details. Also see the Penobscot Bay cruise described on the next page.

PUMPKIN ISLAND, EAGLE ISLAND & DEER ISLAND THOROFARE

DEER ISLAND THOROFARE LIGHTHOUSE (MARK ISLAND).
CHARACTERISTIC: Flashing white 6s
HAW: 52' **RANGE**: 8 nm

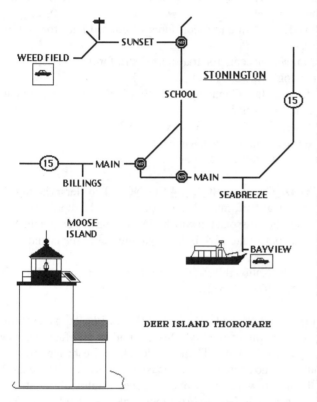

DEER ISLAND THOROFARE

In 1857 the station consisted of the present square brick light tower, the main dwelling, an oil house, bell tower, boathouse and support buildings. The keeper's residence, connected to the tower, was a 1 1/2-story, wooden structure that had a one-story kitchen annex. All of the station's structures were demolished after the Coast Guard watch crew was withdrawn. Today only the 25-foot tall lighthouse remains.

The original optic installed in the Federal Design-styled lighthouse was a fourth-order Fresnel lens. The light was automated in 1958 when the presently active modern plastic lens was introduced.

OWNER. On December 15, 1997, the Maine Lighthouse Selection Committee, formed to oversee the transfer of 36 Maine lighthouse properties under the Maine Lights Program, announced that Deer Island Thorofare Light would be turned over by the Coast Guard to the Island Heritage Trust. The Trust plans to maintain the island as a wildlife refuge. Mark Island's birds include bald eagles and nesting eider ducks. The U.S. Coast Guard still maintains the active beacon.

Marnie Reed Crowell of the Island Heritage Trust has written a booklet on the history of Deer Island Thorofare Light. To obtain the booklet send $18 plus $3 shipping to: Deer Island Granite Company, Deer Isle, ME 04627. Email: digranite@aol.com. Portions of the proceeds will be used for the maintenance of the lighthouse.

- Island Heritage Trust, P.O. Box 42, Deer Isle, ME 04627
Website: http://www.mltn.org/trusts/IHT.HTM
Email: SFMMWM@acadia.net

PRESERVATION. Not listed in the National Register of Historic Places.

TOWN PARKING. Daytime or overnight parking available at the boat docks on Bayview Street or at Steve Robbins Garage & Transportation, Weed Field Road, Stonington, ME 04681. Phone: (207) 367-5548.

PENOBSCOT BAY CRUISE. The Isle au Haut Mail Boats offer cruises among the islands of east Penobscot Bay south of Deer Isle. These feature a view of the lighthouse on Mark Island and a narrative of the history and folklore of the island region.
The boat is docked off Sea Breeze Avenue in Stonington.
SCHEDULE. Mid-June to Mid-September Day, daily at 2. Returns at 3.
FARES. Reduced fare for children under 12.

- Isle au Haut Company, P.O. Box 709, Sea Breeze Avenue, Stonington, ME 04681.
Phone: (207) 367-5193. Fax: (207) 367-6503
Website: http://www.isleauhaut.com/   Email: staige@together.net

ISLE AU HAUT

FERRY TO TOWN LANDING. The mail boats make scheduled 40 minute trips from Stonington to the Isle Au Haut Town Landing, which is about a mile from the lighthouse. Passengers bound for The Keeper's House are disembarked at the inn's private boat landing on Robinson Point.

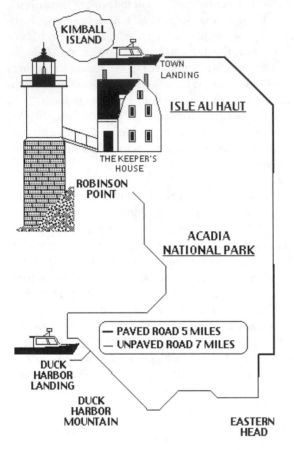

SCHEDULE. Call or check website for current schedule. One hour crossing time.

FARES. Cash and credit fares. Reduced Fare for children under 12.

Company accepts for transport (extra fare) bicycles, canoes, boats and dogs, cats and other pets.

- Isle au Haut Company, P.O. Box 709, Sea Breeze Avenue Stonington, ME 04681.

Phone: (207) 367-5193. Fax: (207) 367-6503

Website: http://www.isleauhaut.com/

Email: staige@together.net

TO DUCK HARBOR LANDING. Travelers visiting the Acadia National Park must disembark at Duck Harbor. There are certain restrictions associated with hiking, biking and camping. Visitors should contact the park before heading out to the island's wilderness.

- Acadia National Park, PO Box 177, Bar Harbor, ME 04609. Phone (207) 288-3338.

THE ISLAND. Isle Au Haut ("island with a high elevation") has but one overnight facility. Not all homes and facilities have electricity or a telephone. There is a delightful freshwater pond for swimming, but no swimming off the island's beaches. There are 12 miles of roads, of which only five are paved. Automobiles are few, since there is no auto ferry to bring more onto the island. Bring your own bicycles; there are no rentals on the island.

In past years Isle Au Haut had a sizable population and its economy flourished with a lobster and seafood cannery, a boatbuilding industry and summer visitors. Today there are about 50 permanent residents and the few that remain are mighty proud of their unspoiled island.

THE KEEPER'S HOUSE. This overnight facility in the old lighthouse keeper's dwelling is a bed and breakfast inn owned and operated by Jeffrey and Judi Burke. Judi Burke, by the way, is the daughter of a lighthouse keeper.

The inn's four guest rooms (double beds) are comfortably furnished in antiques and coastal memorabilia. There are also rustic accommodations in the light station's old oil house and barn. The inn has hot water for guests, but no television, telephone or electricity. Guests read and eat by the light of candles, gaslights and kerosene lamps. The Burkes serve fresh native seafood and chicken (no red meat) with the gourmand in mind. VHF radio is available for emergency communications.

If you plan to visit with the Burkes, write for their brochure describing accommodations, current rates, boat schedules and planning tips.

OPEN. May to October.

COST. Daily tariff plus tax includes room, all meals, special diet requests, extra bed if requested, box lunches for day hikes and use of the inn's bicycles. Single, double and triple rates. There is a two day minimum stay during July and August.

- The Keeper's House, PO Box 26, Isle Au Haut, ME 04645.

Phone: Off-island only (207) 367-2261.

Website: http://media5.hypernet.com/~KEEPERS/keepers.html

ISLE AU HAUT

ISLE AU HAUT LIGHTHOUSE (ROBINSON POINT).
CHARACTERISTIC: Flashing red 4s (white sector)
HAW: 48' **RANGES**: Red 6; white 8 nm

Construction of this light station was authorized by Congress in June 1906 with an appropriation of $14,000. The station is built on Robinson Point, a volcanic ledge overlooking the Isle Au Haut Thorofare between Isle Au Haut and Kimball Island. The light was first exhibited on December 24, 1907.

The white 16-foot tall, cylindrical brick tower rests on a gray 20-foot tall conical granite base. The tower's design along with its approach ramp closely resembles Maine's Marshall Point Lighthouse in Port Clyde. The 2 1/2-story, L-shaped Victorian residence is the original gambel-roof structure built in 1907. The station also includes a small stucco and slate-roofed oil house located near the boathouse and a wooden storage building standing in back of the dwelling.

Isle Au Haut's Fresnel lens was removed in 1959 when it was replaced by an automated modern lens.

OWNER. In 1934 the dwelling, outbuildings and grounds were sold at public auction. The keeper's house remained a private summer retreat until the Burkes purchased it. Under the Maine Lights Program the lighthouse was turned over to the Town of Isle Au Haut in April 1998. The U.S. Coast Guard maintains the active beacon.

PRESERVATION. Listed in the National Register of Historic Places.

In 1989 the Burkes received the Coast Guard's permission to remove the wire fencing around the ramp connecting the house and the lighthouse and to restore the walkway to its original appearance.

A complete restoration of the lighthouse was finished in June 1999. $62,000 was raised for the overhaul by concerned residents of Isle Au Haut, who formed the Isle Au Haut Lighthouse Committee. Workers from the Campbell Construction Company of Beverly, Massachusetts, repaired a bulge in the exterior of the lighthouse and removed a concrete shell that had been added to the tower's base. The lantern railing, windows and doors were replaced with carefully crafted replicas of the originals, and the entire structure was repainted. The lighthouse now looks much as it did when it was built, and it is considered to be in good shape for its second century.

VIEWS FROM THE ISLAND. One can see on a clear night the lights of three lighthouses from The Keeper's Inn (Burnt Coat Harbor is visible from the island's east side):
- Matinicus Rock to the south southwest.
- Saddleback Ledge to the southwest.
- Heron Neck to the west southwest.

Here's a challenge for you hardy hikers. Pick a full moonlit night and hike up Duck Harbor Mountain. Jeff Burke believes that as many as eight lighthouse beacons should be visible. That item raises a question you prospective Sir Hillarys might be able to answer: "How many lighthouses can be seen on a crisp, clear day?"

Isle Au Haut Lighthouse

Egg Rock Lighthouse

EGG ROCK

The route to view the lighthouses on and offshore of Mount Desert Island follows a clockwise loop from Ellsworth to Bar Harbor, to Northeast Harbor, to Bass Harbor, and returns to Ellsworth.

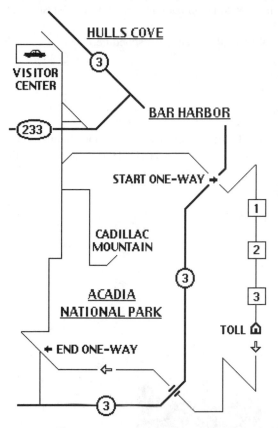

ACADIA NATIONAL PARK. In Ellsworth take ME 3 to the entrance to the park, three miles south of Hulls Cove. There is ample free parking. Steps and paved ramps lead up to the Visitor Center. Three handicapped parking spaces, located topside near the center's main entrance, are reached from the parking lot via a service road to the right of the building.

The center offers a free 15-minute film about Acadia. An informational brochure with map is free for the asking. A self-guiding tape tour and cassette player (or tape alone) can be rented.

OPEN. Winter visitor center hours: 8:00 AM - 4:30 PM daily, November 1 to mid-April, except Thanksgiving Day, December 24 and 25, and January 1.

Summer visitor center hours: Mid-April through June and October, daily 8:00 AM - 4:30 PM. July-August, daily 8:00 AM-6:00 PM. September, daily, hours vary.

FEES. Weekly pass for person or vehicle. Free for holders of Golden Pass and Golden Access passports.

- Acadia National Park, PO Box 177, Bar Harbor, ME 04609.

Phone: (207) 288-3338.

Website: http://www.nps.gov/acad/home.htm

TO PARK LOOP ROAD. The 20-mile route, connecting Mount Desert Island's lakes, mountains and seashore, provides panoramas of the coast and island studded Frenchman, Blue Hill and Penobscot Bays.

The Egg Rock Lighthouse can be seen from this loop road. A side road takes the motorist up onto Cadillac Mountain, the highest elevation (1,530') on the Atlantic Coast. Head east out of the Visitor Center's parking area and pass a sign marking the road. The Egg Rock Lighthouse, offshore in Frenchman Bay, can be viewed at these locations: Champlain Mountain Overlook, the Precipice, and the Scenic Overlook.

EGG ROCK LIGHTHOUSE.
CHARACTERISTIC: Flashing red 5s
HAW: 64'   **RANGE**: 14 nm

The 40-foot tall lighthouse proper is a square brick tower that rises through the center of a 1 1/2-story square wood framed keeper's dwelling. Built in 1875, it was extensively damaged by storms in 1876 and again in 1877. The original shallow hip roof was replaced around 1899 with the present high hip roof with dormers. The light marks the upper reaches of Frenchman Bay.

After it was automated and unmanned in 1976, the Coast Guard tore down the station's ancillary structures, removed the lantern and its fourth-order Fresnel lens and installed back-to-back aerobeacons on the tower's stump. The brick fog signal building built in 1875 was untouched. The disfiguring was not unlike that done to towers in Connecticut and Massachusetts as well as Maine's Wood Island and Mount Desert Lighthouses. In 1986, at the urging of the public, the Coast Guard refitted the tower with an octagonal aluminum lantern and a protective balustrade on the service gallery.

OWNER. Under terms of the Maine Lights Program the lighthouse was officially turned over to the U.S. Fish and Wildlife Service, but it may eventually become the property of the National Park Service. The U.S. Coast Guard still maintains the beacon.

PRESERVATION. Listed in the National Register of Historic Places.

TO BAR HARBOR. If a rented tape requires a return to the Visitor Center leave the park via the Hulls Cove Exit, turn right and follow ME 3 into Bar Harbor. Otherwise, depart via the ME 233 interchange.

FRENCHMAN BAY LIGHTHOUSE CRUISE. A two-hour Lighthouse Cruise offered by the Bar Harbor Whale Watch Company features the Egg Rock Lighthouse. The Bar Harbor Whale Watch Company is located at 1 West Street at Harbor Place on the Town Pier in Bar Harbor.

SCHEDULE. Two to four cruises daily from mid-May to late October. Call for the latest schedule.

FARES. Discounts for children 12 and under and seniors.

- Bar Harbor Whale Watch Co., 1 West St. Bar Harbor, ME 04609.

Phone (207) 288-2386. In USA toll-free (800) 508-1499.

Website: http://www.whalesrus.com

A ride on the Bar Harbor Ferry provides views of mountains, mansions, fishing villages and lobstermen hauling their traps, as well as the Egg Rock Lighthouse. You can take the ferry to visit other locations near Bar Harbor, such as Little Cranberry Island and Southwest Harbor. Contact Captain Steven Pagels for schedule information.

- Capt. Steven F. Pagels, P. O. Box 28, Cherryfield, Maine 04622.

Phone: Summer: (207) 288-2984 Winter: (207) 546-2927.

Website: http://www.downeastwindjammer.com/which_cruise.html

Bear Island Lighthouse

MOUNT DESERT

WHALE WATCH CRUISES. There are whale watch cruises that may occasionally pass this lighthouse. Lighthouse sightings are not guaranteed. The cruises go where the whales are, which is not necessarily where the lighthouses are.

- The four-hour, narrated whale watching excursion aboard the 149-passenger *Acadian Whale Watcher* departs from the Bar Harbor Regency Holiday Inn Marina.

SCHEDULE. Sails May to October. There's no set schedule; call ahead for departure days and times.

FARES. Ticket office is on West Street at the corner of Cottage and Main Streets. Discounts for seniors 62+, children 7-15. Under 7 free.

- Acadian Whale Watcher, PO Box 954, Bar Harbor, ME 04609.

Phone: (207) 207-288-9776. In USA toll-free (800) 421-3307 (year round).

Acadian Whale Adventures offers whale watches on the *Royal Miss Belmar*, a jet-powered catamaran. There are daily departures from the Golden Anchor Pier at 55 West Street.

- Acadian Whale Adventures, (207) 288-9800 or toll free (866) 710-9800.

MOUNT DESERT LIGHTHOUSE (MOUNT DESERT ROCK).
CHARACTERISTIC: Flashing white 15s
HAW: 75' **RANGE:** 18 nm

Mount Desert Rock, a disturbed pile of granite boulders, lies some 26 miles south of Mount Desert Island. Its first aid to navigation, built in 1830, was a short octagonal wooden tower placed atop one end of a two-story rubble stone keeper's house.

The tower was replaced in 1847 by the present 58-foot tall conical, granite structure, which looks a bit out of proportion with its wide base and thick-walled trunk. There is a plaque above the tower's main entrance that bears the date "1847."

The original keeper's dwelling remained in use until 1876, when a second keeper's house was erected to the south of it. That second dwelling was dismantled after the present colonial duplex residence was completed in 1893. The station's brick fog signal building built in 1891 also has disappeared.

The first lighting apparatus was the rather inefficient Lewis optic, consisting of eight whale oil-burning lamps each fitted with a parabolic reflector. The light's focal point was 56 feet above the water. In 1858, after a new lantern was in place, a single oil-burning lamp and a LePaute third-order Fresnel lens were installed. A bell tower was also added. Both the revolving light and the fog bell were operated by clockwork mechanisms that had to be rewound several times each night. The fog bell was replaced in 1889 by a steam-driven fog whistle. The modern plastic lens installed in 1977 is now solar powered.

Between 1974 and its automation in 1977 when the Coast Guard withdrew its personnel, the tower's lantern was removed to accommodate a sizable drum-type aerobeacon. Reportedly, public objection to the scalping moved the Coast Guard to recap the tower with a new lantern in 1985. Although it has not been publicly stated as a contributing factor to the recapping of the light towers, a compelling reason, according to a former member of the Coast Guard, was that the service's aids to navigation teams found that the exposed aerobeacons had a higher than expected damage rate from storms and high winds, thus increasing operations and maintenance costs beyond those experienced in maintaining lantern-protected optics.

In a testimonial to the power of the sea, Maine's Superintendent of Lighthouses reported in 1842 that a storm had moved a 57-ton granite boulder the size of a mobile home onto the island. And to top that one, the same report also mentioned that in another storm the sea moved a 75-ton boulder a distance of 60 feet. Mount Desert Rock's worse damage occurred during Hurricane Daisy in October 1962.

While the crew huddled in the tower, the hurricane and the sea cleaned the rock of two empty 1,500-gallon fuel tanks, a paint locker, concrete walkway and the covered walkway between the tower and the keepers dwelling. After the storm, the keepers found a 4-ton boulder resting inside the boathouse, having been washed onto the Rock over the boathouse and released as the wave passed over the roof.

Mount Desert Rock, like Boon Island, Matinicus Rock and Saddleback Ledge, does not have any topsoil. Nevertheless when manned, fishermen referred to the island as "God's Rock Garden," because each spring the lighthouse keepers would bring to the barren outcropping barrels and bags of soil to establish flower and vegetable gardens. During fall and winter, the soil and plantings invariably were washed away by restless and stormy seas. But each spring, the hauling and planting ritual was repeated.

Today the station's old engine room stores survival gear for wrecked or lost mariners. The keeper's dwelling has been boarded up and the soil has long vanished. At various times of the year up to 70 species of migrating birds drop in to rest.

OWNER. In February 1998 under the Maine Lights Program coordinated by the Island Institute of Rockland, Mount Desert Rock Lighthouse, along with Great Duck Island Lighthouse, became the property of the College of the Atlantic in Bar Harbor. The U.S. Coast Guard still maintains the beacon.

During summer months, the lighthouse has been used as an observation post and living quarters by marine scientists from the College of the Atlantic, engaged in the study of the large number of whales cavorting offshore while scooping up the area's plentiful plankton.

- College of the Atlantic, Bar Harbor, Maine 04609.
Phone: Toll free (800) 528-0025. Fax: (207) 288-4126
Website: http://www.coa.edu/
Email: inquiry@ecology.coa.edu

PRESERVATION. Listed in the National Register of Historic Places.

BEAR ISLAND
BAKER ISLAND

TO NORTHEAST HARBOR. Take scenic ME 3 to ME 198 and then head south to Northeast Harbor. In Northeast Harbor turn left off ME 198 (Harborside Road) at Harbor Drive. The turn is marked by a "Marina" sign. Drive to the first stop sign, turn right and continue on Harbor (one way) past the tennis courts to Clifton Dock Road (on the left).

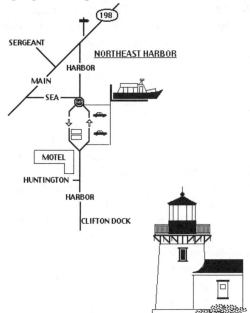

Because of the dock's small parking space and its tight turnaround, it is recommended that you park along Harbor Drive and walk the short distance to the dock. The Bear Island Lighthouse lies off to the southeast at the entrance to Northeast Harbor.

For a better view of Bear Island Lighthouse a boat ride is necessary. The ferry to the Cranberry Isles and the Somes Sound cruise described below, as well as the Baker Island cruise described on the next page, all offer good views of Bear Island and its lighthouse.

FERRY TO THE CRANBERRY ISLES.

Beale & Bunker operate a passenger and mail ferry to Great Cranberry and Islesford from Northeast Harbor's municipal pier. During the trip the 49-passenger *Sea Queen* (open deck with enclosed cabin) passes close by Bear Island, allowing for the taking of photographs of the lighthouse. Islesford has the Islesford Historical Museum, The Islesford Market for groceries, snacks, pizza and ice cream, a variety of shops, an art gallery and the Islesford Dock restaurant.

SCHEDULE. Runs year round; call or check website for current schedule.

FARES. One way and round trip. Discount for children under 12, under 3 free. Bicycles extra.

- Beale & Bunker, Inc., PO Box 33, Cranberry Isles, ME 04625.
Phone: (207) 244-3575.
Website: http://www.cranberryisles.com/ferry.html

SOMES SOUND FJORD CRUISE.

Sea Princess Cruises, a sightseeing cruise company in Northeast Harbor, offers a narrated cruise that passes Bear Island Lighthouse. The cruise also visits Southwest Harbor and Manset Harbor, and provides an opportunity to view some of the area's wildlife.
- Sea Princess Cruises, Box 545, Mount Desert, ME 04660.
Phone: (207) 276-5352.
Website: http://www.barharborcruises.com/   Email: rliebow@acadia.net

BEAR ISLAND LIGHTHOUSE.
CHARACTERISTIC: Flashing white 5s
HAW: 100'

The first Bear Island Lighthouse, constructed in 1839, consisted of a stone dwelling surmounted by a short tower and lantern. In 1852-53, a new brick tower was built off one end of the original keeper's residence.

Contrary to some published histories, the light station was not repaired or refurbished in 1889, but totally rebuilt. This fact is borne out in an October 1984 Inventory of Structures Report by the National Park Service's Division of Cultural Resources. In that report, the surveying architectural conservator states that the present lighthouse, although recorded as having been rebuilt from the earlier 1853 tower, appears to incorporate virtually none of the earlier lighthouse construction components. He also mentions that the two-story brick tower is built on a granite rubblestone foundation. The main entry attached to the tower has a granite lintel over the doorway showing the year "1889." The report also states that, except for the replacement of a window sash with glass block masonry, the lighthouse of 1889 remains essentially unchanged.

The light station consists of the 33-foot tall lighthouse with an attached workroom, the detached 1 1/2-story, gambrel-roofed house, barn (1889), a stone oil house (1905) and a boathouse.

Bear Island's electrified fifth-order Fresnel optic (1858) was extinguished in April 1982 after offshore lighted buoys had been placed in service. The aid was reestablished in 1989 using a modern plastic lens.

OWNER. The station property was transferred to the National Park Service in 1987 and incorporated into Acadia National Park. Leased to a private party in 1989.

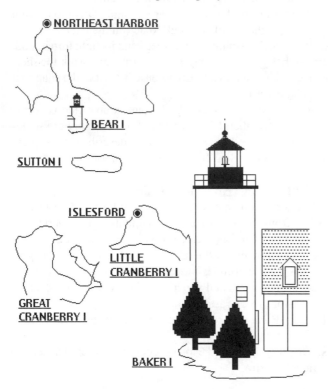

PRESERVATION. Eligible for listing in the National Register of Historic Places.

In 1989, after the nonprofit Friends of Acadia spent $17,000 for repairs to the keeper's house, the National Park Service gave the Friends its permission to restore the light station. The Friends, using funds received from contributions and through a financial grant, repaired the dwelling's roof and the tower's entryway and reestablished the light as a private aid.

The National Park Service threw a monkey wrench into the Friends' plans for the station, when in 1991 it granted a Philadelphian a 60-year lease. Under terms of the National Park Service's Historical Leasing Program, the contract had a five-year clause that called for the new owner to make specified repairs, estimated to cost $200,000, to the station's five buildings. For his partially tax deductible financial commitment to restore a historic place, the light station became the lessee's summer vacation chalet. Accordingly, the Friends of Acadia withdrew from any involvement in the station's preservation.

Meanwhile, with public support, especially from fishermen and lobstermen, the Coast Guard decided in 1996 to keep the light shining.

VISITING THE BAKER ISLAND LIGHTHOUSE. Acadia National Park sponsors a naturalist-led cruise (weather permitting) to and a natural history walk on Baker Island, including a visit to the lighthouse located about a half mile from the boat landing. Expect moderate physical exertion from the landing by rowed dory and the island hike.

Transportation is aboard the Islesford Ferry (two open decks) docked at Northeast Harbor's Municipal Marina at the end of Sea Street. The cruise passes close by the Bear Island Lighthouse on the outbound leg. Reservations are recommended.

SCHEDULE. Sailings depend upon the weather and the popularity of the excursion.
July and August, daily at 1. Returns at 5:30. September, weekends only at 1.
FARES. Discounts for seniors 65+ and children 4-12. Under 4 free.
- Islesford Ferry Company, Box 451, RFD 2, Ellsworth, ME 04605.
Phone (207) 276-3717. Off-season (207) 422-6815.

BAKER ISLAND LIGHTHOUSE.
CHARACTERISTIC: Flashing white 10s
HAW: 105' **RANGE**: 10 nm
The island's first tower, a wood framed structure erected in 1828, was rebuilt in 1855.

The Maine Historic Preservation Commission reports that documentary photographs of the station show that the existing tower and keeper's house have undergone several alterations since 1855, such as the replacement of the 1 1/2-story cape cod dwelling's original board-and-batten siding with clapboards and the removal of the narrow connecting passageway between the house and the tower.

In 1903, in order to strengthen its framework, the 43-foot tall brick lighthouse was sheathed in an extra course of brick. Inside the tower is a cast-iron open staircase that spirals up to the octagonal lantern.

During the 1855 refurbishing, the light was fitted with a fourth-order Fresnel lens and its fuel changed from whale oil to lard oil. The Fresnel lens was replaced in 1966 by an automated and solar powered plastic lens.

BEAR ISLAND & BAKER ISLAND

OWNER. U.S. Coast Guard (lighthouse). The dwelling, a brick oil house (1895) and a storage shed (1905) belong to the National Park Service.

PRESERVATION. Listed in the National Register of Historic Places.

As part of Maine's continuing effort to salvage and restore its lighthouses, the State's Historic Preservation Commission in 1989 spent $3,600 for structural analyses of the station's tower, keeper's house and outbuildings. Since then, necessary repairs have been made.

In 1991 the Coast Guard, declaring that the surrounding trees had obscured the light, announced it was about to deactivate the beacon. The Friends of Acadia sought a delay in the Coast Guard's plans, while trying to get the National Park Service to trim the trees. Despite published reports to the contrary, the trees were not trimmed. Since then, the Friends of Acadia have withdrawn from any involvement in the preservation of the light station.

Then in 1996, after a show of hands and written protests, especially from fishermen, the Coast Guard decided not to deactivate the light.

WALKING TO BAKER ISLAND.[1] According to Captain Ted Spurling, one can walk at low tide across the bar that stretches some 0.75 mile between Little Cranberry and Baker Island. Check the tidal calendar, ask questions and then let someone on Little Cranberry know you are going. To avoid deep wading, take the slippery hike during morning or evening lowest low tides. For real lighthouse buffs the walk across the spit and a few hours on the island to visit the lighthouse should be quite an experience.

Bass Harbor Head Lighthouse

---

1. Spurling, Captain Ted, Sr., Cranberry Report, "Strolling dry-shod to Bakers Island with Hemmingway the poodle", *Inter-Island News*, Island Institute, April 1996.

BASS HARBOR HEAD
BURNT COAT HARBOR - GREAT DUCK ISLAND

TO BASS HARBOR. From Northeast Harbor take ME 198 north and ME 102 and ME 102A south through the town of Bass Harbor to the entrance of the Coast Guard Bass Harbor Head Station. Since RVs and trailers are not allowed into the station, park along ME102A and walk the short distance to the lighthouse.

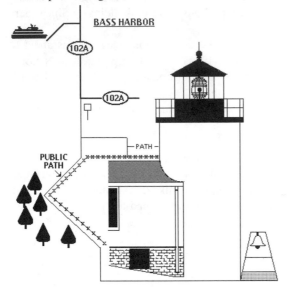

OPEN. All year, 9 to sunset.

FREE ADMISSION. The keeper's house is a Coast Guard family residence. Visitors are requested to be considerate of the occupants' privacy and to remain outside of the fenced area when walking to the lighthouse.

On the east side of the station there is a trail that leads from the parking lot to the granite-strewn shore. Expect moderate to heavy physical exertion and by all means, be careful. The first part of the trail is covered with bare roots and rocks. A steep two-flight stairway descends to another rocky path. Once at the water's edge, one must climb out on large granite boulders to see the lighthouse.

BASS HARBOR CRUISES.

Two local companies offer sightseeing cruises that offer chances to see this lighthouse from the water. Call for the latest schedules.

- Bass Harbor Cruise, Swan's Island Ferry Terminal, Bass Harbor, ME. Phone: (207) 244-5365

- Island Cruises, Little Island Marine, Shore Road, Bass Harbor, ME. Phone: (207) 244-5785

BASS HARBOR HEAD LIGHTHOUSE.
CHARACTERISTIC: Occulting red 4s
HAW: 56' **RANGE:** 13 nm
The lighthouse abuts a steep and picturesque granite ledge to mark the Bass Harbor Bar, which stretches across the eastern entrance to Blue Hill Bay and Bass Harbor.

This cylindrical Federal Design brick tower is connected to its T-shaped keeper's dwelling by an L-shaped passageway. Both structures were erected in 1858. In 1878 the house was raised some 10 feet on a rebuilt foundation and given a clapboard exterior that is now covered by vinyl siding. East of the lighthouse is a detached brick bell house (1876), a brick oil house (1902) and a barn (1905). The station's bell tower has been dismantled.

OWNER. U.S. Coast Guard.

PRESERVATION: Listed in the National Register of Historic Places. Bass Harbor Head Lighthouse is a jewel among the Coast Guard's lighthouse properties.

FERRY TO SWAN'S ISLAND. Return to Swan's Island Road and the ferry landing. Ferry service to Swan's Island is available all year. The 12-car ferry makes the six mile crossing in 40 minutes. Make vehicle reservations through the Bass Harbor office. Note this sign at the Bass Harbor ferry terminal:
"Swan's Island is not for everyone. No movies. No hotels. No entertainment. Only peace and quiet."

FARES. Round trip vehicle + passengers. Discount for children 5-11.

SCHEDULE. Two or three departures from Bass Harbor daily. Call or check website for the latest schedule.
- Maine State Ferry Service, PO Box 114, Bass Harbor, ME 04653.
Phone: In Bass Harbor (207) 244-3254. On Swan's Island (207) 526-4273. Schedule information (207) 624-7777. Daily operations update in Maine toll-free (800) 491-4883.
Website: http://www.state.me.us/mdot/opt/ferry/ferry_1.htm

BASS HARBOR HEAD, BURNT COAT HARBOR & GREAT DUCK ISLAND

<u>ON SWAN'S ISLAND.</u> There are no road signs on the island. Leave the ferry landing and turn right (start 0.0 miles). Then:

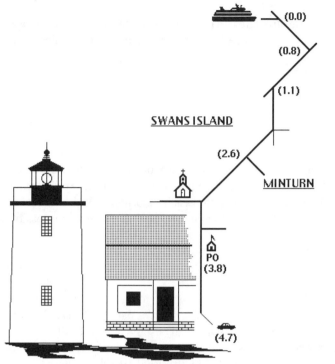

-> Right again at the next T-head intersection (0.8 miles),

-> Continue on the main unmarked road southeast,

-> Bear left at fork in the road (1.1 miles),

-> Continue south and southeast past the Minturn turn-off (2.6 miles) into the town of Swan's Island (locally called Harbor),

-> At the road's end, bear left and continue straight ahead on a narrow lane to a small parking area next to the lighthouse (4.7 miles).

Restaurant meals are available during the summer months at Sheila's Bakery on the ferry road and the Boat House Restaurant in Minturn. The General Store in the Harbor is open all year. In case you miss your return ferry, overnight lodging is available year round in the Harbor (Swan's Island) at Jeannie's B&B, (207) 526-4116. For information on lodging in Minturn, call (207) 526-4350.

BURNT COAT HARBOR LIGHTHOUSE
(HOCKAMOCK HEAD).
CHARACTERISTIC: Occulting white 4s.
HAW: 75'   **RANGE:** 9 nm

To mark the entrance to Burnt Coat Harbor two towers were erected to serve as range lights at Hockamock Head in 1872. In 1884, after numerous complaints that the range lights were confusing, the front range light was discontinued, although the tower remained standing for some years.

The present square brick tower is the former rear range light. The light tower was originally connected to an L-shaped keeper's dwelling by a covered passageway. The slightly tapered tower is architecturally of the Federal Design genre.

Today the station consists of the tower, now separated from the 1 1/2-story wood frame Cape Cod residence, a bell house (1911) that has four trapezoidal elevations, and a brick oil house (1895).

The Coast Guard closed the lighthouse in 1975, removed the original fifth-order Fresnel lens and transferred the aid's warning responsibility to a nearby 24-foot skeletal steel tower. At that height the beacon could be seen only out to a distance of some seven nautical miles. Vocal complaints, letters to Washington and a petition to the Coast Guard's district office in Boston brought the lighthouse back into service.

OWNER. U.S. Coast Guard (lighthouse). In November 1995 the keeper's dwelling and grounds were turned over to the Town of Swan's Island.

PRESERVATION. Listed in the National Register of Historic Places.

In 1982 Burnt Coat Harbor's normally white lighthouse was a paint-peeling shabby mess. To save maintenance costs the Coast Guard removed the peeling paint and covered its exposed brown exterior with a colorless sealant. This was not appreciated by the local lobstermen and fishermen who also use the tower as a daymark. They complained that the brown exterior could not be readily identified against the equally brown landscape. The Coast Guard relented and gave the old lighthouse and house a fresh coat of white paint. Note that the tower's windows have been sealed with glass blocks, the same treatment seen on the Spring Point Ledge Lighthouse in South Portland.

Although it will eventually be transformed into a public park managed by the Swan's Island Educational Society, the town will have to find the funds to maintain a balanced preservation program for the lighthouse and the island's other historic structures. Despite financial problems, the town is determined to keep and maintain the light station. On March 6, 1995, a committee was formed to oversee the care of the lighthouse property. Then on May 19, 1995, Swan's Island's selectmen and the lighthouse committee developed plans for the upkeep of the station's grounds, including the clearing of trails and placement of benches donated by local businesses.

In 1996 the International Masonry Institute, at no cost to Swan's Island, sent a team of four masons to repair the lighthouse and the keeper's house. The tower's walls were repaired by sealing a crack and eliminating a bulge, then repointed and painted. The dwelling's stone foundation was also repaired.

There is still more to be done before the public can visit these structures. The dwelling's interior is in poor shape, having been stripped by the Coast Guard when it left the station in 1975. Also, a septic tank will have to be installed. And of course there's the cost of liability insurance.

Donations for the preservation of the light station are welcomed.

- Board of Selectmen, Swan's Island, ME 04685.

GREAT DUCK ISLAND LIGHTHOUSE
CHARACTERISTIC: Flashing red 5s
HAW: 67' **RANGE:** 19 nm

Great Duck Island lies some 5.5 miles southeast of Bass Harbor Head. There is no ferry or scheduled boat cruises to the island. Perhaps the main reason for the lack of transportation is that the island is off limits to visitors from April through August. It is during these months that Great Duck Island becomes the nesting site for Leach's storm petrels, black backed gulls, black guillemots, and eider ducks. An active bald eagle nest is also on the island. For information on possible birdwatching trips to the island:

- Maine Audubon Society, Gilsland Farm, PO Box 6009, Falmouth, ME 04105-6009.

Phone: (207) 781-2330.

In his important report on the nation's lighthouses in 1843, I. W. P. Lewis called attention to the need for a beacon on Great Duck Island to help show the entrance to Mount Desert as well as Bass Harbor. The decades passed. The Lighthouse Board recommended a lighthouse on Great Duck Island in 1885, and the beacon was finally established in 1890.

The white cylindrical tower is constructed of granite stone and brick. Its three small windows have been sealed with glass blocks. The lantern deck is an ornate, bracketed cast-iron parapet, surmounted by the usual 10-sided lantern.

Some distance north of the tower is a 1 1/2-story wood framed keeper's cottage, the lone survivor from among three dwellings built in 1890. Other existing structures include a brick fog signal building (1890), a small stone oil house (1901) and a storage shed (1890). Besides the two houses, the station has also been stripped of its boathouse, boatslip, rain water collection shed, engine house, coal bunkers and several smaller buildings. The original fifth-order Fresnel lens was replaced in 1986 by an automated modern plastic lens.

OWNER. In February 1998 Great Duck Island Lighthouse, along with Mount Desert Rock Lighthouse, became the property of Bar Harbor's College of the Atlantic under the Maine Lights Program. The College of the Atlantic will work in cooperation with the Nature Conservancy, the largest land holder on Great Duck, to study Great Duck Island's flora and fauna. The college will pay $100,000 for the repair of the lighthouses, and must see that the properties' condition meets state historical preservation guidelines.

- College of the Atlantic, Bar Harbor, Maine 04609.

Phone: toll-free (800) 528-0025. Fax: (207) 288-4126.

Website: http://www.coa.edu

Email: inquiry@ecology.coa.edu

PRESERVATION. In 1984 most of the 265-acre island was purchased by the Maine Chapter of the Nature Conservancy. In 1994 the Nature Conservancy renovated the island's remaining keeper's house. The renovation of the light tower was one tough task. The island, a relatively flat piece of land, is almost constantly buffeted by gale-strength winds and high seas. The first contractor yanked his men off the island after they had experienced the wrath of winter cold, gales and 18-foot waves. The second contractor had the same problem of keeping workers on the job. In the spring of 1994 the International Chimney Corporation returned to the task of practically rebuilding the light tower. The workers found that the inner courses of brick were in unrepairable condition. Although of double wall construction, the space between the walls was found to be stuffed with all sorts of debris rather than the usual rubblestone. The project, at a cost of over $250,000, was completed in 1996.

Burnt Coat Harbor Lighthouse

Winter Harbor Lighthouse

BLUE HILL BAY

BLUE HILL BAY LIGHTHOUSE (EGGEMOGGIN).

This lighthouse cannot be seen from any public cruises in the area, but it can be seen via a flight out of the Hancock County / Bar Harbor Airport off ME 3 in Trenton. When searching for this inactive station, look for a patch of green grass, the white house with a tan roof and the white tower connected to the house by a red brick passageway. See flight details below.

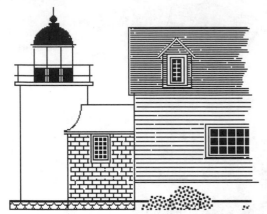

The Blue Hill Bay Light Station was constructed in 1856-57 on Green Island, at high tide mere patch of rocks and grass. Nearby lies Flye Island, which can be reached over a sand and rock formation at low tide.

The light station consists of a white cylindrical brick tower (1857) of the Federal Design genre connected to a 1 1/2-story gable-roofed keeper's colonial cape quarters (1856) with attached kitchen, a barn, a boathouse and an outside privy. A brick oil house for storage of kerosene was added in 1905.

The original optic was a whale oil-fed fourth-order Fresnel lens. It was removed in 1935 when the lighthouse's warning responsibility was transferred to an automated fifth-order Fresnel lens placed atop a skeletal streel tower. That beacon is ow solar powered.

OWNER. After automation the Coast Guard sold the property to a private party. A gray boathouse and a steel dock with a float at its end were added by Edith and Wilbur Trapp, who purchased the property in 1976. In May of 1995, Edith Trapp placed the island and its properties on the real estate market for an asking price of $975,000.

PRESERVATION. Eligible for listing in the National Register of Historic Places. The island and the light station are superbly restored and maintained.

LIGHTHOUSE SIGHTSEEING FLIGHTS.

To add a bit of spice to your lighthouse tour, consider taking one or more aircraft flights to view several lighthouses. The sight of these lighthouses from an airplane circling at low altitude is an unforgettable experience. The single engine aircraft is normally flown at altitudes of from 1,000 feet to 1,500 feet, which affords ease of spotting and excellent clarity. If requested and conditions permit, the pilot will fly at slightly lower altitude at no extra charge. He will even dip his wing for the benefit of photographers or on some occasions allow a window to be opened.

The scenic flights featuring lighthouses offered by Acadia Air are from 20 minutes to an hour. There is a per person fare, and there is a minimum of two passengers. Scenic flights are available all year, but in the winter they are by appointment only. A number of area lighthouses can be seen on these flights; call to find out about possible itineraries.

To reach the Hancock County/Bar Harbor Airport from Bass Harbor: ME 102A -> ME 233 -> ME 3. Flights depart from an aircraft parking area (with ticket booth) on the airport's perimeter adjacent to ME 3.

- Acadia Air Inc., Bar Harbor Airport, Trenton, ME 04605.
Phone: (207) 667-5534
Website: http://www.acadiaair.com
Email: acadiaair@acadia.net

Prospect Harbor Point Lighthouse

Petit Manan Lighthouse

WINTER HARBOR

NORTH OR SOUTH ON ME 186 Between Birch Harbor and Winter Harbor turn off ME 186 at the marked road leading to the entrance to Acadia National Park's Schoodic Peninsula. The lighthouse stands on four-acre Mark Island across Winter Harbor. It can be seen quite clearly from the park's perimeter road. Very good viewing spots are the off-road lookouts (parking permitted) located about 0.8 to 1.2 miles south of the park entrance.

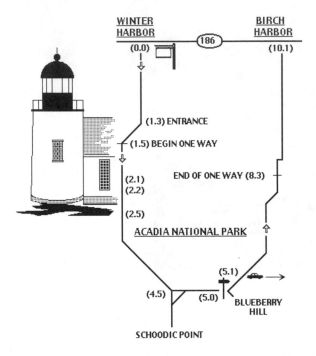

OPEN, All year, daily 8 to 5.

ADMISSION FEES. From Memorial Day to Labor Day, everyone must show passes to enter. A one-time entry pass is good for seven days. Annual and other National Park passes are accepted.

For a closer view from the water, a Winter Harbor company offers a great opportunity to sail close to this lighthouse and to enjoy some of Maine's most beautiful seacoast aboard the 27-foot Bristol Sloop *Bon Hiver.* There are two trips daily in the summer.

- Salty Dog Sailing, Capt. Jeff Prosser.

Phone: (207) 963-2674.

Website: http://www.oceaninn.com/saltydogsailing/

WINTER HARBOR LIGHTHOUSE.

The white brick light tower, built in 1856, is connected to the one-story extension of the 1876 Victorian keeper's dwelling by means of a narrow brick workroom. Auxiliary buildings include a storage shed, stone oil house (1905) and a boathouse (1878).

OWNER. The station was decommissioned in 1934 and sold a year later to the same Bar Harbor gentleman who purchased Pumpkin Island off Little Deer Isle. Three years later the buyer, George Harmon, sold the property to author Bernice Richmond and her husband. Mrs. Richmond, who was the organist in Thornton Wilder's *Our Town*, wrote about her lighthouse experiences in two published books, *Winter Harbor* and *Our Island Lighthouse*. Rene Prud-Hommeaux, a writer of children's books, purchased Mark Island and the lighthouse complex in the 1950s. The Prud-Hommeauxes, in turn sold the island in 1983 to Connecticut playwright Gerald Kean. Today the owner is William C. Holden III, a retired banker, former animal farmer, mariner and novelist.

PRESERVATION. Listed in the National Register of Historic Places.

When Mr. Holden bought the station in July 1995, he found the property in poor condition. The dwelling had a leaking roof and collapsed ceilings. All of the lighthouse windows were broken. The tower's staircase was thoroughly rusted. The two water cisterns were nonfunctioning. By the end of that year all had been repaired or restored.

CONTINUE ON. Continue south on the park's one way loop road and take the two way road to Schoodic Point, where a magnificent 400-foot headland affords sweeping views of the Bay of Fundy (east) and Mount Desert Island (west). Return to the loop road and motor east to a beach road marked with a "Blueberry Hill" sign. Continue past the intersection, up a slight rise, pull over and park. If you have a clear day, take your binoculars and look eastward. There, way out in the Atlantic, at a distance of about eight miles, stands the gracefully tall Petit Manan Lighthouse. You will be able to discern the station's brown ledge and a small white equipment building at the tower's base.

PROSPECT HARBOR POINT

NORTH OR SOUTH ON ME 186

From Winter Harbor enter Prospect Harbor on ME 186. If southbound, both ME 195 and ME 186 converge on the town.

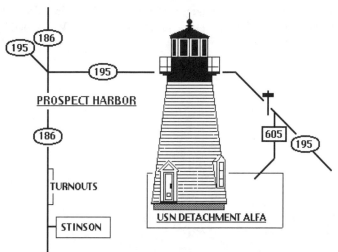

There are three places from which the motorist can view the lighthouse.

1) South of Prospect Harbor from the grounds of the Stinson Canning Company. It is suggested that you take the few minutes needed to pay a courtesy call at the company's office and ask permission to enter to view the lighthouse. You might also want to purchase some of Stinson's canned fish products.

2) From the shoulder of ME 186 just north of Stinson Canning.

3) From Lighthouse Point Road leading to a restricted U.S. Navy station. Just past a "Detachment Alpha" sign drive straight ahead where ME 195 bears left towards Corea.

In May 1989 the U.S. Navy, in cooperation with the Prospect Harbor Women's Club, sponsored an open house celebration with both the lighthouse and the old keeper's residence opened to the general public. The event became an annual affair, but has been discontinued in recent years. Hopefully the open houses will return in the future.

The keeper's dwelling is used as a guest house for official visitors and Navy personnel, and on a year-round basis as a vacation rental (five days maximum) for active and retired military families. Reservation priorities: 1) active Navy, 2) other active military services, 3) retired Navy, and 4) other retired service personnel.

And wouldn't you know — there's an eerie something inhabiting the house! People who have stayed there say that a small statue of a sea captain, sitting out of reach on a high ledge at the top of the stairs, moves at will — facing the sea one time, then turning around to view the staircase.

For information or to make a reservation (not more than one month in advance):
- Detachment Alpha, Naval Satellite Operations Center, Prospect Harbor, ME 04669-9999.
Phone: (207) 963-7700.

PROSPECT HARBOR POINT LIGHTHOUSE.

CHARACTERISTIC: Flashing red 6s (2 white sectors)
HAW: 42' **RANGE:** Red 7, white 9 nm.

Although its construction was authorized in 1847, the light station was not completed until 1850. The first lighthouse was a granite stone tower attached to one end of a stone keeper's dwelling. Although these structures were renovated in 1871, they continued to deteriorate until they were dismantled and replaced in 1891 by the present tower and the 1 1/2-story wood framed house.

The two structures exhibit a certain handsomeness not often seen in Maine's lighthouse architecture. The 38-foot tall wood framed lighthouse is shingled with a simple exterior showing but one door and a pedimented window. The tower is capped with a 10-sided lantern and the usual polygonal roof and ventilator ball. The gable roof dwelling has an asymmetrical five-bay facade, sheltered by a covered porch. Its first story is sheathed in clapboard while the upper floor's exterior has wood shingles. The oil house on the north side was built in 1905 with stone collected from along the shore.

The light and fog signal were first established to mark the inner harbor's east side entrance for the town's large fishing fleet. Although the Lighthouse Board deactivated the aids in 1859, because the harbor was not being used as an anchorage during storms, the station was reopened in 1870.

The lighthouse's 1870 fifth-order Fresnel lens was automated in 1934 and replaced with a modern lens in 1951.

OWNER: U.S. Coast Guard (light). Station dwelling and grounds belong to the U.S. Navy. The Navy also takes care of the light tower.

PRESERVATION. Listed in the National Register of Historic Places as the Prospect Harbor Light Station. Both structures are in excellent condition.

TO COREA. Now for another peek at the distant Petit Manan Lighthouse. From Lighthouse Point Road follow ME 195 for 2.8 miles east and south to Corea. In Corea center where ME 195 turns to the left, drive straight ahead into an unmarked road. Corea's post office is located on the southeast corner. Follow this road south past the entrance to "Young Bros. Boats" company and to a westward turn in the road. From this turn, continue west for about 0.2 mile. The Petit Manan tower and its blinking light can be seen with the naked eye, some six miles away, jutting up inside a "V" formed by the vegetation on intervening Outer Bar Island.

Machias Seal Island Lighthouse

PETIT MANAN

NORTH OR SOUTH ON US 1. Between Steuben and Milbridge, at a "Pigeon Hill Rd." sign, turn south off US 1 into Pigeon Hill Road. The turn is about 2.9 miles east of the Unionville-Steuben road intersection and three miles west of Milbridge's US 1 and US 1A intersection.

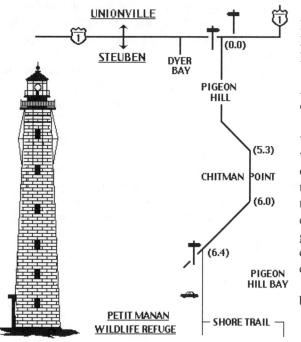

Continue south on Pigeon Hill to the Chitman Point area, location of a fishermen's cooperative and a large lobster pound. Petit Manan can be seen quite clearly without the use of binoculars.

Petit Manan Island supports colonies of common terns, Arctic terns and roseate terns, and there is also a breeding colony of puffins as well as common eiders.

PETIIT MANAN BIRDWATCHING CRUISE Closer views of Petit Manan Lighthouse are possible from narrated bird watching cruises leaving the Regency Holiday Inn, one mile north of Bar Harbor (before Bar Harbor on ME 3, inbound traffic should turn into the lot marked Bar Harbor Regency Hotel next door to the Ferry Terminal). The trips, aboard a high-speed catamaran capable of speeds over 40 mph, do not land at the island but do go close enough for excellent photographs of the lighthouse. The cruises are offered once daily from June to August; call for the current schedule.

- Bar Harbor Whale Watch Co., 39 Cottage St., Bar Harbor, ME 04609.

Phone: (207) 288-2386 or toll-free (800) WHALES-4.
Website: http://www.whalesrus.com/

PETIT MANAN NATIONAL WILDLIFE REFUGE. Farther south is the entrance to the Petit Manan National Wildlife Refuge's Petit Manan Point Unit. Continue straight ahead at the park sign to an unpaved parking lot. A short distance south of the parking lot is the beginning (marked with a small sign) of the refuge's five-mile Shore Trail. The improved section of the trail (about two miles) leads to the eastern side of the Petit Manan Point peninsula and the best mainland views of the lighthouse.

OPEN. All year, sunrise to sunset.
FREE ADMISSION.

PETIT MANAN LIGHTHOUSE.
CHARACTERISTIC: Flashing white 10s.
HAW: 123' **RANGE:** 26 nm

Petit Manan's first light station, established in 1817, consisted of a rubblestone keeper's dwelling, an outdoor privy and a 25-foot tall rubblestone tower. In 1852 the station was given a 1,200 pound brass fog bell. Sometime between 1870 and 1889 (based on photographs) the old stone tower was torn down, probably to provide foundations for two houses built in 1876 and 1899.

Because of the beacon's low elevation and short range, the Lighthouse Board decided in 1854 to build the present tower on the eastern end of the four-acre island, whose highest elevation is but 16 feet above mean high water. It has no soil and very little vegetation. An apt description is that the ledge is all shoals and tides.

The gray ashlar granite lighthouse is a slender 119-foot tall shaft, whose height is surpassed in Maine only by Boon Island's 133 feet. The tower was built by the U.S. Army Corps of Engineers. The granite blocks were cut in Trenton, Maine, and assembled, numbered, put together and then taken apart and shipped to the island for construction. The brick-lined tower, traversed via a 147-step spiral cast-iron staircase, is capped with a watchroom and a 12-sided lantern. The tower's two lower windows have been sealed, and the other nine are secured with glass blocks.

Petit Manan's graceful looks may appear to have been designed on a computer and built with the wisdom of King Solomon. Unfortunately this was not the case. The most serious engineering mistake was to opt for a slender shaft. The tower's diameters (20 feet at the base, 12 feet at the top) either prevented or discouraged the dovetailing of the walls' dressed granite blocks. Lacking the built-in squeezing effect when dovetailed walls are subjected to external pressures of wind and wave, the lighthouse was literally tailored for the problems it would experience in later years.

Meanwhile storms continued to weaken the tower. During an 1856 storm wall blocks were knocked loose. The tower swayed violently and a portion of the shaft near the top actually separated from the lower section. In 1869 the tower swayed so much during a storm that the Fresnel lens' clockwork weights broke loose and fell to the ground floor, taking along a large section of the tower's cast-iron stairway. Finally, in 1887 the loosened upper section, including the watchroom and the lantern, was refastened to the more solid lower portion of the tower. Six sets of 1/2-inch cast-iron rods were slipped through holes bored through the granite walls and anchored to embedded bolts. The strengthening job did the trick. Although the slim tower still sways in violent storms, it has passed numerous structural surveys.

The first lighting apparatus at Petit Manan was one of Winslow Lewis' multi-lamp devices. It was 53 feet above mean high water and could be seen out to 14 nautical miles. During 1823-25, the tower received extensive repairs and an improved lighting apparatus, with the number of lamps reduced from 13 to eight. In 1843 the number of lamps was again raise to thirteen.

In 1855 the new lantern was fitted with a rotating second-order Fresnel lens powered by a whale oil-fed lamp. Over the years the illuminant changed from whale oil to colza, to lard oil, in 1917 to kerosene and in 1938 to electricity. The Fresnel lens was replaced in 1972 by an automated modern lens. The second-order lens is now on display in Rockland's Shore Village Museum. A fog bell from Petit Manan is at the elementary school in the town of Milbridge.

Petit Manan's number of foggy days does not quite measure up to those experienced on Maine's Seguin Island and Saddleback Ledge, but over 30 years the island was recorded to have been fogged in for an annual average of 70 days.

The station once consisted of the tower and the following structures:
1855. Mechanism-operated fog bell tower.
1868. Boathouse (removed in 1993).
1869. Brick steam whistle building, replaced in 1889; rebuilt in 1892.
1875. Main 1 1/2-story Greek Revival keeper's dwelling.
1876. Engine house.
1876. Assistant keeper's residence, dismantled after 1985.
1899. Coal tramway for coal delivery, rebuilt in 1909 and removed in 1938.

Prior to the optic's automation, the rainspouts on the main service gallery were removed. One of the cast-iron gargoyles is on display in Rockland's Shore Village Museum.

OWNER. After the light was automated Petit Manan Island, except for the tower, was turned over to the U.S. Fish and Wildlife Service. It is part of 3,335-acre Petit Manan National Wildlife Refuge, which includes Petit Manan Point and parts of Bois Bubert and Nash islands. Under the Maine Lights Program the tower has also become the property of the U.S. Fish and Wildlife Service. Fish and Wildlife staff and students from Bar Harbor's College of the Atlantic use the tower as an observation post and live in the keeper's house. The beacon is still maintained by the U.S. Coast Guard.

PRESERVATION. Listed in the National Register of Historic Places.

The Maine Historic Preservation Commission has been involved in the restoration of the tower. For the second phase of the preservation project, the Commission awarded $14,500 for repairs to the keeper's residence's exterior and the repointing and rerouting of two support buildings. Meanwhile the Coast Guard, through a $40,000 contract with the International Chimney Corporation, had the strengthening rods coated (sleeved) to protect them from corrosion.

In 1997 the Campbell Construction Group of Beverly, Massachusetts, did further restoration of the lighthouse. The job included repointing, lead paint removal and repainting. In September 1998 the company returned to the island to replace 11 decorative cast iron treads on the interior spiral staircase. The treads were replaced by decorative treads that matched the original design.

MOOSE PEAK - MACHIAS SEAL ISLAND
NARRAGUAGUS - NASH ISLAND - LIBBY ISLAND

If the day is clear and without haze, motor down to Great Wass Island for a distant peak at the Moose Peak Lighthouse. Whether or not Great Wass Island is visited, the traveler has in Jonesport the opportunities to (1) cruise out to Machias Seal Island to view or visit the Canadian lighthouse there, and (2) to charter a cruise to view three of easternmost Maine's otherwise inaccessible lighthouses.

NORTH ON US 1. Just west of Columbia Falls take ME 187 south through Indian River and West Jonesport to Jonesport.

SOUTH ON US 1. West of Jonesboro take ME 187 to Jonesport.

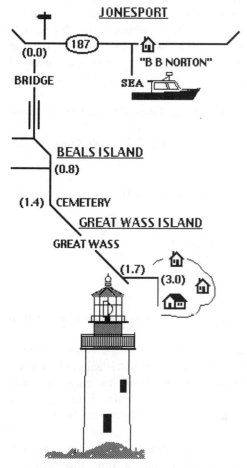

In Jonesport at a "Bridge Street" and a "Beals Island" sign turn south off ME 187 into Bridge Road. Cross over a causeway and a bridge to Beals Island. Upon reaching the island turn left and continue on Great Wass Road across Beals Island to its terminus on Great Wass Island. Parking is free at the road's end. Walk straight ahead to the top of a rocky knoll or, if tall weeds prevent movement in that direction, walk along the shore to the point. The white Moose Peak Lighthouse can be seen to the east across Mud Hole Channel nestled in a V-shaped section of the island's elevation.

MOOSE PEAK LIGHTHOUSE.
CHARACTERISTIC: Flashing white 30s
HAW: 72' **RANGE:** 25 nm

Moose Peak Lighthouse is located at the eastern end of Mistake Island, an outcropping that rivals Maine's Seguin Island, Matinicus Rock and Egg Rock for being fog enshrouded, averaging 2,000 hours annually.

Erected in 1827, the 57-foot tall brick lighthouse was rebuilt in 1851 and fitted with a second-order Fresnel lens in 1856.

In 1901 the keeper's house was in disrepair. Two years later a new two family house was completed and linked to the lighthouse tower by a walkway. A fog signal house was added in 1912.

In 1972 the Coast Guard replaced the Fresnel lens with an automated plastic lens. The dwelling was almost sold to a private party, but the high cost of a sewage system that would meet Environmental Protection Agency standards caused the sale to fall through.

In 1982 a team of Green Berets blew up the keeper's house as a training exercise. The demolition didn't go exactly as planned; panes in the lighthouse lantern were broken and the helicopter pad was damaged.

The lighthouse was converted to solar power in 1999.

OWNER. U.S. Coast Guard. Under the Maine Lights Program coordinated by the Island Institute of Rockland in 1997, the lighthouse was expected to be turned over to a local community or organization, but none applied.

PRESERVATION. Not listed in the National Register of Historic Places.

CRUISES TO MACHIAS SEAL ISLAND. There are two boat captains who take birdwatchers to Machias Seal Island.

- Captain Andrew Patterson operates out of Cutler, Maine. Information on his excursions can be found in the Little River Light chapter on page 409.

- Captains Barna B. and John E. Norton are licensed tour operators whose office is located on Jonesport's main street about 0.4 mile east of Bridge Road (or 0.3 mile west of the post office on ME 187). There is a white "B. B. Norton" sign painted on the west side and front roof of the house.

Mid-June to July is the best time period to see the puffins. The crossing from Jonesport takes approximately two hours. Maximum time on the island is three hours.

SCHEDULE. Approximately Memorial Day to August, daily at 7 AM. Returns between 12 and 1 PM. Call for current dates.

RESERVATIONS. Not less than six passengers must take the trip. Reservations with full payment are required. More than a single day reservation is advisable. If the trip does not materialize, reservation deposits will be refunded.

Once a reservation has been made, the passenger <u>must</u> call the night before between 7 and 8 to learn the time of the departure. These communications are necessary because weather conditions can change quickly, and if it can be avoided the Nortons do want to have their passengers endure otherwise predictable heavy squalls or high winds.

Landing on the island is dependent on the weather, sea conditions and visitation restrictions imposed by the Canadian government. Landings can be hazardous and at each individual's risk. Dress warmly, carry or wear rain gear, wear a hat as protection against tern squirts and bring your own water and food. A warden from the Canadian Wildlife Service orients and supervises all visitors.

Lodging with kitchenettes is available in Jonesport at the Puffin House and its two cottages.

- Captains Barna B. and John E. Norton, RR 1, Box 990, Jonesport, ME 04649-9704.

Phone: (207) 497-5933.

Website: http://vbirder.iserver.net/vbirder/onLoc/onLocDirs/DOWNEAST/bg/MSI.html

MACHIAS SEAL ISLAND LIGHTHOUSE.
CHARACTERISTIC. Flashing white 3s
HAW: 82' **RANGE:** 17 nm

This 60-foot tall lighthouse, a white octagonal tower with a red lantern, is located on a treeless 18-acre island about 10 miles southeast of Cutler. It was built in 1832.

Although the Canadian Government has operated this lighthouse since 1832, ownership of the two-island group remains a sore point in American-Canadian relations. The State Department in Washington claims the islands belong to and have been a part of the United States since the American Revolution. Not so, says Ottawa. While the quiet diplomatic quarrel continues, American and Canadian lobstermen and fishermen have skirmished over harvesting rights. Canadian Fisheries patrol boats on several occasions have stopped, boarded, searched and even cut loose lobstering floats to keep American lobstermen out of the disputed territorial waters.

A few years ago, a new aspect of this American-Canadian disagreement appeared. Besides flocks of terns, razorbill auks and storm petrels, the main attraction, at least for bird watchers, is the colorful puffin. In late spring these ungainly, tuxedoed "sea parrots" seek the rugged granite shores to nest and produce little puffins. The flocking of mainland bird watchers, tourists and the curious to the island has caused quite a bit of fussing. Canada has restricted daily visits to 25 persons.

In 1986 a new controversy arose. Barna B. Norton, claiming his great-grandfather, "Barna "Tall Barney" Beal, took possession of the islands when, in 1865, he foiled an attempt by Canadian authorities to take over the islands and the fishing grounds. Norton even formed a quasi-government and renamed his claimed real estate the "Territory of Machias Seal Island and North Rock, Atlantic Ocean, U.S.A." Interestingly, Captain Norton has a letter from the Department of State wherein the department restates the American claim to the islands and informs Captain Norton that he has every right to disregard Canadian laws and regulations regarding the two islands.

VIEWING EASTERNMOST MAINE LIGHTHOUSES.
The Nortons will also plan a chartered (hourly rate for 1-6 persons) cruise to view the Narraguagus, Nash Island and Libby Island Lighthouses. None of them can be seen from the mainland.

MOOSE PEAK - MACHIAS SEAL ISLAND
NARRAGUAGUS - NASH ISLAND - LIBBY ISLAND

NARRAGUAGUS LIGHTHOUSE (POND ISLAND)

This lighthouse is located southeast of Milbridge on a rock ledge on the seaward side of Pond Island in Narraguagus Bay.

The tower is constructed of dressed granite and is reinforced with brick. Base to center of the lantern is 31 feet. When erected in 1853 the tower rested upon a five-bay dwelling. In 1875, when the present 1 1/2-story wooden keeper's house was built, the tower remained on the original building. In 1882 one end of the original house was removed, leaving the tower exposed. In 1894 the tower was strengthened by the addition of an exterior wall of coursed brick.

The white tower is joined to the main house (gray roof) by an L-shaped brick workroom (gray roof) built in 1887. The station also has a brick oil house built in 1905.

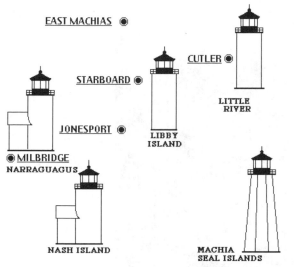

The light station was deactivated and sold to a privated party in 1934. Thereafter, Pond Island became a posh resort with its own golf course and a large comfortable inn. All except the lighthouse station have disappeared.

OWNER. Privately owned since 1934.

PRESERVATION. Listed in the National Register of Historic Places.

NASH ISLAND LIGHTHOUSE.

The Nash Island Lighthouse lies off Cape Split south of South Addison on the east side entrance to Pleasant Bay. It is further isolated by a 13-foot tide, ocean swell and tidal currents.

It was erected in 1838 and rebuilt in 1874. This white square and slightly tapered brick lighthouse with protruding covered entry duplicates the Federal Design architecture styling seen in at least 15 other New England lighthouses.

When active, the station consisted of the tower connected to a 1 1/2-story wood frame main keeper's house by three one-story structures that served as a kitchen, equipment shed, and workroom. There were also quarters for three families (1875), a fog whistle house, an oil house that stored both coal and lamp oil, a boathouse, and a one-room schoolhouse.

The lighthouse's original lamps and reflectors were replaced by a Fresnel lens in 1856.

In 1958, when the beacon was automated, the Coast Guard withdrew its personnel and dismantled all structures except the tower and its entryway (former workroom). The light was discontinued in 1982 and replaced by an offshore buoy.

OWNER. The Friends of Nash Island Light applied for the property under the Maine Lights Program. In December 1997 the Maine Lighthouse Selection Committee announced the transfer of the lighthouse to the nonprofit group. The Friends of Nash Island Light have done much restoration of the tower's exterior, and they hope to restore the interior as well.

- Friends of Nash Island Light, RR 1, Box 490, Addison, Maine 04606.

PRESERVATION. Not listed on the National Register of Historic Places.

LIBBY ISLAND LIGHTHOUSE

CHARACTERISTIC: Group flashing white 20s

HAW: 91'   **RANGE:** 25 nm

This lighthouse at the entrance to Machias Bay, scene of the American Revolution's first naval battle, is located on the southernmost island of the two Libby Islands. It marks a treacherous bar that joins the islands.

Libby Island's first lighthouse, a wooden tower erected in 1817, was toppled over during a storm in April 1824. Before the old tower was lost to the sea a new light station was constructed in 1822, consisting of the present 42-foot tall lighthouse and a 1 1/2-story wood frame house. While the old keeper's dwelling was improved in 1949, the sturdy granite tower and the keeper's house, rain shed (1856), boathouse (1856), masonry fog signal house (1884) and brick oil house (1893). All except the tower and the fog signal house have been destroyed.

OWNER: Under the Maine Lights Program the lighthouse was turned over to the U.S. Fish and Wildlife Service. The U.S. Coast Guard still maintains the beacon.

PRESERVATION. Listed in the National Register of Historic Places.

Little River Lighthouse

LITTLE RIVER

NORTH OR SOUTH ON US 1. In East Machias take ME 19 to Cutler (12 miles). Continue through the town around a circular rock-trimmed platform and to the dock across from the town's white Methodist Church. The light station's old fog bell is displayed on the platform.

This lighthouse, located on the seaward side of Little River Island, is not visible from the shoreline. It can be seen and photographed aboard the following cruises.

CRUISE TO MACHIAS SEAL ISLAND. Captain Andrew Patterson's *Barbara Frost* (single open deck) is a 40-foot passenger vessel that transports birdwatchers and others to Machias Seal Island, principally to view the Maine coast's largest puffin colony. The round trip lasts about five hours.

Landing on the island is dependent on weather, sea conditions and visitation restrictions imposed by the Canadian Government. Landings can be hazardous and at each individual's risk. Dress warmly, carry or wear rain gear, wear a hat as protection against tern squirts and bring your own water and food. A warden from the Canadian Wildlife Service orients and supervises all visitors.

SCHEDULE. May to late August, daily at 7 or 8 AM.

FARES. Round trip per person fare. Advance reservations are recommended and require one-half fare deposits. Deposits are returned if the trip is canceled. There are discounts for children and groups. Captain Patterson shares proceeds with the National Audubon Society.

COASTAL CRUISES. Captain Patterson also offers two additional cruises that pass the Little River Lighthouse. One is a two-hour sightseeing excursion along the coast. The other is either a half-day or full-day nature cruise in the Cross Island Wildlife Refuge located at the entrance to Machias Bay.

SCHEDULE. Call for schedule. May to October, most days at 2 PM.

FARES. Round trip per person. No discounts.

- Bold Coast Charter Company, PO Box 364, Cutler, ME 04626.

Phone: (207) 259-4484.

Website: http://www.boldcoast.com

Email: info@boldcoast.com

LITTLE RIVER LIGHTHOUSE

The island's first aid was established in 1847, not only to mark the harbor's entrance, but also to provide an intermediate beacon between West Quoddy Head to the north and Machias Seal Island Light to the southeast.

The station was simply built with a rubblestone tower and a small stone keeper's house.

In 1876 the lighthouse was rebuilt. The 41-foot tower still stands. The four-section tower has a plated cast-iron skin supported by an iron and brick frame. The station consists of the light tower, the red-roofed, 1 1/2-story, L-shaped wood frame Victorian keeper's house (1888), a brick oil house (1905), a storage building (1879), and a boathouse (1881). The station's fog signal building has been dismantled.

Inn 1855 the lantern received a fifth-order Fresnel lens. The light was automated in 1975. In 1980 the Fresnel lens was removed and a modern lens was posted to a nearby skeletal tower.

OWNER. Leased to the American Lighthouse Foundation in January 2000.

- **American Lighthouse Foundation**, PO Box 889, Wells, Maine 04090.

Phone: (207) 646-0515.

Website: http://www.lighthousefoundation.org

PRESERVATION. Listed in the National Register of Historic Places.

In 2000 and 2001 the Coast Guard and volunteers of the American Lighthouse Foundation have done a great deal of work at this station. The walkway across the island has been rebuilt. At this writing (August 2001) there are plans to return the light to the restored lighthouse tower before the end of 2001. Much work remains to be done on the keeper's house, but the American Lighthouse Foundation plans a complete restoration.

Lubec Channel Lighthouse

West Quoddy Head Lighthouse

LUBEC CHANNEL
WEST QUODDY HEAD

TO LUBEC In Whiting turn off US 1 into ME 189 and continue towards Lubec. About 4.1 miles east of US 1 turn right into South Lubec Road marked with a "Quoddy Head State Park" sign. The best views of the Lubec Channel Lighthouse occur between 0/3 to 0.6 miles from ME 189.

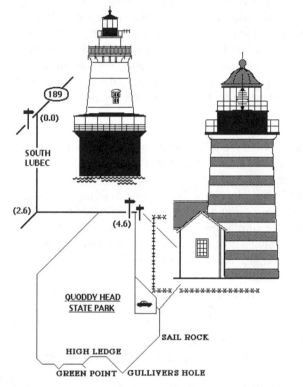

Some of the sightseeing cruises offered by Island Cruises of Campobello Island provide water views of Lubec Channel Lighthouse and other area lighthouses. It may also be possible to charter a cruise with this company to get excellent views of several American and Canadian light stations, including the picturesque Head Harbour Lighthouse, also known as East Quoddy Head Lighthouse. Departures are from Head Harbour Wharf, Campobello Island, New Brunswick. Campobello is connected by the FDR International Bridge to Lubec.
- Island Cruises, Wilson's Beach, Campobello, New Brunswick, Canada E0G 3L0
  Phone: (506) 752-1107 or toll-free (888) 249-4400.
  Email: islcrus@campnet.nb.ca

LUBEC CHANNEL LIGHTHOUSE (SPARK PLUG, CHANNEL LIGHT)
CHARACTERISTIC: Flashing white 6s
HAW: 53'   **RANGE:** 6 nm
In the 1800s the river ports at Calais (cal' iss), Eastport and Lubec were commercial centers whose livelihoods were dependent on navigation on the St. Croix River and through the Lubec Channel.

After Lubec Channel had been dredged, the Lighthouse Board recommended that the channel be marked with a lighted beacon to facilitate night navigation. With an initial appropriation of $20,000, construction of the light station began in the spring of 1889.

Lubec Channel Lighthouse's white conical cast-iron and brick-lined tower rests on a circular concrete-filled caisson constructed from 160 cast-iron plates arranged in five courses of 32 plates each. The bottom gallery deck originally had a roof with rain gutters that fed the storage cisterns inside the foundation pier. Hanging over the side of the gallery was a fog bell activated by a 700-pound weight housed in a small wooden shed. The weight had to be would each day. The fog bell now rests in the Lubec Historical Society's museum.

Inside the main door there are two sets of stairs. One on the right leads to the upper decks; the left one gives access to the circular basement (same diameter as the tower above) 12 feet below. The cisterns are reached through the basement floor's manholes. When occupied, the first deck housed the crew's quarters and galley. The second and third levels contained the crew's bedrooms, the fourth deck the watchroom and service balcony and the fifth the lantern.

The original optic, established on December 31, 1890, was a kerosene-powered fourth-order Fresnel bullseye lens that was rotated by a weight-powered clockwork mechanism. The weights descended through a 24-inch diameter cast-iron tube positioned vertically in the center of the superstructure. The light was automated in 1939 after one of the keepers was asphyxiated during a damaging oil fire. The Fresnel lens was replaced in 1968 by a plastic lens. The optic is now solar powered. Note the solar panel attached to the watchroom's service gallery.

Unfortunately, as a result of corrosion and storm damage, the tiny brass lighthouses set on the support columns of the canopy disappeared two decades ago when the Coast Guard removed the canopy. The little lighthouses were similar to those remaining on the gallery balusters of Nobska Point and Cape Neddick Lighthouses.

OWNER. U.S. Coast Guard.
PRESERVATION. Listed on the National register of Historic Places.

In 1989 the Coast Guard, lacking the estimated $1 million needed to repair the superstructure (including a six-degree starboard list) and fully restore a badly rusted caisson foundation, announced that the optic and its lantern were to be moved to a shore location and the tower abandoned. Public concern and efforts of the Lubec Historical Society and Maine Historic Preservation Commission were instrumental in saving "Old Spark Plug." One campaign ploy by Lubec citizens was to send engine spark plugs to their congressmen and legislators with the plea "Save the Spark Plug."

The decision not to abandon the lighthouse was made after an engineering study concluded that a restored structure would be able to withstand projected ice loads and tides. Work began in October 1992 and was slowed by the severe deterioration of the concrete-filled caisson. New steel plates were emplaced and a couple of hundred yards of concrete pumped into a dry cofferdam built with twelve 120-foot long H-piles driven through the caisson and mud bottom into the bedrock. Thereafter the following repairs were made: 1) the superstructure was sandblasted and repainted; 2) the brick lining was repointed and repaired; 3) new landing platforms were built; 4) the canopy roof around the first deck was rebuilt and 5) windows were replaced. The restoration cost about $700,000.

TO WEST QUODDY HEAD. Motor south on Lubec Road to a fork in the road marked by a "Quoddy Head State Park" sign. Bear left and continue on to the light station. At the entrance to the station and another "Quoddy Head State Park" sign, turn right into the road leading to the parking area within the park.

Enroute (on the left) is Carrying Place Cove, the site of a former lifesaving station. The cove was so named because lifesaving boats could be hand carried across the spit of land and launched in either a north or south direction. In 1972 the station, which belonged to the Coast Guard, was closed and declared to be surplus government property. The refurbished real estate is now occupied by the West Quoddy Biological Research Station, a nonprofit organization devoted to research on every marine subject from mammals to jellyfish to intertidal ecology, algae, and the maritime society.

QUODDY HEAD STATE PARK. Visitors are permitted to walk about the light station. The lighthouse and keeper's house are not open to the public.

OPEN. Memorial Day to September, daily 9 to sunset.

ADMISSION FEES. Discounts for children 5-12, under 5 free. Seniors 65+ free.

TRAILS. From the parking area there are two finished trails that will interest the lighthouse seeker. The shorter one to the left takes the visitor to the light station.

The coastal trail takes the hiker to Carrying Place Cove (2.0 miles), across a field to the road (2.5 miles) and on the road back to the parking area (4.0 miles). Sail Rock, the easternmost point in the United States, and the lighthouse can be viewed from along the first 0.5 mile of the trail. About 0.25 mile farther on is Gulliver's Hole, a wave eroded cave surrounded by 90-foot high cliffs. Farther on are High Ledge and Green Point, which offer excellent views of Grand Manan and New Brunswick Islands, some nine miles offshore.

- Quoddy Head State Park, RR #2, Box 1490, Lubec, ME 04652.

Phone: (207) 733-0911. Off-season (207) 941-4014.

Website: http://www.state.me.us/doc/prkslnds/quoddy.htm

WEST QUODDY HEAD LIGHTHOUSE
CHARACTERISTIC: Group flashing white 15s
HAW: 83' **RANGE:** 18 nm

The first lighthouse on West Quoddy Head was a rubblestone tower completed in 1808. Its light was established the following year. The structure was rebuilt in 1853.

Five years later, because of the poor condition (probably due to a faulty mortar mix and moisture) of the rebuilt tower, the present 49-foot brick lighthouse was erected. Added at the same time was the present 1 1/2-story, gable roofed Victorian dwelling. The oil house was built in 1892 and a fog signal building in 1887.

In 1820 West Quoddy Head became the first of two light stations to receive a large 500-pound fog bell. That so called "silent" signal was replaced by a higher-pitched 240-pounder, which was replaced by a heftier and disturbingly resonant 1,565 pound bell. None of the bells could produce a sound that could be heard far enough out to sea to warn ships off the rocks. A hand-struck metal triangle (1837) was also a failure. Finally, in 1869, West Quoddy Head, Cape Elizabeth and Matinicus Rock received steam-operated fog whistles (Daboll trumpets) that were at the time the world's most powerful fog signals.

LUBEC CHANNEL & WEST QUODDY HEAD

The station originally operated another type of fog signal. It was a light iron cannon that on foggy days was repeatedly muzzle-loaded with gunpowder and fired as a ship approached the entrance to Quoddy Roads. Signaling with ships' whistles for the gunners to fire and then sensing the direction of the sound of each cannon shot, captains were able to lay a safe course past West Quoddy Head. The fog cannon did not endure, primarily because of safety considerations, handling problems and directional inaccuracies.

West Quoddy Head Lighthouse's third-order Fresnel optic was automated in 1988. The station is on the easternmost point of the continental United States, marking the southwest entrance to Quoddy Roads. Its companion station, the East Quoddy Head Lighthouse, is located on the northeastern tip of Canada's Campobello Island.

OWNER. In 1998, under the Maine Lights Program, the station became the property of the State of Maine. The light itself is still maintained by the Coast Guard. Managed by the Department of Conservation's Bureau of Parks and Lands.

PRESERVATION. Listed in the National Register of Historic Places.

The keeper's dwelling and grounds were leased to Maine for use as housing for the park manager. The Bureau of Parks and Lands has stated its awareness of and concern for the dwelling's deteriorating condition and is looking for ways to secure the funds needed to perform major repairs. In 1994 and again in 1996 the resident park ranger made minor repairs to the keeper's house.

A nonprofit organization called the West Quoddy Head Lighthouse Keepers Association has been formed, with these stated purposes: 1) To enhance the experience of visitors to the West Quoddy Head Lighthouse; 2) To create exhibits and displays that link the history of the lighthouse with the community of Lubec and the maritime world; 3) To become a resource center for Lubec and the region; 4) To make space available for relevant community activities and educational programs; 5) To engage in any other activities that further the promotion of a thriving community and a natural environment. Hopefully this group will work with the State of Maine to insure a positive future for this historic station.

And there's exciting news -- a Lighthouse Visitors Center is under construction in the keeper's house at this writing in the summer of 2001, with a full opening planned for the 2002 summer season.

- West Quoddy Head Lighthouse Keepers Association, PO Box 378, Lubec, ME 04652.

Website: http://lighthouse.cc/westquoddylightkeepers/

Canada's inactive Mullholland Lighthouse can be seen clearly from Lubec's riverfront. Follow ME 189 (Washington Street) into Lubec and before the approach to the international bridge bear left into Water Street. Before Commercial Street there is a small parking area (free). Beyond Commercial Street there is a larger parking lot (free).

WHITLOCKS MILL

This lighthouse is located just east of Whitlocks Mill off US 1 between Calais and Red Beach. Since it stands on private property, the tower can be viewed (distantly, largely obscured by trees is summer) from the St. Croix View Rest Area located about 4.9 miles northwest of the entrance to the St. Croix Island International Historic Site. The park is announced by a "Rest Area 1,500 Ft" sign.

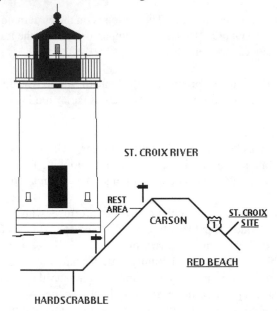

ST. CROIX RIVER LIGHTHOUSES Since the early 1800s the St. Croix River has been a well-traveled waterway, serving both American and Canadian fishing, trade, and manufacturing industries. Calais, for example, was an important lumber transshipment point. In recognition of the river's commercial importance American and Canadian lighthouse authorities built five light towers between Eastport and Calais. Three active Canadian aids are located on Cherry Islet east of Eastport and on Spruce Point and Mark Point farther upstream. All are 25 feet tall and are painted with alternating red and white bands. Maine's St. Croix Lighthouse, established on Dochet Island in 1856, was destroyed by a carelessly tended campfire in 1976.

WHITLOCKS MILL LIGHTHOUSE
CHARACTERISTIC: Equal interval green 6s
HAW: 32' **RANGE:** 5 nm

Beginning in 1892 a lantern was displayed from a tree at this spot. Complaints that the light was inadequate led to the construction of the present Federal Design lighthouse in 1910. The 25-foot cylindrical tower is lined with ceramic tile. The extant two-story, stuccoes and gambrel roof, Dutch colonial cottage was completed in 1909. Added also in 1920 were the brick oil house and a pyramidal bell tower.

The 1892 fourth-order Fresnel lens was replaced in 1969 by an automated modern lens.

OWNER. Under the Maine Lights Program the lighthouse was transferred to the St. Croix Historical Society in December 1997. In the 1970s the station had been leased to the Washington County Vocational Technical Institute. The station, except for the lighthouse tower, was then sold to a private party.

PRESERVATION. Listed in the National Register of Historic Places.

INDEX

INDEX

INDEX

INDEX

INDEX

INDEX OF LIGHTHOUSE PRESERVATION ORGANIZATIONS

INDEX OF LIGHTHOUSE PRESERVATION ORGANIZATIONS, cont.

Notes

Notes

Notes

Notes

Help Save Our Lighthouses!

Help us save our nation's endangered lighthouses from the approaching seas, violent storms, and sheer neglect. The American Lighthouse Foundation has been directly responsible for projects such as the total restoration of the Race Point Lighthouse on Cape Cod Massachusetts and the restoration of the grave-sites of Abbie Burgess and the Grant family of famous lighthouse keepers.

The American Lighthouse Foundation has given financial assistance to different lighthouse groups throughout the United States and Canada, including the Friends of Doubling Point Lighthouse, the Nauset Lighthouse Preservation Society, the Crisp Point Historical Society, Minot's Lightkeepers' Memorial, the Lightship Sailors' Memorial, the Avery Point Lighthouse (the only lighthouse memorial to lighthouse keepers), and the Grand Island East Channel Light.

The Foundation has formed the Friends of the Rockland Breakwater Light to guide and help the City of Rockland in their preservation efforts of their recently acquired landmark. The Friends group has raised donations from all over the United States and even enlisted the US Navy in their restoration efforts.

Time is running out for many lighthouses. If money is not raised **now**, many of our historic lighthouses may soon be gone. We need your financial support to save, restore, and maintain lighthouses and their artifacts before they are lost forever.

Please make your checks payable to:

The American Lighthouse Foundation
PO Box 889, Wells, Maine 04090

Yearly membership dues are:

❑ **Commissioner $1000**   ❑ **Inspector $500**   ❑ **Keeper $100**
❑ **Assistant Keeper $20**   ❑ **Supporting Membership $10**

Name: _____

Address: _____

City: _____ State: ____ Zip: _____

Phone: _____

❑Check enclosed.
❑Charge my credit card # _____ Exp _____

Memberships and donations can be made by check, Visa, or MasterCard.

Please help us save America's Maritime Heritage by becoming a member today!